Collected poems of
Sir Thomas Wyatt

LIVERPOOL ENGLISH TEXTS AND STUDIES

GENERAL EDITOR: KENNETH MUIR

Other titles in this Series

THE POEMS OF WILLIAM HABINGTON

EDITED BY KENNETH ALLOTT

ROLLO, DUKE OF NORMANDY

or THE BLOODY BROTHER

EDITED BY J. D. JUMP

THE POEMS OF JOSEPH HALL

BISHOP OF EXETER AND NORWICH

EDITED BY ARNOLD DAVENPORT

POEMS OF NICHOLAS BRETON

EDITED BY JEAN ROBERTSON

JOHN KEATS: A REASSESSMENT

EDITED BY KENNETH MUIR

THE POEMS OF HENRY CONSTABLE

EDITED BY JOAN GRUNDY

THE POEMS OF JOHN MARSTON

EDITED BY ARNOLD DAVENPORT

LIFE AND LETTERS OF SIR THOMAS WYATT

BY KENNETH MUIR

SAMUEL DANIEL

BY JOAN REES

Collected poems of
Sir Thomas
Wyatt

EDITED BY
KENNETH MUIR
AND
PATRICIA THOMSON

LIVERPOOL UNIVERSITY PRESS

1969

Published by
LIVERPOOL UNIVERSITY PRESS
123 Grove Street, Liverpool 7

Copyright © *1969 by Kenneth Muir and Patricia Thomson*

Printed and bound in England by
Richard Clay (The Chaucer Press) Ltd
Bungay, Suffolk

85323 110 9

This edition first published 1969

PREFACE

THIS edition includes nearly all the poems contained in the Muses' Library edition (1949), together with most of the poems from *Unpublished Poems of Sir Thomas Wyatt and his Circle* (1961). It is not implied that all the poems included are Wyatt's but most readers would regret the absence of many good poems for which there is no real evidence of Wyatt's authorship, for example, 'Forget not yet', 'Blame not my lute', 'With serving still', and 'Once in her grace'.

The text has been greatly improved. This has been made possible by a fresh scrutiny of the MSS., by reference to Professor Ruth Hughey's notes in her edition of the Arundel MS., and, above all, by the use of Dr. R. Southall's unpublished thesis (Birmingham University, 1961), which includes accurate transcripts of the Egerton and Devonshire MSS. Dr. Southall has increased our indebtedness by letting us use his transcripts of the Wyatt poems in the remaining MSS. He has also given us valuable advice, though we have reluctantly disagreed with him on editorial policy.

The text and collations have been prepared by Kenneth Muir; Patricia Thomson has provided the notes to poems translated or imitated from the Italian; and the two editors have, of course, criticized each other's work. We have not included a critical study of Wyatt's poetry as we have both published our views on it in recent years.

It will be obvious that this edition owes a great deal to the work of previous editors; most to the first, Nott, but a great deal to Rollins and Hughey, and some to Foxwell. It owes much to Wyatt's critics, especially Sergio Baldi, H. A. Mason, and O. Hietsch. We are likewise indebted to many colleagues and correspondents in both hemispheres for their assistance, especially to Professor Emeritus R. G. Austin, Professor C. A. Mayer, Professor J. E. Cross, Mr. R. T. Davies, and Mr. N. F. Blake of Liverpool University; Professor G. Kane, Professor J. C. Maxwell, Mr. H. A. Mason, Mr. W. Tydeman, Mr. J. Stevens, and others mentioned in the Commentary.

Acknowledgements are due to the Trustees of the British

Museum and to the Board of Trinity College, Dublin, for permission to reproduce pages of manuscripts in their possession and to the Henry E. Huntington Library for permission to include Wyatt's one prose translation.

K. M.

P. T.

CONTENTS

PREFACE   v

LIST OF ILLUSTRATIONS   ix

INTRODUCTION   xi

SIGLA   xxvii

   I. Poems from the Egerton Manuscript   1

  II. Satires   88

 III. Penitential Psalms   98

  IV. Poems from the Blage Manuscript   126

   V. Poems from the Devonshire Manuscript   189

  VI. Poems from the Arundel Manuscript   237

 VII. Poems from Minor Manuscripts   241

VIII. Poems from Tottel's *Songes and Sonettes*   245

  IX. Poems from *The Court of Venus*, etc.   254

COMMENTARY   263

APPENDICES

  A. A rejected poem   439

  B. *The Quyete of Mynde*   440

GLOSSARY   465

INDEX OF FIRST LINES   473

INDEX OF VERSE IN COMMENTARY   481

ILLUSTRATIONS

1. Egerton MS. 2711. f. 26^v *facing page* 68
2. Egerton MS. 2711. f. 69^v 84
3. Egerton MS. 2711. f. 90^v 100
4. Royal MS. 17^A, xxii. f. 14^v, 15^r 116
5. Blage MS. f. 108 196
6. Add. MS. 17492. f. 54^v 212

No. 5 is reproduced by kind permission of the Board of Trinity College, Dublin. The remainder are reproduced by kind permission of the Trustees of the British Museum.

INTRODUCTION

I. THE MANUSCRIPTS

THE following is a list of the more important manuscripts containing poems by Wyatt. (There are others which contain corrupt texts of single poems.)

1.	Egerton MS. 2711 [B.M.]	E
2.	Blage [Trinity College, Dublin]	B
3.	Devonshire MS. Add.17492 [B.M.]	D
4.	Arundel [Arundel Castle]	A
5.	Hill MS. Add.36529 [B.M.]	P
6.	Harleian MS. 78 [B.M.]	H
7.	Parker MS. 168 [Corpus Christi College, Cambridge]	C
8.	Royal MS. 17ᴬ, xxii [B.M.]	R

I. EGERTON

The Egerton MS. was the poet's own. It consists, for the most part, of fair copies of his poems written in a clear and elegant hand *c*. 1535. A few of these have corrections by the poet himself. Others have corrections by Grimald, as Miss Hughey has demonstrated,[1] made perhaps when he was preparing the text of Tottel's *Songes and Sonettes*. Towards the end of the MS., other hands appear (LXXXVIII–XCIV, XCVII, CIII) and twelve poems, including the Penitential Psalms, are in the poet's own hand. The MS. also contains copies of Wyatt's two letters to his son, Sir John Harrington's rival version of the Penitential Psalms, and a collection of French poems.

Unfortunately the MS. was used by one of the Harrington family in the seventeenth century for jottings on a variety of topics – doctrinal, political, mathematical, medical – and the poems are difficult to decipher beneath the palimpsest. Some sheets, moreover, are missing, and others are torn.

Most of E was copied in 1537, or earlier, before Wyatt left for Spain. There is no reason to think that the poems were copied in the order of composition. But the later poems, including those in

1. *The Library* 1934–5, pp. 388–444.

Wyatt's hand, were written in Spain and afterwards, between 1537 and 1542.[1]

The poems are printed here in the order of the MS., with the following exceptions: the three satires appear in E after LXXIV, LXXVI, and LXXXIII; the Psalms appear on ff. 86–98 and are followed by CIV on ff. 100–1. There are no poems between f. 69ᵛ and Surrey's prefatory sonnet to the Psalms.

2. BLAGE

The Blage MS. was compiled by one of Wyatt's closest friends, Sir George Blage. It includes poems by Blage himself, Wyatt, Surrey, and others. It afterwards passed into the hands of Archbishop Ussher and was bequeathed by him to Trinity College, Dublin. It is written in a variety of hands, but the poems are arranged in approximately alphabetical order of first lines. A partial index is provided in the same hand as that of the copier of most of the first part of the MS. This suggests that it was originally intended to make a fair copy of the whole collection; but, if so, the intention was abandoned after CXLI. Some of the poems listed in the index are missing from the MS.[2]

The following is a list of the poems in the MS:

f. 58 When shall the cruell stormes be past (n) 62 CIX 63 CX 64 CXI 65 CXII 66 CXIII 67 CXIV 68 LI 69 CXV 70 CXVI A sobre maid ... 71 CXVII 72 CXVIII 73 XCV 74 V 75 CXIX 76 CXX 77 CXXI 78 Brome if yow wante yet ought to be loued 80 CXXII 81 CXXIII 82 Cursyd be he that first began (n) 83 CXXIV 84 CXXV 85 CXXVI 86 CXXVII 87 CXXVIII 88 CXXIX 89 CXXX 90 CXXXI 91 Danger thy selff led for nothyng (n) 92 CXXXII 94 From Adams fall to Noes noyfull floudd 95 O Ioue geve eare vnto my cry 96 CXXXIII 97 CXXXIV 98 XXI 99 CXXXV 100 CXXXVI 101 A voyce I have and yk a will to wayle (n) 104 CXXXVII 105 CXXXVIII 106 CXXXIX 107 CXL 108 CXLI 109 LXVII 110 CXLII 111 CXLIII When shall my lyeue ... 112 CXLIV 113 CXLV 114 CXLVI 115 In Sommer season as soune as the sonne (n) 117 LXXXVII 119 CXLVII 120 CXLVIII 121 Love

---

1. H. A. Mason, *Humanism and Poetry in the Early Tudor Period* (1959) believes that the Psalms were written in 1536. It is, of course, possible that Wyatt left a gap for the copying of more secular poems; but if the Psalms were written so early, it is surprising that Wyatt did not polish them and have a fair copy made.

2. See K. Muir, *Unpublished Poems of Sir Thomas Wyatt and his Circle* (1961).

who so wyll whyt bread I best do love browne (n) Alas your
ffondnes makys me smylle (n) 122 LXX 123 CXLIX 124 Let the
hethen whiche trust not in the Lorde (n) If nowe the tyme is this
the dulfull daye (n) 125 LXVI 126 CL 127 CLI, CLII 127 My
lady ys suche one to whom our Lord hath lent 128 XXXIV Of
ffewe words sir ye syme to be 129 CLIII, LXVIII 130 CLIV 131–4
prose 136 O Lord what chance what thyng ys thys 137 CLV 138
CLVI 139 CLVII 140 O Faythfull hart plungyd in distress (n)
141–4 prose 145 CLVII 146 XXXIX 147 XL 148 CLIX 149 prose
150 CLX 151 CLXI 152 Ryd of bondage, free from kaer seven
yeres space and mor (n) 153 Only the Elect on the Sabbath doth
praye. Bragg not of goodes 154 Some men would think of right to
have (T) 155 CLXII 156 LXXII 157 CLXIII 158 CLXIV 159
CLXV 160 CLXVI 161 Sustayne, abstayne, kep well in your mynd
(n) 162 Syns Loue ys founde wythe parfytnes (n) 163–6 prose 167
CLXVII 168 CLXVIII 169 CLXIX 170 CLXX 171 LXXVIII 172
CLXXI 173 CLXXII 174 XVI Repentance ransome of each offence
175 CLXXIII 176 Degrese of lyghtnes lefte behynde (Surrey) He
that spares to speake hath hardly his entent (Surrey ?) 177 Tho I
seyme ded vnto the daslynge Iy (n) 178 Such wayward ways hath
loue (Surrey) 179 Yf Ryght be rakt and ouer Ron (T) 180 When
many dayes and nyghtes in grefe were paste 181 CLXXIV 182
CLXXV 183 CLXXVI 184 CLXXVII 185 VII.

3. DEVONSHIRE

The D MS. is written in a variety of hands and it contains poems
by Surrey, E. Knyvet, Anthony Lee, Henry Stuart, A.I., and
others, as well as extracts from Thomas Hoccleve, Sir Richard
Roos, and Chaucer's *Troylus and Criseyde*, apparently adapted to
suit the feelings of the copyist.

Accounts of the MS. are to be found in A. K. Foxwell's *A Study
of Sir Thomas Wyatt's Poems* (1911), Ruth Hughey's *The Arundel
Harington Manuscript* (1960), K. Muir's 'Unpublished Poems in the
Devonshire Manuscript' (*Proceedings of Leeds Philosophical and
Literary Society* (1947), and Raymond Southall's article *RES*
(1964), pp. 142–50. Ethel Seaton, *RES* (1956), pp. 55–6 and R.
C. Harrier, *RES* (1960), p. 54, identified the medieval poems in
the MS. The vicissitudes of the MS. before it found its way into
the Duke of Devonshire's library before the end of the sixteenth
century are impossible to trace with any certainty; but we know,

at least, that it belonged to Mary Shelton who copied, and probably composed, some of the poems, and to whom one poem is acrostically addressed.

Those poems printed in my article are indicated by the letters PLPLS.

The contents of D are as follows:

f. 2 CLXXVIII 2ᵛ O cruell causer of vndeservede chaynge v 3 XIV 3ᵛ CLXXIX 4 CXIV 5 CLXX 6 CLXXX 6ᵛ CLXV 7ᵛ My ferefull hope from me ys fledd PLPLS 8 Yowre ferefull hope cannot prevayle PLPLS 8ᵛ Bownd am I now and shall be styll PLPLS 9ᵛ CLXXXI 10ᵛ May not thys hate from the estarte (Anthony Lee) PLPLS 11 Yff I had sufferd thys to yow vnware CXXIII 11ᵛ CLXXXII 12 LI 12ᵛ CLXXXIII 13ᵛ XXXIX 14 CLXXXIV 14ᵛ LXVI 15ᵛ CLXXXV 16ᵛ LII 17 CLXXXVI 17ᵛ CLXXIII 18 CLXXXVII 18ᵛ All women have vertues noble and excelent (Richard Hattfeld) PLPLS 19 XLV 19ᵛ XVI 20 CLXXXVIII 20ᵛ CLXXXIX 21 CXCI 21ᵛ In faythe methynkes yt ys no Ryght (A. I.) Muses 119 and PLPLS 22ᵛ The knot which fyrst my hart dyd strayn (fragment) cf. CLXXII (John Hall ?) He Robyn gentyll robyn (fragment) LV Wel I hawe at other lost (Mary Shelton) 23 CLXXII 24 LV 24ᵛ CXCII 26 Now may I morne as one off late PLPLS 26ᵛ My hart ys persed sodaynly (Margret) PLPLS 27 What thyng shold cawse me to be sad PLPLS 27ᵛ Alas that men be so vngent PLPLS 28 Who hath more cawse for to complayne PLPLS 28ᵛ I may well say with Joyfull hart PLPLS 29 To yowr gentyll letters an answere to resyte PLPLS 29ᵛ And now my pen alas/wyth wyche I wryte (Chaucer) PLPLS 30ᵛ CXCII 31 LVI 32 CXCIII 33 CLXXII 34ᵛ XLIII 35ᵛ XLVI 36ᵛ XLVII 37ᵛ LVII 38ᵛ LIX 39ᵛ LXIII 40 CXCIV 40ᵛ CXCV 41 Ther ys no cure ffor care off mynd PLPLS As ffor my part I know no thyng PLPLS 42 CLXXI 43 CXCVI 43ᵛ What nedythe lyff when I requyer PLPLS 44ᵛ Too yoye in payne my will PLPLS 45 Yff reason govern fantasye (T.H.) PLPLS 46ᵛ What helpythe hope of happy hape (T.H. ?) PLPLS 47ᵛ This rotyd greff will not but growe (T.H.) PLPLS CCXXXIV 49 XCVIII 51 CXCVII 51ᵛ CXCVIII 52ᵛ CXCIX 53 CC, CCI 53ᵛ LXXXIX 54 CCII 54ᵛ CCIII 55 O happy dames that may embrayes (Surrey) 57 My hope is yow for to obtaine (Henry Stuart) PLPLS 58 When I bethynk my wonted ways, see f. 59 58ᵛ CCIV sum say I love sum say I moke PLPLS My hart ys se not to remove

PLPLS 59 Wan I be thyng my wontyd was PLPLS 59ᵛ Wyly no
dought ye be a wry (E. Knyvet) PLPLS To dere is bowght the
doblenes PLPLS For thylke grownde that bearyth the wedes wycke
(Chaucer) 60 To men that knows ye not PLPLS 60ᵛ Myn vnhappy
chaunce to home shall I playn PLPLS 61ᵛ xx Fanecy framed my
hart ffurst PLPLS 62ᵛ In places where that I company PLPLS 63ᵛ
If that I cowlde in versis close (E. Knyvet) PLPLS 64 CCV 65 My
hart is set nat to remoue (Margaret Douglas) PLPLS I ame not she
be proweff off syt PLPLS 65ᵛ Myght I as well within my song be
lay CLIII (fragment) To cowntarffete a mery mode 66 Might I as
well within my songe belay (fragment) The pleasaunt beayt of
swet Delyte Dothe blynd PLPLS 67ᵛ The sueden glance ded mak
me mues PLPLS 68 My ywtheffol days ar past 69 LXXVII, CCVI
69ᵛ I, XIX, XXXVII 70 III 70ᵛ LXVII, CLVIII 71 XL 71ᵛ LXIX,
LXVIII, LVIII, LV (fragment) 72 XXII, CCVII 72ᵛ LXXII, LXXVI,
LXXI 73 LXX, CCVIII, LXXV, LIV, XLII 73ᵛ XLI, CCIX, LXV 74
LXXIV, LXIII, LX 74ᵛ LXII, CCX 75 XIII, XV, CCXI 75ᵛ XIV,
CCXII, X, CCXIII 76ᵛ CCXIV 77 CCXV, CXCVI 77ᵛ CCXVI,
CCXVII, CCXVIII 78 CCXIX 78ᵛ CCXX, CCXXI, CXIII, CXXXVI
79 CCXXII 79ᵛ CCXXIII, CCXXIV 80 CCXXV 80ᵛ CXLVIII 81
CLXXIV, CCXXVI 81ᵛ CXXVIII, CCXXVII, CCXXVIII 82 XXVI
82ᵛ CCXXIX, CCXXX 83 CCXXXI 84 CCXXXII 84ᵛ CCXXXIII
85 CXL 85ᵛ CV 87ᵛ CVI 88 Now that ye be assemblled heer PLPLS
89ᵛ Womans harte vnto no creueltye (Hoccleve) Ys thys afayre
avaunte/ys thys honor (Hoccleve) 90 Yff all the erthe were parch-
ment scrybable ('The Remedy of Love') O marble herte/and yet
more harde perde (Roos) Alas what shuld yt be to yow preiudyce
(Roos) 91 How frendly was Medea to Jason (Chaucer) For
thowgh I had yow to morow agayne (Chaucer) Yff yt be so that ye
so cruel be (Chaucer) 91ᵛ Wo worth the fayre gemme vertulesse
(Chaucer) For loue ys yet the moste stormy lyfe (Chaucer) Alas
wyckyd tonges byn so prest (Chaucer) 92 And who that sayth that
for to love ys vyce (Chaucer)

4. ARUNDEL

As Ruth Hughey's edition is readily available, it is not necessary
to give an account of this MS. The Wyatt poems mostly appear
between ff. 60 and 119, in the following order: CCXXXVI,
CCXXXVII, XVI, IV, VII, IX, X, XLIV, CV, XII, XIII, XVI, XXIV,
XXV, XXVII–XXXIII, XLVII, XLIX, LVI, LXXIX, XCII, XCVII,

XLII, XLVIII, LIV, LIX, LXI, XLIII, XXXIX, XL, LVIII, LXII, LIII, LVII, LXXXII, LXXXIII, XCVIII, CIV, CVII, CVI, VIII, CVIII, XCIV. Later in the MS. (f. 216ᵛ) occur two poems ascribed to Wyatt by T (CCXXXVIII, CCXL) and on f. 217ʳ a poem often thought to be his (CCXXXIV). It should be added that CCXXXIX follows XCIV, and that on f. 105ʳ, following VIII, the following fragment appears, which I previously printed as a doubtful poem.

> But Lorde how straunge is this/that to the iust befall,
> To end with shame lyke synfull folke/and lyue to slaunder thrall!
> Theise Impps lyke wyse of death/as maskers weare for synne,
> Disguysed walke in vertues Cloke/and hyde their measlid skynne.
> Such fruteles travayles then/vnto my thought commend
> Their nature mylde and harmles hart/that gladsome life entend;
> That myngle drincke with sporte,/and sawce their food with myrt[h]
> Convert their sower into sweete,/what wold they more on earthe?
> Thus whyle I sweate in searche/of wisdomes vncowthe leere,
> And to discipher the vnrest/whearein man walketh heare;
> Then with such hongrie thrust/as greedynes forbadd,
> The head to seace, the eye to wynck,/in sifting good from badd.
> When in that shoreles floode/long tyme my shipp had ronne,
> I fownde by state of mortall spryte/soche secreasye not wonne;
> Suche mysteries to revaile/what with doth moste endevour
> Shall waste his tyme, as I have done,/and deeper doutes discever.

A is the primary text for several poems ascribed to Wyatt by Tottel and for the missing lines of three Egerton poems.[1] It is probable, as Miss Hughey argues, that some missing poems were printed in *Nugae Antiquae*.

5. HILL

Miss Hughey has shown that P originally belonged to the Harrington family; that in 1663 it was in the possession of Sir James Tyrrell, in 1791 of the Rev. William Sayle, in 1800 of Thomas Park (who used it for his edition of *Nugae Antiquae*). It was borrowed by Chalmers and Nott, and before it was acquired by the British Museum it belonged successively to Longmans, Heber, and Sir Thomas Phillipps.

The MS. contains part of Phaer's Virgil, a group of Surrey's poems (ff. 50–65ᵛ), some translations from Petrarch,[2] and the

1. Nos. VIII, XCIV, CVIII.
2. Printed in *Proceedings of Leeds Philosophical and Literary Society*, vol. vi (1950) 464–71.

following Wyatt poems: 30 CV   32 XXVI, LXXVI, LX, CCXLI, CXVIII, XLV 33 CCXLII, CCXLIII.

6. HARLEIAN 78

The following Wyatt poems are contained in this MS.: f. 27^r LXVIII, LXXVI, CCXLIV, LIX (first four lines) 27^v CCXLV (possibly Surrey's) 28^r LXXXVI, CXLIII 29^v CIII, CCXXXV (variant version followed by an answer). On the previous page is Surrey's poem 'Of thie lyff Thomas'.

7. PARKER

The Parker MS. contains the text of a poem ascribed to Wyatt by Tottel (CCXLVI) and the first satire, including lines missing from E.

8. ROYAL

This MS., beautifully written, contains only the Penitential Psalms, and it supplies the one line which is missing from both E and A.

II. PRINTED SOURCES

1. Tottel's *Songes and Sonettes* (1557)   T
2. *The Court of Venus*   V
3. *A Boke of Balettes*   BB
4. *Certayne Psalmes* (1550)   Q
5. *Nugae Antiquae* (1769, 1775, 1804)   N

1. TOTTEL

Tottel printed more than ninety poems which he ascribed to Wyatt, and these include fifteen for which no manuscript source has been discovered. (In the second edition he added a few Wyatt poems, and he removed one poem from the Wyatt section.) Where comparison is possible with E – and even with A, B, D, H – it is clear that Tottel's texts are unreliable: the lines have been made smoother and feebler.

   All editors of Wyatt must be indebted to H. E. Rollins' splendid edition of Tottel's *Miscellany* (1929; revised 1965) but his critical judgement on Wyatt as a poet is, I believe, too severe.

2, 3. THE COURT OF VENUS and A BOKE OF BALETTES

These consist of two fragments of *The Court of Venus* – fragment *c.* 1538, the Folger fragment *c.* 1563 – and one fragment of *A Boke of Balettes* (*c.* 1548). The two books, which overlap in contents, are anthologies which contain poor texts of some Wyatt poems, together with songs of doubtful authorship. They have been admirably edited by Russell A. Fraser (1955). Several doubtfully authentic poems are printed from this source.

4. CERTAYNE PSALMES

The Penitential Psalms were first published in 1550 – the printing was completed on 31 December 1549 – with the following title-page and epistle dedicatory:

> Certayne psal/mes chosen out of the psal/ter of Dauid/
> commonly/called thee. vii. penytentiall psal-/mes, drawen
> into englyshe me-/ter by Sir Thomas Wyat/Knyght, whereunto
> is ad-/ded a prologue of yᵉ auc-/tore before euery psal-/
> me, very pleasaunt &/profettable to the/godly reader./
> Imprinted/at London in Paules/Churchyarde, at the signe/
> of the Starre, By/Thomas Ray-/nald. /and Iohn Harryngton.

To the right honorable and his singuler good Lord William, Marqueshe of Northampton, Earle of Essex, Barone of Kendal, Lord Parre, & knight of the most noble ordre of the Garter, youre moste bonden orator at commaundement, Iohn Harrington, wysheth helth, & prosperite wyth encrease of vertue & the mercy of God for euer.

Consyderyng the manyfolde dueties and aboundant seruice that I owe vnto your good Lordeshyp (ryghte honorable, & my Singuler good Lord) I cannot but see infinite causes, why I chiefely of all others oughte (wyth all cherefull and ready endeuoure) to gratifye your good Lordshyp by all meanes possyble, and to applye my selfe wholye too thee same, as one that woulde gladly, but can by no meanes be able to do accordinglye as his bonden duetie requireth: I cannot, I say, but se & acknowledge my selfe bounden, and not able to doo soche seruice as I owe, both for the inestimable benefittes yᵗ your noble progenitors, and also your good Lordeship hath shewed vnto my parents & predycessors: & also to my selfe, as to one least able to do anye acceptable seruice, though the wil be at all tymes most ready, In token wherof, youre lordship shal at all tymes perceaue, by simple thinges, that my littel wit shal be able to inuent that yf myne harte coulde do you any seruice: no labour or trauayle shulde witholde me from doynge my duetie, & that yf busy labour & the hert myght be able to paye the duetye that loue oweth: your lordship shulde in no point fynde me ingrate or vnthankful. And to declare this my redye wyll: I haue dedicated vnto your name, thys little treatyse, whyche after I had perused and by thaduise of others (better learned then my self) determined to put it in printe, that the noble fame of so worthy a knighte, as was thee Auctor hereof, Syr Thomas Wyat, shuld not perish but remayne as wel for hys synguler learning, as valiant dedes in mercyal feates: I thought that I could not find a more worthy patron for soch a mans worke then your Lordship, whom I haue alwayes knowen to be of so godlye a zeale, to thee furtheraunce of gods holy & a secrete gospel, most humbly besechynge your good Lordshippe, herin to accepte my good wyll, and too esteme me as one that wisheth vnto the same al honour, healthe, and prosperous successe.

AMEN

Your good Lordshyppes most humble at commaundement

Iohn Harrington.

The only authentic text of the Penitential Psalms is provided by E, though ll. 100–53 have to be taken from A and R because of a missing leaf in E. A, R, and Q all have unique readings, as one would expect from the habits of copyists in the sixteenth century. It appears[1] that A, R, and Q all had access to E; that R was copied after 1550 since it accepts some of Q's readings; and that some changes were made in A after the publication of Q.

5. NUGAE ANTIQUAE

Since, for a few poems, *Nugae Antiquae* was printed from pages of A, torn out for the purpose, it can be used as a check on the text of four poems which are not in E.

III. THE CANON

This edition contains poems which are certainly by Wyatt, poems which have been ascribed to him either by one of the MSS., Tottel, or modern editors, and poems which are by Wyatt or one of his contemporaries. Everyone would allow that the twelve Egerton poems in the poet's handwriting, and six others with corrections in his hand, are authentically his. Nearly everyone accepts Wyatt's authorship of the seventy-two poems which have 'Wyat' or 'Tho' in the margin, and it is reasonably certain that twenty-four other poems in E, not so authenticated, are his. One

1. Cf. K. Muir, *NQ* (1967), pp. 442–4.

poem in B is certainly Wyatt's (CLXXVI). T ascribes ninety-two poems to Wyatt, including thirty which are not in E. The fact that in the second edition one poem, previously ascribed to Wyatt, was placed among uncertain authors, suggests that Tottel's ascriptions are generally reliable, especially as most of them are confirmed by E and not a single ascription has been proved wrong.

The authorship of the remaining poems is less certain. Wyatt's authorship of some poems is suggested by the fact that they are to be found in A, D, P, or H in groups of his known poems. Five poems in D, not in the 'Wyatt' group, are ascribed to 'W' or 'Wyatt', including 'Blame not my lute' and 'And wilt thou leave me thus?'

The external evidence for Wyatt's authorship is given where possible. Stylistic evidence, though in some cases more convincing than contemporary ascriptions, is apt to be subjective. We know comparatively little about the work of the other Court poets of the period, but we may suspect that they, as well as Wyatt, drew on a stock of poetic clichés. Parallels with known Wyatt poems, therefore, despite his tendency to repeat himself, must be used with caution. On the other hand, Tottel, in his section of uncertain authors, was drawing on the work of Wyatt's contemporaries, and there is hardly a single poem which could be mistaken for Wyatt's.

IV. THE RELATION BETWEEN THE MSS

Although it is impossible to date the various handwritings in D with any accuracy, it may be said that some of the poems, at least, could have been copied in Wyatt's lifetime, and, as several critics have observed, D sometimes preserves earlier versions of the poems in E. Nearly half the E poems are contained in D, but only one of these was written after 1537. Some of the differences between the texts of E and D are due merely to carelessness on the part of the copyists responsible for D. The text of No. XCVIII, for example, incorporates Wyatt's own alterations, but does not incorporate any of the deleted readings. It is therefore safe to say that the copy must have been made after Wyatt's return to England in 1539 and that the variant readings have no authority. But it can be shown by an examination of poems which were corrected by Wyatt himself that some at least of the D poems are based on a text earlier than that of E. In many cases the D text corresponds with that of the E scribe, and it does not incorporate Wyatt's corrections which may have been made at any time between 1536 and 1542. The following may be given as examples – W represents Wyatt's corrected version:

No. XLII   1 Who hath herd of suche tyranny before?   (E)
  Who hathe harde of sich tyrannye before   (D)
  Who hath herd of such crueltye before?   (W)

  5 Had prykt my hert, for to encrese my sore   (E)
  had prickid my herte for tencrese my sore   (D)
  Had prykt myn hert, for to encrese my sore (W)

No. LVI   9 Twixt hope and drede lacking my libertie   (E)
  twyxt hope and drede lakyng my lybertye   (D)
  Twixt hope and drede locking my libertie   (W)

No. LVII   16 Ffor I se well that your high disdain   (E)
  Ffor I se wele that yowr hey dysdayne   (D)
  But I se well that your high disdain   (W)

  20 to rew vpon my pain   (E)
  to rewe apon my payne   (D)
  Reioyse not at my pain   (W)

No. LIX   2 by hilles and dales, by water and by wynd   (E)
  by hyllys by dales by water and by wynd   (D)
  by see, by land, by water and by wynd   (W)

No. LX   1 I ame not ded all though I had a fall   (E)
  I am not ded altho I had a falle   (D)
  He is not ded that somtyme hath a fall   (W)

No. LXIII   3 My worldly joye and blys   (E)
  my worldly joy my blysse   (D)
  My wele, my joye, my blys   (W)

  19 Thus doeth my torment gro   (E)
  Thys doth my torment groo   (D)
  Thus doth my torment goo   (W)

No. LXVIII 2 To get hony of so wondrous fashion (E)
to gett honnye of so wonderous fasshion (D)
To fynd honnye of so wondrous fashion (W)

It can hardly be doubted that these seven poems were derived from a MS. written before E, or from E before Wyatt made his alterations. In another case, however, the second alternative is impossible, for D does not agree with the uncorrected version in E. It is apparent that Wyatt revised the poem twice, the first version being preserved, more or less accurately, in D (No. LXXV):

> Cruell desire my master and my foo
> thy self so chainged for shame how maist thou see
> that I have sought doth chase me to and froo
> whom thou didst rule now rulith the and me
> what right is to rule thy subiectes soo
> and to be rulid bye mutabilitye
> lo where bye the I doubted to have blame
> even now bye dred againe I doubt the same.

In the version Wyatt copied into E he left only one line unchanged:

> Desire, alas, my master and my foo,
> so sore alterd thi selff, how mayst thou se?
> Whome I did seke now chasith me to and fro,
> whom thou didst reule now rewlyth the and me.
> Tyrant it is to rewle thy subiectes so
> by forcyd law and mutabilite?
> For where by the I dowtyd to have blame,
> evyn now by hate agayne I dowt the same.

He was still not satisfied, and in his final version he made changes in three lines, in line 5 reverting almost to the D version:[1]

> Some tyme I sowght that dryvys me to and fro;
> some tyme thow ledst that ledyth the and me.
> What reason is to rewle thy subiectes so
> by forcyd law and mutabilite?

If we turn to the poems in E in which Wyatt himself made no corrections, the difference between these versions and those in D,

1. Perhaps *right* (D) was a mistake.

in the light of the above evidence, may in some cases be due to revision. Two examples may be given. The first is No. III, of which D gives the following version:

> Caeser whan the traytor of egipte
> with thonorable hed ded him presente
> Covering his gladnesse ded represente
> plaint with his tearis outwarde as it is writ.
> And Annyball eke whan fortune ded flitt
> from him and to Rome ded her whele relente
> ded laugh among them whom tearis had besprent
> her cruell dispight inwardelye to shitt.
> soo chaunsith yt oft that everye passhion
> the minde hideth bye collour contrarye
> with faynid visage now sad now merye
> whereby if I laugh at eny season
> yt is by cause I have none other waye
> to cloke my care but vndre sporte and playe.

The differences between this version and that in E can hardly be explained by the assumption that the former derives from the latter or by an ordinary process of textual deterioration. It is surely obvious that D represents an earlier version of the poem. We can see that Wyatt rewrote the second quatrain and made some changes in the last three lines of the sonnet:

> And Hannyball eke, when fortune him shitt
>   Clene from his reign and from all his intent,
>   Laught to his folke, whome sorrowe did torment,
>   His cruell dispite for to disgorge and qwit.
> Whereby if I laught, any tyme or season
>   It is for bicause I have nother way
>   To cloke my care, but vnder sport and play.

The other sonnet is No. XVI. The following is the D version:

> Was neuer yet fyle half so well fylyd
> to fyle a fyle to any smythys intent
> as I was made a fylyng instrument
> to frame other whyle I was begylyd.
> But Reason at my foly hathe smylyd
> And pardond me syns that I me Repent
> my lytyll perseyvyng and tyme myspent
> ffor yowthe dyd lede me and falshed gydyd.

But thys trust I haue by gret aparans
syns that dyscayte ys ay Retournable
of very force yt ys Agreable
that therwithall be done the Recompence
And gylys Reward is small trust for euer
gyle begyld shuld be blamyd neuer.

Here again the only possible explanation of the major differences between D and E is that D represents an earlier version. Wyatt, it would seem, made some radical changes:

There was never ffile half so well filed,
   to file a file for every smythes intent,
   as I was made a filing instrument
   to frame othres, while I was begiled.
But reason hath at my follie smyled,
   and pardons me syns that I me repent
   of my lost yeres and tyme myspent;
   for yeuth did me lede and falshode guyded.
Yet this trust I have of full great aperaunce:
   syns that decept is ay retourneable,
   of very force it is aggreable;
That therewithall be done the recompence.
   Then gile begiled plained should be never,
   And the reward little trust for ever.

These examples are enough to show that the majority of the versions in D preceded those in E. But as more than half the D poems were copied in a single hand at one time, and as this group includes at least six of the poems Wyatt afterwards revised as well as one of the poems written in Spain, it is clear that this group of poems was copied after 1537, and probably after 1539. For most of the poems – and perhaps for all except No. xcviii – the copyist was using an earlier MS. than E.

It is a reasonable hypothesis that the poems peculiar to D were also written early and it is strange that Wyatt did not include them in his own MS. Some pages have been torn from E, but not enough to have contained all the D poems assumed to be Wyatt's. One can only suppose that he had another MS. from which the poems in D, A, P, H, T, and B were ultimately derived.

Fifteen of the E poems appear also in the Blage MS. (B), and of these nine are also in D. Many of the B variants are obviously mistakes.[1] In some poems B agrees with E more than with D:[2] but in others D and E tend to agree against B.[3] The text of one poem, however, not in D, appears to incorporate some of Wyatt's own corrections (No. xcv):

> From thes hye hilles as when a spryng doth fall,
> It tryllyth downe with small and suttyll corse;
> Off this and that it gaders still and shall . . .
> His rayne is rage, then botyth no deny;
> The first estew is only remedy.　　　　(E)

> From these hye hilles as when a spryng doth fall,
> It tryllyth downe with still and suttyll corse;
> Off this and that it gaders ay, and shall . . .
> His rayne is rage, resistans vaylyth none;
> The first estew is remedy alone.　　　　(W)

> As from theys hylles when that a spryng doth fall,
> hyt tryllyth down by styll and suttyll cours;
> and of ech thyng hyt gaders aey and shall . . .
> Hys rayne is rage, resistans ys ther none;
> the furste extwe ys remedy alone.　　　　(B)

Although there are several variants in the B version, it clearly derives from Wyatt's revision. This is particularly apparent in the last two lines. It will be recalled that Blage was with Wyatt in Spain. It seems, therefore, that although B may sometimes be derived from an earlier MS., it is never sufficiently different from E for us to be sure that it preserves earlier versions of the poems.

The variants in the remaining MSS. – A, H, P, C – seem to be without authority though for the passage in cv no longer extant in E, the readings of C are sometimes superior to those of D.

V. EDITORIAL PRINCIPLES

The poems, apart from exceptions mentioned above, are printed in the order in which they appear in the MSS. Where a poem appears in more than one MS., the readings of E are accepted in

---

1. In No. v, e.g. B reads *stykyd* for *soked*, and *serve* for *sterue*. But two readings, *present* (24) and *lyst* (30) correspond to those of D.
2. XVI, XL.
3. LI, LXXII. LI. 10 *wepe* E, D: *sighe* B. LXXII. 4 *relese* E, D; *redres* B. 19 *oon slain* E, D: me you'v slain/me your slaue B. 34 Defamed E, D: disdayned B.

almost every case. For poems not in E, some eclecticism is inevitable; but indifferent readings of B are preferred to those of D; and, for the reason given above, the readings of the MSS. are preferred to those of T and V.

The spelling of the original texts has been retained, but the following changes have been made. (1) The lines have been provided with initial capitals. (2) Proper names have also been capitalized (3) Abbreviations in the MSS. (e.g. &, ō) have been expanded. (4) Where appropriate, the poems have been divided into stanzas. (5) Most of the punctuation has been added.

The early poems in E are heavily punctuated, but in a way which would be misleading to a modern reader. Many of the later poems in the MS. have no stops at all (e.g. xxxv–xli) and it is by no means certain that Wyatt was responsible for all or most of the two hundred punctuation marks in the first hundred lines of the MS.

A case could be made for retaining the solidus employed both by Wyatt and his scribe in many of the poems, e.g.

I.	14	and, as his lorde,/the lowly, entreath
II.	7	true meanyng hert/is had in disdayn
VIII.	130	by mortall thinges/,above the starry skye:
XI.	14	thus to sustain/of eche a part

These exhaust the examples in the first twenty-one poems. They may, perhaps, indicate pauses. (It may be mentioned that in 1.14 there is no/in D; and in the eleven poems of the first twenty-two in E which appear also in D there are nineteen solidi, and in no case do they correspond to those in E.)

An exact transcription of lxxx, one of the poems in Wyatt's hand, will show the kind of changes which have been made in this edition:

> In dowtfull brest,/whilst moderly pitie,/
> w^t furyous famyn/stondyth at debate:/
> sayth thebrew moder/o child vnhappye
> retorne thi blowd/where thow hadst milk of late.
> yeld me those lyms/y^t I made vnto the.
> and entre there where y^u wert generate.
> for of on body agaynst all nature/
> to a nothr must I mak sepulture.

SIGLA

A.   Arundel MS.
B.   Blage MS.
C.   Parker MS. 168
D.   Devonshire MS. 17492
E.   Egerton MS. 2711
F.   Foxwell's edition (1913)
G.   Grimald
H.   Harleian MS. 78
J.   Tillyard's edition (1929)
K.   Kökeritz, 'Dialectal Traits in Sir Thomas Wyatt's Poetry' in *Franciplegius* ed. J. B. Bessinger, Jr. and R. P. Creed (London, 1965)
L.   Muir, *Life and Letters of Sir Thomas Wyatt*
M.   Muir, Muses' Library edition of Wyatt
N.   *Nugae Antiquae*
O.   Nott's edition (1815–16)
P.   Hill MS. 36529
Q.   *Certayne Psalmes*
R.   Royal MS. 17^A, xxii
S.   Southall, *The Courtly Maker*, and private communications
T.   Tottel's *Songes and Sonettes*
U.   Muir, ed. *Unpublished Poems*
V.   *The Court of Venus*
W.   *Wyatt*
X.   Ashmole MS. 48
Z.   B.M. Add. MS. 18752
BB.   *A Boke of Balettes*
CC.   Cambridge University MS., ff. 5, 14
GG.   *The Gorgeous Gallery of Gallant Inventions*
WMT. W. M. Tydeman

I

Poems from the Egerton Manuscript

I

BEHOLD, love, thy power how she dispiseth!
My great payne how litle she regardeth!
The holy oth, wherof she taketh no cure
Broken she hath: and yet she bideth sure,
Right at her ease: and litle she dredeth.   5
Wepened thou art: and she vnarmed sitteth:
To the disdaynfull, her liff she ledeth:
To me spitefull, withoute cause, or mesure.
       Behold, love!

I ame in hold: if pitie the meveth,   10
Goo bend thy bowe: that stony hertes breketh:
And, with some stroke, revenge the displeasure
Of thee and him, that sorrowe doeth endure,
And, as his lorde, the lowly entreath.
       Behold, love!   15

II

WHAT vaileth trouth? or, by it, to take payn?
To stryve, by stedfastnes, for to attayne,
To be iuste, and true: and fle from dowblenes:
Sythens all alike, where rueleth craftines

I. D, T.   2 great] greuous T. payne] grief D.   3 holy] solemne T. taketh] takes T.
4 + beholde love D.   5 she] thee she T.   6 Wepened thou art] thou haste weapon D.
7 her] all her T.   8 spitefull] dispitefull D. cause] iust cause T.   9 Behold Loue,
how proudly she triumpheth T.   10 pitie the] thee pitie T. meveth] me with D.   12
displeasure] great displeasure T.   13 sorrowe] sorrowes D.   14 lowly] lowly here
T. entreath] E; entreathe D; entreateth T.
  [*Authorship:* 'Tho.', marginal ascription E; ascribed to W by T.]

II. T.   3 To . . . true] How to be iust T.   4 Sythens] since T,

Rewarded is boeth fals, and plain.   5
Sonest he spedeth, that moost can fain;
True meanyng hert is had in disdayn.
Against deceipte and dowblenes
          What vaileth trouth?

Decyved is he by crafty trayn   10
That meaneth no gile and doeth remayn
Within the trapp, withoute redresse,
But, for to love, lo, suche a maisteres,
Whose crueltie nothing can refrayn,
          What vaileth trouth?   15

III

CAESAR, when that the traytour of Egipt
     With th'onourable hed did him present,
     Covering his gladness did represent
     Playnt with his teeres owteward, as it is writt:
And Hannyball eke, when fortune him shitt   5
     Clene from his reign and from all his intent,
     Laught to his folke whome sorrowe did torment,
     His cruell dispite for to disgorge and qwit.
So chaunceth it oft that every passion
     The mynde hideth by colour contrary   10
     With fayned visage, now sad, now mery:
Whereby, if I laught, any tyme, or season
     It is for bicause I have nother way
     To cloke my care but vnder spoort and play.

---

5 fals] crafty false T. 6 spedeth] spedes T. fain] lye and fayn T. 7 disdayn] hye disdain T. 8 dowblenes] cloked doublenesse T. 9 trouth] troth, or parfit stedfastnesse T. 10 by] by false and T. 11 meaneth] meanes T. and] and faithfull T. 12 without] without help or T. 13 maisteres] sterne maistresse T. 14–15 Where cruelty dwelles, alas it were in vain T.

[*Authorship:* Ascribed to W by T. Probably Tho. beside no. I refers also to this poem.]

III. D, T.   1 when that] whan D. 3 gladness] hartes gladnesse T. 5 And ... eke] Eke Hannibal T. him shitt] ded flitt D; him outshyt T. 6–8 from him and to Rome ded her whele relente/ded laugh among thim whom teares had besprent/her cruell dispight inwardelye to shitt D. 9 it oft] me T. 12 if I ... or] if that I laught at my (any) T. laught, any tyme or] laught at eny D. 13 for ... nother] by cause I have none other D; because I haue none other T.

[*Authorship:* Ascribed to W by T.]

IV

THE longe love, that in my thought doeth harbar
　　And in myn hert doeth kepe his residence
　　Into my face preseth with bold pretence,
　　And therin campeth, spreding his baner.
She that me lerneth to love and suffre　　　　　　　5
　　And will that my trust, and lustes negligence
　　Be rayned by reason, shame, and reverence
　　With his hardines taketh displeasure.
Wherewithall, vnto the hertes forrest he fleith,
　　Leving his entreprise with payne and cry　　　　10
　　And there him hideth and not appereth.
What may I do when my maister fereth,
　　But, in the felde, with him to lyve and dye?
　　For goode is the liff, ending faithfully.

V

ALAS the greiff, and dedly wofull smert,
The carefull chaunce, shapen afore my shert,
The sorrowfull teres, the sighes hote as fyer,
That cruell love hath long soked from myn hert,
And for reward of ouer greate desire　　　　　　　5
Disdaynfull dowblenes have I for my hiere!

O lost seruise! O payn ill rewarded!
O pitiful hert with payn enlarged!
O faithfull mynd, too sodenly assented!
Retourne, Alas, sethens thou art not regarded;　　10
Too great a prouf of true faith presented
Causeth by right suche faith to be repented.

IV. A, T.　4 therin] there T.　5 suffre] to suffer T.　6 will] wills A; willes T.
lustes] *G's correction*, A, T; lust E　8 taketh] takes A, T.　9 Wherewithall] Wher-
with loue T. vnto] to T.
　　[*Authorship:* Ascribed to W by T; in W section of A.]

V. B, D.　1-12] *omitted* D.　3 the sighes] sethes B.　4 soked] stykyd B. myn]
my B.　5 ouer] *later correction* E; oᴿ E, B.　6 have I] I have now B.　7 ill] euyll B.
9 too] so B.　10 sethens] syns B.　11 prouf] sorrowe B.

O cruel causer of vnderserued chaunge
By great desire vnconstantly to raunge
Is this your waye for prouf of stedfastnes?   15
Perdy you knowe – the thing was not so straunge –
By former prouff to muche my faithfulnes:
What nedeth, then, suche coloured dowblenes?

I have wailed thus weping in nyghtly payne
In sobbes, and sighes, Alas! and all in vayne,   20
In inward plaint and hertes wofull torment;
And yet, Alas, lo! crueltie and disdayn
Have set at noght a faithfull true intent
And price hath priuilege trouth to prevent.

But though I sterue and to my deth still morne,   25
And pece mele in peces though I be torne,
And though I dye, yelding my weried goost,
Shall never thing again make me retorne:
I qwite th'entreprise of that that I have lost
To whome so euer lust for to proffer moost.   30

VI

BUT sethens you it asaye to kyll
By crueltie and dowblenes,
That that was yowers, you seke to spill
Against all right and gentilnes;
And sethens you will, euen so I will.   5

And then, helas, when no redresse
Can be, to late ye shall repent,
And say your self with woordes expresse:
Helas, an hert of true intent
Slain haue I by vnfaithfulnes!   10

13 chaunge] chaunce B.   16 you] ye B; I D.   19 nyghtly] myghty D.   24 prevent]
present B; presentt D.   25 sterue] serue B.   26 mele] me B.   28 retorne] to torne B.
30 lust] liste B, D.
   [*Authorship:* Between two W poems in D.]

VI. A leaf is missing with the earlier stanzas of this poem. Four lines, in a different
(?) hand, follow:

I plede, and reason my selffe emonge
agaynst reason, howe I suffer
but, she that doethe me all the wronge
I plede and reason my sealffe emonge.

VII

WHO so list to hounte I know where is an hynde;
    But as for me, helas, I may no more:
    The vayne travaill hath weried me so sore,
    I ame of theim that farthest cometh behinde;
Yet may I by no meanes my weried mynde   5
    Drawe from the Diere: but as she fleeth afore
    Faynting I folowe; I leve of therefore,
    Sithens in a nett I seke to hold the wynde.
Who list her hount I put him owte of dowbte,
    As well as I may spend his tyme in vain: 10
    And graven with Diamondes in letters plain
There is written her faier neck rounde abowte:
    'Noli me tangere for Cesars I ame,
    And wylde for to hold though I seme tame'.

VIII

MYNE olde dere En'mye, my froward master,
Afore that Quene I caused to be acited;
Which holdeth the divine parte of nature:
That, lyke as goolde, in fyre he mought be tryed.
Charged with dolour, theare I me presented   5
With horrible fear, as one that greatlye dredith
A wrongfull death, and iustice alwaye seekethe.

And thus I sayde: 'Once my lefte foote, Madame,
When I was yonge I sett within his reigne;
Whearby other than fierlye burninge flame   10
I never felt, but many a grevous payne;
Tourment I suffred, angre and disdayne,
That myne oppressed patience was past
And I myne owne life hated at the last.

Thus hytherto have I my time passed   15
In payne and smarte. What wayes proffitable,

VII. B, A.   1 an] a B.   2 helas] alas B.   6 fleeth] flyth B.   7 leve] must leve B.   8 Sithens] sens B; sins *later correction* E.   11 And graven] and grave A; Igravyn B   14 And . . . hold] wyld to be caught B.
    [*Authorship:* 'Wyat' is written in the margin. The poem also appears in the W section of A.]

VIII. A, T.   1–21] A; *omitted* E.   3 nature] our nature T.
    C

How many pleasant dayes have me escaped
In serving this false lyer so deceaveable?
What witt have wordes so prest and forceable,
That may contayne my great myshappynesse,   20
And iust complayntes of his vngentlenesse?

O small hony, much aloes, and gall,
In bitterness have my blynde lyfe taisted
His fals swetenes, that torneth as a ball,
With the amourous dawnce, have made me traced: 25
And where I had my thought and mynde araced
From all erthely frailnes and vain pleasure,
He toke me from rest, and set me in errour.

He hath made me regarde god muche less then I ought
And to my self to take right litle heede: 30
And, for a woman, have I set at nought
All othre thoughtes, in this onely to spede:
And he was onely counceillour of this dede,
Always wheting my youthely desyere
On the cruell whetstone, tempered with fiere.   35

But (helas) where, nowe, had I ever wit?
Or els any othre gift geven me of nature?
That souner shall chaunge my weryed sprite
Then the obstinate will that is my rueler.
So robbeth my libertie with displeasure   40
This wicked traytour whom I thus accuse
That bitter liff have torned me in pleasaunt vse.

22 O] So A, T.   23 have . . . taisted] my blynde Lif hath ytasted A, T.   24 swetenes]
semblaunce A, T.   25 the] faire and A, T. have made me] made me be A, T.   26
araced] A, T; ataced E.   27 From all] from A, T. vain] from vayne A, T.   28 He
. . . rest] Me from my rest he toke A, T. set me] sett A, T.   29 God made he me
regard, lesse than I oughte A, T.   30 take right] take A.   34 Whetting all wayes my
youthlye frayle desyre A, T.   35 On the] On A, T.   36 helas] oh alas A, T. where,
nowe,] wheare A, T.   37 Or . . . othre] Or other A, T. geven me] geuen to me T.
38 chaunge] be chaunged A, T.   40 my libertie] he my freedome A, T.   41 whom]
A, T; whon? E.   42 have torned me] hath turned A, T.

He hath chased me thorough dyvers regions,
Thorough desert wodes and sherp high mountaignes,
Thorough frowarde people and straite pressions,   45
Thorrough rocky sees, over hilles and playnes,
With wery travaill and labourous paynes,
Always in trouble and in tediousnes,
In all errour and daungerous distres.

But nother he, nor she, my tother ffoo,   50
For all my flyght, did ever me forsake:
That though tymely deth hath ben to sloo
That, as yet, it hath me not overtake;
The hevynly goodenes of pitie do it slake
And not this his cruell extreme tyranny   55
That fedeth hym with my care and mysery.

Syns I was his, owre rested I never,
Nor loke for to do, and eke the waky nyghtes
The bannysshed slepe may no wyse recouer.
By decept and by force over my sprites   60
He is rueler; and syns there never bell strikes
Where I ame, that I here not my playntes to renewe;
And he himself, he knoweth that that I say is true.

Ffor never wormes have an old stock eaten
As he my hert, where he is alwaye resident;   65
And doeth the same with deth daily thretyn.
Thens com the teres and the bitter torment,
The sighes, the wordes, and eke the languisshement
That annoye boeth me and, peraduenture, othre;
Iudge thou, that knowest th'one and th'othre'.   70

43 chased me] me hasted A, T. thorough] throughe A, T. 44 Thorough] Throughe A, T. 45 Thorough] Throughe A, T. straite pressions] through bitter passions A, T. 46 Thorrough] Throughe A, T. over] and over A, T. 47 and] and with A, T. 49. In all] All in A, T. 52 though] though my A, T. 53 as] me as A, T. hath me not T. 54 goodenes] Goddz G; gods A; goddes T. slake] G, A, T; shake E. 55 not] note G, A, T. this] they this A, T. cruell extreme] cruell A, T. 56 fedeth] feedes A, T. 58 for to] to A, T. 59 no] in no A, T. 60 By . . . sprites] by guyle and force, over my thralled sprites A, T. 61 and . . . bell] syns whiche bell never A, T. strikes] G, A, T; strekes ?E. 62 That I heare not, as sownding to renewe A, T. 63 And . . . say is] My playntes/hym self, he knowes, that I say A, T. (knoweth T). 64 have . . . stock] olde rotten stocke have A, T. 65 alwaye resident] is resydent A, T. 67 the bitter] thence the bitter A, T. 69 annoye] noye A, T. 70 th'one and th'othre] thone & thothre E; the one and eke the tother A, T.

Myn aduersary, with grevous reprouff,
Thus he began: 'here, lady, th'othre part:
That the plain trueth from which he draweth alowff,
This vnkynd man, shall shew ere that I part.
In yonge age I toke him from that art   75
That selleth wordes, and maketh a clattering knyght;
And of my welth I gave him the delight.

Nowe shameth he not on me for to complain
That held him evermore in pleasaunt game
From his desire that myght have ben his payne;   80
Yet onely thereby I broght him to some frame,
Which, as wretchednes he doth greately blame:
And towerd honour I qwickened his wit,
Where els, as a daskard, he myght have sitt.

He knoweth that Atrides, that made Troye frete   85
And Hannyball, to Rome so trobelous;
Whome Homere honoured, Achilles that grete,
And the Affricane Scipion, the famous,
And many othre, by much vertue glorious,
Whose fame and honour did bryng theim above   90
I did let fall in base dishonest love.

And vnto him, thoughe he no deles worthy were
I chose right the best of many a mylion,
That, vnder the mone, was never her pere,
Of wisdome, womanhode, and discretion;   95
And of my grace I gave her suche a facon
And eke suche a way I taught her for to teche,
That never base thought his hert myght have reche.

71 aduersary] aduersair T. with] with suche A, T.   72 th'othre] thothre E.   73 trueth] trothe A, T.   74 This] Thus A. shall] may A, T. ere] G, T; err A; here E. 75 yonge] his yonge A, T.   76 maketh] makes A, T.   77 the delight] my delight A, T.   78 shameth] shames A, T.   79 game] gayne A. T.   80–147] *omitted* A.   81 onely thereby] therby alone T.   82 Which, as] Which now, as T. greately] so T.   83 I qwickened] quicknd I T.   84 Where ... daskard] Where: as a daskard els T. myght] mought T.   85 that Atrides] how great Atride T.   89 vertue] nurture Tl; honour T2.   92 no deles worthy] vnworthy T.   93 chose right] chose T.   94 That, vnder sonne yet neuer was her pere T.   95 discretion] of discrecion T.   97 a way] way T.   98 myght have reche] so hye might reche, T.

Evermore thus to content his maistres
That was his onely frame of honeste.   100
I sterred him, still, towerd gentilnes,
And caused him to regard fidelitie;
Patiens I taught him in aduersite:
Suche vertues he lerned in my great schole,
Wherof he repenteth, the ignoraunt ffole.   105

These were the deceptes and the bitter gall
That I have vsed, the torment and the anger;
Sweter then for to injoye eny othre in all.
Of right good seede ill fruyte I gather
And so hath he that th'unkynd doeth forther.   110
I norisshe a Serpent vnder my wyng
And of his nature nowe gynneth he to styng.

And for to tell at last my great seruise
From thousand dishonestes I have him drawen:
That by my meanes in no maner of wyse   115
Never vile pleasure him hath overthrawen
Where in his dede shame hath him alwaies gnawen
Dowbting repoort that should com to her eere;
Whome now he accuseth, he wonnted to fere.

What soever he hath of any honest custume   120
Of her and me, that holdeth he every wit;
But, lo, there was never nyghtely fantome
So ferre in errour as he is from his wit;
To plain on vs he stryveth with the bit,
Which may ruell him and do him pleasure and pain,   125
And in oon Oure make all his greif remayn.

But oon thing there is above all othre:
I gave him wynges wherewith he myght flye

101 sterred] stirred T. 104 he lerned] learned he T. 105 he repenteth] repenteth, now T. 106 deceptes and the] same deceites and T. 108 then . . . all] then euer dyd to other fall T. 109 I] loe thus I T. 110 hath] shall T. th'unkynd] thunkynd E; the vnkinde T. 111 I . . . Serpent] A Serpent nourish I T. vnder] T; vnger E. 112 And . . . nowe] And now of nature T. 114 I have] have I T. 115 in . . . of] him in no maner T. 116 him] once T. 119 accuseth, he] blames, her T. to] he to T. 120 soever] euer T. 121 holdeth] holdes T. 122 there was never] yet never was there T. 126 remayn] his gayn T. 128 flye] vpflie T.

To honour and fame, and if he would farther
By mortall thinges above the starry skye;   130
Considering the pleasure that an Iye
Myght geve in erthe by reason of his love
What should that be, that lasteth still above?

And he the same himself hath sayed, or this,
But now forgotten is both that and I   135
That gave her him his onely welth and blisse'.
And, at this worde, with dedly shright and cry:
'Thou gave her me' (quod I) 'but, by and by
Thou toke her streight from me, that wo worth thee!'
'Not I' (quod he) 'but price, that is well worthy.'   140

At last, boethe, eche for himself, concluded,
I trembling; but he, with small reverence:
'Lo, thus, as we have nowe eche othre accused,
Dere lady, we wayte onely thy sentence'.
She, smyling: 'after thissaid audience,   145
It liketh me' (quod she) 'to have herd your question:
But lenger tyme doth aske resolution.'

IX

WAS I never, yet, of your love greeved:
    Nor never shall, while that my liff doeth last:
    But of hating myself that date is past:
    And teeres continuell sore have me weried.
I will not yet in my grave be buried: 5
    Nor on my tombe your name yfixed fast:
    As cruell cause, that did the sperit sone hast
    Ffrom th'unhappy bonys, by great sighes sterred.
Then, if an hert of amourous faith and will

---

129 farther] to higher T. 130 By] Than T. 134 or] ere T. 137 shright] shreke T.
138 me] once T. 139 streight] ayen T. 140 Not I but price: more worth than thou
(quod he) T. worthy] Flügel; worth E. 141 boethe, eche] eche other for T. 142
trembling] trembling still T. 143 as . . . othre] as we eche other haue T. 144 we . . .
they] now we waite thyne onely T. 145 after thissaid] at the whisted T. 147 aske]
ask a T.

[*Authorship:* In W sections of A and T.]

IX. A, T. 1 Was . . . yet] Yet was I neuer T. yet . . . love] of your love yet A. 6
yfixed] haue fixed T. 7 the sperit] my sprite T.

May content you, withoute doyng greiff,   10
Please it you so, to this to doo releiff:
Yf, othre wise, ye seke for to fulfill
Your disdain, ye erre, and shall not as ye wene:
And ye yourself the cause therof hath bene.

X

ECHE man me telleth I chaunge moost my devise.
And on my faith me thinck it goode reason
To chaunge propose like after the season,
Ffor in every cas to kepe still oon gyse
Ys mytt for theim that would be taken wyse,   5
And I ame not of suche maner condition,
But treted after a dyvers fasshion,
And therupon my dyvernes doeth rise.
But you that blame this dyvernes moost,
Chaunge you no more, but still after oon rate   10
Trete ye me well, and kepe ye in the same state;
And while with me doeth dwell this weried goost,
My word nor I shall not be variable,
But alwaies oon, your owne boeth ferme and stable.

XI

FFAREWELL, the rayn of crueltie!
Though that with pain my libertie
Dere have I boght, yet shall surete
Conduyt my thoght of Joyes nede.

Of force I must forsake pleasure   5
A goode cause just syns I endure
Thereby my woo, which be ye sure
Shall therewith goo, me to recure.

10 withoute] withouten T.   13 disdain] wrath T.   14 ye] you A, T.
[*Authorship:* 'Wyat' in margin of E; among W poems in A and T.]

X. D, A, T.   1 me telleth] tells me D; me tellth T. moost] of D.   3 propose] pur-
pose D, A, T. like] even D.   4 every] ech T.   8, 9 dyvernes] dyversnes D, A, T.   9
that . . . dyvernes] this diuersnesse that blamen T.   11 ye me] you me T. ye in the]
ye the D; you in that T.   13 not] never D.   14 oon, your] as your D. your] you A.
[*Authorship:* 'Wyat' in margin; in W sections of A and T.]

XI. T.   1 rayn] hart T.   3 yet . . . surete] and wofully T.   4 Finisht my fearfull
tragedy T.   5 pleasure] such pleasure: T.

I fare as oon escaped that fleith,
Glad that is gone yet still fereth,   10
Spied to be cawght, and so dredeth
That he for nought his pain leseth.

In joyfull pain reioyse myn hert,
Thus to sustain of eche a part;
Let not this song from the estert;   15
Welcome emong my plaisaunt smert.

XII

Y F amours faith, an hert vnfayned,
    A swete languor, a great lovely desire,
    Yf honest will kyndelled in gentill fiere,
    Yf long errour in a blynde maze chayned,
Yf in my visage eche thought depaynted,   5
    Or else in my sperklyng voyse lower or higher,
    Which nowe fere, nowe shame, wofully doth tyer,
    Yf a pale colour which love hath stayned,
Yf to have an othre then my selfe more dere,
    Yf wailing or sighting continuelly   10
    With sorrowful anger feding bissely,
Yf burning a farre of and fresing nere
    Ar cause that by love my self I distroye,
    Yours is the fault and myn the great annoye.

XIII

F F A R E W E L L , Love, and all thy lawes for ever;
    Thy bayted hookes shall tangill me no more;
    Senec and Plato call me from thy lore,
    To perfaict welth my wit for to endever.

10 that] he T.   13 myn] my T.   14 a part] T; apart E.
    [*Authorship:* In W section of T.]

XII. A, T.   1 amours] amorous A, T. faith, an] fayth, or if an T.   5 depaynted] dis-
tayned T.   6 Or else in] Or if T.   7 nowe . . . shame] fear and shame, so T.   8 a pale]
pale T. love hath] loue alas hath T.   10 sighting] sighing A, T.   12 farre] fall A, T.
13 Ar] T; or E, A. distroye] stroy T.
    [*Authorship:* 'Wyat' in margin of E; among W poems in A and T.]

XIII. A, D, T.   1 Ffarewell . . . thy] Nowe farewell love and thye D.   3 Senec . . .
call] to sore a profe hathe called D.   4 perfaict . . . to] surer welthe my wyttes to D.

In blynde errour when I did perseuer,   5
   Thy sherpe repulce that pricketh ay so sore
   Hath taught me to sett in tryfels no store
   And scape fourth syns libertie is lever.
Therefore, farewell; goo trouble yonger hertes
   And in me clayme no more authoritie;   10
   With idill yeuth goo vse thy propertie
And theron spend thy many britill dertes:
   For hetherto though I have lost all my tyme,
   Me lusteth no lenger rotten boughes to clyme.

XIV

Mɣ hert I gave the not to do it payn,
   But to preserue it was to the taken;
   I serued the not to be forsaken,
   But that I should be rewarded again.
I was content thy seruant to remayn,   5
   But not to be payed vnder this fasshion.
   Nowe syns in the is none othre reason,
   Displease the not if that I do refrain.
Vnsaciat of my woo and thy desire,
   Assured be craft to excuse thy fault;   10
   But syns it please thee to fain a default,
Farewell, I say, parting from the fyer:
   For he that beleveth bering in hand
   Plowith in water and soweth in the sand.

---

5 when I] when last I D. 6 ay so] so D. 7 Taught me in trifles that I set no store T.
8 And] but D, T. syns] for D; thence: since T. 11 thy] A, D, T; they E. 12
theron . . . many] thereupon go spende thy D. 13 though I] I D. lost all] lost D, T.
14 lusteth] liste D, T. lenger rotten] longe & rottyn D.
   [*Authorship:* 'Tho.' in E; in W sections of A and T.]
XIV. A, D (iii), D (lxxv), T. 2 it] lo it T. 3 to be] that I should be T. 4 be re-
warded] receiue reward T. 5 thy seruant] thy slave D (iii). 6] And, not to be repayd
after this fashion T1; on this fashion T2. this] suche D. 7 syns] sins that D (lxxv).
is] is there T. none othre] no maner of D (iii). 8 if that] tho D (iii). refrain] restraine
D (lxxv). 9 thy] my D (iii). 10] *omitted* D (iii). be] by D (lxxv), T. 11] *omitted*
D. a] *omitted* T. 12 parting] departing T. 13 beleveth] beleves D (iii); doth beleue T.
14 Plowith . . . soweth] D (lxxv); . . . with E (*torn*); ploues in the water and sows D
(iii); Ploweth in the water: and soweth T. the sand] sand D (lxxv).
   [*Authorship:* 'Wyat' in margin; in W section of T.]

XV

FFOR to love her for her lokes lovely
My hert was set in thought right fermely,
Trusting by trought to have had redresse;
But she hath made an othre promes
And hath geven me leve full honestly   5
Yet do I not reioyse it greatly,
For on my faith I loved to surely;
But reason will that I do sesse
      For to love her.

Syns that in love the paynes ben dedly,   10
Me thinck it best that reddely
I do retorne to my first adresse;
For at this tyme to great is the prese,
And perilles appere to abundauntely
      For to love her.   15

XVI

THERE was never ffile half so well filed
To file a file for every smythes intent,
As I was made a filing instrument
To frame othre while I was begiled.
But reason hath at my follie smyled   5
And pardond me syns that I me repent
Of my lost yeres and tyme myspent,
For yeuth did me lede and falshode guyded.
Yet this trust I have of full great aperaunce:
Syns that decept is ay retourneable   10
Of very force it is aggreable;
That therewithall be done the recompence.
Then gile begiled plained should be never
And the reward litle trust for ever.

XV. D.   4 an othre] anodre D.   7 to] so D.   8 will] woll D. sesse] leesse D.   10
ben] be D.   11 thinck] thinckes D.   14 perilles] perells D.

XVI. A (2) B, D, T.   1 Was neuer yet fyle [file yet T] half so well fylyd D.   2 for
every] for anye A, B, T; to any D.   4 othre] othres G; a nother B. while I] while that
I T.   5 reason] reason, loe T. hath . . . follie] at my foly hathe D.   6 pardond] G, D,
T; pardons B; pardon E.   7 Of . . . yeres] my lytyll perseyvyng D. tyme] of my
time T.   8 did me lede] did lede me D; led me T. guyded] me gyded B; me mis-
guided T; gylyd D.   9 Yet] But D. of full great] off gret B; by gret D.   11 very]

XVII

HELPE me to seke for I lost it there:
And if that ye have founde it, ye that be here,
And seke to convaye it secretely,
Handell it soft and trete it tenderly
Or els it will plain and then appere,   5
But rather restore it mannerly,
Syns that I do aske it thus honestly;
For to lese it it sitteth me to neere:
      Helpe me to seke.

Alas, and is there no remedy,   10
But I have I thus lost it wilfully?
I wis it was a thing all to dere
To be bestowed and wist not where.
It was myn hert: I pray you hertely
      Help me to seke.   15

XVIII

YF it be so that I forsake the,
As banysshed from thy company,
Yet my hert, my mynde and myn affection
Shall still remain in thy perfection;
And right as thou lyst so order me.   5
But some would saye in their opinion
Revoulsed is thy good intention;
Then may I well blame thy cruelte,
      Yf it be so.

But myself I say on this fasshion,   10
I have her hert in my possession,

euery B.   13–14 & gylys Reward is small trust for euer/gyle begyld shuld be blamed
neuer D.   13 Then] the B. plained] blamyd B.   14 litle] but lyttyl B.
  [*Authorship:* 'Tho' in E; 'tv' in D; among W poems in A and T.]

XVII. [*Authorship:* 'Wyat' in margin.]

XVIII.   7 Revoulsed] revoultid G.
  [*Authorship:* 'Wyat' in margin.]

And of it self there cannot, perdy,
By no meanes love an herteles body;
And, on my faith, good is the reason,
　　　　If it be so.　　　　　　　　　　15

XIX

THOU hast no faith of him that hath none,
But thou must love him nedes by reason;
For as saieth a proverbe notable,
Eche thing seketh his semblable:
And thou hast thyn of thy condition.　　　　5
Yet is it not the thing I passe on,
Nor hote nor cold of myn affection;
For syns thyn hert is so mutable,
　　　　Thou hast no faith.

I thought the true withoute exception,　　　　10
But I perceve I lacked discretion
To fasshion faith to wordes mutable:
Thy thought is to light and variable,
To chaunge so oft withoute occasion,
　　　　Thou hast no faith.　　　　　　　　15

XX

GOO burnyng sighes Vnto the frosen hert!
Goo breke the Ise which pites paynfull dert
Myght never perse, and if mortall prayer
In hevyn may be herd, at lest I desire
That deth or mercy be end of my smart.　　　　5
Take with the payne wherof I have my part,

XIX. D.　1 that] that eke D.　2 reason] good reason D.　3 For as the proverbe saith right notable D.　4 Eche] everye D.　5 thy] thy owne D.　6 on] vppon D.　7 Nor] nother D. of] is G, D.　8 thyn] thi D. is] is thus D.　12 fasshion] fasten D. mutable] so dobtable D.
　　[*Authorship:* 'Tho,' in margin.]

XX. D, T.　2 which pites] G, T; with pite E; with piteus D.　3 if] if that T.　4 may . . . lest] be herd, at lest yet T.　5 be . . . my] end my wofull T.　6 the] thee T; you D.

And eke the flame from which I cannot stert
And leve me then in rest, I you require:
   Goo burning sighes!

I must goo worke, I se, by craft and art,   10
For trueth and faith in her is laide apart;
Alas, I cannot therefore assaill her
With pitefull plaint and scalding fyer,
That oute of my brest doeth straynably stert:
   Goo burning sighes!   15

XXI

I T may be good, like it who list,
But I do dowbt: who can me blame?
For oft assured yet have I myst,
And now again I fere the same:
The wyndy wordes, the Ies quaynt game,   5
Of soden chaunge maketh me agast:
For dred to fall I stond not fast.

Alas! I tred an endles maze
That seketh to accorde two contraries;
And hope still, and nothing hase,   10
Imprisoned in libertes,
As oon unhard and still that cries;
Alwaies thursty and yet nothing I tast:
For dred to fall I stond not fast.

Assured, I dowbt I be not sure;   15
And should I trust to suche suretie
That oft hath put the prouff in vre
And never hath founde it trusty?

9 sighes] sighes fulfil that I desire T. 14 That from my brest disceiuably doth start T.
  [*Authorship:* 'Wyat' in margin; in W section of T.]
XXI. B, T. 3 assured . . . I] as sure as I haue hit B. 5] The wordes that from your
mouth last came T. Ies] yeche B. 6 maketh] make T. 9 seketh to accorde] seke
taccord T. seketh] seekes B. 10 hope] hope thus T. nothing] naught elles B. 13 yet
nothing I] naught doth T. nothing] naught B. 16 to] vnto T. 18 hath founde] yet

Nay, sir, In faith it were great foly.
And yet my liff thus I do wast: 20
For dred to fall I stond not fast.

XXII

RESOUND my voyse, ye woodes that here me plain,
Boeth hilles and vales causing reflexion;
And Ryvers eke record ye of my pain,
Which have ye oft forced by compassion
As Judges to here myn exclamation;   5
Emong whome pitie I fynde doeth remayn:
Where I it seke, Alas, there is disdain.

Oft ye Revers, to here my wofull sounde,
Have stopt your course and, plainly to expresse,
Many a tere by moystour of the grounde   10
The erth hath wept to here my hevenes;
Which causeles to suffre without redresse
The howgy okes have rored in the wynde:
Eche thing me thought complayning in their kynde.

Why, then, helas, doeth not she on me rew?   15
Or is her hert so herd that no pitie
May in it synke, my Joye for to renew?
O stony hert, who hath thus joyned the
So cruell that art, cloked with beaultie?
No grace to me from the there may procede,   20
But as rewarded deth for to be my mede.

proued B.   19 great] but B.   20 I do] doo I B, T.   21 I] that B.
   [*Authorship:* 'Wyat' in margin; in W section of T.]

XXII. D, T.   1 here] herith D.   2 vales] valeis D. causing] causers of D.   4 have
. . . forced] haue oft forced ye T.   5 myn] my T.   6 pitie I fynde] I finde pitye D;
such (I finde) yet T1; ruth (I finde) yet T2.   7 seke] sought D.   9 to expresse]
txepresse D.   10 a tere] atree D.   12 to suffre] I endure T.   14 complayning in their]
moving in the D.   18 stony] tygres D. who] D; ho E. thus] this E; so D. joyned]
clokid D; framed T.   19 So . . . art] that arte so cruell D; So cruell? that art T.
cloked] couered D.   20 No . . . procede] there is no grace from the that maye pro-
cede D; That from thee may no grace to me procede T.   21 rewarded] reward D, T.
   [*Authorship:* 'Wyat' in margin; in W section of T.]

XXIII

In faith I wot not well what to say,
Thy chaunces ben so wonderous,
Thou fortune, with thy dyvers play
That causeth Joy full dolourous,
And eke the same right Joyus: 5
Yet though thy chayne hath me enwrapt
Spite of thy hap, hap hath well hapt.

Though thou me set for a wounder
And sekest thy chaunge to do me payn,
Mens myndes yet may thou not order,   10
And honeste, and it remayn,
Shall shyne for all thy clowdy rayn;
In vayn thou sekest to have trapped:
Spite of thy hap, hap hath well happed.

In hindering thou diddest fourther,   15
And made a gap where was a stile;
Cruell willes ben oft put vnder,
Wenyng to lowre thou diddist smyle.
Lorde! how thy self thou diddist begile,
That in thy cares wouldest me have lapped!   20
But spite of thy hap, hap hath well happed.

XXIV

Som fowles there be that have so perfaict sight,
Agayn the Sonne their Iyes for to defend,
And som, bicause the light doeth theim offend,
Do never pere but in the darke or nyght.
Other reioyse that se the fyer bright   5
And wene to play in it as they do pretend,
And fynd the contrary of it that they intend.

XXIII. T. 1 not well] not T.   4 Joy full dolourous] O; Joyfull dolours E; joyfull dolourous T. 8 me set] hast set me T. 9 thy] by T. 10 not] not so T. 11 And] For T. and] if T. 13 trapped] me trapt T. 15 thou diddist] me, me didst thou T. 18 lowre thou diddist] lower, then didist thou T. 20 lapped] wrapt? T.

[*Authorship:* 'Tho' in margin; in W section of T.]

XXIV. A, T. 2 Agayn] Against T. 4 Do . . . pere] Neuer appeare T. 5 that] to T. fyer] fire so T. 6 they do] they T. 7 And] But T. the contrary] contrary T.

Alas, of that sort I may be by right,
For to withstond her loke I ame not able;
  And yet can I not hide me in no darke place,   10
  Remembraunce so foloweth me of that face,
So that with tery yen swolne and vnstable,
  My destyne to behold her doeth me lede;
  Yet do I knowe I runne into the glede.

XXV

BICAUSE I have the still kept fro lyes and blame
And to my power alwaies have I the honoured,
Vnkynd tong right ill hast thou me rendred
For suche deserft to do me wrek and shame.
In nede of succour moost when that I ame   5
  To aske reward, then standest thou like oon aferd
  Alway moost cold, and if thou speke towerd,
It is as in dreme vnperfaict and lame.
And ye salt teres again my will eche nyght
  That are with me when fayn I would be alone,   10
  Then are ye gone when I should make my mone;
And you so reddy sighes to make me shright,
  Then are ye slake when that ye should owtestert,
  And onely my loke declareth my hert.

XXVI

I FYNDE no peace and all my warr is done;
  I fere and hope I burne and freise like yse;
  I fley above the wynde yet can I not arrise;
And noght I have and all the worold I seson.

8 I may] may I T.   10 And yet] Yet can T.   11 Remembrance . . . me] So foloweth
me remembrance T.   12 So . . . tery] That with my teary T.   14 Yet do I] And yet I T.
  [*Authorship:* 'Wyat' in margin; in W sections of A and T.]

XXV. A, T.   1 have . . . kept] still kept thee T.   2 have I] I T; have A.   3 right] to
T. ill] well A.   6 then . . . like] then standist thow as A; thou standst like T.   7 if . . .
towerd] if thou speake a worde A; if one word be sayd T.   8 It . . . in] It is in A; As
in a T. and lame] is the same T.   9 again] agaynst A, T.   10 fayn I] I T.   12 you]
ye T.   14 my loke declareth] my Love declareth A; doth my loke declare T.
  [*Authorship:* 'Wyat' in margin; in W sections of A and T.]

XXVI. D, P, T.   3 fley above the wynde] flye aloft T; flye aboute the heaven D.
4 have] haue yet P.

That loseth nor locketh holdeth me in prison   5
  And holdeth me not, yet can I scape no wise;
  Nor letteth me lyve nor dye at my devise,
  And yet of deth it gyveth me occasion.
Withoute Iyen, I se; and withoute tong I plain;
  I desire to perisshe and yet I aske helthe;   10
  I love an othre and thus I hate my self;
I fede me in sorrowe and laugh in all my pain;
  Likewise displeaseth me boeth deth and lyffe;
  And my delite is causer of this stryff.

XXVII

THOUGH I my self be bridilled of my mynde,
  Retorning me backewerd by force expresse,
  If thou seke honour to kepe thy promes,
  Who may the hold, my hert, but thou thy self vnbynd?
Sigh then no more, syns no way man may fynde   5
  Thy vertue to let, though that frowerdnes
  Of ffortune me holdeth: and yet, as I may gesse,
  Though othre be present thou art not all behinde.
Suffice it then that thou be redy there
  At all howres; still vnder the defence   10
  Of tyme, trouth and love to save the from offence;
Cryeng, 'I burne in a lovely desire
  With my dere Maisteres: that may not followe,
  Whereby his absence torneth him to sorrowe.'

XXVIII

MY galy charged with forgetfulnes
  Thorrough sharpe sees in wynter nyghtes doeth pas
  Twene Rock and Rock; and eke myn ennemy, Alas,

---

5 loseth nor locketh] lockes nor loseth T.   6 scape] scrape T.   8 me] none P.   10 I wish to perysh, yet I aske for helth T.   I aske] aske I P.   11 thus] yet P.   12 fede me] feed P.   13 Likewise displeaseth] Likewise pleaseth P; Lo thus displeaseth T. deth and lyffe] D, P; lyffe and deth E.

[*Authorship:* 'Wyat' in margin; among W poems in T.]

XXVII. A.   13 Maisteres:] mystres A.

[*Authorship:* 'Tho.' in margin; among W poems in A.]

XXVIII. A, T.   3 myn ennemy] my fo T.

D

That is my lorde, sterith with cruelnes;
And every owre a thought in redines,   5
   As tho that deth were light in suche a case;
   An endles wynd doeth tere the sayll a pase
   Of forced sightes and trusty ferefulnes.
A rayn of teris, a clowde of derk disdain
   Hath done the wered cordes great hinderaunce,   10
   Wrethed with errour and eke with ignoraunce.
The starres be hid that led me to this pain;
   Drowned is reason that should me confort,
   And I remain dispering of the port.

XXIX

AUYSING the bright bemes of these fayer Iyes,
   Where he is that myn oft moisteth and wassheth,
   The werid mynde streght from the hert departeth
   For to rest in his woroldly paradise,
And fynde the swete bitter vnder this gyse.   5
   What webbes he hath wrought well he perceveth
   Whereby with himself on love he playneth,
   That spurreth with fyer and bridilleth with Ise.
Thus is it in suche extremitie brought:
   In frossen thought nowe and nowe it stondeth in flame;   10
   Twyst misery and welth, twist ernest and game;
But few glad and many a dyvers thought;
   With sore repentaunce of his hardines:
   Of suche a rote commeth ffruyte fruytles.

4 sterith] stirreth A.   5 owre] houre A. 6 light] lif A.   8 sightes] sighes A, T.   11 Wrethed] wretched *original reading* E. and eke] and T.   12 led] leade T.   13 Drowned] Drownde T. me confort] me compforte A; be my comfort T; me consort O, M.
   [*Authorship:* 'Wyat' in margin; in W sections of A and T.]

XXIX. A, T.   1 Auysing] Advysing A. these] those T.   2 is] abides T. moisteth] moistes T.   3 departeth] parteth A.   4 For to] To T.   in] within T.   5 fynde . . . bitter] bitter findes the swete T.   6 webbes] webb A. he hath] there he hath T.   7 Whereby] Wherby then T.   8 spurreth] spurs T.   9 Thus . . . extremitie] In such extremity thus is he T.   10 In . . . stondeth] Frosen now cold, and now he standes T. thought] O; though E, A.   11 misery] wo T. twist ernest] betwixt earnest T.   12 But few] With seldome T.   13 With] In T.   14 rote] roote lo T.
   [*Authorship:* 'Wyat' in margin; in W sections of A and T.]

XXX

E VER myn happe is slack and slo in commyng,
  Desir encresing, myn hope vncertain,
  That leve it or wayt it doeth me like pain,
  And Tigre like, swift it is in parting.
Alas, the snow shalbe black and scalding,   5
  The See waterles, fisshe in the moyntain,
  The Tamys shall retorne back into his fountain,
  And where he rose the sonne shall take lodging,
Ere that I in this fynde peace or quyetenes,
  Or that love or my lady rightwisely   10
  Leve to conspire again me wrongfully;
And if that I have after suche bitternes
  Any thing swete, my mouth is owte of tast,
  That all my trust and travaill is but wast.

XXXI

L OVE and fortune and my mynde, remembre
  Of that that is nowe with that that hath ben,
  Do torment me so that I very often
  Envy theim beyonde all mesure.
Love sleith myn hert; fortune is depriver   5
  Of all my comfort; the folisshe mynde then
  Burneth and plaineth as one that sildam
  Lyveth and rest still in displeasure.
My plaisaunt dayes they flete away and passe,
  But daily yet the ill doeth chaunge into the wours;   10
  And more than the half is runne of my cours.

XXX. A, T.   1 myn] my A, T.   2 myn] my A; ay my T.   3 leve it] loue T. doeth
me like] alike doth me T.   4 swift] so swift T.   5 shalbe black] black shal it be T.   6
fisshe] and fishe T. in] vpon T.   7 retorne back] back returne T.   8 take] take his T.
9 that I] I T.   10 Or] A, T; in E. rightwisely] rightuouslye A.   11 again] against T.
12 if that] if T.
  [*Authorship:* 'Wyat' in margin; among W poems in A and T.]

XXXI. A, T.   1 and fortune] Fortune T.   2 Of that that] Eke that T. with that
that] are that that once T.   3 Do . . . I] Torment my hart so sore that T.   4 Envy]
I hate and enuy T.   5 fortune] while Fortune T.   8 and] in *later correction* E, A, T.
10 But] And T. yet . . . doeth] doth myne yll T. into the] into A; to the T.   11
And . . . runne] While more than half is runne now T.
  [*Authorship:* 'Wyat' in margin; in W sections of A and T.]

Alas, not of steill but of brickell glasse,
  I see that from myn hand falleth my trust,
  And all my thoughtes are dasshed into dust.

XXXII

How oft have I, my dere and cruell foo,
  With those your Iyes for to get peace and truyse,
  Profferd you myn hert: but you do not vse
  Emong so high thinges to cast your mynde so lowe.
Yf any othre loke for it, as ye trowe,   5
  There vayn weke hope doeth greatly theim abuse;
  And thus I disdain that that ye refuse;
  It was ones mine: it can no more be so.
Yf I then it chase, nor it in you can fynde
  In this exile no manner of comfort,   10
  Nor lyve allone, nor where he is called resort,
He may wander from his naturall kynd.
  So shall it be great hurt vnto vs twayn,
  And yours the losse and myn the dedly pain.

XXXIII

LIKE to these vnmesurable montayns
  Is my painfull lyff the burden of Ire,
  For of great height be they, and high is my desire,
  And I of teres, and they be full of fontayns.
Vnder Craggy rockes they have full barren playns;   5
  Herd thoughtes in me my wofull mynde doeth tyre;
  Small fruyt and many leves their toppes do atyre;
  Small effect with great trust in me remayns.
The boystrous wyndes oft their high bowghes do blast,
  Hote sighes from me continuelly be shed;   10
  Cattell in theim, and in me love is fed;

XXXII. A, T.   2 those ... and] my great pain to get som peace or T.   3 Profferd
... hert] Geuen you my hart? T.   4 Emong] In T.   5 ye] you T.   6 weke] weite A.
7 thus ... ye] that thus I disdayne, that you T.   8 can no more] can more *original
reading* E; may nomore A.   9 I then] you T. nor] that T.
    [*Authorship:* 'Wyat' in margin; in W sections of A and T.]

XXXIII. A, T.   1 to] vnto T.   2 Is] So is T.   3 of ... they] hye be they T.   5
have full] have T.   8 Small ... with] With small effect T.   9 boystrous] boyst'ous
A; boyseus E.   10 from] in T.   11 Cattell] Wilde beastes T. and ... love] fierce

Immoveable ame I, and they are full stedfast;
Off the restles birdes they have the tune and note,
And I alwayes plaintes that passe thorough my throte.

XXXIV

MADAME, withouten many wordes,
Ons I am sure ye will or no:
And if ye will, then leve your bordes,
And vse your wit and shew it so.

And with a beck ye shall me call,   5
And if of oon that burneth alwaye
Ye have any pitie at all,
Aunswer him faire with yea or nay.

Yf it be yea, I shalbe fayne;
If it be nay, frendes as before;   10
Ye shall an othre man obtain,
And I myn owne and yours no more.

XXXV

YE old mule that thinck your self so fayre,
Leve of with craft your beautie to repaire,
For it is true withoute any fable
No man setteth more by riding in your saddell;
To muche travaill so do your train apaire,   5
        Ye old mule!
With fals savours though you deceve th'ayer,
Who so tast you shall well perceve your layer
Savoureth som what of a Kappurs stable,
        Ye old mule!   10

love in me T.   12 Immoveable] Vnmoueable T. they are full] they T.   13 the restles] that restless E, A; singing T. tune] A, T; tone E.   14 that passe] passing T. thorough] through A, T.

[*Authorship:* 'Tho.' in margin; in W sections of A and T.]

XXXIV. B, T.   1 Madame, withouten] Mistres what nedis B.   2 ye] you T.   3 And if] yf B.   5 And] For T.   6 burneth] burns B, T.   7 any pitie] pity or ruth T.   8, 9 Yea] T; ye B; & E.   11 Ye] You T. obtain] retayne B.   12 myn] my B.

[*Authorship:* 'Tho.' in margin; among W poems in T.]

XXXV. [*Authorship:* 'Tho.' in margin.]

Ye must now serve to market and to faire,
All for the burden for pannyers a paire:
For syns gray heres ben powdered in your sable,
The thing ye seke for you must your self enable
To pourchase it by payment and by prayer,   15
          Ye old mule!

XXXVI

SUCHE happe as I ame happed in
Had never man of trueth I wene;
At me fortune list to begyn
To shew that never hath ben sene
A new kynde of vnhappenes;   5
Nor I cannot the thing I mene
          My self expres.

My self expresse my dedely pain
That can I well, if that myght serue;
But why I have not helpe again   10
That knowe I not vnles I starve;
For honger still a myddes my foode
So graunted is that I deserue
          To do me good.

To do me good what may prevaill?   15
For I deserve and not desire,
And stil of cold I me bewaill
And raked ame in burnyng fyere;
For tho I have, suche is my lott,
In hand to helpe that I require,   20
          It helpeth not.

It helpeth not, but to encrese
That that by prouff can be no more:
That is the hete that cannot cesse,
And that I have to crave so sore,   25
What wonder is this greedy lust
To aske and have, and yet therefore
          Refrain I must.

XXXVI. [*Authorship:* 'Tho.' in margin.]

Refrain I must; what is the cause?
Sure, as they say, so hawkes be taught.   30
But in my case laieth no suche clause,
For with suche craft I ame not caught;
Wherefore I say and good cause why,
With haples hand no man hath raught
        Such happe as I.   35

XXXVII

THEY fle from me that sometyme did me seke
With naked fote stalking in my chambre.
I have sene theim gentill tame and meke
That nowe are wyld and do not remembre
That sometyme they put theimself in daunger   5
To take bred at my hand; and nowe they raunge
Besely seking with a continuell chaunge.

Thancked be fortune, it hath ben othrewise
Twenty tymes better; but ons in speciall
In thyn arraye after a pleasaunt gyse   10
When her lose gowne from her shoulders did fall,
And she me caught in her armes long and small;
Therewithall swetely did my kysse,
And softely said 'dere hert, how like you this?'

It was no dreme: I lay brode waking.   15
But all is torned thorough my gentilnes
Into a straunge fasshion of forsaking;
And I have leve to goo of her goodeness,
And she also to vse new fangilnes.
But syns that I so kyndely ame serued,   20
I would fain knowe what she hath deserued.

XXXVII. D, T.   1 They] Thye D.   2 in] within T.   3 I have] once haue I T.
theim] them both D.   4 not] not once T.   5 they] thye D. put theimself] haue put
them selues T.   7 seking with a] seking D; sekyng in T.   9 in speciall] in esspiall D;
especiall T.   11 from . . . did] from her shoulders T.   13 Therewithall] but there-
withall D; And therwithall, so T.   15 I] for I D, T.   16 torned thorough] tornd
thorowe D; turnde now T.   17 straunge] bitter T.   18 goo] parte D.   19 also]
like wise D.   20 so kyndely] so gentillye D; vnkyndly so.   21 I . . . hath] what
think you bye this that she hat D; How like you this, what hath she now T.
   [*Authorship:* 'Tho.' in margin; among W poems in T.]

XXXVIII

THERE was never nothing more me payned,
Nor nothing more me moved,
As when my swete hert her complayned
That ever she me loved.
     Alas the while!   5

With pituous loke she saide and sighed
'Alas what aileth me
To love and set my welth so light
On hym that loveth not me?
     Alas the while!   10

'Was I not well voyde of all pain,
When that nothing me greved?
And now with sorrous I must complain
And cannot be releved.
     Alas the while!   15

'My restfull nyghtes and Joyfull daies
Syns I began to love
Be take from me; all thing decayes
Yet can I not remove.
     Alas the while!'   20

She wept and wrong her handes withall,
The teres fell in my nekke.
She torned her face and let it fall;
Scarsely therewith could speke.
     Alas the while!   25

Her paynes tormented me so sore
That comfort had I none,
But cursed my fortune more and more
To se her sobbe and grone.
     Alas the while!   30

XXXVIII. [*Authorship:* 'Tho.' in margin.]

XXXIX

PATIENCE, though I have not
The thing that I require,
I must of force, god wot,
Forbere my moost desire:
For no ways can I fynde   5
To saile against the wynde.

Patience, do what they will
To worke me woo or spite,
I shall content me still
To thyncke boeth day and nyte,   10
To thyncke and hold my peace,
Syns there is no redresse.

Patience, withouten blame,
For I offended nought;
I knowe they knowe the same,   15
Though they have chaunged their thought.
Was ever thought so moved
To hate that it haith loved?

Patience of all my harme,
For fortune is my foo;   20
Patience must be the charme
To hele me of my woo:
Patience, withoute offence,
Is a painfull patience.

XL

PATIENS for my devise,
Impaciens for your part;
Of contraries the gyse

XXXIX. A, B, D. [In B the stanzas are printed in the following order: 3, 1, 2, 4.]
2 require] desyryd D.   4 my moost desire] that I Requiryd D.   5 ways] way B. can]
not *original reading* E.   7 they] she D; ye B.   10 boeth . . . nyte] that ons I myght B,
D.   13 withouten] off all my B; without A.   15 I . . . same] I wyshe she knoyth the
same B; I know she knows the same D.   16 they . . . their] she . . . her B, D.   18
that] where D. it] she B.   20 For] sith B.   21 must be] shalbe B.   22 hele] ease D.
  [*Authorship:* 'Tho.' in margin; in W section of A; ascribed 'fnys qᵈ Wyatt' in D.]
XL. A (1–8), B, D.   *Note in* D: patiens tho I had nott the &c/to her that saide this
patiens was not for her but that the contrarye of myne was most metiste for her
pourposse.   3 contraries] contrarve D.

Is ever the overthwart:
Paciens, for I ame true,   5
The contrary for yew.

Paciens, a good cause why
You have no cause at all;
Therefore yours standeth awry,
Perchaunce sometyme to fall: 10
Paciens, then take him vp
And drynck of paciens cupp.

Pacience, no force for that,
But brusshe your gowne again;
Pacience, spurne not therat;   15
Let no man knowe your payne:
Pacience, evyn at my pleasure,
When youres is owte of mesure.

Th'othre was for me,
This pacience is for you;   20
Chaunge when ye list, let se,
For I have taken a new;
Pacience, with a good will
Is easy to fulfill.

XLI

YE know my herte, my ladye dere,
That sins the tyme I was your thrall
I have bene yours both hole and clere,
Tho my reward hathe bene but small;
So am I yet and more then all   5
And ye kno well how I have seruid,

---

4 Is ever the] is ever B; must nedes be D. 8 You have] Yours hathe D. 9 truste me
that stondes awrye D. yours] your E; yowrs B. standeth] standes B. 10 Perchaunce]
May chaunce B. sometyme to] maye some tyme D. 11 then . . . vp] the saye and
supp D. 12 And drynck] a taste D. 14 But] Yet D. 16 Let . . . knowe] lest folkes
percyve D. 17 evyn at] at D. 18 is owte of] hathe no D. 19 Th'othre] the tother
B, D. 22 taken] tane D.
  [*Authorship:* Clearly a sequel to XXXIX.]
XLI. D. 1–23] D; *a leaf is missing in* E.

As yf ye prove it shall apere
   Howe well, how longe,
   How faithefulye
   And soffred wrong   10
   How patientlye!
Then sins that I have neuer swarfde
Let not my paines be ondeseruide.

Ye kno also, though ye saye naye,
That you alone are my desire   15
And you alone yt is that maye
Asswage my fervent flaming fire;
Soccour me then I you require.
Ye kno yt ware a just request,
Sins ye do cause my heat, I saye,   20
   Yf that I bourne
   That ye will warme
   And not to tourne
   All to my harme
Sending suche flame from frosen brest   25
Against all right for my vnrest.

And I knowe well how frowerdly
Ye have mystaken my true Intent
And hetherto how wrongfully
I have founde cause for to repent;   30
But deth shall ryd me redely
Yf your [hard] hert do not relent;
And I knowe well all this ye knowe
   That I and myne
   And all I have   35
   Ye may assigne
   To spill or save.
Why are ye then so cruel ffoo
Vnto your owne that loveth you so?

---

26 all right] nature D.   27 frowerdly] scornefullye D.   28 mystaken] mistane D.
31–3 But if your herte doth not relente/Sins I do kno that this ye kno/Ye shall sle
me all wilfullye D.   32 hard] *conj*. F; *space in* E.   34 That I] For me D.
   [*Authorship:* The authentication would probably have been on the missing leaf.]

XLII

W HO hath herd of suche crueltye before?
That when my plaint remembred her my woo
That caused it, she cruell more and more
Wisshed eche stitche, as she did sit and soo,
Had prykt myn hert, for to encrese my sore;   5
And, as I thinck, she thought it had ben so:
For as she thought this is his hert in dede,
She pricked herd and made her self to blede.

XLIII

I F fansy would favour
As my deseruing shall,
My love, my paramour,
Should love me best of all.

But if I cannot attain   5
The grace that I desire,
Then may I well complain
My seruice and my hiere.

Fansy doethe knowe how
To fourther my trew hert   10
If fansy myght avowe
With faith to take part.

But fansy is so fraill
And flitting still so fast,
That faith may not prevaill   15
To helpe me furst nor last.

For fansy at his lust
Doeth rule all but by gesse;

XLII. A, D, T.   1 Who ... of] What man hath hard T. crueltye] W; tyranny E, D.
2 remembred] remembre D.   5 prykt] W; pricked E, A, D. myn] W; my E, A, D, T.
to encrese] tencrese D.   8 herd] her D.
   [*Authorship:* Corrections in W's hand in E; in W sections of A and T.]
XLIII. A (9–36), D, V.   1 fansy] fantasy V.   2 my deseruing] I deserue and V.   3
paramour] lady paramour V.   5 cannot] not V.   9 Fansy doethe knowe] Fantasy
knoweth V.   10 fourther] forbeare V.   11 fansy] fantasye V.   12 to] for to D.
13–6] *omitted* D.   13 fansy is so] fantasy is V.   14 flitting] fletynge V.   17 For fansy]
Since fantasy V.   18 but by] by V.

Whereto should I then trust
In trouth or stedfastnes? 20

Yet gladdely would I please
The fansy of her hert,
That may me onely ease
And cure my carefull smart.

Therefore, my lady dere, 25
Set ons your fantasy
To make som hope appere
Of stedfast remedy.

For if he be my frend
And vndertake my woo, 30
My greife is at an ende
If he continue so.

Elles fansy doeth not right,
As I deserue and shall,
To have you daye and nyght 35
To love me best of all.

XLIV

ALAS madame for stelyng of a kysse
Have I so much your mynd ther offended?
Have I then done so greuously amysse,
That by no meanes it may be amended?
Then revenge you, and the next way is this: 5
An othr kysse shall have my lyffe endid.

19 then] put V. 20 or] and V. 21 Yet gladdely] Yet A. 22 The fansy] The fantasy V1; That fantasy V2. 24 cure] helpe V. 26 Set ons] Let se V. 28 stedfast] D; stedfastnes, E, A; helpe and V. 29 he] ye V. 32 he] ye V. 33 fansy] fantasy V. 34 As I] as D. 35 To have you] To haue her V1; To her V2.
    [*Authorship:* In W section of A.]
XLIV. A, T.   1 stelyng] W; robbing E.   2 ther] W; then E; therin *correction* E, A, T.   3 Have I then] or haue I T.   4 it may be amended] the matter may be mended *later correction* E, A; it may not be amended T.   5 Then . . . this] W; Reuenge you then and sure you shall not mysse E, A; Reuenge you then, the rediest way is this T. 6 An . . . endid] W; to have my liff with an othre ended E; Another kisse my life it shall haue ended T; an other kisse shall haue my lief throughe endid A (W inserted

For to my mowth the first my hert did suck,
The next shall clene oute of my brest it pluck.

XLV

W H A T no, perdy, ye may be sure!
Thinck not to make me to your lure,
With wordes and chere so contrarieng,
Swete and sowre contrewaing;
To much of it were still to endure.   5
Trouth is trayed where craft is in vre;
But though ye have had my hertes cure,
Trow ye I dote withoute ending?
    What no, perdy!

Though that with pain I do procure   10
For to forgett that ons was pure
Within my hert shall still that thing,
Vnstable, vnsure and wavering,
Be in my mynde withoute recure?
    What no, perdye!   15

XLVI

THE wandering gadlyng in the sommer tyde,
That fyndes the Adder with his recheles fote,
Startes not dismayd so soudenly a side
As jalous dispite did, tho there ware no bote,
When that he sawe me sitting by her side   5
That of my helth is very croppe and rote,
It pleased me then to have so fair a grace
To styng that hert that would have my place.

'thoughe' in E and then deleted it). 7 first] W; ton E. 8 next shall clene] W; tother shall E.
    [*Authorship:* 'Tho.' in margin; corrections in W's hand; in W sections of A and T.]
XLV. D.   6 trayed] D; tryed E.   12 hert] ♡ D.
    [*Authorship:* 'Tho.' in margin; ascribed 'fynys qᵈ Wyatt' in D.]
XLVI. D, P, T, N.   2 recheles] restlesse N.   4 As . . . did] As did gelosy P, N.   7 It . . . then] it pleased me P, N.   8 that . . . have] the wight that would have had P N.   have] have had N, T.
    [*Authorship:* 'Tho.' in margin; in W section of T.]

XLVII

T HE lyvely sperkes that issue from those Iyes
    Against the which ne vaileth no defence
    Have prest myn hert and done it none offence
    With qwaking pleasure more then ons or twise.
Was never man could any thing devise   5
    The sonne bemes to torne with so great vehemence,
    To dase mans sight as by their bright presence.
    Dased ame I much like vnto the gyse
Of one I-stricken with dynt of lightening,
    Blynded with the stroke, erryng here and there,   10
    So call I for helpe, I not when ne where,
The pain of my fal patiently bering :
    For after the blase, as is no wounder,
    Of dedly nay here I the ferefull thoundere.

XLVIII

W HA T nedeth these thretning wordes and wasted wynde ?
All this cannot make me restore my pray.
To robbe your good, I wis, is not my mynde,
Nor causeles your faire hand did I display.
Let love be judge, or els whome next we meit,   5
That may boeth here what you and I can say.
She toke from me an hert and I a glove from her :
Let vs se nowe, if th'one be wourth th'othre.

XLIX

R YG HT true it is, and said full yore agoo :
Take hede of him that by thy back the claweth,
For none is wourse then is a frendly ffoo.

XLVII. A, D, T. 2 ne] there T. 3 prest myn] prest my A; perst my T. 6 The]
omitted T. 9 I-stricken] I stricken E, D; ystreken A; striken T. 10 Blynded] Blind
T. erryng] and erryng T. 11 ne] nor T. 12 fal] ?W; fals E; fall A; faute D.
bering] learnying T1. 13 after] streight after T. 14 Of dedly nay] Geue I the nay
deleted D ; of deadly noyse T.
   [*Authorship:* 'Tho.' in margin ; in W sections of A and T.]
XLVIII. A, T. 1 nedeth] nedes A, T. thretning] threning E; threatning A, T. 5
meit] finde T. 7 toke . . . an] reft my T. 8 nowe] then T. th'one] thone E, A; one
T. th'othre] A; thothre E; the other T.
   [*Authorship:* 'Tho.' in margin ; in W sections of A and T.]

Though they seme good, all thing that the deliteth,
Yet knowe it well, that in thy bosom crepeth: 5
For many a man such fier oft kyndeleth,
That with the blase his berd syngeth.

L

W HAT wourde is that that chaungeth not,
Though it be tourned and made in twain?
It is myn aunswer, god it wot,
And eke the causer of my payn.
A love rewardeth with disdain,   5
Yet is it loved. What would ye more?
It is my helth eke and my sore.

LI

A T moost myschief
I suffre greif
For of relief
Syns I have none
My lute and I   5
Continuelly
Shall vs apply
To sigh and mone.

Nought may prevaill
To wepe or waill   10
Pitie doeth faill
In you Alas
Morning or mone
Complaint or none
It is all one   15
As in this case.

XLIX. A, T.   4 Though they] Thought he T.   6 such fier oft] oft tyme suche fyer
A; such fire oft times he T.   7 berd syngeth] berd him self he singeth T.
    [*Authorship:* 'Tho.' in margin; in W sections of A and T.]
L. A, T.   3 It] yf A. aunswer] Anna T.   4 And . . . causer] and the cause A; The
only causer T.   5 A love rewardeth] A Love A; My love that medeth T.   6 would
ye] will you.   7 helth eke and] salue, and eke T.
    [*Authorship:* 'Tho.' in margin; in W sections of A and T.]
LI. B, D.   4 Syns] sith B.   8 sigh] (i) vale (ii) sythe B.   9 may] doth B.   10 wepe]
sighe B.   11 Pitie] (i) sens pety (ii) pety B.   15 all one] Alone D.

For crueltie
Moost that can be
Hath soveraynte
Within your hert　　　　　20
Which maketh bare
All my welfare
Nought do ye care
How sore I smart.

No Tigres hert　　　　　25
Is so pervert
Withoute dessert
To wreke his Ire
And you me kyll
For my good will　　　　　30
Lo how I spill
For my desire!

There is no love
That can ye move
And I can prove　　　　　35
None othre way;
Therefore I must
Restrain my lust
Banisshe my trust
And welth away.　　　　　40

Thus in myschief
I suffre greif
For of relief
Syns I have none,
My lute and I　　　　　45
Continuelly
Shall vs apply
To sigh and mone.

18 can] may B.　19 soveraynte] sufferaunte B; suffraynte D.　23 ye] you B.　29 you]
ye B.　34 ye] you B.　36 None othre] no nother B.　38 Restrain] refrayne B, D. my]
me D.　39 Banisshe my] and banyshe B; banysshe me D.　40 And welth away] frome
me alway B.　41 Thus] B, D; ffor E.　42–8] B, D; *omitted* E.
　　[*Authorship:* 'Tho.' in margin.]
　　E

LII

MARVAILL no more, all tho
The songes I syng do mone,
For othre liff then wo
I never proved none;
And in my hert also   5
Is graven with lettres diepe
A thousand sighes and mo,
A flod of teres to wepe.

How may a man in smart
Fynde matter to rejoyse,   10
How may a morning hert
Set fourth a pleasaunt voise?
Play who that can that part,
Nedes must in me appere
How fortune overthwart   15
Doeth cause my morning chere.

Perdy, there is no man,
If he never sawe sight,
That perfaictly tell can
The nature of the light;   20
Alas, how should I then
That never tasted but sowre
But do as I began
Continuelly to lowre?

But yet perchaunce som chaunce   25
May chaunce to chaunge my tune,
And when suche chaunce doeth chaunce,
Then shall I thanck fortune;
And if I have souche chaunce,

LII. D, T, V, N.   7] And many thousands mo V.   8 A flod] The flouds V.   11
morning] woful V.   13 who that] who D; who so T.   13 part] depart V.   14
Nedes . . . me] In me must nedes V.   16] *omitted* V.   21 Alas, how] How V. how
should I do than D.   22 tasted] taste D, T.   25 som] from T.   25] Such chaunce
perchaunce may chaunce V.   26 May chaunce to] To cause me V.   27 suche]
(souch) T.   29] and yf suche chance do chawnce D, V; And if I have (souch) chance
T. souche] *later insertion* E.

Perchaunce ere it be long,   30
For such a pleasaunt chaunce
To syng som plaisaunt song.

LIII

WHERE shall I have at myn owne will
Teres to complain? Where shall I fett
Suche sighes that I may sigh my fill
And then again my plaintes repete?

For tho my plaint shall have none end,   5
My teres cannot suffice my woo.
To mone my harme have I no frend
For fortunes frend is myshappes ffoo.

Comfort (god wot) els have I none,
But in the wynde to wast my wordes.   10
Nought moveth you my dedly mone,
But all you torne it into bordes.

I speke not now to move your hert
That you should rue vpon my pain;
The sentence geven may not revert: 15
I know such labour were but vayn.

But syns that I for you, my dere,
Have lost that thing that was my best,
A right small losse it must appere
To lese thes wordes and all the rest.   20

But tho they sparkill in the wynde,
Yet shall they shew your falsed faith
Which is retorned vnto his kynde,
For like to like the proverbe saieth.

---

31 such] (souch) T.

    [*Authorship:* 'Tho.' in margin; in W section of T; ascribed 'ffnys q^d Wyatt' in D. LIII. A, T.   3 that] as A.   4 plaintes] plaintes (to) *deleted* E.   12 all] stil T.   14 rue] *inserted in another hand* E.   17 syns that I] syns for you I *original reading* E.   22 your] thie A.   23 vnto] to T.

Fortune and you did me avaunce; 25
Me thought I swam and could not drowne;
Happiest of all, but my myschaunce
Did lyft me vp to throwe me downe.

And you with your owne crulnes
Did set your fote vpon my neck, 30
Me and my welfare to oppresse,
Without offence your hert to wreke.

Where are your plaisaunt wordes, alas,
Where your faith, your stedfastnes?
There is no more but all doth passe, 35
And I ame left all comfortles.

But forbicause it doeth you greve
And also me my wretched liff,
Have here my trouth: shall not releve,
But deth alone my wery striff. 40

Therefore farewell my liff, my deth,
My gayn, my losse, my salve, my sore!
Farewell also with you my breth!
For I ame gone for evermore
Podra esser che no es

LIV

S HE sat and sowde that hath done me the wrong
Wherof I plain, and have done many a daye;
And whilst she herd my plaint in pitious song
Wisshed my hert the samplar as it lay.
The blynd maister whome I haue serued so long, 5
Grudging to here that he did here her saye,
Made her owne wepon do her fynger blede,
To fele if pricking were so good in dede.

---

25 avaunce] advaunce A. 29 with your owne] E; with hir of *later correction* E, T; with [ ] of A. 34 Where] Where is *later correction* E, A, T. 37 forbicause] E; syns so moche *later correction* E, A, T. 39 trouth: shall not] trouth naught shall *later correction* E, A, T. 40 wery] very E; verye A; wretched T. 45] E; *omitted* A, T.
 [*Authorship:* 'Tho.' in margin; in W sections of A and T.]
LIV. A, D, T. 3 whilst] while D. in] W; and E. 4 Wisshed] She wisht T. as] that T. 5 so] *deleted* A. 7 Made] W; With E, D. do] W; did make E, D. 8 in] W; a E
 [*Authorship:* 'Tho.' in margin; corrections in W's hand; in W sections of A and T.]

LV

'A ROBYN
Joly Robyn
Tell me how thy leman doeth
And thou shall knowe of myn.'

'My lady is vnkynd, perde!'   5
   'Alack, whi is she so?'
'She loveth an othre better than me,
   And yet she will say no.'

Responce

I fynde no suche doublenes,
   I fynde women true.   10
My lady loveth me dowtles,
   And will chaunge for no newe.

Le plaintif

Thou art happy while that doeth last,
   But I say as I fynde,
That womens love is but a blast   15
   And torneth like the wynde.

Responce

Yf that be trew yett as thou sayst
   That women turn their hart,
Then spek better of them thou mayst
   In hope to hau thy partt.   20

Le plaintif

Suche folkes shall take no harme by love
   That can abide their torne,
But I alas can no way prove
   In love but lake and morne.

LV. D xxii (1–8), xxiv (See Commentary).   1 A] Hey D.   2 Joly] gentyll D1.   3
leman] lady D. doeth] dose D2.   7 me] I D.   8/9 Etc. D *omits speech headings.*   10 I]
for I D.   13 while that] yff ytt D.   16 like] as D.   17–20 yf … partt] D; *omitted* E,
with consequent dislocation of speech-headings.   21 shall … harme] that tak no hurt D.
23 no way] noways D.

Responce

But if thou wilt avoyde thy harme   25
   Lerne this lessen of me,
At othre fires thy self to warme
   And let theim warme with the.

LVI

SUCHE vayn thought as wonted to myslede me
   In desert hope by well assured mone,
   Maketh me from compayne to live alone,
   In folowing her whome reason bid me fle.
She fleith as fast by gentill crueltie;   5
   And after her myn hert would fain be gone,
   But armed sighes my way do stoppe anone,
   Twixt hope and drede locking my libertie.
Yet, as I gesse, vnder disdaynfull browe
   One beame of pitie is in her clowdy loke,   10
   Which comforteth the mynde that erst for fere shoke:
And therewithall bolded I seke the way how
   To vtter the smert that I suffre within,
   But suche it is, I not how to begyn.

LVII

THO I cannot your crueltie constrain,
For my good will to favour me again;
   Tho my true and faithfull love,
   Have no power your hert to move,
      Yet rew vpon my pain.   5

Tho I your thrall must evermore remain,
And for your sake my libertie restrain,

---

25 But . . . thy] Yet . . . the D.   27 othre] others D.   warme] warne D.   28 warme]
warn D.
   [*Authorship:* 'Wyat' in margin.]

LVI. A, D, T.   3 Maketh] Makes T.   4 bid] bids T.   5 fleith] flyeth D.   She . . .
fast] So fleeth she T.   6 myn] my A.   7 do] doth D.   8 locking] W, T; lacking E,
A.   9 disdaynfull] W; that scornfull E; the skornfull D.   10 pitie] ruth T.   11
comforteth] comfortes T.   12 And . . . how] That bolded straight the way then seke
I how T.   13 vtter the] vtter forth the T. that I suffre] I bide T.
   [*Authorship:* 'Wyat' in margin; in W sections of A and T.

The greatest grace that I do crave
Is that ye would vouchesave
    To rew vpon my pain.   10

Tho I have not deserued to obtain
So high Reward but thus to serue in vain,
Tho I shall have no redresse
Yet of right ye can no lesse
    But rew vpon my pain.   15

But I se well that your high disdain
Wull no wise graunt that I shall more attain;
Yet ye must graunt at the lest
This my poure and small request:
    Reioyse not at my pain.   20

LVIII

To wisshe and want and not obtain,
To seke and sew esse of my pain,
Syns all that ever I do is vain,
    What may it availl me?

All tho I stryve boeth dey and howre,   5
Against the streme with all my powre,
If fortune list yet for to lowre,
    What may it availl me?

If willingly I suffre woo,
If from the fyre me list not goo,   10
If then I burne to plaine me so,
    What may it availl me?

And if the harme that I suffre
Be runne to farre owte of mesur,
To seke for helpe any further   15
    What may it availl me?

LVII. A, D.   12 So ... but] so hey reward D.   16 But] W; ffor E, D.   17 Wull]
Will A. more] that *deleted* E.   18–20] *omitted* A.   20 Reioyse not at] W; to rew vpon
E, D.
  [*Authorship:* 'Tho.' in margin; two corrections in W's hand; in W section of A.]
LVIII. A (11–36), D.   4 it] that D.   5 dey] *inserted by later hand* E.   5 howre] night D.

What tho eche hert that hereth me plain
Pitieth and plaineth for my payn,
If I no les in greif remain
    What may it availl me?   20

Ye tho the want of my relief
Displease the causer of my greif,
Syns I remain still in myschiefe,
    What may it availl me?

Such cruell chaunce doeth so me threte,   25
Continuelly inward to frete,
Then of relesse for to trete,
    What may it availl me?

Fortune is deiff vnto my call,
My torment moveth her not at all,   30
And though she torne as doethe a ball
    What may it availl me?

For in despere there is no rede;
To want of ere speche is no spede;
To linger still alyve as dede,   35
    What may it availl me?

LIX

SOME tyme I fled the fyre that me brent
By see, by land, by water and by wynd;
And now I folow the coles that be quent
From Dovor to Calais against my mynde.
Lo! how desire is boeth sprong and spent!   5
And he may se that whilome was so blynde;
And all his labor now he laugh to scorne.
Mashed in the breers that erst was all to torne.

17 hereth] heares A, D. 18 Pitieth] pitis D. 27 relesse] relef D. trete] entreat A, D.
30 moveth her not] moves not her A.
   [*Authorship:* 'Tho.' in margin; in W section of A.]
LIX. A, D, H (1-4), T. 1 me] me so T. 2 By ... land] W; by hilles and dales E.
3 I ... coles] the coales I folow T. 4 against my mynde] with willing minde T. 5
boeth sprong] both furth sprong T. 7 now he laugh] laughes he now T. 8 all to]
onely T.
   [*Authorship:* 'Tho.' in margin; a correction in W's hand; in W sections of A and
T, headed 'Tho. W' in H.]

LX

HE is not ded that somtyme hath a fall.
The Sonne retorneth that was vnder the clowd
And when fortune hath spitt oute all her gall
I trust good luck to me shalbe allowd.
For I have sene a shippe into haven fall   5
After the storme hath broke boeth mast and shrowd;
And eke the willowe that stowpeth with the wynde
Doeth ryse again, and greater wode doeth bynd.

LXI

THE furyous gonne in his rajing yre,
When that the bowle is rammed in to sore,
And that the flame cannot part from the fire,
Cracketh in sonder, and in the ayer doeth rore
The shevered peces; right so doeth my desire   5
Whose flame encreseth from more to more,
Wych to let owt I dare not loke nor speke:
So now hard force my hert doeth all to breke.

LXII

MY hope, Alas, hath me abused,
And vain rejoysing hath me fed;
Lust and Joye have me refused
And carefull plaint is in their stede;
To muche avauncing slaked my spede;   5
Myrth hath caused my hevines,
And I remain all comfortles.

Whereto did I assure my thought
Withoute displeasure stedfastly?

LX. D, P, T, N.   1 He . . . fall] W; I am not ded all though I had a fall E, D, P.
hath] had T.   2 retorneth] W; retornes E, D, T. was vnder the] hid was vnder T.
was] was hid P.   4 to me shalbe] shalbe to me P.   5 into] in T. haven] the haven P.
6 After the] when P.   6 the] that T. shrowd] also shrowde P.   7 And . . . willowe]
The willow eke T. stowpeth] D, P. T; stoppeth E.
   [*Authorship:* 'Tho.' in margin: corrections in W's hand; in W section of T.]
LXI. A, T.   1 The furyous gonne] W; Like as the canon E (i); Like as the bombard
E (ii).
   [*Authorship:* 'Tho.' in margin; a correction in W's hand; in W sections in A and
T.]
LXII. A, D.   8 Whereto] Whereof D.

In fortunes forge my Joye was wrought,   10
And is revolted redely.
I ame mystaken wonderly,
For I thought nought but faithfulnes,
Yet I remain all comfortles.

In gladsom chere I did delite,   15
Till that delite did cause my smert
And all was wrong where I thought right;
For right it was that my true hert
Should not from trouth be set apart,
Syns trouth did cause my hardines;   20
Yet I remain all comfortles.

Sometyme delight did tune my song,
And led my hert full pleasauntly;
And to my self I saide among:
My happe is commyng hastely.   25
But it hath happed contrary;
Assuraunce causeth my distres,
And I remain all comfortles.

Then if my note now do vary
And leve his wonted pleasauntnes,   30
The hevy burden that I cary
Hath alterd all my Joyefulnes.
No pleasure hath still stedfastnes,
But hast hath hurt my happenes,
And I remain all comfortles.   35

LXIII

WHAT deth is worse then this
        When my delight,
My wele, my joye, my blys,
        Is from my sight?
        Boeth daye and nyght   5
My liff, alas, I mys.

12 wonderly] wonderuslye D.   13 thought] A, D; though E.   17 where] were D.
19 from] for D.   19, 20 trouth] trothe A.   20 my]A, D; me E.   23 led] A, D; leds E.
29 do] doth A, D.
    [*Authorship:* 'Tho.' in margin; in W section of A.]
LXIII. D. xxxix, lxxiv.   3] my wordly Joy my blysse D1; my wordly Joye and blise
D2.

For though I seme alyve,
  My hert is hens
Thus botles for to stryve
  Oute of presens   10
  Of my defens,
Towerd my deth I dryve.

Hertles, alas, what man
  May long endure?
Alas, how lyve I then?   15
  Syns no recure
  May me assure
My liff I may well ban.

Thus doeth my torment gro
  In dedly dred.   20
Alas, who myght lyve so,
  Alyve as deed
  Alyve to lede
A dedly lyff in woo.

LXIV

TH'ENMY of liff, decayer of all kynde,
That with his cold wethers away the grene,
This othre nyght me in my bed did fynde,
And offered me to rid my fiever clene;
And I did graunt, so did dispayre me blynde.   5
He drewe his bowe with arrowe sharp and kene,
And strake the place where love had hit before,
And drave the first dart deper more and more.

LXV

ONS as me thought fortune me kyst
And bad me aske what I thought best,
And I should have it as me list
Therewith to set my hert in rest.

12] Towerd] towardes D2. 19 Thus] Thys D1.
  [*Authorship:* 'Tho.' in margin.]
LXIV. T. 1 Th'enmy] Thenmy E; The enmy T. 2 wethers] wythers T. 6
arrowe] arrowes T.
  [*Authorship:* 'Tho.' in margin of E; in W section of T.]
LXV. D lxxi (1-8), lxxiii, T, N. 4 in] at N.

I asked nought but my dere hert   5
To have for evermore myn owne;
Then at an ende were all my smert,
Then should I nede no more to mone.

Yet for all that a stormy blast
Had overtorned this goodely day;   10
And fortune semed at the last
That to her promes she saide nay.

But like as oon oute of dispere
To soudden hope revived I;
Now fortune sheweth herself so fayer   15
That I content me wonderly.

My moost desire my hand may reche,
My will is alwaye at my hand;
Me nede not long for to beseche
Her that hath power me to commaund.   20

What erthely thing more can I crave?
What would I wisshe more at my will?
No thing on erth more would I have,
Save that I have to have it still.

For fortune hath kept her promes   25
In graunting me my moost desire:
Of my sufferaunce I have redres,
And I content me with my hiere.

LXVI

My lute, awake! perfourme the last
Labour that thou and I shall wast
And end that I have now begon;
For when this song is sung and past,
My lute be still, for I have done.   5

5 nought . . . dere] but my ladies T. 8 to mone] D, T, N; mone E. 16 wonderly]
wonderslye T, N. 27 sufferaunce] soueraigne T.
  [*Authorship:* 'Tho.' in margin; in W section of T.]
LXVI. B, D, T, V, N. 1 last] last labor D. 4 sung] B, N; songe, D, T; song E.

As to be herd where ere is none,
As lede to grave in marbill stone,
My song may perse her hert as sone;
Should we then sigh, or syng, or mone?
No, no, my lute, for I have done.   10

The Rokkes do not so cruelly
Repulse the waves continuelly
As she my suyte and affection,
So that I ame past remedy,
Whereby my lute and I have done.   15

Prowd of the spoyll that thou hast gott
Of simple hertes thorough loves shot,
By whome, vnkynd, thou hast theim wone,
Thinck not he haith his bow forgot,
All tho my lute and I have done.   20

Vengeaunce shall fall on thy disdain
That makest but game on ernest pain;
Thinck not alone vnder the sonne
Vnquyt to cause thy lovers plain,
All tho my lute and I have done.   25

Perchaunce the lye wethered and old,
The wynter nyghtes that are so cold,
Playnyng in vain vnto the mone;
Thy wisshes then dare not be told;
Care then who lyst, for I have done.   30

And then may chaunce the to repent
The tyme that thou hast lost and spent,
To cause thy lovers sigh and swoune;
Then shalt thou knowe beaultie but lent
And wisshe and want as I have done.   35

---

9 sigh . . . syng] syng or walle B. 11 Rokkes] Rok B, D. 16–20] *omitted* N. 17
thorough] through B, T. 18 By whome, vnkynd] vynkynd althoughe B. 21 shall]
may B, D. 22 makest] makes D. on] of B. 23 Thinck] Trowe D. 26 Perchaunce]
May chaunce B, D, T. the] they D, T, N. the lye] W; they lay E. 27 nyghtes] B, D,
T, N; nyght E. 30 Care then] but care B. 33 lovers] louer B.

Now cesse, my lute; this is the last
Labour that thou and I shall wast,
And ended is that we begon;
Now is this song boeth sung and past;
My lute, be still, for I have done.   40

LXVII

If chaunce assynd
Were to my mynde
By very kynd
Of destyne,
Yet would I crave   5
Nought else to have
But only liff and libertie.

Then were I sure
I myght endure
The displeasure   10
Of crueltie,
Where now I plain
Alas in vain,
Lacking my liff for libertie.

For withoute th'one   15
Th'othre is gone
And there can none
It remedy;
If th'one be past,
Th'othre doeth wast,   20
And all for lack of libertie.

And so I dryve
As yet alyve

36 Now . . . lute] my lute be styll B.   38 is that we] that I have now B. we] I D.
39 Now . . . both] ffor when this song ys B. sung] B; song E, T; songe D; sunge N.
    [*Authorship:* 'Tho.' in margin; ascribed 'fynys qᵈ Wyatt' in D; in W section of T;
but ascribed to Rochford by N.]
LXVII. D.   7 only] D; *omitted* E.   15 th'one] thone E; ton D.   16 Th'othre]
thothre E; tother D.   19 th'one] thone E; ton D.   20 Th'othre] thothre E; tother D.

All tho I stryve
With myserie,   25
Drawing my breth,
Lowking for deth
And losse of liff for libertie.

But thou that still
Maist at thy will   30
Torne all this ill
Aduersitie,
For the repare
Of my welfare
Graunt me but liff and libertie.   35

And if not so,
Then let all goo
To wretched woo,
And let me dye;
For th'one or th'othre   40
There is none othre,
My deth or liff with libertie.

LXVIII

NATURE, that gave the bee so feet a grace
To fynd hony of so wondrous fashion
Hath taught the spider owte of the same place
To fetche poyson, by straynge alteration.
Tho this be straynge, it is a straynger cace   5
With oon kysse by secret operation
Boeth these at ons, in those your lippes to fynde,
In chaunge whcrof, I leve my hert behinde.

LXIX

I HAVE sought long with stedfastnes
To have had som ease of my great smert,
But nought availleth faithfulnes
To grave within your stony hert.

40 th'one . . . th'othre] thone . . . thothre E; ton . . . tother D.
    [*Authorship:* 'Tho.' in margin.]
LXVIII. B, D, H, T.   1 feet] fayre B; fatt H.   2 fynd] W; featch B; seche H; get D,
E. of] aftre B. wondrous] strange a B.   6 by] of B.   7 your] thy B; our H.
    [*Authorship:* 'Tho.' in margin; a correction in W's hand; in W section of T.]

But happe and hit or els hit not,   5
As vncertain as is the wynde,
Right so it fareth by the shott
Of love, alas, that is so blynd.

Therefore I plaid the foole in vain,
With pitie, when I first began   10
Your cruell hert for to constrain,
Syns love regardeth no doulfull man.

But, of your goodenes, all your mynde
Is that I should complain in vain:
This is the favor that I fynde,   15
Ye list to here how I can plain.

But tho I plain to please your hert,
Trust me, I trust to temper it so,
Not for to care which do revert:
All shalbe oon in welth or woo.   20

For fansy rueleth, tho right say nay,
Even as the goodeman kyst his kowe;
None othre reason can ye lay
But as who saieth, I reke not how.

LXX

LYKE as the Swanne towardis her dethe
Doeth strayn her voyse with dolefull note
Right so syng I with waste of brethe,
I dy! I dy! and you regarde yt note.

I shall enforce my faynting breth   5
That all that heris this dedlye note
Shall knowe that you dothe cause my deth:
I dy! I dy! and you regarde yt note.

LXIX. D.   12 regardeth] regardes D.   17 please] eese D.   19 do] side D.   21
rueleth] Rulis D.
    [*Authorship:* 'Tho.' in margin.]
LXX. B, D. [*The leaf is torn in E and the ends of the lines are supplied from B and D.*]
6 heris] here B. dedlye] B; delye D.   7 dothe] do B.

Your vnkyndnes hath sworne my dethe,
And chaunged hathe my plesaunte note   10
To paynfull sighes that stoppis my brethe:
I dy! I dy! and you regarde yt note.

Consumeth my lif, faileth my brethe;
Your fawte is forger of this note,
Melting in tearis, a cruell dethe: 15
I dy! I dy! and you regarde yt note.

My faith with me after my dethe
Bured shalbe, and to this note
I do bequethe my wery brethe
To cry 'I dyede and you regardid note'.   20

LXXI

In eternum I was ons determed
For to have louid and my mynde affermed,
That with my herte it should be confermed
    In eternum.

Forthwith I founde the thing that I myght like,   5
And sought with loue to warme her hert alike,
For as me thought I shuld not se the like
    In eternum.

To trase this daunse I put my self in prese;
Vayne hope ded lede and bad I should not cese   10
To serue, to suffer, and still to hold my pease
    In eternum.

With this furst Rule I fordred me a pase
That as me thought my trowghthe had taken place
With full assurans to stond in her grace   15
    In eternum.

It was not long er I by proofe had found
That feble bilding is on feble grounde,
For in her herte this worde did never sounde
    In eternum.   20

11 stoppis] stoppe B.   19 wery] B; verye D.   20 regardid] B; regarde yt D.
  [*Authorship:* 'Tho.' in margin.]
LXXI. D. [*The first part of each line is missing from E on account of a torn leaf.*]
  F

In eternum then from my herte I keste
That I had furst determind for the best;
Now in the place another thought doeth rest
    In eternum.

LXXII

Syns ye delite to knowe
That my torment and woo
    Should still encrese
    Withoute relese,
I shall enforce me so   5
That liff and all shall goo,
    For to content your cruelnes.

And so this grevous trayne
That I to long sustayn
    Shall sometyme cese   10
    And have redresse;
And you also remain
Full pleased with my pain,
    For to content your cruelnes.

Onles that be to light   15
And that ye would ye myght
    Se the distresse
    And hevines
Of oon slain owte right,
Therewith to please your sight,   20
    And to content your cruelnes.

Then in your cruell mode
Would god fourthwith ye woode
    With force expresse
    My hert oppresse   25
To do your hert suche good
To se me bathe in blode,
    For to content your cruelnes.

LXXII. B, D. 3 Should] shall B. 4 relese] redres B. 7–14] *omitted* B. 16 that]
yf B. 19 oon slain] me your slaue (? me you'v slane) B. slain] I slayne D. 24
expresse] exprest B. 26 suche] some B. 27 me bathe] bathe D.

Then cowld ye aske no more
Then should ye ease my sore, 30
And the excesse
Of myn excesse;
And you should evermore
Defamed be therefore,
For to repent your cruelnes. 35

LXXIII

HEVYN and erth and all that here me plain
Do well perceve what care doeth cause me cry,
Save you alone to whome I cry in vain:
'Mercy, madame, alas, I dy, I dy!'

Yf that you slepe, I humbly you require 5
Forbere a while and let your rigour slake
Syns that by you I burne thus in this fire:
To here my plaint, dere hert, awake, awake!

Syns that so oft ye have made me to wake
In plaint and teres and in right pitious case, 10
Displease you not if force do now me make
To breke your slepe, crieng 'alas, alas!'

It is the last trouble that ye shall have
Of me, madame, to here my last complaint:
Pitie at lest your poure vnhappy slave 15
For in dispere, alas, I faint, I faint!

It is not now, but long and long ago
I have you serued as to my powre and myght
As faithfully as any man myght do,
Clayming of you nothing of right, of right. 20

Save of your grace only to stay my liff,
That fleith as fast as clowd afore the wynde;
For syns that first I entred in this stryff
An inward deth hath fret my mynde, my mynd.

31-2 And . . . excesse] & exsese of my B. 32 myn] my D. 33 you] Ye B. 34
Defamed] disdayned B. 35 For] for for D; So B.
  [*Authorship:* 'Tho.' in margin.]
LXXIII. D (25-36). 24 my mynd] me mynd E.

Yf I had suffered this to you vnware,   25
Myn were the fawte and you nothing to blame;
But syns you know my woo and all my care
Why do I dy? Alas, for shame, for shame!

I know right well my face, my lowke, my teeres,
Myn Iyes, my Wordes, and eke my drery chiere   30
Have cryd my deth full oft vnto your eres;
Herd of belefe it doeth appere, appere!

A better prouff I se that ye would have
How I ame dede; therefore when ye here tell
Beleve it not all tho ye se my grave.   35
Cruell, vnkynd! I say farewell, farewell!

LXXIV

COMFORT thy self my wofull hert
Or shortly on thy self the wreke,
For length redoubleth dedly smert:
Why sighes thou, hert, and woult not breke?

To wast in sighes were pitious deth;   5
Alas, I fynd the faynt and weke.
Enforce thy self to lose thy breth:
Why sighes thou then, and woult not breke?

Thou knowest right well that no redresse
Is thus to pyne, and for to speke,   10
Pardy, it is remediles:
Why sighes thou then, and woult not breke?

It is to late for to refuse
The yoke when it is on thy neck;
To shak it of vaileth not to muse: 15
Why sighes thou then, and woult not breke?

To sobbe and sigh it were but vain,
Syns there is none that doeth it reke;

29 my teeres] teeres E; my terys D. 30 drery] dere D. 31 my] me D.
  [*Authorship:* 'Tho.' in margin; ascribed 'ffynys qᵈ Wyatt' in D.
LXXIV. D. 3 length] lenght E; lengthe D. 5 sighes] sight E; sighis D.

Alas, thou doyst prolong thy pain:
Why sighes thou then, and woult not breke? 20

Then in her sight, to move her hert,
Seke on thy self thy self to wreke,
That she may knowe thou sufferdst smert:
Sigh there thy last, and therewith breke!

LXXV

DESIRE, alas, my master and my foo,
So sore alterd thi sellff how mayst thou se?
Some tyme I sowght that dryvys me to and fro;
Some tyme thow ledst that ledyth the and me.
What reson is to rewle thy subiectes so 5
By forcyd law and mutabilite?
For where by the I dowtyd to have blame,
Evyn now by hate agayne I dowt the same.

LXXVI

VENEMUS thornes that ar so sharp and kene
Sometyme ber flowers fayre and fresh of hue;
Poyson offtyme is put in medecene
And cawsith helth in man for to renue;
Ffyre that purgith allthing that is vnclene 5
May hele, and hurt: and if these bene true,

23 sufferdst] suffirid D.
  [*Authorship:* 'Tho.' in margin.]
  This poem is followed by a gap in the MS, and then by part of the First Satire.
LXXV. D, T. 1 Desire, alas] cruell desire D. 2 So . . . sellff] thy silf so chaungid
for shame D. 3 Some . . . dryvys] Where thou didst seke which chaseth *deleted* W;
that I have sought dothe chase D. I sowght] thou sekest D. 4 Some . . . ledyth]
Whome thow didst rule now rulyth *deleted* W, D. 5 What reson] tyrant it *deleted* W;
what right D. 6 By . . . and] And to be rulid by D. 7 For] lo D. 8 hate] dred D.
  [*Authorship:* In W's handwriting; 'Tho.' in margin; in W section of T.]
LXXVI. D, P, H, CC, T, N. 1 ar so] be both P, N; are bothe CC. 2 Sometyme
ber] Beare somtymes N. Sometyme . . . hue] Beare flowers we se full fresh and faire
of hue T. 3 Poyson offtyme] And poyson ofte P, N. offtyme] oft tymes D, CC;
oftayne H; is also T. 4] And to his helthe dothe make the man renue D; And vnto
man his helth doth oft renue T; *omitted* CC. And] Which H. 5] The fyre, eke, that
all consumeth cleene P, N: fyre that all thing consumith so clene D; The fier that all
thinges eke consumeth cleane T. 6 hele] helpp N. hele, and hurt] hurt and heale T.
and then T. these bene] that this be P, T, N; this be H, CC.

I trust somtyme my harme may be my helth,
Syns every wo is joynid with some welth.

LXXVII

To cause accord or to aggre,
Two contraries in oon degre,
And in oon poynct as semeth me
To all mens wit it cannot be:
    It is impossible.   5

Of hete and cold when I complain
And say that hete doeth cause my pain,
When cold doeth shake me every vain,
And boeth at ons, I say again
    It is impossible.   10

That man that hath his hert away
If lyff lyveth there as men do say
That he hertles should last on day
Alyve and not to torne to clay,
    It is impossible.   15

Twixt lyff and deth, say what who sayth,
There lyveth no lyff that draweth breth;
They joyne so nere and eke i' feith
To seke for liff by wissh of deth,
    It is impossible.   20

Yet love that all thing doeth subdue
Whose power ther may no liff eschew
Hath wrought in me that I may rew
These miracles to be so true
    That are impossible.   25

7 I . . . be] I trust my harme to be H.   8 with] to H.
[*Authorship:* In W's handwriting; 'Tho.' in margin; in W section of T.]
The poem is followed in the MS. by the Second Satire.

LXXVII. D.   4 mens] mennis D; mans E.   12 lyveth] lyve D. do] dothe D.   13 That he] that D.   14 torne] tone D.   18 i'] I E, D.   21 thing] things D.   24 These] this D.
[*Authorship:* 'Tho.' in margin.]

LXXVIII

THOUGH this thy port and I thy seruaunt true
And thou thy self doist cast thy bemes from hye
From thy chieff howse promising to renew
Boeth Joye and eke delite, behold yet how that I
Bannysshed from my blisse carefully do crye: 5
'Helpe now Citherea, my lady dere,
My ferefull trust en vogant la galere.'

Alas the dowbt that dredfull absence geveth;
Withoute thyn ayde assuraunce is there none;
The ferme faith that in the water fleteth   10
Succour thou therefor; in the it is alone.
Stay that with faith that faithfully doeth mone,
And thou also gevest me boeth hope and fere,
Remembre thou me en vogant la galere.

By Sees and hilles elonged from thy sight,   15
Thy wonted grace reducing to my mynde
In sted of slepe thus I occupy the nyght;
A thowsand thoughtes and many dowbtes I fynde,
And still I trust thou canst not be vnkind
Or els dispere my comfort, and my chiere   20
Would fle fourthwith en vogant la galere.

Yet on my faith full litle doeth remain
Of any hope whereby I may my self vphold,
For syns that onely wordes do me retain,
I may well thinck the affection is but cold;   25
But syns my will is nothing as I would
But in thy handes it resteth hole and clere,
Forget me not en vogant la galere.

LXXIX

VNSTABLE dreme according to the place
    Be stedfast ons: or els at leist be true:
    By tasted swetenes make me not to rew

LXXVIII. B.   1 this thy porte] B; this port E. I thy] I the B.   7, 14, 21, 28 en] in B.
13 gevest] gevys B.   14, 21, 28 galere] galerie E.   15 elonged] elongyd B.   21 fle]
Nott *conj*; she E, B.   22 on] in B.   23 Of any] off B.

The sudden losse of thy fals fayned grace.
By goode respect in such a daungerous case   5
   Thou broughtes not her into this tossing mew
   But madest my sprite lyve my care to renew,
My body in tempest her succour to embrace.
The body dede, the spryt had his desire;
   Paynles was th'one: th'othre in delight.   10
   Why then, Alas, did it not kepe it right,
Retorning to lepe into the fire,
   And where it was at wysshe it could not remain?
   Such mockes of dremes they torne to dedly pain.

LXXX

In dowtfull brest, whilst moderly pitie
With furyous famyn stondyth at debate,
Sayth thebrew moder: 'O child vnhappye,
Retorne thi blowd where thou hadst milk of late.
Yeld me those lymmis that I made vnto the,   5
And entre there where thou wert generate;
For of on body agaynst all nature
To a nothr must I mak sepulture.'

LXXXI

Off Cartage he that worthie warrier
Could ouercome, but cowld not vse his chaunce,
And I like wise off all my long indeuor
The sherpe conquest tho fortune did avaunce
Cowld not it vse: the hold that is gyvin ouer   5
I vnpossest. So hangith in balaunce
Off warr, my pees, reward of all my payne;
At Mountzon thus I restles rest in Spayne.

LXXIX. A, T.   6 broughtes] broughtest A, T. this . . . mew] these tossing seas T.
7 lyve] to liue T. to renew] tencrease T.   8 succour to embrace] delight timbrace T.
10 th'one] thone E, A, T. th'othre] thothre E; th'other A; the other T.   12 Retorn-
ing] But thus return T.   13 it could] could T.   14 they] do T.
   [*Authorship:* In W sections of A and T.]
LXXX. T.   1 whilst] whiles T.   3 Sayth . . . moder] The mother sayth T.   6 wert]
were T.   8 a nothr] an other T. must I] I must *deleted* W.
   [*Authorship:* In W's handwriting; 'Tho.' in margin; in W section of T.]
LXXXI. T.   4 avaunce] aduance T.   5 Cowld . . . vse] Ne could I vse T.   8 thus]
lo *deleted* W.
   [*Authorship:* In W's handwriting; 'Tho.' in margin; in W section of T.]

LXXXII

PROCESSE of tyme worketh such wounder
That water which is of kynd so soft
Doeth perse the marbell stone a sonder
By litle droppes falling from aloft.

And yet an hert that sems so tender   5
Receveth no dropp of the stilling teres,
That alway still cause me to render
The vain plaint that sowndes not in her eres.

So cruel, alas, is nowght alyve,
So fiers, so frowerd, so owte of fframe,   10
But some way, some tyme, may so contryve
By mens the wild to tempre and tame.

And I that alwaies have sought and seke
Eche place, eche tyme for some lucky daye
This fiers Tigre lesse I fynde her meke   15
And more denyd the lenger I pray.

The lyon in his raging furour
Forberis that sueth mekenes for his boote:
And thou, Alas, in extreme dolour
The hert so low thou tredist vnder thy foote.   20

Eche fiers thing lo! how thou doest excede
And hides it vnder so humble a face,
And yet the humble to helpe at nede
Nought helpeth tyme, humblenes, nor place.

LXXXIII

AFTER great stormes the cawme retornis
And pleasanter it is thereby;
Fortune likewise that often tornis
Hath made me now the moost happy.

LXXXII. A. 12 the] of A.   18 boote] O; *omitted* E, A.   20 tredist] A; tredis E.
   [*Authorship:* 'Tho.' in margin.]

Thevin that pited my distres,   5
My iust desire and my cry,
Hath made my languor to cesse
And me also the most happy.

Whereto dispaired ye, my frendes?
My trust always in hevin did ly   10
That knoweth what my thought intends
Whereby I lyve the most happy.

Lo! what can take hope from that hert
That is assured stedfastly?
Hope therefore ye that lyve in smert,   15
Whereby I ame the most happy.

And I that have felt of your paine
Shall pray to god continuelly
To make your hope, your helth retayne,
And make me also the most happy.   20

LXXXIV

ALL hevy myndes
Do seke to ese their charge
And that that moost theim byndes
To let at large.

Then why should I   5
Hold payne within my hert
And may my tune apply
To ese my smart?

My faithfull lute
Alone shall here me plaine,   10
For els all othre sute
Is clene in vaine.

For where I sue
Redresse of all my grieff

LXXXIII. A.   5 Thevin] The heaven A.   10 hevin did] M; hid E; her did O.
11 thought] though E; thoughte A.   16 happy] vnhappie A.
[*Authorship:* In W section of A.]
LXXXIII is followed by the Third Satire.

Lo! they do most eschew 15
My hertes relieff.

Alas, my dere,
Have I deserued so
That no help may appere
Of all my wo? 20

Whome speke I to,
Vnkynd and deff of ere?
Alas, lo, I go,
And wot not where.

Where is my thoght? 25
Where wanders my desire?
Where may the thing be soght
That I require?

Light in the wynde
Doth fle all my delight 30
Where trouth and faithfull mynd
Are put to flyght.

Who shall me gyve
Fetherd wynges for to fle
The thing that doeth me greve 35
That I may se?

Who would go seke
The cause whereby to playne?
Who could his foo beseke
For ease of payne? 40

My chaunce doeth so
My wofull case procure
To offer to my ffoo
My hert to cure.

What hope I then 45
To have any redresse?

LXXXIV. 38 playne] J.; payne E.
  [*Authorship:* 'Tho.' in margin.]

Of whome, or where, or when,
Who can expresse?

No, sins dispaire
Hath set me in this case   50
In vain oft in the ayre
To say Alas,

I seke nothing
But thus for to discharge
My hert of sore sighing,   55
To plaine at large;

And with my lute
Sumtyme to ease my pain,
For els all othre sute
Is clene in vain.   60

LXXXV

To seke eche where, where man doth lyve,
The See, the land, the Rock, the clyve,
Fraunce, Spayne and Ind and every where
Is none a greater gift to gyve,
Lesse sett by oft and is so lyff and dere,   5
Dare I well say than that I gyve to yere.

I cannot gyve browches nor Ringes,
Thes goldsmythes work and goodly thinges,
Piery nor perle oryente and clere,
But for all that is no man bringes   10
Leffer Juell vnto his lady dere,
Dare I well say, then that I gyve to yere.

Nor I seke not to fetche it farr,
Worse is it not tho it be narr,
And as it is it doeth appere   15
Vncontrefaict mistrust to barr,

LXXXV. 4 a gift] *deleted* E.   5 and dere] dere *original reading* E.   9 oryente] orent
original reading E.   10 is . . . bringes] can no man bring *later correction* E.
   [*Authorship:* 'Tho.' in margin.]

Left hole and pure withouten pere,
Dare I well say the gift I gyve to yere.

To the therefore the same retain,
The like of the to have again;   20
Fraunce would I gyve if myn it were;
Is none alyve in whome doeth rayne
Lesser disdaine; frely, therfore, lo here,
Dare I well gyve, I say, my hert to yere.

LXXXVI

O GOODELY hand,
Wherin doeth stand
My hert distrast in payne,
Faire hand, Alas,
In litle spas   5
My liff that doeth restrayne.

O fyngers slight,
Departed right,
So long, so small, so rownd,
Goodely bygone,   10
And yet alone
Most cruell in my wound.

With Lilis whight
And Roses bright
Doth stryve thy colour faire;   15
Nature did lend
Eche fyngers ende
A perle for to repayre.

Consent at last,
Syns that thou hast   20
My hert in thy demayne,
For seruice trew
On me to rew,
And reche me love againe.

LXXXVI. H.   4 Faire] dere H.   6 that doeth] thou dost H.   15 stryve] strayne H.

And if not so,   25
Then with more woo
Enforce thiself to strayne
This simple hert,
That suffereth smart,
And rid it owte of payne.   30

LXXXVII

Lo what it is to love!
Lerne ye that list to prove
At me, I say,
No ways that may
The growndyd greiff remove,   5
My liff alwaie
That doeth decaye:
Lo what it is to love!

Fle alwaye from the snare,
Lerne by me to beware   10
Of suche a trayne
Which dowbles payne,
And endles woo and care,
That doth retayne;
Which to refrayne   15
Fle alwaye from the snare.

To love and to be wise,
To rage with good aduyse,
Now thus, now than,
Now of, now an,   20
Vncertyn as the dyse;
There is no man
At ons that can
To love and to be wise.

---

29 suffereth] suffered H.
  [*Authorship:* 'Tho.' in margin.]
LXXXVII. B.   4 No ways that] that no wyse B.   5 growndyd] B; grownd is E.
10 by] att B.   12 Which dowbles] and dubbyll B.   13 And] wyth B.   14–15] wych to
refrayne/and nott retayne B.

Suche are the dyvers throws,   25
Suche that no man knows
That hath not profd
And ons have lofd;
Suche are the raging woos,
Soner reprofd   30
Then well remofd:
Suche are the dyvers throwes.

Love is a fervent fire,
Kendeld by hote desire,
For a short pleasure   35
Long displeasur;
Repentaunce is the hire;
A poure tresoure
Withoute mesure,
Love is a fervent fire.   40

Lo what it is to love!

        *   *   *

Leve thus to slaunder love!
Though evill with suche it prove
Which often vse
Love to mysuse   45
And loving to reprove;
Such cannot chose
For their refuse
But thus to slaunder love.

Fle not so much the snare;   50
Love sildom causeth care,
But by deserftes
And crafty partes
Some lese their owne welfare;
Be true of hertes   55
And for no smartes
Fle not so much the snare.

27 That hath not] But he have B. 35 For a short] a small B. 41] *omitted* B. 41 +] the
answer B. 43 evill] yll B. 49 thus] thys B.

> To love and not to be wise
> Is but a mad devise;
> Such love doeth last   60
> As sure and fast
> As chansys off the dise
> A bitter tast
> Coms at the last
> To love and not to be wise.   65
>
> Suche be the plaisaunt daies,
> Suche be the honest wayes;
> There is no man
> That fully can
> Knowe it but he that sayes   70
> Loving to ban
> Were folly then:
> Such be the plaisaunt daies.
>
> Love is a plaisaunt fire
> Kyndled by true desire,   75
> And though the payne
> Cause men to playne,
> Sped well is oft the hiere;
> Then though som fayne
> And lese the gayne   80
> Love is a plaisaunt fyer.

*   *   *

> Who most doeth slaunder love
> The dede must alwaye prove;
> Trouth shall excuse
> That you accuse   85
> For slaunder and reprove;
> Not by refuse
> But by abuse
> You most do slaunder love.

58 to be] be B.   59 Is but] hytt were B.   62 chansys off] B; chaunce on E.   65 to be] be B.   69 That fully] fully that B.   70 it] them B.   77 men] sum B.   79 som] ye B.   80] plesuer for payn B.   81 +] the answer to thys B.   83 must] shall B.   89 You] ye B.

They fle from me / that sometyme did me seke
wyth naked fote stalking in my chambre
I have sene them gentill tame and meke
that nowe are wyld and do not remembre
that sometyme they put themself in daunger
to take bred at my hand & nowe they raunge
besely seking wyth a continuell chaunge

Thanked be fortune it hath ben othrewise
twenty tymes better but ons in speciall
in thyn arraye after a pleasaunt gyse
when her lose gowne from her shoulders did fall
and she me caught in her armes long & small
therewithall swetely did me kysse
and softely saide dere hert howe like you this

It was no dreme I lay brode waking
but all is torned thorough my gentilnes
into a straunge fasshion of forsaking
and I have leve to goo of her goodnes
and she also to vse new fangilnes
but syns that I so kyndely ame serued
I would fain knowe what she hath deserued

1. Egerton MS
(*poem* XXXVII, *page* 27)

Ye graunt it is a snare   90
And would vs not beware;
Lest that your trayne
Should be to playne
Ye colour all the care;
Lo how you fayne   95
Pleasure for payne
And graunt it is a snare!

To love and to be wise,
It were a straunge devise;
But from that tast   100
Ye vow the fast;
On zyns tho runne your dise,
Ambs as may hast
Your payne to wast:
To love and to be wise!   105

Of all suche pleasaunt dayes,
Of all suche pleasaunt playes,
Without deserft
You have your part,
And all the worould so sayes;   110
Save that poure hert
That for more smert
Feleth yet suche pleasaunt dayes.

Such fire and suche hete
Did never make ye swete,   115
For withoute payne
You best obtayne
To good spede and to great;
Who so doeth playne
You best do fayne   120
Such fire and suche hete.

Who now doeth slaunder love?

90 Ye] Yow B. 92 Lest that] and lest B. 94 Ye] yow B. 95 you] ye B. 101 the] to
B. 102 tho] ye B. 113 Feleth] feles B. suche] sum B. 114 and] nor B. 115 ye] yow
B. 117 You best] ye did B. 119 so] most B. 120 You] ye B. 122] *omitted* B.
    [*Authorship:* 'Tho.' in margin.]
    G

LXXXVIII

I LEDE a liff vnpleasant, nothing glad;
Crye and complaynt offerre, voydes Joyfullnesse;
So chaungethe vnrest that nought shall fade;
Payne and dyspyte hathe altered plesantnes
Ago, long synnys, that she hathe truly made,   5
Dysdayne for trowght sett lyght yn stedfastnes,
I haue cause goode to syng this song:
Playne or reioyse, who felythe wele or wrong.

LXXXIX

YF in the world ther be more woo
Then I haue yn my harte,
Wher so ytt is itt doithe come fro,
And in my brest there doithe itt groo,
For to encrease my smarte.   5
Alas I ame recepte of euery care
And of my liff eche sorrow claymes his part.
Who list to lyue in quyetnes
By me lett hym beware,
For I by highe dysdayne   10
Ame made withoute redresse;
And vnkyndenes, alas, hath slayne
My poore trew hart all comfortles.

XC

TH'ANSWERE that ye made to me, my dere,
Whann I did sewe for my poore hartes redresse,
Hathe so appalld my countenaunce and my chere,
That yn this case I ame all comfortelesse,
Sins I of blame no cawse can well expresse.   5

LXXXVIII. 3 chaungethe vnrest] *between these words is inserted in W's* (?) *handwriting
what looks like* re; *possibly it is meant for* y^e = the.
   [*Authorship:* 'Tho.' in margin.]

LXXXIX. D.   2 yn] now within D.   10 highe] gret D.   12 alas, hath] hathe D.
13 My poore trew] a symple D.
   [*Authorship:* 'Tho.' in margin.]

XC. T.   1 Th'answere] The answere T.

I haue no wrong wher I cann clayme no right;
Nowght tane me fro wher I nothing haue had;
Yete of my wo I cann nott so be quyte,
Namely sins that another may be glad
With that that thus in sorowe makethe me sad.   10

Another? why, shall lyberty be bond?
Fre hart may not be bond but by desert.

*   *   *

Nor none cann clayme, I say, by former graunte
That knowithe nott of any graunt att all;
And by deserte I dare well make avaunte,   15
Of faythfull will ther is no wher that shall
Bere you more trowthe, more redy att your call.

Now good then call agayne that frendly word
That seithe your frende in saving of his payne;
And say, my dere, that itt was sayde in borde;   20
Late or too sone lett that nott rule the gayne,
Wherwith fre will doth trew deserte retayne.

XCI

Most wretchid hart most myserable,
Syns the comforte is from the fled,
Syns all the trouthe is turned to fable,
Most wretchid harte why arte thou nott ded?

No, no, I lyve and must doo still,   5
Whereof I thank god and no mo;
Ffor I me selff have all my will,
And he is wretchid that wens hym so.

Butt yete thow hast bothe had and lost
The hope so long that hathe the fed,   10
And all thy travayle and thy cost:
Most wretchid harte why arte thow nott ded?

---

7 nothing haue] haue nothing T.   10 makethe] makes T.   11–12] *omitted* T.   13 Nor]
Yet T.   18 frendly] bitter T.   19] That toucht your frende so nere with panges of
paine T.   22 doth] T; *omitted* E.
  [*Authorship:* T. W. in margin; in W section of T.]

Some other hope must fede me new;
Yff I haue lost I say 'what tho?'
Dyspayr shall nott throwghe it ynsew   15
For he is wretchid that wenys hym so.

*   *   *

The sonne, the mone doth frowne on the;
Thow hast darkenes in daylightes stede;
As good in grave as soo to be:
Moost wretched hert why art thou not ded?   20

Some plesant sterre may shewe me light,
But tho the heven wold worke me woo,
Who hath himself shal stande vp right,
And he is wretched that wens him soo.

Hath he himself that is not sure?   25
His trust is like as he hath sped;
Against the streme thou maist not dure:
Most wretched herte, why art thou not ded?

The last is worst, who feres not that?
He hath himself where so he goo;   30
And he that knoweth what is what
Sayeth he is wretched that wens him soo.

Seist thou not how they whet their teth,
Which to touche the somtime ded drede?
They finde comforte for thy mischief: 35
Moost wretched hert, why art thou not dede?

What tho that currs do fal by kinde
On him that hathe the overthrow?
Al that can not opresse my minde,
For he is wretched that wens him soo.   40

Yet can it not be thenne denyd,
It is as certain as thy crede;
Thy gret vnhap thou canst not hid:
Vnhappy thenne why art thou not dede?

XCI. 15 throwghe it] J; throwghe E; therewith O.
 [*Authorship:* 'Tho.' in margin.]

Vnhappy, but no wretche therfore,   45
For happe doth come again and goo;
For whiche I kepe my self in store,
Sins vnhap cannot kil me soo.

XCII

You that in love finde lucke and habundance
    And live in lust and joyful jolitie,
    Arrise for shame! do away your sluggardie!
    Arise, I say, do May some obseruance!
Let me in bed lye dreming in mischaunce;   5
    Let me remembre the happs most vnhappy
    That me betide in May most commonly,
    As oon whome love list litil to avaunce.
Sephame saide true that my natiuitie
    Mischaunced was with the ruler of the May: 10
    He gest I prove of that the veritie.
In May my welth and eke my liff I say
    Have stoude so oft in such perplexitie:
    Reioyse! let me dreme of your felicitie.

XCIII

And if an Iye may save or sleye,
    And streke more diepe then wepon longe,
    And if an Iye by subtil play
    May move on more thenne any tonge,
    How canne ye say that I do wrong   5
    Thus to suspect without deserte?
    For the Iye is traitour of the herte.

To frame all wel I am content
    That it were done vnwetingly;

XCII. A, T.   4, 7, 10, 12 May] may E.   1 habundance] swete abundance T.   2 lust
and] lust of T.   3 away] way T.   5 in] of T.   6 the happs most] my missehappes T.
9 Sephame] Sephances A; Stephan T.   10 Mischaunced] Mischaunce A.   11 I . . .
that] of that I prove A.   12 liff] wittes T.   14 Reioyse] Ioye T.
    [*Authorship:* 'Tho.' in margin; in W sections of A and T.]
XCIII. Two versions in E, the earlier deleted.   1 an Iye] an Ie E; that ye E1.   2
streke] stryke E1.   7 For] from E1.

But yet I say who wol assent,   10
To do but wel, do nothyng whie
That men shuld deme the contrary,
For it is said by menn expert
That the Iye is traitour of the hert.

But yet, alas, that loke all sowle   15
That I doo clayme of right to haue,
Shuld not, methinkes, goo seke the scole
To plese alle folke; for who canne crave
Frendlier thing thenne hert witsaue?
By loke to give in frendely parte,   20
For the Iye is traitour of the hert.

And my suspect is without blame,
For, as ye saye, not only I
But other moo haue demyd the same;
Thenne is it not of Jelowsye   25
But subtille loke of rekeles Iye
Did rainge to farre to make me smart,
For the Iye is traitour of the hert.

But I your freende shall take it thus,
Sins you wol soo, as stroke of chaunce;   30
And leve furder for to discus
Wither the stroke did sticke or glaunce;
But scuse who canne, let him avaunce
Dissembled lokes; but for my parte
My Iye must still bitray my harte.   35

And of this grief ye shalbe quitte
In helping trowth stedfast to goo;
The time is longe that doth sitt
Feble and weike and suffreth woo,
Cherish him wel, continewe soo,   40
Let him not fro your hart astart;
Thenne fere not the Iye to shewe the hert.

11 nothyng] E1; not thing E2. 17 methinkes] me thynkethe E1. 25 of] E1; *omitted*
E2. 29–42 *omitted* E1.

XCIV

Psalm 37. *Noli emulare in maligna*

ALTHO thow se th'owtragius clime aloft,
　Envie not thowe his blinde prosperitye;
　The welth of wretches tho it semith soft,
Move not thy hert by theyre felicitye.
　They shalbe found like grasse turnd into hay,　　　　5
　And as the herbes that wither sodenlye.
Stablisshe thy trust in god, seke right allway,
　And on the yerth thowe shalte inhabite longe;
　Fede and encreace such hope from day to day,
And if with god thow time thy hartie songe　　　　10
　He shal the giue what soo thy hart can lust.
　Cast vppon god thy will that right thy wrong;
Gyve him the charge for he vpright and iust
　Hath cure of the and of thy cares all,
　And he shall make thy trowgh to be discust　　　　15
Bright as the sonne, and thy rightwisnes shall
　(The cursids welth, tho now do it deface)
　Shine like the daylight, that we the none call.
Paciently abide the Lordes assured grace;
　Bere with even minde the trouble that he sendes　　　　20
　Dismay the not tho thou se the purchace
Encresse of some, for such like lucke god sendes
　To wicked folke . . .
　Restrayne thy mind from wrath that ay offendes;
Do way all rage, and se thou do eschew　　　　25
　By theire like dede suche dedes for to committ:
　For wikked folke theire overthrow shal rewe.
Who pacientlie abid and do not flitt,
　They shall possede the world from heire to hayre:
　The wikked shall of all his welth be quitt　　　　30
So sodainly and that without repaire
　That all his pompe and his staring aray
　Shall from thyn Iye departe as blast of ayre.
The sobre thenne the world shall weld, I say,

XCIV. A.　3 semith] seemythe A; senith E.　14 and] and eke A.　16 Bright as] O; vpright all E; upright as A. rightwisnes] rightuosnes A.　20 sendes] A; sende E. 25 eschew] A; estewe E.　28 abid] abydes A.　32 and] and eke A. staring] straunge A.

And live in welth and pes soo plentifull.   35
Him to distroy the wikked shall assay
And gnasshe his teethe eke with girninge yrefull.
    The Lord shall scorne the threatninges of the wretche,
    Ffor he doth know the tyde is nighe at full
When he shall syncke and no hand shall hym seeche.   40
    They have vnsheathed eke their blouddy bronds
    And bent theire bowe to prove if they might reach
To overthrowe the . . .
    Bare of relief the harmelesse to devoure.
    The sworde shall pearce the hart of suche that fonds;   45
Their bow shall breake in their moste endevoure.
    A litle Livinge gotten rightfullie
    Passithe the ritchesse and eke the highe powre
Of that that wretches have gatherd wickedlye.
    Pearishe shall the wickedes posteritie,   50
    And god shall stablishe the iuste assuredlye.
The iust mans dayes the Lorde doth know and see,
    Their heritage shall laste for evermore,
    And of their hope beguylde they shall not be.
When dismolde dayes shall wrappe the tother sore,   55
    They shall be full when other faynte for foode;
    Thearwhyl'ste shall faile theise wicked men thearfore.
To godes ennemyes suche end shall be allowdd
    As hath lambs greace wastinge in the fyre,
    That is consumde into a smokye clowde.   60
Borow'th th'vniust without will or desyre
    To yelde agayne; the iuste freelye dothe geve,
    Wheare he seethe neede as marcye dothe requyre.
Who will'the hym well for right thearfore shall leve;
    Who bannythe hym shall be rooted awaye;   65
    His steppes shall god directe still and relieve,
And please hym shall what lyf hym lust assaye;
    And though he fall vnder foote lye shall not he,
    Catchinge his hand for god shall streight hym staye.

                  *   *   *   70

Nor yet his sede foodelesse seene for to be.
The iuste to all men mercyfull hathe bene,

37–112] A; *omitted* E.   43 To overthrowe the iust; stretched forth their honds *conj.* F.
58 To] O; The A.   65 bannythe] Mason *conj.*; bannyshe A.   70–1] *omitted* A.

Busye to do well, thearfore his seede, I saye,
Shall have habundaunce all waye fresshe and grene.   75
Fflee yll, do good, that thow mayste last all waye,
    Ffor god dothe love for evermore th' vpright:
    Never his Chosen dothe he cast awaye;
Ffor ever he them myndeth daye and night,
    And wicked seede alwaye shall waste to nought: 80
    The iust shall welde the worlde as their owne right,
And longe thearon shall dwell as theye have wrought.
    Withe wisdome shall the wyse mans mowthe hym able;
    His tongue shall speake alwaye even as it ought;
With godes learning he hathe his harte stable;   85
    His foote thearfore from slydinge shall be sure.
    The wicked watchethe the iust for to disable,
And for to se hym dothe his busye cure;
    But god will not suffer hym for to quaile
    By tyrannye nor yet bye faulte vnpure   90
To be condemn'd in iudgement without faile.
    Awayte thearfore the commynge of the Lorde;
    Live withe his lawes in pacience to prevayle,
And he shall raise the of thyne owne accorde
    Above the earth in suretye to beholde   95
    The wickedes deathe that thow maye it recorde.
I have well seene the wicked sheene lyke goolde,
    Lustie and greene as lawrell lasting aye;
    But even anon and scantt his seate was colde:
When I have paste agayne the self same waye,   100
    Wheare he did raigne he was not to be fownde;
    Vanyshte he was for all his fresshe arraye.
Let vprightnes be still thie stedfast grownde.
    Ffollowe the right suche one shall alwaye fynde
    Hym self in peace and plentie to habounde.   105
All wicked folke reversyd shall vntwynde,
    And wretchidnes shall be the wickedes end:
    Healthe to the iuste from god shall be assignde.
He shall them strengthe whome troble shoulde offend.
    The Lord shall helpp, I saye, and them delyver   110
    Ffrom curssed handes, and healthe vnto them send,
For that in hym they sett their trust for ever.

XCV

F ROM thes hye hilles as when a spryng doth fall
It tryllyth downe with still and suttyll corse;
Off this and that it gaders ay and shall
Tyll it have just off flowd the streme and forse,
Then at the fote it ragith ouer all: 5
So faryth love when he hath tan a sorse;
His rayne is rage, resistans vaylyth none;
The first estew is remedy alone.

XCVI

P ROVE wythr I do chainge, my dere,
Or if that I do still remayne
Lik as I went or ferre or nere
And if ye fynde . . .

XCVII

I F waker care if sodayne pale Coulour
If many sighes with litle speche to playne
Now ioy, now woo, if they my chere distayne,
For hope of smalle, if muche to fere therfore,
To hast, to slak my pase lesse or more,   5
  Be signe of love then do I love agayne.
If thow aske whome, sure sins I did refrayne
Brunet that set my welth in such a rore,
Th' unfayned chere of Phillis hath the place
  That Brunet had: she hath and ever shal.   10
  She from my self now hath me in her grace:
She hath in hand my witt, my will, and all
  My hert alone wel worthie she doth staye,
  Without whose helpe skant do I live a daye.

XCV, B, T. 1 From . . . when] as from theys hylles when that B. 2 with] by B.
still] *later correction* W; small W. 3 ay] *later correction* W; still W. Off . . . that] and
of ech thyng B. 4 off flowd] downflowed T. 7 His . . . rage] Rage is his raine T.
7 resistans . . . none] *later correction* W; then botyth no deny W. vaylyth] ys ther B.
8 remedy alone] *later correction* W; only remedy W.
  [*Authorship:* In W's handwriting.]
XCVI. This fragment is apparently in W's handwriting.
XCVII. A, T. 5 to slak] or slack T. pase] A; passe E; pace to T. 6 Be] T; by E,
A. 8 Brunet . . . rore] W; her that did set our country in a rore E.
  [*Authorship:* 'Tho.' in margin; in W sections of A and T; corrections in W's hand-
writing.]

XCVIII
In Spayne

So feble is the threde that doth the burden stay
Of my pore lyff, In hevy plyght that fallyth in dekay,
That but it have elles where some aide or some socours,
The runyng spyndell off my fate anon shall end his cours.
Sins thunhappy howre that did me to depart   5
From my swete wele, one only hope hath staide my lyff apart,
Wych doth perswade such wordes vnto my sory mynd.
'Mayntene thy sellff, o wofull spryte, some better luk to fynd:
Ffor tho thou be depryffd from thy desyerd syght
Who can the tell iff thi retorne be for thy most delyght?   10
Or who can tell thy losse if thou ons maist recover?
Some plesant howre thy wo may rape and the defend and cover.'
This is the trust that yet hath my lyff sustaynid;
And now alas I se' it faint and I by trust ame trainid.
The tyme doth flete and I perceyve thowrs how thei bend   15
So fast that I have skant the space to marke my comyng end.
Westward the sonne from owt th'est skant doth shew his lyght,
When in the west he hyds hym straite within the darke of nyght;
And coms as fast where he began his path a wrye
From est to west, from west to thest so doth his jornei ly.   20
The lyff so short, so fraile, that mortall men lyve here,
So gret a whaite, so hevy charge, the body that we bere,
That when I thinke apon the distance and the space
That doth so ferr devid me from my dere desird face,
I know not how t'attayne the wynges that I require,   25
To lyfft my whaite that it myght fle to folow my desyre.
Thus off that hope, that doth my lyff some thing sustayne,

XCVIII. A, D, T.   2 hevy] sory E. in dekay] with his sway E.   3 have] hathe A.
elles . . . or some] frome elles where some aide or E.   5 Sins] ffore sins E, A, T; syns D.
that did] did D.   6 one] and A, T. staide] held E.   7 Wych] That E. such wordes] with
such like E. sory] wofull E; sored A, T.   8 spryte] wight A, T.   10 most] more A, T.
11 ons maist] maist ons E, A, T; ons must D.   12 rape] wrape E; wrapp A, T.   13
This is the] Thus is this T. that] as A, T. hath] that hath A; it hath T.   14 and] but A,
T. I by] by D.   15 flete] passe E. perceyve] se T. thowrs how thei bend] the howres
. . . bend A, D; how the howers do bend T. bend] flye E.   16 that] alas that E.   17
th'est] thest W, D; the easte A, T. skant doth shew] dothe scantlye shew A; scant
shewes T.   18 When] Butt A. straite] sellff E.   19 as fast] agayne E. where he]
where D.   20 from west] to est. E. jornei] viage E.   22 body] bodies A, T.   26 my
whaite] me vp T. it] I A, T. fle] flye A, T.   27 hope] hope as yet A. lyff some thing]

Alas, I fere and partly fele full litill doth remayne.
Eche place doth bryng me grieff, where I do not behold
Those lyvely Iyes wich off my thowghtes were wont the kays to
    hold.   30
Those thowghtes were plesaunt swete whilst I enioyd that grace;
My plesure past, my present payne, wher I myght well embrace.
But for becawse my want shold more my wo encresse,
In wache, in slepe, both day and nyght, my will doth neuer cesse
That thing to wish wheroff, sins I did lese the syght,   35
I neuer saw the thing that myght my faytfull hert delyght.
Th'vnesy lyff I lede doth teche me for to mete
The flowdes, the sees, the land and hilles that doth them entremete
Twene me' and those shining lyghtes that wontyd to clere
My darke panges off clowdy thowghtes as bryght as Phebus
    spere;   40
It techith me also what was my plesant state,
The more to fele by such record how that my welth doth bate.
If such record, alas, provoke th'enflamid mynd
Wich sprang that day that I did leve the best of me byhynd;
If love forgett hym sellff by lenght of absence let,   45
Who doth me guyd, o wofull wrech, vnto this baytid net
Where doth encresse my care? much better were for me
As dome as stone, all thing forgott, still absent for to be.
Alas the clere crystall, the bryght transparant glas,
Doth not bewray the colour hyd which vnderneth it has,   50
As doth th'accomberd sprite thowghtfull throws discover
Off fiers delyght, off fervent love, that in our hertes we cover.
Owt by thes Iyes it shewth that euer more delyght
In plaint and teres to seke redresse, and that both day and nyght.
Thes new kyndes off plesurs, wherein most men reioyse,   55
To me thei do redowble still off stormye syghes the voyce;

lyf A.   28 fele] fle D.   29 me] my A.   30 lyvely] lovelye A. wich] that E.   32
wher] that E; when A, T. myght well] myght D.   33 But] And T.   34 in slepe] and
sleepe A, T.   35 sins I] I D.   36 I . . . hert] Was neuer thing that mought in ought
my woful hart D. the] that A.   38 land and hilles] Landes the Hilles A; land, the hylles
T.   39 shining] shene T. to] for to A, T.   40 darke] darked A, T. spere] spheare A.
41 also] also to know E.   43 mynd] my mynd E.   44 Wich] that E. that day] the
daye A.   46 doth] did A.   48 all thing forgott, still] to think on nowghte and E.
forgott] forgeat A.   49 the bryght transparant] that bright transplendaunt A; the
bright transplendant T.   50 bewray] declare E. colour] colours T. vnderneth] vnder
it E.   51 th'accomberd] A; thaccomberd E. sprite] sprite now A; sprite the T;   54 and
teres] of teares A. and that] to seke E; and eke A.   55 new] *omitted* T. kyndes] kynde

Ffor I ame one off them whom plaint doth well content:
It sittes me well, myn absent welth meseems me to lament,
And with my teris for to' assay to charge myn Iyes tweyne,
Lyke as myn hert above the brink is frawtid full of payne;   60
And for by cawse therto off those fayre Iyes to trete,
Do me provoke, I shall retorne, my plaint thus to repete;
For there is nothing elles that towches me so within
Where thei rule all, and I alone nowght but the cace or skyn.
Wherfore I do retorne to them as well or spryng,   65
From whom decendes my mortall wo above all othr thing.
So shall myn Iyes in payne accompagnie min hert,
That were the guydes that did it lede of love to fele the smert.
The cryspid gold that doth sormount Apollos pryd,
The lyvely strenes off plesaunt sterres that vnder it doth glyd,   70
Where in the bemes off love doth still encresse theire hete,
Wich yet so farre towch me so nere in cold to make me swete;
The wise and plesaunt talk, so rare or elles alone,
That did me gyve the courtese gyfft that such had neuer none,
Be ferre from me, alas, and euery other thing   75
I myght forbere with better will then that that did me bryng
With plesant word and chere redresse off lingerd payne,
And wontyd oft in kendlid will to vertu me to trayne.
Thus ame I dryven to here and herken affter news
My confort skant, my large desire, in dowtfull trust renewes;   80
And yet with more delyght to mone my wofull cace
I must complaine; those handes, those armes, that fermely do
    embrace
Me from my sellff, and rule the sterne of my pore lyff,
The swete disdaynes, the plesant wrathes, and eke the lovely
    stryff
That wontid well to tune in tempre just and mete   85

A. wherein most] wherein all E; most wherein T.   57 them] those A.   58 me to] for
to A, T.   59 for to' assay] to geve assaye A; tassay T. myn] my D.   60 lyke as] sins
that E. myn] my A, T. above] ... ouer (?) E. payne] A; pa (*torn*) E.   63 towches]
toucheth A, D, T.   65 do] shall T.   67 min] my A, D, T.   68 were ... guydes ...
the smart] wher ... gooides ... smart D.   70 strenes] streames A, D, T.   71 doth
still] dothe so A; doe styll T.   72 me so] so D.   74 did me gyve] gave to me A, T
courtese] Curteist A; curteis T. such] erst E, A, T.   75 Be] are E.   76 that that] it
that A; that I D; this that T.   77 lingerd] all my E; linger D.   78 And] whiche A.
in] with E. to] in E.   79 dryven] forst T.   80 renewes] A; renew (*torn*) E.   81 mone]
playne E; morn D.   83 sterne] streme D.   84 eke the lovely] the eke louyth D.
85 well] offt E.

The rage that offt did make me erre by furour vndiscrete:
All this is hid me fro with sharp and craggyd hilles.
At other will my long abode my diepe dispaire fulfilles.
But if my hope somtyme ryse vp by some redresse,
It stumblith straite, for feble faint, my fere hath such excesse.   90
Such is the sort off hope, the lesse for more desire,
Wherby I fere and yet I trust to see that I requyre,
The restyng place of love where vertu lyves and grose,
Where I desire my wery lyff also may take repose.
My song, thou shalt ataine to fynd that plesant place   95
Where she doth lyve by whome I lyve; may chaunce the have
    this grace:
When she hath red and seene the dred wherein I sterve
By twene her brestes she shall the put there shall she the
    reserve.
Then tell her that I come she shall me shortly se;
Yff that for whayte the body fayle, this sowle shall to her fle.   100

XCIX

TAGUS, fare well, that westward with thy stremes
Torns vp the grayns off gold alredy tryd:
With spurr and sayle for I go seke the Tems
Gaynward the sonne, that shewth her welthi pryd
And to the town which Brutus sowght by drems   5
Like bendyd mone doth lend her lusty syd.
My kyng, my Contry, alone for whome I lyve,
Of myghty love the winges for this me gyve.

86 rage] Charge D. 87 craggyd] Craggie A; ragged T. 88 At other will] my fayntyng
hope E; att others will A, T. long abode] brytill lyff E. my diepe dispaire] welling
despaire E. 89 But] And T. somtyme] some tymes D. 90 excesse] A; exs (*torn*) E;
express D. 91 sort] fere E. 92 Whereby . . . trust] And yet I trust ere that I dye T.
93 lyves] dwelles T. 94 Where] There T. wery] wearyd A. also may take] may
sometyme take E (*the word* sometyme *is underlined apparently for deletion*) somtyme may
take A, T; also may somtyme take D. 96 may chaunce] perchaunce E. the have] she
shew E; the have D. 97 dred] dreede A, D; grief T. sterve E, D; serve A, T. 99 tell
her that] say E; tell her D. she shall me shortly se] for here I may not tary E. 100 Yff
that for] and yf for A, T. this sowle] my sowle E; the Sowle A, T. fle] flye A, D.
    [*Authorship:* In W's handwriting with many corrections; in W sections of A and
T.]
XCIX. T.   3 With . . . I] For I with spurre and saile T.   6 doth lend] that leanes T.
7 alone . . . lyve] W; for whome only alone E. alone] I seke T.   8 Of] O T. love the
winges] Ioue the windes T.
    [*Authorship:* In W's handwriting; in W section of T.]

C

O FF purpos Love chase first for to be blynd,
For he with sight of that that I behold
Vanquisht had bene against all godly kynd;
His bow your hand and trusse shold have vnfold,
And he with me to serve had bene assind.   5
But for he blind and rekelesse wold him hold,
And still by chaunse his dedly strokes bestow,
With such as see I serve and suffer wow.

CI

W H A T rage is this? What furour of what kynd?
What powre, what plage, doth wery thus my mynd?
Within my bons to rancle is assind
        What poyson, plesant swete?

Lo, se myn iyes swell with contynuall terys;   5
The body still away sleples it weris;
My fode nothing my faintyng strenght reperis,
        Nor doth my lyms sustayne.

In diepe wid wound the dedly strok doth torne
To curid skarre that neuer shalle retorne.   10
Go to, tryumphe, reioyse thy goodly torne,
        Thi frend thow dost opresse.

Opresse thou dost, and hast off hym no cure,
Nor yett my plaint no pitie can procure,
Fiers tygre fell, hard rok withowt recure,   15
        Cruell rebell to love!

C. T.   1 chase] chose T.   2 For . . . that] W; For yff he myght have sene E.   4 His
. . . hand] W; Your hand his bow E.   6 he blind and] W; by cawse he E.   8 wow]
wo T.
    [*Authorship:* In W's handwriting with corrections; in W section of T.]
CI. T.   1 what kynd] excesse E.   2] What powre, what poyson doth my mynd
opresse E.   3 my] the E. is assind] doth not cesse E.   4] the poysond plesantnesse E.
5 myn iyes] my chekes E. swell] flow T.   6 away sleples] sleples away E.   8 sus-
tayne] ssustaine E (i); redresse E (ii).   9 In . . . wound] The strok doth stretche E
(i); Into wid wound E (ii).   10 To] In E curid] cureles T.   13 cure] ruthe E.   14
plaint] woos E (i); deth E (ii).   16 rebell] vnkynd E.

Ons may thou love, neuer belovffd agayne;
So love thou still and not thy love obttayne;
So wrathfull love with spites of just disdayne
        May thret thy cruell hert.   20

CII

FROM thowght to thowght from hill to hill love
                                doth me lede,
Clene contrary from restfull lyff thes comon
                                pathes I trede

CIII

VULCANE bygat me; Mynerua me taught;
Nature my mother craft norischt me yere by yere;
Thre bodyes ar my fode; my strength is in naught;
Angre, wrath, wast, and noyse, are my children dere.
Gesse, frend, what I ame and how I ame wrought: 5
Monstre of see or of lande or of els where?
Know me and use me and I may the defende,
And if I be thine enmye I may thy life ende.

CIV

Jopas' Song

WHEN Dido festid first the wandryng Troian knyght,
Whom Junos wrath with stormes did force in Lybyke sandes
    to lyght,
That myghty' Atlas did teche, the souper lastyng long,
With cryspid lokkes, on golden harpe, Jopas sang in his song.
That same, quod he, that we the world do call and name,   5
Off hevin and yerth with all contentes it is the very frame.

17 Ons . . . love] Myghtst thou so love E.   18 Myghtst thou so love and neuer
more attayn E.   19 Myght wrathfull love so threte you with disdayne E.   20] thy
cruell hert to prove E (i); thy cruellty reprove E (ii).
    [*Authorship*. In W's handwriting; deleted readings are followed above by E.]
CII. In W's handwriting.
CIII. H, T.   3 strength is in] strengh is in E; strength is H.   4 Angre] slawghter H.
5 and] or H.   6 of see . . . els] of land see or els H.   7 Know] have H.
    [*Authorship:* In W sections of H and T.]
CIV. A, T.   2 lyght] light A, T; lygh (*torn*) E.   3 did teche] taught A, T.   4 on]

2. Egerton MS
(*poem* CI, *page* 83)

Or thus: off hevinly powrs, by more powre kept in one
Repugnant kyndes, in myddes of whome the yerth hath place
   alone;
Firme, round, off liuing thynges the moder place and nourse,
Withowt the wych in egall whaight this hevin doth hold his
   course;   10
And it is calld by name the first moving hevin,
The firmament is next containing othr sevyn.
Off hevinly powrs that same is plantid full and thikk,
As shyning lyghtes wych we call steres that therin cleve and
   stikk;
With gret swifft sway the first and with his restles sours   15
Caryth it sellff and all those eight in evin continuall cours.
And off this world so rownd within that rollyng case
There be two pointes that neuer move, but fermely kepe ther
   place:
The t'one we se alway, the t'othr stondes obiect
Against the same deviding just the round by line direct;   20
Wich by' ymagination draune from t'on to t'othr
Towchith the centre of the yerth, way there is no nothr;
And thes bene calld the poles, discribd by sterres not bryght
Artyke the t'one northward we se, Antartyke t'othr hight.
The lyne that we devise from t'on to t'othr so   25
As Axell is, apon the wich th'evins abowt doth go;
Wych off water nor yerth, of Ayre nor fyre have kynd:
Therfore the substance of those same were herd for man to
   fynd.
But thei ben vncorrupt, symple and pure, vnmixt;

and E. his] *omitted* T. 8 Repugnant] the dyuerse E. alone] alo (*torn*) E. 9 liuing]
lyvely E. 11 first] first and A, T. 12 firmament . . . containing] stery skye vnder the
wich that movith E; firmament is placed nexte conteyning A, T. 13 that same] this
skye E. 14 therin] therto E. 15 the first] thys hevin E. his restles sours] restles
recours E. 16 eight] seven E. 18 There . . . pointes] there be ii signs E; Two
poyntes there be A, T. place] plac (*torn*) E. 19 t'one . . . t'other] tone . . . tother E,
A, T. obiect] direct E. 20 round] grownd A, T. 21 t'on to t'othr] ton to tothr E;
the one to th'other A, T. 22 Towchith] passeth E; Touche A. way] for way E, A, T.
no nothr] none other A, T. 23 discribd . . . bryght] as axell is the lytt E; discryde
bye starres not bright A, T. 24 t'one] tone E; the one A, T. northward we se] that
we do se E. t'othr] tothr E; thother A, T. 25 t'on to t'othr] ton to tother E; thone
to th'other A. T. 26 thevins] thevin E (i); the hole E (ii). doth] do A, T. 27 have]
hath E. 28 those] the E. 29 But thei ben] ffor it is E. symple . . . vnmixt] vnmixt
symple and pure E.

And so we say bene all those sterrys that in those same bene
    fixt;   30
And eke those errying sevin in cyrcles as thei stray
So calld by cawse against that first thei have repugnant way.
And smaller by ways to, skant sensible to man
To busy work for my pore harp, let sing them he that can!
The widest, saff the first, off all these nyne above   35
On hunderd yere doth aske of space for on degre to move:
Off wich degres we make In the first moving hevin
Thre hunderd and thre skore in partes, justly devidid evin.
And yet there is an othr by twene those hevins tow,
Whose moving is so sli, so slake, I name it not for now.   40
The sevent hevyn, or the shell next to the starry skye,
All those degres that gaderth vp with agid pas so slye,
And doth performe the same, as elders compt hath bene,
In nyne and twenty yeres complete and days almost sixtene,
Doth cary in his bowght the sterr off Saturne old,   45
A thretner of all lyving thinges with drowfft and with his cold.
The sixt whom this containes doth staulk with yonger pase,
And in twelff yere doth sum what more then t'othrs viage wase.
And this in it doth bere the sterre of Jove benigne,
Twene Saturns malice and vs men frendly deffendyng signe.   50
The fift berth blody Mars that in three hundred days
And twise elefn with on full yere hath finisht all those ways.
A yere doth aske the fourt, and houres thereto six,
And in the same the day his yie the sonner therein he stix.
The third that governd is by that that governth me,   55
And love for love and for no love provokes as offt we se.
In like space doth performe that cours that did the t'othr,
So doth the next to the same that second is in order,

30 those same] the same E. bene] be T. 31 errryng] wandryng E. cyrcles] circle A, T.
32 that first] the heven E. 35 nyne above] nyne that above E. 40 sli, so slake] slow
to prove E. name it not] let it passe E. 41 next . . . skye] that mouethe vnder that
E (i); vnder the firmament E (ii). 46 and with] and eke E. 48 t'othrs viage was]
tothrs Iorney was E; thothers vyoage was A, T. 49 in it doth bere] is it that beares
A. 50 men . . . deffendyng] deffence and frendly E. 51 berth] hath Cruell E;
beares A, T. in iii hundred days] movithe all this warre E. *At the foot of this page are
scribbled two lines after a large gap:*

      Nor is it lyke that man may think thes sters all
      Streyis ther path as thei do passe within that hevinly hall.

53 A] the E. therto howres] howres therto E. 54 day his] dayes T. he] her T. 55
governth] governs A, T. 58 So] and so E. to] vnto A, T.

But it doth bere the sterr that calld is Mercury,
That mayni' a craffty secret stepp doth tred as calcars try.   60
That skye is last and first, next vs those ways hath gone
In sevin and twenty comon days, and eke the third of one;
And beryth with his sway the diuerse mone abowt,
Now bryght, now browne, now bent, now full, and now her
    light is owt.
Thus have thei of thire owne two movinges all those sevin: 65
One, wherin they be carid still eche in his sevrall hevin;
An othr, of hym sellffes where theire bodis ben layd
In by ways and in lesser rowndes, as I afore have sayd.
Saff of them all, the sonne doth stray lest from the straight,
The sterry sky hath but on cowrse that we have calld the eight; 70
And all these movinges eight ar ment from west to th'est,
Altho thei seme to clymb aloftt, I say, from est to west.
But that is but by force of the first moving skye,
In twise twellff howres from est to th'est that caryth them bye
    and bye.
But mark we well also thes movinges of these sevin   75
Be not about that axell tre of the first moving hevin;
For thei have theire two poles directly t'one to t'other . . .

61 first] fyxte A, T. next . . . gone] and next therwith E. 64 now bent] A, T; no bent
E. out] ou (*torn*) E. 65 have . . . owne] have thei of them sellffes E; of their owne
have they A. 67 hym sellffes] hym sellffes his body E (i); hym sellffes as he E (ii);
them selves A, T. ben] be A, T. 69 lest] still A. 71 to thest] to east A; to the east T.
72 aloftt] thevin E. 74 est to th'est] east to east A, T. 75 these] the A. 76 about
that] bout that W; ap bout E; about the A, T. 77 t'one to t'other] to the tother A;
tone to the tothr T.

[*Authorship:* In W's handwriting with many corrections; in W sections of A and
T.]

II

Satires

CV

Myne owne John Poyntz, sins ye delight to know
  The cawse why that homeward I me draw,
  And fle the presse of courtes wher soo they goo
Rather then to lyve thrall vnder the awe
  Of lordly lookes, wrappid within my cloke,   5
  To will and lust lerning to set a lawe,
It is not for becawsse I skorne or moke
  The power of them to whome fortune hath lent
  Charge over vs, of Right, to strike the stroke;
But trew it is that I have allwais ment   10
  Lesse to estime them then the common sort
  Off owtward thinges that juge in their intent
Withowte Regarde what dothe inwarde resort.
  I grawnt sumtime that of glorye the fyar
  Dothe touche my hart: me lyst not to report   15
Blame by honowr and honour to desyar;
  But how may I this honour now atayne
  That cannot dy the coloure blake a lyer?
My Poyntz, I cannot frame my tonge to fayne
  To cloke the trothe for praisse, withowt desart,   20
  Of them that lyst all vice for to retayne.
I cannot honour them that settes their part
  With Venus and Baccus all their lyf long,
  Nor holld my pece of them alltho I smart.

CV. D, C, P, A, T (See Commentary). 1–52 D; *omitted* E. 1 Iohn poyntz D, C, T;
I. P. A. ye] you A. 2 cawse] causes C. me] do me A, P. 3 fle] flye A. they] I C. 6
lawe] lowe A, P. 7 not for] not A, P, C. 8 to whome] whome T. fortune] powre
A. fortune here T. 8 Charge] chargde A. 10 allwais] ever A. 13 what dothe
inwarde] that dothe inwarde C; what inward doth T. 14 that of glorye] of glory that
T. 15 touche] A, P, C, T. twyche D. me ... reporte] my lyst not to report D; and
me lust not repent C. 17 this ... now] nowe this honour A, P. 18–19 *omitted*
A, P. 18 coloure blake] colour of blak C. 19 frame my tonge] C; from me tune D;
frame my tune T. fayne] sayne? C. 21 lyst] lust C. vice for] vices to C; nice for T.
22 settes] sett C. 24 alltho] though that A, P.

I cannot crowche nor knelle, nor do so great a wrong   25
   To worship them like God on erthe alone,
   That ar as wollffes thes sely lambes among.
I cannot with my wordes complayne and mone
   And suffer nought; nor smart wythout complaynt,
   Nor torne the worde that from my mouthe is gone.   30
I cannot speke and lok lyke a saynct,
   Vse wyles for witt and make deceyt a plesure,
   And call crafft counsell, for proffet styll to paint.
I cannot wrest the law to fill the coffer,
   With innocent blode to fede my sellff ffat,   35
   And doo most hurt where most hellp I offer.
I am not he that can alow the state
   Off highe Cesar and dam Cato to dye,
   That with his dethe dyd skape owt off the gate
From Cesares handes, if Lyvye do not lye,   40
   And wolld not lyve whar lyberty was lost:
   So did his hart the commonn wele aplye.
I am not he suche eloquence to boste,
   To make the crow singing as the swanne,
   Nor call the lyon of cowarde bestes the moste,   45
That cannot take a mows as the cat can:
   And he that diethe for hunger of the golld
   Call him Alessaundre, and say that Pan
Passithe Apollo in musike manyfolld;
   Praysse Syr Thopas for a noble tale,   50
   And skorne the story that the knyght tolld;
Praise him for counceill that is droncke of ale;
   Grynne when he laugheth, that bereth all the swaye,
   Frowne when he frowneth and grone when he is pale;

25 nor . . . a] to such a A; nor do suche C; to such A, T.   26 like] as A.   27 as] like C.   28] *omitted* D. my wordes] T; wordes A; my worde C. 29–30] C, T; *omitted* D, A, P. lyke a] like as a T. and . . . lyke] with loke ryght C.   32 wyles] A, C, P, T; willes D. make] vse C.   33 And call] call T. proffet] lucre T.   36 most] my self A. most hellp] my self A, P. that most helpe T.   38 highe] A, P, T; him D, C. dam] deme C. 39 with] by C. his] is D.   40 do] A; can D; doth P, T; did C.   41 wolld] will A, P (*original*).   42 his] is D. wele] wealth C, T.   44 make] marke C. crow singing] singing crowe C; crow is singyng T.   45 lyon] A; lyond D. cowarde] cowardes D; Coward A, P.   47 of the] of C.   49 manyfolld] many a fold C.   50 Thopas] Topias P.   52 droncke] drounkin D.   53 laugheth] laughes A, P, T. bereth] beres C. all the] the A, P.   54 frowneth] frownes D T. he] *omitted* E.

On othres lust to hang boeth nyght and daye: 55
  None of these poyntes would ever frame in me.
My wit is nought, I cannot lerne the waye:
And much the lesse of thinges that greater be,
  That asken helpe of colours of devise
  To joyne the mene with eche extremitie,   60
With the neryst vertue to cloke always the vise;
  And as to pourpose like wise it shall fall
  To presse the vertue that it may not rise;
As dronkenes good felloweshippe to call,
  The frendly ffoo with his dowble face   65
  Say he is gentill and courtois therewithall;
And say that Favell hath a goodly grace
  In eloquence, and crueltie to name
  Zele of Justice and chaunge in tyme and place;
And he that sufferth offence withoute blame   70
  Call him pitefull and him true and playn
  That raileth rekles to every mans shame.
Say he is rude that cannot lye and fayn,
  The letcher a lover, and tirannye
  To be the right of a prynces reigne.   75
I cannot, I; no, no, it will not be,
  This is the cause that I could never yet
  Hang on their slevis that way as thou maist se
A chippe of chaunce more then a pownde of witt.
  This maketh me at home to hounte and hawke   80
  And in fowle weder at my booke to sitt.
In frost and snowe then with my bow to stawke;
  No man doeth marke where so I ride or goo;
  In lusty lees at libertie I walke,
And of these newes I fele nor wele nor woo,   85
  Sauf that a clogg doeth hang yet at my hele:

55 lust] lustes A, P. nyght and daye] day and night P.   56 poyntes] poyntz C. would]
will A, P. ever] neuer D. in] wyth C.   57 the waye] to waye A, P.   59 asken] aske
A, P. of] to A, P, T.   61 With the] With T. to cloke alwaye] ay to cloke T.   62 it
shall] may C.   65 dowble] faire double T.   66 he] this C.   67 And say that] and that
A, P. Affirme that T.   72 to every] vnto ech T.   76 no, no, it] nor it A. no nor yet]
P.   77 that I] I C. could] wold A, D, P.   78 maist] may D.   80 and hawke] A; and
to hawke E.   81 fowle] the fowle C.   83 where so] wheare that A, P; where to C.
84 lees] leases A, P.   85 these] theire D. nor] nother A, P; no D. nor woo] ne woo C.
86 that] of C. doeth hang yet] doth hang yet still A; that yet doth hang C; dothe hang

No force for that for it is ordered so,
That I may lepe boeth hedge and dike full well.
 I ame not now in Fraunce to judge the wyne,
 With saffry sauce the delicates to fele;   90
Nor yet in Spainge where oon must him inclyne
 Rather then to be owtewerdly to seme.
 I meddill not with wittes that be so fyne,
Nor Flaunders chiere letteth not my sight to deme
 Of black and white, nor taketh my wit awaye 95
 With bestlynes, they beestes do so esteme;
Nor I ame not where Christe is geven in pray
 For mony, poisen and traison at Rome,
 A commune practise vsed nyght and daie:
But here I ame in Kent and Christendome   100
 Emong the muses where I rede and ryme;
 Wherc if thou list, my Poynz, for to come,
Thou shalt be judge how I do spend my tyme.

CVI

M Y mothers maydes when they did sowe and spynne,
 They sang sometyme a song of the feld mowse,
 That forbicause her lyvelood was but thynne,
Would nedes goo seke her townyssh systers howse.
 She thought her self endured to much pain, 5
 The stormy blastes her cave so sore did sowse,
That when the forowse swymmed with the rain
 She must lye cold and whete in sorry plight;

yet D, P, T. 88 dike] dytche A, C, D, P. 89 ame not now] am not A, P. 90 With]
what A, D, P. sauce] sawces C. the] these A, C, P, D; those T. 91 oon] ay D. him]
so D. 92 owtewerdly] vtterlye D. 94 letteth] lettes A, D, P. my] me D. sight]
wittes A; wyt C. 95 and] nor A, D, P. taketh] takes A, D, C, P, T. wit] wittes A, C,
P, T. 96 they . . . esteme] the beastes do so esteeme A, P; they bestes do esteme D;
those beastes do esteme C; such do those beastes esteme T. 97 I ame not] am I C.
Christe] truth T. 98 at Rome] of some T. 99 practise] plague A; place P. 100
here I ame] I am here T. 101 rede] do rede C. 102 list] lust C. my] myne owne T.
Poynz] poynz E; I P. A., P.; Iohn Poyns T. for to] to T. 103 do spend] dispende C;
spend *original* P.
 [*Authorship:* In W sections of A and T.]
CVI. A, D (1–18), T. 1 did] do A, T. and] or D. 2 sang . . . mowse] sing a songe
made of the fieldishe mowse A, T; sang somtyme a sonng of the fild mowsse D. 4
seke] se A, T. 5 much] greevous A, T; myche D.

And wours then that, bare meet then did remain
To comfort her when she her howse had dight,   10
    Sometyme a barly corn, sometyme a bene,
    For which she laboured hard boeth daye and nyght,
In harvest tyme whilest she myght goo and glyne;
    And when her stoore was stroyed with the flodd,
    Then well aweye, for she vndone was clene.   15
Then was she fayne to take in stede of fode
    Slepe if she myght her hounger to begile.
    'My syster', quod she, 'hath a lyving good,
And hens from me she dwelleth not a myle.
    In cold and storme she lieth warme and dry,   20
    In bed of downe the dyrt doeth not defile
Her tender fote; she laboureth not as I;
    Richely she fedeth and at the richemans cost,
    And for her meet she nydes not crave nor cry.
By se, by land of delicates the moost   25
    Her Cater sekes and spareth for no perell;
    She fedeth on boyled bacon, meet and roost,
And hath therof neither charge nor travaill;
    And when she list the licour of the grape
    Doeth glad her hert, till that her belly swell'.   30
And at this Journey she maketh but a Jape;
    So fourth she goeth, trusting of all this welth
    With her syster her part so for to shape
That if she myght kepe her self in helth
    To lyve a Lady while her liff doeth last,   35
    And to the dore now is she come by stelth
And with her foote anon she scrapeth full fast.
    Th'othre for fere durst not well scarse appere,
    Of every noyse so was the wretche agast.
At last she asked softly who was there;   40
    And in her langage as well as she cowd,
    'Pepe', quod the othre, 'syster I ame here'.

---

13 whilest] when A; while T. 14 when her] wher E. 17 myght] cowlde A. 18 quod]
omitted D. 22 laboureth] labours A, T. 23 fedeth] feedes A, T. 24 nydes] neede A.
25 delicates] A, T; the delicates E. 27 She . . . roost] she fedes on boylde meat,
bake meat, and on roste A; she . . . boyle . . . rost T. 28 therof neither] therfore
no whitt of A, T. 31 she maketh] makes she A, T. 32 goeth] goes T. 34 kepe]
theare kepe A, T. 37 scrapeth] scrapes A, T. 38 well scarse] well A. 40 At last] At
the last *original* E.

'Peace', quod the towne mowse, 'why spekest thou so lowde?'
　And by the hand she toke her fayer and well.
'Welcome', quod she, 'my sister, by the Rood'.　　　　　　　45
She fested her, that Joy it was to tell
　　The faere they had; they drancke the wyne so clere,
　　And as to pourpose now and then it fell,
She chered her with 'how syster, what chiere?'
　　Amyddes this Joye befell a sorry chaunce　　　　　　　50
　　That well awaye the straunger bought full dere
The fare she had, for as she loked ascaunce
　　Vnder a stole she spied two stemyng Ise
　　In a rownde hed with sherp erys; in Fraunce
Was never mowse so ferd, for tho th'unwise　　　　　　　55
　　Had not I-sene suche a beest before,
　　Yet had nature taught her after her gyse
To knowe her ffoo and dred him evermore.
　　The towney mowse fled: she knewe whether to goo.
　　Th'othre had no shift but wonders sore　　　　　　　60
Ferd of her liff; at home she wyshed her tho,
　　And to the dore, alas, as she did skipp,
　　Thevyn it would, lo, and eke her chaunce was so,
At the threshold her sely fote did tripp,
　　And ere she myght recover it again　　　　　　　65
　　The traytour Catt had caught her by the hipp,
And made her there against her will remain,
　　That had forgotten her poure suretie and rest
　　For semyng welth wherin she thought to rayne.
Alas, my Poynz, how men do seke the best　　　　　　　70
　　And fynde the wourst by errour as they stray!
　　And no marvaill, when sight is so opprest,
And blynde the gyde; anon owte of the way
　　Goeth gyde and all in seking quyete liff.
　　O wretched myndes there is no gold that may　　　　　　　75

---

43 towne] townysshe *original* E.　45 by] my *original* E.　46 Joy it was] Joye was A.
48 pourpose] poupsse E.　50 Amyddes] Amyd A, T.　52 loked ascaunce] loke a
scaunce E; lookt a scaunce A, T.　53 stole] stoole A. spied] espyed A.　55 tho th'un-
wise] tho E; for the vnwyse A, T.　59 towney] Towne A, T. whether] whyther A, T.
60 Th'othr] The other A, T.　63 Thevyn] The heaven A, T.　65 recover it again] it
recover again *original* E.　68 forgotten] forgote A, T.　69 semyng] seeking A.
71 wourst] worsse A.　73 blynde] blyndes A, T.

Graunt that ye seke, no warre, no peace, no stryff,
　　No, no, all tho thy hed were howpt with gold,
　　Sergeaunt with mace, hawbert, sword, nor knyff
Cannot repulse the care that folowe should.
　　Eche kynd of lyff hath with him his disease.   80
　　Lyve in delight evyn as thy lust would,
And thou shalt fynde when lust doeth moost the please
　　It irketh straite and by it self doth fade.
　　A small thing it is, that may thy mynde apese.
Non of ye all there is that is so madde   85
　　To seke grapes vpon brambles or breers,
　　Nor none I trow that hath his wit so badd
To set his hay for Conys over Ryvers,
　　Ne ye set not a dragg net for an hare,
　　And yet the thing that moost is your desire   90
Ye do mysseke with more travaill and care.
　　Make playn thyn hert that it be not knotted
　　With hope or dred and se thy will be bare
From all affectes whome vice hath ever spotted;
　　Thy self content with that is the assigned   95
　　And vse it well that is to the allotted.
Then seke no more owte of thy self to fynde
　　The thing that thou haist sought so long before,
　　For thou shalt fele it sitting in thy mynde.
Madde, if ye list to continue your sore,   100
　　Let present passe and gape on tyme to come
　　And diepe your self in travaill more and more.
Hens fourth, my Poynz, this shalbe all and some:
　　These wretched fooles shall have nought els of me
　　But to the great god and to his high dome   105
None othre pain pray I for theim to be
　　But when the rage doeth led them from the right
　　That lowking backward vertue they may se

76 ye] you A, T.   77 howpt] hoope A.   with] of A.   78 hawbert] with hawlberd A,
T.   nor] or A, T.   79 Cannot] That can A, T.   81 delight] delightes A.   82 doeth . . .
please] thee most doth please A.   84 it is] is it A, T.   85 ye] you A, T.   86 grapes]
for grapes A, T.   vpon] on A, T.   or] or on A, T.   87 his] a A.   89 Ne ye set] Nor
ye sett A, T; ne ye se E.   91 Ye] you A, T.   mysseke] myslyke A.   92 thyn] thye A.
94 From] ffor A.   euer] never A.   99 sitting] stickinge A, T.   100 Madde] Made A.
102 your] thie A.   105 his high] his A, T.   107 them] A, T; then E.   108 vertue
they] they A.
　[*Authorship:* In W sections of A and T.]

Evyn as she is so goodly fayre and bright;
   And whilst they claspe their lustes in armes a-crosse,   110
   Graunt theim, goode lorde, as thou maist of thy myght,
To frete inward for losing such a losse.

CVII

A SPENDING hand that alway powreth owte
   Had nede to have a bringer in as fast,
   And on the stone that still doeth tourne abowte
There groweth no mosse: these proverbes yet do last.
   Reason hath set theim in so sure a place   5
   That lenght of yeres their force can never wast.
When I remembre this and eke the case
   Where in thou stondes I thowght forthwith to write,
   Brian, to the, who knows how great a grace
In writing is to cownsell man the right.   10
   To the, therefore, that trottes still vp and downe,
   And never restes: but runnyng day and nyght
From Reaulme to Reaulme, from cite, strete and towne;
   Why doest thou were thy body to the bones,
   And myghtst at home slepe in thy bed of downe   15
And drynck goode ale so nappy for the noyns,
   Fede thy self fat and hepe vp pownd by pownd?
   Lykist thou not this? 'No'. 'Why?' 'For swyne so groyns
In stye and chaw the tordes molded on the grownd,
   And dryvell on pearles, the hed still in the maunger,   20
   Then of the harp the Asse to here the sownd.
So sackes of durt be filled vp in the cloyster,
   That servis for lesse then do thes fatted swyne.
   Tho I seme lene and dry withoute moyster,
Yet woll I serve my prynce, my lord and thyn,   25
   And let theim lyve to fede the panche that list,
   So I may fede to lyve both me and myn.'
By god, well sayde, but what and if thou wist
   How to bryng in as fast as thou doest spend?

CVII. A, T. 4 groweth] growes A. 8 stondes] stand'st A, T. 15 myghtst] mightest A, T. 16 nappy] A, T; noppy E. 19 the tordes] donge A, T. 20 pearles, the] perilles the E; pearells with A; pearles with T. 21 Then of] So, on A; So of T. to] dothe A, T. 22 filled . . . cloyster] fild. The neat Courtyer A, T. 23 That] So A, T. 24 withoute] withouten A, T. 25 woll] will A, T. 27 fede to lyve] lyve to feede A, T.

'That would I lerne'; and it shall not be myst   30
To tell the how: now hark what I intend.
    Thou knowest well first who so can seke to plese
    Shall pourchase frendes where trowght shall but offend.
Fle therefore trueth: it is boeth welth and ese.
    For tho that trouth of every man hath prayse,   35
    Full nere that wynd goeth trouth in great misese.
Vse vertu as it goeth now a dayes:
    In word alone to make thy langage swete,
    And of the dede yet do not as thou sayse;
Elles be thou sure thou shalt be farre vnmyt   40
    To get thy bred, eche thing is now so skant.
    Seke still thy proffet vpon thy bare fete.
Lend in no wise for fere that thou do want,
    Onles it be as to a dogge a chese;
    By which retorne be sure to wyn a kant   45
Of half at lest, it is not good to lese.
    Lerne at Kittson that in a long white cote
    From vnder the stall withoute landes or feise
Hath lept into the shopp; who knoweth by rote
    This rule that I have told the here before.   50
    Sumtyme also riche age begynneth to dote:
Se thou when there thy gain may be the more.
    Stay him by the arme where so he walke or goo;
    Be nere alway: and if he koggh to sore,
When he hath spit, tred owte and please him so.   55
    A diligent knave that pikes his maisters purse
    May please him so that he withouten mo
Executour is, and what is he the wourse?
    But if so chaunce you get nought of the man,
    The wedow may for all thy charge deburse.   60
A ryveld skyn, a stynking breth, what than?
    A tothles mowth shall do thy lips no harme:
    The gold is good, and tho she curse or ban,
Yet where the list thou maist ly good and warme;
    Let the old mule byte vpon the bridill,   65

34 boeth] for A.   35 hath] have A.   37 a dayes] A, T; a day so E.   39 the] thie A.
44 dogge] calf A, T.   45 By which retorne] but yf thow can A.   46 it] I A.
47 Kittson] the Ladde A, T.   48 withoute] withouten A, T.   49 knoweth] knowes
A, T.   51 also riche age] ryche age also A. begynneth] begynnes A, T.   55 When]
what A, T.   59 you] thow A, T.   60 charge deburse] payne disbursse A.   65 mule]

Whilst there do ly a swetter in thyn arme.
In this also se you be not Idell:
    Thy nece, thy cosyn, thy sister or thy doghter,
    If she be faire, if handsom be her myddell,
Yf thy better hath her love besoght her,   70
    Avaunce his cause and he shall help thy nede.
    It is but love, turne it to a lawghter.
But ware I say so gold the helpe and spede,
    That in this case thow be not so vnwise
    As Pandare was in suche a like dede;   75
For he the ffooll of conscience was so nyse
    That he no gayn would have for all his payne.
    Be next thy self, for frendshipp beres no prise.
Laughst thou at me? Why do I speke in vayne?
    'No, not at the, but at thy thrifty gest.   80
    Wouldest thou I should for any losse or gayne
Chaunge that for gold that I have tan for best,
    Next godly thinges, to have an honest name?
    Should I leve that? then take me for a best?'
Nay, then, farewell, and if you care for shame   85
    Content the then with honest pouertie
    With fre tong what the myslikes to blame
And for thy trouth sumtyme aduersitie:
    And therewithall this thing I shall the gyve –
    In this worould now litle prosperite,   90
And coyne to kepe as water in a syve.

---

moyle A.   66 do] dothe A. thyn] thye A.   67 you] that thow A; thou T.   68 cosyn
. . . doghter] cosen, or thye doughter A.   69 handsom be] handsam by E; handsome
be A, T.   71 Avaunce] Advaunce A.   72 turne] turne thow A.   75 As] and *original*
E.   85 you] thow A, T.   89 thing] guifte A, T.
   [*Authorship:* In W section of A and T.]

III

Penitential Psalms

THE great Macedon that out of Perse chasyd
Darius of whose huge power all Asy Rang,
In the riche arke of Homers rymes he placyd,
Who fayned gestes of hethen Prynces sang;

What holly grave, what wourthy sepulture
To Wyates Psalmes shuld Christians then purchase?
Wher he dothe paynte the lyvely faythe and pure,
The stedfast hope, the swete returne to grace

Of iust Dauyd by parfite penytence,
Where Rewlers may se in a myrrour clere
The bitter frewte of false concupicense,
How Jewry bought Vryas deathe full dere.

In Prynces hartes goddes scourge yprynted depe
Myght them awake out of their synfull slepe.

HENRY HOWARD, EARL OF SURREY

CVIII

LOVE to gyve law vnto his subiect hertes
Stode in the Iyes off Barsabe the bryght;
And in a look anone hymsellff convertes,
Cruelly plesant byfore kyng David syght;
First dasd his Iyes and forder forth he stertes   5
With venemd breth as sofftly as he myght
Towcht his sensis and ouer ronnis his bonis
With creping fyre, sparplid for the nonis.

CVIII. A, R, Q. 1 subiect] subiectes A, Q. 3 hymsellff] hymselfes Q. 4 David] Davides
A, R, Q. 5 dasd] David A. 6 venemd] poyson E. 7 Towcht his sensis] Touche his
senewes Q. ronnis] ranne A. 8 creping] sparplyd E. sparplid] spark'led A, R, Q.

And when he saw that kendlid was the flame,
The moyst poyson in his hert he launcyd,   10
So that the sowle did tremble with the same;
And in this brawle as he stode and trauncyd,
Yelding vnto the figure and the frame
That those fayre Iyes had in his presens glauncid,
The forme that love had printyd in his brest   15
He honorth it as thing off thinges best.

So that forgott the wisdome and fore-cast
(Wych wo to Remes when that thes kynges doth lakk)
Forgettyng eke goddes maiestie as fast,
Ye and his own, forthwith he doth to mak   20
Vrye to go in to the feld in hast,
Vrye I say, that was his Idolles mak,
Vnder pretence off certen victorye
For enmys swordes a redy pray to dye.

Wherby he may enjoy her owt of dowte,   25
Whom more then god or hymsellff he myndyth;
And after he had browght this thing abowt
And off that lust posest hym sellff, he fyndyth
That hath and doth reuerse and clene torn owt
Kynges from kyndomes and cytes vndermyndyth: 30
He blyndyd thinkes this trayne so blynd and closse
To blynd all thing that nowght may it disclosse.

But Nathan hath spyd out this trecherye
With rufull chere, and settes afore his face
The gret offence, outrage and Iniurye,   35
That he hath done to god as in this Case,
By murder for to clok Adulterye;

---

10 moyst] warme E; noysome Q. he] *omitted* A.   11 the sowle] his Sowle A.   12 this]
his R, Q. he] at E.   15 that . . . printyd] wheroff love printyd E.   16 thing] a thing
A, Q.   17 the . . . cast] and owt off mynd clene cast E1; the wisdome ouer all E2.
forgott] he forgotte. Q.   18 to] the E. thes] this A; the Q. kynges] kynge Q. doth]
do A, R.   20 Ye and] and ye E. forthwith] anone E.   21 Vrye . . . feld] vnder
pretence of victorye E.   22 I say] to go E. Idolls] Ieweles Q.   24 For . . . swordes]
on the foes swordes ?E. dye] be Q.   25 owt of dowte] all alone E.   26] Whome he
doth Love more then hym sellff or god E1; whom more then god or elles hymsellff
he lovth E2.   27 after] when E.   28 that lust] this delyght E; that his lust E2.   29
torn] tornd E.   30 from] and E.   31 this] his A.   32 thing] thynges Q. nowght]
nothing Q.   33 this] his R. trecherye] gret E.   34 rufull] ruthfull A. settes] set A.

He shewth hym ek from hevyn the thretes, alas,
So sternly sore, this prophet, this Nathan,
That all amasid this agid woofull man.   40

Lyke hym that metes with horrour and with fere,
The hete doth strayte forsake the lyms cold,
The colour eke drowpith down from his chere,
So doth he fele his fyer maynifold.
His hete, his lust and plesur all in fere   45
Consume and wast, and strayt his crown of gold,
His purpirll pall, his sceptre he lettes fall,
And to the ground he throwth hym sellff withall.

The pompous pryd of state and dygnite
Fortwith rabates repentant humblenes;   50
Thynner vyle cloth then clothyth pouerty
Does skantly hyde and clad his nakednes;
His faire hore berd of reverent gravite
With ruffeld here, knowyng his wykednes:
More lyke was he the sellff same repentance   55
Then statly prynce off worldly governance.

His harpe he taketh in hand to be his guyde,
Wherewith he offerth his plaintes his sowle to save,
That from his hert distilles on euery syde,
Withdrawyng hym into a dark Cave   60
Within the grownd wherin he myght hym hyde,
Fleing the lyght, as in pryson or grave:
In wych as sone as David enterd had,
The dark horrour did mak his fawte a drad.

---

38 hym] *omitted* R, Q. from] how E. thretes alas] sore menace E. 40 amasid . . .
woofull] amased was thys wofull aged Q. 41 metes] mete A; meateth Q. 42 hete]
colour E. lyms] lymyttes Q. 43 drowpith] droppeth R, Q. 44 his fyer] the fyre E.
45 hete] helth R. and] his R, Q. fere] fyre A. 47 His . . . pall] his pall, his purpull E.
pall] pauler Q. lettes] letteth Q. 49 The] Then Q. of state and] and statelie R.
rabates] rebates A; rebate R, Q. 51 Thynner . . . cloth] a thyn vile cloth E. Thynner]
Th'inner A. clothyth] clothed Q. 53 His . . . berd] his hore his berd E. of] with R. 54
here] hears A. knowyng his wykednes] repentyng his excesse E. wykednes]
wyknednes W. 55 was he] he was E. sellff] *omitted* Q. 57 taketh in hand] hathe
taken in his hand E. taketh] takes A. 58 his plaintes . . . save] the plaintes and the
Cryis E. his plaintes] playnts Q. 59 distilles] dystylleth Q. 60 hym] hym selfe Q.
dark] darke depe A. 61 grownd] growndes A. wherin] wher Q; whenne R. 62
as . . . or] in pryson or in E. 64 did mak] mad E.

3. Egerton MS
(*poem* CVIII, *pages* 107–8)

But he withowt prolonging or delay 65
Rof that that myght his lord, his god, apese,
Fallth on his knees, and with his harp, I say,
Afore his brest, frawtyd with disese
Off stormy syghes, his chere colourd lyk clay,
Dressyd vpryght, sekyng to conterpese 70
His song with syghes, and towching of the strynges
With tendre hert, lo thus to god he synges.

Psalm 6. *Domine ne in furore*

O LORD, sins in my mowght thy myghty name
Sufferth it sellff, my lord to name and call,
Here hath my hert hope taken by the same, 75
That the repentance wych I have and shall
May at thi hand seke marcy as the thing,
Only confort of wrechid synners all.
Wherby I dare with humble bymonyng
By thy goodnes off the this thing require: 80
Chastyse me not for my deserving,
Acordyng to thy just conceyvid Ire.
O lord, I dred, and that I did not dred
I me repent, and euermore desyre
The, the to dred. I open here and spred 85
My fawte to the, but thou, for thi goodnes,
Mesure it not in largenes nor in bred,
Punish it not, as askyth the grettnes
Off thi furour, provokt by my offence.
Tempre, O lord, the harme of my excesse 90
With mendyng will, that I for recompense
Prepare agayne; and rather pite me,
For I ame wek and clene withowt defence:
More is the nede I have of remede,

---

65 he] *omitted* Q. or] of E. 66 Rof that] the thing E; of that A, R, Q. that] whyche Q.
68 frawtyd] yfraughted A. 69 his . . . clay] depe draughtes of hys decaye Q; and
touching of the stringes R. 70 Dressyd] dressing R. sekyng to conterpese] he tunes
his god to plese E. 71 song] songes Q. 73 in] off E; *omitted* R, Q. 74 call] to call Q.
75 hert] harpe Q. hope taken] cawght confort E; he taken Q. 77 marcy as the] euer
the same E. 78 Only confort of] Of onely comfort to Q. wrechid] vs E. 80 thy] the
Q, R. the this thing] the thing E. 85 The, the] thee for A; Thee Q. open] knolege E.
87 it not in] it in A. largenes] lenghe E. 89 provokt] provoketh E. furour] furie R.
my] myne R, Q. 90 my] mine R. 91 for recompense] prepare agayne E. 94 More . . .
remede] And have more nede of the for remede E.

I

For off the hole the lech takyth no cure.   95
The shepe that strayth the sheperd sekes to se:
I lord ame strayd: I, sek withowt recure,
    Fele al my lyms, that have rebelld for fere,
    Shake in dispayre, onles thou me assure.
Mye flesshe is troubled, my hart doth feare the speare;   100
    That dread of death, of death that ever lastes,
    Threateth of right and draweth neare and neare.
Moche more my sowle is trowbled by the blastes
    Of theise assawltes, that come as thick as hayle,
    Of worldlye vanytie, that temptacion castes   105
Agaynst the weyke bulwarke of the flesshe frayle:
    Wheare in the sowle in great perplexitie
    Ffeelethe the sensis, with them that assayle,
Conspyre, corrupte by vse and vanytie;
    Whearby the wretche dothe to the shade resorte   110
    Of hope in the, in this extreamytie.
But thow, O Lord, how long after this sorte
    Fforbearest thow to see my myserye?
    Suffer me yet, in hope of some comforte,
Ffeare and not feele that thow forgettest me.   115
    Returne, O Lorde, O Lorde, I the beseche,
    Vnto thie olde wonted benignitie.
Reduce, revyve my sowle: be thow the Leche,
    And reconcyle the great hatred and stryfe
    That it hath tane agaynste the flesshe, the wretche   120
That stirred hathe thie wrathe bye filthie life.
    Se how my sowle doth freat it to the bones,
    Inward remorce so sharp'the it like a knife;
That but thow helpp the caitife, that bemones
    His great offence, it turnes anon to dust.   125
    Heare hath thie mercye matter for the nones,
Ffor if thie rightwise hand that is so iuste
    Suffer no Synne or stryke with dampnacion,
    Thie infinyte marcye want nedes it must

96 strayth] strays R. sekes] sekth E. 97 I sek] and seke Q. 98 Fele] for E. 99 in] for
E. unles] of E. me] me not E. 100–53] *omitted* E. 102 Threateth] Tretith R. 105
worldlye] worlds R. vanytie] vanities Q. 106 weyke] *omitted* Q. 109 vse] pleasure Q.
110 shade] R, Q; shadowe A. 116 O . . . beseche] I beseche thee o lorde Q. 117 thie]
thine R. 120 hath] had Q. tane] had Q. 121 wrathe] wroth R. 125 great] *omitted* R.
turnes] turnith R, Q. 127 rightwise] R; rightuous A, Q.

Subjecte matter for his operacion: 130
   For that in deth there is no memorie
   Amonge the Dampnyd, nor yet no mencion
Of thie great name, grownd of all glorye.
   Then if I dye and goe wheare as I feare
   To thinck thearon, how shall thie great mercye   135
Sownde in my mowth vnto the worldes eare?
   Ffor theare is none than can thee lawde and love,
   Ffor that thow wilt no love among them theare.
Suffer my Cryes thie marcye for to move,
   That wonted is a hundred yeares offence   140
   In momente of repentaunce to remove.
How ofte have I calde vpp with diligence
   This slowthful flesshe longe afore the daye,
   Ffor to confesse his faulte and negligence,
That to the done for ought that I coold say   145
   Hath still returnd to shrowde it self from colde;
   Whearbye it suffers nowe for suche delaye.
By nightlye playntes in stede of pleasures olde
   I wasshe my bed with teares contynuall,
   To dull my sight that it be never bolde   150
To stirr mye hart agayne to suche a fall.
   Thus drye I vpp among my foes in woe,
   That with my fall do rise and grow with all,
And me bysett evin now where I am so
   With secrett trapps to troble my penance.   155
   Sum do present to my weping yes, lo,
The chere, the manere, beaute and countenance
   Off her whose loke alas did mak me blynd;
   Sum other offer to my remembrans
Those plesant wordes, now bitter to my mynd;   160
   And sum shew me the powre of my armour,
   Tryumph, and conquest, and to my hed assind
Dowble diademe: sum shew the favour

131] R, Q; *omitted* A.   139 thie] thee Q. for] *omitted* Q.   141 In momente] In a momente Q.   145 done] denne Q.   146 it] hym Q.   147 suffers] sufferth R; suffreth Q. nowe] none Q.   148 nightlye] R; mightye A, Q.   151 stirr] stere Q.   154 bysett] besettes A.   155 trapps] gye E.   156 Sum do] the and doth E. to my weping] vnto myn E; to me, my wepinge Q. lo] *omitted* R, Q.   157 the manere] manere R. and] or Q.   160 Those] these Q.   161 my] myne R.   162 my] myne R.   163 the] *omitted* Q.

Of people frayle, palais, pompe and ryches:
To thes marmaydes and theyre baytes off errour   165
I stopp myn eris with help of thy goodnes;
    And for I fele it comith alone of the
    That to my hert thes foes have non acces
I dare them bid: 'avoyd wreches and fle!
    The lord hath hard the voyce off my complaint;   170
    Your engins take no more effect in me.
The lord hath herd, I say, and sen me faynt
    Vnder your hand, and pitith my distres.
    He shall do mak my sensis by constraint
Obbey the rule that reson shall expres,   175
    Wher the deceyte of yowr glosing baite
    Made them vsurp a powre in all exces'.
Shamid be thei all that so ly in whaite
    To compas me, by missing of theire pray!
    Shame and rebuke redound to suche decayte!   180
Sodayne confusion's stroke withowt delay
    Shall so defface theire craffty sugestion
    That they to hurt my helthe no more assay,
Sins I, o Lord, remayne in thi protection.

*   *   *

Who so hathe sene the sikk in his fevour,   185
Affter treux taken with the hote or cold
And that the fitt is past off his faruour,
Draw faynting syghes, let hym, I say, behold
Sorowfull David affter his langour,
That with the terys that from his iyes down rold,   190
Pausid his plaint, and laid adown his harp,
Faythfull record of all his sorows sharp.

---

164 ryches] glory E.   165 thes] the R, Q.   166 myn] my A, Q.   167 comith] comes A.
168 hert] harpe Q.   thes] those A.   169 I dare] Dare Q.   172 herd . . . and] pitid for
to E.   sen] seme R.   175 the rule] thee rule Q; therefore A.   176 the] by E; that thee Q.
glosinge] glawncynge A.   baite] venem E.   177 made them] that had E.   vsurp] vsurpt
E; vsurpp A.   178 ly] do lye Q.   in] in and E.   180 decayte] decaye A.   181 confusion's]
confusion is; confusion as ? W/E, A, R, Q.   182 sugestion] entreprise E.   185
fevour] dolour E.   186 Affter] affter the E.   the hote] thete E; heat A, R; the heate Q.
or] or with A.   187 faruour] feruour R; furour A; fevour Q.   188 let . . . behold] with
sobbyng double fold E.   189 Sorowfull] let hym E.   190 the] his Q.   iyes] eyen Q.
191 adown] downe Q.

It semid now that of his fawt the horrour
Did mak aferd no more his hope of grace,
The thretes whereoff in horrible errour   195
Did hold his hert as in dispaire a space
Till he had willd to seke for his socour,
Hym selff accusing, beknowyng his cace,
Thinking so best his lord for to apese,
Eesd, not yet heled, he felith his disese.   200

Semyth horrible no more the dark Cave
That erst did make his fault for to tremble,
A place devout or refuge for to save
The socourles it rather doth resemble:
For who had sene so knele within the grave   205
The chieff pastor of thebrews assemble
Wold juge it made by terys of penitence
A sacrid place worthi off reuerence.

With vapord iyes he lokyth here and there,
And when he hath a while hym selff bethowght,   210
Gadryng his sprites that were dismayd for fere,
His harp agayne in to his hand he rowght.
Tunyng accord by Jugement of his ere:
His hertes botum for a sigh he sowght,
And there withall apon the holow tre   215
With straynid voyce agayne thus cryth he.

Psalm 32. *Beati quorum remisse sunt*

O H happy ar they that have forgiffnes gott
   Off their offence (not by their penitence
   As by meryt wych recompensyth not
Altho that yet pardone hath non offence   220
   Withowte the same) but by the goodnes

195 errour] terrour Q. 197 willd] wyll Q. 198 beknowyng] and knoleging E. 199 for
to] to A, Q. 200 Eesd] esed? E; And Q. heled] held W. felith] filleth A. 201 Semyth]
Now semyth E, Q. horrible] fearefull Q. 202 for to tremble] to be adrad E. 203 or]
of Q. 204 doth] dyd Q. 205 had] hathe A. so] so him *later insertion* E. knele] kneeling
Q. the] a A. 206 thebrews] the hebrewes Q. 209 lokyth] loked Q. 210 a . . . sellff]
himself a while R. bethowght] besought A. 211 Gadryng] Gatheringe A, Q. were]
R; weare A; where W. 212 agayne] agayne and E. into] vnto Q. rowght] caught A.
216 straynid] lowd E. agayne] lo E. cryth] oferyth E; cryed Q. 217 that] that that E.
220 non] not R, Q.

Off hym that hath perfect intelligens
Off hert contrite, and coverth the grettnes
　　Off syn within a marcifull discharge.
　　And happy ar they that have the willfullness　　　　225
Off lust restraynd, afore it went at large,
　　Provokyd by the dred of goddes furour
　　Wherby thei have not on theyre bakes the charge
Of othrs fawte to suffer the dolour;
　　For that thire fawte was neuer excecute　　　　　230
　　In opyn syght, example of errour;
And happi is he to whom god doth impute
　　No more his faut by knoleging his syn
　　But clensid now the lord doth hym repute,
As adder freshe new stryppid from his skin;　　　　　235
　　Nor in his sprite is owght vndiscoverd.
　　I for by cawse I hidd it still within,
Thynking by state in fawte to be preferd,
　　Do fynd by hyding of my fawte my harme,
　　As he that feels his helth to be hinderd　　　　　240
By secrete wound concelid from the charme
　　Of lechis cure that elles had had redresse,
　　And fele my bonis consume and wax vnfarme
By dayly rage roryng in excesse.
　　Thy hevy hand on me was so encrest　　　　　　245
　　Both day and nyght and held my hert in presse
With priking thowghtes byreving me my rest,
　　That wytherd is my lustynes away
　　As somer hettes that hath the grene oprest;
Wherfore I did an othr way assay,　　　　　　　250
　　And sowght forthwith to opin in thi syght
　　My fawt, my fere, my filthines, I say,

223 and] that E. coverth] covereth R; couert Q. 224 with in . . . discharge] vnder the
mantell off mercy E. 225 And] oh E. the willfullness] forgiff E. 229 Of] off E1; with
E2. othrs fawte] other faultes Q. to . . . dolour] examplid theire errour E. 230 was]
did E. excecute] it extend E. 232 is he] is E. 234 But] And Q. 235 freshe . . .
stryppid] new ystryppid E. new] and new A. 236 owght] nothing E. 237 I for] In
for R. by cawse] that E. hidd] had A. 238] And for to shew my fawte have bene
aferd E. 239 Do] do E1; and E2. fynd] fyndes E. 240 feels] feeles A; fells W;
feleth R. feels . . . hinderd] fyndeth, hys healthe hyndered Q. 242 lechis] Leathis A.
243 and] Dyd E. 244] by dayly plaint that I by force expresse E. 245 Thy] and for
thy E; The Q. was] hath E. 247 priking] restles E. 248 That] That I am E. 249
hath] haue R, Q.

And not to hide from the my gret vnryght.
   I shall (quod I) agaynst my sellff confesse
   Vnto the lord all my synfull plyght;   255
And thou forthwith didst washe the wikkednes
   Off myn offence, of trowgth ryght thus it is.
   Wherfor they that have tastid thi goodnes
At me shall take example as of this,
   And pray and seke in tyme for tyme of grace.   260
   Then shall the stormes and fluddes of harme him miss,
And hym to rech shall neuer have the space.
   Thow art my refuge and only savegard
   From the trobles that compasse me the place.
Such Joy as he that skapis his enmis ward   265
   With losid bondes hath in his libertie,
   Such Joy, my Joy, thow hast to me prepard,
That as the seman in his Jeopretie
   By soden lyght perceyvid hath the port,
   So by thy gret marcifull propertie   270
Within thi lok thus rede I my confort.
   I shall the tech and gyve vnderstondyng,
   And poynt to the what way thou shalt resort;
For thi adresse to kepe the from wandryng,
   Myn iye shall tak the charge to be thy guyde.   275
   I aske therto of the alone this thing:
Be not like horse or Mule that man doth ryde,
   That not alone doth not his master know,
   But for the good thou dost hym must be tyde
And brydeld, lest his guyd he bite or throw.   280
   Oh dyuerse ar the chastysinges off syn!
   In mete, in drynk, in breth that man doth blow,
In slepe, in wach, in fretyng styll within,
   That neuer soffer rest vnto the mynd;
   Filld with offence, that new and new begyn   285

---

253 from] to E. 254 quod] quoth Q. confesse] bemone E. 260 tyme] tyms ?E. 261 him miss] *omitted* Q. 265 Joy] Ioyes Q. scapis] scapeth Q. 266 bondes] bandes Q. his] *omitted* Q. 267 Joy, my] is my Q. 269 lyght] sight R, Q. port] light R, Q. 271 lok] booke R, Q. 274 adresse] redresse A. 275 Myn] My R, Q. iye] yIe W; eyes A. 276 I] E. alone] onelye Q. 277 Mule] moyle A. man doth] men do R, Q. 278 doth not] doth R, Q. 279 the . . . tyde] thee good, thou must hym betide Q. 280 guyd] maister R. lest] yt lest E. 281 ar the] there are Q. 282 in drynk] and drynke Q. 283 in wach] and watche Q. 285 that] but E. Filld] Feld R.

With thowsand feris the hert to strayne and bynd.
   But for all this he that in god doth trust
   With mercy shall hym sellff defendid fynd.
Joy and reioyse, I say, ye that be just
   In hym that makth and holdyth yow so still;   290
   In hym your glory alwey set yow must,
All ye that be off vpright hert and will.

*   *   *

This song endid, David did stint his voyce,
And in that while abowt he with his iye
Did seke the Cave with wiche withowten noyce   295
His sylence semid to argew and replye
Apon this pees, this pees that did reioyce
The sowle with mercy, that mercy so did Crye,
And fownd mercy at mercyes plentifull hand,
Neuer denid but where it was withstand.   300

As the servant that in his masters face
Fyndyng pardon of his passid offence,
Consyderyng his grete goodnes and his grace,
Glad teris distills, as gladsome recompence;
Ryght so David that semid in that place   305
Marble ymage off singuler reuerence
Carffd in the rokk with Iyes and handes on hygh,
Made as by crafft to plaine, to sobbe, to sygh.

This while a beme that bryght sonne forth sendes,
That sonne the wych was neuer clowd cowd hide,   310

286 hert] mynd E. to] so A. bynd] blynde A, Q. 289 Joy] Ioyce Q. I say] saye
A; o A. ye] you Q. be] bene E. 290 makth and holdyth] doth contynew E. 291
your . . . must] I say set all your glory yow must E. alwey] alwayes Q. 292 All ye]
All A; All you Q. off] of an A. 293 This . . . David] This endid did our David E.
David . . . voyce] David held his pece E. stint] skant R. 294 abowt he] did seke E;
he aboute Q. 295 Did seke the Cave] A; Did seke the dark Cave W, R, Q; the darke
Cave E. [*W, in revising the line, neglected to delete 'dark'.*] withowten] withoute Q.
296 to] his to E. 297 pees . . . that] marcy whereon he E. this pees hys harpe Q.
298 sowle] hert for E. Crye] cal R, Q. 299 mercyes . . . hand] mercy plenty full hand
W; mercy full hand E; mercie at plentifulles hand R; plentifull mercyes hand A, Q.
300 where] whi R. 301 As] And as E. that] *omitted* Q. 302 Fyndyng pardon] fynds
pardons ?E; ffynding the pardon A. 305 that] and E. that semid] did seme as R;
semed Q. that] thee Q, R. 306 Marble ymage] and ymage E; A marble image Q.
307 in the rokke] in Rock A. handes] hande Q. on hygh] lyfft vp E. 308 Made as]
semyng E. as] is Q. plaine . . . sygh] syghe to sobbe to supp E. 309 This] The A.
that . . . sendes] down from that sonne discendes E. sendes] sendeth Q. 310 was]

Percyth the cave and on the harpe discendes,
Whose glauncyng light the cordes did ouerglyde,
And such luyster apon the harpe extendes
As lyght off lampe upon the gold clene tryde:
The torne wheroff into his Iyes did sterte,   315
Surprisd with Joye by penance off the herte.

He then Inflamd with farr more hote affect
Of god then he was erst of Bersabe,
His lifft fote did on the yerth erect,
And just therby remaynth the tothr kne;   320
To his lifft syde his wayght he doth direct.
Sure hope of helth, and harpe agayne takth he;
His hand, his tune, his mynd sowght his lay,
Wyche to the Lord with sobre voyce did say.

Psalm 38. *Domine ne in furore tuo arguas me*

O LORD, as I the have both prayd and pray,   325
   (Altho in the be no alteration
   But that we men, like as our sellffes we say,
Mesuryng thy Justice by our Mutation)
   Chastice me not, o lord, in thi furour,
   Nor me correct in wrathfull castigation.   330
Ffor that thi arrows off fere, off terrour
   Of sword, of sekenes, off famine and fyre
   Stikkes diepe in me. I, lo, from myn errour
Ame plongid vp, as horse owt of the myre
   With strok off spurr: such is thi hand on me,   335
   That in my fleshe for terrour of thy yre
Is not on poynt of ferme stabilite,

theare was A. clowd] sonne R, Q. cowd hide] hide E.   311 on the] on his A. des-
cendes] descendethe Q.   312 Whose . . . glyde] and with the luster on the cordes it
glyde E. cordes] world Q.   313 luyster] glister A. extendes] extendethe Q.   315
sterte] stette Q.   317 then] more Q. affect] desire E.   318 he . . . off] off his Idolle E.
319 lifft] list R.   320 And] *omitted* Q. tothr] other Q.   321 his] thee Q.   322 Sure]
assured E; for Q. and] hys Q.   323 mynd] mynde eke A.   324 voyce] looke A.
325 the have] have the Q.   326 in] be in E no] no such E; none R. alteration] altera-
tions E.   327 like as] as we E.   328 Mesuryng] And mesuryng E. by our] by the E.
mutation] Mutations E.   330 castigation] castigations E.   331 thi] thine R.   332
famine and fyre] derth and deth E. off famine] a famin R. and] of A, Q.   333 Stikkes
diepe] ar stykyt E.   334 plongid] plucked Q. as] like R.   336 terrour] fere E. thy]
thine R.   337 ferme] helthe E.

Nor in my bonis there is no stedfastnes:
Such is my drede of mutabilite,
Ffor that I know my frailefull wykednes.   340
    For why? my sinns above my hed ar bownd,
    Like hevi wheyght that doth my force oppresse
Vnder the wych I stopp and bowe to grownd,
    As whilow plant haled by vyolence;
    And off my fleshe ech not well curyd wound,   345
That festred is by foly and neclegens,
    By secrete lust hath ranklyd vnder skyn,
    Not duly Curyd by my penitens.
Perceyving thus the tyranny off sin,
    That with his wheit hath humblid and deprest   350
    My pryd, by gruging off the worme within
That neuer dyth, I lyve withowten rest.
    So ar myn entrayles infect with fervent sore,
    Fedyng the harme that hath my welth oprest,
That in my fleshe is lefft no helth therfore.   355
    So wondrus gret hath bene my vexation
    That it hath forst my hart to crye and rore.
O lord thow knowst the inward contemplation
    Off my desire, thou knowst my syghes and plaintes
    Thow knowst the teres of my lamentation   360
Can not expresse my hertes inward restraintes.
    My hart pantyth, my force I fele it quaile,
    My syght, myn Iyes, my lok dekays and fayntes.
And when myn enmys did me most assayle,
    My frendes most sure, wherein I sett most trust,   365
    Myn own vertus, sonest then did ffaile,
And stoud apart, reson and witt vniust,

339 drede] fere E. 340 frailefull] sinfull E. 341 For why] by Cawse E. above . . .
bownd] ar clome above my hed E1; ar . . . my crowne E2. 342 wheyght] weightes
Q. 343 stopp] stoupe R, Q; shrincke A. to grownd] a down E; to the grounde Q.
343 + by force wheroff the evill Curid skarris E. 344 whilow plant] doth a bow E.
345 and] that E. not well] evyll E. 346 That festred is] festred by E. 347 vnder
skyn] styll with sin E1; styll within E2. ranklyd] ranked Q. 350 his] *omitted* Q.
351 gruging] gnawying E. worme] wounde R. 353 myn] mye A. 354 the] my
R, Q. hath] *omitted* Q. welth] helth E. 357 it hath forst] forcyd hath E; it forsced
Q. to crye] for to E. 358 the inward] inward R; thinward Q. 362 hart] force E.
quaile] faile E. 363 myn] my A, Q. 364 myn] mye A. 365 My . . . sure] myn owne
vertus E. most] my E. 366 Myn own vertus] as frendes most sure E. vertus]
acquaintance *later correction* E. did] did me A. 367 and] did E. stoud] stode Q;
stond A, R.

As kyn vnkynd were fardest gone at nede.
So had thei place theire venim owt to thrust
That sowght my deth by nowghty word and dede: 370
   Theire tonges reproche, theire wittes did fraude aplye,
   And I like deffh and domme forth my way yede,
Lyk one that heris not, nor hath to replye
   One word agayne, knowyng that from thi hand
   Thes thinges procede and thow o lord shalt supplye   375
My trust in the wherein I stikk and stand.
   Yet have I had gret cawse to dred and fere
   That thou woldst gyve my foos the ouerhand;
Ffor in my ffall they shewd suche plesant chere,
   And therwithall I alway in the lashe   380
   Abyd the strok: and with me euery where
I bere my fawte, that gretly doth abashe
   My dowlfull chere; ffor I my fawt confesse,
   And my desert doth all my conffort dashe.
In the mene while myn Enmys saffe encresse   385
   And my provokars herby do augement,
   That withowt cawse to hurt me do not cesse.
In evill for good agaynst me they be bent,
   And hinder shall my good pursuyte off grace.
   Lo now, my god, that seist my hole Intent,   390
My lord, I ame, thow knowst well, in what case.
   Fforsak me not, be not farre from me gone:
   Hast to my help, hast, lord, and hast apace,
O lord, the lord off all my helth alone.

     *   *   *

Lik as the pilgryme that in a long way   395
Fayntyng for hete, provokyd by some wind

368 As kyn vnkynd] as naturall kyn E. were fardest gone] were gone farr off E; fardest gone A. 371 reproche] deceyte E. wittes] wit Q. 374 One] not one Q. knowyng . . . hand] ffor that to the o Lord E. thi hand] thyne hande Q. 375 Thes . . . supplye] I me dyrect thow shalt my hope supplye E. o lord] *omitted* R; lorde Q. supplye] replye Q. 376 My trust in] the trust off E. the] that Q. wherein] where R. 377 to] to off E. 378] That myn enmys shold have the ouerhand. 379 shewd] shew A. such . . . chere] reioysing chere E. 380 And] That Q. 382 that] and A. 383 my . . . confesse] confesse my fawt E. 385 saffe] styll Q. 386 provokars] evill willers E; provokes A. do] do moche A. 387 hurt] harme E. 388 he bent] shall assent E. 389 pursuyte] presente Q. 390 god] lord my E. seest] knowst E. 391 lord] god E. well] *omitted* Q. 392 be . . . gone] nor be not from me farr E. 395 in] hath E. 396 wind] shaad E.

In some fresh shaade lith downe at mydes off day,
So doth off David the weryd voyce and mynd
Tak breth off syghes when he had song this lay,
Vnder such shaad as sorow hath assynd;   400
And as the tone still myndes his viage end,
So doth the tother to mercy still pretend.

On sonour cordes his fingers he extendes,
Withowt heryng or Jugement off the sownd;
Down from his Iyes a storme off terys discendes,   405
Withowt feling, that trykill on the grownd,
As he that bledes in baigne ryght so intendes
Th'altryd sensis to that that thei ar bownd;
But syght and wepe he can non othr thing,
And lok vp still vnto the hevins kyng.   410

But who had bene withowt the Cavis mowth,
And herd the terys and syghes that he did strayne,
He wold have sworne there had owt off the sowth
A lewk warme wynd browght forth a smoky rayne;
But that so close the Cave was and vnkowth   415
That none but god was record off his payne:
Elles had the wynd blowne in all Israelles erys
The wofull plaint and off theire kyng the terys.

Off wych some part, when he vpp suppyd hade,
Like as he whom his owne thowght affrays,   420
He torns his look; hym semith that the shade
Off his offence agayne his force assays
By violence dispaire on hym to lade;

---

397 shaade . . . day] wynd restyth at myd day E. off day] of the day Q.   398
weryd] wery Q.   401 still myndes] sekys still E. viage] voyage A, R.   402 tother]
other Q. to mercy still] still to marcye A.   403 On . . . extendes] his fyngers strik
apon the sonour cordes E. sonour] Sower A; foure Q. extendes] pretendes Q.
405 from] of Q. storme] streame A, Q.   407 baigne] vayne Q.   408 Thaltryd sensis]
his sensis sparplid E. to that that] so that A.   409 syght] sighe A, R.   410 vp] on E.
hevins] heauen Q.   411 who] who so A. had] hath Q. withowt] forth of E. Cavis]
caue Q.   412 terys and syghes] syghes and terys E. did strayne] powrd out E. he]
hym Q.   415 so . . . and] the Cave close was and eke A.   417 in all] in to all E.
Israelles] Israell Q.   418] of theyr kynge, the wofull playnte and teares Q.   419 some]
sonne Q. vpp suppyd hade] had suppyd E.   420 affrays] affayres Q.   421 semith]
semed Q.   423 violence] vyolente Q.

Stertyng like hym whom sodeyne fere dismays,
His voyce he strains, and from his hert owt brynges   425
This song that I not wyther he crys or singes.

Psalm 51. *Miserere mei domine*

REW on me, lord, for thy goodnes and grace,
    That off thy nature art so bountefull,
    Ffor that goodnes that in the world doth brace
Repugnant natures in quiete wonderfull,   430
    And for thi mercys nomber withowt end
    In hevin and yerth perceyvid so plentefull
That ouer all they do them sellffes extend:
    Ffor those marcys much more then man can synn
    Do way my synns that so thy grace offend.   435
Agayne washe me but washe me well within,
    And from my synn that thus makth me affrayd
    Make thou me clene as ay thy wont hath byn;
Ffor vnto the no nombre can be layd
    For to prescrybe remissions off offence   440
    In hertes retornd, as thow thy sellff hast sayd.
And I beknow my ffawt, my neclegence,
    And in my syght my synn is fixid fast,
    Theroff to have more perfett penitence.
To the alone, to the have I trespast,   445
    Ffor none can mesure my fawte but thou alone;
    For in thy syght I have not bene agast
For to offend, juging thi syght as none,
    So that my fawt were hid from syght of man,
    Thy maiestye so from my mynd was gone: 450
This know I and repent; pardon thow than,
    Wherby thow shalt kepe still thi word stable,

---

424 Stertyng] he stertes E. fere dismays] dispayre dismayde Q. 425 His] with his E. voyce] herte R, Q. his hert] the same R. 426 that] *omitted* R. not] note A, Q. Crys] cryeth Q. 427 lord] good lorde. 429 in] all E. the world] thy worde Q. 434 those marcys] hys mercye Q. 435 way] a way Q. synns] synne Q. so] *omitted* Q. 436 Agayne] offttyme E; oft times R, A; ofte tymes agayne Q. 437 synn] synnes Q. makth] makes A, R, Q. 438 ay] euer Q. 439 no nombre] nowe, none Q. 440 remissions off offence] remysyon of synne Q. 441 hertes] harte Q. 442 ffawt, my] faulte and my Q. 443 And] *omitted* Q. synn] synnes Q. is fixid fast] shall still remayne E. 444 Theroff] Thearfore A. 445 alone] aboue Q. 446 mesure] cure Q. 450 mynd] sight Q. 452 shalt . . . stable] hold ferme and fast thi word still and E.

Thy justice pure and clene; by cawse that whan
I pardond ame, then forthwith Justly able,
　Just I ame jugd by justice off thy grace.　　　　455
　Ffor I my sellff, lo thing most vnstable,
Fformd in offence, conceyvid in like case,
　Ame nowght but synn from my natyvite;
　Be not this sayd for my excuse, alase,
But off thy help to shew necessite;　　　　　　　460
　Ffor lo thou loves the trowgh off inward hert,
　Wich yet doth lyve in my fydelite;
Tho I have fallen by fraylte ouerthwart,
　Ffor willfull malice led me not the way,
　So much as hath the flesh drawn me apart.　　　465
Wherfore, o lord, as thow hast done alway,
　Tech me the hydden wisdome off thy lore,
　Sins that my fayth doth not yet dekay;
And as the Juyz to hele the liepre sore
　With hysope clense, clense me, and I ame clene.　470
　Thow shalt me wash, and more then snow therfore
I shall be whight, how fowle my fawt hath bene.
　Thow off my helth shalt gladsome tydynges bryng;
　When from above remission shall be sene
Descend on yerth, then shall for Joye vp spryng　　475
　The bonis that were afore consumd to dust.
　Looke not, o lord, apon myn offendyng,
But do a way my dedes that ar vnjust.
　Make a clene hert in the myddes off my brest
　With spryte vpryght, voydyd from fylthye lust.　480
Ffrom thyn Iys cure, cast me not in vnrest,
　Nor take from me thy spryte of holynesse.
　Rendre to me joye off thy help and rest;

453 pure] stable E.　454 then] and E. Justly able] iusticiable Q.　455 I ame] to be E.
458 from my natyvite] by corrupt nature E.　458+ yet lo thou loves so the hertes
trowgh in Inward place E.　459 this] these Q. not] nat R. my] myne A, R, Q. alase]
ah alas Q.　460 necessite] necessitie inwarde Q.　461 loves] lov'ste A, R, Q. inward]
the Q.　462 my] mooste Q.　463 fraylte] fraile R, Q.　464 led . . . way] led me no
the way W; hath not led me a way E. led] leade Q.　468 fayth] t E. yet] as yet A, R.
469 Juyz] Iewes Q.　471 Thow] do thow E.　474 When] when he E.　475 shall]
shalte Q.　476 afore] before Q.　479 a clene] clene E. in the myddes] in myd ?E].
myddes] middell Q.　480] With vpryght spryte purgid from all vile lust E. voydyd].
voyde A. fylthye] all filthie A.　481 thyn] thye A.　482 thy] thee Q.　483 Rendre to]
retourne E. rest] heste Q.

My will conferme with spryte off stedfastnesse:
　　And by this shall thes goodly thinges ensue.　　485
　　Sinners I shall in to thy ways adresse:
They shall retorne to the and thy grace sue.
　　My tong shall prayse thy Justification,
　　My mowgh shall spred thy gloryus praysis true.
But off thi sellff, o god, this operation　　490
　　It must proced, by purging me from blood,
　　Among the just that I may have relation;
And off thy lawdes for to let owt the flood;
　　Thow must, o lord, my lypps furst vnlose:
　　Ffor if thou hadst estemid plesant good　　495
The owtward dedes that owtward men disclose,
　　I wold have offerd vnto the sacryfice.
　　But thou delyghtes not in no such glose
Off owtward dede, as men dreme and devyse.
　　The sacryfice that the lord lykyth most　　500
　　Is spryte contrite: low hert in humble wyse
Thow dost accept, o god, for plesant host.
　　Make Syon, lord, accordyng to thy will,
　　Inward Syon, the Syon of the ghost:
Off hertes Hierusalem strength the walles still.　　505
　　Then shalt thou take for good these vttward dedes,
　　As sacryfice thy plesure to fullfyll.
Off the alone thus all our good procedes.

　　　　*　　　　*　　　　*

Off diepe secretes that David here did sing,
Off mercy, off fayth, off frailte, off grace,　　510
Off goddes goodnes and off Justyfying,
The grettnes dyd so astonne hymselff a space,
As who myght say who hath exprest this thing?

484 My will] And me E. with] wyth the Q.　486 ways] waie R.　487 They] Theise A.
489 spred] speed ?W; spread A, R, Q. praysis] prayse Q.　490 operation] repenta ?E
(reputa *Hughey*).　494 furst] at furst A.　498 delyghtes] delyghtest A, R, Q.　500 the
lord lykyth] plesith god E.　504 ghost] host Q.　505 Hierusalem] I Hierusalem E.
strength] strengh E. the] thy Q.　506 these] the Q.　507 As] of a Q.　508 Off . . .
procedes] *omitted* Q.　509 Off] the E. here] ther Q.　510 off grace] and grace E.　511
and] eke, and A.　512 The . . . so] did with the wonder E. The] Thy Q. grettness]
goodnesse Q. astonne] astony Q. hymselff] hym E. a space] apace Q.

I synner, I, what have I sayd alas?
That goddes goodnes wold within my song entrete,   515
Let me agayne considre and repete.

And so he doth, but not exprest by word:
But in his hert he tornith and paysith
Ech word that erst his lypps might forth aford.
He poyntes, he pawsith, he wonders, he praysyth   520
The marcy that hydes off justice the swourd,
The justice that so his promesse complysyth,
For his wordes sake to worthilesse desert,
That gratis his graces to men doth depert.

Here hath he confort when he doth mesure   525
Mesureles marcys to mesureles fawte,
To prodigall sinners Infinite tresure,
Tresure termeles that neuer shall defawte.
Ye, when that sinn shall fayle and may not dure,
Mercy shal reygne, gaine whome shall no assaute   530
Off hell prevaile, by whome, lo, at this day,
Off hevin gattes Remission is the kay.

And when David hath ponderd well and tryd,
And seith hym sellff not vtterly deprivid
From lyght of grace that dirk of sinn dyd hyde,   535
He fyndes hys hope muche therewith revivid;
He dare Importune the lord on euery syde,
(For he knowth well to mercy is ascrybid
Respectles labour) Importune, crye and call:
And thus begynth his song therwithall.   540

---

514 alas] ah alas Q. 515 song] me E. 517 not] *omitted* Q. 519 erst] *omitted* Q. forth
aford] foorde abrode Q. 520 poyntes . . . wonders] pointeth . . . wondreth Q.
521 hydes] hydeth Q. 522 complysyth] accomplysheth Q. 524 That gratis his] so
gratis doth his E. men doth] men E. graces] grace Q. 526 Mesurles] this mesureles
E. marcys] mercye Q. to] and E. fawte] fautes Q. 527 sinners] synnes A, Q. Infinite]
Infinitye Q. tresure] mercie R. 528 termeles] celestyall Q. 529 dure] endure Q. 530
gaine] gaynste A; agayne Q. no] not A, Q; none R. 533 David] that David E. hath]
had Q. ponderd well] considerd this E. 535 From] for Q. dirk . . . hyde] sinn had
mad hym mis E. dirk] dark A, Q. 536 fyndes] fyndeth Q. muche] so much E. there-
with] therewith all A. 537 He dare Importune] Importunth he E. dare Importune]
importeth on Q. 538 to] that to Q.

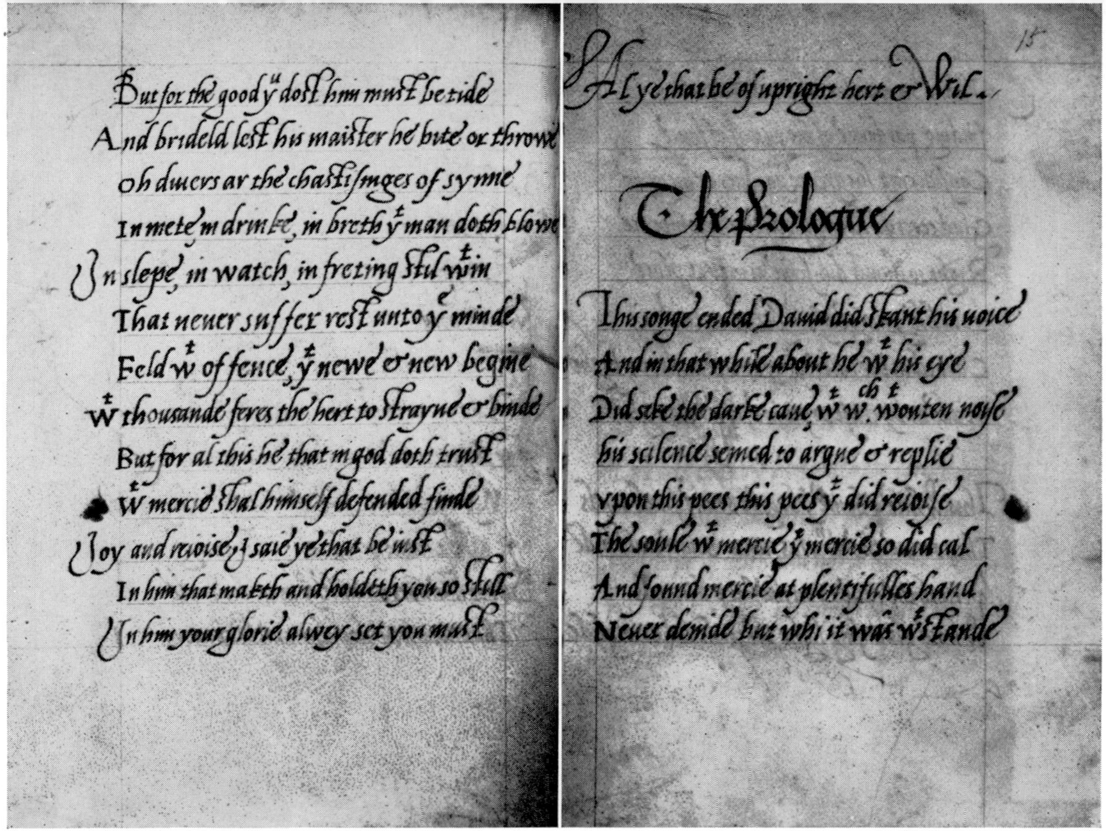

But for the good yu dost him must betide
And brideld lest his maister he bite or throwe
Oh divers ar the chastisinges of synne
In mete, in drinke, in breth yt man doth blowe
In slepe, in watch, in freting stil wtin
That never suffer rest unto ye minde
Feld wt offence, yt newe & new begine
Wt thousande feres the hert to strayne & binde
But for al this he that in god doth trust
Wt mercie shal himself defended finde
Joy and reioise, I said ye that be iust
In him that maketh and holdeth you so still
In him your glorie alwey set you must
Al ye that be of upright hert & wil.

15

The Prologue

This songe ended David did stint his voice
And in that while about he wt his eye
Did seke the darke cave, wt wch wtouten noyse
his scilence semed to argue & replie
upon this pees this pees yt did reioise
The soule wt mercie yt mercie so did cal
And found mercie at plentifulles hand
Never denide but whr it was wtstande

4. Royal MS 17A
(*poem* CVIII, *pages* 107–8)

Psalm 102. *Domine exaudi orationem meam*

L O R D here my prayre and let my crye passe
Vnto the lord withowt impediment.
Do not from me torne thy mercyfull fase,
Vnto my sellff leving my government.
In tyme off troble and aduersitye 545
Inclyne to me thyn ere and thyn Intent;
And when I call help my necessitye;
Redely graunt th'effect off my desyre.
Thes bold demaundes do plese thy maiestye,
And ek my Case such hast doth well require. 550
Ffor like as smok my days bene past awaye,
My bonis dryd vp as forneis with the fyre.
My hert, my mynd is wytherd vp like haye,
By cawse I have forgot to take my brede,
My brede off lyff, the word off trowthe, I say. 555
And ffor my plaintfull syghes, and my drcde,
My bonis, my strenght, my very force of mynde
Cleved to the flesh, and from thi spryte were flede,
As dispairate thy mercy for to fynd.
So made I me the solaine pelycane, 560
And lyke the owle that fleith by propre kynd
Lyght of the day and hath her sellff betane
To ruyne lyff owt of all companye.
With waker care that with this wo bygane,
Lik the sparow was I solytarye, 565
That sittes alone vnder the howsis effes.
This while my foes conspird continually,
And did provoke the harme off my dises.
Wherfor lik ashes my bred did me savour,
Of thi just word the tast myght not me ples; 570

542 withowt impediment] withowten stopp or lett E. 546 to] vnto Q. thyn . . . thyn] thye . . . this A. 547 when] when so E. help my necessitye] ffor help vnto the E. my] myne Q. 549 Thes . . . do] Boldelye too Q. 551 as smok] a synke Q. bene] are Q. 552 as] as a Q. 554 By cawse] But Q. brede] food E. 555 brede] foode E. 556 plaintfull] paynfull Q. syghes] my syghes E. and] and eke R; and for A. 557 of] and R. 558 thi] the A, Q. 559 as dispairate] R, Q; In diepe dispaire E; I as dispairate W, A. 560 me] am Q. solaine] solemne A; soden Q. 561 fleith] flyeth A, R, Q. 563 To . . . lyff] to lyve alone E. lyff] lief R. 565 was I] I ame E. 566 effes] eaves A. 568 provoke] assaut E. 569 me] *omitted* R. 570 Of . . . ples] In trowgh I fownd no tast that myght me ples E. me not] not me R, Q.

K

Wherfore my drynk I temperd with lycour
  Off weping teris that from myn Iyes do rayne.
By cause I know the wrath off thy furour,
Provokt by ryght had off my pride disdayne;
  For thou didst lyfft me vp to throw me downe,   575
  To tech me how to know my sellff agayne;
Wherby I knew that helples I shold drowne.
  My days lik shadow declyne and I do drye;
  And the for euer eternite doth crowne;
World withowt end doth last thy memorye.   580
  Ffor this frailte that yokyth all manekynd,
  Thou shallt awake, and rue this misery,
Rue on Syon, Syon that as I ffynd
  Is the peple that lyve vnder thy law;
  For now is tyme, the tyme at hand assynd,   585
The tyme so long that doth thy servantes draw
  In gret desyre to se that plesant day,
  Day off redeming Syon ffrom sins Aw.
Ffor they have ruth to se in such dekay
  In dust and stones this wrechid Syon lowr.   590
  Then the gentilles shall dred thy name alway;
All erthly kinges thy glory shall honour,
  Then, when thi grace this Syon thus redemith,
  When thus thou hast declard thy myghty powre.
The lord his servauntes wishis so estemith   595
  That he hym tornth vnto the poores request.
  To our discent thys to be wrytten semith,
Off all confortes as consolation best;
  And thei that then shalbe regenerate
  Shall praise the lord therfore both most and lest.   600
Ffor he hath lokt from the heyght off his astate,

---

571 Wherfore] Within her fore E. 572 that . . . rayne] that haile down from myn yIes E. myn A. do] downe A; dyd R, Q. 577 knew] knowe R, Q. 578 drye] crie R, Q. 579 crowne] drowne Q. 580 doth] shall E. 581 frailte] misery E. all mane kynd] euery mane E. 583 ffynd] assynd E. 584 is] ffor E. thy] the Q. 586 doth] *omitted* Q. servantes] seruaunt R. 588 sins] the E; his R. 590 In] off E. stones] stines E. lowr] ly E; lore Q. 591 Then] And so E. 592 thy . . . honour] shall honour thy glory E. 593 thi . . . thus] thou hast thi Syon thus savid E. this] thi R, Q. 594 myghty] R, A, Q; myght W. 595 The lord] E1; He lord W, A; he hath E2. wishis so estemith] cryes estemid E. wishis] wishes and Q. 596 he] *omitted* Q. poores] power Q. 597 our discent] all mankynd E. to be wrytten] publysht me E. 598 consolation] conffor E. 599 And] wherb E. 601 heyght] high Q.

The lord from hevyn in yerth hath lokt on vs,
  To here the mone off them that ar algate
In fowle bondage, to lose and to discus
  The sonns off deth owt from theire dedly bond,   605
  To gyve therby occasion gracius,
In this Syon hys holy name to stond
  And in Hierusalem hys laudes lastyng ay.
  When in one chirche the peple off the lond
And remes bene gaderd to serve, to lawd, to pray   610
  The lord aboue so just and mercyfull.
  But to this samble runnyng in the way
My strenght faylyth to rech it at the full.
  He hath abrigd my days, they may not dure,
  To se that terme, that terme so wonderfull,   615
Altho I have with herty will and Cure
  Prayd to the lord; take me not lord away
  In myddes off my yeres, tho thyn euer sure
Remayne eterne, whom tyme can not dekay.
  Thow wrowghtst the yerth, thy handes the vyns did mak; 620
  Thei shall peryshe and thou shalt last alway,
And althinges age shall were and ouertake
  Like cloth, and thou shalt chainge them lik aparell,
  Tourne, and translate, and thei in worth it tak.
But thou thy sellff the sellff remaynist well   625
  That thou wast erst, and shalt thi yeres extend.
  Then sins to this there may nothing rebell,
The gretest confort that I can pretend
  Is that the childerne off thy servantes dere
  That in thy word ar gott, shall withowt end   630
Byfore thy face be stablisht all in fere.

*   *   *

602 in] on Q. vs] vs men E.   604 fowle] soche Q. to discus] o₁ discus Q.   606
gracius] glorious Q. 607 hys] thy E; thys R, Q. name] to name E. 608 hys] thys E.
610 bene gaderd] shall range E1; been ranged E2. to pray] and pray E. 611 aboue]
that is E; that is above Q; that aboue R. 612 to] *omitted* R, Q. this] these Q. samble]
sample A; feble Q; semble R. 614 may not dure] are not sure Q. 615 that] the E.
terme so] tyme so Q. 616 herty] hart Q. 617 take . . . lord] lord take me not A;
take me not Q. 618 In] In the Q. off my yeres] of yeares A. 621 alway] ay R. 622
age] aye Q. 623 shalt chainge] shalt E. them] the R. 624 Tourne] torne E. 625 the]
thy Q. well] hole Q. 626 wast] waste A; was Q. shalt] shall Q. thi yeres] withouten E.
yeres] yere R, Q. 630 thy word] the world Q. 631 stablisht] stabisht W; stablishte
A.

When David had perceyvid in his brest
The sprite off god retournd that was exild,
By cause he knew he hath alone exprest
Thes grete thinges that greter spryte compilde,   635
As shalme or pype letes owt the sownd inprest
By musikes art forgid to fore and fyld,
I say when David had percyvid this
The sprite of confort in hym revivid is.

Ffor therapon he makyth argument   640
Off reconsiling vnto the lordes grace,
Altho sometyme to prophecy have lent
Both brut bestes and wikkyd hertes a place;
But our David jugith in his intent
Hym sellff by penance clene owt off this cace,   645
Wherby he hath remission off offence,
And gynnyth to Alow his payne and penitence.

But when he weyth the fawt and recompense
He damth his dede and fyndyth playne
A twene them to no whitt equivalence,   650
Wherby he takes all owtward dede in vayne
To bere the name off ryghtfull penitence;
Wich is alone the hert retornd agayne
And sore contryt that doth his fawt bymone,
And owtward dede the sygne or fruyt alone.   655

With this he doth deffend the slye assault
Off vayne alowance off his voyde desert,
And all the glory off his forgyven fault
To good alone he doth it hole convertt.

---

633 retournd] retourne Q. 634] ffor that he knew off hym were not exprest E. 635 greter] same great A. that] by E. spryte] thinge E. 637 musikes] musyke Q. 638 this] that I wys Q. 642 have] hathe Q. 644 our] he E. 645 this] his R. 647 gynnyth] begynneth Q. 648 he] that he E. the] tho E. 649 damth] dampnethe A, Q. and] and this A. 650 whitt] what R, Q. 651 takes] takethe Q. all . . . in] all recompense as E. dede] dedes Q. 653 Wich] that E. 654 that] hart, that Q. 655 sygne or fruyt] fruyt theroff E. sygne] synne Q. 657 voyde] worde A; owne Q. 658 glory] meryt E. 659 good] god A, Q, R.

His owne merytt he fyndyth in deffault; 660
And whilst he ponderd thes thinges in his hert,
His knee, his arme, his hand, susteind his chyn,
When he his song agayne thus did begynn.

Psalm 130. *De profundis clamavi*

FFROM depth off sinn and from a diepe dispaire,
  Ffrom depth off deth, from depth off hertes sorow, 665
  From this diepe Cave off darknes diepe repayre,
The have I cald o lord to be my borow;
  Thow in my voyce o lord perceyve and here
  My hert, my hope, my plaint, my ouerthrow,
My will to ryse, and let by graunt apere 670
  That to my voyce, thin eres do well entend.
  No place so farr that to the it is not nere;
No depth so diepe that thou ne maist extend
  Thin ere therto; here then my wofull plaint.
  Ffor, lord, if thou do observe what men offend 675
And putt thi natyff mercy in restraint,
  If just exaction demaund recompense,
  Who may endure o lord? who shall not faynt
At such acompt? dred, and not reuerence,
  Shold so raine large. But thou sekes rather love, 680
  Ffor in thi hand is mercys resedence,
By hope wheroff thou dost our hertes move.
  I in the, lord, have set my confydence;
  My sowle such trust doth euermore approve
Thi holly word off eterne excellence, 685
  Thi mercys promesse, that is alway just,
  Have bene my stay, my piller and pretence;

---

661 whilst] whyles Q. ponderd] ponderth A, E. 662 knee] arme E. 663 his] the E.
664 a] *omitted* Q. diepe] dirk R. 666 off . . . repayre] where darknes doth repayre E.
repayre] dispayre A. 667 The . . . lord] To the o lord have I cald E. 671 entend;
attende Q. 672 that] but E. it is not] is E; is not A, Q, R. 674 Thin ere] thi sellff E;
Thine eare self R; Thyne eare sette Q. 675 Ffor, lord] ffor E. do observe] observe A.
offend] doo offende Q. 676 And . . . mercy] Thy natyff mercy to put E. thy] the Q.
677 recompense] a recompence A. 679 dred, and not] dede, and no Q. 680 raine
large] runne at large Q. sekes] seekest A, Q. 681 in thi hand] mercy is with the E.
mercyes] mercye A. 682 dost] doth E. move] eke move A. 683 set my confydence]
euer set my trust E. 684 trust] trueth Q. 685 eterne] excellence E. 686 mercys . . .
alway just] just . . . infallible E.

My sowle in god hath more desyrus trust
　　Then hath the wachman lokyng for the day,
　　By the releffe to quenche of slepe the thrust.　　690
Let Israell trust vnto the lord alway,
　　Ffor grace and favour arn his propertie;
　　Plenteus rannzome shall com with hym, I say,
And shall redeme all our iniquitie.

*　　　*　　　*

This word redeme that in his mowght did sownd,　　695
Did put David, it semyth vnto me,
As in a traunce to starre apon the grownd,
And with his thowght the heyght of hevin to se;
Where he beholdes the word that shold confownd
The sword off deth, by humble ere to be　　700
In mortall mayd, in mortall habitt made,
Eternall lyff in mortall vaile to shade.

He seith that word, when full rype tyme shold come,
Do way that vayle by fervent affectione
Torne off with deth, for deth shold have her dome.　　705
And leppeth lyghter from such coruptione
The glint of lyght that in the Ayre doth lome.
Manne redemid, deth hath her distructione,
That mortall vaile hath immortalite,
David assurance off his iniquite.　　710

Wherby he frames this reson in his hert:
That goodnes wych doth not forbere his sonne
From deth for me and can therby convert
My deth to lyff, my synn to salvation,
Both can and woll a smaller grace depert　　715

689 wachman] wach that E. lokyng] lokyth E. 690 by the] for his E; by this his A;
by thy Q. of slepe] of the slepe E. thrust] thurst A. 691 Let] Let all E. vnto] in E;
to Q. alway] I say E. 692 arn] are A, Q. 693 Plenteus . . . com] plentefull rannzome
is E1; plentefull rannzome comth E2. 694 shall redeme] he shall rannzome E. 696
Did] hath E. it] into a diepe as E. vnto] to E. 698 heyght] hyg E. 699 confownd]
resownd E. 700 sword] worde Q. humble ere] humilitie here Q. 702 Eternall lyff]
Eternallye Q. 703 full rype] plenne ?E. sholde] was E. 704 Do way] shake off E;
Doo awaye Q. 707 glint] glutt A, R; glute Q. in the Ayre] in th Ayre E; in ayre A;
in the ayre R, Q. 708 Manne] sine E. redemid] redemeth Q. 710 David] Too Dauid
Q. 712 his sonne] the deth E; his some R. 713 From . . . me] of his dere sonne E.
714 my] our E. 715 can] may E.

To hym that suyth by humble supplication;
And sins I have his larger grace assayd,
To aske this thing whi ame I then affrayd?

He grauntyth most to them that most do crave,
And he delyghtes in suyte withowt respect;   720
Alas my sonne, poursuys me to the grave,
Sufferd by god my sinne for to correct;
But of my sinne sins I my pardonne have,
My sonnis poursuyt shall shortly be reiect;
Then woll I crave with suryd confidence.   725
And thus begynns the suyt off his pretence.

Psalm 143. *Domine exaudi orationem meam*

HERE my prayer o lord, here my request,
  Complyshe my bone, answere to my desire,
  Not by desert, but for thyn own byhest,
In whose ferme trowgh thou promest myn empyre   730
  To stond stable. And after thy Justyse,
  Performe, o lord, the thing that I require;
But not off law after the forme and guyse
  To entre judgement with thy thrall bond slave,
  To plede his ryght, for in such maner wyse   735
By fore thy syght no man his ryght shall save.
  Ffor off my sellff lo this my ryght wisenes,
  By skourge and whipp and prykyng spurrs I have
Skante rysen vp, such is my bestlynes;
  Ffor that my enmy hath pursuyd my lyff,   740
  And in the dust hath foyld my lustynes;

---

717 And . . . have] since I have then E. have his] have thys Q. grace] brute E. 719
most do crave] aske hym most E. 720 he] *omitted* R. suyte . . . respect] forceable
request E. 721 to the grave] with his ost E. 722 sinne] synnes Q. 723 sinne] synnes
Q. my] may Q. 724 poursuyt] suyte Q. 725 suryd] sure Q. 726 begynns] begynnethe
A; begynne Q. 728 answere to] supply thou E, R, Q. 729 by] for my Q. 730 In]
Inw E. 731 after thy] for thyn own E. 732 the] that Q. 733 not] *omitted* Q. off
. . . and] accordyng to just ryght in the E1; off justise aftre suche the forme and E2.
734 bond] thrall bond E. thy thrall] thee thrall Q. 735 his] thy E1; my E2. 736 By
fore] Before A, Q. 737 right wisenes] rightuousnes A, Q. 738 prykyng spurrs]
suffrans that E; pricking sourrs A. I have] have A. 739 Skante rysen] skantly rysn
E; scante rysyng A. 740 my enmy] myne enmye A, R; myne enemyes Q. 741 foyld]
soyled Q.

Ffor that in heins to fle his rage so ryff,
   He hath me forst as ded to hyd my hed;
   And for by cawse within my sellff at stryffe
My hert and spryte with all my force were fled.   745
   I had recourse to tyms that have ben past,
   And did remembre thy dedes in all my dred;
And did peruse thi workes that euer last,
   Wherby I knew above those wondres all
   Thy mercys were. Then lyfft I vp in hast   750
My handes to the, my sowle to the did call
   Like bareyne soyle for moystre off thy grace.
   Hast to my help, o lord, afore I fall;
Ffor sure I fele my spryte doth faynt a pace
   Torne not thi face from me, that I be layd   755
   In compt off them that hedlyng down do pase
In to the pitt. Shew me by tyms thyn Ayde,
   Ffor on thy grace I holly do depend.
   And in thi hand sins all my helth is stayde
Do me to know what way thou wolt I bend,   760
   Ffor vnto the I have reysd vp my mynd.
   Rydd me, o lord, from that that do entend
My foos to me, ffor I have me assind
   Allway within thi secrette protection.
   Tech me thy will, that I by the may fynd   765
The way to work the same in affection.
   Ffor thou my god, thy blyssyd spryte vp right,
   In lond off trowght shalbe my dyrection.
Thow for thy name, lord, shalt revive my spryte
   Within the ryght that I receyve by the,   770
   Wherby my lyff off danger shalbe quyte.

---

742 Ffor . . . heins] fforreyne Realmes A, Q; for in hernes R. to . . . ryff] as man in mortal stryff E1; to fle his furyus stry E2; to flye . . . ripe A. 743 me forst as ded] constrained me for E. 744 by cawse] because A. 745 hert and spryte] harte, spirite Q. 746 to] vnto the E; two R. have] *omitted* Q. 747 dedes] workes E. 749 knew] knowe Q. those] these Q. 750 were] ar E. 751 did] doth E. 752 bareyne] bare Q. 754 sure] euer Q. 755 that . . . layd] to make me seme E. 756 hedlyng] headlonge A. 758 I holly do] holly do I E. 759 and . . . hand] do me to know E; And in thy handes Q. 760 wolt] wilt A. 762 Rydd] Do E. that that] those that A; them that Q. 763 to me] on me E; to be A, Q. me] bene E. 764 within vnto E. 765 me thy] my w E. 766 affection] effection R. 767 spryte vp ryght] vpryght spryte W, A; spirite vpryght Q, R; spryte shall guyde E. 768 lond off] lawde ot A; laude of Q; laude and R. 769 name, lord] name E, R. shalt] shal Q.

Thow hast fordon theire grete Iniquite
   That vext my sowle, thou shalt also confownd
   My foos, o lord, for thy benignite,
Ffor thyn ame I, thy servant ay most bownd.   775

772–5 There whilst thow shalt off thi benignite
       confownd my foos and them distroy that sek
       to hurt my lyff by theyre iniquite
       sins [thus E2] I thi servant humbly the besek.

772 theire] the Q.   773 thou shalt also] A.   775 ay] *omitted* Q.

IV
Poems from the Blage Manuscript

***

CIX

ALAS! dere herte, what happe had I,
  Yf that I myght youre grace attayne!
  And sens I loue you faythfully,
  Why should ye not loue me agayne?

Me thynkes of right ye should me loue,   5
  For well ye know I doo not fayne,
  Nor neuer shall ye other proue;
  Therfore, swete hart, loue me agayne.

I dare well say, yf that ye knew
  How long that I haue suffered payne,   10
  Ye wold not chaunge me for no new,
  But euyn of ryght loue me agayne.

For as youre owne, ye may be sure,
  Ye haue my hart styll to remayne;
  Hyt lyeth in you me to recure: 15
  Therefore, swet hart, loue me agayne.

In hopp I lyve, and haue doone long,
  Trustyng yet styll for to optayne;
  And sure, me thynkes, I haue great wrong,
  Yf that I be not loved agayne.   20

This poem preceded by the first two stanzas of CL is also in Z.
CIX. 1 dere] swet Z. happe] hoppe B; hap Z.   2 I ... grace] your grace I myght Z.
3 sens] syeng Z. faythfully] faytfully B.   4 ye ... me] not I be lovyd Z.   5 Me
thynkes] My thynkes B; ye ought Z. ye should me] one fore to Z.   6 know] wot Z.
7] Nor ye shall neuer otherwise proue Z.   8 Therfore] Wherefore Z.   9 ye] you Z.
10 How long] Saw Z.   12 euyn] euyer Z.   13 ye] you Z   14 Ye] you Z.   18 yet
styll] styll Z.

CX

ALONE musyng,
Remembryng
The woofull lyfe that I doo lede;
Then sore sythyng,
I lye crying   5
As one for payne nere dede.

The vnkyndnes
Of my mystres
In great distres hath me brought;
Yet disdayneth she   10
To take petye
And settith my hart right naught.

Whoo wold haue thought
She wold haue wrought
Such sorow vnto my hart,   15
Seyng that I
Indeuered me
Frome her neuer to depart?

CXI

ABSENCE, alas,
Causeth me pas
Frome al solas
   To great grevans:
Yet though that I   5
Absent must be,
I trust that she
   Hath remembraunce.

Where I her fynd
Lovyng and kynd,   10
There my poore mynd
   Eased shalbe;
And for my parte
My loue and harte
Shall not reverte,   15
   Though I shuld dye.

CX. 10 Yet] yt B.

Beawty, pleasure,
Riches, treasure,
Or to endure
    In pryson stronge,   20
Shall not me make
Her to forsake,
Though I shuld lak
    Her neuer soo long.

For ones trust I,   25
Or that I dy,
For to aspye
    The happy owre –
At lyberty
With her to be,   30
That pytys me
    In this dolowre.

CXII

ALAS, fortune, what alith the
Thus euermore to turment me?
Although that I onworthy be
    Thow wylt not chaunge.

Faynest when I wold obteyne,   5
Then thow hast me still in disdayne,
Wylt thow thus styll increase my payne,
    And wylt not chaunge?

Alas! doth this not the suffice?
What prouf yet canste thow more devyse   10
Then styll to turment me in this wise
    And yet not chaunge?

What shuld I more to thee now saye?
Sum hoppe in me doth rest alwaye,
Yet bound to thee I doo obey;   15
    When wylt thou chaunge?

CXI.   22 forsake] for sake B.

CXII. 2 Thus] Thys B. 4 wylt not chaunge] wylnot B (*torn*). 7 thus] this B. payne]
omitted B (torn). 8] *omitted* B (*torn*). 12, 16 chaunge] *omitted* B (*torn*).

Seyng there ys noo remedy,
I wyll the suffer paciently,
Euer in trust at last, perdy,
  That thow wylt chaunge.   20

CXIII

A! MY harte, A! what aleth the
To set soo light by libertye,
Makyng me bounde where I was fre?
  A! my harte, A! what ayleth the?

Where thow warte ryd from all distres,   5
Voide of all payne and pensyfnes,
To chouse agayne a new mistress,
  A! my harte, A! what ayleth the?

When thow warte well, thow couldest not hold;
To turne agayne thow warte to bolde;   10
Thus to renew my sorowes olde,
  A! my harte, a! what ayleth the?

Thow knowest full well that but of late
I was turned owt of loues gate,
And now to gyde me to this mate,   15
  A! my harte, a! what ayleth the?

I hopte full well all had ben doone,
But now my hope is tane and wone,
To my turment to yeld soo sone,
  A! my hart, a! what ayleth the?   20

CXIV

A T last withdraw youre crueltye,
  Or let me dy at ons;
Hit ys to mych extremety
  Devysid for the nons,

CXIII. D.   2 by] be B; my D.   5 ryd] ryde B. distres] dist B.   7 chouse] chaunge
original B.   9 warte] ware D. couldest] couldes B; could D.   10 thow warte] that
ware D.   17 hopte] D; hopped B.   18 hope] D; hoppe B,
CXIV. D.   2 at ons] D; a tons B,

To hold me styll alyve   5
    In paynes styll for to stryve.
What may I more susteigne?
Alas! that dy wold fayne,
And cannot dy for payne.

For to the flame wherwith I burne   10
    My thought and my desyre,
When into ashes hit shuld turne
    My harte by faruent fyer,
        You send a stormy rayne
            That doth yt quench agayne   15
    And makes my Eyes expresse
    The teyres that do redresse
    My lyffe in wretchednes.

Then when they shuld haue drowned
    And ouerwhelmed my harte,   20
The hete doth them confound,
    Renewyng all my Smarte;
        Then doth the flame encresse,
            My turment cannot seasse;
    My paynes doth than revyve,   25
    And I remayne alyve,
    With deth styll for to stryve.

But yf that you wyll haue my deth,
    And that you wold no nother,
Then shortly for to stope my breth   30
    Withdrawe the one or other;
        For this youre cruelnes
            Doth let yt self doughtles,
    And yt ys reason why
    No man a lyve nor I   35
    Of dowble deth canne dy.

---

6 paynes] paine D. stryve] dryve D.   16 my Eyes] myn eys D.   17 that do redresse]
D; doth than redresse B; that dothe opres *later correction* B.   19 they] these D.   20
ouerwhelmed] D; ouer whelmed B.   21 them] then D.   25 My paynes] My woo D.
28 that you wyll] thatt that he wolde D.   29 you] ye D.   30 stope] spein D.   31 one
or other] touwn or tother D.   32 cruelnes] cruelte *later correction* B.   33 doughtles]
perde *later correction* B; doubles D.

CXV

ALLE ye that knowe of care and heuynes,
　My wofull fatte when ye haue hard,
　Then judge the truthe in this my great distresse,
　Yf any woo may be therto compared;
　And marke my thought as I shall yt expresse,　　　5
　For cause hit self doth nother mar nor make,
　But euyn as the pacyent doth hit take.

I thyncke whoo soo doth behold my payne
　Sees the Soule of Sorow grounded in gryff,
　The rotte of woo portred in payne,　　　10
　The cloude of care dispayred in Relyff,
　The lothed lyff thorow dartyd with dysdayne,
　Sorow ys I and I evyn the same,
　Ine that all men do call me by that name.

When I doo cast my careful lok doun Right　　　15
　Vpon the ground, as thoo that I wolld fall,
　Theryn me thynckes ys gravyn with my sight
　The pyctour of my Sorowfull thoughtes all;
　Ye, and the wormes that appere agaynst the nyght,
　As me Semes, they thynck that deth doth mych yll　　　20
　To leve me thus to lyve agaynst my wyll.

Where I do vse to lye Right secretly,
　Apon a banck ouer a Ryuer clere,
　Soo ofte I there be wayle my desteyne
　That the water disdayneth hit to here,　　　25
　And at my wepyng takes great envy,
　Lest the teres that ffrome my nyes do rayne
　Shuld cause the fysshe theryn to morne and playne.

Alone when I doo walke the woodes wandryng,
　Vttryng my care with paynefull sighes and groans,　　　30
　The birdes, which on the bowes syt syngyng,
　To here my Cry then ses they all attons,
　Hauyng great grudge at me and my wellyng,
　By cause yt was so grevous shyrle and lowde,
　That hit stonnyd their song thorow all the woode.　　　35

CXV. 20 they] the B. 21 thus] this B. 30 groans] J. C. Maxwell *conj.*; grevans B.

CXVI

Accusyd thoo I be without desert,
  Noone can hit proue, yet ye beleue hit treue;
Nor neuer yet, sens that ye had my hart,
  Entended I to be false or untrewe.
Soner I wold of deth sustayne the Smart   5
  Than breke one thyng of that I promast you;
Accept therfore my seruyce in good parte;
  Noon ys a lyve that yll tonges can Extew.
Hold them as false and let not vs depart
  Oure frendship old in hope of any new.   10
Put not thy trust in suche as vse to fayne,
Except thow mynd to put thy frynds to payne.

CXVII

Agaynste the Rock I clyme both hy and hard,
  When at the foote the ford doth bray so lowde
That saue the hart So faythfully had vowyed,
  Seith frome the foote in medeway I was forward,
No hart soo hardy nor corryge that cowld   5
  Aventure to clyme Soo hy a Shrowd:
Hoppe byddes me hoppe of payne the right reward.
Now past the vale of Daunger and Dispyt,
  Mounted the Rock of Loue and perfit Joye;
Bayned in the forde, Dispere to washe awaye,   10
  Hoppyng hereafter frome Darke to fynd the Light,
Brought to the hyiste, am of the Deptyst agast,
For Dred to falle, my hand now hold the fast.

CXVIII

A face that shuld content me wonders well
  Shuld not be faire but cumley to behold,
Wyth gladsum loke all gref for to expell;

CXVI. T.   2 Sith none can proue, beleue it not for true T.   3 Nor] For T. ye] you
T.   4 Entended] Intended B, T.   6 thyng] word T.   8 that ... can] than can yll
tonges T. Extew] eschew T.   10 hope] T; hoppe B.
  [*Authorship:* Ascribed to W by T.]
CXVII.   3 faythfully] faytfully B.   8 vale] valeis *original reading* B.
CXVIII. P, T, N.   1 wonders] wond'rous N; wonderous T.   2 faire] P; fere B.
cumley] louelie P, T, N.   3 Wyth gladsum loke] with gladsome cheare P, N; Of

With sober chere so wold I that yt shuld
Speke withowt wordes, such wordes as non can tell; 5
    The tresse also shuld be of cryspyd goold;
With wytt, and these myght chance I myght be tyed,
And knytt agayne the knott that shuld not slyde.

CXIX

ALAS! my Dere, the word thow spakest
    Hath smotte the Stroke within my brest
Of Cruell Deth, sens thow forsackyst
    Me and my faithfull ment behest.
Too long I Shewed that word to here, 5
That doth renew my great onrest
        And mornyng Chere.

And mornyng Chere, which by dispayre
    For wante of hoppe ys myche increst,
So that now past both hoppe and fere, 10
    Of my judgement I know the best
Ys Lyf a while in paynefull woo;
And how soon Deth wyll pers my brest,
        I doo not know.

I do not know when, nor how sone, 15
    The stroke thow smast within my hart
Wyll blede me to a dedely sowne,
    But well I know, tho thow revert,
Till yt do blede and I stark dede,
I shall renew with dayly smart 20
        This Lyffe I Lede.

This Lyffe I Lede and Lyve to Long,
    Agayn my wyll in ters to melt,
Sens none ther ys may ryght my wrong;

liuely loke T. expell] repell T.   4 With sober chere] with sober lookes P, N; With
right good grace T.   5 wordes] word T.   7 these] T; theys B; thus P, N. myght
chance] perchance T. be tyed] betyde P, N; be tryde T.
    [*Authorship:* Ascribed to W by T.]
CXIX.   2 smotte] stroke *original* B.   5 Too] to B.   7 Chere] *omitted* B (*torn*).   13
soon] shuld *original* B.   14 know] *omitted* B (*torn*).   19 do] doth *original* B.   24 may]
ma B.
    L

But I must fele that I haue felt   25
The Stroke of Deth, and cannot Dy,
Gaylyd within the strongist belt
  Of Crueltie.

Of Crueltie and cruell Deth,
 Forst to abyde Extremytie,   30
And yet do lyve, thoo I want breth,
To Show further how cruelly
My hope ys turned to murnyng chere,
And ye the cause thereof onely,
  Alas, my dere.   35

CXX

By belstred wordes I am borne in hand,
 As whoo saith, byddyn I shuld obbey.
Ye may thret twys, er ons ye maye
Prevayle by poure to vnderband,
That I shuld yeld and nat withstand.   5
Youre wordes doo well, your wittes bewraye
Wenyng to bere so great a Swaye,
To wene my will when ye commaunde.
The ffre ye fforse by ffere,
To seke obedyens of the thrall.   10
Youre thretnyng wordes of poer but small
Ys wasted wynd to vse them here;
For lyke aquytaunce of lyke scathe
Ys my noo force of your no faith.

CXXI

Beyng as noone ys I doo complayne
 Of my myshapp, turment, and my woo,
Wysshyng for Dethe with all my myght and mayne,
For Lyffe ys to me as my Chief Deadly foo.
Alas, alas, of Comford I haue noo moo;   5
Left but onely to syng this Dulphull song:
Paciens, parforce content thy self with wrong.

31 yet] yt B. do] doth *original* B.
CXX.   1 By] Be B.   11 poer] po^r B.

Euer I hoppe sum faver to obteyne,
   Trustyng that she wyll recompence at Last,
   As reason were, my passyng deadly payne;   10
   And styll I percevered, and they increse soo fast,
   That hoppe me Left, and I, as all agaste,
   Had noo comford, but Lernd to syng this song:
   Paciens, parforce content thy self with wrong.

I Burne and boyle withoute redres;   15
   I syegh, I wepe, and all in vayne.
   Now Hotte, now Cold, whoo can expresse
   The thowsaund parte of my great payne?
   But yf I myte her faver Atteigne,
   Then wold I trust to chaunge this song,   20
   With pety for paciens, and consciens for wrong.

CXXII

COMPLAYNYNG, alas, without redres,
   Thus wofully do I my Lyfe Lede,
   My harte Lamentyng in heuynes,
   Through whose mekenes I am nere dede.

This I induer alwayes in payne,   5
   Dewoyd of pyty as in this Case,
   Yet my pore Harte cannot refrayne;
   Wherfore, Alas, I Dy, Alas!

Soo vnkynd, alas, saw I never noone,
   So hard hartid, so mych without pyty   10
   As she to whome I make my mone;
   Wherefore, alas, I Dy, I Dy.

Where I Love best, I am refused;
   Where I am Louyd, I doo not passe;
   Where I wold faynest, I am dysdayned;   15
   Wherefore I Dy, alas, alas!

Comforthles, complaynyng, thus I remayne;
   Merceles, remaynyng without remedy;

CXXI.   11 they] the B.
CXXII. 2 Thus] This B.

Cruelnes incressyng through fals dysdayne,
Pytyles remaynyng, alas, I Dy, I Dy.   20

But from hensforth I hold it best
    Them for to loue that loueth me;
    And then my hart shall haue sum rest,
    Where now for payne I Dy, I Dy.

CXXIII

"COMEFORTHE at hand, pluck vp thy harte!
    Lok Lowe! se where hit doth stand!
    Synes the redresse of all thy smart
    Douth Ley soo good a hand,
        Pluck vp thy hart.   5

Pluck vp thy harte! why Droupest thow soo?"
    So Sayde I me thought;
    And frome the Hile I loked Loo
    And with myn eye I Sought
        Comforth at hand.   10

Comeforth at hand myn eye hath found;
    My thought, therfore be glade;
    Yf she be there may hele thy wounde,
    Why shuldyst thou then be sad?
        Pluck vp thy hart.   15

Pluck vp thy hart! A mornyng man
    Doth gett noo good by woo.
    Be glad alway, for whoo soo can
    Shall fynd, wher soo He goo,
        Comeforth at hand.   20

Comeforth at hand! goo seecke and fynd!
    Loke yf there be redresse:
    Yf not, abyde a better wynd,
    In hope of Sum reles,
        Pluck vp thy hart.   25

CXXIII.   1, 3, 5, 6, 13, 16 thy] they B.   6, 14 why] whey B.   7 me] my B.   9 myn eye] my nye B.   11 myn eye] my nye B.   18 Be] By B.   24 In] In soo B.

CXXIV

DURESE of paynes and grevus Smarte
   Hath brought me Low and wonderusse weke,
That I cannot cumfort my hart:
   Why Syest thou, hart, and wilt not breke?

Thy syghes, thy playntes ar all in vayne;   5
   The teres that from thyne eyes doo Leke;
This Lyffe ys Dethe, this joye ys payne:
   Why Syest thow, hart, and wil not breke?

Thow clymest to catche where ys noo hold,
   Thow stryves where strength ys all to weke,   10
Thy carefull lyff cannot be told:
   Why Syest thow, hart, and wyll not breke?

The faithfuller thow dust endure,
   Les she regards to here the speke;
And seyng pety will not the Cure,   15
   Why Syest thow, hart, and wyll not Breke?

As good thow wart asvnder ryve,
   As thus in thought thy self to breke;
Better were dethe then thus alyve
   Euer to sighe and never breke.   20

Wherefore, pety, now shew redresse,
   Or elles cum Dethe, thy vengeance wreke!
And sens thow fyndes noo gentylnes,
   Harte, syghe no more, I pray the Breke.

CXXIV. V. 1 Durese of paynes] During of payne V. 4 wilt] wil V. 5 Thy] The
V. thy] and V. 6 that] V; voide that B. thyne eyes] V; thy yes B. doo] doth V. 9
clymest] V; clymes B. 10 Thow ... all] Thou pullest the stringes that be V. 11
told] V; toll B. 14 regards] regard B; regarded V. 15 seyng] V; seith B. not the]
the not V. 17 wart] were V. asonder ryve] a sunder to ryve V. 18 thus] V; this B.
19 were dethe] to dy V. thus] V; this B. 20] Why syghest thou, hart, and will not
breake? V. 21 Wherefore] I pray the V. shew] V; shuld B. 22 Or elles] Orellse B;
Or else V. vengeance] selfe V. wreke] awreake V. 23 sens] if V. fyndes] fynd V.
24] Syth no more but, hart, thou breake! V.

CXXV

Do way, do way, ye lytyll wyly prat!
  Youre slyly slynkyng cannot you excuse,
  Nor wordes Dysymmblyd cannot hid that
  That wyll pere owt, yf oftyn ye yt vse.
  Yf ye thynke other, youre self ye do abuse,   5
  For hartly Loue unspyd Long to Last,
  Yf ye asay, youre wyttes sore ye waste.

Yff yt be possible, that frome a fyer gret
  The blak Smoke shall not yssu owt,
  Or a fore a Cryppyll to halt and countefet   10
  And be not spyd, then quycly goo aboute
  Vs to begyle; for truly without dowte
  We know the craft, the Lokys and the prys.
  Wherfore trust me yt ys hard to blere our yes.

Yff that we to you of this do speke,   15
  For good wyll to make ye leue your folly,
  Then wyll ye not stynt till ye be wreke;
  And redy to swere and styll wyll deny
  That that ys trew, yet wyll ye neuer apply
  To youre own fawtes, but alwayes ye excuse.   20
  Leve, fy for shame! ye make men to thynk and muse.

Ye thynck to cloke that cloked cannot be,
  And thincke to hide that open ys in sight.
  Alas! my thynckith yt ys a great pety
  Youre self to bryng in suche a plyght,   25
  That shuld vs cause to thynck ye Light.
  Leue of, therfore: in faith ye ar to blame;
  Ye hurt your self and lesyth your good name.

CXXVI

Desyre to Sorow doth me constrayne,
Dayly incressyng my Smart and payne;
I Se there ys no remedy playne,
    But paciens.

CXXV. 3 Dysmmblyd] Dysmmlyd B. 5 self] felt B. 10 halt] half B. 11 then]
them B. 17 till] tell B. 24 a great] agreat B.

Dispayre doth put hym self in prese 5
To cause my sorows to encrese:
I trust at Last that yt wyll sesse
    By paciens.

Good hoope doth byd me be content,
And not my self thus to torment, 10
Promassyng me my hole intent
    Through paciens.

I wyll not stryve agaynst the tyde,
For well I Se who doth abide;
That sufferans to hartes desyre ys gyde 15
    By pacyens.

CXXVII

DEFAMED gyltynes by sylens vnkept,
My name alle slaunderus, my faut detect,
Gylty, I graunt that I haue don amys.
Shall I neuer do soo agayne, forgyve me this.

Betrayed by trust and soo begyled, 5
By promas vnjust my name defyled;
Wherfore I graunt that I haue done amys.
Wyll I neuer do so agayne, forgyue me this.

Accept myne Excuse for this Offens,
And spare not to refuse me your presens, 10
Onles ye perceyue ye do refrayne
From doyng amys, wyle I Lyue agayne.

CXXVIII

DRYVEN by Desire I Dyd this Dede,
To Daunger my self without cause why:
To trust the vntrue, not Lyke to sped,
To speke and promas faithfully;
But now the prouf Doth verefy 5

CXXVI.   8 By] But *original* B.   10 thus] this B.
CXXVII.   4, 8 forgyve] for gyue B.
CXXVIII. D (1–7), T (1–7). 3 the vntrue] thuntrue T.

That whoo soo trustith ere he knoo
Doth hurt hym self and pleas his foo.

*   *   *

Sens that my Language without eloquence
  Ys playne vnpaynted and not vnknowen,
  Dyspache myn answere with redy vtteraunce: 10
  The question ys youres or elles my owne.
  To be vpholdyn and styll to fawne,
  I know non cause of such obedyence.
  To haue suche corne as sede was sowen,
  That ys the worst: therfore gyve centaunce.   15

But yf youre wyll be in this case
  To vphold me Styll, what nedith that?
  Seith ye or nay my question was:
  So Long delay yt nedith not.
  Yf I haue ye, than haue I that   20
  That I haue sought to bryng to pas;
  Yf I haue nay, yet reke I nat:
  Where aught ys got, ther ys no lose.

The ye desyred, the nay not;
  No gref so gret, nor desire so sore   25
  But that I may forbere to dote.
  Yf ye, for euer; yf nay, no more
  To trubbyll ye thus: speke on therfore.
  Yf that ye wyll, say ye; yf not,
  We shalbe frendes euyn as before,   30
  And I myn own, that yours may not.

CXXIX

Dryuyn to Desyre, a drad also to Dare,
  Bitwene two stoles my tayle goith to the ground.
  Dred and desire the reson doth confound,
  The tonge put to sylence, the hart in hope and fere,
  Doth Dred that hit Dare and hyde that wold appere.   5

6 ere] T; or D; ar B.   11 or elles] orelles B.   23 aught] naught *original* B.   28 thus]
this B.   on] in B.   31 myn own] my nown B.
CXXIX.   1 Dryuyn] Druyng *original* B.

Desyrus and Dredfull, at Lybertye I goo bound,
For presyng to proffer me thynckes I here the sonde.
Back of thy Boldnes, thy corage passith care.
This Daungerus Dought whether to obey
My Dred or my Desire soo sore douthe me troubyll,   10
That cause causith for Dred of my Dekey.
In thowght al wone, in dedes to shoo me Dobyll,
Ferefull and faithfull, yet take me as I am,
Though Dowbell in Dedes, a inward perfit man.

CXXX

DOBELL, dyuerse, soleyn and straunge,
   But I haue sped and skappt vnspyd.
   Thancked be fortune of frendly chaunge,
   The Dede ys Don and I not Denyed.
   My traught mystakyn, and I vntryed,   5
   Yf Dobbell Drabbes were soo Defyed,
   As worthy ys therc waudryng wyt.
   I wysse with reson doth not sit:
   To Do and vndo, and Scapp vnquyt.
   For youre noo faith, such faute were fyt,   10
   Forborne for fere, nay Loue ys hit
   Wherby ys bound the body soo.
   Thancked be fortune of euery chaunce,
   Of my myshappe I thanck my self.
   Payne or pleasure, woo or welth.   15
   Wounded by wordes, and Lackes avaunce.

CXXXI

DYDO am I, the fownder first of Cartage,
   That as thou seyst my nowne deth do procuer
   To saue my fayth, and for no new loues rage
   To fley Iarbes, and kepe my promes suer.
   But se fortune, that wold in nother age   5
   Myne honest wyll in perfayte blisse assuer;
   For while I lyuyd, she made my day short;
   And now with Lyes my shame she doth report.

7 me] my B. 12 thowght] wordes *original* B.
CXXX. 3 chaunge] chaunce B. 8 sit] set B. 13 be] by B.
CXXXI. 2 thou] thu B. 3 loues] lowes B.

CXXXII

DYSDAYNE not, madam, on hym to louke,
   Whom sumtyme you haue louyd;
And, tho you forswar yt on a bouke,
   Error yt may be prouyd:
Tho now your loue be gon and spent,   5
   May happe you may yt soon repent.

Syns that hieraufter coums not yet,
   Nor now ys so good as than,
Yet throw hym not doun, but let hym syt,
   That so longe hathe been your man: 10
The tym may comm he may you ees,
   Wyche now so soor dothe you dysplees.

Onys I was he that now I am not;
   Your selff knos thys full well.
My mynd you kno wel enou by rot –   15
   You nyd no fashion to spell:
Feyr wourds to you I use,
   Tho that you cruelly me refuse.

What tho nu broum suype very clyne,
   Yet cast not the olde awey;   20
That seruys not sumtym ys often syen
   To serue well a nouther dey:
And stoer of housolde ys well had,
   To kype the best and leue the bad.

CXXXIII

HAD I wiste that now I wott,
   For to haue found that now I fynd,
I wold haue Don that I Dyd not;
   But fayned faith dyd make me blynd,
And by great othes fixed in my mynd,   5
   His faith to be faithfull to trust,
The Dede now proued, I fynd vnjust.

CXXXII. 1 to] too B. 2 Whom] wohem B. 5 now] nou B. 9 throw] thro B.
10 longe] logne B. 12, 13 now] nou B. 16 fashion] fashn B. 17 wourds] wourd
B. to] too B. 20 awey] auey B. 24 bad] bade B.

Hit ys not the thing that I pas on:
  Of his faith though I had assuraunce,
  Of that no more I wyll trust one   10
  Then of a thyng that Lyeth in balance.
  Truth Laide aparte falsed ys: his mayntenaunce,
  Euer Dubbell, neuer wyll be true;
  Roted at the hart must nedes contynew.

CXXXIV

HORRYBELL of hew, hidyus to behold,
  Carefull of countenaunce, his here all clustred,
  With dead dropy blude that down his face rowled,
  Pale, paynefull, and petyvsly persyd,
  His hart in sunder sorofully Shyvered,   5
  Me thought a man, thus marvelyusly murdred,
  This night to me Came and carefully cryed.

'O man mysfortunate, more then any Creytour,
  That paynefully yet lyues more payne to perceyue,
  What hardenyd hath thy hart this harme to suffer?   10
  Thy Doughtfull hope, hit doo the but disceyue.
  No good nor grace to glade the shalt receyve,
  By payne frome thy payne then payne to procure,
  Soo bitter hit were then endles Deth to endure.

'Folowe me', Seith he, 'hold here my hand.   15
  To longe ys Dethe in ters to Proue.
  The se shall Soner quenche the brand
  Of the Desyre that hath the thus ondon;
  Or soner send the to a deadly sowne.
  Hold in thy hand the hafte herof this knyfe,   20
  And with the blade boldely bereyve thy lyffe.'

'Cum of', quod he. 'I cum', quod I.
  Then therwith as me thought
  My brest I persyd paynefully,
  My hart right sowne I hit raught.   25
  But, lord! alas! hit was for naught:
  For with that stroke I dyd awake.
  My hart for sorow yet fele I quake.

CXXXIV. 1 behold] be hold B. 6, 23 me] my B. 6, 18 thus] this B. 9 yet] yt B.

CXXXV

HAPPE happith ofte vnloked for,
  As men may se before theire yes;
  For he that Dayly Doth labour
  And studith all he can Devyse
  To bryng his purpose to affect,   5
  Yet by myshap most commenly
  From his entent he ys abiect;
  And happe doth happe clene contrary,
  So that the prouf Doth verefye,
  As I haue wryttyn here before,   10
  That happ happes ofte vnloked for.

Some to myshapp when they ar borne,
  Ar prefate by there Distyne;
  To sume, tho all the world had sworn,
  Fortune wyl not be contrary: 15
  This happ doth happ at his own lust.
  Sum men to welth and sum to woo;
  Sum tyme the stronge he throyth yth Dust;
  Sum tyme the lame he maketh goo,
  And the Starke blynd to se alsoo;   20
  Sum tyme the hole he maketh sore:
  Alle this happs ofte vnloked for.

Sum by good happe ar braught alofte,
  And sum by myshap ar throwen doun;
  And sum by hap ar set full softe,   25
  That thynck neuer for to come downe.
  But I wyll rede them to take hede,
  Seith hap doth turne soo sodenly,
  Lest he by chaunge do chaunce them lede
  Into sum trade clene contrary,   30
  And bryng hym low that was full hy,
  And set hym hard that set full softe:
  Vnloked for all this happs ofte.

CXXXV. 6, 24 myshap] mys hap B.   27 to] for to *original* B.   29 he] hym *original*
B.   33 Vnloked] and loked *original* B. ofte] softe B.

CXXXVI

HATE whome ye lyste, I care not;
Loue whome ye lyste and spare not;
Doo what ye lyst and fere not;
Sey what ye lyst and dred not;
For as for me, I am not   5
But euyn as one that rekyth not
Whether ye hate or hate not,
For in youre loue I dote not;
Wherfore I pray you forget not,
But loue whome ye lyst and spare not.   10

CXXXVII

Your lokes so often cast,
Your eyes so frendly rold,
Your syght fyxid so fast,
All ways one to behold:
Thoughe hyd yt fayne you would,   5
Yet playnly dothe declaer
Who hathe your hart in hold,
And wheer goudwil ye baer.

Fayne woulde you fynde a cloke
Your byrninge fier to hyde,   10
Yet bothe the flame and smoke
Brekes out on euery syed:
Ye can not Love so gide
That yt not issue wynn;
Abrode nydes must it glide   15
That burnes so hot within.

For cawse your selff dothe winke,
Ye iuge all other blynde;
And that Secret you thinke
That euery man dothe fynde;   20

CXXXVI. D.   1 I] for I D, *original* B.   3 fere] drede D.   4 Sey] Think D; make
original B. dred] fere D.   6 rekyth] reckes D.   7 Whether] whither B, D.   9 forget]
for get B.   10 and spare not] ffor I care not D.
CXXXVII. T.   6 Yet] It T.   9 you] ye T.   10 byrninge] brennyng T.   14 not]
no T.   16 burnes] brens T.   17 dothe] do T.   19 that Secret] secret it T.   20 That]

In wast oft spend your wynde,
Your selfe from Loue to quitt,
For agues of that kynde
Wyl sho who hathe the fytt.

Cawses you fet from far,   25
And all to wrap your wo;
Yet ar you neuer the nar;
Men ar not blyndyd so.
Dyply oft swer you no,
But all thos othes ar vayne,   30
So wel your eye dothe sho
The cawse of all your payne.

Thynke not therfor to hyde
That styll yt selffe betrays,
Nor syek menes to prouid   35
To darke the sounny deys.
Forget thos wontyd weys,
Leue of dyssemblynge chyer:
Theer woul be found no steys
To stop a thynge so cleer.   40

CXXXVIII

The answere

EVYN when you lust ye may refrayne
    To payne youre self thus wilfully.
    Nother new nor old I doo retayne:
    Hit ys naught but your fantesy.

Youre profferd seruice ys nothing Swete,   5
    Yet wold you fayne yt properly.
    I doo not love but where yt ys mete:
    I chaunge nothing my fantesy.

Youre meate and Drynke though hit be gone,
    Ye toke enouff when yt was by: 10

which T.   21 your] ye T.   22 from] in T.   25 Cawses] your sighes T.   26 wrap]
wry T.   27 neuer] nere T.   29 you] ye T.   32 Who puttes your hart to paine T.
38 dyssemblynge] such frowning T.   39 woul] will T.
    [*Authorship:* Ascribed to W by T.]
CXXXVIII.   2, 18, 29 Thus] This B.

Or ye may call for more a noone,
When hit shall please your fantesy.

Hit was youre febyll founded love
    That fancy, founded fowlyshely,
    That made me love, lenger to prove   15
    Shuch fowlyshe fayned fantesy.

Yf that youre fancy, as you say,
    Doth cause you playne thus petiously,
    Esely to turne, perdy you may,
    When hit shall please your fantesy.   20

Your chaine ys long, thow you be bound,
    For ye leppe far and Diversly;
    To small effect your wordes doth sound:
    They come but of your fantesy.

As ye Dyd knyt, soo Dyd I knyt.   25
    Evyn slack for slack right wisely:
    I Dought yt mych your new fangled wyt,
    Which proued ys by your fantesy.

Thus to comeplayne withouten gryffe,
    Therto ye lust your self Apply.   30
    The Smartles nedith no relyff:
    I am not Rulyd by fantesy.

CXXXIX

I AM redy and euer wyll be
    To doo you seruice with honeste.
    Ther ys nothing that lackys in me
        But that I haue not.

My pore hart alwayes and my mynd   5
    Fixed in youres you shall styll fynd;
    To Loue you best reson doth bynd,
        Although I haue not.

24 They] the B.   29 comeplayne] come playne B.
CXXXIX. 8 Although] althought B.

And for youre sake I wold be glad
　To haue myche more then I haue had,　　　　10
　The Lacke wherof doth make me sad,
　　Because I haue not.

For I doo loue ye faithfully,
　And ye me agayne right secretly;
　Of let ther ys no cause why,　　　　15
　　But that I haue not.

Yff I you ons of that myght suer,
　Oure loue shuld increse and induer;
　To study therfore hit ys my cure
　　How I myght haue.　　　　20

Such ar cald frendes now a Dayes,
　Which do muse and study alwayes
　Bitwixt yong Lovers to put Dylayes
　　By cause they haue not.

But this resisteth all my trust verely,　　　　25
　That ye agayne wyll love me stedfastly,
　And let thy word pas as yt hath don hardely,
　　Till that we haue.

But for this tyme, swete hart, adew.
　Contynew faithfull, and I wylbe true:　　　　30
　And loue thee styll, what soeuer insew,
　　Although I haue not.

CXL

I AM as I am and so wil I be,
But how that I am none knoith trulie;
Be yt evill, be yt well, be I bonde, be I fre,
I am as I am and so will I be.

I lede my lif indifferentelye,　　　　5
I meane no thing but honestelie,
And thoughe folkis judge full dyverslye,
I am as I am and so will I dye.

25 verely] werely B.
CXL. D. 1–8] D; *omitted* B.

I doo not rejoise nor yet complayne;
Both myrth and sadness I do refrayne;   10
And vse the mene sens folkys wyll fayne;
Yet I am as I am, be hit pleasure or payne.

Men doo juge as they doo trow,
Sum of pleasure, and sum of woo;
Yet for all that nothing they know;   15
But I am as I am wheresoeuer I goo.

But sens that Judgers take that way,
Let euery man his judgement say;
I wyll hit take in sport and play,
Yet I am as I am whoosoeuer say nay.   20

Who Judggis well, god well them send;
Whoo Judgith yll, god them amend;
To juge the best therefore intend;
For I am as I am and soo wyll I end.

Yet sum therbe that take delyght   25
To Judge folkes thowght by outward sight;
But whether they Judge wrong or Right,
I am as I am and soo doo I wright.

I pray ye all that this doo rede,
To trust hit as ye doo your cred,   30
And thynck not that I wyll change my wede,
For I am as I am how sooeuer I spede.

But how that ys I leue to you;
Judge as ye lyst, false or trew;
Ye know no more then afore ye knew;   35
But I am as I am whatsoeuer insew.

And frome this mynd I wyll not flee;
But to all them that mysejudge me

13, 15, 27 they] the B. 13 Men] Dyvers D. 16 I am] am D. 17 take that way] do
thus dekaye D. 20 Yet] for D. whoosoeuer] woosoeuer B. 21 Judggis . . . them]
Judgith . . . him D. 22 yll] evill D. 26 by outward sight] for envye and spight D.
27 Judge] Jude D. wrong] me wrong D. 29 I pray ye] prayeng you D. 31 thynck
. . . wyll] not to think I D. 32 how sooeuer] howe ever D. 36 whatsoeuer] whatever
D. 37 flee] D; flye B.

M

I do protest, as ye doo se,
That I am as I am and soo wyll I dy.   40

CXLI

I MUSTE go walke the woodes so wyld,
    And wander here and there
    In dred and Dedly fere;
For wher I trust, I am begilyd,
    And all for your Loue, my dere.   5

I am banysshed from my blys
    By craft and fals pretens,
    Fawtles, without offens,
And of return no certen ys,
    And all for your Loue, my dere.   10

Banysshed am I, remedyles,
    To wildernes alone,
    Alone to sigh and mone,
And of relefe all comfortles,
    And all for your Loue, my dere.   15

My house shalbe the grene wood tre,
    A tuft of brakys my bede,
    And this my lyf I lede
As one that from his Joy doth fly,
    And all for your Loue, my dere.   20

The runnyng stremes shalbe my drynke,
    Akehornes shalbe my foode;
    Naught Elles shall doo me good,
But on your beawty for to thynke,
    And all for your Loue, my dere.   25

And when the Dere draw to the grene
    Makys me thynke on a row,
    How I haue sene ye goo
Aboue the fayrest, fayrest besene,
    And all for your Loue, my dere.   30

39 doo] maye D.   40 dy] bee D.
CLXI. 19 one] on B.

But where I se in any cost
  To turkylles set and play,
  Rejoysing all the day,
  Alas, I thinck this haue I lost,
      And all for your Loue, my dere.   35

No Byrd no bushe, no bowgh I se
  But bryngith to my mynd
  Sumthing wherby I fynd
  My hart far wandred, far fro me,
      And all for your Loue, my dere.   40

The tune of byrdes when I doo here,
  My hart doth bled, alas,
  Remembryng how I was
  Wont for to here your wayes so clere,
      And all for your Loue, my dere.   45

My thought doth please me for the while:
  While I se my Desire
  Naught Elles I do requyer.
  So with my thought I me begyle,
      And all for your Loue, my dere.   50

Yet I am further from my thought
  Then yerth from hevyn aboue:
  And yet for to remoue
  My payne, alas, avayleth naught,
      And all for your Loue, my dere.   55

And where I ly Secret, alone,
  I marke that face a none,
  That stayith my Lyff, as one
  That other comfort can get non,
      And all for your Loue, my dere.   60

The Sumer Dayes that be so long,
  I walked and wandred wyde,
  Alone, without a gyde,
  Always thynkyng how I haue wrong,
      And all for your loue, my dere.   65

46 me] *omitted* B.   58 one] won B.   62 walked] walke B.

The wynter nyghtes that ar so cold,
  I ly amyd the
  Vnwrapt in pryckyng thornes,
  Remembryng my sorowes old,
      And all for your loue, my dere.   70

A wofull man such desprat lyfe
  Becummyth best of all;
  But wo myght them befall
  That are the causers of this stryfe,
      And all for your Loue, my dere.   75

CXLII

Y ғ I myght hau at myne owne wyll
  Suche fflud of tearis wherwith to drowne
  Or ffyer so hott as Ætna hyll
  With fervent ffyere that I myght burne,
  Then shulde I ende this carffull paygne   5
  That fforce perforce I do sustayne.

Or yf the syghis of woffull hart
  Could cause my selffe a sonder brake,
  Then by that means I shulde departe
  My mornynge dayes, and so to wreake   10
  My weryede lyfe and carffull payne
  That fors perforce I do sustayne.

Or yf my hand suche happe myght ffinde,
  With sword or knyfe to ese my woo,
  Then shulde I ease my paynffull mynd;   15
  But syns my hap cannote hap soo,
  I must Abyd this carffull payne
  That fforce perforce I do sustayne.

Or yf I myght haue at my wyshe
  The hevyn to ffall to short my lyfe,   20
  So by suche chaunce I coulde not myse
  But I shuld ende this carfull stryfe

CXLII.   3 Ætna] Ethena B.   10 mornynge] morninges B.   12 That fors] perforce

That dothe increase the woffull payne
That ffors perforce I do sustayne.

Or yf the yerthe at my request 25
Had powere to opyne, as in my wyll,
I know Ryght well my weryed breast
Shuld ned no more to syghe his ffyll,
For then shulde end this carffull payne
That fforce perforce I do sustayne. 30

CXLIII

I wyll allthow I may not,
The more yt ys my paygne;
What thow I wyll, I shall not,
Wherffor my wyll ys vayne.

My wyll wylling ys vayne, 5
This Ryght well may I see,
Tho wyll wold neuer so ffayne,
Yet my wyll wyll not be.

By cawse I will and may not,
My will is not my owne; 10
For lacke of will I can not,
The cawse wherof I mone.

Ffor that I wyll and cannot,
The more I wyll certayne:
Thus betwene wyll and shall not 15
My wyll I may optayne.

Thus wyshyrs want ther wyll
And they that wyll do crave;
But they that wyll not wyll
Ther wyll they soonest have. 20

original B.   23 the] my *original* B.

CXLIII. H.   1 allthow] and yet H.   3 thow] thynge H.   5 My wyll] will H.   6
This] H; Thus B. Ryght well may I] Ryghght well ma I B; may I rightwell H.   7]
Althoughe my will wolde fayne H.   8 Yet my wyll wyll] Yet my wyll wyll wyll B; my
will it may not be H.   9–12] H; *omitted* B.   14] Yet styll I do sustayne H.   15 Thus
betwene] betwene I H.   16 My wyll I may] my love came not H.   17 wyll] willes H.
19 they] H; thay B.   20 they] thay B; the H.

Syns that I will and shall not,
My will I will refrayne,
Thus for to will and will not
Will willinge is but vayne.

CXLIV

I KNOWE not where my heuy syghys to hyd
My sorrowffull hart ys so vexed with paygne
I wander fforthe as one without a gyd,
That sekythe to ffynd a thyng partyd in twaine,
And sse fforthe ronne that skant can torne Agayne;   5
Thus tyme I passe and wast ffull petuslye,
Ffor Dethe yt ys owte off thy syght to bee.

I skantlye know ffrome whome commys all my greff,
But that I wast as one dothe in seknes,
And cannot tell whiche way commes my mescheff;   10
Ffor All I tast to me ys betyrnes,
And of my helthe I have no sykernes
Nor shall not have tyll that I do the see:
Yt ys my Dethe out of thy syght to be.

I leve in yerthe as one that wold be dead,   15
And cannot dye: Alas! the more my payne.
Ffamyshed I am, and yet Alwayes am ffed:
Thus contrary all thyng dothe me constrayne
To laugh, to morne, to walke, to joye, to playne,
And shall do styll, ther ys no remedye,   20
Vntyll the tyme that in thy syght I be.

Ther nys syknes but helth yt dothe desyer,
Nor povertye but Ryches lyke to haue,
Nor shypp in storme but stering douthe Requyer
Harbor to fynd, so that she may her saue;   25

21-4] H; *omitted* B.
  [*Authorship:* On the same page as LXXXVI in H.]
CXLIV. 1 heuy] hartye *original* B. 6 Thus] This B. 18 Thus] Thys B. all] dyd all
original B. 22 nys] helthe *original* B. helth] helt B. 23 lyke] ffor *original* B. 24 Nor]
but *original* B. stering douthe] that my dethe *original* B. 25 fynd] have *original* B. she]
they *later correction* B.

And I, Alas, nought in thys world do craue
Save that thow lyst on hym to haue mercye,
Whose dethe yt ys out of thy syght to be.

CXLV

I HAVE benne a lover
  Ffull long and many days,
  And oft tymes a prover
  Of the most paynffull wayes;
  But all that I have past   5
  Ar tryffylles to the last.

By prouffe I know the payne
  Of them that serue and serue;
  And nothyng can attayne
  Of that whiche they deserue;   10
  But those payngys haue I past
  As tryffylles to this last.

I haue er this bene thrall
  And durst yt neuer shewe;
  But glad to suffer all,   15
  And so to clok my woo;
  Yet that pang haue I past
  As tryffelles to this last.

By lenthe of tyme or nowe
  I haue attayned grace;   20
  And or I west well howe
  A nothyr had my place;
  Yet that pang haue I past
  As tryffelles to this last.

My loue well ner ons wonne,   25
  And I ffull lyk to sped,
  Evyll tonges haue then begonne

---

26 do] doth *original* B. 27 Save that] Saving *original* B. haue] tak *original* B. 28 Whose]
That *original* B.
CXLV. 6 tryffylles] tryffyll B.

With lyes to let my med;
Yet that pang haue I past
As tryfflles to thys last.   30

Somtyme I lovyd one
    That lykyd well my suete;
    But of my dedly mone
    Ffayr wordys was all the ffruite;
    Yet that pang haue I past   35
    As tryfflles to this last.

My stedffast ffaythe and wyll
    With ffayr wordes haue I told;
    Yet haue I ffownd them styll
    In ther beleve to colde;   40
    But that pang haue I past
    As tryfflles to thys last.

In love when I haue benne
    With them that loved me,
    Suche daunger haue I senne   45
    That we wold not Agree;
    Yet that pang haue I past
    As tryffelles to this last.

Abssence of tymes or this
    Hathe doblyd my deasease   50
    In causying me to mysse
    That thing that myght me please;
    Yet that pang haue I past
    As tryfflles to this last.

To promys love ffor love,   55
    And mak to long delayes,
    Hath mad me ffor to prove
    Of love the paynffull wayes;
    Yet that pang haue I past
    As tryfflles to this last.   60

31 lovyd] wold *original* B.   32 lykyd] *conj*. Zandvoort; lakyd B.   34 ffruite] *conj*.
Zandvoort] ffawte B.

Ffull many tormentes more
  In lovyng I haue ffound,
  Whiche oft hathe payned sore
  My hart when yt was bound;
  Yet all that haue I past   65
  As tryfflles to this last.

Nowe gesse all ye that lyst
  And jug enow as ye please;
  For oftymes haue ye myst
  In Jugyng my dessease;   70
  Be nothyng then agast,
  Tho ye mysiug these last.

CXLVI

In mornyng wyse syns daylye I Increas,
  Thus shuld I cloke the cause of all my greffe;
So pensyve mynd with tong to hold his pease,
  My reasone sayethe there can be no relyeffe:
Wherffor geve ere, I vmble you requyre,   5
  The affectes to know that thus dothe mak me mone.
The cause ys great of all my dolffull chere,
  Ffor those that were, and now be dead and gonne.

What thoughe to Dethe Desert be now ther call,
  As by ther ffautis yt dothe apere ryght playne, 10
Of fforce I must lament that suche a ffall
  Shuld lyght on those so welthy dyd Raygne;
Thoughe some perchaunce wyll saye of crewell hart,
  A tratores dethe why shuld we thus bemone?
But I, Alas, set this offence apart,   15
  Must nedis bewayle the dethe of some begonn.

As ffor them all I do not thus lament,
  But as of Ryght my Reason dothe me bynd;
But as the most doth all ther dethes repent,
  Evyn so do I by fforce of mornyng mynd.   20
Some say: 'Rochefford, hadyst thou benne not so prowde,

68 jug] g Iug B.
CXLVI. 2, 6, 17, 32 Thus] this B. 14 bemone] be mone B.

Ffor thy gryt wytte eche man wold the bemone;
Syns as yt ys so, many crye alowde:
Yt ys great losse that thow art dead and gonne.'

A ! Norrys, Norres, my tearys begyne to Rune   25
To thynk what hap dyd the so led or gyd,
Wherby thou hast bothe the and thyn vndone.
That ys bewaylyd in court of euery syde;
In place also wher thou hast neuer bene
Both man and chyld doth petusly the mone.   30
They say: 'Alas, thou art ffar ouer seene
By there offences to be thus ded and gonne.'

A ! Weston, Weston, that pleasant was and yonge;
In actyve thynges who myght with the compayre?
All wordis exsept that thou dydyst speake with tonge;   35
So well estemyd with eche wher thou dydyst fare.
And we that now in court dothe led our lyffe
Most part in mynd doth the lament and mone;
But that thy ffaultis we daylye here so Ryffe
All we shuld weppe that thou art dead and gone.   40

Brewton, ffarwell, as one that lest I knewe.
Great was thy love with dyuers as I here;
But common voyce dothe not so sore the Rewe,
As other twayne that dothe beffore appere.
But yet no dobt but thy frendes thee lament   45
And other her ther petus crye and mone.
So dothe eche hart ffor the lykwyse Relent,
That thou gevyst cause thus to be ded and gonne.

A ! Mark what mone shuld I ffor the mak more?
Syns that thy dethe thou hast deseruyd best,   50
Save only that myn eye ys fforsyd sore
With petus playnt to mone the with the Rest.
A tym thou haddyst aboue thy poore degree,
The ffall wherof thy frendis may well bemone.
A Rottyn twygge apon so hyghe a tree   55
Hathe slepyd thy hold and thou art dead and goonn.

31 seene] seenne B.   45 thee lament] *conj.* Maxwell; lament yee B.   51 myn eye]
my ny B.

And thus ffarwell eche one in hartye wyse!
   The Axe ys home, your hedys be in the stret;
   The trykklyngge tearys dothe ffall so from my yes,
   I skarse may wryt, my paper ys so wet.   60
   But what can hepe when dethe hath playd his part,
   Thoughe naturs cours wyll thus lament and mone?
   Leve sobes therffor, and euery crestyn hart
   Pray ffor the sowlis of thos be dead and goone.

CXLVII

    Longer to troo ye
       What may hyt avayle me?
       For ryght well knoo ye
       Ye sware hyt vnto me
       Styll for to loue me   5
       Alone and no moo;
       But ye haue deceyvd me:
       Who cold haue thowght soo?

    Yowr fayth and yowr othe
       Fly abrode in the wynd;   10
       I woold be ryght loth
       To stay that by kynde
       Cold never yet fynd
       In change to say whoo:
       Thys mene I by your mynd.   15
       Who cold haue thowght soo?

    Your gret assuerance
       Full oftyms dyd glade me;
    But the parformance
       Hath as well made me,   20
       As reson bade me,
       To lett your loue goo.

CXLVII. A (*seven stanzas in a different order:* 1, 1a, 3, 2, 2a, 4, 5). 1 troo] prove A.   4
sware] tolde A.   7 ye] now ye A.   8, 16, 24, 32 cold] wold A.   10 Fly abrode in]
dothe flye as A.   11 ryght loth] lothe A.   12 stay] chaunge A.   15 Thys mene I] I
meane A.   18 Full] *omitted* A. oftyms] oftmys B.   20 Hath as well] therof hathe A.

Wyth lyse ye haue lade me:
Who cold haue thowght soo?

But trust well that I   25
Shall neuer mystrust ye;
I care not a fley;
Go loue wher hyt lust ye,
For nedes change must ye
In wele and in woo –   30
In that most I trust ye.
Who cold haue thowght soo?

Farewell, vnstabyll,
For here I forsake thee;
Tru love ys not abyll   35
Tru louer to make the.
Therfore betake the
To them that do knoo
The ways how to brake the,
Where I cold not soo.   40

Youre faire wordes caught me
And made me your mickell,
But tyme hath taught me,
Their truthe is to tickell,
Sence faithe is fickell   45
And flitted you froe
Your ware is to brickell;
Whoe wolde have thought soe?

Sence waxe nor wryting
Can certain assure ye   50
Nor Love nor lyking
Can no waies allure ye
Once to procure ye
To staidnesse to growe,
I can not endure ye,   55
I care not whoe knowe.

23 me] *omitted* A. 25 But] *omitted* A. 26 Shall] will A. 30 In wele and in] for waile
or for A. 37 Therfore] Wherfore A. 38 do knoo] can shewe A. 39 ways] waye A.
40 cold] doe A. 41–56] A (in two four-line stanzas); *omitted* B.

CXLVIII

LOVE hathe agayne
Put me to payne,
 And yet all ys but lost:
I serue in vayne
And am certayne   5
 Of all myslyked most.

Bothe het and cold
Dothe so me holde,
 And combres so my mynd
That when I shuld   10
Speak and be bold
 Yt draweth me styll behynd.

My wyttes be past,
My lyfe dothe wast,
 My comffort ys exyled;   15
And I in hast
Am lyk to tast
 How love hathe me begylled.

Onles that Ryght
May in her syght   20
 Optayne pety and grace,
Why shuld a wyght
Haue bewty bryght
 Yf marsye haue no place?

Yet I Alas   25
Am in suche case
 That bak I cannot goo;
But styll forthe trace
A pacient pace
 And suffer seckret woo.   30

Ffor wythe the wynde
My fyered mynd
 Dothe styll incres in flame,

CXLVIII. D. 1 hathe] doth D. 8 so me holde] D; me behold B. 9 combres]
combrid D. 11 be bold] behold D. 12 draweth] dryvith D. 33 incres in flame]
inflame D.

And she vnkynd
That dyd me bynd   35
　　Dothe torne yt all to game.

Yet can no paygne
Make me reffrayne
　　Nor here nor ther to range;
I shall Retayne   40
Hope to obtayne
　　A hart that ys so strange.

But I requyer
The paynffull ffyre
　　That oft dothe mak me swete   45
For all my hyer
With lyk desyere
　　To geve here hart a hette.

Then shall she prove
How I her love,   50
　　And what I haue her offeryd,
Whiche shuld her move
Ffor to Remove
　　The payne that I haue sufferd.

A better ffee   55
Then she gave me
　　She shall of me attayne;
Ffor wher as she
Showyd creweltye
　　She shall my hart optayne.   60

CXLIX

L YUE thowe gladly, yff so thowe may;
Pyne thou not in loukynge for me;
Syns that dispayr hathe shut the wey,
Thoue to see me, or I to see the.

41 Hope] D; hop B. obtayne] D; attayne B. 45 swete] D; swere B. 46 hyer] yre D.
51 her] *omitted* D. 52 her] D; here B. 55 A] And D. 56 gave] D; geve B. 60 my]
D; me B.
CXLIX. 3 the] they B.

Make thoue a vertu of a constreynte; 5
    Deme no faulte wer non ys wourthy;
    Myns ys to muche, what nedes thy playnt?
    God he knoythe who ys for me.

Cast apon the Lorde thy cuer,
    Prey ounto hym thy cause to iuge; 10
    Beleuye, and he shall send recur:
    Vayne ys all trust of mans refuge.

CL

MORNYNG my hart dothe sore opres,
    That ffors constraynethe me to complayne;
    Ffor wher as I shuld haue redres,
Alas, I cannot be lovyd Againe.

I serue, I sewe, all of one sorte; 5
    My trust, my trayvell ys all in vayne;
    As in dispere without comfforte:
    Alas, I cannot be lovyd Agayne.

Perdye, yt ys but now of late,
    Not long ago ye knew my paygne; 10
    Wyll your Rygore neuer Abate?
    Alas, when shall I be louyd agayne?

It ys bothe dethe and dedlye smart,
    No sharp sorrow can now susstayne,
    Then ffor to love with ffaythffull harte, 15
    Alas, and cannot be lovyd agayne.

CLI

MADAME, I you requyere
    No longer tyme detract;
    Let truth in you aper,
    And geve me that I lak.

8 God] Grd ?B. for me] me for me B.
  [*Authorship:* Signed T. W.]

CL. B.M. MS. 18752 = Z. 1 Mornyng] Moaning Z. 3 as] *omitted* Z. 5 I sewe]
and sue Z. 6 My . . . all] Yet me thynketh all is Z. 7 As in dispere] And so I leue
Z. 8 Alas, I cannot] can not yet Z. 16 agayne] gayne B. See No. CIX.

Ye wot as well as I   5
   That promys ye dyd mak,
   When tyme I cold aspye
   I shuld haue that I lak.

Bothe tyme and place ye haue
   My fervent paygnes to slak;   10
   Nothyng, Alas, I crave,
   But onlye that I lak.

Whyche thyng me thynk ys deue,
   Remembryng what ye spake;
   Ffor yf your wordes be trewe,   15
   I must haue that I lake.

CLII

The Aunswere

Your ffolyshe fayned hast
   Ffull small effecte shall tak;
   Your wordes in vayne ye wrast;
   Ye get not that ye lack.

I wot, as ye shall ffind,   5
   The promys I dyd mak;
   No promys shall me bynd:
   Ye get not that ye lack.

Tho tyme and place I haue
   To slyd yf truthe wer slacke,   10
   Tho styll ye crye and crave,
   Ye get not that ye lacke.

Bycause ye thynck yt deue,
   I spek that that I spake;
   And this word shalbe trewe: 15
   Ye get not that ye lacke.

CLIII

Myght I as well within my songe belaye
   The thing I wolde, as in my hart I mave.

CLI.   13 deue] deve B.
CLII.   13 deue] deve B.   16 not] no B.
CLIII.   D (1–4 only).   2 wolde] me ne D.

Repentens shulde drawe frome those eyes
Salt tearis, with cryes, remorce, and grudge of harte,
Causles by cause that I haue ssuffred smart.   5

Or myght I ellis enclose my paynfull breast,
    That that myght be in syght, my great vnrest,
    Ther shulde ye see tormentes Remayn
As hell of payne to move your crewell hart,
Causles by cause that I haue suffred smart.   10

Ther ys in hell not such a feruent fyere
    As secret hete of inward hotte desyere,
    That wyll not let the flame appayre
That I haue here within my wastyd hart,
Causles by cause that I haue suffred smart.   15

Yet you cause yt, and ye may cause my welthe;
    Ons cause yt, then retorne vnto my helthe;
    And of all mene releve that man
That nothyng can but crye: 'Releve this hart,
Causles by cause that I haue suffred smart.'   20

Redres ye ought that harme that ye haue donne,
    Yt ys no game that ye nowe haue bygonne;
    But worthye blame ye shall remayne
To do hym payne that knowythe not thought of hart,
Causeles by cause that I haue suffred smart.   25

CLIV

My swet, alas, fforget me not,
    That am your owne ffull suer posseste;
And ffor my part, as well ye woot,
    I cannot swarue ffrome my behest;
Sens that my lyffe lyethe in your lott,   5
    At this my pore and just request,
        Fforget me not.

Yet wott how suer that I am tryed,
    My menyng clene, devoyde of blott;

---

4 grudge of harte] growes D.   6 Or] or yf *original* B.   8 tormentes Remayn] the tor-
mentes remayn *later correction* B; tormentes Remaygine *original* B.   11 Ther] or
myght *deleted* B. not] no B.

N

Yours ys the proffe; ye haue me tryed, 10
And in me, swet, ye ffound no spott;
Of all my welthe and helth is the gyd,
That of my lyff doth knyt the knot,
    Fforget me not.

Ffor yours I am and wilbe styll, 15
Although dalye ye se me not;
Sek ffor to saue, that ye may spyll,
Syns of my lyffe ye hold the shott;
Then grant me this ffor my goodwyll,
Which ys but Ryght, as god yt wot, 20
    Fforget me not.

Consyder how I am your thrall,
To serue you bothe in cold and hott;
My ffawtes ffor thinking nought at all;
In prysone strong tho I shuld Rott, 25
Then in your earys let petye ffall,
And leste I peryshe, in your lott
    Fforget me not.

CLV

O WHAT vndeseruyd creweltye
Hathe ffortune shewed vnto me!
When all my welthe, joye and ffelycytie
Ar tornyd to me most contrarye.

My joye ys woo, my pleasure payne, 5
My ease ys trayvell – what remedye?
My myrthe ys mornyng, hoppe ys in vayne:
Thus all thyng tornythe clen contrayrye.

The place of slepe that shuld my rest restore
Ys vnto me an vnquyet enymye, 10
And most my woo reuiuythe euermore;
Thus all thyng tornythe to me contrayrye.

CLIV. 11 me] my B. 15 wil be] welbe B. 19 Then] Than B. 23 hott] heatt B.
27 leste] lesse B.
CLV. 2 shewed] shewᵗ B. 10 vnquyet] vnquyed B.

I borne ffor cold, I sterve ffor hete;
    That lust lykythe desyre dothe yt denye;
    I ffast ffrom joye, sorrow ys my meate;   15
    Thus euery joy tornythe to me contrayrye.

The place of my reffuge ys my exylle;
    In desdaynes pryson desperat I leye,
    Therto abyd the tyme and wooffull whyle,
    Till my carffull lyfe may torne contrarye.   20

CLVI

Ons in your grace I knowe I was,
    Evyn as well as now ys he;
    Tho ffortune so hath tornyd my case,
    That I am doune, and he ffull hye,
        Yet ons I was.   5

Ons I was he that dyd you please
    So well that nothyng dyd I dobte;
    And tho that nowe ye thinke yt ease
    To take him in and throw me out,
        Yet ons I was.   10

Ons I was he in tyms past
    That as your owne ye did Retayne;
    And tho ye haue me nowe out cast,
    Shoyng vntruthe in you to Raygne,
        Yet ons I was.   15

Ons I was he that knyt the knot,
    The whyche ye swore not to vnknyt;
    And tho ye fayne yt now fforgot,
    In vsynge yowr newffanglyd wyt,
        Yet ons I was.   20

Ons I was he to whome ye sayd:
    'Welcomm, my joy, my hole delight!'
    And tho ye ar nowe well apayd

20 Till] tell B.
CLVI. 11 tyms] *the last letter is doubtful.*

Of me, your owne, to clame ye quyt,
    Yet ons I was.   25

Ons I was he to whome ye spake:
'Haue here my hart, yt ys thy owne!'
And tho thes wordis ye now fforsake,
Sayng therof my part ys none,
    Yet ons I was.   30

Ons I was he before Reherst,
And nowe am he that nedes must dye;
And tho I dye, yet at the lest,
In your Remembrance let yt lye
    That ons I was.   35

CLVII

O CREWELL hart, wher ys thy ffaythe?
Wher ys become thy stedffast vowe?
Thy sobbyng syghys, with ffayntyng breathe,
Thy bitter tearys, where ar theay now?

Thy carffull lokys, thy petus playnte,   5
Thy woffull wordis, thy wontyd chere?
Now may I see thou dydst but paynt,
And all thy craft does playn Appere.

For now thy syghes ar out of thought,
Thyn othe thou dost no thyng Regard,   10
Thy tears hathe quenchet thy lov so hote,
And spyt ffor love ys my Reward.

Yet love ffor love I had Awhyle,
Tho thyn were ffalse and myn were true;
Thy ffayned tearys dyd me begylle,   15
And causyd me trust the most vntrue.

To trust why dyd I condyssend,
And yeld my selffe so ernystlye
To her that dyd nothyng intend
But thus to trappe me craftyllye?   20

29 Sayng] syns *original* B.
CLVII.   2 vowe; voyve B.   4 bitter] better B.   5 playnte] playntis *original* B.   18
ernystlye] crewelye *original* B.

O ffalshed ffaythe, hast thou fforgot
    That ons of latte thou wart myn owne?
    But slaklye tyed may slepe the knot,
    No marvell then tho thou arte gonne.

Myn owne but late assuredlye,   25
    With ffaythe and truthe so justlye bounde,
    And thus to chaung so sodenlye,
    Eche thyng vpon thy shame shall sownd.

Eche thyng shall sownd vppon thy shame;
    Syns that thy ffaythe ys not to trust,   30
    What mor Reproche ys to thy name
    Then of thy word to prove vnjust?

And ffrom thy wordis yf thow wylt swerue,
    And swere thou dydst them neuer seye,
    Thy letters yet I do Reserve,   35
    That shall declare the owre and daye.

The owre and day, the tyme and where
    That thou thy selffe dyddyst them indyte,
    Wherin thou showdyst what dred and ffeare
    Thou haddyst ons spyed thy byllys to wrytte.   40

Thys proffe I thynk may well ssuffyse
    To prove yt tru that her I speake;
    No fforgyd taylis I wyll devyse,
    But with thy hand I shall me wreake.

When tyme and place therto I see,   45
    No dobt ther ys, but thou shalt know
    That thou dydst payn me wrongffully,
    Without offence to fforge my woo.

And thus ffarwell, most crewell hart;
    Ffarwell, thy falshyd ffayth also;   50
    Ffarwell my syghes, ffarwell my smart;
    Ffarwell my love, and all my woo.

---

24 arte gonne] be gonne *original* B. 25 but] fface *original* B. 28 Eche] Eke *original* B.
29 Eche] Eke B. 34 dydst] dyst B. 35 letters] tokens *correction* B. 44 me] my B.
47 dydst] dyst B.

CLVIII

PERDY I sayd hytt nott,
Nor never thought to doo,
As well as I ye wott
I haue no powr thertoo;
And yff I dyd, the lott   5
That furst dyd me inchayne
Do never slake the knoott
But strayter to my payne.

And yff I dyd, ech thyng
That may do harm or woo   10
Contynually may wryng
My hart wher so hytt goo;
Report may alway ryng
Off shame on me for aye,
Yf in my hart dyd spryng   15
Theys wordes that ye do say.

And yff I dyd, ech starr
That ys in heavyn aboue
May frown on me to mar
The hope I haue in loue;   20
And yff I dyd, such war
As they browght in to Troy
Bryng all my lyfe afar
From all hys lust and joy.

And yf I dyd so say,   25
The bewty that me bound
Incresse from day to day
More cruell to my wound,
Wyth all the mone that may
To playnt may turn my song;   30
My lyfe may sone decay,
Wythowt redresse my wrong.

CLVIII. D, T.   7 Do] May T.   8 strayter] strayt it T.   12 hytt] I D, T.   13 alway] always D, T.   14 on] of D. aye] D; aey B.   16 Theys wordes] the worde D; The wordes T.   22 in to] vnto D, T.   23 afar] as farre T.   24 hys] this D.   32 my] bye

Yf I be clere from thowght,
Why do ye then complayn?
Then ys thys thyng but sowght   35
To put me to more payn.
Then that that ye haue wrowght
Ye must hyt now redresse;
Off ryght therfore ye ought
Such rygor to represse.   40

And as I haue deseruyd,
So grant me now my hyer;
Ye kno I never swarvyd,
Ye never fownd me lyer.
For Rakhell haue I seruyd,   45
For Lya caryd I never;
And her I haue reseruyd
Wythin my hart for euer.

CLIX

P AS fourthe, my wountyd cries,
Thos cruel eares to pearce,
Whyche in most hatful wyse
Dothe styll my playntes reuers.
Doo you, my tears, also   5
So weet hir bareyn hart,
That pite ther may gro
And cruelty depart.

For thoughe hard roks amonge
She semis to haue beyn bred,   10
And wythe tygers ful Longe
Ben norysshed and fed;
Yet shall that natuer change,
Yff pyte wons wyn place,
Whome as ounknown and strange   15
She nowe away dothe chase.

D, T.   34 ye] you T.   37, 38 39 ye] you T.   43, 44, Ye] You T.
   [*Authorship:* Ascribed to W by T.]
CLIX. T.   11] And of the Tigre long T.   16 away] T; auey B.

And as the water soufte,
Wytheout forsinge of strength,
Wher that it fallythe oft,
Hard stonnes dothe perce at Lengthe,   20
So in hyr stony hart
My playntes at Lengthe shall grave,
And, rygor set apart,
Cawse hir graunt that I craue.

Wherfor, my pleyntes, present   25
Styl so to hyr my sut,
As it, through hir assent,
May brynge to me some frut;
And as she shall me proue,
So byd hir me regard,   30
And render Loue for Loue:
Wyche is my iust reward.

CLX

QUONDAM was I in my Ladys gras,
 I thynk as well as nou be you;
And when that you haue trad the tras,
Then shal you kno my woordes be tru,
 That quondam was I.   5

Quondam was I. She sayd for euer:
 That euer lastyd but a short whyl;
Promis mad not to dysseuer.
I thoght she laughte – she dyd but smyl:
 Than quondam was I.   10

Quondam was I: he that full oft lay
 In hyr armes wythe kysses many whon.
Yt is enou that thys I may saey:
Tho amonge the moo nou I be gon,
 Yet quondam was I.   15

18 of] or T. 22 shall] T; shaul B. 24 Cawse hir] Winne T. that] of that T. 27 through] T; throw B. 28 some] T; soum B. 29 shall] T; shaul B. 32 my] a T.
 [*Authorship:* Ascribed to W by T.]
CLX. 11 full] foul B. 12 armes] harmes B. 14 amonge] amogne B.

Quondam was I: yet she wyl you tell
  That syns the ouer she was furst borne
  She neuer louyd non halffe so well
  As you. But what altho she had sworne,
    Suer quondam was I.   20

CLXI

  FFORTUNE what ayleth the
    Thus for to banyshe me
Her company whome I loue best?
    For to complayne me
    Nothyng avaylethe me;   5
Adew, fare well thys nyghtes rest.

    Her demure countenaunce,
    Her womanly pacience,
Hath wounded me thorough Venus darte,
    That I cannot refrayne me   10
    Nother yet abstayne me,
But nedes I must loue her with all my hart.

    Long haue I loued her,
    Ofte haue I prayd her,
Yet, alas, she thorow dysdayn   15
    Nothyng regardes me
    Nor yet rewardes me
But lets me ly in mortall payn.

    Yet shall I loue her styll
    With all my hart and wyl   20
Wher so euer I ryde or go;
    My hart, my seruyce,
    Afore al ladyes
Is hers al onely and no mo.

    She hath my hart and euer shall   25
    In this terrestrial;
What can she more of me require?

CLXI. V.   2 Thus] thys B.   8 womanly] whumly B.   11 Nother] Nor V.   21-end] *omitted* B.

Her whom I loue best,
God send her good rest,
And me hartely my whole desyre.   30

CLXII

Sche that shuld most, percevythe lest
    The vnffayned sufferance of my gret smart;
    Yt ys to her sport to haue me oprest;
    But theay of suche lyffe whiche be expert
    Say that I borne vnsertayne in my hart: 5
    But wher jug ye? no mor! ye kno not.
    Ye ar to blame to saye I cam to late.

To lat? naye, to soon methynke Rather,
    Thus to be intretyd and haue seruyd ffaythffully.
    Lo! thus am I Rewardyd amonge the other.   10
    I thoughe vnvysyd whiche was to besye,
    Ffor ffere of to late I cam to hastylye;
    But thether I cam not, yet cam I ffor all that:
    But whether so euer I cam, I cam to late.

Who hathe mor cause to playn then I?   15
    Ther as I am jugyd to lat, I came;
    And there as I cam, I cam to hastylye.
    Thus may I playn as I that am
    Mysjugyd, mysintretyd more then any man.
    Now juge, let se of this debate,   20
    Whether I cam to hastelye, or to late.

CLXIII

Spytt off the spytt whiche they in vayne
    Do styk to fforce my fantysye,
    I am proffest, ffor losse or gayne,
    To be thyn owne assuredlye.
    Who lyst therat by spytt to sporne: 5
    My ffancy ys to hard to torne.

CLXII.   11 vnvysyd] Kane *conj.*; vnnysyd *or* vnuysyd B.   20 this] thes B.
CLXIII.   1 they] yᵗ B.

Altho that some of bessye witt
 Do babyll styll, ye, ye, what tho?
 I haue no ffeare, nor wyll not flytt
 As dothe the water to and ffroo.   10
 Spytt then ther spytt that lyst to sporne,
 My ffancye ys to hard to torne.

Who ys affrayd? ye, let hym fflee,
 Ffor I full well shall byd the bront,
 May grece ther lyppis that lyst to lye 15
 Of bessye brayns as ys ther wont;
 And yet agaynst the pryk thay sporne:
 My fancy ys to hard to torne.

Ffor I am set and wyll not swerve,
 Whom ffaythffull spetche removyth nought; 20
 And well I may thy grace deserue;
 I think yt ys not derely bought;
 And yf thay bothe do spyt and sporne,
 My ffancy ys to hard to torne.

Who lyst therat to lyst or louere,   25
 I am not he that ought dothe reche;
 Ther ys no payne that hathe the power
 Out of my brest this thought to seche;
 Then though theay spytt therat and sporne,
 My ffancy ys to hard to torne.   30

CLXIV

SYETHE yt ys so that I am thus refusyd,
 And by no meanys I can yt Remedye,
 Me thynckes of Right I ought to be excusyd,
 Tho to my hart I set yt not to nye;
 But now I see, Alas, tho I shuld dye, 5
 Ffor want of truthe and ffaythffull stedfastnes
 Of hym that hathe my hart onlye,
 Yt wold not be but ffals nuffanglydnes.

7 with] wett B. 22 derely] derly B. 29 though] thou B.
CLXIV. 6 want] what B. 8 but] *omitted* B; for *later insertion* B.

I set my hart I thought not to withdrawe,
　The proffe therof ys knowen to well, Alas!　　　　10
But now I se that neuer erst I sawe
Wher I thought gold I fond but brytell glas.
Now yt ys this ye know, somthyng yt was
Not so promysed, the truthe ys so dobtles.
Who ys my fo who brynges me in thys cace?　　　15
I can none blame but ffals newfanglydnes.

Yet Reasone wold that trewe love wer regardyd
Without ffayninge, wher ment ffaythfully,
And not with vnkyndnes ys to be rewardyd.
But this yt ys, Alas, suche hap had I,　　　　20
I can no more but I shall me aplye
My woffull hart to bryng out of distres,
And withdraw my mynd so full of ffollye,
Sythe thus dothe Raygne this false newfanglydnes.

CLXV

SUFFRYNG in sorrowe in hope to Attayne,
Desyring in ffeare I dar not complayne,
Trewe in belyefe in whome ys All my trust,
Do thou aplye to ease me of my payne,
For elys to serue and suffyr styll I must.　　　　5

Hope ys my hold, yet in Dyspayre I speake;
I Dryve ffrom tyme to tyme and do not Recke
How long to love thus after louys lust,
In studye styll of that I dar not brake:
Wherffore to serue and suffyr styll I must.　　　10

Encreas of care I ffynd bothe day and nyght;
I hate that sometyme was my most delyght;
The cause therof ye know I haue dyscust,

18 wher ment] wher ment ys *original* B; wher yt is ment *later correction* B.　19 to] not to *original* B.　24 thus] this B.
CLXV. D.　2 1] and D.　3 in] of D.　5 For elys] els thus D.　6 I] to D.　7 tyme to tyme] D; tyme B. do] dothe D.　8 love] lyve D.　9 studye] D; stody B.　11 Encreas] Increas B; Encrease D.　12 hate] D; hat B. sometyme . . . most] was symtyme all my D.　13 dyscust] D; dyscost B.

And yet to Reffrayne yt passythe my myght:
Wherfor to serue and suffer styll I must.   15

Love who so lyst, at lenthe he shall well saye:
To love and lyve in feare yt ys no playe.
Record that knoweth, yf this be notyd just,
That wher as love Dothe lede, ther ys no nay,
But serue and suffer styll allwaye I must.   20

Then ffor to lyve with losse of lybertye
At last perchaunce shalbe his remedye;
And ffor his truthe quyted with ffals mistrust,
Who wold not Rew to se how wrongfullye
Thus for to serue and suffer styll I must.   25

Vntruthe by trust oft tymes hathe me betrayed,
Mysusyng my hoppe, styll to be Delayed;
Fortune Allway I haue the fownd vniust;
And so with lyk Reward now hast thou me payed:
That ys, to serue and suffer styll I must.   30

Neuer to cesse, nor yet lyke to attayn,
As long as I in fere dare nor complayn;
Trew of beleff hathe allways ben my trust,
And tyll she knowythe the cawse of all my payn,
Content to serve and suffer styll I must.   35

CLXVI

S ᴛ ʜ ᴇ I my selffe dysplease the,
    My ffrend why shuld I blame
    That from the ffawte aduyse me
    That Kynkoryd my good name,
    And mad my mynd to morne   5
    That laughyt my lov to skorne,
    And bownd my hart allwaye
    To thynk this payne a playe,
    That wold and neuer maye?

---

17 lyve] leve B.   18 yf] and yf D.   19 nay] way D.   23 quyted] Requit D.   24 how]
D; who B; whow *later correction* B.   25 for to] D; to B.   26 Vntruthe] Untrew D. by]
be D.   29 so] to D.   31–5] D; *omitted* B.

Too led my lyffe at lybertye,   10
    I lyk yt wonders well,
    Ffor proffe hath tought his propertye
    That allway payne his hell;
    But sythe so well I wott
    Theys kyndes of cold and hott,   15
    Suche ffancyes I fforsake,
    That dothe ther ffredome lake;
    My lyst no more to make.

Grodge one that ffell the greffe,
    I laughe that ffell the gayne   20
    Of ffredome from the lyffe
    Wherby wyld beastys be tayme.
    As ffast and wak a bedde,
    With hart and hevy hed,
    That haue a hongery hart   25
    To mak my selffe well ffed,
    That may Redresse my smart.

Sythe I have slept the knot
    That dothe my hart inchayne,
    I lyk the loky lotte   30
    To well to knyt agayne.
    So newly com to welthe,
    Shall I deceayue my selffe?
    Nay, set thy hart at reast,
    Ffor welthe, my new ffownd gest,   35
    Shall harber in my neast.

To mak a wyllffull band
    Wher I may well Reffus,
    To be a byrde in hand
    And not my ffredome vse,   40
    To syng and sorow not
    Yf wyllyngly I dott,
    To slypp in to the cayge,
    Yt were a wylffull Rage.

CLXVI.   10 Too] Tyll *original* B.   15 theys] y^t *original* B.   34 Nay] May *original* B.
35 new] ne B.   40 not] at *original* B.

CLXVII

THOU slepest ffast; and I with wofull hart
  Stand here alone, syghing, and cannot ffleye.
Thou slepyst ffast, when crewell love his darte
On me dothe cast, Alas! so paynefullye.
Thou slepyst fast, and I all ffull of smart   5
To the my fo in vayn do call and crye.
And yet, methinkes, thou that slepyst ffast,
Thou dremyst styll whiche way my lyf to wast.

CLXVIII

THO some do grodge to se me joye,
  Fforcynge ther spytte to slak my helthe,
Ther false mystrust shall neuer noy
  So long as thou dost wyll my welthe;
Ffor tho theay frowne, ffull well I knowe   5
  No power theaye haue to fforge my woo.
Then grodge who lyst, I shall not sease
  To seke and sew ffor my Redres.

Whylest lyffe doth last and thou content,
  What shulde I dobt, what shuld I dred   10
Ther spyet that daylye do consent
  To make my joy frome me be led?
What shulde I bowe to ffrend or ffoo,
  That wold me so thi syght fforgoo?
What shuld I do, but passe full light   15
  The ffrayle mystrust of all ther spyet?

Yf cause were gevyne of any part
  To cause mystrust in them to spryng,
Nought shuld yt greve me then to smart;
  But I, Alas, know none suche thynge.   20
Then by myshappe and crewell lott,
  Thowe thaye wold so, forsake me not;

CLXVII. 5 Thou] thu B.

CLXVIII. 4 thou dost] you do *original* B. 9 thou] you *original* B. 11 do] doth
original B. 12] my Joy and all frome me to hydde *original* B. 14 thi] your *original* B.
15 light] leght B. 22 wold so] mysing *original* B.

Nor wyll me not my ffoos to please,
To slake the sewte of all my ease.

Thyne owne and thyne for euermore   25
I am and must contynew styll.
No woo nor paynes, no hurt nor sore
Can cause me fflee frome this my wyll
Thy owne to be, and not to start
As long as lyfe ys in my hart.   30
Then graunt me this my lyfe to saue;
As I desyrve, so let me haue.

CLXIX

Tho of the sort ther be that ffayne
And cloke ther craft to serve ther turne,
Shall I, Alas, that trewlye mene,
Ffor ther offence thus gyltles burne;
And yf I bye ther ffawt to dere,   5
That ther vntruthe thus hett my ffyere,
    Then haue I wronge.

Tho ffraylte fayle not to appere
In them that wayle as well as I,
And thoughe the ffals by lycke desyere   10
Dothe swere hym selfe thyn owne to bee,
Yf thou dost judge me one of theys
That so can fayne suche commone ways,
    Then haue I wronge.

Tho chaunse hathe powere to chaunge thy love,   15
That all by chaunce ther wyll dothe gyd,
Suche chaunce may not my hart remove,
For I by choise my selfe haue tryed;
And not by chaunce, wherfore I saye,
Yf thou dost not my wylffare staye,   20
    Then haue I wronge.

25 Thyne] your *original* B. thyne] yours *original* B. 29 Thy] your *original* B. 30] tyll
lyf and all frome me departe *original* B.
CLXIX. 9 wayle] weayle B. 10 thoughe] thou B. by] be B. 11 hym] them hym
B. 12 thou] tho B. 13 ways] wavys B. 15 chaunse] *original* chaunge B. 18
choise] chose B.

Tho stedffastnes in them do lacke,
That do protest the contrayrye,
And tho perfformans none theay mak
Of that theay promyse diuerslye, 25
Yet syns ther ffawtis ar none of myne,
Yf thou Reffussyst me for thyne,
Then haue I wronge.

CLXX

To wette your yee withoutyn teare,
And in good helthe to fayne dyssease,
That you therby myn yee myght bleare,
Therwith your ffrendes to please;
And thoughe ye thynk ye ncd not ffeare, 5
Yet so ye cannot me Apease;
But as you lyst, ffayne, fflatyr or glose,
You shall not wynn yf I do lose.

Prat and paynt and spare not,
Ye knowe I can me wreke; 10
And yf so be ye car not,
Be suer I do not Recke:
And thoughe ye swere yt were not,
I can bothe swere and speake;
By god and by the crosse, 15
If I haue the mocke, ye shall haue the worse.

CLXXI

To my myshap alas I fynd
That happy hap ys dangerus;
And fortune workyth but her kynd
To make the joyfull dolorus.
But all to late hyt cumes in mynd 5

22 Tho] Thow B.
CLXX. D. 3 you therby] thou therbe D. 4 ffrendes] other frendes D. 5 ffeare] fer
feare D. 7 you] ye D. 8 You] ye D. lose] D; losse B. 9 spare] spre D. 10 wreke]
worke D. 11 car] canrrre ?D 15 the] this D. crosse] crosse y *original* B; crvsse D.
16 worse] loss D.
CLXXI. D, T, X. *Order of stanzas* 1, 2, 4, 3, 5, D, T; 2, 3, 6, 4, 5, 1 X. 3 workyth]
workes D. 5 in] to T.

O

To wayle the want that made me blynd,
So often warnyd.

Amydes my myrth and plesantnes
Such chance ys chansyd sodenly,
That in dyspere to haue redres   10
I fynd my chefyst remedy.
No new kynd off vnhappynes
Shuld thus haue left me comfortles,
So oftyn warnyd.

In better case was never none,   15
And yet vnwares thus am I trappt;
My chefe desyer doth cause me mone,
And to my harm my welth ys hapt:
Ther ys no man but I alone
That hath such cause to syghe and mone,   20
So oftyn warnyd.

Who wold haue thowght that my request
Shuld bryng me forth such bytter frute?
But now ys hapt that I ferd lest,
And all thys harm cumes by my sute;   25
For when I thought me happyest,
Evyn then hapt all my chefe vnrest,
So oftyn warnyd.

Thus am I tawght for to beware,
And trust no more such plesant chance;   30
My happy hap hath bred thys care,
And browght my myrth to grete myschance.

6 that made] that makes T; whyght make X; wych made D. 7] *omitted* X, T.
8 Amydes] Amid T. 10 to haue] without T. 13 Shuld] Wolde X. thus haue]
thys a D. 14] *omitted* X, T. 16 yet] ye D. 17 me] my X. 18 harm] woo and payne
X; payn D. 19 Ther ys no] was never D. 20] that had sech hap to wayll and grown
D. to] *omitted* X. 21] *omitted* X, T. 22 wold] cold D. 23 bryng me] have broght D.
24 But] For X. 25 harm] greff D. by] be D. 25] And all is com bye myne owné
suyte X. 26 when] wher D. thought] thowgh B. 27 then hapt all] ther I ffownd D.
chefe] cheffest D. 27] Then forthwyth came all myne vnrest. 28] *omitted* X, T.
30 trust no more] not to trust D. 31 My] For X. hath bred] has bred D; bred me
T; has don X. 32 browght] tovrned D. myrth] nyrth B. 32] And tourned my

Ther ys no man that hap wyll spare,
But when she lyst hys welth ys bare,
   Thus am I warnyd.   35

CLXXII

THE knott that furst my hart dyd strayn,
  When that thy servant I becam,
Doth bynd me styll for to remayn
  Always your own, as now I am;
And yff ye fynd that I do fayn,   5
  Wyth just jugement my self I dam
    To haue dysdayn.

Yf other thowght in me do groo,
  But styll to loue the stedfastly,
And yff the proffe do nott forth shoo   10
  That I am yours assuerydly,
Lett euery welth turne me to woo,
  And ye to be contynually
    My chefyst foo.

Yff other thowght or new request   15
  Do sese my hart, but only thys,
Or yff whythin my weryd brest
  Be hyd one thowght that mene amys,
I do desyer that my unrest
  May styll incres and I to mys   20
    That I loue best.

Yff in my loue be hyd one spoot
  Off fals decete and dubbylnes,

welthe to great grevance X.   33 that] whom T. spare] here X.   34 when] weane
X. hys] owr D; *omitted* X.   35] *omitted* T. Thus] thys D. *Additional stanza* in X:
He is in wellth that feleth no woe/But I maye synge and thus reporte/Farewell my
joye and plesure to/Thus maye I sing withought comforte/For sorrowe hath caught
me in her sner/Alas! why colde I not be ware/So often warnd?
   [*Authorship:* T includes the poem among those of uncertain authorship.]
CLXXII. D1 (xxiii), D2 (xxxiii).   1 that] which D.   2 thy] your D.   6] reward me
justlye wythe dysdayn *later correction* B.   9 the] yow D; yᵘo *later correction* B.   10
And yff] or yff *later correction* B: yff that D. forth] well D. That] how *later correction* B.
12] Let all my joys turn all to woo *later correction* B. euery] eure D1. turne] turned
original B.   13 ye] yow D.   15 thowght] love D. request] behest *later correction* B.
16 sese] cesse D2; cese D1.   18 one] D; on B. one thowght] the traynes *later correc-
tion* B.   19 my] myne D.   22 loue] hert *later correction* B. be hyd] ther be D.   23 and]

Or yff I mynd to slyp the knoot
　　By want of fayth or stedfastnes,   25
Let all my servys be forgoot,
　　And when I wold haue chefe redres,
　　　　Esteme me nott.

But yff that I consume in payn
　　Wyth burnyng syghes and farvent loue,   30
And dayly seke non other gayn
　　But wyth my dedes thes wordes to proue,
Me thynkes off ryght I shuld obtayn
　　That ye shuld mynd for to remoue
　　　　Your gret dysdayn.   35

And for an end off thys my song,
　　In to your handes I do submytt
The dedly grefe, the paynes so strong,
　　Wych in my hart be fyrmly shytt;
And when ye lyst, redres my wrong,   40
　　Sens well ye knoo thys paynfull fytt
　　　　Hath last to long.

CLXXIII

THAT tyme that myrthe dyd stere my shypp
Whyche now ys frowght with heuenes,
And fortune bot not then the lypp,
But was Defence off my Dystresse,
Then in my boke wrote my mystresse: 5
'I am yowres you may be well sure,
And shall be whyle my lyff dothe dure.'

But She her selffe whyche then wrote that
Is now myn extreme enemye;
Above all men she dothe me hate,   10
Reioysyng of my myserye;
But thoughe that for her sake I dye,

or D.   24 the] thys D.   25 fayth] trust *later correction* B.   26 servys] frendshyp *later correction* B; sorowys D2; sarwyes D1.   30 Wyth] of D.   32 dedes] dede D.   34 shuld] wulde D.   36 an end] the ende D; a nend B.   37 In to] vnto D.   38 The ... the] my ... and D.   39 in] D; I B.   40 my] me D1.
CLXXIII. D (*spellings from D*).   3 bot] boate D.   7 my] D; that B.   9 myn] D; my

I shall be hyrs she may be sure,
As long as my lyff dothe endure.

It is not tyme than can were out   15
With me that once ys fermly sett;
Whyle nature kepys her cours Abowt
My hate frome her no man can lett;
Thowghe neuer so sore they me thrett,
Yet I am hyrs, she may be sure,   20
And shallbe whyle that lyff dothe dure,

And once I trust to see that day,
Renuer of my joy and welthe,
That She these wordes to me shall say:
'In feythc, welcum to me myselffe,   25
Welcum my hart, welcum my helthe;
Ffor I am thyne, thow mayst be sure,
And shallbe whyle that lyff dothe dure.'

Ho me! alas! What woordes were theyse?
In couenant I myght fynd them so!   30
I Reke not what smart or dysease,
Tourment or troubel, payne or woo
I suffred so that I myght knoo
That she were myn, I myght be sure,
And shuld be whyle that lyff dothe dure.   35

CLXXIV

WYTHE seruyng styll
This haue I wonne,
Ffor my good wyll
To be vndonne.

And ffor redres   5
Of all my payne
Disdaynffulnes
I haue agayne.

B.   18 hate] love D.   20–1 she . . . dure] D; *omitted* B.   23 Renuer] Renuare D.   24
these . . . me] to me theyse wordes D. hart] joy D.   27–8 thow . . . dure] D; *omitted*
B.   30 couenant] coumnant B; comenant D.   32] *omitted* D.   35 be] *omitted* D.

And ffor Reward
　　Of all my smart　　　　　　　　　　　10
　　Lo thus unhard
　　I must departe.

Wherefore all ye
　　That after shall
　　By fortune be,　　　　　　　　　　　15
　　As I am, thrall,

Exempell take
　　What I have wonne,
　　Thus for her sake
　　To be vndone.　　　　　　　　　　　20

CLXXV

W HAT wolde ye mor of me, your slav, Requyere
　　Then ffor to aske and haue that ye desyre?
　　Yet I Remaygne without recure.
　　I insuere ther ys no ffaythffull harte
　　That without cause causles that sufferth smart.　　　5

You haue the joy, and I haue all the payne;
　　Yours the pleasore and I in woo Remaygne.
　　Alas! and why do ye me blame?
　　Yt ys no gam, thus to destroye my hart,
　　Nor without cause thus to cause yt smart.　　　　10

I haue Assayed in all that euer I myght
　　You ffor to please, ffor that was my delyght.
　　All could not serue: ye lyst not see,
　　But crewelly hathe vndone my pore hart,
　　And without cause dothe cause yt suffer smart.　　　15

Ye mak a play at all my woo and greffe,
　　And yet Alas! Amonge all my myscheffe
　　Nothyng at all that ye regard,

CLXXIV. D.　14 shall] me *original* B.
　[*Authorship:* See Commentary.]
CLXXV.　9, 20 thus] this B.

Nor wyll Reward a ffaythfful menyng hart,
But thus causles to cause yt suffer smart.   20

If that ye lyst my paynffull dethe to see
  Ye ned no more but vse this creweltye;
  Ffor shorter dethe cannot be ffownd
Then without grownd by force of crewell hart
  Causeles by cause to cause me suffer smart.   25

A Deue! ffarwell! I ffell my joyes destresse.
  Ffled ys my welthe, my tormentis dothe encres.
  Thus haue I woone ffor all my hyere
To brynne in ffyer sweltyng my woffull hart,
  That without cause causles thus suffreth smart.   30

CLXXVI

V. Innocentia
Veritas Viat Fides
Circumdederunt me inimici mei

W HO lyst his welthe and eas Retayne,
  Hym selffe let hym vnknowne contayne;
    Presse not to ffast in at that gatte
  Wher the Retorne standes by desdayne:
    For sure, *circa Regna tonat.*   5

The hye montaynis ar blastyd oft,
  When the lowe vaylye ys myld and soft;
    Ffortune with helthe stondis at debate;
  The ffall ys grevous ffrome Aloffte:
    And sure, *circa Regna tonat.*   10

These blodye dayes haue brokyn my hart;
  My lust, my youth dyd then departe,
    And blynd desyre of astate;
  Who hastis to clyme sekes to reuerte:
    Of truthe, *circa Regna tonat.*   15

The bell towre showed me suche syght
That in my hed stekys day and nyght;

CLXXVI. 5, 10, 15, 20, 25 *tonat*] *to nat* B.

Ther dyd I lerne out of a grate,
Ffor all vauore, glory or myght,
  That yet *circa Regna tonat*.   20

By proffe, I say, ther dyd I lerne,
Wyt helpythe not deffence to yerne,
  Of innocence to pled or prate;
Ber low, therffor, geve god the sterne,
  Ffor sure, *circa Regna tonat*.   25

CLXXVII

Venus, in sport, to please therwith her dere,
  Dyd on the helm off myghty Mars the red.
  Hys spere she toke, hys targe she myght not stere;
  She lokt as tho her foys shuld all be ded,
  So wantonly she frownyth wyth her chere.   5
  Priapus gan smyle and sayd; 'Doway for dred,
  Do way, maddame, theys wepyns gret and grym.
  I, I for you am wepyn fytt and trym.'

21 ther] the B.
CLXXVII.   6 gan] can B. for dred] fordred B.

V

Poems from the Devonshire Manuscript

CLXXVIII

TAKE hede be tyme leste ye be spyede
Your lovyng eye yee canne not hide
At last the trowthe will sure be tryde,
    Therefore take hede!

For Som there be of craftie kynde   5
Thowe yow shew no parte of your mynde,
Sewrlye there Ies ye cannot blynde,
    Therefore take hede!

For in lyke case there selves hathe bene,
And thowght ryght sure none had theym sene,   10
But it was not as theye did wene,
    Therfore take hede!

All thowgth theye be of dyvers skoolles,
And well can yose all craftye toolles
At leynthe theye prove themselfe bott foolles   15
    Therefore take hede!

Yf theye myght take yow in that trape
Theye wolde sone leve yt in your lape;
To love vnspyed ys but a happe
    Therfore take hede!   20

CLXXVIII.   2 eye yee] I yee D.   3 trowthe] trwthe D.   5 craftie] crafite D.   7 cannot] can te not D.   10 thowght] thowzt D.   11 theye] thye D.   14 well] will D. 15 theye] thye D.   18 yt] yet D.
   [*Authorship:* Signed 'Th. W' in D.]

CLXXIX

My pen, take payn a lytyll space
To folow that whyche dothe me chace,
And hathe in hold my hart so sore;
But when thow hast thys browght to passe,
My pen, I prithe, wryght no more!   5

Remember, oft thow hast me eaysyd,
And all my paynes full well apeaysyd,
But now I know vnknowen before
Ffor where I trust I am dysceavyd,
And yet, my pen, thow canst no more.   10

A tyme thow haddyst as other have
To wryght whyche way my hope to crave;
That tyme ys past; withdrawe therffore!
Syns we do lose that other save,
As good leve off and wryght no more.   15

Yn worthe to vse another waye,
Not as we wold, but as we maye,
For ons my losse ys past Restore,
And my desyre ys my decaye;
My pen, yet wryght a lytyll more.   20

To love in vayn who euer shall
Off worldlye payn yt passythe all,
As in lyke case I fynd. Wherfore
To hold so fast and yet to ffall?
Alas, my pen, now wryght no more!   25

Syns thow hast taken payn thys space
To folow that whyche dothe me chace,

CLXXIX. V.   2 that whyche] the thing that V.   4 But] And V.   5 prithe] pray the
V.   6 oft . . . eaysyd] thou hast oft ple V1; how thou hast oft plesed V2.   7] And
my sorowes also eased V1; And al my sorowes also eased V2.   8] But now vn-
knowne I knew before V.   9 Ffor] That V.   10 no] do no V.   14 that] let V1; and
V2.   16 Yn worthe] And vse V2.   17 we . . . we] ye . . . ye V2.   18 ons] els V.   20
omitted V1; And yet my pen now wryt no more V2.   21 who euer] Who so euer V.
25 Alas] Alak V1.   27 me] the V1.

And hathe in hold my hart so sore,
Now hast thow browght my mynde to passe:
My pen, I prithe, wryght no more.   30

CLXXX

I LOVE lovyd and so doithe she,
And yet in love wee sufer still;
The cause is strange as semeth me,
To love so will and want our will.

O deadly yea! O grevous smart!   5
Worse than refuse, vnhappe gaine!
I love: whoeuer playd this part,
To love so will and leve in payn.

Was euer hart soo well agrede,
Sines love was love as I do trowe,   10
That in ther love soo evell dyd sped,
To love so will and leve in woo?

Thes morne wee bothe and hathe don long,
With wofull plaint and carefull voice:
Alas! it is a grevous wrowng   15
To love so will and not reioice.

And here an end of all our mone!
With sighinge oft my brethe is skant,
Sines of myshappe ours is alone –
To love so will and it to wantt.   20

But they that causer is of this,
Of all owr cares god send them part!
That they may trowe what greve it is
To love so will and leve in smart.

29 Now . . . mynde] nd A now thou hast this brought V1; And now to haue brought
this V2.   30 prithe] pray the V2.

CLXXX.   1 love] lowe D.   3 semeth] simeth D.   4 love] lowe D. our] or D.   7
love] lowe D. this] thes D.   8 love] lovve D.   10 love] lowe D.   11 love] lowe D.
12 love] low D.   13 wee] we te D.   15 Alas!] alas alas D.   17 our] or D.   18 oft]
of D.   20 love] lowe D.   21 this] thes D.   23 is] ies D.   24 love] lowe D.

CLXXXI

FAREWELL all my wellfare,   9
My shue is trode awry;
Now may I karke and care
To syng lullay by by.
Alas! what shall I do thereto?   5
There ys no shyffte to helpe me now.

Who made hytt such offence
To love for love agayn?
God wott that my pretence
Was but to ease hys payn;   10
Ffor I had Ruthe to se hys wo;
Alas, more fole, Why did I so?

For he frome me ys gone
And makes thereat a game
And hathe leffte me Alone   15
To suffer sorow and shame.
Alas! he is vnkynd dowtles
To leve me thus all comfortles.

Hytt ys a grevows smarte
To suffer paynes and sorrowe;   20
But most it grevyd my hart
He leyde hys feythe to borow;
And falshode hathe hys feythe and trowthe,
And he forsworne by many an othe.

All ye lovers, perde,   25
Hathe cawse to blame hys dede,
Whyche shall example be
To lett yow off yowre spede;
Let neuer woman Agayn
Trust to suche wordes as men can fayn.   30

For I vnto my coste
Am warnyng to yow all,
That they whom you trust most

CLXXXI.   7 offence] a fence D.   14 thereat] there at D.   21 it] M; *omitted* D.   24
an othe] a nothe D.   29 Agayn] A gayn D.

Sonest dysceyve yow shall;
But complaynt cannot redresse 35
Of my gret greff the gret excesse.

CLXXXII

THE hart and servys to yow profferd
With ryght good wyll full honestly,
Refuce yt not syns yt is offerd
But take yt to yow jentylly.

And tho yt be a small present, 5
Yet good, consyder gracyowsly
The thowght, the mynd, and the entent
Of hym that lovys you faythfully.

Yt were a thyng of small effecte
To worke my wo thus cruelly, 10
Ffor my good wyll to be abiecte:
Therfore accepte yt lovyngly.

Payn or travell, to rune or ryde,
I vndertake yt plesawntly;
Byd ye me go and strayte I glyde 15
At your commawndement humbly.

Payn or plesure now may yow plant
Evyn whyche it plese yow stydfastly;
Do whyche yow lyst, I shall not want
To be your servant secrettly. 20

And syns so muche I do desyre
To be your owne Assuryddly,
Ffor all my servys and my hyer
Reward your servante lyberally.

CLXXXIII

WHAT menythe thys when I lye alone?
I tosse, I turne, I syghe, I grone,
My bedd me semys as hard as stone:
    What menys thys?

I syghe, I playne contynually;   5
The clothes that on my bedd do ly
Always methynks they lye awry:
    What menys thys?

In slumbers oft for fere I quake;
Ffor hete and cold I burne and shake;   10
Ffor lake of slepe my hede dothe ake;
    What menys thys?

A mornynges then when I do rysse
I torne vnto my wontyd gysse;
All day after muse and devysse: 15
    What menys thys?

And yff perchanse by me there passe
She vnto whome I sue for grace,
The cold blood forsakythe my face:
    What menythe thys?   20

But yff I sytte nere her by,
With lowd voyce my hart dothe cry,
And yet my mowthe ys dome and dry:
    What menys thys?

To aske ffor helpe no hart I have   25
My tong dothe fayle what I shuld crave,
Yet inwardly I Rage and Rave:
    What menys thys?

Thus have I passyd many a yere,
And many a day, tho nowght Apere;   30
But most of that that most I fere:
    What menys thys?

CLXXXIV

Ys yt possyble
That so hye debate,
So sharpe, so sore, and off suche rate

CLXXXIII.   7 methynks] methynk D.   29 a] A D.   30 a] A D.
    [*Authorship:* D concludes 'fynys q^d Wyatt S'.]

Shuld end so sone and was begone so late?
Is it possible? 5

Ys yt possyble
So cruell intent,
So hasty hete and so sone spent,
Ffrom love to hate, and thens ffor to Relent? 10
Is it possyble?

Ys yt possyble
That eny may fynde
Within on hert so dyverse mynd,
To change or torne as wether and wynd?
Is it possyble? 15

Is it possyble
To spye yt in an Iye
That tornys as oft as chance on dy?
The trothe wheroff can eny try?
Is it possyble? 20

It is possyble
Ffor to torne so oft,
To bryng that lowyste that wasse most Alofft,
And to fall hyest yet to lyght sofft:
It is possyble. 25

All ys possyble,
Who so lyst beleve;
Trust therfore fyrst, and after preve;
As men wedd ladyes by lycence and leve,
All ys possyble. 30

CLXXXV

ALAS, poor man, what hap have I
That must fforbeare that I love best
I trow yt be my desteny
Neuer to lyve in quiet Rest.

CLXXXIV. 17 Iye] yIe D.
 [*Authorship:* D concludes 'fynys q^d Wyatt'.]

No wonder ys tho I complayn,   5
Not withowt cawse ye may be sure;
I seke ffor that I cannot attayn
Whyche ys my mortall dysplesure.

Alas, pore hart, as in thys case
With pensyff playntes thow art opprest,   10
Vnwysse thow were to desyre place
Where as another ys possest.

Do what I can to ese thy smart,
Thow wylt not let to love her styll;
Hyrs and not myn I se thow art   15
Let her do by the as she wyll.

A carefull carkace full of payn
Now hast thow lefft to morne for the;
The hart ons gone the body ys slayn;
That euer I saw her, wo ys me!   20

Myn Iye, alas, was cawse of thys
Whyche her to se had neuer hys ffyll;
To me that syght full bytter ys
In Recompence of my good wyll.

She that I sarve all other above   25
Hathe payd my hyre as ye may se;
I was vnhappy and that I prove
To love aboue my poore degre.

CLXXXVI

And wylt thow leve me thus?
Say nay, say nay, ffor shame,
To save the from the Blame
Of all my greffe and grame;
And wylt thow leve me thus?   5
   Say nay, Say nay!

And wylt thow leve me thus,
That hathe lovyd the so long,
In welthe and woo Among?

I muste go walke the wodes so wyld
and wander here & there
in dred and dedly feir
for where I trust I am begylyd } and all for yo[ur] loue my dere

I am banysshed from my blys
by craft & fals pretence
fawtles wout offence
& of retorn no certenys } and all for yo[ur] loue my dere

Banysshed am I remydyles
to wyldarnes alone
alone to sighe & mone
& of relefe all recheles } and all for yo[ur] loue my dere

My house shalbe the grene wood tre
a tuft of brakys my bede
and thus my lyf I lede
as on that fro hys Ioy dothe fle } and all for yo[ur] loue my dere

The runnyng stremes shalbe my drynke
the hornes shalbe my fode
naught els shall do me good
but on yo beauty for to thynke } and all for yo[ur] loue my dere

And when the dere draw to the grene
makythe me thynke on a rowe
how I haue sene ye goo
aboue the fayrest fayrest besene } and all for yo[ur] loue my dere

But where I se in any cost
to frysk & set and play
reioysyng all the day
alas I thynke there haue I lost } and all for yo[ur] loue my dere

No byrd no busshe no bowghe I se
but bryngithe to my mynd
sumthyng wherby I fynd
my hart far wandred far from me } and all for yo[ur] loue my dere

The tune of byrdes when I do here
my hart dothe bled alas
remembryng how I was
wont for to here yo wayes so clere } and all for yo[ur] loue my d[ere]

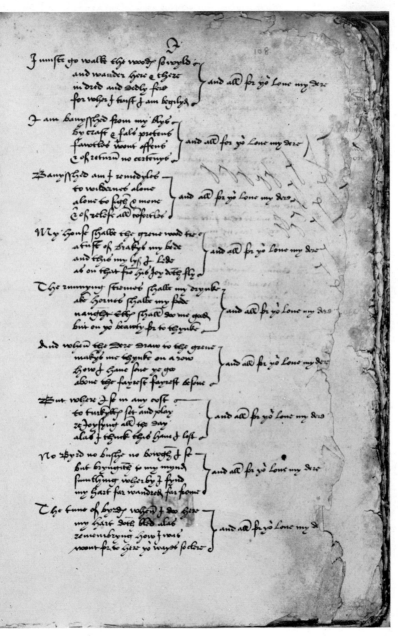

5. Blage MS
(*poem* CXLI, *page* 150)

And ys thy hart so strong   10
As for to leve me thus?
   Say nay, Say nay!

And wylt thow leve me thus,
That hathe gevyn the my hart,
Neuer for to Depart,   15
Nother for payn nor smart;
And wylt thow leve me thus?
   Say nay, Say nay!

And wylt thow leve me thus
And have nomore Pyttye   20
Of hym that lovythe the?
Helas thy cruellte!
And wylt thow leve me thus?
   Say nay, Say nay!

CLXXXVII

The restfull place, Revyver of my smarte,
The labors salve incressyng my sorow,
The body ese and trobler off my hart,
Quieter of mynd and my vnquiet foo,
Fforgetter of payn, Remembrer of my woo,   5
The place of slepe wherein I do but wake
Besprent with teres my bed I the forsake.

The frost, the snow, may not redresse my hete
Nor yet no heate abate my fervent cold.
I know nothyng to ese my paynes mete,   10
Eche cure cawsythe increse by twenty fold;
Revyvyng carys vpon my sorows old.
Suche overthwart affectes they do me make
Bysprent with terys my bed for to forsake.

CLXXXVI. [*Authorship:* D concludes 'fynys qᵈ W'.]

CLXXXVII. E (1–7), T.   1 The] O E. Revyver] reneewer E, T.   2 The] O E.   3 The] O E. and] O E.   4 Quieter] Peaser E. and my] of myne E; myne T.   5 Fforgetter] Refuge E. Remembrer of] E, T; Remembryng D.   5] Of care coomefort, where I dispayer my part E.   8 The ... snow] The frosty snowes T.   9 yet my heate] heat of sunne T.   10 mete] so great T.   11 cure] T; care D.   12 Revyvyng] Renewyng T.   13 affectes] effectes T.

P

Yet helpythe yt not I fynd no better ese   15
In bed or owt thys moste cawsythe my payn,
Where most I seke how beste that I may plese,
My lost labor, Alas, ys all in vayn;
Yet that I gave I cannot call agayn;
No place fro me my greffe away can take,   20
Wherfor with terys my bed I the forsake.

CLXXXVIII

As power and wytt wyll me Assyst
My wyll shall wyll evyn as ye lyst.

Ffor as ye lyst my wyll ys bent
In euery thyng to be content
To serve in love tyll lyff be spent   5
And to Reward my love thus ment
    Evyn as ye lyst.

To fayn or fable ys not my mynd
Nor to Refuce suche as I fynd
But as a lambe of humble kynd   10
Or byrd in cage to be Assynd
    Evyn as ye lyst.

When all the flokk ys cum and gone
Myn eye and hart agreythe in one
Hathe chosyn yow only Alone   15
To be my joy or elles my mone
    Evyn as ye lyst.

Joy yf pytty apere in place
Mone yf dysdayn do shew hys face
Yet crave I not as in thys case   20

15 Yet . . . not] But all for nought T.   17 most I] I do T.   19 My heart once set, I
can not it refrayne T.   20 fro] from T.
   [*Authorship:* Ascribed 'ffnys q^d Wyatt' in D; in W section of T.]

CLXXXVIII. Z.   1–2] *omitted* Z.   3 Ffor as ye] Evyn as you Z.   6 thus ment]
yncontynent Z.   7 ye] you Z.   10 of humble] humbull and Z.   12 ye] you Z.   13
flokk] folke Z.   14 eye] joye Z.   15] And hartly chosen you only alone Z.   17 ye]
you Z.   18 Joy yf] Yf Z. in] yu his Z.   19 Mone . . . do] Or yf dysdayn Z.   20 not
as] nothyng Z.

But as ye lede to follow the trace
    Evyn as ye lyst.

Sum in wordes muche love can fayn
And sum for wordes gyve wordes agayn;
Thus wordes for wordes in wordes Remayn,   25
And yet at last wordes do optayn
    Evyn as ye lyst.

To crave in words I wyll exchew
And love in dede I wyll ensew;
Yt ys my mynd bothe hole and trew   30
And for my trewthe I pray yow rew,
    Evyn as ye lyst.

Dere hart, I bydd you now farewell
With better hart than tong can tell;
Yet take thys tale as trew as gospell;   35
Ye may my lyff save or expell
    Evyn as ye lyst.

CLXXXIX

Sᴜᴍ tyme I syghe, sumtyme I syng,
Sumtyme I lawghe, sumtyme mornynge,
As one in dowte thys ys my ssayyng:
Have I dysplesyd yow in anythyng?

Alake, what aylythe you to be grevyd?   5
Ryght sory am I that ye be mevyd;
I am your owne yf trewthe be prevyd
And by your dyspleasure as one myschevyd.

When ye be mery, than am I glad;
When ye be sory, than am I sad;   10
Suche grace or fortune I would I had,
Yow for to plese how euer I were bestad.

---

21 lede] lyst Z. 22 ye] you Z. 23 can] doth Z. 27 ye] you Z. 30] Wythe the my hole hart faythfull and trew Z. 31 for] of Z. 32 ye] you Z. 33 you now] Z; your hart D. 34 better] as good Z. than] as Z. 35] Thys tale take trew as the gospell Z. 36] My lyfe you may both saue and spylle Z. 37 ye] you Z.

When ye be mery, why shuld I care?
Ye are my joye and my wellfare;
I wyll you love; I wyll not spare   15
Into yowre presens as farr as I dare.

All my poore hart and my love trew
Whyle lyff dothe last I gyve yt yow;
And yow to serve with servys dew,
And neuer to change yow for no new.   20

CXC

PACYENCE of all my smart,
Ffor fortune ys tornyd awry;
Pacyence must ese my hart
That mornes contynually;
Pacyence to suffer wrong   5
Ys a pacyence to long.

Pacyence to have a nay
Of that I most Desyre;
Pacyence to haue all way
And euer burne lyke fyre;   10
Pacyence withowt desart
Ys grownder of my smart.

Who can with mery hart
Set forthe sum plesant song,
That allways felys but smart   15
And neuer hathe but wrong?
Yet pacyence euermore
Must hele the wownd and sore.

Pacyence to be content
With froward fortunes trayn;   20
Pacyence to the intent
Sumwhat to slake my payn;
I see no Remedy
But suffer pacyently.

To playn wher ys none ere   25
My chawnce ys chawnsyd so

Ffor yt dothe well apere
My frend ys tornyd my foo;
But syns there ys no defence
I must take pacyence.   30

CXCI

W ho would haue euer thowght
A hart that was so sett
To have suche wrong me wrowght,
Or to be cownterfett?
But who that trustythe most   5
Ys lyke to pay the cost.

I must of force, god wott,
Thys paynfull lyff susteyen,
And yet I know nott
The chefe cawse of my payn;   10
Thys ys a strange dyssese
To serve and neuer plese.

I must of force endure
Thys drawght drawyn Awry,
Ffor I am fast and sure   15
To have the mate therby;
But note I wyll thys texte,
To draw better the nexte.

CXCII

I t was my choyse, yt was no chaunce,
That browght my hart in others holde,
Wherby ytt hath had sufferaunce
Lenger perde then Reason wold;
Syns I ytt bownd where ytt was ffree,   5
Me thynkes, ywys, of Ryght yt shold
        Acceptyd be.

Acceptyd be withowte Refuse
Vnles that fortune hath the powere
All Ryght of love for to abuse   10

CXCI.   3 wrowght] wrowgt D.   11 dyssese] dyssase D.

For, as they say, one happy howre
May more prevayle then Ryght or myght.
Yf fortune then lyst for to lowre,
    What vaylyth Right?

What vaylyth Ryght yff thys be trew?   15
Then trust to chaunce and go by gesse;
Then who so lovyth may well go sew
Vncerten hope for hys redresse.
Yett some wolde say assueredly
Thou mayst appele for thy relesse   20
    To fantasy.

To fantasy pertaynys to chose;
All thys I knowe, for fantasy
Ffurst vnto love dyd me Induse;
But yet I knowe as stedefastly   25
That yff love haue no faster knott
So nyce a choyse slyppes sodenly—
    Yt lastyth nott.

Itt lastyth not that stondes by change;
Fansy doth change, fortune ys frayle;   30
Both these to plese, the ways ys strange;
Therfore me thynkes best to prevayle,
Ther ys no way that ys so Just
As trowgh to lede, tho tother fayle,
    And therto trust.   35

CXCIII

So vnwarely was never no man cawght
With stedefast loke apon a goodly face,
As I of late; for sodenly me thowght
My hart was torne owte of hys place.

Thorow myn Iye the strock frome hyrs dyd slyde,   5
Dyrectly downe vnto my hert ytt ranne;
In helpe wherof the blood therto dyd glyde,
And left my face both pale and wanne.

CXCII. The first two stanzas appear also on f. 24.
CXCIII. T. 1 So vnwarely] Vnwarely so T. 4 hys] D, T2; hys proper T. 6 vnto]
into T. 7 glyde] T; slyde D. 8 face] T; place D.

Then was I leke a manne for woo amasyd,
Or leke the byrde that flyeth in to the fyer;　　10
For whyll that I vpon her beaulte gasyd
The more I burnt in my desyre.

Anon the blowd stert in my face agayne,
Enflamde with hete that yt had att my hart,
And browght therwith thorowt in euery vayne　　15
A quakyng hete with plesaunt smert.

Then was I leke the strawe whan that the flame
Ys drevyn therin by force and rage off wynd;
I can nott tell, alas, what I shall blame,
Nor what to seke, nor what to fynd.　　20

But wele I wote the greffe holdes me so sore
In hete and cold betwyxt hope and drede,
That but her helpe to helth doth me restore
Thys restles lyff I may nott lede.

CXCIV

THY promese was to loue me best,
And that thy hart with myn shold rest,
And nat to brek thys thy behest,
Thy promese was, thy promese was.

Thy promese was not to aquyt　　5
My ffathfulnes with such despyt,
But recompense it yff thou myght,
Thy promese was, thy promese was.

Thy promese was, I tel the pleyn,
My ffayth shold not be spent in vayne,　　10
But to haue mor shold be my gayne,
Thy promese was, thy promese was.

---

10 byrde] fowle T.　11 vpon] T; on D.　21 holdes me so] doth hold me T.　22 hope]
both hope T.　23 doth] to T.
　[*Authorship:* Ascribed 'W' in D; in W section of T.]
CXCIV.　3 behest] be hest D.　5 aquyt] a quyt D.　6 such] sech D.　7 recompense
it] recompenset D.　thou] thau D.　10 vayne] wene D.　11 hauel hawe D.

Thy promese was to haue obsarued
My ffayth lyke as yt hath deserued,
And nat casles thus to a' swarued,   15
Thy promese was, thy promese was.

Thy promese was, I dar avow,
But yt ys changyt I wot well how,
Tho then wer then and now ys now,
Thy promese was, thy promese was.   20

But sens to change thou dost delyt
And that thy ffayth hath tayn his fflyghte,
As thou desaruest I shall the quyt,
I promese the, I promese the.

CXCV

I s E the change ffrom that that was
And how thy ffayth hath tayn his fflyt
But I with pacyense let yt pase
And with my pene thys do I wryt
To show the playn by prowff off syght,   5
        I se the change.

I se the change off weryd mynd
And sleper hold hath quet my hyer;
Lo! how by prowff in the I ffynd
A bowrnyng ffath in changyng ffyer.   10
Ffarwell my part, prowff ys no lyer!
        I se the change.

I se the change off chance in loue;
Delyt no lenger may abyd;
What shold I sek ffurther to proue?   15
No, no, my trust, ffor I haue tryd
The ffolloyng of a ffallse gyd:
        I se the change.

13 haue obsarued] hawe obsarwed D.   14 deserued] deserwed D.   15 thus to a'
swarued] thys to a sward D.   17 avow] a woe D.   21 thou dost] tho doos D.   22
ffayth] ffatyth D.   his fflyghte] hes fflythe D.   23 desaruest] desarwest D.

CXCV.   2 fflyt] fflyth D.   9 by] be D.   11 Ffarwell] Ffar well.   14 abyd] a byed D.
15 proue] prowe D.   16 haue] hawe D.

I se the change, as in thys case,
Has mayd me ffre ffrom myn avoo,   20
Ffor now another has my plase,
And or I wist, I wot ner how,
Yt hapnet thys as ye here now:
       I se the change.

I se the change, seche ys my chance   25
To sarue in dowt and hope in vayn;
But sens my surty so doth glanse,
Repentens now shall quyt thy payn,
Neuer to trust the lyke agayn:
       I se the change.   30

CXCVI

H o w E shulde I
Be so plesunte
In my semblaunt
As my fellowes bee?

Not long agoo   5
It chaunsed soo
As I ded walke alone
I harde a man
That now and than
Hymselff ded thus bemone: 10

Alas (he saide)
I am betraide
And vttrelye ondone;
Whom I dede trust
And think so iuste   15
Another man hath wonne.

Mye servise due
And herte so true
On her I ded bestowe;

20 avoo] a woo D. 21 another] a novder D. 22 wist] west D. 26 sarue] sarwe D.
vayn] weyn D. 29 agayn] a gayn D.
CXCVI. D. xlliii (1), lxxvii (2). 8 a man] D1; aman D2. 10 Hymselff] D1; him-

I never ment   20
For to repente
Yn welthe nor yet in woo.

Love ded asyen
Her to be myn
And nat to love non new;   25
But who can bynd
Ther ffeckell kynd
That never wyll be tru?

The westerne winde
Hath turnid her minde
And blowen it clene awaye;   30
Therebye my welthe,
My mirth and helthe
Are dryven to grete dekaye.

Ffortune ded smyle   35
A right shorte while
And never saide me naye,
With plesaunte plaes
And joyfull dayes
My tyme to passe awaye.   40

Alas! ah las!
The tyme so was,
So never shall it be,
Sins she is gone,
And I alone   45
Armeles as ye maye see.

Where is the othe,
Where is the trothe
That she to me ded gyve?
Such fayned wordes   50
Withe silie boordes
Lett no wise man beleve.

silf D2. 23–8] D1; *omitted* D2. 25 new] nwe D1. 30 Hath] D2; has D1. her] D1;
his D2. 33 and] my D1. 34 are dryven] ys turnd Dr. 35–46] *omitted* D1. 47 othe]
trowth D1. 48 trothe] owth D1. 49 she] ye D1. 50 fayned] craffty D1. 51 silie]
wyly D1. 52 wise] young D1.

Ffor even as I
Thus wofullye
Vnto my self complaine,   55
Yf ye then truste
Nedes lerne ye muste
To sing my song in vayne:

How shulde I
Be so plesunte   60
In my semblaunt
As my fellowes be?

CXCVII

Ffull well yt maye be sene
To suche as vnderstand
How some there be that wene
They haue theyre welthe at hand
Throughe loues abusyd band;   5
But lytyll do they see
Th'abuse wherin they be.

Of loue there ys a kynd
Whyche kyndlythe by abuse,
As in a feble mynd   10
Whome fansy may enduce
By loues dysceatfull vse
To folowe the fond lust
And profe of a vayne trust.

As I my self may saye   15
By tryall of the same
No wyght can well bewraye
The falshed loue can frame;
I saye twyxt grefe and game
Ther ys no lyvyng man   20
That knows the crafte loue can.

53–8] *omitted* D1.   59–62] D1; how shulde I &c D2.
CXCVII.   5 Throughe] Thruhe D.   7 Th'abuse] Thabuse D.

Ffor loue so well can fayne
To favour for the whyle
That suche as sekes the gayne
Ar servyd with the gyle;   25
And some can thys concyle
To gyue the symple leave
Them sellffes for to dysceave.

What thyng may more declare
Of loue the craftye kynd?   30
Then se the wyse, so ware,
In loue to be so blynd,
Yf so yt be assynd
Let them enjoye the gayn,
That thynkes yt worthe the payn.   35

CXCVIII

SYNES loue ys suche that, as ye wott,
Cannot allways be wysely vsyd,
I say therfore then blame me nott,
Tho I therin haue ben abusyd;
Ffor as with cause I am accusyd.   5
Gyllty I graunt, suche was my lott;
And tho yt cannot be excusyd,
Yet let suche folye be forgott.

Ffor in my yeres of Rekles youthe
Me thought the power of loue so gret   10
That to her lawes I bound my treuthe
And to my wyll there was no lett.
Me lyst nomore so farr to fett
Suche frute, lo, as of loue ensewthe;
The gayn was small that was to gett,   15
And of the losse the lesse the reuthe.

And few there ys but fyrst or last
A tyme in loue ones shall they haue
And glad I am my tyme ys past,
Henceforthe my fredome to withsaue.   20

CXCVIII.   10, 13 Me] my D.

Now in my hart there shall I grave
The groundyd grace that now I tast;
Thankyd be fortune that me gave
So fayre a gyfft, so sure and fast.

Now suche as haue me sene or thys,   25
Whan youthe in me sett forthe hys kynd,
And foly framd my thought amys,
The faute wherof now well I ffynd,
Loo, syns that so yt ys assynd
That vnto eche a tyme there ys,   30
Then blame the lott that led my mynd
Sometyme to lyue in loves blys.

But frome henceforth I do protest
By proffe of that that I haue past
Shall neuer ceace within my brest   35
The power of loue so late owt cast;
The knott therof ys knytt ffull fast,
And I therto so sure proffest,
Ffor euermore with me to last
The power wherin I am possest.   40

CXCIX

Lo! how I seke and sew to haue
That no man hathe and maye be had.
There ys no more but synk or saue,
And bryng thys doute to good or bad.
To lyue in sorows allways sad,   5
I lyke not so to lynger fforthe;
Hap evyll or good I shall be glad
To take that comes as well in worthe.

Shold I sustayne thys gret dystres,
Styll wandryng forthe thus to and froo,   10
In dredfull hope to hold my pese,
And fede my sellff with secret woo?
Nay, nay, certayne I wyll not soo,
But sure I shall my self aply

CXCIX.   3 no more] O; more D.

To put in profe thys doute to knoo   15
And Rydd thys daunger Redely.

I shall assay by secret sute
To show the mynd of myn entent
And my desertes shall gyue suche frute
As with my hart my wordes be ment.   20
So by the profe of thys consent
Sone owt of doute I shall be sure;
For to rejoyce or to Repent
In joye or payne for to endure

CC

My loue ys lyke vnto th'eternall fyre,
And I as those whyche therin do remayne
Whose grevous paynes ys but theyre gret desyre
To se the syght whyche they may not attayne.
So in helles heate my self I fele to be,   5
That am restraynd by gret extremyte
The syght of her whyche ys so dere to me.
O puissant loue and power of gret avayle,
By whome hell may be fellt or dethe assayle!

CCI

Synes so ye please to here me playn,
And that ye do reioyce my smart,
My lyst no lenger to Remayne
To suche as be so overthwart.
But cursyd be that cruell hart   5
Whyche hathe procuryd a careles mynd
Ffor me and myne vnfaynyd smart,
And forcythe me suche fautes to fynd.
More than to muche I am assuryd
Of thyne entent wherto to trust: 10
A spedles proffe I haue enduryd,
And now I leve yt to them that lust.

CC.   1 th'eternall] theternall D.

CCII

Now must I lerne to lyue at rest
And weyne me of my wyll,
Ffor I repent where I was prest
My fansy to ffullfyll.

I may no lenger more endure   5
My wontyd lyf to lede,
But I must lerne to put in vre
The change of womanhede.

I may not se my seruys long
Rewardyd in suche wyse,   10
Nor I may not sustayne suche wrong
That ye my loue dyspyce.

I may not syghe in sorows depe,
Nor wayle the wante of loue
Nor I may nother cruche nor crepe,   15
Where hyt dothe not behoue.

But I of force must nedes forsake
My faythe so fondly sett
And frome henceforthe must vndertake
Suche foly to fforgett.   20

Now must I seke some otherways
My self for to withsaue,
And as I trust by myne assays
Some Remedy to haue.

I aske none other Remedy   25
To recompence my wrong,
But ones to haue the lyberty
That I haue lakt so long.

CCIII

Fforget not yet the tryde entent
Of suche a truthe as I haue ment,
My gret travayle so gladly spent
          Fforget not yet.

Fforget not yet when fyrst began　　　　5
The wery lyffe ye know syns whan,
The sute, the seruys none tell can,
　　　Fforgett not yet.

Fforget not yet the gret assays,
The cruell wrong, the skornfull ways,　　　10
The paynfull pacyence in denays,
　　　Fforgett not yet.

Fforget not yet, forget not thys,
How long ago hathe bene and ys
The mynd that neuer ment amys,　　　　15
　　　Fforget not yet.

Fforget not then thyn owne aprovyd
The whyche so long hathe the so louyd,
Whose stedfast faythe yet neuer movyd,
　　　Fforget not thys.　　　　20

CCIV

O MYSERABLE sorow withowten cure!
Yf it plese the, lo, to haue me thus suffir,
At lest yet let her know what I endure,
And this my last voyse cary thou thether
Wher lyved my hope now ded for euer;　　　5
For as ill grevus is my banyshement
As was my plesur when she was present.

CCV

BLAME not my lute, for he must sownd
Of thes or that as liketh me;
For lake of wytt the lutte is bownd
To gyve suche tunes as plesithe me;
Tho my songes be sume what strange　　　5
And spekes such words as toche they change,
　　　Blame not my lutte.

CCV. 5 sume] sune D.

fforget not yet the tryde entent
of such a truthe as I have ment
my gret travayle so gladly spent
    fforget not yet

fforget not yet when furst began
the wery lyffe ye know syns when
the sute the servis none tell can
    fforgett not yett

fforget not yet the gret assays
the cruell wrong the skornefull wayes
the paynefull pacyence in denays
    fforgett not yet

fforget not yet forget not thys
howe long ago hathe ben & ys
the mynd that never ment amys
    fforget not yet

fforget not then thyn owne aprovyd
the wyche so long hathe the so lovyd
whose stedfast faythe yet never movyd
    fforget not thys

6. Devonshire MS
(*poem* CCIII, *pages* 211–12)

My lutte, alas, doth not ofend
Tho that perfors he must agre
To sownd such teunes as I entend   10
To sing to them that hereth me;
Then tho my songes be some what plain,
And tocheth some that vse to fayn,
    Blame not my lutte.

My lute and strynges may not deny   15
But as I strike they must obay;
Brake not them than soo wrongfully,
But wryeke thy selffe some wyser way;
And tho the songes whiche I endight
To qwytt thy chainge with Rightfull spight,   20
    Blame not my lute.

Spyght askyth spight and changing change,
And falsyd faith must nedes be knowne,
The faute so grett, the case so strange,
Of Right it must abrod be blown: 25
Then sins that by thyn own desartte
My soinges do tell how trew thou artt,
    Blame not my lute.

Blame but thy selffe that hast mysdown
And well desaruid to haue blame;   30
Change thou thy way so evyll bygown
And then my lute shall sownd that same;
But if tyll then my fyngeres play
By thy desartt their wontyd way,
    Blame not my lutte.   35

Farewell, vnknowne, for tho thow brake
My strynges in spight with grett desdayn
Yet haue I fownd owt for thy sake
Stringes for to strynge my lute agayne;
And yf perchance this folysh Rymyme   40
Do make the blush at any tyme
    Blame nott my lutte.

---

9 perfors] perforus D. 11 hereth] herth D. 22 change] changes D. 23 nedes]
indes D. 29 thy] the D. 33 if] ef D. 39 agayne] a gayne D. 40 folysh] folys D.
  [*Authorship:* 'W' at foot of third stanza.]
  Q

CCVI

ALL yn thi sight my lif doth hole depende,
Thou hidist thyself and I must dye therefore;
But sins thou maiste so easelye saue thy frende
Whye doste thou styk to heale that thou madist sore?
Whye doo I dye sins thou maist me diffende?   5
For if I dye then maiste thou lyve no more,
Sins ton bye tother dothe lyve and fede thy herte,
I with thye sight, thou also with my smerte.

CCVII

THE fructe of all the seruise that I serue
Dispaire doth repe, such haples hap have I;
But tho he hath no powre to make me swarve
Yet bye the fire for colde I fele I dye;
In paradis for hunger still I sterve   5
And in the flowde for thurste to deth I drye;
So Tantalus ame I and yn worse payne
Amydes my helpe, and helples doth remayne.

CCVIII

YF with complaint the paine might be exprest
That inwardelye dothe cause me sigh and grone,
Your harde herte and your cruell brest
Shulde sighe and playne for my vnreste;
And tho yt ware of stone   5
Yet shulde Remorse cause yt relent and mone.

But sins yt ys so farre out of mesure
That with my wordes I can yt not contayne,
My ouerlye truste, my hertes tresure,
Alas, whye doo I still indure   10
This restles smerte and payne,
Sins yf ye list ye maye my woo restraine?

CCVI. T.   1 sight] loke T.   3 saue] helpe T.   4 heale] salue T.   6 For] And T.
then . . . lyue] thy life may last T.   7] For ech by other doth liue and haue reliefe T.
8] I in thy loke, and thou most in my griefe T. thou] then D.
     [*Authorship:* In W section of T.]
CCVII.   6 in] In D.

CCIX

S I N S you will nedes that I shall sing,
Take yt in worth siche as I have,
Plentye of plaint, mone and morning,
Yn depe dispaire and dedlye payne,
Boteles for bote, crying to crave,   5
     To crave yn vayne.

Such hammers worke within my hed
That sounde nought els vnto my eris
But faste at borde and wake abed:
Suche tune the tempre to my song   10
To waile my wrong, that I wante teris
     To waile my wrong.

Dethe and dispaire afore my face,
My dayes dekaes, my grefe doth gro;
The cause thereof is in this place,   15
Whom crueltye dothe still constraine
For to reioise, tho yt be wo
     To here me plaine.

A brokin lute, vntunid stringes
With such a song maye well bere parte,   20
That nether pleasith him that singes
Nor theim that here, but her alone
That with her herte wold straine my herte
     To here yt grone.

Yf it greve you to here this same   25
That you do fele but in my voyse,
Considre then what plesaunt game
I do sustaine in everye parte
To cause me sing or to reioyse
     Within my herte.   30

CCX

    M E list no more to sing
    Of love nor of suche thing,

CCIX.   1 you] yon D (*also* in 25, 26).   4 dedlye] delye D.

Howe sore that yt me wring;
For what I song or spake
Men dede my songis mistake.   5

My songes ware to defuse,
Theye made folke to muse;
Therefore, me to excuse,
Theye shall be song more plaine,
Nother of joye nor payne.   10

What vailith then to skippe
At fructe over the lippe?
For frute withouten taste
Dothe noght but rott and waste.

What vailith vndre kaye   15
To kepe treasure alwaye.
That never shall se daye?
Yf yt be not vsid
Yt ys but abusid.

What vayleth the flowre   20
To stond still and wither?
Yf no man yt savour
Yt servis onlye for sight
And fadith towardes night.

Therefore fere not t'assaye   25
To gadre ye that maye
The flower that this daye
Is fresher than the next:
Marke well, I saye, this text.

Let not the frute be lost   30
That is desired moste;
Delight shall quite the coste.
Yf hit be tane in tyme,
Small labour is to clyme.

And as for siche treasure   35
That makithe the the Richer,

CCX.   10 Nother] Nothr D.   21 wither] whither D.   25 t'assaye] tassaye D.

And no dele the poorer,
When it is gyven or lente
Me thinckes yt ware well spente.

Yf this be undre miste,   40
And not well playnlye wyste,
Vndrestonde me who lyste;
For I reke not a bene,
I wott what I doo meane.

CCXI

To Rayle or geste ye kno I vse it not
   Though that such cause some tyme in folkes I finde:
   And tho to chaung ye list to sett your minde,
   Love yt who liste, in faithe I like yt not.
And if ye ware to me as ye are not,   5
   I wolde be lothe to se you so unkinde;
   But sins your faithe muste nedes be so be kinde,
   Tho I hate yt, I praye you leve yt not.
Thinges of grete waight I neuer thought to crave:
   This is but small – of right denye yt not.   10
   Your fayning wayis as yet forget them not,
But like rewarde let other lovers have:
   That is to saye, for seruis true and faste,
   To long delaies and changing at the laste.

CCXII

THE Joye so short, alas, the paine so nere,
The waye so long, the departure so smarte,
The furst sight, alas, I bought to dere,
That so sodainelye now from hens must parte;
The bodye gone, yet remaine shall the herte   5
With her, wiche for me salte teris ded Raine,
And shall not chaunge till that we mete againe.

Tho tyme doth passe, yet shall not my love;
Tho I be farre, always my hert is nere;
Tho other chaunge, yet will not I remove;   10

CCXI.   14 delaies] delaees D.

Tho other care not, yet love I will and fere;
Tho other hate, yet will I love my dere;
Tho other woll of lightnes saye adewe,
Yet woll I be founde stedefast and trewe.

When other laughe, alas, then do I wepe;   15
When other sing, then do I waile and crye;
When other runne, perforcyd I am to crepe;
When other daunce, in sorro I do lye;
When other Joye, for paine welnere I dye;
Thus brought from welthe, alas, to endles paine,   20
That undeseruid, causeles to remayne.

CCXIII

PAYNE of all payne, the most grevous paine
Ys to loue hartelye and cannot be loued againe.

Love with vnkindenesse is causer of hevenis,
Of inwarde sorro and sighis painefull.
Whereas I love is no redresse   5
To no manner of pastime, the sprites so dull
With prive morninges and lookes Rufull:
The boddye all werishe, the collor pale and wan,
More like a gost then lyk a lyving man.

Whan Cupido hath inflamid the hertes desires   10
To love there as ys disdayne,
Of good or ill the minde obliuyous,
Nothing regarding but love t'attaine;
Alwais imagining by what meane or traine
Yt may be at rest; thus in a momente   15
Now here, now there, being never contente.

Tossing and torning, whan the body wold rest
With dreamis opprest and visions fantastycall,
Sleping or waking love is ever preste,
Some tyme to wepe, some tyme to crye and call,   20
Bewayling his fortune and lif bestiall;
Nowe in hope of recure and now in dispaire,
This ys a sorye lyf to lyve alwaye in care!

CCXII.   20 to endles] tendles D.

Recorde of Therence in his commedis poeticall
Yn love ys Jelosye and iniuris mannye one   25
Angre and debate with mynde sensuall
Nowe warre, nowe peace, musing all alone,
Some tyme all morte and colde as enye stonne
This causith unkindenesse of siche as cannot skill
Of trewe love assurde with herte and good will.   30

Lucrese the Romaine for love of her lord
And bye cause perforce she had commit advowtrye
With Tarquinus, as the storye doth recorde
Her silf ded slee with a knif most pituoslye
Among her nigh frindes bye cause that she   35
So falslye was betrayed, lo this was the guardon,
Where as true love hathe no domynyon.

To make rehersall of old antiqitye
What nedith it ? We see by experience
Among lovers yt chaunsith daylye   40
Displeasour and variaunce for none offens;
But if true love might gyve sentens
That vnkindenes and disdayne shuld have no place
But true harte for true love yt ware a grete grace.

O Venus, ladye, of love the goddesse   45
Help all true lovers to have love againe!
Bannishe from thye presens disdayne and vnkindnesse,
Kyndnesse and pytie to thy seruice Retayne;
For true love, ons fixid in the cordiall vayne,
Can never be revoulsid bye no manner of arte,   50
Vnto the sowle from the boddye departe.

CCXIV

LAMENT my losse, my labor, and my payne,
All ye that here mye wofull playnte and crye,
Yf ever man might ons your herte constrayne
To pytie wordes of right, yt shulde bee I;
That sins the time that youthe yn me ded rayne   5
My plesaunte yeris to bondage ded aplye,

CCXIII.   31 her] F; our D.

Whiche as yt was I pourpose to declare,
Wherebye my frindes hereafter maye be ware.

And if perchaunce some redres list to muse
What menith me so playnlye for to wright   10
My good entente the fawte of yt shall skuse,
Whiche meane nothing but trulye t'endyght
The crafte and care, the greef and long abuse
Of lovers lawe and eke her puisshaunte might,
Wiche though that menn oft tymes bye paynis doth
        kno,   15
Lyttle theye wot wiche wayes the gylis doth growe.

Yet well ye know yt will renue my smarte
Thus to reherse the paynes that I have past;
My hand doth shake, my penn skant dothe his parte,
My boddye quakes, my wyttis begynne to waste;   20
Twixt heate and colde in fere I fele my herte
Panting for paine, and thus as all agaste
I do remayne skant wotting what I wryte:
Perdon me then rudelye tho I indyte.

And patientelye, o Redre, I the praye   25
Take in good parte this worke as yt ys mente,
And greve the not with ought that I shall saye,
Sins with good will this boke abrode ys sent
To tell men how in youthe I ded assaye
What love ded mene and nowe I yt repente: 30
That musing me my frindes might well be ware,
And kepe them fre from all soche payne and care.

CCXV

WHAT shulde I saye   *a*
Sins faithe is dede   *b*
And truthe awaye   *a*
From you ys fled?   *b*
Shulde I be led   *b*   5
With doblenesse? *double ness*
Naye, naye, mistresse!   *c*

CCXIV.   9 redres] redrs D.   17 renue] renwe D.   23 wryte] wrytt D.   25 Redre]
Rerdre D.   31 musing] Chambers *conj.*; moving D.

I promisid you
And you promisid me
To be as true 10
As I wolde bee,
But sins I se
Your doble herte
Farewell, my perte.

Though for to take 15
Yt ys not my minde
But to forsake
One so unkind
And as I finde
So will I truste. 20
Farewell, uniuste!

Can ye saye naye?
But you saide
That I allwaye
Shulde be obeide; 25
And thus betraide
Or that I wiste,—
Fare well, unkiste!

CCXVI

GYVE place all ye that doth reioise
And loves panges dothe clene forgett;
Let them drawe nere and here my voyse
Whom love dothe force in paynes to frett.
For all of playnte my song is sett 5
Wiche long hathe seruid and nought can gett.

A faithefull herte so trulye mente
Rewardid is full slenderelye,
A stedfaste faithe with good entente
Ys recompensid craftelye 10
Such happe dothe happe vnhappelye
To them that mene but honestelye.

CCXV. 18] *conj.* O; *omitted* D.
CCXVI. 2 dothe] hathe D.

With humble sute I have assayde
To tourne her cruell-hertid minde
But for rewarde I am delaide   15
And to mye welthe her eyes be blinde
Lo thus bye chaunse I am assignid
With stedfaste love to serue the vnkinde.

What vaylithe trothe or stedfastness
Or still to serue without repreffe?   20
What vaylith faithe or gentilnesse,
Where crueltie dothe raine as chefe?
Alas there is no greter greef
Then for to love and lake releffe.

Care dothe constraine me to complaine   25
Of love and her vncertaintye,
Wich grauntith nought but grete disdayne
For losse of all my libretye;
Alas, this is extremytye,
For love to finde suche crueltye!   30

For hertye love to finde suche hate,
Alas, it is a carefull lott
And for to voide so fowle a mate
There is no waye but slipp the knott;
The gayne so colde, the paine so hott   35
Prayse yt who list, I like yt not.

CCXVII

D Y V E R S dothe vse as I have hard and kno,
  Whan that to chaunge ther ladies do beginne
  To mourne and waile and neuer for to lynne
  Hoping therbye to pease ther painefull woe.
And some therbe that whan it chansith soo   5
    That women change and hate where love hath bene,
    Thei call them fals and think with woordes to wynne
    The hartes of them wich otherwhere dothe gro.

14 cruell-hertid] cruell hertid D. 16 her] here D. eyes] eris D. 31 hate] crueltye D.
33 mate] mote D.
CCXVII.   2 ladies] lades D.

But as for me though that by chaunse indede
 Change hath outworne the favour that I had,   10
 I will not wayle, lament, nor yet be sad,
Nor call her fals that falsley ded me fede,
 But let it passe and think it is of kinde
 That often chaunge doth plese a womans minde.

CCXVIII

 T HE losse is small to lese such one
 That shrynckith for a slendr naye;
 And wyt thei lak that wolde mak mone
 Tho all suche peakes ware wipid awaye.

CCXIX

 SPIGHT hath no powre to make me sadde,
 Nor scornefulnesse to make me playne
 Yt doth suffise that ons I had,
 And so to leve yt is no payne.

 Let theim frowne on that leste doth gaine   5
 Who ded reioise must nedes be gladd
 And tho with wordis thou wenist to rayne,
 Yt doth suffise that ons I had.

 Sins that in chekes thus overthwarte
 And coylye lookis thou doste delight,   10
 Yt doth suffise that myne thou wart;
 Tho change hathe put thye faith to flight.

 Alas it is a pevishe spight
 To yelde thi silf and then to parte;
 But sins thou settst thie faithe so light,   15
 Yt doth suffise that myne thou warte.

 And sins thy love dothe thus declyne
 And in thye herte suche hate dothe grow
 Yt dothe suffise that thou warte myne
 And with good will I quite yt soo.   20

CCXIX. 2 scornefulnesse] scorenefulnesse D. 6 must] most D. 9 overthwarte]
overthawrte D. 15 settst] M; seiste D.

Some tyme my frinde, fare well my fooe
Sins thou change I am not thyne,
But for relef of all my woo
Yt doth suffise that thou warte myne.

Prayeng you all that heris this song   25
To iudge no wight, nor none to blame;
Yt dothe suffise she dothe me wrong,
And that herself doth kno the same.

And tho she change, it is no shame;
Theire kinde it is, and hath bene long;   30
Yet I proteste she hathe no name:
Yt dothe suffise she dothe me wrong.

CCXX

GRUDGE on who list, this ys my lott,
No thing to want if it ware not.
My yeris be yong even as ye see;
All thinges thereto doth well agre;
Yn feithe, in face, in eche degre,   5
No thing doth want as semith me,
          If yt ware not.

Some men dothe saye that frindes be skace,
But I have founde as in this cace
A frinde wiche gyvith to no man place   10
But makis me happiest that euer was,
          Yf yt ware not.

Groudge on who list, this is my lot,
No thing to want if yt ware not.
A hart I have besides all this   15
That hathe my herte and I have his;
If he dothe well yt is my blis
And when we mete no lak there is,
          Yf yt ware not.

29 change] chang D.
CCXX. 12, 19, 24, 31 yt ware not] & D.

Yf he can finde that can me please   20
A thinckes he dois his owne hertes ease,
And likewise I coulde well apease
The chefest cause of his misease
        Yf yt ware not.

Groudge on who list, this is my lot,   25
No thing to want if yt ware not.
A master eke god hath me sente
To whom my will is hollye bente
To serue and love for that intente
That bothe we might be well contente,   30
        Yf yt ware not.

And here an ende that dothe suffise
To speke few wordes among the wise;
Yet take this note before your eyes,
My mirthe shulde doble ons or twise,   35
        Yf yt were not.

Groudge on who liste, this my lot
No thing to want if it ware not.

CCXXI

FFORTUNE dothe frowne:
What remedye?
I am downe
Bye destenye.

CCXXII

GRETING to you bothe yn hertye wyse
As vnknowen I sende, and this mye entente
As I do here, you to aduertyse,
Lest that perchaunce your deades you do repente.
The unknowen man dredes not to be shente,   5
But sayes as he thinckes: so fares yt bye me
That nother ffere nor hope in no degree.

25–6, 37–8 this . . . not] & D.   28 whom] hom D.
CCXXI.   3 downe] done D.

The bodye and the sowle to holde togiddre,
Yt is but right and resone woll the same,
And ffryndelie the one to love the other   10
Yt incresith your brute and also your fame.
But marke well my wordes, for I fere no blame:
Truste well your selves but ware ye trust no mo,
For such as ye think your frinde maye fortune be your ffoe.

Beware hardelye ere ye have enye nede,   15
And to frindes reconsilide trust not greatelye;
Ffor theye that ons with hasty spede
Exilid them selves out of your companye,
Though theye torne againe and speke swetlye,
Fayning them selves to be your frindes faste,   20
Beware of them for theye will disseyeve you at laste.

Fayre wordes makis ffoolys fayne,
And bering in hande causith moche woo,
For tyme tryeth trothe, therefore refrayne:
And from suche as be redye to doo –   25
None doo I name but this I kno,
That bye this faute cause causith moche,
Therefore beware if ye do kno anye suche.

'To wise folkes fewe wordes' is an old sayeng;
Therefore at this tyme I will write nomore,   30
But this short lesson take fore a warninge:
Bye soche light frindes sett littill store;
Yf ye do othere wise ye will repent yt sore.
And thus of this lettre making an ende,
To the boddye and the sowle I me commend.   35

Wryting lyfles at the manner place
Of him that hathe no chave nore no were dothe dwell,
But wandering in the wilde worlde, wanting that he hase,
And nother hopis nor ffearis heven nor hell;
But lyvith at adventure, ye kno him full well,   40
The twentie daye of marche he wrote yt yn his house,
And hathe him recommendyd to the kat and the mowse.

CCXXII.   8 togiddre] to giddre D.   15 ere] are D.   22 wordes] woodes D.   36
Wryting] Wrytin D.

CCXXIII

MYE love toke skorne my servise to retaine
 Wherein me thought she vsid crueltie:
 Sins with good will I lost my libretye
 To follow her wiche causith all my payne.
Might never care cause me for to refrayne   5
 But onlye this wiche is extremytie,
 Gyving me nought, alas, not to agree
 That as I was, her man I might remayne.
But sins that thus ye list to ordre me
 That wolde have bene your seruaunte true and faste, 10
 Displese the not, my doting dayes bee paste,
And with my losse to leve I must agre;
 For as there is a certeyne tyme to rage,
 So ys there tyme suche madnes to asswage.

CCXXIV

 TANGLID I was yn loves snare,
 Opprest with payne, tormente with care,
 Of grefe right sure, of Joye full bare,
 Clene in dispaire bye crueltye;
 But ha, ha, ha, full well is me,   5
 For I am now at libretye.

 The wofull dayes so full of paine,
 The werye night all spent in vayne,
 The labor lost for so small gayne,
 To wryt them all yt will not bee;   10
 But ha, ha, ha, full well is me,
 For I am now at libretye.

 Everye thing that faire doth sho,
 When prof is made yt provithe not soo,
 But tournith mirthe to bittre woo,   15

CCXXIII. T. 1 toke] to T. 2 Wherein] Therin T. she] you T. 4] *omitted* T. her] here D. 5 care . . . for] wo yet cause me T. 7 Gyving] To geue T. not] nor T. 8 her] your T. 11 the] you T. dayes be] time is T. 14 to asswage] T; tasswage D.
 [*Authorship:* In W section of T.]
CCXXIV. 8 werye] verye D.

Wiche in this case full well I see;
But ha, ha, ha, full well is me,
For I am now at libretye.

To grete desire was my guide,
And wanton will went bye my syde;   20
Hope rulid still and made me byde
Of loves craft th'extremitye.
But ha, ha, ha, full well is me,
For I am now at libretye.

With faynid wordes wich ware but winde   25
To long delayes I was assind;
Her wylye lokes my wyttes ded blinde;
Thus as she wolde I ded agree.
But ha, ha, ha, full well is me,
For I am now at libretye.   30

Was never birde tanglid yn lyme,
That brake awaye yn bettre tyme,
Then I that rotten bowes ded clyme,
And had no hurte, but scaped fre.
Now ha, ha, ha, full well is me,   35
For I am nowe at libretye.

CCXXV

LENGRE to muse
On this refuse
I will not vse,
But studye to forget;
Letting all goo,   5
Sins well I kno
To be my foo
Her herte is fermelye sett.

Sins my entent
So trulye mente   10
Cannot contente
Her minde as I doo see,

To tell you playne
Yt ware yn vayne
For so small gaine   15
To lese my libretie.

For if he thryve
That will goo stryve
A shippe to dryve
Againste the streme and winde,   20
Vndoutedlye
Then thryve shuld I
To love trulye
A cruell-hertid mynde.

But sithe that so   25
The worlde dothe goo
That everye woo
Bye yelding doth incresse,
As I have tolde
I wilbe bolde   30
Therebye my paynis to cese.

Prayeng you all
That after shall
Bye fortune fall
Ynto this folishe trade,   35
Have yn your minde,
As I do finde,
That oft be kinde
All womens love do fade.

Wherefore apace,   40
Come, take my place,
Some man that hase
A lust to berne the fete;
For sins that she
Refusith me,   45
I must agre
And studye to forgett.

CCXXV.   36 Have] O; Howe D.
R

CCXXVI

Now all of chaunge
Must be my songe
And from mye bonde nowe must I breke,
Sins she so strange
Vnto my wrong   5
Doth stopp her eris to here me speke.

Yet none doth kno
So well as she
My greefe wiche can have no restrainte;
That faine wolde follo   10
Nowe nedes must fle
For faute of ere vnto my playnte.

I am not he
Bye fals assayes
Nor faynid faith can bere in hande,   15
Tho most I see
That such alwaies
Are best for to be vndrestonde.

But I that truth
Hath alwaies ment   20
Dothe still procede to serue in vayne;
Desire pursuithe
My tyme mispent,
And doth not passe vppon my payne.

O fortunes might   25
That eche compellis,
And me the most yt dothe suffise,
Now for my right
To aske nought ells
But to withdrawe this entreprise.   30

And for the gaine
Of that good howre,
Wiche of my woo shalbe relefe,

CCXXVI. A.   3 bonde] bownd A.   6 to] A; to to D.   11 nedes] *omitted* A.   13–24] *omitted* A.   31 for the] so for A.

I shall refrayne
Bye paynefull powre   35
The thing that most hathe bene my grefe.

I shall not misse
To exersyse
The helpe therof wich doth me teche,
That after this   40
In any wise
To kepe right within my reche.

And she vniuste
Wich ferithe not,
Yn this her fame to be defilyd,   45
Yett ons I truste
Shalbe my lott,
To quite the crafte that me begild.

CCXXVII

I ABIDE and abide and better abide,
    And after the olde prouerbe the happie daye;
    And ever my ladye to me dothe saye
    'Let me alone and I will prouyde'.
I abide and abide and tarrye the tyde   5
    And with abiding spede well ye maye;
    Thus do I abide I wott allwaye,
    Nother obtayning nor yet denied.
Aye me! this long abidyng
    Semithe to me as who sayethe   10
    A prolonging of a dieng dethe
Or a refusing of a desyrid thing:
    Moche ware it bettre for to be playne,
    Then to saye abide and yet shall not obtayne.

CCXXVIII

ABSENS absenting causithe me to complaine;
    My sorofull complayntes abiding in distresse
And departing most pryvie increasithe my paine;
    Thus lyve I vncomfortid, wrappid all in hevines.

37-42] *omitted* A.   43 vniuste] A; oniuste D.   44 Wich] that A.

In hevenes I am wrapid, devoyde of all solace,   5
    Nother pastyme nor plesure can revyve my dull wytt;
My sprites be all taken, and dethe dothe me manace,
    With his fatall knif the thrid for to kitt.

Ffor to kit the thrid of this wretchid lif
    And shortelye bring me owt of this cace;   10
I se yt avaylith not, yet must I be pensif,
    Sins fortune from me hathe turnid her face.

Her face she hathe turnid with cowntenance contrarious,
    And clene from her presens she hathe exilid me,
Yn sorrowe remayning as a man most dolorous,   15
    Exempte from all pleasure and worldelye felicitie.

All worldely felicitye nowe am I pryvate,
    And left in deserte moste solitarilye,
Wandring all about, as one withowt mate:
    My dethe aprochithe – what remedye?   20

What remedye, alas, to reioise my wofull herte,
    With sighis suspiring most rufullie?
Nowe wellcome! I am redye to deperte.
Fare well all plesure, welcome paine and smerte!

CCXXIX

    PATIENS, for I have wrong
    And dare not shew whereyn;
    Patiens shalbe, my song,
    Sins truthe can no thing wynne;
    Patiens then for this fytt,   5
    Hereafter comis not yett.

CCXXX

    WHAN that I call vnto my mynde
    The tyme of hope that ons I hade,
    The grete abuse that ded me blinde
    Dothe force me allwaies to be sad;

CCXXVIII.   16 worldelye] wordelie D.

Yet of my greef I fayne me glad 5
But am assurid I was to bolde
To truste to such a slipper holde.

I thought yt well that I had wrought
Willing forthewith so to ensue,
But he that sekis as I have sought 10
Shall finde most trust oft tymes vntrue;
For lest I reckte that most I rue,
Of that I thought my silf most sure
Ys nowe the wante of all mye cure.

Amiddes my welthe I dede not reke 15
But sone alas or that I wiste
The tyme was come that all to weake
I had no powre for to resiste.
Nowe am I prof to theim that liste
To flee such woo and wrongfull paine 20
As in my herte I doo sustayne.

Ffor faynid faithe is alwaies free
And dothe inclyne to bee oniuste,
That sure I thinck there can none bee
To muche assurid without mistruste, 25
But happe what maye, to theim that muste
Sustaine suche cruell destenye
Wythe paitens for remedye.

As I am on wich bye restrainte
Abides the tyme of my retourne 30
Yn hope that fortune by my playnte
Wyll slake the fire wherewith I bourne
Sins no waies els may serue my tourne
Yet for the dowt of this distresse
I aske but right for my redresse. 35

CCXXXI

To make an ende of all this strif,
    No lenger tyme for to sustaine,
But now withe dethe to chaung the lif

CCXXX.   6 am] on D.   32 bourne] boururne D.

Of him that lyves alwaies in payne;
Dispaire suche powre hathe yn his hande,   5
That helpith most I kno certeyne
Maye not withstonde.

May not withstande that is electe
Bye fortunis most extremytie;
But all in worthe to be excepte   10
Withouten lawe or libretye;
What vaylithe then vnto my thought?
Yf right can have no remedie,
There vaylith nought.

There vaylithe nought, but all in vaine;   15
The fawte thereof maye none amende,
But onlie dethe, for to constraine
This spightfull happe to have an ende:
So grete disdaine dothe me provoke
That drede of deth cannot deffende   20
This dedelye stroke.

This dedelie stroke, wherebye shall seace
The harborid sighis within my herte,
And for the gifte of this relese
My hand in haste shall playe his parte,   25
To doo this cure againste his kinde,
For chaunge of lif from long deserte
To place assignid.

To place assignid for ever more,
Nowe bye constrainte I do agre   30
To loose the bonde of my restore,
Wherein is bounde my liberte;
Dethe and dispaire doth vndretake
From all mishappe now hardelye
This ende to make.   35

CCXXXII

Wyll ye se what wonders love hathe wrought?
Then come and loke at me;

CCXXXII. 1 wonders] O; wonderous D.

There nede no where els to be sought,
Yn me ye maye theim see.

Ffor vnto that that men maye see   5
Most monstruous thing of kinde
My self maye beste compared bee:
Love hathe me soo assignid.

There is a Rok in the salte floode,
A Rok of suche nature   10
That drawithe the yron from the woode
And levithe the shippe vnsure.

She is the Rok, the shippe ame I.
That Rok my dedelie ffoo,
That drawithe me there, where I muste die   15
And Robbithe my harte me ffroo.

A burde there fliethe and that but one,
Of her this thing enswethe,
That when her dayes be spent and gone,
Withe fyre she renewithe.   20

And I withe her may well compare
My love that is alone
The flame whereof doth aye repare
My lif when yt is gone.

CCXXXIII

DEME as ye list vpon goode cause
    I maye and think of this or that,
But what or whye my self best knowes,
    Wherebye I thinck and fere not;
But there vnto I maye well link   5
    The doubtefull sentence of this clause:
I wolde yt ware not as I think,
    I wolde I thought yt ware not.

---

5 see] ssee D. 7 compared] comparad D. 10 Rok]Rook D. 21 her] here D; fire F.
CCXXXIII. GG. 2 I] yee GG. 5 But there vnto] Wher vnto GG. link] Rollins
conj.: think D; like GG. 8 not] not so GG.

Ffor if I thought yt ware not soo,
   Though yt ware so yt greved me not;   10
Vnto my thought yt ware as tho
   I harkenid tho I here not.
At that I see I cannot wynk,
   Nor from mye thought so let it goo:
I wolde yt ware not as I think,   15
   I wolde I thought yt ware not.

Lo how my thought might make me free
   Of that perchaunce that nedeth nott;
Perchaunce no doubte the drede I see,
   I shrink at that I bere not;   20
But in my harte this worde shall sink
   Vnto the proffe maye better be:
I wolde yt ware not as I think,
   I wolde I thought yt ware not.

Yf yt be not, shewe no cause whye   25
   I shoulde so think, then care I not;
For I shall soo my self applie
   To bee that I apere not;
That is as one that shall not shrink
   To be your owne vntill I dye: 30
And if yt be not as I think,
   Lyke wyse to think yt is not.

9 Ffor if] If that GG. 11 thought] hart GG. 12 tho] and. 14 from . . . so] for my hart to GG. 16 not] not so GG. 18 nedeth] reedeth GG. 19 Perchaunce . . . the drede] For though . . . in deede GG. 21 But] Yet GG. 22 Vnto] Vntill GG. 25–32] *omitted* GG.

VI
Poems from the Arundel Manuscript

CCXXXIV

HART oppressyd with desp'rat thought
Ys forced ever to lament,
Whiche now in me so sore hath wrought
That needes to it I must consent:
Whearfore all ioy I must refuse,   5
And crewell will thearof accuse.

Yf crewell will had not been guyde
Dispayre in me had had no place;
Ffor my trew meaning she well espied
And for all that wold give no grace;   10
Thearfore all ioye I must refuse
And crewell will thearof accuse.

Shee well moght see and yet wolde not,
And may daylye, if that shee will,
How paynfull is my haples lott   15
Ioyn'de with dispayre me for to spill;
Whearby all ioye I must refuse
Sence Crewell will doth me so vse.

CCXXXV

WHAT thing is that, that I both have and lack
With good will grawnted and yet is denyde?
How may I be receav'd and putt aback,

CCXXXIV. D. 1 thought] thoughtes D. 2 Ys] D; Yf A. 5 must] do D. 8 had had] had D. 10 And] but yett D. 11 Thearfore] Wherffor D. must] do D. 13 well moght] mowt well D. 17 Whearby] Wherffor D. must] do D. 18] and cruell wyll theroff acvys D.
   [*Authorship:* followed in A by two W poems and in D by another.]
CCXXV. H, T. 1 that, that] that which T. 2 yet is] yet yt is H, T. 3] Always forwarde and yet full fare put backe H.

Alway doing and yet vnoccupy'de,
Moste slow in that I have moste applyde?   5
Thus may I say I leese all that I wynne,
And that was readye is new to begynne.

In wilfull Riches I have found povertie,
And in great pleasure I lyved in heavynes;
In too moche freedome I lacked libertie;   10
Nothing but plentie caused my scarsenes:
Thus was I both in ioye and in distresse;
And in few woordes if I shuld be playne,
In a Paradyse I suffred all this payne.

CCXXXVI

THE piller pearisht is whearto I Lent
The strongest staye of myne vnquyet mynde;
The lyke of it no man agayne can fynde
From East to west still seking though he went.
To myne vnhappe, for happe away hath rent   5
Of all my ioye the vearye bark and rynde;
And I (alas) by chaunce am thus assynde
Dearlye to moorne till death do it relent.
But syns that thus it is by destenye
What can I more but have a wofull hart,   10
My penne in playnt, my voyce in wofull crye,
My mynde in woe, my bodye full of smart,
And I my self my self alwayes to hate
Till dreadfull death do ease my dolefull state?

CCXXXVII

A LADYE gave me a gyfte she had not
And I receyvid her guifte I toke not.

4 Alway] Ever more H.   5 that] that which T; that that H.   6 Thus . . . I] Still thus
to seke, and T; whearby I H.   7 And] ffor H. that] that that H. new] newest T;
now H.   8–14] *omitted* H.   8 wilfull . . . found] riches finde I wilfull T.   9 And]
omitted T. I lyved] liue I T.   10 too] *omitted* T. lacked] lacke my T.   11 *omitted* T.
12 was] am T.   13 I shuld] that I shall T.   14 a] *omitted* T. suffred] suffer T.
   [*Authorship:* See Commentary.]
CCXXXVI. T.   11 wofull] carefull T.   14 ease] T; cause A.
   [*Authorship:* In W section of T.]
CCXXXVII. T.   2 I] which I *original* A, T.

She gave it me willinglye, and yet she wold not,
And I receyvid it, albeit I coulde not.
If she geve it me, I force not;   5
And, yf she take it agayne, she cares not.
Conster what this is and tell not,
Ffor I am fast sworne, I maye not.

CCXXXVIII

T HE flaming Sighes that boile within my brest
   Somtyme brake forthe and they can well declare
   The hartes vnrest and how that it doth fare,
   The payne thearof, the greef and all the rest.
The watrid eyes from whence the teares do fall   5
   Do feele some force or ells they wolde be drye;
   The wasted flesshe of cowlour dead can trye
   And Some thing tell what Sweetnes is in gall;
And he that list to see and to discerne
   How care can force within a weried mynd   10
   Come hee to me, I am that place assynd.
But for all this no force; it dothe no harme
   The wound, alas, happ in some other place
   Ffrom whence no toole away the skarr can race.
But you that of suche like have had your part   15
   Can best be iudge, whearfore, my frend so deare,
   I thought it good my state shuld now appeare
   To you, and that there is no great desert;
And whear as you in weightie matters great
   Of ffortune saw the shadow that you know,   20
   Ffor trifling thinges I now am stryken soo
   That thoughe I feele my hart doth wound and beat,
I sitt alone, save on the second day
   My ffeaver comes with whome I spend the tyme
   In burning heat whyle that she list assigne;   25
And whoe hath health and libertie alwaye,
   Let hym thanck god and lett hym not provoke
   To have the lyke of this my paynefull stroke.

[*Authorship:* In W section of T.]
CCXXXVIII. T.   5 eyes] eyen T.   8 Some thing] sometime T2.   9 list] lust T.   16
iudge,] iudge: T2.   21 trifling] T; tasting A.
   [*Authorship:* In W section of T.]

CCXXXIX

Th' Argument

SOMTYME the pryde of mye assured trothe
Contemned all helpp of good and eke of man:
But when I saw man blyndlye how goi'the
In demyng hartes, whiche none but god there can,
And his domes hyd wheareby mans Malyce growth,   5
Myne Earle, this doute my hart did humble than
Ffor errour so might murder Innocence.
Then sang I thus in god my confydence.

CCXL

STOND who so list vpon the Slipper toppe
Of courtes estates, and lett me heare reioyce;
And vse me quyet without lett or stoppe,
Vnknowen in courte, that hath suche brackish ioyes.
In hidden place, so lett my dayes forthe passe,   5
That when my yeares be done, withouten noyse,
I may dye aged after the common trace.
For hym death greep'the right hard by the croppe
That is moche knowen of other, and of him self alas,
Doth dye vnknowen, dazed with dreadfull face.   10

CCXXXIX. A.   7 Innocence] O; Innocentes A.
  [*Authorship:* See Commentary.]

CCXL. T.   1 toppe] whele T.   2 courtes] hye T. estates] astate T.   3 vse . . .
stoppe] vse my life in quietnesse eche dele T.   4 Vnknowen] T; Vnknowe A. suche
brackishe ioyes] the wanton toyes T.   5 so . . . forthe] my time shall slowly T.   6
That] And T. done] past T.   7 I . . . aged] Let me dye olde T. For] T; Ffrom A. hym
. . . croppe] gripes of death doth he to hardly passe T.   9 is . . . other] knowen is to
all T. and of] but to T.   10 Doth dye] He dyeth T.
  [*Authorship:* In W section of T.]

VII
Poems from Minor Manuscripts

CCXLI

LUCKES, my faire falcon, and your fellowes all,
How well pleasaunt yt were your libertie!
Ye not forsake me that faire might ye befall.
But they that somtyme lykt my companye
Like lyse awaye from ded bodies thei crall: 5
Loe what a profe in light adversytie!
But ye my birdes, I swear by all your belles,
Ye be my fryndes, and so be but few elles.

CCXLII

PLAYN ye, myn eyes, accompany my hart
For, by your fault, Loe! here is death at hand.
Ye brought him first into this bytter band,
And of his harme as yet ye felt no part;
But now ye shall: Loe! here begyns your smart,   5
Wet shall ye be – ye shall yt not withstand –
With weeping teares that shall make dymm your sight,
And mistie clowdes shall hang still in your light.
Blame but your selves that kyndyld have this brand,
Withe such desire to straine that past your might.   10
But synce by yow the hart hathe cawght his harme,
His flamed heate shall sometyme make ye warme.

CCXLI. P, T, N.   1 your] thy T.   3 might . . . befall] mought you fall T.   5 thei]
omitted N.   8 so be but] very T.
   [*Authorship:* In W section of T.]
CCXLII. P, N.   1 myn eyes] my neyes P; myne eyes N.

CCXLIII

I SEE my plaint with open eares
Ys heard, alas, and lawghing eyes;
I see that scorne beholds my teares,
And all the harme hap can devyse;
I se my lyfe away so weares   5
That I my self my self dispyse;
And most of all wherewith I stryve
Ys that I see my self alyve.

CCXLIV

SYGHES ar my foode, drynke are my teares;
Clynkinge of fetters suche musycke wolde crave;
Stynke and close ayer away my lyf wears;
Innocencie is all the hope I have.
Rayne, wynde, or wether I iudge by myne eares.   5
Mallice assaulted that rightiousnes should have.
Sure I am, Brian, this wounde shall heale agayne,
But yet, alas, the scarre shall styll remayne.

CCXLV

LYKE as the wynde with raginge blaste
Dothe cawse eche tree to bowe and bende,
Even so do I spende my tyme in wast,
My lyff consumynge vnto an ende.

Ffor as the flame by force dothe quenche the fier   5
And runnynge streames consume the rayne,
Even so do I my self desyer
To augment my greff and deadly payne.

Whear as I fynde that hot is hot,
And colde is colde by course of kynde,   10
So shall I knet an endeles knott;
Suche fructe in love, alas, I fynde.

CCXLIII. P, N.   2 heard] N, hard P.   3 beholds my] N; beholding P.
CCXLIV. H, T.
  [*Authorship:* In W sections of T and H.]
CCXLV. H.   9 hot is hot] whot is whott H.

When I forsaw those Christall streames
Whose bewtie dothe cawse my mortall wounde
I lyttyll thought within those beames 15
So swete a venim for to have founde.

I fele and se my owne decaye
As on that bearethe flame in his brest
Forgetfull thought to put away
The thynge that breadethe my vnrest. 20

Lyke as the flye dothe seke the flame
And afterwarde playethe in the fyer,
Who fyndethe her woe and sekethe her game
Whose greffe dothe growe of her owne desyer:

Lyke as the spider dothe drawe her lyne, 25
As labor lost so is my sute,
The gayne is hers, the lose is myne,
Of euell sowne seade suche is the frute.

CCXLVI

LIKE as the byrde in the cage enclosed,
The dore vnsparred and the hawke without,
Twixte deth and prison piteously oppressed
Whether for to chose standith in dowt.
Certes so do I, wyche do syeke to bring about 5
Wyche shuld be best by determination,
By losse off liefe libertye or liefe by preson.

Oh myscheffe by myschieffe to be redressed,
Wher payne is the best their lieth litell pleasure,
By schort deth out off daunger yet to be delyuered 10
Rather then with paynfull lieffe thraldome and doloure,
Ffor small plesure moche payne to suffer
Soner therfore to chuse me thincketh it wysdome
By losse off life lybertye then liefe by preson.

[*Authorship:* 'T. Wyat of Love' in H. See Commentary]
CCXLVI. C, T. 1 in] within T. 2 and] her foe T. 5 Certes] Lo T. do syeke] seke
T. 9 the best] best T. litell] but little T. 10 out . . . be] better to be T. 11 Rather
then with] Than bide in T. 12] Small is the pleasure where much payne we suffer T.
13 Soner] Rather T. thincketh it] thinketh T.

By leynght off liefe yet shulde I suffer,   15
Adwayting time and fortunes chaunce;
Manye thinges happen within an hower;
That wyche me oppressed may me avaunce;
In time is trust wyche by deathes greuaunce
Is vtterlye lost, then were it not reson   20
By deathe to chuse libertye, and not lieffe by preson.

But deathe were deliueraunce and liefe lengthe off payne:
Off two ylles, let see nowe chuse the lest:
This birde to deliuer youe that here her playne,
Your aduise, yowe louers, wyche shalbe best   25
In cage thraldome, or by the hauke to be opprest
And which for to chuse? Make playne conclusyon
By losse off liefe libertye or liefe by prison

15] And yet me thinkes allthough I liue and suffer T. 16 Adwayting] I do but wait
a T. 17] Oft many thinges do happen in one houre T. 18 me oppressed] oppressed
me T. 20 vtterlye] wholy T. 22 and . . . off] where life lengthes T. 23 Off two
ylles] of these two euyls T. lest] *conj.* Lovelock; best C, T. 24 youe that here her]
that here dothe T. 25 Your . . . yowe] What saye ye T. best] the best T. 26 to be
opprest] opprest T. 27 for to] to T.
   [*Authorship:* In W section of T.]

VIII
Poems from Tottel's *Songes and Sonettes*

CCXLVII

WITHIN my brest I neuer thought it gain,
Of gentle mindes the fredom for to lose.
Nor in my hart sanck neuer such disdain,
To be a forger, faultes for to disclose.
Nor I can not endure the truth to glose,   5
To set a glosse vpon an earnest pain.
Nor I am not in nomber one of those,
That list to blow retrete to euery train.

CCXLVIII

FOR want of will, in wo I playne
Vnder colour of sobernesse,
Renewyng with my sute my payne,
My wanhope with your stedfastnesse.
Awake therfore of gentlenesse.   5
Regard at length, I you require,
The sweltyng paynes of my desire.

Betimes who geueth willingly,
Redoubled thankes aye doth deserue.
And I that sue vnfaynedly,   10
In frutelesse hope (alas) do sterue.
How great my cause is for to swerue!
And yet how stedfast is my sute
Lo, here ye see: where is the frute?

CCXLVII.   2 mindes] T2; mynde T1.
   [*Authorship:* All the poems in this section are ascribed to W by T.]
CCXLVIII.   7 The] My T2.

As hounde that hath his keper lost,   15
Seke I your presence to obtayne:
In which my hart deliteth most,
And shall delight though I be slayne.
You may release my band of payne.
Lose then the care that makes me crye   20
For want of helpe, or els I dye.

I dye, though not incontinent,
By processe yet consumingly
As waste of fire, which doth relent,
If you as wilfull wyll denye.   25
Wherfore cease of such crueltye:
And take me wholy in your grace:
Which lacketh will to change his place.

CCXLIX

I F euer man might him auaunt
Of fortunes frendly chere,
It was my selfe I must it graunt,
For I haue bought it dere.
And derely haue I helde also   5
The glory of her name:
In yelding her such tribute, lo,
As did set forth her fame.

Some tyme I stode so in her grace:
That as I would require,   10
Ech ioy I thought did me imbrace,
That furdered my desire.
And all those pleasures (lo) had I,
That fansy might support:
And nothing she did me denye,   15
That was to my comfort.

I had (what would you more perdee?)
Ech grace that I did craue.
Thus fortunes will was vnto me
All thing that I would haue.   20
But all to rathe alas the while,

She built on such a ground:
In little space, to great a guyle
In her now haue I found.

For she hath turned so her whele: 25
That I vnhappy man
May waile the time that I did fele
Wherwith she fedde me than.
For broken now are her behestes,
And pleasant lokes she gaue: 30
And therfore now all my requestes
From perill can not saue.

Yet would I well it might appere
To her my chiefe regard:
Though my desertes haue ben to dere 35
To merite such reward.
Sith fortunes will is now so bent
To plage me thus, pore man,
I must my selfe therwith content:
And beare it as I can. 40

CCL

SUCH is the course, that natures kinde hath wrought,
That snakes haue time to cast away their stynges.
Ainst chainde prisoners what nede defence be sought?
The fierce lyon will hurt no yelden thinges.
Why shoulde such spite be nursed then in thy thought? 5
Sith all these powers are prest vnder thy winges:
And eke thou seest, and reason thee hath taught
What mischief malice many waies it bringes.
Consider eke, that spight auaileth naught,
Therfore this song thy fault to thee it singes: 10
Displease thee not, for saiyng thus my thought
Nor hate thou him from whom no hate forth springes,
    For furies, that in hell be execrable,
    For that they hate, are made most miserable.

CCL.   11 my thought] O; (me thought) T.

CCLI

Suffised not (madame) that you did teare
My wofull hart, but thus also to rent
The weping paper that to you I sent,
Wherof eche letter was written with a teare.
Could not my present paines, alas, suffise　5
Your gredy hart? and that my hart doth fele
Tormentes that prick more sharper then the stele,
But new and new must to my lot arise?
Vse then my death. So shall your cruelty,
Spite of your spite, rid me from all my smart,　10
And I no more such tormentes of the hart
Fele as I do. This shalt thou gain thereby.

CCLII

When first mine eyes did view, and marke,
Thy faire beawtie to beholde:
And when mine eares listned to hark
The pleasant wordes, that thou me tolde:
I would as then, I had been free　5
From eares to heare, and eyes to see.

And when my lips gan first to moue,
Wherby my hart to thee was knowne;
And when my tong did talk of loue,
To thee that hast true loue down throwne:　10
I would my lips, and tong also,
Had then bene dum, no deale to go.

And when my handes haue handled ought,
That thee hath kept in memorie:
And when my fete haue gone and sought　15
To finde and geat thy company:
I would eche hand a foote had bene,
And I eche foote a hand had sene.

And when in mynde I did consent
To folow this my fansies will:　20
And when my hart did first relent,

To tast such bayt, my life to spyll:
I would my hart had bene as thyne:
Or els thy hart had bene as mine.

CCLIII

SYNCE loue wyll nedes that I shall loue,
Of very force I must agree;
And since no chance may it remoue,
In welth, and in aduersitie,
I shall alway my self apply　　　　　　　5
To serue, and suffer paciently.

Though for good will I finde but hate,
And cruelty my life to wast;
And though that still a wretched state
Should pine my dayes vnto the last:　　　10
Yet I professe it willingly
To serue, and suffer paciently.

For since my hart is bound to serue,
And I not ruler of mine owne,
What so befall, tyll that I sterue,　　　15
By proofe full well it shall be knowne:
That I shall still my selfe apply
To serue and suffer paciently.

Yea though my grief finde no redresse,
But still increase before mine eyes:　　　20
Though my reward bé cruelnesse,
With all the harme happe can deuise:
Yet I professe it willingly
To serue, and suffer paciently.

Yea, though fortune her pleasant face,　　　25
Should shew, to set me vp a loft:
And streight, my wealth for to deface,
Should writhe away, as she doth oft:
Yet would I styll my self apply
To serue and suffer paciently.　　　　　30

CCLII.　24 Or els] Orels T.

There is no grief, no smart, no wo,
That yet I fele, or after shall,
That from this mynde may make me go;
And whatsoeuer me befall,
I do professe it willingly,   35
To serue and suffer paciently.

CCLIV

MYSTRUSTFULL mindes be moued
To haue me in suspect.
The troth it shalbe proued,
Which time shall once detect.

Though falshed go about   5
Of crime me to accuse,
At length I do not doute
But truth shall me excuse.

Such sawce, as they haue serued
To me without desart,   10
Euen as they haue deserued,
Therof god send them part.

CCLV

Louer. It burneth yet, alas, my hartes desire.
Lady. What is the thing that hath inflamde thy hert?
Louer. A certain point, as feruent as the fyre.
Lady. The heate shall cease, if that thou wilt conuert.
Louer. I cannot stoppe the feruent raging yre.   5
Lady. What may I do, if thy self cause thy smart?
Louer. Heare my request, and rew my weeping chere.
Lady. With right good wyll, say on: lo, I thee here.

Louer. That thing would I, that maketh two content.
Lady. Thou sekest, perchance, of me, that I may not.   10
Louer. Would god thou wouldst, as thou maist, well assent.
Lady. That I may not, thy grief is mine, God wot.
Louer. But I it fele, what so thy wordes haue ment.

CCLV.   3–31] The speech prefixes have been expanded to conform with ll. 1, 2.   7
and . . . chere] T2; alas, with weping chere T2.

Lady. Suspect me not: my wordes be not forgot.
Louer. Then say, alas, shall I haue help, or no?　　15
Lady. I see no time to answer yea, but no.

Louer. Say ye, dere hert, and stand no more in dout.
Lady. I may not grant a thing that is so dere.
Louer. Lo, with delayes thou drieues me still about.
Lady. Thou wouldest my death: it plainly doth appere.　　20
Louer. First may my hart his bloode and life blede out.
Lady. Then for my sake, alas, thy will forbere.
Louer. From day to day, thus wastes my life away.
Lady. Yet, for the best, suffer some small delay.

Louer. Now good, say yea: do once so good a dede.　　25
Lady. If I sayd yea, what should therof ensue?
Louer. An hart in pain of succour so should spede;
　　Twist yea and nay, my doute shall styll renew.
　　My swete, say yea and do away this drede.
Lady. Thou wilt nedes so; be it so; but then be trew.　　30
Louer. Nought would I els, nor other treasure none.
　　Thus hartes be wonne by loue, request, and mone.

CCLVI

I SEE that chance hath chosen me
　　That secretely to liue in paine;
And to an other geuen the fee
　　Of all my losse, to haue the gayn.
By chance assinde, thus do I serue:　　5
And other haue, that I deserue.

Vnto my self sometime alone
　　I do lament my wofull case.
But what auaileth me to mone?
　　Since troth and pitie hath no place　　10
In them, to whom I sue and serue:
And other haue, that I deserue.

To seke by meane to change this minde,
　　Alas, I proue it will not be;
For in my hart I cannot finde　　15

Once to refrain, but still agree
As bounde by force, alway to serue:
And other haue, that I deserue.

Such is the fortune that I haue,
    To loue them most that loue me lest;   20
And to my pain to seke and craue
    The thing that other haue possest.
So thus in vain alway I serue:
And other haue, that I deserue.

And till I may apease the heate,   25
    If that my happe will happe so well,
To waile my wo my hart shall freate,
    Whose pensif pain my tong can tell.
Yet thus vnhappy must I serue:
And other haue, that I deserue.   30

CCLVII

FOR shamefast harm of great and hatefull nede,
In depe despayre, as did a wretch go
With ready corde out of his life to spede,
His stumbling foote did finde an hoorde, lo,
Of golde, I say, where he preparde this dede: 5
And, in eschange, he left the corde tho.
He that had hidde the golde and founde it not,
Of that he founde he shapte his neck a knot.

CCLVIII

THROUGH out the world, if it wer sought,
Faire wordes ynough a man shall finde:
They be good chepe, they cost right nought;
Their substance is but onely winde:
But well to say and so to mene,   5
That swete acord is seldom sene.

CCLIX

IN court to serue decked with freshe aray,
Of sugred meates felyng the swete repast,
The life in bankets, and sundry kindes of play

Amid the presse of lordly lokes to waste
Hath with it ioynde oft times such bitter taste,   5
   That who so ioyes such kinde of life to holde,
   In prison ioyes, fettred with cheines of gold.

CCLX

SPEAKE thou and spede where will or power ought helpthe,
Where power dothe want will must be wonne by welth.
For nede will spede, where will workes not his kinde,
And gayne, thy foes, thy frendes, shall cause thee finde.
For sute and golde, what do not they obtaine: 5
Of good and bad the triers are these twaine.

CCLXI

IF thou wilt mighty be, flee from the rage
Of cruell wyll, and see thou kepe thee free
From the foule yoke of sensuall bondage,
For though thy empyre stretche to Indian sea,
And for thy feare trembleth the fardest Thylee,   5
If thy desire haue ouer thee the power,
Subiect then art thou and no gouernour.

If to be noble and high thy minde be meued
Consider well thy grounde and thy beginnyng,
For he that hath eche starre in heauen fixed,   10
And geues the Moone her hornes and her eclipsyng:
Alike hath made the noble in his workyng,
So that wretched no way thou may bee
Except foule lust and vice do conquere thee.

All were it so thou had a flood of golde,   15
Vnto thy thirst yet should it not suffice.
And though with Indian stones a thousande folde,
More precious then can thy selfe deuise,
Ycharged were thy backe: thy couitise
And busye bytyng yet should neuer let   20
Thy wretchid life, ne do thy death profet.

Poems from
The Court of Venus
and *A Boke of Balettes*

CCLXII

D RYUEN by dissyr to set affection
A great way, alas, above my degre,
Chosen I am, I thinke by election
To couet that thing that will not be.

I serue in loue, not lyke to sped;   5
I loke, alas, a lytell to hye;
Agaynst my will I do in ded
Couet that thing that will not be.

My fanzy, alas, doth me so bynd
That I can se no remedy,   10
But styll to folow my folych mind,
And couet that thing that wyll not be.

I hopyd well whan I began;
And, sens the proue is contrary,
Why shold I any longer than   15
Couet that thing that wyll not be?

But rather to leaue now at the last
Then styll to folowe fantasy,
Content with the payn that is past
And not couet that thing that will not be.   20

CCLXII. VI.   6 a lytell] alytell VI.   18 fantasy] fanzy VI.

CCLXIII

LOUE whom you lyst and spare not
Therwyth I am content;
Hate whom you lyst and spare not,
For I am indifferent.

Do what you lyst and dread not   5
After your owne fantasye,
Thynke what you lyst and feare not
For al is one to me.

But as for me I am not
Wauering as the wind,   10
But euen as one that reketh not
Whych way you turne your mind.

For in your loue I doubt not,
But as one that reketh not,
Whether you hate or hate not   15
Is least charge of my thought.

Wherfore I pray you forget not
But that I am wel content
To loue whom you list and spare not,
For I am indyfferent.   20

CCLXIV

SHALL she neuer out of my mynde,
Nor shall I neuer out of this payn,
Alas her loue doth me so blinde,
Except her helpe I am now slayne.

I neuer told her of my mynde   5
What payne I suffer for her sake:

CCLXIII. V2, BB. 1] *torn* BB. 3 you] ye BB. 4 I] euen I BB. 5 you] ye BB. 8 to] BB; with V2. 12 you] ye BB. 15 you] yon BB. 16 Is] In BB. thought] thou BB. 19 you] ye BB. Cf. No. CXXXVI.
CCLXIV. BB, V2, Z. 1 my] *omitted* Z. 2 this] my V2. 3 loue] ioy V2; yee Z. me] *missing* V2. blinde] bynde Z. 4] For lacke of helpe now am I slayne V2. now] nere Z. 4–5 *extra stanza*: She hath myne hart al other before/So hath she my body she may be sure/nothyng on erth maye glade me more/then to spende them both to do her plesur Z. 6 payne] paynes Z. her] his V2.

Alas! what meanes might I now find
That no displeasure with me she take.

Yf I speake fayre, she sayth I flatter,
And if I dare not I shall not spede,   10
Yf I to her do wryte a letter,
Then wyll she say she can not rede.

Shall I despayre yet for all this?
Nay, nay, my hart wyll not do so.
I wold ones my swete hart kys,   15
A thousand times to bynd more wo.

I am abashed when I shuld speake
Alas! I can not my mind expresse.
Yt maketh my hart in peces breake
To se her louing gentelnes.   20

CCLXV

To whom should I sue to ease my payne?
To my mystres? Nay, nay, certayne!
For feare she should me then disdayne
I dare not sue, I dare not sue.

When I should speake to my mystres   5
In hope for to get redres
. . . .
When I should speake, when I shold speake.

What hap had I that suffereth payne
And if I myght her grace attayne?   10
Or els she would here me complayne:
What hap had I, what hap had I?

I fly for feare to be espyed
Or of euil wil to be destroyed

7 meanes] paynes V2. now] *omitted* Z. 9 Yf] When Z. flatter] *missing* BB. 10] Yf I speke not I shuld not spede Z. dare] V2; do BB. 11 Yf] When Z. do] V2; to BB. 12 she] that she Z. 13 Shall . . . yet] shuld . . . then Z. for all] I V2. 14] nay my pore hart shall neuer do so Z. 15–20] *omitted* V2. 15] but yet rather then she shall mys Z. 16 bynd] suffer Z. 17–20] *omitted* Z.

CCLXV. V2. 2 mystres] mysters V2. 7 *line omitted* V2.

The place wher I would faynest abyde 15
I fly for feare, I fly for feare.

Though I wer bold who should me blame?
Loue caused me to do the same;
Wyth honesty it were no shame,
Though I were bold, though I were bold. 20

And here an end, wyth ful glad wyl,
In purpose for to serue her styl,
And for to part I thinke none yl
And here an end, and here an end.

CCLXVI

DYSDAINE me not without desert
Nor leaue me not so sodeynly
Sence wel ye wot that in my hart
I meane nothing but honestly.
　　　　　Dysdayne me not. 5

Refuse me not without cause why,
Nor thynke me not to be vniust;
Synce that by lot of fantasye
The carefull knot nedes knyt I must,
　　　　　Refuse me not. 10

Mystrust me not though some there be
That fayne would spot my stedfastnes;
Beleue them not, sins that ye se
The profe is not as they expresse.
　　　　　Mystrust me not. 15

Forsake me not til I deserue,
Nor hate me not, tyll I offend,

20 Though] Thouth V2. 23 I thinke] thinke V2.

CCLXVI. V2, T, Z. 2 leaue] payne Z. 3 Sence] syth Z. wot] know Z. 4 honestly] T, Z; honesty V2; faythfully Z. 5] Refuse me not Z; *omitted* T. 7 vniust] vnkynd Z. 8] My hart is yours vntyll I dy Z. 9] And that yn short space ye shall yt fynd Z. The] This T. 10] Mistrust me not Z; *omitted* T. 11 there be] T; therbe V2. 12 my] Z, T; thy V2. 13 sins that] T; seyng that V2; syth well Z. 15] Forsak me not Z; *omitted* T. 17–18] T, Z; Nor hate me not til I swarue V2.

Destroy me not, tyll that I swerue;
But sins ye know what I intend,
Forsake me not.   20

Dysdayne me not that am your owne;
Refuse me not that am so true;
Mystrust me not til al be knowen;
Forsake me neuer for no new:
Disdayne me not.   25

CCLXVII

I MAY by no meanes surmyse
My fantasy to resyst,
But after the old gyse
To call on had I wyst
And thought it to suffyce   5
That agayne I shall haue none.
Yet can I not deuyse
To get agayne myne owne.

It is my hart that I haue lost:
God send it me againe.   10
I should it haue what euer it cost,
Or else I am but slaine.

.   .   .   .

I study day and night
And loud I cry and cal
To be deliuered quyte   15
From her that I am thral.
And yet agaynst al right
Of force I must stil mone,
For it doth passe my might
To get agayne myne owne.   20

19] T; Syth ye well wote what I intend Z; For syth you knew what I entend V2.
20] Dysdayn me not Z; *omitted* T. 21 that am] Z, T; being V2. 22 am] Z, T; I am
V2. 24 neuer] not now Z, T2; not, ne T1. 25 Disdayne me not] Thus leue me not Z;
omitted T.
  [*Authorship:* In W section of T.]
CCLXVII. V2. 12–13 *four lines omitted* V2.

In tormentes I am torne
That no rest find I can,
None so vnhappye borne
Sence that the world began;
I aske but such corne   25
And suche sede that was sowne;
And yet though I had sworne,
I cannot get my owne.

But seyng that I cannot
Attayne my true desyre   30
Nor by no meanes may not
Crepe out of the fyre,

. . . .

Geue ought of your owne
By reason that you should not
Let me to haue myne owne.   35

CCLXVIII

Now must I lern to faine
And do as other do,
Seing no truth doth raine
That I may trust vnto;
I was both true and playne   5
To one and to no mo,
And vnto me againe
Alas! she was not so.

Vnknowen againe my hart
Into my foes hand,   10
And euer I could astart
Out of that careful band.
All the wyt I had
Could scarce the knot vndo,
This careful lyfe I had   15
For one that was not so.

31 meanes] meane V2. 32–3 *line omitted* V2.
CCLXVIII. V2. 14 scarce] scace V2. 16 not] no V2.

The nights right long and heuy,
The dayes of my torment,
The sighes continually
That thorow my hart went,   20
My colour pale and wan
To her dyd playnly shewe
That I was her true man,
And yet she thought not so.

Out of her sight no pleasure   25
But to my hart gret paine,
And teares out of measure
That out of mine eies did raine;
Her absence was my death,
For to depart her fro,   30
And yet alas her fayth
Was fayned and not so.

Not the feuer quartayne
Dothe halfe a man so shake
As dyd the wo and payne   35
That dayly dyd me take.
No slepe could I nor rest,
But tossyng to and fro,
And wheras I loued best,
Alas! she did not so.   40

And seing it is my chaunce
My loue in vaine to wast,
I am not in that daunce
The first nor yet the last;
But wise he is by once   45
That can his foly know,
To reuoke at once
Seyng she wyl not so.

17 nights] night V2. 48 not] no V2.

ABBREVIATIONS
USED IN THE COMMENTARY

Baldi — Sergio Baldi, *La Poesia di Sit Thomas Wyatt*, Florence, 1953.

Berdan — John M. Berdan, *Early Tudor Poetry*, New York, 1920, repr., 1961.

Cecchini — Antonio Cecchini, *Serafino Aquilano e la Lirica Inglese del '500*, Aquila, 1935.

Chambers — E. K. Chambers, *Sir Thomas Wyatt and Some Collected Studies*, London, 1933.

Foxwell, *Study* — A. K. Foxwell, *A Study of Sir Thomas Wyatt's Poems*, London, 1911.

Gesualdo — *Il Petrarcha*, ed. G. A. Gesualdo. Venice 1533. (Quoted from the edition of 1541.)

Guss — D. L. Guss, 'Petrarchism in England: Wyatt and Gascoigne' in *John Donne, Petrarchist*, Detroit, 1966, Ch. III. pp. 34–40, on W's imitations of Petrarch, reproduced in revised form from Guss's article in *HLQ*, XXIX (1965), 1–15.

Hangen — E. C. Hangen, *A Concordance to the Complete Poetical Works of Sir Thomas Wyatt*, Chicago, 1941.

Hietsch — Otto Hietsch, *Die Petrarcaübersetzungen Sir Thomas Wyatts*, Vienna and Stuttgart, 1960.

Hughey — *The Arundel Harington Manuscript of Tudor Poetry*, ed. Ruth Hughey, 2 vols. Columbus, Ohio, 1960.

Koeppel — E. Koeppel, 'Studien zur Geschichte des englischen Petrarchismus im sechszehnten Jahrhundert', *Romanische Forschungen* v (1889) 65–97.

Lever — J. W. Lever, *The Elizabethan Love Sonnet*, London, 1956.

Mason — H. A. Mason, *Humanism and Poetry in the Early Tudor Period*, London, 1959.

Nott — Henry Howard Earl of Surrey and Sir Thomas Wyatt, *Works*, ed. G. F. Nott Vol. II (Wyatt), London, 1816.

Opere (1516) — *Opere dello Elegantissimo Poeta Seraphino Aquilano*, Florence, 1516.

Padelford — F. W. Padelford, *Early Sixteenth Century Lyrics*, Boston and London, 1907.

T

Puttenham	George Puttenham, *The Arte of English Poesie*, ed. G. D. Wilcock and A. Walker. Cambridge, 1936.
Rime	Francesco Petrarca, *Le Rime*, ed. G. Carducci and S. Ferrari, Florence, 1899; repr., 1957.
Rollins	*Tottel's Miscellany*, ed. H. E. Rollins. 2 vols. Cambridge, Mass., 1928–9.
Simonds	W. E. Simonds, *Sir Thomas Wyatt and His poems*, Boston, 1889.
Stagnino	*Li Sonetti Canzone Trivmphi del Petrarcha con li soi Commenti* (incorporating the commentaries of A. da Tempo, F. Filelfo, and G. Squarciafico, and published by B. Stagnino) Venice, 1519.
Stevens	John Stevens, *Music and Poetry in the Early Tudor Court*, London, 1961.
Thomson	Patricia Thomson, *Sir Thomas Wyatt and his Background*, London, 1964.
Tilley	M. P. Tilley, *A Dictionary of the Proverbs in England in the Sixteenth and Seventeenth Centuries*, Ann Arbor, 1950.
Tillyard	*The Poetry of Sir Thomas Wyatt*, ed. E. M. W. Tillyard. London, 1929.
Vellutello	*Le Volgari Opere del Petrarcha con la Espositione di Alessandro Vellvtello da Lvcca*, Venice, 1525.

Commentary

1. Poems from the Egerton Manuscript

1. Source:

> Or vedi, Amor, che giovenetta donna
>   Tuo regno sprezza e del mio mal non cura,
>   E tra duo ta' nemici è sí secura.
> Tu se' armato, et ella in treccie e 'n gonna
>   Si siede e scalza in mezzo i fiori e l' erba,
>   Vèr' me spietata e contra te superba.
> I' son pregion; ma, se pietà ancor serba
>   L' arco tuo saldo e qualcuna saetta,
>   Fa di te e di me, signor, vendetta.

Petrarch, *Rime*, cxxi

The source was identified by Koeppel (67); but, as with xviii, the substance of the Italian may have reached W through a French rondeau. (Cf. xx in which a sonnet by Petrarch becomes a rondeau.) F (11.9–13) notes W's typical dispensing with Petrarch's descriptions of landscape and the physical features of the lady; see especially ll. 4–5 of the Italian, which are virtually omitted by W. Baldi (187, 218) and Hietsch (183–7) discuss W's alterations. Guss (36) argues that W, unlike Petrarch, stresses the mistreatment of virtue. W sometimes expands the Italian: cf. his ll. 11–14 with Petrarch's last two lines.

The metrical reshaping, as well as the omission of rusticity, suggests that W may not have recognized the Italian madrigal as a distinctive lyric kind. (Cf xxxiv and note.) The madrigal varies in form and this one was labelled in contemporary editions as a *canzone* (Stagnino), a *stanza* (Vellutello), and as *amoroso Madrigaletto* (Gesualdo). I. L. Mumford speaks of its popularity with composers (*EM*, xiv (1963), 21) and W may have known it as a song.

Though the 'rondel' was known in England before W, the French version was evidently unusual enough for T to reshape the poem as a sonnet. W's formal model is in the fifteen-line rondeau as used by Jean and Clément Marot and Mellin de Saint-Gelais. Of the nine rondeaux in E, seven are in the exact French form (i, ii, xv, xix, xx, xxv, xlv), one in a variant of this form (xviii), while another follows an original triplet scheme (lxxi). (The triplet scheme is prominent in D which has no example of the exact French form.) T entitles the poem: 'Request to Cupide, for reuenge of his vnkinde loue.'

1 *she*] Cf. the more precise *giovenetta donna*.

10 *I ame in hold*] This phase is frequently found in medieval poetry, e.g. Robbins, *Secular Lyrics*, 136.37, 160.5 (WMT).

14 *entreath*] A syncopation of *entreateth* (F).

11. No source has been discovered for this rondeau, although Nott (545)

says it has the appearance of being a translation. T entitles the poem: 'Complaint for true loue vnrequited.'

3 *iuste and*] iuste &. The ampersand may have been inserted later.

13 *maisteres*] mistress.

III. Source:

> Cesare, poi che 'l traditor d' Egitto
> Li fece il don de l' onorata testa,
> Celando l' allegrezza manifesta,
> Pianse per gli occhi fuor, sí come è scritto;
> Ed Anibàl, quando a l' imperio afflitto
> Vide farsi fortuna sí molesta,
> Rise fra gente lagrimosa e mesta,
> Per isfogare il suo acerbo despitto;
> E cosí aven che l' animo ciascuna
> Sua passïon sotto 'l contrario manto
> Ricopre con la vista or chiara or bruna:
> Però, s' alcuna volta i' rido o canto,
> Faccio 'l perch' i' non ho se non quest' una
> Via da celare il mio angoscioso pianto.
>
> Petrarch, *Rime*, cii

The source of this translation was identified by Nott (539). The story of Caesar's shedding tears when Ptolemy sent him Pompey's head is told by Lucan and by Plutarch and became a literary commonplace. (See Rollins, 11.165.) It is aptly applied to W's enemies in one of Surrey's elegies (ed. Jones, no. 29). The story of Hannibal's cloaking his sorrow when defeated is mentioned in one of Petrarch's letters (*Franc. Petrarchae ... Epistolarum* (Lyons, 1601), VI, iii, 202). The interest of both sonnets is in the psychology of disguised feelings and the classical examples are adapted to this purpose. Neither the Italian nor, in spite of T's title ('Of others fained sorrow, and the louers fained mirth'), the English need be read as a love poem. Da Tempo and Vellutello assume that Petrarch was writing of his feelings about Laura; but Filelfo believes that it concerns the occasion of his brother's death, when he hid his sorrow from Francesco da Carrara.

There are discussions by Berdan (469–70), Lever (19), and Hietsch (77) F. M. Padelford scans it as a pentameter (*SP*, xx (1923), 150). See notes to IV and XXVI with Prince's explanation of the pressure of the Italian hendecasyllabic on the native 'pausing line'.

8] Vellutello's explanation that Hannibal laughed *per celare la gran passione dell' animo* (f. 30ᵛ) has found its way into the D version.

The E version is closer to the Italian than the earlier version in D.

11 *now sad, now mery*] Derived, as Baldi has indicated (*English Studies Today*, ed. I. Cellini and G. Melchiori (Rome, 1966), 122) from Vellutello's paraphrase of *or chiara or bruna* as *hor allegra hora mesta* (f. 31ʳ).

12 *any tyme, or season*] The redundancy and omission of Petrarch's *canto* were probably forced on W by the need to find a rhyme. Hietsch (79), however, remarks on the strength of his expression compared with the original.

iv. Source:

> Amor, che nel penser mio vive e regna
>   E 'l suo seggio maggior nel mio cor tene,
>   Tal or armato ne la fronte vène,
>   Ivi si loca et ivi pon sua insegna.
> Quella ch' amare e sofferir ne 'nsegna,
>   E vòl che 'l gran desio, l' accesa spene,
>   Ragion, vergogna e reverenza affrene,
>   Di nostro ardir fra sé stessa si sdegna.
> Onde Amor paventoso fugge al core
>   Lasciando ogni sua impresa, e piange e trema;
>   Ivi s'asconde e non appar piú fòre.
> Che poss' io far, temendo il mio signore,
>   Se non star seco in fin a l' ora estrema?
>   Ché bel fin fa chi ben amando more.
>
>   Petrarch, *Rime*, cxl

The source of this translation was identified by Nott (537) who considered it 'much inferior' to Surrey's. He was followed in this opinion by Lee, Berdan, and Padelford, and both Berdan and F deplored W's choice of Petrarch's 'conceited' sonnet. Hallett Smith, however, showed that W takes Petrarch's conceit more seriously than Surrey, justified his additions, and found him more energetic and vivid. (*IILQ*, ix (1946), 332–7). See also S (80–3).

The question whether W admitted four-stress lines in a basically pentameter structure has been much debated. Padelford came to the conclusion that he did not (*SP*, xx (1923), 137), but he relied too much on F's system of prosodic variants. A. Swallow, by contrast, believes that W introduces four-stress lines deliberately, adducing, particularly, his tendency to use this device to produce a rushing effect at the end: cf. vii.14, xiv.14, and xxv.14 (*MP*, xlviii (1950), 7).

This is one of nine poems in E with corrections in the hand of Nicholas Grimald, who supplies, *inter alia*, all the punctuation. See R. Hughey *Library*, xv (1935), 415–16, 427–9, 442–3, and in her edition of A, ii.127–9. T entitles the poem: 'The louer for shamefastnesse hideth his desire within his faithful hart.'

1 *longe*] The final 'e' should probably be sounded. Cf. *lustes*, i. 5. A, however, reads *long*.

5–8] W brings out more fully than Surrey Petrarch's main theme, which, according to Vellutello, is desire and restraint, the same theme as that of 'Quando 'l voler' (*Rime*, cxlvii), the sonnet printed immediately before this in his edition.

9 *the hertes forrest*] Nott sees no 'propriety or elegance' in this addition of W's. Smith defends it as 'specific and vivid' and as a successful 'evocation of a picture of the chivalric world' (op. cit., p. 336). There is furthermore a strong precedent for W's addition, and a strong argument for its propriety, in Petrarch's *Rime*. Sometimes he is literally wandering through the forests of the Ardennes, as in 'Per mezz' i boschi inospiti e selvaggi' (clxxvi); and at others the forest is his image for those worldly vanities in which, as a young lover, he got lost: 'Ahi quanti passi per la selva perdi!' (liv).

13 *in the felde*] W's addition is not altogether appropriate, since Love has fled from the battle.

v

2 *shapen afore my shert*] Cf. Chaucer, *CT*, A 1866: 'That shapen was my death erst than my shert' (Nott) and 'Complaint of Black Knight,' 489, 'my dethe shoped or my shert'. The phrase was proverbial (WMT).

5 *ouer*] Despite the agreement of B and E in reading *o*ʳ one would expect *my* rather than *our* in the context. We have therefore accepted the correction in E.

24 *price*] F declares that *price* in northern dialects means 'bargain'; but the meaning seems to be a much-prized and sought-after lady. Nott explains 'such wealth in another as gives him the privilege of purchasing affection, to the injury of true love'. Cf. VIII.140 n.

VI. A leaf is missing in E, containing the opening stanzas of this poem.

VII. Source:

> Una candida cerva sopra l' erba
>> Verde m' apparve, con duo corna d' oro,
>> Fra due riviere, a l' ombra d' un alloro,
>> Levando 'l sole, a la stagione acerba.
> Era sua vista sí dolce superba,
>> Ch'i' lasciai per seguirla ogni lavoro;
>> Come l' avaro che 'n cercar tesoro
>> Con diletto l' affano disacerba.
> "Nessun mi tocchi," al bel collo d' intorno
>> Scritto avea di diamanti e di topazi;
>> "Libera farmi al mio Cesare parve".
> Et era 'l sol già vòlto al mezzo giorno;
>> Gli occhi miei stanchi di mirar, non sazi;
>> Quand' io caddi ne l' acqua, et ella sparve.
>
>>> Petrarch, *Rime*, cxc

Some scholars think that W's sonnet was imitated directly from Petrarch, and others think that it derives from Giovanni Antonio Romanello's fifteenth-century imitation, 'Vna cerva gentil'. This first appeared in his *Rhythmorvm Vvlgarivm* (Verona, n.d., *c.* 1480, sonnet iii) and afterwards in Giusto de' Conti's *La Bella Mano* (Venice, 1531), which supplies W's possible source for LIII. It contains the lines:

> Tocar non lice la mia carne intera
> CAESARIS. Enim sum. . . .

which are closer to W's l. 13 than is Petrarch's l. 11. Accordingly Nott (571) preferred Romanello as W's source. Koeppel (66) preferred Petrarch since in his sonnet, as in W's, the biblical words are inscribed on the hind's collar, and not spoken, as they are by Romanello's 'cerva gentil'. Thus only *for Cesars I ame* seemed dependent on Romanello. F agreed; but Carlo Segré was still inclined to accept Romanello's influence (*Relazioni Letterarie fra Italia e*

Inghilterra (Florence, 1911), 82 n., 92.) Baldi (219) thinks the likeness to Romanello coincidental, Hughey (11.130) that W used both sources, and Thomson (198) that the likeness is accidental, since the well-known Latin motto *Noli me tangere quia Caesaris sum* is to be found in the various early commentaries on Petrarch's sonnets.

The personal reference of Petrarch's sonnet, as understood by the early commentators, is described by Thomson (197–200). Many critics believe that W too was referring to personal circumstances, when Henry VIII claimed Anne Boleyn *c.* 1527. (See Nott, xxiv–v; Chambers, 132; Baldi, 19, 22, 57). Berdan (472) was sceptical.

W adapts Petrarch's description of his symbolic vision of a white hind who then disappears from his view into an account of a love chase in which many are involved and from which he, convinced of its futility, withdraws. He abandons Petrarch's picturesque landscape (cf. 1 n.), his dream-like atmosphere, pathos and symbolism, and develops the metaphor of the hunt, making it central to his meaning. See the comparisons by F. W. Bateson (*English Poetry: a Critical Introduction* (1950), 141–2), Baldi (183), Lever (26–7), Mason (188–90), S (86–9), Thomson (196–200). S's argument against those who believe that W gives a cynical slant to Petrarch's meaning has received indirect support from Guss (37–8).

Grimald's corrections in E are described by Hughey (11.129–30), who also supplies a facsimile in *Library*, xv (1935), 414–15.

6] The deer/dear pun is one of the commonest in sixteenth-century literature.

8] Proverbial. See Tilley, W416; Erasmus, *Adagia*, 1720; Petrarch, 'In rete accolgo l'aura', *Rime*, ccxxxix, 37; Florio, 'pigliar il vento colle reti', *Giardino di Ricreatione* (1591) 4.

11 *Diamondes*] In Petrarch, like the topazes, symbols of chastity. S cites Hawes, *Passetyme of Pleasure*, 169–71:

> Theyr colers were of gold/and of tyssue fyne,
> Wherin their names/appered by scrypture
> Of Dyamondes/that clerely do shyne.
> The lettres were grauen fayre and pure . . .

13 *Noli me tangere*] *John*, xx, 17 is the ultimate origin of the Latin motto, which was said to be inscribed on the collars of Caesar's hinds so that they were left alone (cf. Da Tempo in Stagnino, f. 103ᵛ; Vellutello, f. 149ᵛ). No irreverence need be imputed to either poet since the words, as remarked by Gesualdo (f. 237ʳ), 'sono uenute in prouerbio'.

for . . . ame] cf. *Matthew*, xxii. 21.

14] See note to IV for Swallow's comment on W's use of the four-stress line in dénouements.

VIII. Source:

> Quell' antiquo mio dolce empio signore
>   Fatto citar dinanzi a la reina
>   Che la parte divina
>   Tien di nostra natura e 'n cima sede;
>   Ivi, com' oro che nel foco affina,   5

Mi rappresento carco di dolore,
Di paura e d' orrore,
Quasi uom che teme morte e ragion chiede;
E 'ncomincio – Madonna, il manco piede
Giovenetto pos' io nel costui regno,   10
Ond' altro ch' ira e sdegno
Non ebbi mai; e tanti e sí diversi
Tormenti ivi soffersi,
Ch' al fine vinta fu quell' infinita
Mia pazïenzia, e 'n odio ebbi la vita.   15
Cosí 'l mio tempo in fin qui trapassato
È in fiamma e 'n pene; e quante utili oneste
Vie sprezzai, quante feste,
Per servir questo lusinghier crudele!
E qual ingegno ha sí parole preste   20
Che stringer possa 'l mio infelice stato
E le mie d' esto ingrato
Tante e sí gravi e sí giuste querele?
Oh poco mèl, molto aloè con fele!
In quanto amaro ha la mia vita avezza   25
Con sua falsa dolcezza,
La qual m' atrasse a l' amorosa schiera!
Che, s' i' non m' inganno, era
Disposto a sollevarmi alto da terra.
E' mi tolse di pace, e pose in guerra.   30
Questi m' ha fatto men amare Dio
Ch' i' non deveva, e men curar me stesso:
Per una donna ho messo
Egualmente in non cale ogni pensero.
Di ciò m' è stato consiglier sol esso,   35
Sempr' aguzzando il giovenil desio
A l' empia cote ond' io
Sperai riposo al suo giogo aspro e fero.
Misero! a che quel chiaro ingegno altero
E l' altre doti a me date dal cielo?   40
Ché vo cangiando 'l pelo
Né cangiar posso l'ostinata voglia:
Cosí in tutto mi spoglia
Di libertà questo crudel ch' i' accuso,
Ch' amaro viver m' ha vòlto in dolce uso.   45
Cercar m' ha fatto deserti paesi,
Fiere e ladri rapaci, ispidi dumi,
Dure genti e costumi
Et ogni error ch' e' pellegrini intrica;
Monti, valli, paludi e mari e fiumi;   50
Mille lacciuoli in ogni parte tesi;
E 'l verno in strani mesi,
Con pericol presente e con fatica:
Né costui né quell' altra mia nemica
Ch' i' fuggia me lasciavan sol un punto.   55
Onde, s' i' non son giunto
Anzi tempo da morte acerba e dura
Pietà celeste ha cura

Di mia salute, non questo tiranno,
  Che del mio duol si pasce a del mio danno.   60
Poi che suo fui, non ebbi ora tranquilla,
  Né spero aver; e le mie notti il sonno
  Sbandiro, e piú non ponno
  Per erbe o per incanti a sé ritrarlo.
  Per inganni e per forza è fatto donno   65
  Sovra miei spirti; e non sonò poi squilla,
  Ov' io sia in qualche villa,
  Ch' i' non l' udisse. Ei sa che 'l vero parlo:
  Ché legno vecchio mai non róse tarlo
  Come questi 'l mio core, in che s' annida   70
  E di morte lo sfida.
  Quinci nascon le lagrime e i martíri,
  Le parole e i sospiri,
  Di ch' io mi vo stancando, e forse altrui.
  Giudica tu, che me conosci e lui.–   75
Il mio adversario con agre rampogne
  Comincia – O donna, intendi l' altra parte,
  Che 'l vero, onde si parte
  Quest' ingrato, dirà senza defetto.
  Questi in sua prima età fu dato a l' arte   80
  Da vender parolette, anzi menzogne:
  Né par che si vergogne,
  Tolto da quella noia al mio diletto,
  Lamentarsi di me, che puro e netto
  Contr' al desio che spesso il suo mal vòle   85
  Lui tenni, ond' or si dole,
  In dolce vita ch' ei miseria chiama,
  Salito in qualche fama
  Solo per me, che 'l suo intelletto alzai
  Ov' alzato per sé non fôra mai.   90
Ei sa che 'l grande Atride e l' alto Achille
  Et Anibàl al terren vostro amaro,
  E di tutti il piú chiaro
  Un altro e di vertute e di fortuna,
  Com' a ciascun le sue stelle ordinaro,   95
  Lasciai cader in vil amor d' ancille:
  Et a costui di mille
  Donne elette eccellenti n' elessi una
  Qual non si vedrà mai sotto la luna,
  Ben che Lucrezia ritornasse a Roma;   100
  E sí dolce idïoma
  Le diedi et un cantar tanto soave,
  Che penser basso o grave
  Non poté mai durar dinanzi a lei.
  Questi fûr con costui l' inganni miei.   105
Questo fu il fèl, questi li sdegni e l' ire,
  Piú dolci assai che di null' altra il tutto.
  Di bon seme mal frutto
  Mieto: e tal merito ha chi 'ngrato serve.
  Sí l' avea sotto l' ali mei condutto,   110
  Ch' a donne e cavalier piacea il suo dire;

E sí alto salire
Il feci, che tra' caldi ingegni ferve
Il suo nome, e de' suoi detti conserve
Si fanno con diletto in alcun loco;   115
Ch' or saria forse un roco
Mormorador di corti, un uom del vulgo;
I' l' esalto e divulgo
Per quel ch' elli imparò ne la mia scola
E da colei che fu nel mondo sola.   120
E per dir a l' estremo il gran servigio,
Da mille atti inonesti l' ho ritratto;
Ché mai per alcun patto
Al lui piacer non poteo cosa vile:
Giovene schivo e vergognoso in atto   125
Et in penser, poi che fatto era uom ligio
Di lei ch' alto vestigio
L' impresse al core e fece 'l suo simíle.
Quanto ha del pellegrino e del gentile,
Da lei tène da me di cui si biasma.   130
Mai notturno fantasma
D' error non fu sí pien, com' ei vèr' noi;
Ch' è in grazia, da poi
Che ne conobbe, a Dio et a la gente:
Di ciò il superbo si lamenta e pente.   135
Ancor (e questo è quel che tutto avanza)
Da volar sopra 'l ciel li avea dat' ali
Per le cose mortali,
Che son scala al Fattor, chi ben l' estima:
Ché, mirando ei ben fiso quante e quali   140
Eran vertuti in quella sua speranza,
D' una in altra sembianza
Potea levarsi a l' alta cagion prima:
Et ei l' ha detto alcuna volta in rima.
Or m' ha posto in oblio con quella donna   145
Ch' i' li die' per colonna
De la sua frale vita. – A questo, un strido
Lagrimoso alzo, e grido:
– Ben me la diè, ma tosto la ritolse. –
Responde – Io no, ma chi per sé la volse. –   150
Al fin ambo conversi al giusto seggio,
I' con tremanti, ei con voci alte e crude,
Ciascun per sé conchiude:
– Nobile Donna, tua sentenzia attendo. –
Ella allor, sorridendo: 155
– Piacemi aver vostre questioni udite;
Ma piú tempo bisogna a tanta lite. –

Petrarch, *Rime*, ccclx

The source of this translation was identified by Nott (551). It has not
proved very popular. But Hietsch's careful comparison (124–47) enables him
to claim that W has not always disfigured Petrarch, that he writes freshly at
points where he breaks with him, and that his abuse is often vigorous.
H. Howarth has also found something to praise in this and W's other versions

of Italian canzoni (*Italica*, xli (1964), 79–90). For the most part he works as a conscientious literal translator, anxious to bring out the original meaning. Thus *dolore* is rendered as *dolour* (l.5), *preste* as *prest* (l.19), and a careful explanation of Petrarch's classical references is provided (ll. 85–8). Unfortunately the English is not always comprehensible without reference to the Italian (e.g. ll. 19–21, 22–5, 42, 53–5). And W is sometimes reduced to padding (e.g. *thought and mynde* in l. 26). On the other hand he often finds his own equivalents for the Italian phrasing (e.g. *rest* and *errour* in l. 28, *any honest custume* in l. 120). And he often introduces stronger terms (e.g. *wicked traytour* in l. 41) or more vivid ones (e.g. *clattering knyght* in l. 76, *Serpent* in l. 111).

W omits or reduces material inappropriate to himself and his own poetic purposes. Petrarch's references to God are left out (see ll. 134, 139, and 150 of the Italian), as are the exalted compliments to Laura (ll. 100, 120) and the courtly tribute of her liegeman (ll. 126–8). The references to Petrarch's poetry and poetic fame are missing from the corresponding passages in W (ll. 96–8, 99–105). W also tones down Petrarch's Platonism, though without banishing it altogether (ll. 131–3).

viii is consistent with W's handling of Petrarch's *Rime* in general. He chooses only this canzone and one sonnet (see ccxxxvi) from the group 'In Morte di Madonna Laura'. It is questionable whether, in his version of the canzone, he is talking about the loss of the beloved through death and her translation to Heaven: see l. 140 and note.

In other respects the canzone may not have struck W as particularly novel. The poet calls Love before the judgement seat of Reason, complaining of his mercilessness, and the debate which follows, as well as the allegory itself, stands in the medieval court of love tradition.

W's choice of rhyme royal, though it involves the loss of Italianate lyricism, was probably dictated by its use in medieval English love poetry. It may even have been suggested by Chaucer's use of it in poems, such as *Troylus and Criseyde*, based on Italian sources. W works carefully, allowing two stanzas of rhyme royal for each of Petrarch's stanzas, and one for his coda. Unlike his sonnets, Petrarch's canzoni did not prompt W to exact metrical imitation. Poulter's measure is used in xcviii and cii, light eight-line stanzas in clviii and interwoven quatrains in ccxxxii. He seems rather to have been seeking an English equivalent to the complex Italian stanzas. Only in cxiv, a version of a canzonetta by Bembo, does he attempt to approximate to the original scheme.

A contains an anonymous translation, in poulter's measure, of ll. 1–38 (see Hughey, no. 64). W translates *citar* (l. 2) as *acited*, the anonymous poet as 'Scited'. Both render *schiera* as *dawnce*. But as the first is an obvious translation and the second a medieval cliché (e.g. Chaucer, *Pro.*, l. 476 *T & C*, ii, 1106), the evidence for the dependence of W on the anonymous poet, or of the anonymous poet on W, remains too slight. The poulter's measure of the analogue is of interest in view of W's use of it in his other versions of Petrarch's canzoni (xcviii and cii).

Texts: The only complete early sixteenth-century text is in T. Hughey's collation (ii.188–92) indicates a close relation between A and T 'as opposed to E'. Both attempt conformity with iambic pentameter, whereas E has in many lines a freer rhythm. Hughey (1.44–5 and 11.189) also studies Grimald's corrections in E. T entitles the poem: 'Wiates complaint vpon Loue, to Reason: with Loues answer.'

1] Cited by Puttenham (126) as an illustration of W's frequent use of the dactyl, though he accidentally misplaces the stress in his scansion *master*] The lord of love.

2 *that Quene*] Reason (cf. l. 3).

3 *the divine parte of nature*] The divine part of human nature: cf. *nostra natura* and T's reading. Vellutello (f. 158ᵛ) explains what would, in any case, be clear to most sixteenth-century readers, that this is reason, a nobler thing than sense. W omits *e 'n cima sede*.

4] Baldi (219) suggests that this could be emended, on the strength of Petrarch's l. 5, to 'There, like as gold in fire that mought be tryed'.

5 *Charged*] Cf. xxviii.1.

7 *wrongfull, alwaye*] W's additions, perhaps accounted for by his tendency both to insist on and to persist with his statement of the lover's rights.

8–9] According to Vellutello's note on the original, while the right foot is reason, the left is sense or appetite: 'egli pose il manco piede, cio è l'appetito che mouea l'animo, nel regno d'amore, ne diletti, & piaceri terreni, essendo e gli giouenetto' (f. 158ᵛ).

10, 11 *fierlye burninge flame, many a grevous payne*] W anticipates the phrasing of Petrarch's l. 17.

13 *oppressed*] Substituted for *infinita*, and expressing, as indicated by Hietsch (135), the force of *vinta*.

16 *payne and smarte*] W substitutes this cliché for *fiamma e 'n pene*, which he has already used in ll. 10–11.
wayes proffitable] W includes Petrarch's *utili* but omits his *oneste* (l. 17).

18 *this false lyer so deceaveable*] A free rendering of Petrarch's 'this cruel flatterer'.

19 *forceable*] The adjective is W's addition, suggested by *stringer*.

21] W renders Petrarch's *giuste*, but omits *gravi*, and shortens the phrasing of the original.

22–5] The Italian suggests that W's sense should run 'O small honey, much aloes, and gall! In bitterness has my blind life tasted his [the lord of Love's] false sweetness which has drawn me into (or with) the amorous dance'. W adds the proverbial phrase *that torneth as a ball* (cf. Tilley, W901). See LVIII.31.

25 *dawnce*] Substituted for *schiera*. Cf. *T & C*, ii, 1106 (WMT).
traced]? drawn (*atrasse*).

26] W omits *s' i' non m' inganno* (l. 28), and, evidently in difficulties with Petrarch's ll. 28–9, fills in with the redundant *thought and mynde*.
araced] The E reading *ataced* was accepted by F, who explained it as 'silenced' (11.83), and by Hietsch (136). It is probably a scribal error for *araced* (cf. A and T) which fits the Italian *sollevarmi* better.

27] W's addition, though implied by *alto da terra*.

28] W substitutes an antithesis between *rest* and *errour* (literally, wandering), for Petrarch's antithesis between peace and war.

29] 'A perfect alexandrine' according to Nott (552), but five stresses arise naturally from the sense and rhythm.
He] i.e. the lord of Love.
regarde] Substituted for *amare*.

32 *in this onely to spede*] W's addition, though implied by Petrarch.

35 *tempered with fiere*] Substituted for *ond' io/Sperai riposo al suo giogo aspro e fero* (ll. 37-8).

36 *wit*] W omits the terms qualifying *ingegno*, i.e. *chiaro* and *altero*.

37 *nature*] A logical substitute for *cielo*.

38 *weryed sprite*] Substituted for the metaphor *pelo*.

41 *wicked traytour*] A stronger term than *crudel*.

42] The meaning of the English, which translates the Italian literally, is that the bitter life has become customary and hence pleasurable.

43-9] Render Petrarch's ll. 46-53, which are said to describe his journey through Germany. W omits, transposes, and adds descriptive details, and perhaps derives a few terms from Vellutello. The chief omissions are of *paludi* and *fiumi* (l. 50), and of the description of spring weather at an unusual time of year, that is, of a cold summer (l. 52).

43 *dyvers regions*] Substituted for *deserti paesi*, the adjective coming perhaps from Vellutello's 'diuerse . . . cose' (f. 159ᵛ).

44 *desert wodes*] The adjective is taken from Petrarch's *deserti* (l. 46). The noun is W's, perhaps suggested, since woods and error go together, by *ogni error ch' è pellegrini intrica* (l. 49): cf. W's addition in IV.9.
sherp high mountaignes] Vellutello's gloss on *ispidi dumi*, 'cio è aspri spini' (f. 159ᵛ), perhaps supplies the first adjective. The second is W's. The mountains are transposed from Petrarch's l. 50.

45 *frowarde people*] Cf. *Fiere e ladri rapaci* (l. 47) and *Dure genti* (l. 48).
straite pressions] Literally, 'tight pressures', and derived probably either from Petrarch's description of the errors entangling the pilgrim (l. 49) or from that of the snares laid on all sides (l. 51).

46 *rocky*] W's addition (cf. *mari*, l. 50).
hilles and playnes] Cf. *Monti, valli* (l. 50).

47 *labourous paynes*] Cf. *fatica* (l. 53).

48] Generalizes the meaning of Petrarch's description as a whole.

49 *all errour*] Cf. *ogni error* (l. 49).
daungerous distres] Cf. *pericol* (l. 53).

51 *For all my flyght*] W slightly modifies the Italian 'she from whom I fled' (ll. 54-5).

52 *tymely deth*] W's adjective derives from *tempo*, and he omits Petrarch's two adjectives, *acerba e dura* (l. 57).

53–5] Cf. Petrarch's ll. 56–9. The meaning runs 'If death has not yet over-taken me, it is because heavenly goodness out of pity prevents it, and not because the tyranny of the god of Love has abated.'

54 *goodenes*] *Pietà* suggests that E's reading is correct, and that there was no need for Grimald's correction.

55 *cruell extreme*] W's addition.

58 *to do*] Substituted for *aver*.
waky] W's addition.

59 *bannysshed*] Derived from Petrarch's verb (*sbandiro*). W expands Petrarch's phrase here, and so has to reduce *per erbe o per incanti* to the comparatively colourless *no wyse*.

62 *my playntes to renewe*] W's addition.

64 *stock*] Cf. *legno*.

65] An alexandrine (F, 11.84).

67 *bitter*] W's addition.

68 *and eke the languisshement*] W's addition.

70] An octosyllabic, according to F (11.84); but, more likely, W intended a truncated decasyllabic, with five stresses, the first foot being spondaic. A and T have a smoother iambic pentameter line.
th' one and th' othre] Cf. *me . . . lui* (l. 75), that is, the lover and the lord of Love.

73 *plain*] The adjective is added by W, in order to get the force of *senza defetto* (l. 79).

74 *This vnkynd man*] (*Quest' ingrato*) is the *he* of l. 73, and not the subject of *shall shew*.
ere that I part] W's addition (unlikely to be a mistaken rendering of *onde si parte*, already translated as *from which he draweth alowff*).

75 *I toke him*] Cf. *Tolto* (l. 83).

76 *and maketh a clattering knyght*] W's free rendering of *anzi menzogne* (l. 81).

77–8 W transposes phrases from ll. 82 and 83 of the Italian.

77] Cf. *al mio diletto* (l. 83).

78] Built up from Petrarch's l. 82 and *Lamentarsi di me* (l. 84).

79 *evermore*] Cf. *puro e netto* (l. 84).
in pleasaunt game] Cf. *In dolce vita* (l. 87).

80 *that myght have ben his payne*] A free rendering of *che spesso il suo mal vòle* (l. 85).

81 *frame*] Petrarch's l. 88 suggests that W might have intended *fame* (*fama*). W's *frame* fits the context, however. See Hietsch (140–1).

82] Cf. *ond' or si dole* (l. 86), which W transposes and connects with *frame*.

83, 84 *qwickened, myght have sitt*] W uses his own metaphor in place of *alzai . . . alzato per sé non fòra mai* (ll. 89–90).

84 *daskard*] W's addition, reinforcing the sense of the original.

85 *Atrides*] Agamemnon. W omits the epithet *grande* (l. 91), but communicates its sense by adding *that made Troye frete*. T's *great Atride* is closer to Petrarch: cf. l. 3.

86] W logically supplies *Rome* in place of *terren vostro*.

87] Cf. *l' alto Achille* (l. 91). W, adding *Whome Homere honoured*, again explains and amplifies the classical reference.
grete] W has now transferred the epithet *grande* to Achilles.

88] Cf. Petrarch's ll. 93–4. W adds the name of this hero, *the Affricane Scipion*, as supplied by Velletullo's gloss on *Un altro*: 'lo primo Scipione Aphricano' (f. 160ᵛ).

89] W's addition, suggested by *tutti* (l. 93) and the sense of the whole passage.

90] In saying that their *fame and honour*, not their 'stars', dictated the heroes' destinies, W alters the sense of the corresponding line in Petrarch (95).

92 *thoughe he no deles worthy were*] W's addition.

93 *mylion*] Cf. *mille* (W is unlikely to have misunderstood the literal sense).

95] A free rendering of *Donne elette eccellenti* (l. 98), and of the sense of Petrarch's l. 100. W omits the specific reference to *Lucrezia*.

96–8] A free rendering of Petrarch's ll. 101–4. W omits his references to the *dolce idïoma* and *cantar tanto soave* lavished on Laura, referring, less specifically, to the gifts of *a facon* and *a way*. Line 95 is W's own contribution. In l. 98 he omits *grave*, and applies Petrarch's statement (ll. 103–4) directly to the lover.

99–105] W's first important departure. The lines correspond roughly to ll. 110–28 of the Italian. Though W includes the idea that he learned virtues in the 'school' of Love, he excludes the references to Petrarch's poetic skill and fame. Obviously he could not afford to make such claims so strongly. He also omits the reference to Laura's uniqueness (l. 120).

101 *sterred*] Both E's reading (meaning *steered*) and T's *stirred* would fit in with the general sense of the Italian *salire/Il feci* (ll. 112–13). Some modification of the original is called for here, since W, throughout this passage, deliberately uses terms less exalted than Petrarch's.

106] W now returns to an earlier passage of his source, building this up from l. 105 and the first half of l. 106.

107 *the torment and the anger*] Cf. *li sdegni e l'ire* (l. 106).

108] A clumsy attempt at Petrarch's l. 107. The meaning is that the torment inflicted by Laura is sweeter than the enjoyment given by any other woman.

109] Cf. xxix.14 and note for this proverbial saying.

111 *Serpent*] W's addition.

112] W's addition, making a conclusion different from Petrarch's in the corresponding ll. 110–11.

113] W now moves forward to l. 121 of the Italian.

114 *dishonestes*] i.e. dishonesties (*atti inonesti*, l. 122).

115 *in no maner of wyse*] Cf. *per alcun patto* (l. 123).

117] A free rendering of Petrarch's l. 125, omitting the specific reference to the poet's youth.

118–19] W, having omitted the passage complimenting Laura and describing Petrarch as her henchman (ll. 126–8), provides his own conclusion.

119 *Whome nowe he accuseth*] Cf. *di cui si biasma* (l. 130).

120–1] Cf. *Quanto ha del pellegrino e del gentile,/Da, lei tène e da me* (ll. 129–30). W's *any honest custume* reduces Petrarch's poetic phrasing to plain English, without destroying its meaning.

122] Cf. Petrarch's l. 131.

123 *ferre*] Substituted for *pien* (l. 132).

124–6] W's addition, though *To plain on vs* is suggested by *vèr' noi* (l. 132) and *si lamenta e pente* (l. 135), and Petrarch's idea of the lover's pride (in the corresponding ll. 133–5) is not altogether lost. W omits the references to grace, God, etc.

127–8] W now returns to the Italian at ll. 136–7.

129 *To honour and fame*] W's addition. Petrarch merely says that the poet's wings enable him to fly *Per le cose mortali* (l. 138), and so to mount to God (l. 139). W, as before (see ll. 124–6), omits the reference to God, and so reduces the Platonic transcendentalism.

130] Built up from *Per le cose mortali* (l. 138) and *sopra 'l ciel* (l. 137).

131–3] Virtually independent of the corresponding Italian (ll. 140–3). W takes only hints from Petrarch's description of the Platonic ascent to the *summum bonum*, e.g. the idea of *Considering* (*mirando*), and the antithesis between *erthe* and *above*. W's very obscure statement seems to mean 'considering the pleasure that loving contemplation can give even on earth, how much greater must it be in the eternal realms above'.

134] W returns to the Italian at l. 144. He uses Petrarch's *ha detto*, but omits his *in rima*. Cf. his omissions in ll. 96–8.
or this] i.e. ere this, W's version of *alcuna volta*.

136 *his onely welth and blisse*] Substituted for *per colonna/De la sua frale vita* (l. 146–7).

137] Cf. *A questo . . . grido* (ll. 146–8). W substitutes *dedly* for *Lagrimoso*.

139 *that wo worth thee*] W's addition.

140 *price, that is well worthy*] Stands in place of Petrarch's reference to God as 'he who desired her for himself' (l. 150). The meaning has been much debated. Nott (553) suggested thealt ernatives: (1) 'that the reward she was to receive at her death was the cause of her being removed', and (2) that W 'designedly departed from the original and meant to intimate "that a richer rival had taken his mistress from him" '. Rollins (ii.180) accepts (1), as, virtually, does F (ii.85), who explains *price* as bargain (northern dialect). H. Howarth accepts (2), and goes further than Nott with the suggestions that ' "Price" has filched her' and ' "Price" is a cipher for King

Henry, who took Anne Boleyn' (*Italica*, xli (1964), 80, 81). Cf. the supposed situation in vii. In support of this conjecture is the use of *price* in v.24.

141] W omits *al giusto seggio* (l. 151), and builds up his line from *Al fin ambo* (l. 151) and *Ciascun per sé conchiude* (l. 153).

142 *with small reverence*] W's free version of *con voci alte e crude* (l. 152).

143] W's addition.

144 *wayte*] Used, as in ME, transitively: cf. xxx.3.

147 *resolution*] Cf. *lite* (l. 157).

ix. Source:

> Io non fu' d' amar voi lassato unqu' anco,
>   Madonna, né sarò mentre ch' io viva;
>   Ma d' odiar me medesmo giunto a riva,
>   E del continuo lagrimar so stanco;
> E voglio anzi un sepolcro bello e bianco,
>   Che 'l vostro nome a mio danno si scriva
>   In alcun marmo, ove di spirto priva
>   Sia la mia carne, che po star seco anco.
> Però, s' un cor pien d' amorosa fede
>   Può contentarvi senza farne strazio,
>   Piacciavi omai di questo aver mercede.
> Se 'n altro modo cerca d' esser sazio
>   Vostro sdegno, erra; e non fia quel che crede;
>   Di che Amor e me stesso assai ringrazio.
>
> Petrarch, *Rime*, lxxxii

The source was identified by Nott (537), who remarked that W 'in the second quatrain and the last line, departs a little from his original'. D. G. Rees showed that Petrarch's theme was already one of defiance of love, sorrow, and Laura, citing the interpretations of the Italian commentators (*MLR*, lii (1957), 389–91). See note on ll. 5–8. For other comparisons between the two sonnets, see W. J. Courthope, *History of English Poetry*, 1897 (11.54), F (11.31), Baldi (190, 220), Lever (24–6), and Hietsch (84–9).

Grimald's corrections in E are studied by Hughey (11.131–2). T entitles the sonnet: 'The louer waxeth wiser, and will not die for affection.'

1 *greeved*] Substituted for *lassato*.

3 *that date is past*] Corresponds to *giunto a riva*.

5–6] In the corresponding lines 5–8, Petrarch tells Laura that he would rather not have a tomb inscribed with her name (i.e. recording that he died for love of her); and then goes on to express the wish that his body and spirit should continue together. W brings forward this last idea to l. 5, so that the effect of his defiance is rather more abrupt than Petrarch's, though not contrary to its spirit. To make room for it he omits *bello e bianco*, and freely rephrases the original. Vellutello, as Rees points out, explains that Petrarch gave Laura to understand 'che egli non era tanto dalle amorose passioni oppresso, che anchora non potesse uiuere' (f. 61ᵛ). In fact, his edition, in which the *Rime* are arranged to form a narrative sequence, would assist

U

W's reading of this sonnet as one rebellious against love. It is grouped with a number of other poems in which Petrarch retracts his love, talks of his freedom from his 'uita lasciua' (f. 60ʳ), or finds on returning to it that it lacks 'la forza che prima hauea' (f. 61ʳ).

6 *yfixed*] The southern past participle, derived from Chaucer (K).

8 *by great sighes sterred*] W's addition.

14] W's only marked departure from his original, in that he lays the blame squarely on the lady.

x. No source has been discovered for this sonnet; and, as it expresses one of W's favourite themes, it is probably original. The metrical irregularities (e.g. in l. 9) suggest that these should not be ascribed in the translations to W's difficulties in conveying the sense of the Italian. T entitles the poem: 'Of change in minde.'

3 *propose*] i.e. purpose, which the other texts, perhaps rightly, read.

5 *mytt*] meet.

8, 9 *dyvernes*] diverseness, the reading of the other texts.

xi. This feeble poem, in single rhymed quatrains, 'a type common in Middle English lyrics' (F), puzzled T's editor, who revised some of the lines. T entitles it: 'A renouncing of hardly escaped loue.'

4 *Conduyt . . . nede*] Presumably the final 'e' of *nede* should be pronounced. 'Conduct my thought which is in need of joys'.

6 *A goode cause just*] i.e. a good just cause.

10 *Glad that is gone*] This means, perhaps, 'glad that, the danger, is gone'.

14 *eche*] i.e. joy and pain.

xii. Source:

> S' una fede amorosa, un cor non finto,
>   Un languir dolce, un desïar cortese;
> S' oneste voglie in gentil foco accese,
>   Un lungo error in cieco laberinto;
> Se ne la fronte ogni penser depinto,
>   Od in voci interrotte a pena intese,
>   Or da paura or da vergogna offese;
>   S' un pallor di vïola e d' amor tinto;
> S' aver altrui piú caro che sé stesso;
>   Se sospirare e lagrimar mai sempre,
>   Pascendosi di duol, d' ira e d' affanno;
> S' arder da lunge et agghiacciar da presso
>   Son le cagion ch' amando i' mi distempre;
>   Vostro, donna, il peccato, e mio fia 'l danno.

> Petrarch, *Ríme*, ccxxiv

The source of this close literal translation was identified by Nott (543), though Puttenham (126), commenting on W's use of dactyls, seems to have recognized it as Petrarchan. As in the case of ix, W has chosen a congenial subject from Petrarch's *Rime*, blame of the lady and the injustice done to her lover. Hietsch (88–91) compares the sonnet with its original and points out that W uses the same material in xcvii. T entitles the sonnet: 'Charging of his loue as vnpiteous and louing other.'

1 *amours*] the reading of A and T, *amorous*, is preferred for metrical reasons, by Baldi (220). It is also a more exact rendering of the Italian and in ix.9 W translates *amorosa fede* as *amourous faith*. He does not elsewhere use the word *amours* which is probably a mistake of the E scribe.

2 *great lovely*] Substituted for *cortese*.

4 *Yf*] Early editions of Petrarch read *s' un lungo error* (e.g. Bembo, 1501; Vellutello, 1525) and this doubtless accounts for W's word.
chaynéd] W's addition.

5] Here, and in l. 9, W changes his original into the first person.
depaynted] W's only use of this word (Hangen). Though obviously dictated by *depinto*, it is not un-English: see *Gawain* (649).

6 *sperklyng*] Rollins (11.199), who notes that W 'does not adequately translate' Petrarch's l. 6, says that one would expect *speaking* here, the reading of the fifth (1565) and later editions of T. But as the early texts agree with E here, it must have had a meaning for early readers, and strong support comes from W's mention of *wordes* that *sparkill in the wynde* (liii.20-1). Petrarch's *voci interrotte* means broken or halting tones (being paraphrased 'parole spezzate' by Gesualdo, f. 276ᵛ). Of the *N.E.D.* definitions of *sparkling* and the related *sparpling*, 'scattering' and 'dispersing' (1440, *c.* 1460, 1530) approximate to *interrotte*. Cf. Surrey, *Aeneid*, II. 199, 517. For W's use of *sparplid*, see cviii.8 (*spark'led* A, R, Q) and cviii.408.
lower or higher] Substituted for *a pena intese*.

7 *tyer*] Cf. *offese*, used in the rare sense of 'impaired' (Hietsch, 91). W adds *wofully* to bring out the sense.

8 *pale colour*] Cf. *pallor di vïola*. W omits the flower image.

11] W omits *d' affanno* and adds *bissely*, probably for the rhyme.

14] W omits *donna*, and adds *great*, in order to strengthen *annoye* (cf. *danno*).

xiii. No source has been discovered for this sonnet, which is metrically smoother than most of W's translations. T entitles it: 'A renouncing of loue.'

3 *Senec and Plato*] Neither guide is mentioned in the earlier version of the sonnet in D. W translated some lines of Seneca (see ccxl) and recommended his son to study Seneca's prose (l.43). There is no evidence that W had a direct knowledge of Plato.

14 *rotten boughs to clyme*] Proverbial: see Tilley, B557 and cf. ccxxiv.33 and cxlvi.55–6 (WMT).

xiv. Source:

> El cor ti diedi non che el tormentassi
> Ma che fosse da te ben conseruato,

> Seruo ti fui non che me abandonassi
> Ma che fosse da te remeritato,
> Contento fui che schiauo me acchatassi
> Ma non di tal moneta esser pagato,
> Hor poi che regna in te poca pietate
> Non ti spiaccia sio torno in libertate.
>
> La donna di natura mai si satia
> Di dar effecto à ogni suo desyderio,
> E sempre ti stá sopra con audatia
> Del tuo martyr pigliando refrigerio,
> Quanto piú humil li uai tanto piú stratia
> Perfin che thá sepulto in cymiterio,
> Perche chi pone suo amor in femina
> Zappa nel acqua & nella haren semina.
>
>   Serafino, *Opere* (1516), f. 151 ʳ⁻ᵛ

The source of W's sonnet, which is based on two consecutive strambotti, was identified by Nott (543). The first is literally translated to form the octave, the second more freely manipulated into the sestet. W's adaptation, and experiment in turning strambotti into sonnet form, are discussed by Thomson (219-21). T entitles the sonnet: 'The louer forsaketh his vnkinde loue.'

5 *servant*] D's 'slave' is closer to *schiauo*.
   remayn] Substituted for *acchatassi*, so that W fails to anticipate the money metaphor of l. 6.

6 *vnder this fasshion*] This substitute for *di tal moneta* weakens the money metaphor further.

7 *none othre reason*] Substituted for *poca pietate* and not in itself clear.

8 *refrain*] Cf. *torno in libertate*.

9-10] A free adaptation of the two opening lines of the second strambotto. W, to give continuity, turns the third into the first and second persons, and avoids Serafino's generalization about 'woman'. He follows the drift of the original, but introduces the idea of the lady's crafty excusing of her faults, where Serafino merely says that a woman is by nature insatiable in giving effect to her desires.

11-12] Independent of the corresponding lines (3-6) of the second strambotto, except that W takes over the lady's feigning.

13] A free rendering of l. 7.

14] See IV note for Swallow's remarks about the four-stress line in dénouements.
   soweth in the sand] Proverbial in Italian and English. See Florio, *Giardino di Ricreatione* (1591), 192, and Tilley, S87, S184. WMT cites *Gorgeous Gallery*, ed. Rollins (1926), 65: 'The plowing in Sea, and sowing in Sandes'. Cf. Skelton, *Speke, Parrot*, 342.

xv. F (11.16) suggested that this rondeau was a reminiscence of two of Clément Marot's, 'D'Estre Amoureux' and 'S'il est ainsi'; but the resemblance is very slight.

3 *trought*] truth.

5 *geven me leve*] i.e. to go; 'an idiom purely French' (Nott).
full honestly] irony.

8 *sesse*] cease.

12 *to my first adresse*] to his situation before he loved her.

13 *to . . . prese*] he has too many rivals.

xvi. No source has been discovered. The many variants in D show that W made a thorough revision of this sonnet. T entitles it: 'The abused louer seeth his foly, and entendeth to trust no more.'

1–4] W is quibbling on the various meanings of *file*, the noun and verb concerned with polishing, and the word for deceive and deceiver.

12 *That . . . recompence*] That deceit is the recompense of deceit.

xvii. No source has been discovered, but the idea of the heart leaving the body was a commonplace to be found, as F points out (11.17), in Chrétien de Troyes and Marot: cf. xviii. See also Chaucer, *B of D*, 1152–4.

5 *appere*] appair.

xviii. Source:

> S'il est ainsi que ce corps t'abandonne,
> Amour commande & la raison ordonne
> Que je te laisse en gaige de ma foy
> Le cueur ja tien, car par honneste loy
> Aulcun ne doibt reprendre ce qu'il donne.
> Ne croy jamais qu'aillieurs il s'abandonne!
> Plus tost la mort (sans que Dieu luy pardonne)
> Le puisse prendre & meutrir devant toy
> S'il est ainsi.
>
> Si Faulx rapport qui les amantz blasonne
> Te vient disant que j'ayme aultre personne,
> Tu respondras: Meschant, point ne le croy,
> Car j'ay son cueur; & corps sans cueur, de foy
> Ne peult aymer; la raison y est bonne
> S'il est ainsi
>
> Rondeau, xxx

The source of W's poem is the above rondeau by Jean Marot – it was formerly attributed to Clément Marot (see F, 11.18; C. A. Mayer and D. Bentley-Cranch, *Bib. D'Humanisme et Renaissance*, xxvii (1965), 183–5) – and Marot was imitating a sonnet by Serafino, 'Se questo miser corpo t'abandona'. W takes Marot's refrain, adapts the conceit of the body without a heart, and gives the main argument of the original; but he weakens the second verse by transferring the lady's words to himself.

xix. F (11.23) compares a rondeau by Clément Marot, 'Amor et Foy sont bien appariez'; but this has little resemblance to W's.

4 *Eche ... semblable*] Cf. LIII.24 and Tilley, L 286.

xx. Source:

> Ite, caldi sospiri, al freddo core;
> Rompete il ghiaccio che pietà contende;
> E, se prego mortale al ciel s'intende,
> Morte o mercé sia fine al mio dolore.
> Ite, dolci penser, parlando fore
> Di quello ove 'l bel guardo non s' estende:
> Se pur sua asprezza o mia stella n' offende,
> Sarem fuor di speranza e fuor d' errore.
> Dir si po ben per voi, non forse a pieno,
> Che 'l nostro stato è inquïeto e fosco
> Sí come 'l suo pacifico e sereno.
> Gite securi omai, ch' Amor vèn vosco:
> E ria fortuna po ben venir meno,
> S' a i segni del mio sol l' aere conosco.
>
> Petrarch, *Rime*, cliii

The source was identified by Nott (545); but, as with xvIII, the substance of the Italian probably reached W through a French rondeau: cf. also 1 in which a madrigal by Petrarch becomes a rondeau. W translates the first quatrain of the sonnet, but thereafter diverges. The second quatrain, in which 'thoughts' displace 'sighs' as the lover's intercessors with Laura, is not used, though the repetition of *Ite* probably suggested W's refrain. The sestet supplies only the idea of 'rest' (l. 8). W omits all Petrarch has to say of fortune. A basis for W's free development of the theme is provided by Vellutello who says that Petrarch at this point, having found little cause to hope, is prepared to experiment ('mostra uoler experimentare', f. 55ʳ). But he does not explain l. 11. And, as Hietsch (187) points out, W changes the spirit of the original, ending on a distressed, instead of a hopeful note. Realizing that his sighs may not succeed in melting his mistress, he introduces the idea that craft and art must be used on so faithless a person. Guss (39) develops the thesis that W adapts Petrarch's conceits 'to an emphatic representation of the virtuous man's position in a corrupt world'. W may have known Petrarch's sonnet in the musical setting by Brocco, published by Petrucci in 1505: see I.L. Mumford, *EM*, xiv (1963), 18–19. T, who reconstructs the poem as a sonnet, entitles it: 'The louer sendeth sighes to mone his sute.'

1 *burnyng*] W's alteration of *caldi* prepares the way for *flame* (7) and *fyer* (13).

2 *paynfull dert*] W's addition.

6 *Take with*] i.e. take with you.

8 *rest*] Cf. *inquïeto* (10), and Vellutello's paraphrase, 'senza riposo' (f. 55ᵛ).

11–12] The emphasis is essentially W's, though the lady's cruelty derives from Petrarch's *sua asprezza* (7).

xxi. The first stanzaic poem in E with a refrain. S (74) regards it as one of W's maturest poems which 'has never received its due'. T entitles it: 'The louer taught, mistrusteth allurements.'

9 *to accorde*] The words should be elided.

10 *hase*] has; but Nott suggests we should read *halse* (embrace).

11 *Imprisoned in libertes*] i.e. because he is unable to decide.

15] 'If one line may represent the psychological crisis expressed in W's poetry this is certainly the line' (S).

19 *Nay, sir*] 'might warrant the conjecture that W wrote this piece at the request, or in the person of some lady' (Nott); but this is unlikely.

xxii. Possible source:

> Laer che sente el mesto a gran clamore
> Diuulga in ogni parte la mia doglia
> Tal che per compassione del mio dolore
> Par che ne treme in arbore ogni foglia,
> Ogni fiero animal posa el furore
> Che daiutarmi ognun par chabbia uoglia
> Et con mugito stran uoglion le carmi
> Et uorrian sol parlar per consolarmi.
>
> Serafino, *Opere* (1516), f. 125ʳ

The possibility that W's three stanzas of rhyme royal are based on Serafino's strambotto was suggested by Nott (546), and accepted by Cecchini (99) and Baldi (222). The subject, the lover's complaint and nature's sympathy with it, is common to the tradition in which both poets write. But the lover's 're-sounding' complaint (*gran clamore*) and some of the scenic details (air, leaves) suggest that W may have taken his inspiration from the strambotto. If so, he adds rivers, hills, vales, and rain, as well as a stanza of open complaint against his hard-hearted mistress. Baldi (195) names this among those versions of Serafino in which W improves on his original; and S (78–9) remarks on W's 'sharpening of the personal element'. T entitles the poem: 'The louer com-playneth that his loue doth not pitie him.' One of the poems in B is on a similar theme (cxv).

13 *howgy*] Among those words with 'y' endings (cf. *tery*, xxiv.12), which, according to Veré L. Rubel (*Poetic Diction in the English Renaissance* (1941), 49), give evidence of W's conscious archaism and use of Chaucerian words.

xxiii T entitles the poem: 'The louer reioyseth against fortune that by hindering his sute had happily made him forsake his folly.'

3] Nott compares 'Fortuno sævo læta negotio', Horace, *Odes*, iii.29.

5] The only line in the poem with three stresses.

7 *Spite . . . hapt*] Cf. xxxvi.1.

9 *thy*] The emendation in T, *by*, is an improvement.

11 *and*] i.e. if.

16 *And . . . stile*] Probably a variant of the proverb 'To leap over the hedge before you come at the stile'. Tilley, H363 (WMT).

xxiv. Source:

> Sono animali al mondo di sí altera
>   Vista che 'n contr' al sol pur si difende:
>   Altri, però che 'l gran lume gli offende.
>   Non escon fuor se non verso la sera:
> Et altri, col desio folle che spera
>   Gioir forse nel foco perché splende,
>   Provan l' altra vertú, quella che 'ncende.
>   Lasso! el mio loco è 'n quest' ultima schiera.
> Ch' i' non son forte ad aspettar la luce
>   Di questa donna, e non so fare schermi
>   Di luoghi tenebrosi o d' ore tarde:
> Però con gli occhi lagrimosi e 'nfermi
>   Mio destino a vederla mi conduce:
>   E so ben ch' i' vo' dietro a quel che m' arde.
>
>   Petrarch, *Rime*, xix

The source was identified by Puttenham (241) and Nott (540). Puttenham cited Petrarch's sonnet as an example of the figure of '*Resemblance*, inuring as well by *Dissimilitude* as *Similitude*' adding that it was 'very well Englished' by W. W, though he adds a line of his own (11), and muffles the original sense of l. 7, is working accurately. He follows out the original structure. F (11.36) notes the unusual break, following Petrarch, after l. 7: l. 8 in both sonnets forms a bridge passage, concluding the octave and introducing the sestet. Lever (22–4) compares the two sonnets, noting W's 'great advance in metrical control, the five-foot iambic principle almost superseding the earlier imitations of Italian rhythm'. Hietsch (91–5) also compares them, allowing that W achieves more flexibility than in xii, though he is still forced by the rigidities of the sonnet form to fill out lines. T entitles the sonnet: 'How the louer perisheth in his delight, as the flie in the fire.'

4 *pere*] i.e. appear (cf. *escon fuor*).

5–6] W inverts Petrarch's phrases (ll. 5–6).

6 *as they do pretend*] A gap-filling phrase (Hietsch, 92), but perhaps justified as emphasizing the *desio folle* of those who play with fire.

7] A free and not fully explicit rendering of Petrarch's l. 7 which states that these 'others' who seek out the brightness of fire, in fact find its other *vertú*, burning. W misses the antithesis of *splende* and *'ncende*. Possibly he misread *'ncende* as *'ntende*.

8 *by right*] Cf. *el mio loco*.

9 *her loke*] Cf. *la luce/Di questa donna*. W's terms are less exalted than Petrarch's.

10] W omits *o d' ore tarde*.

11] W's addition, 'an original touch of subjective detail' (Lever, 24).

12 *tery*] See note on xxii.13, and cf. Chaucer, *T & C*, iv, 821.

xxv. Source:

> Perch' io t' abbia guardato di menzogna
> A mio podere et onorato assai,
> Ingrata lingua, già però non m' hai
> Renduto onor, ma fatto ira e vergogna.
> Ché, quando più 'l tuo aiuto mi bisogna
> Per dimandar mercede, allor ti stai
> Sempre piú fredda; e, se parole fai,
> Son imperfette e quasi d' uom che sogna.
> Lagrime triste, a voi tutte le notti
> M' accompagnate, ov' io vorrei star solo,
> Poi fuggite di nanzi a la mia pace.
> E voi, sí pronti a darmi angoscia e duolo,
> Sospiri, allor traete lenti e rotti.
> Sola la vista mia del cor non tace.
>
> Petrarch, *Rime*, xlix

The source was identified by Nott (540). For comparisons with the original, see Lever (20–2), Hietsch (94–9), and Thomson (193–4). W is on congenial ground with this sonnet. In Vellutello's edition it follows 'Mie venture' and precedes 'Mirando 'l sol', both of which W also translated (xxx and xxix), and which also explain Petrarch's grief and frustration. On the tongue-tied lover, the cause of whose grief lies in his inability to express himself, see LVI.12–14 (translated from Petrarch) and CLXXXIII.21–8. A. Swallow takes this as an example of a 'rough' sonnet, though with the reservation that W's roughness has been exaggerated: except for the four-stress ll. 8 and 14 it can be read as iambic pentameter (*MP*, xlviii (1950), 5).

Hughey (11.143) remarks on A's departures from E. The A compiler 'did not understand the sense in ll. 3 and 14 and so altered the lines in such a way as to destroy the point'. T, on the other hand, does, in both lines, convey 'the sense of E'. T entitles the sonnet: 'Against his tong that failed to vtter his sutes.'

1 *and blame*] W's gap-filling addition.

3 *right ill*] A positive statement, substituted for *non . . . onor* (ll. 3–4).

4 *For suche deserft*] W's addition.
wrek] Substituted for *ira*.

6 *reward*] Cf. *mercede*.
like oon aferd] Lever (21) remarks on this 'vivid original touch', added by W.

8 *and lame*] W's addition, made for the sake of the rhyme.

9 *again my will*] W's addition, reinforcing *ov' io vorrei star solo* (l. 10).

11 *when I should make my mone*] Substituted for *di nanzi a la mia pace*. Petrarch's *la mia pace* ('cio è Madonna Laura': Gesualdo, f. 66ᵛ) may not have been clear to W. His alteration of this phrase, though it appears free and has the effect of emphasizing his personal grievance, is sanctioned by Vellutello, whose comment on ll. 9–11 is 'quando egli è alla presentia di lei, & che per muouerla a compassione di lui uorrebbe lagrimare, non ne puo hauer una' (f. 66ʳ).

13] W's repetition of *Then are ye* (cf. l. 11) is his own contribution to the
parallel structure dictated by Petrarch's tercets. Cf. *And ye . . . And you*
(ll. 9 and 12) and *a voi . . . E voi* (ll. 9 and 12).

when that ye should owtestert] W's version of *traete*, making explicit what is
implied in Petrarch's l. 13. As Hietsch (99) notes, the commentators' para-
phrases sanction his rendering (e.g. Filelfo's 'gittare sospiri grandi', in
Stagnino, f. 43ʳ).

14] See Swallow on W's use of a four-stress line in dénouements (note to IV).

XXVI. Source:

> Pace non trovo e non ho da far guerra;
>   E temo e spero, et ardo e sono un ghiaccio;
>   E volo sopra 'l cielo, e giaccio in terra;
>   E nulla stringo, e tutto 'l mondo abbraccio.
> Tal m' ha in pregion, che non m' apre né serra,
>   Né per suo mi riten né scioglie il laccio;
>   E non m' ancide Amor e non mi sferra,
>   Né mi vuol vivo né mi trae d' impaccio.
> Veggio senz' occhi e non ho lingua e grido;
>   E bramo di perir e cheggio aita;
>   Et ho in odio me stesso et amo altrui.
> Pascomi di dolor, piangendo rido;
>   Egualmente mi spiace morte e vita.
>   In questo stato son, donna, per vui.

> Petrarch, *Rime*, cxxxiv

The source was identified by Nott (540). The 'contraries of love' theme, and
with it, the figure of antithesis are much used by Petrarch (e.g. *Rime*, cclii, in
which the phrase in l. 2, *E temo e spero*, recurs). They are also popular with W
(e.g. LXXVII, CLXXXIX). In this translation he is careful to preserve, and
even, as in ll. 7 and 10, to enhance the antitheses. Berdan (474) cites this
example to illustrate his choice of Petrarch's conceited, and most easily imita-
ted, sonnets. It would undoubtedly be more popular in the sixteenth century
than it is now, since its rhetoric was then thoroughly acceptable. See Hietsch
(98–105), who points out that the sonnet brings into the English Renaissance
a whole 'garland' of sonnets using antithesis as their chief rhetorical device.
W may have known the original in its musical settings by an anonymous com-
poser (1470) and by Romano (1514): see I. L. Mumford, *EM*, xiv (1963), 19.
Mumford also notes a probable musical setting of W's version: see *Music and
Letters*, xxxix (1958), 262–4.

Puttenham (123) quotes ll. 1–2 as an example of good iambic verse con-
sisting wholly of monosyllables. F. T. Prince cites the sonnet as an example
of the pressure exerted upon the native 'pausing' line by the Italian form,
hendecasyllabic line, and antithetical structure (*Elizabethan Poetry*, ed. J. R.
Brown and B. Harris (London, 1960), 14). T entitles the sonnet: 'Description
of the contrarious passions in a louer.'

1 *all my warr is done*] Modifies Petrarch's meaning, which is that he lacks
strength to wage war.

3–4] W substitutes *wynde* and *seson* (seize on) for *cielo* and *abbraccio*.

3] Though the line could be scanned as a hexameter, it is probably intended as a pentameter (without stress on the second syllable of *above*): see A. Swallow, *MP*, xlviii (1950), 4.

5 *That*] obscures the sense of *Tal*, which is usually taken to refer to Laura, but which could equally well refer to Love. The latter, to judge by his *it* in l. 8, was W's interpretation.

7] Built up from *E non m' ancide Amor* (l. 7) and *Né mi vuol vivo* (l. 8). W is repeating the earlier and anticipating the later pattern, in which an antithesis is completed within a single line.
at my devise] W's addition.

8] W's addition, used in place of *e non mi sferra* (l. 7) and *né mi trae d' impaccio* (l. 8).

10 *helthe*] Substituted for *aita*, and emphasizing the contrast with *perisshe*.

11] W inverts the antithetical statements in Petrarch's l. 11, and adds *thus*.

14] W abandons the direct address to Laura (l. 14), and uses the comparatively strong *stryff* in place of *stato*.

xxvii. Source:

> Orso; al vostro destrier si po ben porre
>   Un fren che di suo corso in dietro il volga;
>   Ma 'l cor chi legherà che non si sciolga
>   Se brama onore e 'l suo contrario aborre?
> Non sospirate: a lui non si po tôrre
>   Suo pregio, perch' a voi l'andar si tolga;
>   Ché, come fama publica divolga,
>   Egli è già là, che null' altro il precorre.
> Basti che si ritrove in mezzo 'l campo
>   Al destinato di', sotto quell' arme
>   Che gli dà il tempo, amor, vertute e 'l sangue,
> Gridando: D' un gentil desire avampo
>   Co 'l signor mio, che non po seguitarme
>   E del non esser qui si strugge e langue.

Petrarch, Rime, xcviii

The source of W's fairly free translation has been identified by Sergio Baldi, who has also noticed the influence of Vellutello's commentary on it (*English Studies Today*, ed. I. Cellini and G. Melchiori (Rome, 1966), 124). The freedom is exercised in a distinctive and consistent manner. Petrarch addresses Orso, Count of Anguillara, condoling with him because, contrary to his wishes, he has been unable to attend some social or otherwise important event. Vellutello and Gesualdo both read this as a love poem, Vellutello supposing that the event in question is a joust at which Orso's lady will be present. Though he plays down the jousting terms, W also reads it as a love poem. But instead of addressing a friend, he opens in the first person and adapts Orso's situation to himself. Later (l. 4) he turns Petrarch's remarks on the heart into a direct address to his own heart. So he produces a more subjective and introspective poem, turning an outer into an inner debate. Baldi (222) also formerly noted W's echo, in ll. 1–2, of the opening of another sonnet by Petrarch:

> Quando 'l voler, che con duo sproni ardenti
> E con un duro fren mi mena e regge,
> Trapassa ad or ad or l' usata legge.
>
> (*Rime*, cxlvii)

And he gave high praise to W's varied melody (160), numbering this among his 'great' sonnets (186).

1–2] Baldi (op. cit., 125) paraphrases 'Though my mind prevents me *from* returning backwards at once' (not '*while* I am turning back').

1 *be bridilled*] Cf. *si po ben porre/Un fren.*
mynde. Almost certainly used here in the sense of desire: cf. *destrier*, which, according to Vellutello (f. 187ʳ), is 'inteso per lo suo desiderio'.

2 *by force expresse*] Derived from Vellutello's gloss on Petrarch's l. 2. On the horse of desire one can put a *freno* to turn it back, and one can use force – 'farli forza' – to divert it so that it does not go after the beloved (f. 187ʳ).

3–4] W inverts ll. 3 and 4 of the Italian.

3 *to kepe thy promes*] Substituted for *e 'l suo contrario aborre* (l. 4), which merely strengthens the first statement in the line, and may therefore have struck W as inessential. The words substituted are probably influenced by Vellutello, who suggests that Orso was unable to keep his assignment.

5 *no more, no way*] W's additions.

6 *vertue*] Substituted for *pregio* (praise).
let] Substituted for *tôrre.*

6–7 *though that frowerdnes/Of ffortune me holdeth*] A free development of *perch' a voi l' andar si tolga* (l. 6). The idea of fortune is supplied by Petrarch's meaning in general, by *destinato di'* (l. 10) in particular, and by Vellutello's gloss (on l. 10) to the effect that for success nowadays one must add to virtue, fortune: 'Ma hoggi bisognarebbe giungerui la fortuna' (f. 187ᵛ).

7 *as I may gesse*] W's gap-filling substitute for *come fama publica divolga* (l. 7).

8 *Though othre be present*] Substituted for *che null' altro il precorre* (l. 8), and perhaps suggested by Vellutello's comment on this phrase: 'che nessuno de suoi riuali il precorre, ciò è lo auanza' (f. 187ᵛ).

9 *there*] Substituted for *in mezzo 'l campo* (l. 9). W, as in ll. 1–2 and 10, tones down Petrarch's imagery of cavalry and jousting.

10 *At all howres*] Substituted for *Al destinato di'* (l. 10).
defence] Cf. *arme.*

11] W omits *sangue* and adds *to save the from offence.*

12–4 *I burne . . . sorrowe*] the utterance of the heart.

13 *my dere Maisteres*] Petrarch's *signor mio* indicates that E's reading is correct, A's incorrect.

14 *torneth him to sorrowe*] A free and softened version of *si strugge e langue*.

xxviii. Source:

> Passa la nave mia colma d' oblio
>   Per aspro mare, a mezza notte, il verno
>   In fra Scilla e Cariddi; et al governo
>   Siede 'l signore, anzi 'l nimico mio.
> A ciascun remo un penser pronto e rio,
>   Che la tempesta e 'l fin par ch' abbi a scherno:
>   La vela rompe un vento, umido, eterno,
>   Di sospir, di speranze e di desio.
> Pioggia di lagrimar, nebbia di sdegni
>   Bagna e rallenta le già stanche sarte,
>   Che son d' error con ignoranzia attorto.
> Celansi i duo miei dolci usati segni;
>   Morta fra l'onde è la ragion e l' arte:
>   Tal ch' i' 'ncomincio a disperar del porto.
>   Petrarch, *Rime*, clxxxix

The source was identified by Nott (541). W's task, to render as literally as possible the concentrated short love allegory of the ship, was not easy. But, apart from a few omissions and obscurities, he manages it with a fair degree of success. His sonnet has accordingly received qualified praise. W. J. Courthope calls it 'the production of an energetic mind', but adds that 'the means employed are inadequate to the end' (*History of English Poetry* (London, 1897), II, 53). Tillyard (28, 151) calls it 'the best . . . of the immature sonnets' and agrees with Courthope, as does F (11.40–1). D. G. Rees approves of the 'new sense of drama' present in this example of W's translation from Petrarch (*CL*, vii (1955), 17). See also the comparison by Hietsch (105–9).

Hughey (11.145) describes A as copied from E, with later changes in ll. 6 and 8. T entitles the poem: 'The louer compareth his state to a shippe in perilous storme tossed on the sea'.

3 *Rock and Rock*] Substituted for Scylla and Carybdis.

4 *my lorde*] Cf. *signore*, probably the lord of Love, though Vellutello explains it as 'l' appetito, dalquale essa naue uiene ad esser gouernata' (f. 118r).
sterith with cruelnes] W's strong version of *al governo/Siede 'l signore* (ll. 3–4), influenced by *rio* (l. 5).

5–6] 'Every oar is a thought ready to think that death is a small matter in this extremity' (Tillyard, 151). The Italian (ll. 5–6) brings out the meaning of W's rather obscure lines. He omits *rio* and *tempesta*.

5 *owre*] i.e. oar (*remo*). The A and T *houre* is proved wrong by the Italian, but the error is understandable since W also translates the Italian *ora* as *owre* (viii.57).

6 *light*] A's *lif* may be preferred as providing a sharp antithesis with *deth*. The Italian does not determine the correct reading since W translates l. 6 freely.

7–8] As the Italian shows, the terms in l. 8 are attached to *wynd*. W omits *umido*, adds *forced*, represents *speranze* in *trusty*, and changes *desio* to *ferefulnes*.

9 *derk*] W's addition.

10] W omits *Bagna* (l. 10).
cordes] Cf. *sarte* (shrouds).

12 *The starres*] Substituted for *i duo miei dolci usati segni* (l. 12). Petrarch probably refers to Laura's eyes, envisaged as guiding stars. Cf:

> Come a forza di venti
> Stanco nocchier di notte alza la testa
> A' duo lumi c' ha sempre il nostro polo,
> Cosí ne la tempesta
> Ch' i' sostengo d' amor gli occhi lucenti
> Sono il mio segno e 'l mio conforto solo.
>
> (*Rime*, lxxiii, 46–51)

13] W omits *l' arte*, and adds *that should me confort*.
confort] W elsewhere spells 'comfort' in this way; but it is possible that he wrote *consort*, and that this word, carrying on the nautical metaphor, was misread by the scribe. Nott and M read *consort*.

xxix. Source:

> Mirando 'l sol de' begli occhi sereno,
>   Ov' è chi spesso i miei depinge e bagna,
>   Dal cor l' anima stanca si scompagna
>   Per gir nel paradiso suo terreno;
> Poi, trovandol di dolce e d' amar pieno,
>   Quant' al mondo si tesse, opra d' aragna
>   Vede; onde seco e con Amor si lagna
>   C' ha sí caldi gli spron sí duro 'l freno.
> Per questi estremi duo, contrari e misti,
>   Or con voglie gelate or con accese,
>   Stassi cosí fra misera e felice:
> Ma pochi lieti e molti penser tristi;
>   E 'l piú si pente de l' ardite imprese.
>   Tal frutto nasce di cotal radice.
>
> Petrarch, *Rime*, clxxiii

The source was identified by Koeppel (67). W evidently aims at a literal translation, though there are lapses (e.g. ll. 7 and 9), which Baldi (223) would perhaps take as errors of interpretation. W has not generally been considered successful. Padelford, who condemns the 'insincerity and artificiality' of the original, also finds 'incoherency and elusiveness' in W's translation (xxii). Hietsch (109) shows that he is unable to equal the richness of Petrarch's thought. Lever (18) uses this as an example of the 'battle of the metres', the fifteenth-century English stress pattern striving to assert itself under the 'new' formal principles of the decasyllabic line (see especially ll. 8, 11, and 12). On the other hand S (70–2, 83–5) approves of the rhythm, remarking on the 'dramatic momentum', as well as on W's 'characteristic inwardness'. Hughey (II.146) shows that, in spite of variants, A is taken from E. T entitles the poem: 'Of douteous loue.'

1 *bright bemes*] W reduces Petrarch's 'sun' metaphor, but, as Hietsch (110) remarks, finds an equivalent for his alliteration (*sol . . . sereno*).

2 *he*] Cf. *chi*, that is, love (Vellutello, f. 66ʳ) or 'l' amoroso spirto' (Gesualdo, f. 222ᵛ).
moisteth and wassheth] W uses this doublet for *bagna*, omitting *depinge*.

3 *mynde*] Substituted for *anima*.

5 *vnder this gyse*] W's gap-filling addition.

6] W omits *al mondo* and turns the passive (*si tesse*) into the active. The consequent repetition of *he* creates some confusion. The first is the *he* of l. 2 (i.e. love), the second the *mynde* of l. 3 (Petrarch's *anima*, subject of *Vede*.)

8 *Ise*] Substituted for *duro*, and neatly balancing *fyer* (*caldi*).

9] A free translation of Petrarch's line, missing his point that the soul is torn between the 'two extremes' already defined in l. 8.

10 *thought*] Substituted for *voglie*, a change compatible with that from *anima* to *mynde* in l. 3.

11] W omits the verb (*Stassi*) and adds a second antithesis *twist ernest and game*.

12 *dyvers*] differing (i.e. from *glad*), adverse; hence an adequate rendering of *tristi*.

14] Petrarch's line is a variant of the Italian proverb 'Tal é l' arbore, tal é il frutto' (Florio, *His Firste Fruites* (London, 1578), f. 34ᵛ). W's is a variant of the English 'Such is the tree such is the fruit' (see Tilley, T494, and Skelton, 'Replycacion', l. 156; cf. also Tilley, T486 and 497). It is also used, in a slightly different form, in vIII.109.
ffruyte fruytles] A stronger expression than *Tal frutto*, though Rollins (II.170) thinks that W 'unnecessarily adds that the tree bears no fruit'. The addition of *fruytles* 'may have been suggested by Vellutello's comment' (f. 66ᵛ) which ends with a reference to Ovid's description (*Met.* VI) 'D'Aragne & dei suoi sottilissimi ma *inutili* lavori'. (Baldi in article cited in note on xxvII.)

xxx. Source:

> Mie venture al venir son tarde e pigre,
>   La speme incerta, e 'l desir monta e cresce,
>   Onde il lassare e l' aspettar m' incresce;
> E poi al partir son piú levi che tigre.
> Lasso! le nevi fien tepide e nigre,
>   E 'l mar senz' onda, e per l' alpe ogni pesce,
>   E corcherassi 'l sol là oltre ond' esce
> D' un medesimo fonte Eufrate e Tigre;
> Prima ch' i' trovi in ciò pace né triegua
>   O Amor o madonna altr' uso impari,
>   Che m' hanno congiurato a torto in contra:
> E s' i' ho alcun dolce, è dopo tanti amari,
>   Che per disdegno il gusto si dilegua.
>   Altro mai di lor grazie non m' incontra.
>   Petrarch, *Rime*, lvii

The source was identified by Nott (542). W's translation has received more blame than praise. F (11.43) complains that it is 'harsh and irregular' as compared with the 'liquid' Italian, and that 'The whole sonnet is faulty, the conceit overloaded and ungraceful'; Rollins (11.194–5) that 'The rhymes sound rough to a modern ear, and the changes introduced [in T] render them but little more euphonious'. Hietsch (113), who also finds the translation clumsy, nevertheless finds something to admire in W's anglicizing of Petrarch's learned allusions (see l. 7). And it must surely be allowed that he deals effectively with the 'impossibilities' figure (see ll. 5–8). T entitles the poem: 'How vnpossible it is to finde quiet in his loue.'

2] W inverts the statements in Petrarch's l. 2.

3 *leve it or wayt it*] Proverbial (Tilley, T28).
wayt] Used, as in ME, transitively. Cf. VIII.144.

5–8] The use of *impossibilia* is traced back, by E. R. Curtius, to Archilochus, and discussed under the heading 'The World Upsidedown' (*European Literature and the Latin Middle Ages*, trans. W. R. Trask (New York, 1953), 94–8). Hietsch (114) shows that it would be familiar to W not only from Latin sources but from Chaucer, who uses it, and in a love context, in *T & C*, iii, 1495–8.

7–8] W inverts Petrarch's ll. 7 and 8.

7 *Tamys*] W anglicizes the biblical and literary figure of Euphrates and Tigris, which is found in Lucan and Boethius, and which Petrarch may have derived from Dante's 'Eüfratès e Tigri/veder mi parve uscir d' una fontana' (*Purgatorio*, xxxiii, 112–13).

10 *or*] The reading of A, T makes good sense; the reading of E is very awkward.

13] W omits *per disdegno*.

14] W's free version of Petrarch's l. 14. Baldi (223) calls it his addition, but it is not completely out of touch with the original.

XXXI. Source:

> Amor, fortuna e la mia mente schiva
>   Di quel che vede e nel passato volta
>   M' affligon sí, ch' io porto alcuna volta
>   Invidia a quei che son su l' altra riva.
> Amor mi strugge 'l cor, fortuna il priva
>   D' ogni conforto: onde la mente stolta
>   S' adira e piange; e cosí in pena molta
>   Sempre conven che combattendo viva.
> Né spero i dolci dí tornino in dietro,
>   Ma pur di male in peggio quel ch' avanza;
>   E di mio corso ho già passato 'l mezzo.
> Lasso! non di diamante ma d' un vetro
>   Veggio di man cadermi ogni speranza,
>   E tutt' i miei pensier romper nel mezzo.
>
>   Petrarch, *Rime*, cxxiv

The source was identified by Nott (542), who was also the first to heap abuse on W's 'inelegant' translation, and especially on his repetition of *that* in l. 2. F (11.44) followed suit, calling this 'the most faulty sonnet' in the E group. Hietsch (115–16), though not in total disagreement with them, praises W for his attempt at a version which is correct, yet simpler and stronger than the original. It is true that W fails conspicuously, especially in ll. 1–4, to produce the clear literal translation at which he was probably aiming. But the repetition of *that* has perhaps been criticized too harshly: in the monosyllabic l. 2, with its strong central pause, it gives emphasis to the antithesis between present and past. T entitles the poem: 'Of Loue, Fortune, and the louers minde.'

1–4] One of W's most obscure translations, defeating T's editor, who reconstructs it to make a statement remote from the Italian. W's *remembre* is not clarified by *schiva*, but it is best taken with *schiva* as qualifying *mente/mynde* alone. Hietsch (116–17) emends it to *remembrer* (to which there are no objections on the score of rhyme, since *depriver* is the 'a' rhyme in l. 5). W's *theim* creates the greatest difficulty, since it seems to refer grammatically to love, fortune, and mind, and thus to produce nonsense. Its Italian equivalent is *quei*, which quite clearly refers to the dead, whom Petrarch in his sorrow envies. So it seems likely that W intended *theim beyonde all mesure* to stand for *quei che son su l' altra riva*, and that he did not intend *beyonde all mesure* to be an adverbial phrase attached to *Envy*. Thus the intended meaning would run 'Love, fortune, and my minde, remembrer of a past different from the present, torment me so that I often envy the dead'. Baldi (223) suggests that the emendation 'beyond the river' would bring the phrase into line with the Italian. In a comparable translation W does not adopt this Italian metaphor for dying (see xcviii, 4).

7–8 *as ... displeasure*] 'as one that seldom lives and rests, always in displeasure'. W's *sildam ... Lyveth and rest* represents *combattendo viva*, and the corrected E reading, *Lyveth in rest*, was probably meant as a clearer version of the Italian.

9–10] A free version of Petrarch's statement to the effect that he does not expect the return of the happy days of the past, but rather that the future will go from bad to worse.

11 Petrarch's l. 11 refers to his age, 38, which was three years beyond the 'metà del corso' (Vellutello, f. 79ᵛ). W normally adapts specifically personal references, and it is possible, from his retention of this one, that he too was over 35 at the time of writing.

12] W retains the contrast between the indestructible and the fragile, substituting *steill* for *diamante*. The alteration is appropriate since steel was still used for mirrors in the sixteenth century.

xxxii. Source:

> Mille fïate, o dolce mia guerrera,
> Per aver co' begli occhi vostri pace,
> V' aggio proferto il cor; m' a voi non piace,
> Mirar sí basso colla mente altera:

x

E, se di lui fors' altra donna spera,
  Vive in speranza debile e fallace:
  Mio, perché sdegno ciò ch' a voi dispiace,
  Esser non può già mai cosí com' era.
Or, s' io lo scaccio et e' non trova in voi
  Ne l' essilio infelice alcun soccorso,
  Né sa star sol né gire ov' altri il chiama,
Poria smarrire il suo natural corso:
  Che grave colpa fia d' ambeduo noi;
  E tanto piú di voi, quanto piú v' ama.

Petrarch, *Rime*, xxi

The source was identified by Nott (542). Assessments of its success have varied. F (11.45) says that 'The conceit is intricate, and results in confusion of ideas'. Hietsch (119, 121) shows that W keeps to the essentials of the original though in some places he removes or weakens epithets, that he sharpens P's antitheses, and closes with an effective couplet. Muir also compares the translation with its original, noticing particularly the 'magnificent finality' of W's l. 8 and its anticipation of the sestet (L, 225–7). W's handling is, in some ways, uncharacteristic, since he misses opportunities to criticize (see l. 4) and to blame (see ll. 13–14) his mistress. T entitles the poem: 'The louer prayeth his offred hart to be receiued.'

1 *dere and cruell foo*] Cf. *dolce mia guerrera*. The oxymoron is common Petrarchan stock: see *Rime*, clxxix.2 and ccliv.2, and cf. viii.1. W's addition of *cruell* makes him 'more explicit about his mistress's hostility' (L, 226).

2] W omits *begli* and fills the gap with the redundant *truyse*.

4 *high*] Suggests that W may have misread *altera* as *alta*. (He is unlikely to have mistaken the meaning of *altera*, which is translated *disdaynfull* in lvi.9.) The effect to throw emphasis on the lady's high-mindedness rather than her pride (L, 226), and also to create a stronger antithesis than in Petrarch.

5–6 *othre . . . theim*] W turns the singular (*altra donna*) into the plural .

5 *as ye trowe*] W's addition.

6 *weke*] E's reading, as contrasted with A's *weite*, is authenticated by *debile*. *doeth greately theim abuse*] A strengthening of Petrarch's statement (l. 6).

7] The first *that* is the heart.

8] A free and effective version of Petrarch's 'it can never more be as it was' (l. 8).

10] W omits *infelice* and fills the gap with *manner of*.

12] 'He may die.'
   naturall kynd] A redundant phrase, introduced, for the sake of the rhyme, in place of *natural corso*.

13 *hurt*] W perhaps misread *colpa* as *colpo* (Baldi, 223). It is uncharacteristic of him to miss the opportunity of bringing in blame and guilt: cf. l. 14.

14 Nott (543) suggested that this is taken from the last line of Petrarch's 'S' una fede amorosa', the source of xii. If so, it is a free version of it, with *losse* used in place of *peccato*. W's aim here, as in l. 4, is to create a stronger antithesis than is contained in the equivalent line.

xxxiii. Source:

> Simile a questi smisurati monti
>   E l' aspra uita mia colma di doglie
>   Alti son questi, & alte le mie uoglie
>   Di lagrime ambedui, questi di fonti
> Lor han, di scogli, li superbi fronti
>   In me duri pensier, l' anima coglie
>   Lor son di pochi frutti, e molte foglie
>   Io pochi effetti a gran speranza aggiunti
> Soffian sempre fra lor rabbiosi uenti
>   In me graui suspiri, esito fanno
>   In me se pasce Amor: in lor armenti
> Immobile son io, lor fermi stanno
>   Lor, han d' uccelli, liquidi accenti
>   Et io la mente, di superchio affanno.
>
> Sannazaro, *Le Rime* (Venice, 1531), Pt.
> III, No. 3, f. 49^v

Analogue: 'Sonnet par Marot'

> Voyant ces mons de veue si loingtaine,
> Je les compare à mon long desplaisir;
> Hault est leur chef et hault est mon desir,
> Leur pied est ferme et ma foy est certaine.
>   Là maint ruysseau coulle et mainte fontaine;
> De mes deux yeulx sortent pleurs à loysir;
> De grandz souspirs ne me puys dessaysir,
> Et des grandz ventz leur cime est toute plaine.
>   Mille troppeaulx prenent là leur pasture;
> Amour en moy prend vie et nourriture;
> J' ay peu d' effect et assés d' esperance.
>   Là, sans grand fruict, feulhes ont apparence;
> Et d' eulx à moy n'a q' une differance,
> Qu' en ceulx la neige, en moy la flame dure.
>
> Text from Bibliothèque Nationale MS.
> 1700, printed in Clément Marot, *Oeuvres
> Diverses*, ed. C. A. Mayer (London,
> 1966), 275.

The source was identified by Arthur Tilley (*MLQ*, v (1902), 149). The Italian sonnet, now only doubtfully attributed to Sannazaro, was first printed in the 1531 edition of his *Rime* in 'la terza parte nouamente aggiunta', and thereafter in those sixteenth-century editions containing this section (e.g. in the Venice, 1532 edition, but not the Venice, 1534 one). J. M. Berdan discussed dating possibilities, suggesting that W may have seen the sonnet in MS. before 1531 (*MLN*, xxiii (1908), 34–5). This is a careful line by line translation. It contains some successful literal translation, e.g. *smisurati/vnmesurable*, *Immobile son io/Immovable ame I*. And W finds some good English equivalents for Italian words, e. g. *rabbiosi/boystrous*, *armenti/Cattell*. He collapses only in the final couplet, and particularly in the last line.

The French analogue: This sonnet was first printed in Saint-Gelais's *Oeuvres* (Lyons, 1547), but entitled 'Sonnet par Marot'. (Marot's most recent editor, C.

A. Mayer, discusses its authorship, and, while recognizing that there can be no certainty, inclines to the view that it is probably his: op. cit., pp. 48–9). Until Tilley discovered the common Italian original, Koeppel's belief (*Anglia*, xiii (1891), 77–8) that W's sonnet derived from the French prevailed. W is, throughout, much closer to the Italian: see, for example, the translation of *smisurati* in l. 1. Italy was the gleaning ground common to French and English poets of the sixteenth century. And, though it is possible that W and the French poet worked in friendly rivalry, it is equally likely that, as in the case of XXXIV, they produced independent versions of an Italian poem. The question whether the comparatively free French version of Sannazaro's sonnet was influenced by W's translation has, however, been raised. Berdan pointed to the resemblance between *et hault est mon desir* and *and high is my desire* (*MLN*, xxiii (1908), 34–5). This phrasing is, however, dictated by Sannazaro, and, except in the identical rendering of *uoglie*, which may well be coincidental, does not assist Berdan's case. L. E. Kastner rejected it (*MLR*, iii (1907–8), 273–4). Berdan's reply was an attempt to show, contrary to the received opinion, that *petrarchismo* reached England before France, and that accordingly an English poet could have influenced a French one (*MLR*, iv (1908–9), 240–9). Kastner's opinion was not altered by this (*MLR*, iv (1908–9), 249–53). Berdan reiterated his views, adding some comment on the similarity in the rhyme schemes used by W and his French rival (*MLN*, xxv (1910), 1–4). Both use one more rhyme than Sannazaro. But the fact still does not clinch Berdan's case, for the sestet schemes are differently organized.

Metre: Puttenham (129) remarks on the 'superfluous' syllables in ll. 1, 2, and 4 of the T text. In E these are found in ll. 3, 4, 5, 7, 12, 13, and 14. Puttenham adduces the influence of the Italian hendecasyllabic line, but sounds rather baffled as to W's purpose: 'we must thinke he did it of purpose, by the odde sillable to giue greater grace to his meetre'. T entitles the poem: 'The louers life compared to the Alpes.'

1 *vnmesurable*] Cf. *smisurati*; contrast *de veue si loingtaine*.

2] W's rendering is more accurate and concentrated than the French.
the burden of Ire] Substituted for *colma di doglie*. Baldi (224) suggests that W may have read *colma* as a substantive; but even so his rendering would remain free.

4] While W adheres to Sannazaro, the French poet introduces his own elaboration of the theme, deferring fountains to l. 5 and tears to l. 6.

5 *Craggy*] W's addition. The French poet omits the rocks altogether.
full barren playns] Substituted for *li superbi fronti*. The idea of barrenness is, however, sanctioned by the later *pochi frutti* (l. 7).

6 *tyre*] See *N.E.D.*, tire, 11.2, where the term used in falconry is defined as 'seize: of a hawk tearing at flesh', and cf. Marlowe's metaphoric use of it: 'The grief that tires vpon thine inward soule' (*Dido*, l. 1725).

7] W translates accurately. The French poet uses *graui suspiri* from Sannazaro's l. 10, and defers *frutti* to l. 12.

9 *their high bowghes*] W's amplification of *fra lor*. *Lor*/*their* refers throughout to the mountains. But where Sannazaro refers to the mountains among which

winds rage, W (influenced perhaps by l. 7) refers to the mountain trees blasted by winds. In this case the French version (l. 8) is, though comparatively tame, closer to the Italian.

10] W translates accurately. The French poet, having already dealt with *graui suspiri*, starts upon his elaboration of l. 11 of the Italian.

11 *Cattell*] Cf. *armenti*. The Italian does not justify T's *Wilde beastes*, or the later *fierce* introduced to match it. The French poet expands the sense of Sannazaro's l. 11 to fill his first tercet.

12] While W sticks to the Italian, the French poet starts upon a second tercet which is, except in gist, almost completely independent.

13 *restles*] W's addition. T's *singing* gets closer to Sannazaro's sense.
tune and note]. Cf. *liquidi accenti.*

14] W's free rendering misses the force of *la mente, di superchio affanno*, and his *that passe thorough my throte* is a feeble substitute for it, made to secure a rhyme.

xxxiv. Source:

> Madonna non so dir tante parole;
> o uoi uolet' o no; se uoi uolete
> oprat' al gran bisogn' il uostro senno
> che uoi saret' intesa per un cenno
> & se d' un che sempr' arde al fin ui duole
> un bel si un bel no mi rispondete;
> se sar' un si un si scriuero 'n rima,
> se sar' un no amici come prima
> uoi trouerret' un' altr' amante & io
> Non potend' esser uostro saro mio.

> Dragonetto Bonifacio: first printed with Verdelot's music in his first book of madrigals (*c.* 1535). Text, with light punctuation added, from Philippe Verdelot, *Le Dotte, et Eccellente Compositioni de i Madrigalli . . . a Cinque Voci*, (1549), 16.

The source was identified by Joel Newman (*RN*, x (1957), 13–15). His discovery does not establish the date of W's translation with certainty, but makes it likely to have been after *c.* 1535: Bonifacio (1500–26) left a collection of poems in a Venetian MS. of *c.* 1530, and this madrigal was first printed posthumously in Verdelot's collection of *c.* 1535. Formerly W's poem had been taken as an imitation of Saint-Gelais's douzaine (F, 11.87), but it is much closer to the common Italian original. W makes no major additions or omissions though he uses a different form. He uses English interwoven quatrains to render the Italian madrigal, a form which varies considerably, and which he probably did not recognize as a distinctive one (see 1 and note). His reasons for choosing this particular example may be connected with its omission of the pastoralism usually found in madrigals, and with the fact that this, as Alfred Einstein remarks, is one of the rare occasions in the madrigal genre when 'the lover speaks out as frankly as possible' (*The Italian Madrigal*, trans. A. H. Krappe, R. H. Sessions, and O. Strunk (Princeton, 1949). i, 177). There is little internal evidence that W's version influenced Saint-Gelais, the only common factor being that both use twelve lines in place of ten. T entitles the poem: 'To a ladie to answere directly with yea or nay.'

1] A free rendering of Bonifacio's l. 1.

2] Cf. *o uoi uolet' o no.*

3 *if ye will*] Cf. *se uoi uolete.*
  then leve your bordes] W's addition.

4] A free translation of Bonifacio's l. 3.

5–8] Cf. Bonifacio's ll. 4–6. W substitutes *at all* for *al fin.*

8 *yea*] The ampersand in E may stand for a nod.

9 *yf it be yea*] Cf. *se sar' un si* (l. 7).
  I shalbe fayne] Substituted for *un si scriuero 'n rima* (l. 7).

10–11] Cf. Bonifacio's ll. 8–9.

12] Cf. Bonifacio's *& io . . . mio* (ll. 9–10).
  E has the following reply. It is in a different hand and is also given in B.

> Of few wourdes sir you seme to be
> And wher I doutyd what I woulde doo
> Your quik request hathe causyd me
> Quikly to tell you what you shawl trust too.
> For he that wyl be cawlyd wythe a bek
> Makes haste sute on Lyght desier
> Is euer redi to the chek
> And burnythe in no wastynge fyer.
> Therfor whyther you be lywe or lothe,
> And whyther it giue you Lyght or soer
> I am at a poynt I have made a othe
> Content you wythe nay for you get no moer.

4 shawl] shall   6 haste] hasty   9 be lywe] believe   10] Nott emends, rightly, to *grieve.*

xxxv. The poem is difficult to decipher because it is largely covered with later writing. S has restored the original reading in four places. See his article in *ELN*, V (1967), 5–11. G. A. Parry, *MLR*, XX (1925), 461–2, compared a French rondeau from a miscellany compiled by Pierre Sala of Lyons:

> Vielle mulle du temps passé,
> Vostre visaige est effacé;
> Sy portez [en] la vielle myne
> Dedans vostre ville cuisine,
> En regrètant le temps passé.
> On a bien . . . haulsé
> Il n'a garde d'estre empoussé;
> Pour maquerelle vous assigne,
>   Vielle mulle!

> *Requiescant,* las, *in pace,*
> Car vostre bruit est trespassé;
> Plus ne fault trencher de la fine,
> Ne farder museau, ne poectrine,
> Car chascun est de vous lassé,
> Vielle mulle!

This is probably an analogue rather than a source.

1 *mule*] Anne Boleyn was called this by her enemies, but there is no reason to think the poem was addressed to her.

7 *fals savours*] Perfumes (S)

8 *layer*] lair, with a possible quibble on *layre,* meaning 'love' as in Charles D'Orleans (ed. R. Steele (1941), Glossary).

9 *Kappurs*] A kipper is a word for a colt and used in northern dialect for a wanton (F).

14–15] The middle-aged woman now has to pay her lovers to sleep with her.

xxxvi. This is the first example in E of a form of which W was fond, in which the first line of each stanza repeats the last line of the previous one.

11–14] Unless he is made to fast – deprived of love – for his own good.

12 *For . . . foode*] An allusion to Tantalus (F).

20 *In . . . require*] In hand what I need to help me.

xxxvii. This poem may owe something to Ovid, *Amores,* iii.7 and i.5 as C. E. Nelson has suggested (*MLR,* lviii (1963), 60–3). T, who provided a title ('The louer sheweth how he is forsaken of such as he sometime enioyed') made numerous disastrous improvements which have been analysed by Robert Graves and Laura Riding in *A Pamphlet against Anthologies* (1927).
There are discussions of the poem by Thomson (142–3), J. D. Hainsworth (*EC,* vii (1957), 95), A . S. Gérard (*EC,* xi (1961), 365), Ann Berthoff (*Sewanee Review,* lxxi (1963), 477–94), Donald M. Friedman (*SEL,* vii (1967), 1–13) and many others. R. L. Greene, *Bucknell Review,* xii (1964), 17–30, neatly refutes those critics who have deduced from W's imagery that he was writing of falcons, deer, or Fortune. To Friedman, the poem is W's 'most successful attempt to dramatize the moral predicament of the courtly lover'; but perhaps W was more concerned with his sense of desertion than with his moral predicament.

1 *They fle from me*] Cf. Charles d'Orleans, 1347, 'They flee fro me' (WMT).

2 *stalking*] Walking softly.

5 *in daunger*] In (my) power.

19 *new fangilness*] Inconstancy; the word is often used by Chaucer.

20 *kyndely*] Ambiguous (a) according to the law of kind or nature, (b) kindly in the modern sense (Thomson).
serued] 'Topsy-turvy. W, as the orthodox lover, is presumed to have been serving' (Thomson).

XXXVIII. This is one of the few poems in which W expresses the feelings of a woman.

5 *Alas the while*!] Cf. Chaucer, 'Compleynt d'Amours', 9 (WMT).

XXXIX, XL, CXC, CCXXIX. That these four 'patience' poems are related is shown not only by the common theme, but by the metrical form. A fifth (CCLIII) may also be one of the group, though unlike the others it employs a tetrameter line and formal refrain.

Possible source:

'Canzona de la Patientia'

Patientia alla malora
    poi che vòl cosí fortuna;
    non sta sempre el mondo in una,
    che in un punto Dio lavora.
Non si fidi alcuno al mondo,
    egli è pien tutto d'inganni;
    reputato è oggi i panni,
    le virtú son misse al fondo,
    chi sa ben guidare a tondo
    roba aquista a tutta ora.
        Patientia . . .
Chi sa oggi simulare
    dir si può esser beato,
    non pò stare apresso a stato
    chi questa arte non sa fare,
    e chi 'l mal sa ben tramare
    dice ognun che ben lavora.
        Patientia . . .
Chi avesse bon inditio
    di trovare qualche scropulo
    per cavar dinar dal populo,
    non li può mancare offitio;
    cascar possa in precepitio
    questa gente di fama fuora.
        Patientia . . .
Ognun sta su l'ingannare
    per fare trarre li compagni,
    e com hai rotto i panni,
    dice ognun che se' d'affare;
    sí gli vòl la cazza dare
    o lasciarlo in sua bon' ora.
        Patientia . . .
Hor felice chi dispone
    di seguir cose immortale,
    questo fumo poco vale,
    a chi sua vita gli pone;
    egli è morta la ragione,
    però ognuno ci divora.
        Patientia . . .
Spesse volte dico fra me:
    com pò far questo natura?

questa sorte sia sí dura
che non se trova ogi di fé;
ognun saldo sta sul pè
fin che passa questa ora.
        Patientia . . .
Ma in una hora Dio lavora
    in un punto, in un momento,
    però non mi discontento
    di mia sorte e mia fortuna.
Non mi voglio desperare,
    né cercare di morire,
    Dio se quel che l' à a fare
    per le cose ch' à a venire.
Quanti miseri son stati
    combattuti da fortuna
    a l' ultimo condemnati
    in l' aver e in la persona;
    poi son visti con corona
    tutti licti e consolati,
    però non vi disperati
    se mancassi per dimora,
    ché in una ora Dio lavora.

> *Le Rime di Serafino*, ed. Mario
> Menghini (Bologna, 1894),
> I, xxiv–vi

F (II.89) stated that the 'idea' of XXXIX and XL 'is derived from' Serafino, but without citing a particular source. Of CXCI she made the more definite claim that W 'no doubt found his model in the "Canzona de la Patientia" ' (II.149). Baldi (225, 234) takes all four patience poems as re-elaborations of the theme of the canzone. Apart from the theme, the refrain may have struck W, who himself repeats the word 'patience' in a refrain-like manner. But this inspiration could equally well have come to him via Serafino's 'A questa asppra penitentia', a barzelletta, in six-line stanzas, with the refrain

Al fin uince chi supporta
Ogni peso in patientia.
        (*Opere* (1516), f. 290ᵛ)

In substance the only striking likeness between the 'Canzona de la Patientia' and W's patience poems is found when Serafino's opening two lines are compared with XXXIX.19–20 and CX CI.1–2. Otherwise Serafino's and W's grumblings at misfortune are differently directed. The canzone is a complaint against the times: the wicked flourish, deception, and extortion are widely practised, men are irreligious, and only the poet's trust in God's power saves him from despair. W's poems, at least XXXIX and XL, are, by contrast, love poems, and all four are set in a comparatively narrow, personal, and emotional context: only remotely and by implication are they attacks on society. Furthermore, W, without any assistance from Serafino, was familiar with and given to versifying the subject of fortune's remedies. In 1527 he translated part of Petrarch's *De Remediis Utriusque Fortunae*, and his reading of Plutarch, Seneca, and

Boethius supplied similar philosophical ideas. In his light love poems the 'remedies' are also turned to good account by the habitually impatient hero:

> I se no Remedy
> But suffer pacyently.
>
> (CXCI. 23–4)

Cf. ccxxx.28 and cxxvi.3–4. It therefore seems appropriate to admit the 'Canzona de la Patientia' as a possible, but not a certain, source. Mason (172) takes the patience poems as examples of the kind of verse Tudor courtiers would write on themes proposed by ladies and for their albums. Stevens (218) uses them to exemplify Tudor court poems debating set themes. I. L. Mumford discusses xxxix, xl, cxci, and ccliii as a group, commenting on W's adaptation of Serafino's form (the frottola) and his use of the rhyme scheme of the Italian sestina (*EM*, xiv (1963), 12–15).

xxxix, xl. The note appended to xl in D shows that it was intended as a sequel to xxxix. In xl the lover mocks the lady for her impatience, her refusal to respond to the patience he preached in xxxix. The two are companion pieces, and appear as such in the MSS. They make an obvious appeal to the taste for love debates popular in the Middle Ages and, in W's day, with such literary groups as Louise Labé's in France. xxxix has received due praise, Tillyard (157) admiring W's play with the word 'patience', and Baldi (197) quoting the first two stanzas to illustrate W's melodiousness and superiority to Serafino.

xxxix

13 *withouten blame*] When one is blameless.

19 *of all my harme*] In all the evil I suffer. (For this use of *of*, see cxci.1).

23 *withoute offence*] When one has committed no offence.

xl

1 *devise*] W probably has in mind a heraldic device bearing the motto 'Patience' or the motto alone: both senses are possible (*N.E.D.* 9 and 9b). Alternatively, *devise* in the legal sense of 'gift by will' yields sense.

7–8] Simonds (120), taking this as the lady's reply to her lover's taunt in the first stanza, paraphrases: 'Patience! yes; and with good reason. You have no cause at all, and so, great need of patience!'

21 *let se*] Probably an interjection, meaning 'come!', 'go to!' etc. Alternatively, it could bear the meaning 'show', as part of the statement 'Show your change when you like'.

xli. The rhyme scheme of the third stanza differs from that of the first two; but the D version retains the same scheme. It is possible that W revised the other stanzas. Nott comments (584) 'Its greatest merit is the structure of its stanza. It is complicated, and shows great powers and command of language.'

32 *hard*] Despite the gap in E an epithet is not essential, as the line would scan satisfactorily with a stress on *yf*.

34 *I and myne*] S (174) suggests that 'this is an appeal to Anne Boleyn whose own motto was "Me and Mine" '.

37 *spill or save*] 'conventional phraseology of Amour Courtois' (WMT).

XLII. The first of W's epigrams, many of which were versions of Italian poems. F suggested that W was influenced by Skelton's 'Phylyp Sparowe', 26–9, 35–43, but the resemblance is slight. Cf. LIV on the same theme.

2 *remembred her my woo*] reminded her of my woe (F).

XLIII

8 *hiere*] See Glossary.

14 *flitting*] Hughey reads *falling;* but S confirms the reading of Nott and F.

28] The reading of E is awkward, both metrically and in the apposition of 'stedfastnes' and 'remedy'. Despite Hughey's defence of the reading, it seems probable that the E scribe has repeated 'stedfastnes' from l. 20. In his short-lined ballets W is seldom guilty of this kind of roughness. The meaning, however, is the same, since 'stedefast remedy' = the remedy of steadfastness (i.e. either to be constant in love or to cease loving him altogether). Cf. ll. 29–32.

XLIV. Source:

> Incolpa donna amor se troppo io uolsi
>   Aggiungendo alla tua la bocca mia.
> Se pur punir mi uoi di quel chio tolsi
>   Fá che concesso replicar mi sia.
> Che tal dolceza in quelli labri accolsi,
>   Chel spirto mio fú per fugirsi uia.
> Só che al secondo tocco uscira fora
>   Bastar ti dé, che per tal fallo io mora.
>
> Serafino, *Opere* (1516), f. 179ᵛ

The source was identified by Nott (555). He called it a translation, but it is more accurately described by Baldi (225) as a 'free' one, and by Rollins (II.171) as a paraphrase. W remains true to the spirit of his original, but he transposes and rearranges Serafino's ideas freely. His opening, with its added exclamation and recasting in the interrogative mood, is more dramatic than the original, and his conclusion more concentrated and witty. W preserves the Italian form and also imitates the epigrammatic tone characteristic of this and many other of Serafino's strambotti.

Hughey (II.133–4) goes into the revisions in E in W's hand and the relation of E to A and T: 'The texts of the three versions of this little poem offer us a rare and instructive lesson in sixteenth-century textual criticism, for it is not often that we have such an admirable opportunity to check versions with a manuscript showing both authorial and editorial revision.' T entitles the poem: 'To his loue whom he had kissed against her will.'

1] W's free translation combines Serafino's l. 2 with *donna* (l. 1). He modifies the opening by the addition of the mock-serious *Alas*, by representing the idea of blameworthiness contained in Serafino's l. 1 through *stelyng*, and by framing a question in place of a statement.

2] A free version if *Incolpa . . . amor se troppo io uolsi*.

3–4] W's free elaboration, again framed as a question, of Serafino's l. 3, with some influence from *Bastar ti dé* (l. 8).

5 *Then revenge you*] A concentrated version of Serafino's ll. 3–4.
and the next way is this] Virtually an addition, though based on the helpful, concessive tone of Serafino's ll. 3–4.

6 *An othr kysse*] W, who is being more explicit about the repetition suggested by Serafino in l. 4, concentrates in this phrase the meaning of his l. 5.
shall have my lyffe endid] Based on *io mora* (l. 8) rather than on *el spirto mio . . . al secondo tocco uscirá fora* (ll. 6–7).

7] W's free translation of l. 6 of the Italian.

8] Based on *al secondo tocco uscirá fora* (ll. 6–7).

XLV. Nott comments (573) 'a piece written with great liveliness and spirit'.

2 *make me to your lure*] Cf. Hawes, *The Pastime of Pleasure*, ed. Mead (1927) 4532 (WMT).

6 *trayed*] This reading (i.e. 'betrayed') is stronger than *tryed* (E).

XLVI. Possible sources:

W's image of the man who starts back on encountering an adder is a classical one which became a commonplace. Alexander starts back at the sight of Menelaus, as at the sight of a snake (*Iliad*, iii, 33–6); and Adrogeus, on discovering that the men he has greeted in friendly fashion are Trojans, starts back like one who treads on an adder:

> obstipuit retroque pedem cum voce repressit.
> improvisum aspris veluti qui sentibus anguem
> pressit humi nitens, trepidusque repente refugit
> attolentem iras et caerula colla tumentem.
> (*Aeneid*, ii, 378–81)

W may have taken his version direct from Virgil. Koeppel (77–8) tentatively suggests that his source could have been Ariosto's description of Angelica's sudden meeting with a knight in the wood:

> Timida pastorella mai sí presta
> Non volse piede inanzi a serpe crudo,
> Come Angelica tosto il freno torse,
> Che del guerrier, ch' a piè venia, s'accorse.
> (*Orlando Furioso*, I, xi, 5–8)

Koeppel also compares a later passage in which Ariosto uses the same image in a different connection:

> Ma come poi l' imperial augello,
> I Gigli d' oro e i Pardi vide appresso,
> Restò pallido in faccia, come quello
> Che 'l piede incauto d' improviso ha messo
> Sopra il serpente venenoso e fello,
> Dal pigro sonno in mezo l' erbe oppresso;
> Che spaventato e smorto si ritira,
> Fuggendo quel ch' è pien di tosco e d' ira.
>
> (Ibid., XXXIX, xxxii, 1–8)

Despite the fact that Ariosto's personal and literary reputation stood high in W's lifetime, there is little evidence that he studied his poetry. The possibility of a debt in XCV is another suggestion of Koeppel's, but he again makes it with caution. Both XLVI and XCV employ the ottava rima for which Ariosto is renowned, but there is every reason to believe that W derived it, not from the narrative *Orlando Furioso*, but from the witty strambotti of Serafino which he was so ready to translate and imitate. (F 11.61) is virtually alone in accepting the Ariosto source for XLVI. Berdan (456–7 n.), Rollins (II.172), and Thomson (280) reject it, and Baldi (225) is only slightly less categorical. T provides a title: 'Of the Ielous man that loued the same woman and espied this other sitting with her.' Rollins points out that Surrey, in translating the Virgil passage, echoes W:

> Like him that, wandring in the bushes thick,
> Tredes on the adder with his rechlesse foote,
> Rered for wrath, swelling his speckled neck,
> Dismayed, geves back al sodenly for fere. (ll. 486–9).

6 *very croppe and rote*] Nott compares Chaucer, *T & C*, ii, 348.

XLVII. Source:

> Vive faville uscia de' duo bei lumi
>   Vèr' me sí dolcemente folgorando,
>   E parte d' un cor saggio sospirando
>   D' alta eloquenzia sí soavi fiumi,
> Che pur il rimembrar par mi consumi
>   Qual or a quel dí torno, ripensando
>   Come venieno i miei spirti mancando
>   Al variar de' suoi duri costumi.
> L' alma nudrita sempre in doglia e 'n pene
>   (Quanto è 'l poder d' una prescritta usanza!)
>   Contra 'l doppio piacer sí 'nferma fue,
> Ch' al gusto sol del disusato bene,
>   Tremando or di paura or di speranza,
>   D' abandonarme fu spesso en tra due.
>
> Petrarch, *Rime*, cclviii

The source of W's free imitation was identified by Nott (538). He limited himself to the statement that 'The first line is borrowed from Petrarch', with which Baldi (225) and Hietsch (40) agree. In the notes below it is suggested that the debt, though neither extensive nor visible in detail, goes beyond the first line, and that, in the last, W draws on Vellutello's commentary. The chief appeal of Petrarch's sonnet to W was obviously its lightning image and the ideas associated with it. He develops the image far more fully, but uses it to embody the lover's baffling experience, also central to Petrarch's sonnet, of alternating favour and disfavour.

The sonnet has not received much critical comment, though it is rhythmically an interesting one, with W overriding the usual barrier between octave and sestet (cf. XCVII). F (II.47) points to the 'purposely uneven' sestet; and in Lever's discussion (27–8), the sonnet is taken as 'a good example of the flexible new versification'. T provides a title: 'The louer describeth his being striken with sight of his loue.'

1] W translates the first phrase, *Vive faville uscian*, with great precision, but transmutes the common Petrarchan metaphor for eyes, *duo bei lumi*, into the literal.

3–4] Based on the general idea of Petrarch's l. 2, in which he expresses the pleasure given by Laura's welcoming eyes. W's addition, *qwaking*, was perhaps suggested by the later description of the contrary, and more usual, experience of unhappiness, and especially by the *Tremando*, etc. of l. 13. W's *hert* is perhaps influenced by *cor* in l. 3 of the Italian, but where Petrarch refers to Laura's heart, he refers to his own.

5–14] W's development of Petrarch's light image, though very free, is not entirely independent of the original. He omits Petrarch's journey into the past and description of his habitual state of sorrow. But he does communicate the lover's bafflement, which is also well brought out in Vellutello's commentary. His *lightening* is supplied by *folgorando* (l. 2), and this leads on naturally to *stroke* and *thoundere*. His *dedly nay* is supplied by Vellutello's gloss on *fu spesso en tra due* (l. 14); 'fu spesse uolte tra due, cio è fu spesse uolte tra 'l si e 'l no' (f. 82r).

9 *I-stricken*] The southern and Chaucerian past participle (K, 295).

XLVIII. Source:

> À che minacci, à che tanta ira e orgoglio,
>   Per questo non farai chel furto renda.
> Non senza causa la tua man dispoglio
>   Rapir quel daltri non fú mai mia menda.
> Famme citar dauanti amor chio uoglio,
>   Che la ragion de luno & laltro intenda.
> Lei il cor mi tolse, & io gli hó tolto un guanto
>   Vorró saper da te se un cor ual tanto.
>   Serafino, *Opere* (1516), f. 170r–v

The source was identified by Nott (555). Its relation to its original is discussed by Thomson (231–3). The subject is a common Petrarchan one: cf. *Rime*, cc (Petrarch returns a glove), cci (He regrets doing so), and cxcix (W's model for LXXXVI). T provides a title: 'To his loue from whom he hadd her gloues.'

1 *wasted wynde*] Substituted for *tanta ira e orgoglio*.

thretning] The emendation of E's reading, which has the support of *minacci* and of A and T, has been universally accepted.

3–4] W inverts Serafino's ll. 3 and 4.

3 *I wis*] W's addition.
mynde] Substituted for *menda* (fault).

4 *faire*] W's addition.

5] W omits *chio uoglio*, and fills the gap with *or els whome next we meit*. T's emendation, *finde*, supplies a rhyme.

7] An alexandrine.

XLIX T entitles the poem: 'Of the fained frend.'

2 *Take . . . claweth*] Proverbial: cf. Tilley, B17, and Chaucer, *CT*, A 4326 (Nott). It means 'Beware of him that claps you on the back'.

L. The answer to this riddle is 'Anna'. When the word is divided in the middle, and, the second syllable reversed, one is left with 'An' and 'An'. T, who entitles the poem 'Of his loue called Anna', spoils the point by substituting 'Anna' in l. 3. It appeared first in the second edition. Nott, followed by others, suggested the poem was about Anne Boleyn. S (44) thinks that Anne 'may have replied to the riddle with one of her own making' in the inscription in D (f. 67ᵛ):

> am el men
> an em e
> as I have dese
> I ama yours an.

S, by transposing the second and fourth letters of each line, interprets 'a lemmen amene ah I sane desc I ama yours an'. But this riddle is not in Anne Boleyn's handwriting, and may have been written after CLXXIII with its reference to the poet's mistress writing in his book.

LI. One of several poems in which W mentions the lute and probably, though not certainly, it was intended to be sung. Padelford (xxxviii) regards it as an example of the *chanson à personnages* which died out in France in the fourteenth century, though 'most of its characteristic features are preserved in English songs that were committed to writing in the fifteenth and early sixteenth centuries'.

1 *myschief*] See Glossary.

LII. The poem is apparently addressed to Mary Souche, one of Jane Seymour's maids of honour, as Nott suggested. See the last stanza. There is a fine portrait of her by Holbein. In E the eight-line stanza is wrongly divided into two. In T, the poem is entitled: 'The louers sorowfull state maketh him write sorowfull songes, but *Souche* his loue may change the same.'

27 *suche*] The repetition of this word in ll. 29, 31 suggests that W was quibbling on the name of Mary Souche.

29 *souche*] This is a later insertion in E, not in the hand of the usual scribe.

LIII. Possible source:

> Chi dara a gliocchi miei si larga vena
> Di lagrime, ch' i possa il mio dolore
> Sfocar, piangendo si, che poi m' attempre?
> E per quetar il tormentato core
> Chi dara al petto si possente lena
> Che si, com' hor conuen, sospir i sempre?
>
> Giusto de' Conti, *Rime . . . intitolato La
> Bella Mano* (Venice, 1531), f. 30ʳ

Nott (547) believed that W's 'opening might have been suggested' by Conti's canzone (ll. 1–6), and this is accepted as the source by Baldi (226). Objections are that W does not elsewhere give evidence of having read Conti, and that Petrarchan love complaints will inevitably bear a generic resemblance to each other, particularly in the matter of such commonplace items as tears and sighs. Conti asks who will give, first to his tears (ll. 1–3), then to his breast (ll. 4–6), a vent or strength great enough to enable him to work off, and so to assuage, his grief. Though W says nothing of wanting to assuage grief, the two questions of his first stanza are sufficiently like Conti's in substance and tone to justify Nott's tentative claim. Cf. CXLII, 1–6.

Hughey (II.170) shows that the alterations in E in ll. 14, 29, 34, 37, and 39 were made in a contemporary hand, but not, as that in l. 4, by the usual scribe. That in l. 14, however, is inserted in a gap in the MS. and is necessary to the sense. T's title: 'The louer complaineth himself forsaken.'

The tag in the scribe's hand, appended to the poem, and apparently mixing Spanish with Italian ('It should be what it is not') seems unconnected with the poem and it suggests the possibility that it might belong to W's years in Spain (1537–9). The first poem definitely written in Spain, however, is LXXXI.

1–2] Cf. CXLII.1–2.

6 *My . . . woo*] WMT compares *T & C*, iv, 257–9:

> But tho bygonne his teeris more out breste,
> That wonder is the body may suffise
> To half this wo . . .

21 *Sparkill*] See XII.6 and note.

24 *For . . . saieth*] Cf. XIX.4; and for the proverb, see Tilley, L286; Erasmus, *Adagia*, 78D; Barclay, *Ship of Fools*, ii, 35.

25 *Fortune . . . avaunce*] WMT compares Royal MS. App. 58, ed. Flügel, *Anglia*, XII, 267: 'When fortune had me avaunsyd.'

32 *Without offence*] Attached to *Me* (l. 31).

37–40] 'But because the fact that I am dragging out a wretched life grieves me as well as you, you can take my word for it that death alone will be the means of ending my weary struggle.'

40 *wery*] This emendation makes better sense than *very*, which may have been
merely an odd spelling.

LIV. F (11.60) suggests that W's poem was suggested by Maurice Scève's:

> Ouvrant ma Dame au labeur trop ardente
> Son Dé luy cheut, mais Amour le luy dresse:
> Et le voyant sans raison évidente
> Ainsi trouve, vers Delie s'addresse.
> C'est luy dit elle, afin que ne m'oppresse
> L'aiguille aigue, et que point ne m'offence,
> Donc, respond il, je croy que sa deffence
> Fait que par moy ton cœur n'est point vaincu.
> Mais bien du mien, dy ie, la ferme essence
> Encontre toi lui sert toujours d'ecu.

The resemblance is slight.

T entitles the poem: 'Of his loue that pricked her finger with a nedle.'

LV. The first three stanzas, set to music by Thomas Cornishe, have a slightly
different text:

> A robyn gentyl robyn
> tel me how thy leman doth
> and thow shal know off myne
>
> My Lady is vnkynde Iwis
> alas why is she so
> she louyth another better than me
> and yet she will say no.
>
> I can not thynk such doubylnes
> for I fynd women trew
> In faith my lady louith me well
> she will change for no new.

It is probable that W was expanding a popular song. The opening lines are
sung by Feste in *T.N.*

17–20] The accidental omission of this stanza by E upsets the sense since
ll. 21–44 clearly belong to 'Le plaintif'.

LVI. Source:

> Pien d' un vago penser, che mi desvia
>   Da tutti gli altri e fammi al mondo ir solo,
>   Ad or ad ora a me stesso m' involo,
>   Pur lei cercando che fuggir devria;
> E veggiola passar sí dolce e ria
>   Che l' alma trema per levarsi a volo,
>   Tal d' armati sospir conduce stuolo
>   Questa bella d' Amor nemica e mia.

Y

Ben, s' i' non erro, di pietate un raggio
Scorgo fra 'l nubiloso altero ciglio
Che 'n parte rasserena il cor doglioso:
Allor raccolgo l' alma, e, poi ch' i' aggio
Di scovrirle il mio mal preso consiglio,
Tanto gli ho a dir che 'ncominciar non oso.

Petrarch, *Rime*, clxix

The source was identified by Nott (538). Opinions of its success and the extent of its departure from Petrarch have varied. For F (11.48) 'The error of overmuch metaphor is due to the Italian', and she considers the omission of the sky image (*rasserena*) in l. 11 typical of W, who tends to ignore Petrarch's 'nature touches' (cf. 1). Padelford speaks more strongly, considering that the 'figurative element' in W is 'neither clear nor sustained', and that the finer effects, as well as the pictorial quality, of the original is lost (Padelford, xxi-ii, xxiv-v). On the other hand, Lever (28) claims that W 'characteristically gave the sonnet an introspective cast at the expense of romance idealizations'. Hietsch (167–9) also comments on W's individuality, strongly refuting Padelford. Muir finds something to admire, especially in ll. 9–10, in W's translation (L, 228–9). Baldi (226) thinks that W perhaps misunderstood Petrarch's second quatrain, while Thomson (194–6) attempts to explain this and other apparent departures from the source by reference to Vellutello's commentary. T rearranges the lines of the second quatrain in the order 6, 7, 8, 5, and provides a title: 'The waueryng louer wylleth, and dredeth, to moue his desire.'

2] W's addition, though *desert* (lonely) shows that he had Petrarch's ll. 2–3 in mind.
by well assured mone] The meaning is obscure. Hietsch (171) suggests, for *assured*, 'assurded' (Lat. *exsurgere*, break out), and compares Skelton, 'Garland of Laurel', l. 302.

3] A free translation of Petrarch's ll. 2–3.

4 *whome reason bid me fle*] Cf. *che fuggir devria* (l. 4). The idea of moral restraint is contained in *devria*. W's introduction of *reason* is also compatible with Petrarch's moral ideas in general: cf. his translation in IV.7.

5] W omits *veggiola*, and, in *fleith as fast*, strengthens the meaning of *passar*.

6] W's reading of Petrarch's l. 6 as expressing the wish to renew his pursuit of Laura is sanctioned by Vellutello: 'l' anima per leuarsi a uolo, & uolere il suo uago pensiero, il quale è di uolerle parlare, come la dolcezza di lei gli ditta, adempire, trema & non ardisce per la rigidita' (f. 91ʳ).

8] Substituted for Petrarch's l. 8, though the ideas of *hope*, *drede*, and *locking* are supplied by Vellutello's gloss on l. 6.

11 *that erst for fere shoke*] Substituted for *doglioso*, but consistent with Petrarch's *trema* (l. 6) and W's *drede* (l. 8). W omits *'n parte*.

12 *And therewithall bolded*] W's reading of *Allor raccolgo l' alma* is sanctioned by Vellutello's paraphrase, 'allhora ripiglio l' ardire' (f. 91ʳ).

13 *the smert that I suffre within*] A free rendering of *il mio mal preso consiglio*, avoiding its touch of self-condemnation.

14] A rather vague rendering of Petrarch's statement to the effect that he has so much to say that he dare not begin. Cf. the tongue-tied lover of xxv.

LVII. The stanza form is not used by W elsewhere. A couplet with five stresses is followed by one with four and a refrain with three; and the opening couplets and the refrain share a single rhyme. But in the first thirty poems in E, excluding epigrams, sonnets, and rondeaux, there are twenty-two different stanza forms employed.

LVIII

2 *esse*] ease.

5–6] Cf. Tilley, S927 (WMT).

13–15] The rhymes here resemble those to be found in the translations, but are rare in W's ballets.

21 *ye*] yea.

23 *myschiefe*] See Glossary.

31 *torne . . . ball*] Cf. VIII.28 and Chaucer, *Truth*, 9 (WMT).

33 *For . . . rede*] Proverbial. Cf. Despair is a bad counsellor.

34 *To . . . spede*] Probably proverbial, but I can find no exact parallel.

LIX. Written, as Nott (xxiii) suggested in October 1532, when W went over to Calais in Anne Boleyn's train, just before her marriage to Henry VIII. Title in T: 'The louer that fled loue now folowes it with his harme.'

3 *coles that be quent*] W's passion for Anne was now extinguished.

8 *Mashed . . . torne*] Cf. Tilley, B672, 673 (WMT). Nott refers to *T & C*, iii, 1740.

LX. Source:

> Sio son caduto interra inon son morto,
>   Ritorna el Sol benche talhor si cele,
> Spero mi dará el ciel qualche conforto,
>   Poi che fortuna hará sfocato el fele,
> Chi hó uisto naue ritornarsi in porto,
>   Dapoi che rotta há in mar tutte soe uele
> El salce anchora el uento abasso & piega
>   Poi si ridriza, & glialtri legni lega.
>   Serafino, *Opere* (1516), f. 120ʳ

The source was identified by Nott (558). He also conjectured that it was written 'on the subject of [W's] imprisonment in 1541'. F (11.65), who is followed by Rollins (11.184), prefers to relate it to the imprisonment of 1534. W's is a line by line translation, with ll. 3–4 inverted. He makes no alterations of the sense, but on several occasions introduces more concrete or stronger terms (e.g. *clowd, storme, greater*). Title in T: 'The louer hopeth of better chance.'

1 *He . . . fall*] W's correction. His first version, *I . . . fall*, as well as the similar readings in D and P, is closer to Serafino who uses the first person in l. 1.

2] Cf. Tilley, C441, C442 (WMT).

3–6] Quoted by Puttenham (229) as an example of '*Etiologia*, or the Reason rendrer'.

3–4] W inverts Serafino's ll. 3 and 4, and, in *good luck to me shalbe allowd*, modifies the phrasing, though not the sense, of *mi dará el ciel qualche conforto*.

6] W substitutes *storme* for *in mar*, and *boeth mast and shrowd* for *soe uele*.

7–8] Cf. CVIII.343–4.

7 *stowpeth*] Cf. *abasso & piega*, which may have struck W as redundant. The Italian authenticates 'stooping' as against 'stopping'. E's *stoppeth* is probably a spelling for *stowpeth*: cf. the use of *stopp*, in the same context of the bending willow, in CVIII.343.

8 *greater*] Substituted for *altri*.

LXI. Source:

> Se una bombarda è dal gran foco mossa
> Spirando, ció che troua aterra presto.
> Ma segli aduien chella spirar non possa
> Se stessa rompe & poco offende el resto.
> Cosi io dentro ardo, el foco è giunto à lossa
> Sel taccio imor, sel dico altrui molesto.
> Sospeso uiuo, amor me dá tal sorte,
> Che altro non è che una confusa morte.

> Serafino, *Opere* (1516), f. 145ᵛ

The source was identified by Nott (557). W's version is something between a paraphrase and an imitation. He adopts the internal structure of Serafino's strambotto, describing a gun and then applying the details of the description to himself. But he omits several details (e.g. in ll. 1–2) and, in general, he simplifies in order to develop a more violent and single effect. Baldi (195) considers his conceit better constructed than Serafino's.

Hughey (II.160) notes that A is exceptional here in that it varies considerably from E. Title in T: 'The louer compareth his hart to the ouercharged gonne.'

1–5 *The furyous gonne . . . shevered peces*] Cf. Serafino's ll. 1–4. W omits the opening description (ll. 1–2) of a gun fired successfully, though he works phrases from it (*bombarda, foco*) into his own account of the misfiring gun. The substance of this free version is, however, based largely on the equivalent account of the misfiring gun in ll. 3–4 of the Italian. W omits *& poco offende el resto* (l. 4) because he has already omitted the statement which balances it, *ció che troua aterra presto* (l. 2).

1] W's terms, *furyous, rajing yre*, are intentionally stronger than anything in the source, which uses the epithet *gran*, and does not personify *bombarda* in any detail. His revision of the opening phrase indicates this intention. (W did not have to sacrifice the *bombard* of E (ii) as an un-English term: it was used for 'The earliest kind of cannon, usually throwing a stone ball or very large shot' (*N.E.D.*)).

3] W presumably means that the *flame* used for ignition *cannot part from* the ball which is being fired (? or from the fire-ball).

4–5 *and in the ayer . . . peces*] W's amplification of *Se stessa rompe/Cracketh in sonder* not only fills the gap left by the omission of *& poco offende el resto*, but adds further vigour to his description.

5 *right so doeth my desire*] W rejoins Serafino at *Cosi io dentro ardo* (l. 5).

6] A free rendering of Serafino's l. 5.

7] A free rendering of l. 6. W adds *dare* and *loke*, presumably to heighten the sense of danger. He omits *altrui molesto*, because he has already omitted the corresponding passages (ll. 2 and 4) in the description of the gun.

8] Substituted for Serafino's ll. 7–8, though true to their spirit. W's introduction of *hard force* brings a reminder of the opening image.

LXII

5] more haste, less speed.

11 *revolted*] See Glossary.

24 *among*] See Glossary.

33 *No . . . stedfastnes*] 'Quiet fidelity obtains no pleasure'.

LXIII

10–11 *Oute of presens/Of my defens*] i.e. out of the presence of either his heart or his mistress. N. Blake compares Lydgate, *Troy Book*, V, 2621: 'oute of presence of any other man'.

12 *dryve*] Harrier, *NQ* (June, 1953), 235 argues that the word here means 'suffer'; but it can mean *travel, hasten, tend*, or *drift*.

13–14] Cf. XVIII.13.

19 *gro*] The word appears to have been corrected to *goo* in E, and the correction may be W's.

LXIV. Possibly a translation. T entitles this poem: 'The louer complaineth that deadlie sicknesse can not helpe his affeccion.'

1 *Th'enmy of liff*] Death.

LXV. T entitles this poem: 'The louer reioiceth the enioying of his loue.'

24 *Save . . . still*] Save that I continue to have it.

28 *hiere*] See Glossary.

LXVI. One of W's most popular poems, to judge from the six texts in which it appears and its imitation by John Hall in *The Court of Vertue* (ed. R. A. Fraser, (1961), 169). Hall provides a setting for another poem 'My pen obey my wyll a whyle' and suggests that his 'My lute awake' should be sung to the

same tune. It is possible that this was the setting for Wyatt's also. Title in T:
'The louer complayneth the vnkindnes of his loue.'

7 *As . . . stone*] Cf. *T & C*, ii, 1241: 'And hard was it youre herte for to grave'. (Nott).

13 *affection*] Pronounced with four syllables.

26 *the lye*] W's own correction, altering the plural to the singular.

27 *The . . . cold*] Cf. Gower, *Confessio Amantis*, V, 6668: 'The longe nyhtes that ben cold' (WMT) and CLXI.66.
nyghtes] Padelford defends the E reading, *nyght*, as an uninflected plural.

LXVII. A similar stanza to that of LI except that a four-stress line is substituted for the two short ones at the end of the stanza.

22 *dryve*] Suffer, cf. LXIII.12.

LXVIII. This epigram, entitled in T 'How by a kisse he found both his life and death', is based on a common belief. F refers to a sermon by Latimer and to Gascoigne, 'The Epistle to the Reverend Divines' in *Works*, I, ed. J. W. Cunliffe (1907) 6: 'I had alledged of late by a right reverende father, that although in deede out of everie floure the industrious Bee may gather honie, yet by proofe the Spider thereout sucks mischeevous poyson.'

LXIX

6] Cf. Tilley, W412 (WMT).

7] Cf. 'A folys bolt is sone ysholt' (F).

21–2] Cf. Tilley, M103 (WMT).

LXX. Several sources have been suggested. Koeppel (74) compares the dying swan image to the last stanza of Serafino's 'Non mi pesa di morire' (*Opere* (1516), f. 197).

> Pur conosco apertamente
> La mia uana e trista sorte,
> Che cantando corro à morte
> Come el cygno nel finire.

F (11.94) compares the opening of 'The complaynte of Dido' in Pynson's ed. of Chaucer (1526) and Baldi (227) agrees. But the figure was common (e.g. *Anelida and Arcite*, 346 ff.) and even proverbial. Cf. Tilley, S1028 (WMT). Ivy Mumford (*EM*, xiv 1963), 10, 23) argues that there are striking resemblances to the following anonymous lyric, first printed with Marchetto Cara's music in Ottaviano Petrucci's first book of Frottole (1504). (The text given is from Raffaello Monterosso's ed., Cremona (1954), I, 11).

> [Si] come chel biancho cigno
> Per natural costume
> Morendo in qualche fiume
> el corpo lascia

> E mentre lalma pascia
> De quel corporeo uelo
> Dun amoroso zelo
>   Se empie el pecto
> E par chabbia dilecto
> e de morir se auanti
> e piu suaui canti
>   Alhor che prima
> Tal chio faccio stima
> sol col mio lachrymare
> De farmi intorno un mare
>   senza riua
> Doue che un tempo uiua
> Ne potendo partirme
> Forza fia sepelirme
>   Alfin nel aque
> E come che al ciel piacque
> Amando io uo morire
> e cantando scoprire
>   I mei pensieri
> No*n* gia per che mai speri
> Coi mio angoscioso pianto
> Ne col mio amaro canto
>   El cor placare.

The last two lines have some resemblance to W's refrain.

LXXI. Thomson (135–6) says that the poem 'is dominated by Chaucer's antithesis between convention and experience . . . Where there is no gentle heart or womanly pity, there is, in fact, no groundwork for the courtly love routine. . . . Irony is the chief of the effects achieved'.

9 *trase this daunse*] Cf. VIII.25 and note.
   I . . . prese] Cf. Lydgate, 'Servant of Cupid', 9; *La Belle Dame sans Merci*, 63 (WMT).
15 *to stond in her grace*] Cf. *T & C*, iii, 472, 1176 (WMT).

LXXII. Nott (577) remarks that 'The chief merit of this piece consists in its measure, which is novel and agreeably varied.'

29–35] Nott (577) points out that the argument used by the affectionate lover would be 'If you desert me, you will reflect discredit on your name' whereas W says that if she kills him, he will be eased and she will be defamed.

LXXIII. Possible sources:

> Gridato ho nocte e giorno tanto forte
>   che tutto il ciel e offeso da mia uoce
>   ho tanto suspirato e con tal sorte
>   che laere dal mio foco se arde e coce
>   ho pianto tanto ognor chiamando morte
>   chel troppo humor a tutta terra noce
>   hor tacer uoglio e tolerar mia guerra
>   per non turbar piu il ciel laer ne terra.
>   Marcello Filosseno, *Sylve*
>   (Venice, 1507), sig. b 5ʳ

316   *Commentary*   [LXXIII

> Il ciel contra me intona guerra guerra
> & io fugendo uo de sasso in sasso
> ma la fortuna exclama serra serra
> unde preso i me ritrouo a passo apasso
> amor sta inanti e dice a terra a terra
> e la morte risponde al basso al basso
> cosi il ciel e fortuna dhora in hora
> e amor e morte gridan mora mora.
> Ibid., d 4^r

This lover's complaint against a merciless lady is a tissue of W's favourite
Petrarchanisms. He burns with the fire of love (st. 2), sheds tears and cannot
sleep (st. 3). He brings up his long, faithful service (st. 5). He is dying (sts. 4,
6, 8, 9), and blames the lady for it (st. 7). The poem has not been assigned with
any certainty to a particular source, and is probably an original composite of
familiar notions. F (11.220) related it to the above strambotti by Filosseno,
though without explaining their importance as possible sources. W's first
stanza contains an idea similar to that of 'Gridato ho nocte e giorno', in
which heaven, air, and earth are affected by the lover's cries, sighs, and tears.
Unlike Filosseno, he suggests that the reaction of 'nature' is compassionate,
and this he may owe rather to Serafino's strambotto 'Laer che sente' (quoted
above as a possible source for XXII). Filosseno's 'Il ciel contra me' is not very
like W's poem in substance, but presumably F cited it for the sake of its repe-
tition of the last word of each line, and more especially of the final line. W
uses this device in the last line of each stanza, and 'gridan mora mora' could
have suggested his *I cry . . . I dy, I dy!*' (ll. 2, 4). The device itself would, how-
ever, be familiar to him from Serafino, who sometimes, as Koeppel (75) re-
marks, employs it in a final line. Serafino also has a group of three strambotti,
prominently labelled 'echo', and technically similar to Filosseno's 'Il ciel
contra me'; e.g.

> Ahime che haró del mal che io porto, porto
> Son spirti qui che odo uno accento, cento
> E tú dí, chi sei, uiuo ó morto, morto
> Palpar ti posso, ó sei pur uento, uento.
> (*Opere* (1516), f. 139^r)

There is insufficient evidence that W read Filosseno (see note to LXXIX), and
Baldi (227) is probably right to reject F's case. Serafino, a favourite with him,
is more likely to have suggested his themes and techniques.

18 *to my powre*] Cf. XXV.2.

21–2 *my liff . . . wynde*] Koeppel (70) compares Petrarch's

> Ma non fuggío giammai nebbia per venti,
> Come quel dí . . .
> (*Rime*, lxvi, 37–8)

and

> Ché, come nebbia al vento si dilegua,
> Cosí sua vita súbito trascorse
> Quella . . .
> (*Rime*, cccxvi, 5–7)

Baldi (227) also cites the first of these analogies, but thinks that the likeness may be coincidental.

LXXIV. Almost the same refrain is used in CXXIV and many of the same rhymes are used – smart/hart, vaine/payne, weake/breke, speke/wreke.

15 *To . . . muse*] 'It is of no avail to consider how the yoke may be shaken off, after it is once fastened on the neck' (Nott, 577).

LXXV. In W's handwriting, with numerous corrections. See Introduction, p. xx, for a discussion of the relationship of the texts in D and E. No source has been discovered, though F (11.67) suggests that it is imitated from Scève's dizaine 'Tant est Nature en volonté puissante'. T entitles the poem: 'The louer blameth his instant desyre.'

LXXVI. Source:

> Ogni pungente & uenenosa spina
> Se uede à qualche tempo esser fiorita,
> Crudel ueneno posto in medicina,
> Piú uolte torna lhom da morte uita,
> El foco che ogni cosa arde & ruina,
> Spesso risana una mortal ferita,
> Cosi spero el mio mal me fia salute,
> Chogni cosa che noce há pur uirtute.
>
> Serafino, *Opere* (1516), f. 117^r

The source was identified by Nott (558). W's translation is a line by line one. There are a few omissions and additions, which do not significantly alter the sense. W's translation is briefly compared with its original by Berdan (475–6).

Analogue: A French rondeau based on Serafino's strambotto, 'A Quelque temps la venimeuse espine', appears in Jean Marot's *Recueil des Oeuvres* (Lyons, 1537), (rondeau, No. 40). W is not in debt to it. See E. M. Rutson, *MLR*, lxi (1966), 26–8. The poem also appears, with one line missing, in a commonplace book, Cambridge University MS. ff. 5, 14, ff, 5^v–7^v: see F. D. Hoeniger, *NQ*, ccii (1957), 103–4. Title in T: 'That pleasure is mixed with euery paine.'

1–2] Cf. the proverbial 'Da le spine nascon le rose' (Florio, *Second Frvtes* (London, 1591), 180).

1 *sharp and kene*] W doubles *pungente*.

2 *fayre and fresh of hue*] W's addition.

3] W omits *Crudel* and fills the gap with *offtyme* (taken from *Piú uolte* in l. 4).

4] A free version of *torna lhom da morte uita*.

5 *purgith*] Cf. *arde & ruina*.
that is vnclene] W's addition.

6 *May hele, and hurt*] A free rendering of Serafino's l. 6 .
and if thes bene true] Substituted, as a transitional phrase, for *Cosi* (l. 7).

8] W's *welth*, meaning 'general state of well-being, the opposite of *woe*, is one of his important abstract words' (H. Smith, *HLQ*, ix (1946), 353).

LXXVII. Thomson (140) comments on this poem that W 'associates the lost
heart with other conventional love themes in a more rigorous piece of logic.
. . . Using his stiffest and most academic manner, he expounds the argument
that, in accordance with reason and nature, it is impossible for a man to live
without a heart, or in a state of contrariety such as is expressed in the stock
heat–cold antithesis. . . . Having carefully led his argument this way, W, by
an unexpected stroke of ingenuity, provides a solution to the contradiction
between experience and bookish doctrine – a solution the neater in that it
gives final authority to the religion of love. There is always an appeal open
from the natural to the supernatural. Miracle is W's solution'. Koeppel (70)
thought that there were echoes of Petrarch's 'Io mi rivolgo in dietro a ciascun
passo' (*Rime*, xv) in the third and fifth stanzas (cf. ll. 9–11, 12–14 of the sonnet).
But Baldi (228) rightly rejects Koeppel's suggestion. The contraries of st. 1
and 2, the lost heart of st. 3 and the idea that love can perform miracles in st. 5
are all Petrarchan commonplaces.

11 *That . . . away*] Cf. XVIII.13 and note.

LXXVIII. Although Nott (574) suggests that this is a translation, no source
has been discovered. F (11.113) thinks the poem was written when W was
crossing the Channel on his way to Spain in 1537.

1 *thy*] i.e. Venus's.

3 *chieff howse*] The first and seventh houses, of the twelve into which the
celestial sphere was divided, were regarded as propitious. The reference
here is almost certainly to the seventh.

5 *Banysshed from my blisse*] W, in Spain, was separated from his mistress,
Elizabeth Darrell.

7 *en vogant la galere*] 'a refrain of a French boat song' (F), but I have not been
able to trace it. *Et vogue la galere* means 'Come what may!' and W doubtless
refers to this as well as to rowing the galley.

15 *thy sight*] Apparently W is now thinking of his mistress.

21 *fle*] Nott's emendation makes easier sense, especially as Venus is elsewhere
called 'thou'.

LXXIX. Possible source:

> Pareami in questa nocte esser contento
> che teco iunxi al disiato effecto
> deh fossio sempre in tal dormir attento
> poi che il ciel non mi porge altro dilecto
> ma il gran piacer mutosse in gran tormento
> quando che solo me trouai nel lecto
> ne duolmi gia chel sonno mha ingannato
> ma duolmi sol che sonno sogno e stato.
>
> Marcello Filosseno, *Sylve* (Venice, 1507),
> sig. i 2ʳ

Koeppel (76–7) pointed out that W's sonnet expresses the same thought
as Filosseno's strambotto, which in consequence has been accepted as the

source by F (11.50), Rollins (11.163), and Hughey (11.154). Baldi (228) rejects it. W at most got his idea from Filosseno: the dream of love fulfilled, its delights, brevity, and agonizing deceptiveness. No other poems give evidence of his having read *Sylve* (see note to LXXIII). His ideas might have come to him from the common Petrarchan stock. Petrarch wrote several 'dream' sonnets (e.g. *Rime*, ccxl, cccxli, cccxlii). The Caritean Petrarchans often give the dreams an erotic slant (e.g. Cariteo, *Le Rime*, ed. E. Pèrcopo (Naples, 1892), sonnet xv, and the strambotto immediately following 'Pareami in questa nocte' in Filosseno's *Sylve*).

F (11.27) thinks that W's sonnet was 'written in Spain in 1537', though she later (11.50) expresses less certainty. Her case is based on its position in E, immediately following the sea-going LXXVIII and preceding LXXXI, which mentions a visit of W's to Monçon. It receives support from Fucilla's discovery of the source of LXXX in a Spanish MS. But its validity as a whole depends on whether the E poems are, as F believes, in chronological order.

The poem has not been given much detailed attention, but Baldi (168, 186) praises it and numbers it among W's 'great' sonnets. Title in T: 'The louer hauing dreamed enioying of his loue, complaineth that the dreame is not either longer or truer.'

1 *according to the place*] This, presumably, qualifies *Vnstable*, and means that the dream accords with *this tossing mew* (l. 6).

5 *By goode respect*] ? with proper consideration.

6] W is probably thinking of the bed on which he tosses. The sense seems not to have been clear to T's editor, whose emendation, *seas*, is introduced to fit both *tossing* and the metaphor in l. 8. T's further emendation in l. 7 regularises the rhyme, and so produces an un-Italianate octave (abba, acca), which W never uses.

8 *succour*] The ME sense 'refuse' (*N.E.D.*, 4) fits the metaphor, but 'help' is perfectly possible, besides being a known usage of W's (e.g. XCVIII.3). T's editor seems, again, not to have found this clear.

11 *it*] i.e. the spirit.
kepe it right] keep on in the same straight or satisfactory course.

LXXX. Source:

> Mentre nel duro petto e dispietato
> l'ira, la fame et il furor combatte,
> disse la madre hebrea, figliuol mal nato,
> ritorna il sangue dove suggesti il latte.
> Queste membra mi torna, che io te ho dato
> si come da me fur fatte sian disfatte;
> che rompendo ogni legge di natura
> farò del corpo al corpo sepoltura.
>
> Biblioteca Nacional, Madrid, MS.
> 4117, f. 227ᵛ

The source was identified by J. G. Fucilla (*RN*, ix (1956), 187–8). The text quoted above is taken from his transcription of the anonymous Italian strambotto, ascribed in the Spanish MS to Leone Ebreo, but not thought to be his work. The story of Mary, who devoured her child at the siege of Jerusalem comes originally from Josephus's *Jewish War* (VI, ii, 4), and this was formerly taken as W's source (Nott, 555). W's translation is close, except for his modification of ll. 1–2 and complete alteration of l. 6. F (11.69) believes this to have been 'written in Spain': see note to LXXIX. Title in T: 'Of the mother that eat her childe at the siege of Ierusalem.'

1–2] W throws the emphasis on to the mother's doubt, and, instead of describing her as utterly pitiless (cf. *duro petto e dispietato*) creates a conflict between her pity and her hunger. He omits *ira* and makes *furor* into an adjective qualifying *famyn*.

4 *of late*] W's addition.

5 *made vnto the*] Brought into your possession or power (see *N.E.D.*, 9b)

6] Substituted for the Italian reference to the mother's unmaking the limbs she made.

7] Built up from l. 7 of the Italian and *del corpo* (l. 8).

8 *must*] W's addition, perhaps intended to suggest the mother's compulsive action, as distinct from the determined or willed action of the Italian *farò*.

LXXXI. Source:

> Vinse Anibàl, e non seppe usar poi
>   Ben la vittorïosa sua ventura.
>   Però, signor mio caro, aggiate cura
>   Che similmente non avegna a voi.
> L'orsa, rabbiosa per gli orsacchi suoi
>   Che trovaron di maggio aspra pastura,
>   Rode sé dentro, e i denti e l' unghie endura
>   Per vendicar suoi danni sopra noi.
> Mentre 'l novo dolor dunque l' accora,
>   Non riponete l' onorata spada;
>   Anzi seguite, là dove vi chiama
> Vostra fortuna, dritto per la strada,
>   Che vi po dar, dopo la morte ancora
>   Mille e mille anni, al mondo onor e fama.

> Petrarch, *Rime*, ciii

The source was identified by Nott (11.557); but it is, of course, possible that the content of Petrarch's sonnet reached him through an earlier imitation, perhaps one in strambotto form. He translates Petrarch's first two lines. From the rest he derives only a few hints, for the most part altering the original drastically. The warning to Stefano Colonna to follow up his victory over the Orsini could have no more personal meaning for W than the reference to Giovanni Colonna in the source-poem of CCXXXVI. So he applies Petrarch's opening illustration, Hannibal's failure to follow up victory, to his own situation when in Spain, and he refers it, not to what may happen, but to what has happened. This form of imitation is paralleled in Agnolo Firenzuola's 'Vinse Hanniballe, & mal seppe usar poi', in which the same illustration is adapted to fit an address to his own friend (*Le Rime*, Florence (1549), f. 6ʳ).

The strambotto must belong to W's embassy in Spain (1537–9), and was perhaps written during his only recorded visit to Monçon: see his letter of 16 October 1537, written 'At Barbastra, bysydes Mountzon' (*L*, 47). Internal evidence does not reveal whether W refers to his public or to his domestic life, though the former seems the more likely. W's brief as ambassador was to further Princess Mary's marriage to the infant of Portugal, to make the Emperor Charles V join Henry VIII against Rome, and to promote Henry's offer to mediate between the Emperor and the King of France (*L*, 38–94). These impossible projects were already floundering in October 1537, and W may be describing the frustration and uncertainty which seemed the only result of his endless diplomatic negotiations. His private life also contains possible source material. Before leaving England W had repudiated his wife, and it is generally assumed that his liaison with Elizabeth Darrell was formed at about the same time (see Chambers, 141–5). He may accordingly be describing the frustration caused by his inability to follow up the 'fortune' which had given him a mistress he loved. There could also be some allusion to his irritation at his agents in England, who were negligent in dealing with his finances (see *L*, 54–5). Title in T: 'Of disapointed purpose by negligence.'

1–2] A free translation of Petrarch's ll. 1–2. W's description of *Anibàl* as warrior of Carthage indicates that he knew this well-known story, told in Livy's *History*, xii, 51.

3–5 *And I . . . vse*] Based on Petrarch's ll. 3–4. Where he points the moral of the Hannibal story to his *signor . . . caro*. W applies it to himself.

4–5 *tho fortune . . . vse*] Influenced by Petrarch's ll. 11–12.

5–6 *the hold . . . vnpossest*]? 'I did not possess the hold [over events] which is now abandoned altogether.'

6–8 *So hangith . . . Spayne*] Virtually independent of the source, though the idea of a situation that *hangith in balaunce* is implicit in it.

LXXXII. Possible sources:

> Col tempo el uilanello al giogo mena
>   El tor si fiero, e si crudo animale
>   Col tempo el falcon susa à menar lale
> E ritornare à te chiamando à pena,
> Col tempo si domestica è in chatena
>   El bizarro orso, el feroce cinghiale,
>   Col tempo lacqua che è si molle e frale
> Rompe il dur sasso come fosse harena,
> Col tempo ogni robusto arbore cade,
>   Col tempo ogni alto monte si fá basso
>   Et io col tempo non posso à pietade
> Mouer un cor dogni dolceza casso
>   Vnde auanza dorgoglio e crudeltade
>   Orso, toro, leon, falcone, e sasso.
>   Serafino, *Opere* (1516), sonnet ciii

Con fede e con speranza io uiuo anchora
    Placar col ben seruir la tua dureza,
Ogni animal, che in boscho si dimora
    Col tempo abassa e tempra ogni fiereza,
Vedo una goccia dacqua adhora adhora
    Dar sopra el marmo tal che al fino lo speza,
Cosi spero il tuo cor si humilie e tempre,
    Pregando, amando, & lachrymando sempre.

Ibid., f. 116ᵛ

Se da poca acqua consumar si uede
    Per longa pioggia il marmor duro e forte,
Perche non debbio anchor sperar mercede
    Di tanti affani, & mia si dura sorte,
Che só pregando amando ognhor con fede,
    Leal seruendo, & sospirando forte,
E lachrimando ognhor con piú ferueza
    Non è si duro cor che non si speza.

Ibid., f. 116ᵛ

Col tempo al fier caual si mette el freno
    E se dispiana ogni superba alteza,
Col tempo se addolcisce ogni ueneno
    Et la molle acqua el duro marmo speza,
Col tempo se fá in poluer venir meno
    El diamante & tanta sua dureza.
Et solo in te non pó far cosa alcuna
    Ne seruitù, ne tempo, ne fortuna.

Ibid., f. 117ʳ

Soglion li canti humiliar serpenti,
    Placar le stelle, & linfernal furore,
Et io con gliaspri & graue mei lamenti
    À far humil costei non hó uigore
Suole una gotta dacqua à colpi lenti
    Cauare el marmo in longo tempo & hore
E quel suo freddo cor turbato e obscuro
    Al mio gran lachrymar sempre è piú duro.

Ibid., f. 124ᵛ

F (ii.116) states that the poem is 'Based on Petrarch and full of the usual conceits'. This is true in so far as the origin of the water-stone image in Petrarchan love poetry is probably Petrarch's optimistic supposition that since water eventually wears away stone, no heart, however hard, can fail to yield at last to the lover's entreaty:

Vivo sol di speranza, rimembrando
    Che poco umor già per continua prova
    Consumar vidi marmi e pietre salde.
Non è sí duro cor che, lagrimando,
    Pregando, amando, tal or non si smova,
    Nè sí freddo voler che non si scalde.

(*Rime*, cclxv, 9–14)

The image passed to W either directly, or indirectly through Serafino. In LXXXII.1–8 it expresses the complete disillusion with which Serafino frequently connects it, while in CLIX.17–24 it bears Petrarch's originally hopeful meaning. Koeppel (73–4) suggested that LXXXII derives from Serafino's sonnet 'Col tempo', the first stanza being based on ll. 7–8 and 11–12, while his list of 'fierce things' in ll. 13–14 supplies W's l. 21. This finding is endorsed by Cecchini (109), Baldi (195–6, 228), and Hughey (II.172). It is questionable on the grounds that the strambotti contain images even closer to W's, and that, whereas he does not elsewhere imitate Serafino's sonnets, the strambotti are among his favourite sources. A group concerns the changes wrought by Time in all things but the hard heart of his mistress. Four of these are quoted above, and the memory of them could account for W's poem.

(1) *Con fede e con speranza*] *Eche fiers thing* (l. 21) is rather closer to *Ogni animal, che in boscho si dimora* than to the array of animals listed in the last line of the sonnet.
Marbell stone (l. 3) is closer to *marmo* than to the *dur sasso* of the sonnet.

(2) *Se da poca acqua*] This strambotto, which immediately follows (1) in the 1516 edition, actually starts, like W's poem, with the water-stone image.

(3) *Col tempo al fier caual*] This strambotto, the next but one after (2) in the 1516 edition, combines the water-marble image with that of the *fier caual* (cf. W's *fiers* in ll. 10, 15, 21).

(4) *Soglion li canti*] This later strambotto is relevant because, as in W's poem, an immediate and specific connection between the water drops and the lover's tears, the marble and the mistress's heart, is made.

12 *mens*] means.

18 *that sueth mekenes for his boote*] one that sues for meekness as a reward (for some service).

23–4 *And yet*] i.e. and still (which makes intelligible the transition to the idea that time, humbleness and place – all dealt with in the preceding stanzas – are ineffective in inducing the proud to help the humble).

LXXXIII

5 *Thevin*] The heaven.

6 *My . . . cry*] Cf. Ps. XXXIV.17

10 *in hevin did ly*] R. C. Harrier (*NQ* (June 1953), 234) urged the retention of the reading of E and A, meaning *in occulto*; and he argued that 'If the scribal phrase is unacceptable the proper emendation is "My trust alway in hiding lay" '. This emendation gives a bad rhyme; and the original reading is open to two objections: it makes a very halting line, and it is grammatically awkward. The 'That' of l. 11 would then refer to 'My trust', and the feeble sense would be 'My trust knows what my thought intends'. Nott emended to 'in her did lie', perhaps assuming that W was referring to his mistress, rather than to heaven. It may be suggested that W wrote 'in heaven did lie', (referring back to l. 5) or 'in him did lie', referring to God. That W should put his trust in God, and that God should know what his thought intended

makes excellent sense – better sense, surely, than either of Harrier's suggestions.

LXXXIV. This remarkably skilful handling of a difficult stanza does not require the accompaniment of the lute since the lines can stand without. But it is one of the poems which seems to be written for the lute.

33–4] Koeppel (70) and Baldi (228) compare Petrarch's 'Io sono sí stanco', (*Rime*, lxxxi, 12–14):

> Qual grazia, qual amore, o qual destino
> Mi darà penne in guisa di colomba,
> Ch' i' mi riposi e levimi da terra?

LXXXV. Probable sources:

(1)
> Donar non ti possio uago lauoro
> Doro, di perle, ne riccheza alcuna,
> Ma à me par doni assai riccho thesoro,
> Chi lalma sua col cor franco ui dona,
> Perche riccheza, stato, argento, & oro
> Tutti son sottoposti alla fortuna
> Sola è la fede al mondo un uero lume,
> Chognaltra cosa si risolue in fume.
>
> Serafino, *Opere* (1516), f. 119^r

(2)
> Se dare non ti posso gran tesoro,
>   Signora, dar ti posso lo mio core;
> se povero son io d' argento & d' oro
>   son ricco verso te di grande amore
> se per te vivo al mondo & per te moro
>   ché non m' aiuti & non mi dài favore?
> ma d' una cosa, misero, m' acore
>   ch' un povero è mal visto a tutte l' hore.
>
>   Reprinted from a fifteenth-century
>   collection of 'Strambotti dogni sorte:
>   & Sonetti' in *Le Rime di Serafino*, ed.
>   M. Menghini (Bologna, 1894), I, xli

(3)
> Se povero m' ha fatto la natura
>   d' oro, d' argento & delli beni soi,
> signora il mio tesoro in te s' aduna,
>   richo può farmi & pover gli ochi toi;
> tu vita mi puo' dar & tu sol una
>   mi puoi dar morte, piglia qual tu vòi;
> io dar non ti posso gran richeza,
>   ti dono il core ch' è grande a chi l' apreza.
>
>   Ibid., I, xlii

Padelford (xxxiv) thought the poem was translated from the French and F (11.116) that it was an imitation of Marot's 'Ce nouvel an pour etrenne vous donne'; but Cecchini (106) put forward (1) and (2), which are also accepted by Baldi (229). W may have known all three of Serafino's strambotti, and have worked ideas from them into the equivalent passages of his own more extensive treatment of the common theme: see especially ll. 7–12 and 22–4. In all three strambotti the lover offers his heart as a gift richer than treasure, jewels, etc. Strambotto (1), with its specific mention of *goldsmythes worke* and *perle*, seems to supply W's ll. 7–9, but he neglects its later argument that all riches but faith are subject to fortune. Strambotto (2), because it develops into a love complaint, seems the least like W's unusually happy poem. Strambotto (3) may have suggested the climax of his poem, for in both the heart is mentioned for the first time in the last line. W makes no attempt to imitate the concentrated style of Italian strambotti. Nott (574), without reference to any model, considered his poem 'too much protracted'. But Baldi (195) thinks it improves on Serafino. I. L. Mumford, taking it as an instance of an English lute song derived from an Italian source, also rates it higher than Serafino's strambotti (*EM*, xiv (1963) 15–16).

Date: In the opinion of F (*Study*, 58) Padelford (p. xxxiv) and Stevens (209–10), W's is a New Year's gift poem. F (11.118) also believed that it was composed in Spain, and, if so, the gift belongs to the New Year of either 1538 or 1539.

3] W uses an ascending scale, taking India, as did his medieval predecessors, to stand for the farthest end of the earth: cf. CCLXI.4.

LXXXVI. Source:

> O bella man che mi destringi 'l core
>   E 'n poco spazio la mia vita chiudi,
>   Man ov' ogni arte e tutti loro studi
>   Poser natura e 'l ciel per farsi onore;
> Di cinque perle orïcntal colore,
>   E sol ne le mie piaghe acerbi e crudi,
>   Diti schietti soavi, a tempo ignudi
>   Consente or voi, per arricchirmi, Amore.
> Candido, leggiadretto e caro guanto,
>   Che copria netto avorio e fresche rose;
>   Chi vide al mondo mai sí dolci spoglie?
> Cosí avess' io del bel velo altrettanto!
>   O incostanzia de l' umane cose!
>   Pur questo è furto, e vien ch' i' me ne spoglie.
>
> Petrarch, *Rime*, cxcix

The source of W's imitation was identified by Koeppel (67–8). Possibly the material came to him from an earlier imitation of the sonnet. But it certainly did not come from Giusto de' Conti's *La Bella Mano* (Venice, 1531), as formerly supposed by Nott (575). W builds on the octave of Petrarch's sonnet. When he reaches its end he transmutes the indicative *Consente* into the imperative *Consent*. In Petrarch Love 'consents' to display the naked hand, but W uses the term to introduce a characteristically urgent, personal plea addressed to his mistress. This carries him through to the end of his poem, and, apart from a descriptive detail (see note to ll. 13–15), he takes nothing from the nostalgic and elegiac sestet. He also omits the popular glove motif. See XLVIII and n. Hietsch (190–5) compares W's poem with its model.

z

1–3] A free translation of Petrarch's l. 1.

4 *Faire hand*] W re-uses *bella man*.

5–6] Cf. Petrarch's l. 2.

7–10] This eulogy of the fingers, though largely independent of Petrarch's, roughly corresponds to *Diti schietti soavi* (l. 7).

10 *Goodely bygone*] 'either "beautifully adorned (with rings, etc.)" or "exquisitely fashioned in itself"' (Tillyard, 167): Cf. Chaucer's 'with gold bygoon' ('Romaunt', 943).

11–12] Cf. Petrarch's l. 6.

13–14] Based on Petrarch's l. 10, but omitting the reference to the glove. W retains *rose*, but substitutes *Lilis whight* for *avorio*.

16–18] W combines the comment on nature's artistry in Petrarch's ll. 3–4 with his description of the *cinque perle* in l. 5.

19] Cf. *Consente or* (l. 8).

24 *reche me*] extend to me. Hietsch (195) suggests that W echoes *arricchirmi* (l. 8), Guss (39 and 195) that he perhaps misunderstood Petrarch's phrase ('enrich me').

LXXXVII. This three-part poem (consisting of thesis, antithesis, and synthesis) is carefully constructed: e.g. in the second stanza of each part there is a reference to a snare; in the third stanza to the proverbial idea that one cannot be wise and love, and to dice; and in the last stanza to fire.

A poem ascribed to Alexander Scott (*STS* (ed. 1896), 81) consisting of ll. 1–8, 33–40, 17–24, 9–16, is presumably derivative, although W's could, if improbably, be an expansion of a Scottish original.

No. LXXXVII is the last poem copied in the elegant hand of the scribe responsible for most of the E MS; and it is possible that the remaining poems in the MS were copied into it after W left England.

17 *To ... wise*] An allusion to the popular saying, quoted by Spenser and Shakespeare, the earliest form of which appears to be *Amare et sapere vix deo conceditur* (Pubilius Syrus).

20 *of ... an*] off ... on.

102–3 *zyns ... Ambs as*] Five is a lucky throw, the double ace the unluckiest. Cf. Chaucer, *CT*, B 124–5:

> Youre bagges been nat fild with amber as,
> But with sys cynk, that renneth for youre chaunce.

(WMT)

LXXXVIII

2 *voydes Joyfullnesse*] joyfulness avoids.

3 *So ... fade*] So unrest, that nothing shall alleviate, changes my life.

4–5] Pain and scorn have altered the pleasantness that she made long since.

lxxxix. The stanza, not used elsewhere by W, has a complicated rhyme scheme and a varying length of line, perhaps suggested by Italian *canzoni*.

xc. The unfinished third stanza and the obscurity of the last suggest that this is an early draft. T, who provides a title ('To his loue that had geuen him answere of refusell') rewrote ll. 18–19.

18 *call . . . word*] The answer (l. 1) was obviously not friendly, though the word could be used ironically. But presumably W is asking the lady to revert to her previous attitude, before the harsh answer, when she said 'I am your friend'. This is R. C. Harrier's interpretation (*NQ* (June, 1953), 234).

xci. The first four stanzas are in a different hand from the remainder of the poem. It was suggested (cf. F 11.121) by Chaucer's 'The Playnte to Fortune' ('Fortune') and was probably written 'towards the close of W's residence in Spain' when he was worried by the political situation in England and by his lack of success in his diplomacy. But it appears rather to be a love poem, 'an orderly, stanza by stanza argument between W and his heart' (Thomson, 139).

8 *And . . . so*] Cf. Chaucer, 'Fortune', 25: 'No man is wrecched, but himself it wene' (F).

31 *he*] Chaucer.

xcii. This sonnet, entitled in T 'The louer vnhappy biddeth happy louers rejoice in Maie, while he waileth that moneth to him most unlucky', has a number of Chaucerian echoes. W refers to his imprisonments in May 1534 and 1536. See *L*, 25, 28. There is a discussion by Thomson (275–6) and two by W. H. Wiatt (*NQ*, cxcvii, (1952), 244; *ELN*, iv (1966), 89–92).

2 *lust . . . jolitie*] Cf. Chaucer, 'Complaint unto Pity', 39, 'Lust and Jolyte' (WMT).

3 *Do . . . sluggardie*] Cf. Chaucer, *CT*, A 1042, 'For May wol have no slogardie a-nyght' (F).

4 *Arise . . . obseruance*!] Cf. *T & C*, ii, 112, 'And lat us don to May some observaunce' (F).

8 *As . . . avaunce*] Cf. *T & C*, i, 518, 'Of hem that Love lest febly for to avaunce (WMT).

9 *Sephame*] He has been identified as Edward Sephame by Flügel and by W. H. Wiatt. Sephame cast a horoscope for Edward VI.

11 *gest*] Wiatt suggests Sephame was wise after the event, casting W's horoscope after his troubles in 1534 and 1536.

12 *welth*] Thomson (276) points out that W sometimes refers to the happiness of love as wealth. Cf. xcv.8.

xciii. The first four stanzas of this poem, deleted, are also in E after lxxxviii – not, however, as Nott states, in W's handwriting. The poem is discussed by Thomson (138–9).

1 *Andif*] If.

4 *on*] one.

17 *seke the scole*] seek to study (how to please all).

XCIV. F (II.129–30) suggested that this version of Psalm 37 (36 in the Vulgate) was written in 1538 and that it reflects W's disappointment at his failure to prevent the truce between the Emperor and Francis I. F also argued that W used the Psalter published by Francis Foye (an error for Foxe) in 1530. Mason, however (*TLS*, 27 February 1953), argued that W used the Latin version by Ioannes Campensis (Nuremberg, 1532) and that 'he does not appear to have used the English translation', *A Paraphrasis vpon all the Psalmes of Dauid* (Antwerp, 1535). The English translation, however, is so close to the original that it is difficult to know which W used. In a few places there appear to be echoes of the translation (cited here in the 1539 edition). Some readings are given from the Foxe edition (1530) and from Joye's version (1534) for comparison.

1–4] Cf. Vulgate: 'Noli æmulari in malignantibus; neque zelaueris facientes iniquitatem'.

5–6] Cf. Vulgate: 'Quoniam tamquam fœnum uelociter arescent; et quemadmodum olera herbarum cito decident'.
'Ffor they shalbe founde lyke the grasse, whych when it is rysen, endureth but a shorte tyme and they shalbe lyke vnto a grene herbe that sodenly withereth away' (1539); 'For even lyke grasse anon shall they be kut downe: and lyke the grene fresshe beaute of the flower shall thei wyther a waye' (1530); 'For sodenly lyke heye are they kut downe/and lyke the green grasse be thei witherd' (1534).

7–9] Cf. Vulgate: 'Spera in Domino, et fac bonitatem; et inhabita terram, et pasceris in diuitiis eius'.

8 *And . . . longe*] 'so shalt thou inhabyte the erth a long season' (1539).

10–11] Cf. Vulgate: 'Delectare in Domino; et dabit tibi petitiones cordis tui'.

10 *time*] See Glossary.

12–14] Cf. Vulgate: 'Reuela Domino uiam tuam, et spera in eo; et ipse faciet'.

15–18] Cf. Vulgate: 'Et educet quasi lumen iustitiam tuam, et iudicium tuum tamquam meridiem'.
'Et faciet ut tam sit conspicua iustitia tua, quam est lumen solis: & aequitates tuae, licet nunc nonnihil obscurentur impiorum felicitate, tam clarę fient, quam est sol in ipso meridie' (1532); 'And he shall make thy ryghtuousnesse to be as cleare as the lyght of the sonne, and thy true dealinges (though now they be somthynge darkned thorow the prosperyte of the vngodly) to be as openly sene as the sonne is at the noone daye' (1539); 'He shall lede forth opunly thy rightwisnes even lyke the light: and thi right livinge shall he make to shyne lyke the middaye' (1530); 'he shal set forth thy good dedis like the morninge/and thy iuste dealinge lyke the middaye' (1534).

16 *Bright*] Nott's emendation, supported by Mason as close to the original.

19–23] Cf. Vulgate: 'Subditus esto Domino, et ora eum. Noli æmulari in eo qui prosperatur in uia sua, in homine faciente iniustitias'.

19 *Paciently abide*] 'Abyde pacently' (1539); 'Geue thy selfe hole' (1534).

23 *To wicked folke*] There is a gap after these words in both MSS. Mason suggests that W found he had used up his material too soon. F conj. 'so prosper the untrue'.

24–6] Cf. Vulgate: 'Desine ab ira, et derelinque furorem; noli æmulari ut maligneris'.

24 *Restrayne . . . wrath*] 'Refrayne thy mynde from wrathe' (1539); 'Refrayne (Restraine F) thy selfe from wrathe' (1530); 'Remitte wrath' (1534).

25 *way*] See Glossary.

27–9] Cf. Vulgate: 'Quoniam qui malignantur, exterminabuntur; sustinentes autem Dominum, ipsi hæreditabunt terram'.

28 *pacientlie abid*] 'pacently abyde' (1539, 1534).

29 *They . . . hayre*] 'shall possesse the earth as by ryght herytage' (1539); 'shall inheret the lande' (1530); 'shall possesse the lande' (1534).
hayre] The spelling is influenced by the rhyme.

30–3] Cf. Vulgate: 'Et adhuc pusillum, et non erit peccator; et quæres locum eius, et non inuenies'.

32 *staring*] Hughey reads 'starung', a copyist's error for 'straung'. But *staring*, meaning 'ostentatious' is coupled with *araie* in a story about Julia and Augustus, who was 'offended with hir ouer wanton and staryng araie', in Udall's translation of Erasmus' *Apophthegmes* (1542) 252 (Mason).

34–5] Cf. Vulgate: 'Mansueti autem hæreditabunt terram, et delectabuntur in multitudine pacis'.

36–7] Cf. Vulgate: 'Obseruabit peccator iustum; et stridebit super eum dentibus suis'.

37 *And . . . teethe*] 'gnashe vpon hym with hys teth' (1539); 'grinne vpon hym with his teth' (1530), 'grinneth upon him with his tethe' (1534).

38–40] Cf. Vulgate: 'Dominus autem irridebit eum; quoniam prospicit quod ueniet dies eius'.

38 *The . . . threatninges*] 'The Lorde shall laugh hys threatnynges to scorne' (1539); 'But the Lorde shall laughe him to scorn' (1530); 'But the Lorde laugheth him to scorn' (1534).

41–4] Cf. Vulgate: 'Gladium euaginauerunt peccatores; intenderunt arcum suum, ut deiiciant, pauperum et inopem, ut trucident rectos corde'.

42 *bent . . . bowe*] 'bent theyr bowe' (1539); 'bende their bowes' (1530); 'bende theyr bowe' (1534).

45–6] Cf. Vulgate: 'Gladius eorum intret in corda ipsorum; et arcus eorum confringatur'.
'Theyr swerde shall pearse theyr owne harte, and theyr bowe shalbe

broken' (1539); 'But their swerde shall smite thorowe their owne hartes; and their bowes shalbe broken' (1530); 'But their owne swerde shal perse their owne herte: and their bowes shalbe broken' (1534).

47–9] Cf. Vulgate: 'Melius est modicum iusto super diuitias peccatorum multas'.

47 *gotten rightfullie*] 'well gotten' (1539).

50–1] Cf. Vulgate: 'Quoniam brachia peccatorum conterentur, confirmat autem iustos Dominus'.

52–4] Cf. Vulgate: 'Nouit Dominus dies immaculatorum; et hæreditas eorum in æternum erit'.

53 *for evermore*] 'everlastynge' (1539); 'perpetual' (1530, 1534).

55–7] Cf. Vulgate: 'Non confundentur in tempore malo, et in diebus famis saturabantur'.

55 *When … sore*] 'when myschaunce of tyme shall lappe other men in' (1539); 'In time of adversite they shalnot be shamed (1530); 'Thei shalnot be shamed in the perellouse tyme' (1534). Here *lappe* may have suggested W's *wrappe*.

58–60] Cf. Vulgate: 'Quia peccatores peribunt. Inimici uero Domini mox ut honorificati fuerint et exaltati, deficientes quaemadmodum fumus deficient'.

60 *consume*] 'consume' (Coverdale); 'vanyshe away' (1539).

61–2] Cf. Vulgate: 'Mutuabitur peccator, et non soluet; iustus autem miseretur et tribuet'.

63–5] Cf. Vulgate: 'Quia benedicentes ei hæreditabunt terram; maledicentes autem ei disperibunt'.

64–5] 'Quare qui bene precantur or iustitiam ei, terram possidebunt: qui vero maledicunt, extirpabuntur' (1532): 'Wherfore they that speake good of hym for ryghtousnesse sake, shall possesse the earth, but they that speak euell of hym shalbe destroyed' (1539). Mason shows that *bannyshe* is a scribal error since *bannythe* translates *maledicunt*. (Cf. 'do evel' (1530); 'abhorre' (1534).)

66–7] Cf. Vulgate: 'Apud Dominum gressus hominis dirigentur; et uiam eius uolet'.

68–9] Cf. Vulgate: 'Cum cederit, non collidetur; quia Dominus supponit manum suam'.

68 *though he fall vnder foote*] 'Though he fall, he shall not lye vnder' (1539); 'When he shall fall he shall not be hurte' (1530); 'When he falleth he shall not be hurte' (1534).

70–2] The equivalent of the missing lines is given in the Vulgate: 'Iunior fui, etenim senui; et non uidi iustum derelictum, nec semen eius quærens panem'; 'I was younge and after a longe lyfe am become an olde man, yet haue I not sene a rightuous man desolate, nor hys seade peryshe for want of foode' (1539).

73–86] Cf. Vulgate: 'Tota die miseretur et commodat: et semen illius in bene-
dictione erit.
Declina a malo, et fac bonum; et inhabita in sæculum sæculi.
Quia Dominus amat iudicium et non derelinquet sanctos suos; in æternum
conseruabantur.
Iniusti punientur; et semen impiorum peribit.
Iusti autem hæreditabunt terram; et inhabitabunt in sæculum sæculi super
eam.
Os iusti meditabitur sapientiam; et lingua eius loquetur iudicium.
Lex Dei eius in corde ipsius; et non supplantabuntur gressus eius.'

87–8] Cf. Vulgate: 'Considerat peccator iustum; et quærit mortificare eum'.

89–91] Cf. Vulgate: 'Dominus autem non derelinquet eum in manibus eius;
nec damnabit eum cum iudicabitur illi'.

89–90] 'But the lorde wyl not suffre hym to be opprest thorow his tyranny'
(1539). This is the only version which mentions tyranny (cf. 'in his hande'
(1530, Coverdale); 'in his powr' (1534).

92–6] Cf. Vulgate: 'Expecta Dominum, et custodi uiam eius; et exultabit
te ut hæreditate capias terram; eum perierint peccatores, uidebis.

97–8] Cf. Vulgate: 'Uidi impium superexaltatum, et eleuatum sicut cedros
Libani'. 'I sawe the wycked in great power & in his floures, & lyke vnto the
laurel tre which is euer grene' (1539). Mason contrasts 'euen as the Cedar
trees of Libanus' (from the Vulgate, 1540); 'like a grene baye tre' (Cover-
dale); 'lyke the grene baye tree' (1534). Cf. also 'lyke a tree neuer-remoued
from his naturall fyrst soyle freshly spredyng his branches' (1530).

97 *lyke goolde*] added for the rhyme (F).

99–102] Cf. Vulgate: 'Et transiui, et ecce non erat; et quæsiui eum, et non est
inuentus locus eius'.

102 *fresshe arraye*] Cf. CCLIX.1.

103–5] Cf. Vulgate: 'Custodi innocentiam, et uide æquitatem; quoniam sunt
reliquiæ homini pacifico'.

106–7] Cf. Vulgate: 'Iniusti autem disperibunt simul; reliquiæ impiorum
interibunt'.

106 *All wicked folke*] 'all wycked men' (1539); 'theis sinfull men' (1530); 'the
transgressours' (1534).

108–9] Cf. Vulgate: 'Salus autem iustorum a Domino; et protector eorum
in tempore tribulationis'.

108 *Healthe . . . iuste*] 'Health . . . ryghtous' (1539); 'Helthe . . . rightwise'
(1530); 'helthe . . . iuste' (1534).

109] 'he shalbe ther strength in tyme of trouble' (1539); 'he is their strength
in tyme of tribulacion' (1530); 'he that is their strength in the article of
distresse' (1534).

110–12] Cf. Vulgate: 'Et adiuuabit eos Dominus et liberabit eos; et eruet eos
a peccatoribus et saluabit eos, quia sperauerunt in eo'.

110] 'And the Lorde shall helpe them he (I saye) shall delyuer them' (1539);
  'The lorde for a suretie wyll helpe theym & wyll delyuer them' (1530);
  'The Lorde bringethe them helpe and delyuerth them' (1534). Only W and
  1539 insert 'I saye'.

xcv. Possible sources:

> Rapido fiume, che d' alpestra vena,
>   Rodendo intorno, onde 'l tuo nome prendi,
>   Notte e dí meco disïoso scendi
> Ov' Amor me, te sol Natura mena;
> Vattene innanzi: il tuo corso non frena
>   Né stanchezza né sonno: e pria che rendi
>   Suo dritto al mar, fiso, u' si mostri, attendi
> L' erba piú verde e l' aria piú serena.
> Ivi è quel nostro vivo e dolce sole
>   Ch' adorna e 'nfiora la tua riva manca;
>   Forse (oh che spero?) il mio tardar le dole.
> Basciale 'l piede o la man bella e bianca:
>   Dille (el basciar sia 'n vece di parole)
>   – Lo spirto è pronto, ma la carne è stanca. –
>
>   Petrarch, *Rime*, ccviii

> Vdito hó giá che una acqua se è ueduta
>   Cader duno alto monte in basso loco
> Et per la uiolente alta caduta
>   Talhor nel fondo generar gran foco,
> Tal cosa è pur in me non cognosciuta,
>   Che ogni gran cosa apresso amore è poco
> Lachrymo sempre, el pianto há tal furore,
> Che percotendo el pecto marde el core.
>
>   Serafino, *Opere* (1516), f. 145^(r–v)

> Come torrente che superbo faccia
> Lunga pioggia talvolta o nievi sciolte,
> Va ruinoso, e giú da monti caccia
> Gli arbori, e i sassi, e i campi, e le ricolte:
> Vien tempo poi che l' orgogliosa faccia
> Gli cade, e si le forze gli son tolte,
> Ch' un fanciullo, una femina per tutto
> Passar lo puote, e spesso a piede asciutto:
> Cosí già fu che Marganorre . . . . &c.
>
>   Ariosto, *Orlando Furioso*, XXXVII,
>   cx and cxi, 1

> Forza è alfin che si scuopra, e che si veggia
> Il gaudio mio dianzi a gran pena ascoso,
> Ancor ch' io sappia che tacer si deggia,
>   E quanto a dirlo altrui sia periglioso;
> Perchè sempre chi ascolta è più proclive
> Ad invidiar, che ad esserne gioioso;
>   Ma, come quando alle calde aure estive

Si risolvono i ghiacci e nevi alpine,
Crescon i fiumi al par delle lor rive,
  Et alcun dispregiando ogni confine
Rompe superbo gli argini, et inonda
Le biade, i paschi e le città vicine:
  Così quando soverchia, e sovrabbonda
A quanto cape e può capire il petto,
Convien che l' allegrezza si diffonda,
  E faccia rider gli occhi, e nell' aspetto
Gir con baldanza. . . .

    Ariosto, 'Capitoli Amorosi,' v. 1-17,
    in *Works*, VIII (Florence, 1824), 82-3

All the above passages employ W's image of a raging torrent (an image which perhaps derives ultimately from *Aen.* II. 305-8). and all, except for the stanza from *Orlando Furioso*, in a love context. None bears exactly W's sense. Ariosto's capitolo describes how, as a river bursts its bank, so joy bursts out in the lover. In *Orlando Furioso* he describes parallel diminutions of force in a river and in Marganorre. Petrarch uses the raging Rhône to define the course of his love. Serafino thinks in terms of the incredible phenomenon by which a lover's tears, like torrents, generate firc. Koeppel (77) first suggested, though tentatively, that W was imitating Ariosto's capitolo. Berdan (457 n.) was sceptical: the *Capitoli* were not published till *c.* 1537, and so 'either W's epigram is very late, or he learned it verbally, or [the similarity] is merely a coincidence'. F (11.71) put forward the stanza from *Orlando Furioso*. Rollins (11.175-6) and Baldi (230) cite both Ariosto parallels, but without comment on their possible value as sources. W gives few, if any, signs elsewhere of having read Ariosto, and his use of the ottava rima stanza is traceable to Serafino's strambotti rather than to *Orlando Furioso* (see XLVI and note). The following are therefore offered as alternative suggestions: (1) that W took his hint from Serafino's 'Vdito hó gia', (2) that the combination of his knowledge of Petrarch's imagery and his practice in writing Serafinesque strambotti accounts for his poem. For a fuller discussion of the relative value of all four passages as possible sources, see Thomson (281-3). Title in T: 'Comparison of loue to a streame falling from the Alpes.'

1 *thes hye hilles*] The poem in E stands between LXXXI, with its description of W in Monçon (in view of the Pyrenees), and XCVIII entitled 'In Spayne'. F (11.71) therefore thinks that W here refers to the Pyrenees, as does Rollins (11.176), and Tillyard (169) is inclined to agree. Baldi (230) rejects the idea firmly. Nothing can be inferred from the *Alpes* in T's title, since the word in the sixteenth century denoted any high mountains as well as the Alps.

3 *ay*] W's correction avoids the original repetition of *still*.

4] Possible meanings are: (1) 'Till it has just made the waters of the river and main current overflow', (2) 'Till it has flowed right away from the waters of the river and main current', (3) 'Till it has flowed past the rapids and falls' (Tillyard's paraphrase (169), in which he takes *streme* to mean 'fast flowing stretch' and *forse* as 'waterfall'). T's reading suggests that his editor took it to mean 'Till it has just flowed down to the waters of the river and main current'. Various interpretations of individual words make modifications of the above possible:

off flowd] Overflowed, flowed off from. W, it seems likely, uses *off* as a verbal prefix.

streme] River waters, force or volume of river. (In the latter case, *streme and forse* could be a redundant phrase, not impossible in W.)

forse] Strength of current, 'the spring or fountain whence [the current] is derived' (Nott, 556), waterfall (northern dialect; ON *fors*). Of the latter K (295), who rejects the idea that W's vocabulary in general shows northern influence, says 'The exclusively northern word *force* "waterfall" ... does not occur at all in W', and he therefore takes this as 'clearly the modern word "force".'

6 *sorse*] fountain-head or origin of river, spring: cf. l. 1 and the main image of the poem. Nott (556) suggests 'impetuous flight', from the hawking term *source* (the act of rising on the wing). Cf. Chaucer, *H of F*, 544.

7 *rayne*] rein, i.e. restraint. (Since love's restraint is *rage*, there is in effect no restraint.)

resistans vaylyth none] H. Smith comments on W's correction, presumably made for the sake of the rhyme (*HLQ*, ix (1946), 331).

8] 'The only remedy is to eschew love from the first.' Cf. Chaucer, 'Parlement of Foules', 140: 'Th' eschewing is only the remedye' (WMT).

xcvi. This fragment was omitted in error from the 1949 edition.

xcvii. Possible source:

Petrarch's *S' una fede amorosa*. For the text, see note to xii. Nott (539) identified the source of W's imitation in the first six lines of Petrarch's sonnet. This has not been unreservedly accepted. Hughey (11.156) describes this source as 'probable'. F (11.52), Baldi (230), and Hietsch (180–2) all think that Petrarch supplied no more than hints and a theme. W translated the sonnet in xii, so that he may well be freely working out the same idea, but without much reference to Petrarch's text. The chief influence seems to be structural, and both sonnets use the figure of *Irmus* (suspension): 'the whole sence [of W's ll. 1–5] is suspended till ye come to ... *then do I loue againe*' (Puttenham, 176). W, like Petrarch, uses a series of conditional clauses, describing symptoms of love, the conclusion of which is delayed. Then, on their completion, the long suspended main clause follows (see note to l. 6). Hietsch (182) also indicates some similarities of detail (see notes to ll. 1, 2, and 3). But as these concern the conventional signs of love sickness, they should be treated with caution as evidence of a direct debt. W owes nothing to ll. 7–14 of Petrarch's sonnet, except perhaps to *tinto* (see note to l. 3). His own conclusion, developed from l. 6 on, that he has found a new and better mistress to love, has no counterpart in Petrarch. Title in T: 'The louer confesseth him in loue with Phillis.'

1 *waker care*] Cf. cviii.564.
pale Coulour] Hietsch (182) compares *un pallor di vïola* (l. 8).

2 *litle speche*] Hietsch (182) compares *voci interotte* (l. 6).

3 *they*] i.e. *ioy* and *woo*.
my chere distayne] W, taking up *sodayne pale Coulour*, probably refers to his alternate blushing and paling.
distayne] Cf. *depinto* (l. 5) and *tinto* (l. 8). Hietsch (182) compares *depaynted* and *stayned* (xii.5 and 8).

4] Guss (35) contrasts W's stress on rewards with the 'confessional quality' of Petrarch's *error* and *cieco*.

4–5] ? 'If for hope of small gain to seem much to hasten or to slacken my pace.'

6 *Be signe of love*] As the completion of the earlier conditional clauses this corresponds to *Son le cagion* (l. 13).

6 *then do I love agayne*] As the main clause this corresponds to Petrarch's l. 14.

7–9] Chambers (139), after a careful weighing of the evidence for W's affair with Anne Boleyn, decides in favour of her claim to be *Brunet*. In that case, W's correction to l. 8 in E may have been intended to cover up the tracks. Chambers (140–5) rejects the romantic claim, made by F (ii.52–3), that *Phillis* is Mary, Duchess of Richmond, and puts forward the claims of Elizabeth Darrell, the mistress of W's later years.

8] Cf. *T & C*, v, 45 'al Troie upon a roore' (WMT).

xcviii. Source:

> Sí è debile il filo a cui s' attene
>   La gravosa mia vita,
>   Che, s' altri non l' aita,
>   Ella fia tosto di suo corso a riva:
>   Però che, dopo l' empia dipartita   5
>   Che dal dolce mio bene
>   Feci, sol una spene
>   È stato in fin a qui cagion ch' io viva;
>   Dicendo "Perché priva
>   Sia de l' amata vista,   10
>   Mantienti, anima trista:
>   Che sai s' a miglior tempo anco ritorni
>   Et a piú lieti giorni?
>   O se 'l perduto ben mai si racquista?"
>   Questa speranza mi sostenne un tempo: 15
>   Or vien mancando, e troppo in lei m' attempo.
> Il tempo passa, e l' ore son sí pronte
>   A fornire il viaggio,
>   Ch' assai spazio non aggio
>   Pur a pensar com' io corro a la morte.   20
>   A pena spunta in orïente un raggio
>   Di sol, ch' a l' altro monte
>   De l' adverso orizonte
>   Giunto il vedrai per vie lunghe e distorte.
>   Le vite son sí corte,   25
>   Sí gravi i corpi e frali
>   De gli uomini mortali,

Che, quando io mi ritrovo dal bel viso
Cotanto esser diviso,
Col desio non possendo mover l' ali 30
Poco m' avanza del conforto usato;
Né so quant' io mi viva in questo stato.
Ogni loco m' atrista, ov' io non veggio
Quei begli occhi soavi
Che portaron le chiavi 35
De' miei dolci pensier, mentre a Dio piacque
E perché 'l duro essilio piú m' aggravi,
S' io dormo o vado o seggio,
Altro già mai non cheggio,
E ciò ch' i' vidi dopo lor mi spiacque. 40
Quante montagne et acque,
Quanto mar, quanti fiumi
M' ascondon que' duo lumi,
Che quasi un bel sereno a mezzo 'l die
Fêr le tenebre mie, 45
A ciò che 'l rimembrar piú mi consumi
E quant' era mia vita allor gioiosa
M' insegni la presente aspra e noiosa!
Lasso, se ragionando si rinfresca
Quell' ardente desio 50
Che nacque il giorno ch' io
Lassai di me la miglior parte a dietro,
E s' Amor se ne va per lungo oblio,
Chi mi conduce a l' esca
Onde 'l mio dolor cresca? 55
E perché pria, tacendo, non m' impetro?
Certo, cristallo o vetro
Non mostrò mai di fore
Nascosto altro colore,
Che l' alma sconsolata assai non mostri 60
Piú chiari i pensier nostri
E la fera dolcezza ch' è nel core,
Per gli occhi, che di sempre pianger vaghi
Cercan dí e notte pur chi glie n' appaghi.
Novo piacer, che ne gli umani ingegni 65
Spesse volte si trova,
D'amar qual cosa nova
Piú folta schiera di sospiri accoglia!
Et io son un di quei che 'l pianger giova;
E par ben ch' io m' ingegni 70
Che di lagrime pregni
Sien gli occhi miei sí come 'l cor di doglia;
E, per che a ciò m' invoglia
Ragionar de' begli occhi
(Né cosa è che mi tócchi 75
O sentir mi si faccia cosí a dentro),
Corro spesso e rientro;
Colà donde piú largo il duol trabocchi
E sien co 'l cor punite ambe le luci
Ch' a la strada d' Amor mi furon duci. 80

Le trecce d' òr che devrien fare il sole
  D' invidia molta ir pieno,
  E 'l bel guardo sereno
  Ove i raggi d' Amor sí caldi sono
  Che mi fanno anzi tempo venir meno,   85
  E l' accorte parole,
  Rade nel mondo o sole,
  Che mi fèr già di sé cortese dono,
  Mi son tolte: e perdono
  Piú lieve ogni altra offesa,   90
  Che l' essermi contesa
  Quella benigna angelica salute,
  Che 'l mio cor a vertute
  Destar solea con un voglia accesa:
  Tal ch' io non penso udir cosa già mai   95
  Che mi conforte ad altro ch' a trar guai.
E, per pianger ancor con piú diletto,
  Le man bianche sottili
  E le braccia gentili,
  E gli atti suoi soavemente alteri   100
  E i dolci sdegni alteramente umili,
  E 'l bel giovenil petto
  Torre d' alto intelletto,
  Mi celan questi luoghi alpestri e feri.
  E non so s' io mi speri   105
  Vederla anzi ch' io mora:
  Pero ch' ad ora ad ora
  S' erge la speme e poi non sa star ferma,
  Ma ricadendo afferma
  Di mai non veder lei che 'l ciel onora,   110
  Ov' alberga onestade e cortesia
  E dov' io prego che 'l mio albergo sia.
Canzon, s' al dolce loco
  La donna nostra vedi,
  Credo ben che tu credi   115
  Ch' ella ti porgerà la bella mano
  Ond' io son si lontano:
  Non la toccar; ma reverente ai piedi
  Le di' ch' io sarò là tosto ch' io possa,
  O spirto ignudo od uom di carne e d' ossa.   120

          Petrarch, *Rime*, xxxvii

The source was identified by Nott (553). W for the most part translates, often line by line, and mainly successfully. His care in bringing out the sense is evident, for example, in the passage describing the sun's 'journey' (ll. 17–20), and his use of phrases such as *by such record* (l. 42) and *Thes new kyndes off plesurs* (l. 55) which reinforce the continuity of the argument. He sometimes simplifies Petrarch's grammar, breaking up his long complex sentences (as in ll. 49–54 and 61–8). In at least one other place (ll. 81–7), he could probably, however, have afforded to simplify more, and here, as in the rendering of individual lines (e.g. l. 10), he is obscure, so that his sense is difficult to follow without the aid of the Italian. The effort of translation, coupled with his comparatively long lines, also sometimes forces him into tautologies which have no counterpart in Petrarch's canzone, e.g. *some aide or some socours* in l. 3 (and cf. ll. 64 and 65).

W's alterations and additions, are, except in one feature, typical. The exception is his introduction of the classical references to which he is not given in his original poetry and which he sometimes excises from his translations (e.g. XXVIII.3 and CV.50–1). Thus he elaborates the myth of the spinning Fates (l. 4), and brings in Phoebus (l. 40) and Apollo (l. 69). Otherwise his alterations generally draw attention to himself and his own circumstances. In rendering the description of the mistress's charming features, he adds descriptions of their effect on him (see ll. 83 and 86). But the most marked difference between W and Petrarch comes in the coda, as remarked by Nott (553). Petrarch's addresses Laura with Dantesque reverence and the traditional humility of the lover. W's is no less loving, but it is more confident, more expectant of an ordinary womanly response. Mason (192) comments on the adult, human, 'and therefore moral' love relation W is trying to describe.

The most extensive and detailed comparison of the two poems is by Hietsch (146–67).

The title 'In Spayne' makes it certain that the poem was written between June 1537 and June 1539, and likely that the mistress addressed is Elizabeth Darrell. W's alteration of l. 88 to read *At other will my long abode* probably, as remarked by Nott (553), relates to the King's will that he should remain at the Imperial court in spite of his own desire to return home. And this makes it likely that he was revising the poem early in 1539, at which point his frustration and anxiety to be recalled reached their peak (see his letter of 2 January and Cromwell's reply: *L*, 86–7).

The canzone is divided into seven sixteen-line stanzas, followed by an eight line coda, and, like all its kind, interweaves long and short lines. In none of his versions of Petrarch's canzoni does W attempt exact metrical imitation: see note to VIII. He is however, aware of the stanzaic divisions of his original. And his translation falls into seven sections (the lines being grouped 14 + 14 + 14 + 12 + 14 + 12 + 14) followed by a coda (of six lines). W's choice of poulter's measure may have struck him as an appropriate counterpart to the Italian, since its lines vary in length, and as being, in itself, lyrical: see I. L. Mumford on its 'connection . . . with lyrics intended for singing' (*EM*, xiv (1963), 21), and her account of W's experiments in rendering canzoni (*EM*, xi (1960), 21–32). Probably the modern ear has lost the tune of poulter's measure, the least admired of W's innovations. C. S. Lewis condemns it as 'terrible', citing the present example, and its totally un-Petrarchan sound (*English Literature in the Sixteenth Century* (Oxford, 1954), 224–5). And Mason (191) speaks of W's choice of this metre as 'a sickening lapse'.

Hughey (II.177–8) shows that E is the source for A, D, and T, 'for the three copies present the text in most lines according to W's revised readings, but, at the same time, the three have independent variants'. She also comments on W's revisions. Title in T: 'Complaint of the absence of his loue.'

2 *pore*] W's addition.

In hevy plyght that fallyth in dekay] W's expansion of *gravosa* (l. 2), which he has already rendered in *burden* (l. 1).

3 *some aide or some socours*] A gap-filling redundancy (cf. *aita*).

4] Cf. Petrarch's l. 4. W brings in the common classical metaphor of the spinning Fates, neatly matching the *threde* of l. 1, in place of Petrarch's 'shore' image. Cf. his handling of the Italian in xxx1.4.

5 *did me*] i.e. caused me (cf. Chaucer, *T & C*, iv, 250). W's addition.

6 *one only hope hath staide my lyff apart*] Renders *sol una spene . . . viva* (ll. 7–8), and, in its phrasing particularly, anticipates Petrarch's l. 15.

7] W's expansion of *Dicendo* (l. 9).

8 *Mayntene thy sellff, o wofull spryte*] Translation of Petrarch's l. 11.
some better luk to fynd] Anticipates *miglior tempo* and *più lieti giorni* in Petrarch's ll. 12–13.

9] Translation of *Perché priva . . . vista* (ll. 9–10).

10] A free rendering of Petrarch's ll. 12–13, and rather obscure. W means 'Who can tell you that delight will not return to you ?'

11] Cf. Petrarch's l. 14.

12 *Some plesant howre*] Renders *più lieti giorni* (l. 13). The rest of W's line is a rather puffy reiteration of Petrarch's ll. 12–13.

13 *yet*] Substituted for *un tempo* (i.e. for some time) in Petrarch's l. 15.

14 *I se*] W's addition.
and I by trust ame trainid] Cf. *e troppo in lei* [i.e. *speranza*] *m' attempo* (l. 16). Petrarch expresses the endless waiting which eventually leads him to lose hope in hope, and *attempo* finds a good English equivalent in *trainid*.

15 *The tyme doth flete*] Cf. *Il tempo passa* (l. 17).
I perceyve] W's addition to Petrarch's l. 17.

15–16 *thowrs . . . fast*] Cf. *l'ore . . . viaggio* (ll. 17–18). Petrarch describes the 'voyage' of the hours', i.e. of the sun through the zodiac. Hence W's *bend* doubtless means 'incline', and he, too, uses 'hours', poetically, for the sun.

16 *that I . . . end*] Cf. Petrarch's ll. 19–20.

17–20] A free rendering of Petrarch's ll. 21–4, to which W adds, in l. 20, a careful explanation of the sun's journey based on Petrarch's earlier reference to it (l. 18). W omits *l' altro monte*, and in place of *l' adverso orizonte* reiterates *west*.

21–2] Render ll. 25–7. W applies *fraile* to *lyff* instead of, as in the original, to *body*. The result is some puffy repetition in l. 22.

23–4] Cf. Petrarch's ll. 28–9.

23 *thinke apon*] Substituted for *ritrovo* (l. 28), a change which necessitates the introduction of *the distance and the space*.

24 *my dere desird face*] A subjective substitute for *bel viso* (l. 28).

25–6] W reconstructs Petrarch's dependent phrase (l. 30) as a main statement, and expands it.

27–8] Correspond roughly to ll. 31–2. But W, instead of translating them literally, harks back to l. 15 of the Italian (cf. his own l. 13), and modifies it to fit the present gloomy context.

29] Cf. Petrarch's l. 33.

30] Cf. *Quei begli . . . pensier* (ll. 34–6). E's *lyvely* is a less accurate rendering of *begli* than A's *lovelye*.

31 *Those thowghtes were plesaunt swete*] An amplication of *dolci pensier* (l. 36).
whilst I enioyd that grace] Substituted for *mentre a Dio piacque* (l. 36). W's *grace* is not the grace of God, but that of his mistress.

32] W's addition, though true to the spirit of Petrarch's contrast between past and present.

33 *want*] Substituted for *duro essilio* (l. 37).

34 *In wache, in slepe, both day and nyght*] A free translation of l. 38. W omits *o vado o seggio*, and builds upon *dormo* an effective double antithesis.

34–5 *my will . . . wish*] Cf. Petrarch's l. 39.

35–6 *wheroff . . . delyght*] An expansion of Petrarch's l. 40, the main addition being *my faytfull hert*.

37] W brings forward *mia vita . . . noiosa* (ll. 47–8).

38] The scenic details come from ll. 41–2, though W substitutes *land* for *acque*. (His *flowdes* renders *fiumi*, not *acque*).

38–9 *that doth . . . lyghtes*] Cf. Petrarch's l. 43.

38 *them entremete*] i.e. put themselves (between).

39 *those shining lyghtes*] W strengthens Petrarch's usual description of Laura's eyes, *que' duo lumi* (l. 43).

39–40 *that wontyd . . . spere*] Cf. Petrarch's ll. 44–5. *Phebus* is W's contribution: cf. *Apollo* in l. 69.

41–2] Cf. ll. 46–8. W re-emphasizes *M' insegni* (already used in l. 37).

42 *how that my welth doth bate*] A generalized version of Petrarch's statement, details from which W has already used (see l. 37).

43] Cf. ll. 49–50. W substitutes *such record* for *ragionando*.

44] Cf. Petrarch's ll. 51–2.
sprang] i.e. sprang to life (in reference to *mynd*): cf. *nacque*.

45] Cf. Petrarch's l. 53.

46–7 *Who doth . . . care?*] Cf. Petrarch's ll. 54–5.

46 *o wofull wrech*] W's addition.
baytid net] Strengthens *esca* (bait).

47–8 *much better . . . be*] W turns the question (l. 56) into a statement, and adds *still absent for to be*. His reconstruction of the metaphor, *tacendo . . . m' impetro*, as a simile might have been suggested by Vellutello's gloss, 'tacendo non diuento a similitudine d' una statua di petra, che non parla mai' (f. 84ᵛ). The simile itself, as Hietsch (160) points out, is Chaucerian; see *H of F*, 656.

48] Mason (195) draws attention to the genuine improvement in W's correction in E.

49–54] W, as in ll. 61–8, simplifies the grammar of Petrarch's long complex sentence (ll. 57–64).

49] Cf. Petrarch's l. 57. W substitutes *Alas* for *Certo*, and adds the adjectives, *transparant* being taken from Vellutello's gloss, 'cristallo o trasparente uetro' (f. 84ᵛ).

50] Cf. Petrarch's ll. 58–9.

51] Cf. Petrarch's ll. 60–1. W's *thowghtfull throws* (i.e. throes) renders *i pensier*.

52] Cf. l. 62. W adds *off fervent love* (implied by Petrarch), and in *cover* strengthens the 'hiding' metaphor.

53–4] Cf. Petrarch's ll. 63–4.

55] Cf. Petrarch's ll. 65–6. W's addition of *Thes* and *kyndes off* provides continuity and helps to emphasize the ensuing point that the lover feels pleasure in his pain.
  most men] Substituted for *gli umani ingegni,* and containing the idea of *Spesse volte.*
  reioyse] Substituted for the passive (*si trova*).

56–7] Cf. ll. 67–9. W's *To me* introduces immediately the idea of self, delayed by Petrarch till l. 69.

58–60] Cf. ll. 70–2. W's metaphor (*charge, brink, frawtid*) is based on *pregni,* and anticipates *trabocchi* (l. 78).

58 *It sittes me well*] i.e. it suits me well (*N.E.D.,* 11, 17c), W's addition.

59 *tweyne*] W's addition, anticipating *ambe le luci* (l. 79).

61–8] Cf. Petrarch's ll. 73–80. W, as in ll. 49–54, simplifies the grammar. He also rearranges the order of the statements.

61] Built up from *per che a ció* (ll. 73) and l. 74.

62] Built up from *m'invoglia* (l. 73) and, with the omission of *Corro spesso,* from ll. 77–8. W's *provoke* renders *m'invoglia* and his *repete rientro*. In *my plaint* he shortens the sense of Petrarch's l. 78, from which he has already used a detail in ll. 58–60.

63] Renders the parenthetical statement of ll. 75–6.

64] W's addition to Petrarch's parenthetical statement. His *thei* refers to the lady's eyes.

65–6] A free translation of ll. 77–8, and, in the case of *rientro* (see W's l. 62), retranslation.

65 *well or spryng*] Substituted for, though suggested by, *trabocchi*.

67–8] Cf. ll. 79–80. W's *in payne accompagnie* and *to fele the smert* both render the idea of and strengthen *punite*.

69] Cf. Petrarch's ll. 81–2.
  The cryspid gold] W adds *cryspid* to *Le trecce d' òr*. Cf. CXVIII.6.
  Apollos] Cf. l. 40 and note.

70] A free rendering of Petrarch's l. 83. W's *sterres* are his mistress's eyes (cf. *guardo*), which are, quite literally, *vnder* her golden curls.

AA

strenes]? strains, i.e. light from stars; alternatively, W's error for *stremes*, which would fit the metaphor *glyd* (cf. A, D, and T).

71] Translation of l. 84.

72] Free translation of l. 85, W's terms being suggested by the previous line, and the common Petrarchan descriptions of the feverish lover (e.g. XXVI.2).

73–86] Mason (193–4) discusses W's intention and metre. The passage is not quite so remote from Petrarch as he seems to suggest.

73] Cf. Petrarch's ll. 86–7.
wise and plesaunt] Cf. *accorte* (used in the sense of 'seemly', and not in its more usual rather pejorative sense).
so rare or elles alone] so rare or even unique (*Rade . . . o sole*).

74] Cf. Petrarch's l. 88. W adds *that such had neuer none*, thus intensifying *cortese*.

75] Built up from *Mi son tolte* (l. 89) and *ogni altra offesa* (l. 90). W adds *alas*.

76–7] A free version of *e perdono . . . salute* (ll. 89–92). W's use of *word and chere* is justified by the older commentators, who interpreted *salute* in the sense of *saluto*; e.g. 'Ma sopra tutto della sua benigna & angelica uoce, dallaquale alcuna uolta soleua esser dolcemente salutato' (Vellutello, f. 85ʳ). In *that did me bryng . . . redresse off lingerd payne* W adds a comment, typical of him and merely implicit in the original, on the effect of his mistress's *plesant word and chere*.

78] Translation of ll. 93–4, with *trayne* substituted for *Destar*.

79–80] Free translation of ll. 95–6, in which Petrarch says that he never expects to hear of any other 'comfort' but what will make him lament. W contributes the compulsion (*dryven, herken affter*), and the reference to his *large desire*.

81–7] Based on ll. 97–104, which suggest that *those handes* is not the object of *complaine*, but one of the subjects of *is hid*.

81–2 *And yet . . . complaine*] Translation of l. 97. W strengthens *pianger* by using both *mone* and *complaine*, and by adding *my wofull cace*.

82–3 *those handes . . . lyff*] W's elaboration of Petrarch's ll. 98–9. He preserves *man* and *braccia*, omitting their epithets, and adding the description of their power over him (cf. l. 86). The phrase *that fermely . . . sellff* was traced by Nott (553) to Horace's 'quae me surpuerat mihi' (*Odes*, IV, xiii, 20).

84] A free rendering of Petrarch's paradoxes in ll. 100–1. Various suggestions for alternative sources have been made (e.g. *Rime*, ccccli; *T & C*, ii 1099). But, most likely, W draws on the common Petrarchan stock of antitheses and oxymora.

85] W's addition or, perhaps, intended to represent Petrarch's l. 103.

86] W's addition, substituted for the omitted l. 102 of the Italian. As in l. 83, he adds a description of the effect of his mistress on him.

87] Translation of l. 104.

88] A free rendering of ll. 105–6. Petrarch despairs of seeing Laura again before he dies, whereas W's despair is probably the result of his having to remain in Spain: see introductory note.

89] Cf. ll. 107–8. W adds *by some redresse*.

90–1] W's elaboration of l. 109, the idea of fear being suggested by *afferma/Di mai non veder*, etc. (ll. 109–10).

91 *the lesse for more desire*]? the more desire the less hope.

92] Built up from *afferma* (l. 109) and l. 110. W's *to see that I requyre* is vaguer, less exalted, and more self-centred than *veder lei che'l ciel onora*.

93] Free translation of l. 111. W substitutes *love* for *cortesia*, and adds *lyves and grose*.

94] Translation of l. 112. W adds *my wery lyff*.

95–6 *My song . . . I lyve*] Cf. ll. 113–14. Changing the conditional clause to a main one, W at once sounds more confident, while the change from the first person plural (*nostra*) to the singular (*My, I*) suggests a greater possessiveness.

96–8 *may chaunce . . . reserve*] substituted for ll. 115–18, which describe Laura's gracious reception of the song, in its writer's absence, and the song's reverence for her. W's description is in a different and more human key. *By twene her brestes* was perhaps suggested by Petrarch's l. 102, which W has omitted.

99–100] Translation of ll. 119–20.

99 *she shall me shortly se*] Substituted for *tosto ch'io possa*, and, in effect, a confident repetition of *I come*.

100 *whayte*] Renders *carne* and *ossa*. Cf. ll. 22 and 26.

XCIX. Entitled by T 'Of his returne from *Spaine*'. W left Spain early in June 1539.

1–2 *Tagus . . . gold*] Cf. Chaucer, 'Boethius', III, Metrum 10: 'Alle the thinges that the ryver Tagus yveth yow with his goldene gravelis' (F).Cf. also Skelton, 'Phyllyp Sparowe', 875–81:

> Of Thagus, that golden flod,
> That passeth all earthly good;
> And as that flod doth pas
> Al floodes that euer was,
> With his golden sandes . . .

4 *that*] Refers back to the Tagus.

5 *the town which Brutus sowght*] London. Brutus, Æneas's descendant, was told by Diana to sail to Albion and there found a kingdom. See Geoffrey of Monmouth.

8 *winges*] T substituted the more prosaic *windes*.

c. T entitles this epigram 'Why loue is blinde'. F suggests that it was an adaptation of a French or Italian poem.

CI. T entitles it 'To his vnkind loue'.

This is one of the most interesting of the poems in E because we can see W at
work. It is probably, though not certainly, a first draft. He composed the first
stanza on a single rhyme:

> What rage is this? What furour of excesse?
> What powre what poyson doth my mynd opresse?
> With in the bonis to rancle doth not cesse
> The poysond plesantnesse

Then W decided that the syntax could be improved, that the repetition of
poyson-poysond was weak, and that it would be better not to have the short line
rhyming with the other three. He therefore altered the first three lines:

> What rage is this? what furour of what kynd?
> what powre, what plage doth wery thus my mynd?
> with in my bons to rancle is assind
> the poysond plesantnesse.

Then he began the second stanza:

> Lo se my chekes swell with countynuall terys
> the body still sleples away it weris
> my fode my . . .

He changed *my chekes* to *myn iyes*, reversed the order of *sleples away*, and
changed *my* in the third line to *nothing*:

> my fode nothing my fainting strength reperis
> nor doth my lyms ssustaine.

Then he changed the last word to *redresse* to rhyme with the last word of the
first stanza.

   He began the third stanza:

> The strok doth stretche . . .

He crossed out these four words and tried:

> Into wid wound the deadly strok doth torne
> in curid skarre that neuer (*illegible word*) to . . .

The third version runs:

> In diepe wid wound the dedly strok doth torne
> to curid skarre that neuer shalle retorne.
> Go to, tryumphe, reioyce thy goodly torne
> thi frend thow dost opresse.

   The next stanza came more easily:

> Opresse thou dost, and hast off hym no ruthe . . .

This was a difficult rhyming word, and he changed it to *cure*, and then continued:

> nor yet my woos no pitie can procure
> fiers tygre fell, hard rok withowt recure
> cruell vnkynd to love!

In the second line he then changed *woos* to *death*, and afterwards to *plaint*; and in the last line he changed *vnkynd* to *rebell*.

The first version of the last stanza ran:

> Myghtst thou so loue, neuer belovffd agayne
> myghtst thou so love and never more attayne
> myght wrathefull love so threte you with disdayne
> thy cruell hert to prove.

He changed the last line to:

> thy cruellty reprove

and rewrote the other three lines so as to avoid excessive repetition:

> Ons may thou love, never belovffd agayne;
> so love thou still and not thy love obttayne,
> so wrathefull love with spites of just disdayne.

Then, finally, W felt that it was unsatisfactory to rhyme the concluding lines of the first three stanzas, and the concluding lines of the last two. It would be better to have all five lines rhyming, or all five unrhyming. He did not wish to sacrifice, perhaps, the admirable line 'cruell rebell to love!' so the other rhymes had to go. He changed *plesantnesse* to *plesant swete*, *redresse* to *sustayne* (the original word), and *thy cruelltie reprove* to *may thret thy cruell hert*. The unrhymed lines provide an original and striking effect.

CII. Source:

> Di pensier in pensier, di monte in monte
>   Mi guida Amor; ch' ogni segnato calle
>   Provo contrario a la tranquilla vita.
>
>   Petrarch, *Rime*, cxxix, ll. 1–3

The source of this fragment was identified by Nott (ii). As in XCVIII, W uses poulter's measure to render Petrarch's canzone, and, as far as one can tell, intends to keep close to his original. But it is possible that the lines struck W as appropriate to his situation in Spain and that he never intended to continue with the translation.

CIII. This riddle, on the same page as CII, was copied into E, possibly by Mary Harrington (F 11.73), and probably from T, where it is entitled 'Discripcion of a gonne'. H may therefore be the earlier text, but its variants in ll. 2 and 3 seem inferior. H gives the source 'Latine ex Pandulpho', i.e. Pandolfo Collinutio. According to Nott (cxxvii) it is taken from a dialogue in which he urged the citizens of Siena to purchase artillery for the defence of the town. The Latin given in H is nearer to W's translation than that given by Nott:

> Vulcanus genuit, peperit Natura, Minerva
> Edocuit: Nutrix Ars fuit, atque genitrix
> Vis men de Nihilo est; tria dant mihi corpora pastum;
> Sunt nati, Strages, Ira, Ruina, Fragor.
> Dic hospes, qui sim: num terræ an bellua ponti
> An neutrum: an prosint facta, vel orta modo.

7–8] W's addition.

CIV. David Scott, 'Wyatt's Worst Poem', *TLS*, 13 September 1963, p. 696, claims that W used the version of Joannes de Sacrobosco's *De Sphaera*, published in Paris in 1527, 1534, and 1538 with commentary by J. Faber Stapulensis, 'which includes a corrected table of the periods of revolution of each of the spheres, with values agreeing in detail with those W gives even to a misprint of 29 years 16 days (instead of 29 years 163 days, as in the otherwise identical edition of 1507, and as the table itself requires for internal consistency) for the sphere of Saturn.' Cf. l. 44. Scott argues that the poem was written in October 1539 to coincide with the completion of the clock, once in St. James's Palace and now at Hampton Court, as a welcome for Anne of Cleves; and that the poem was left unfinished because W was sent to the Emperor's court in the middle of November. We cannot, however, assume from the position of the poem in E – after the Psalms – that this was the order of composition. In T the poem is entitled 'The song of Iopas vnfinished'.

1 *When Dido*] The reference is to *Aeneid*, I, 723–47, where Iopas sings of the moon, the sun, and the constellations.

2 *Junos wrath*] Cf. *Aeneid*, I, 4.

3 *myghty' Atlas taught*] Cf. *Aeneid*, I, 741.

4 *golden harpe*] Cf. *Aeneid*, I, 740–1. 'Cithara . . . aurata'.

8–10 *in myddes . . . course*] Cf. Sacrobosco, f. 5ʳ: 'quæ vt centrum mundi, ponderositate sui magnum extremorum motum vndique æqualiter fugiens, rotundæ sphæræ medium possidet'.

36 *On . . . move*] Cf. Sacrobosco, f. 5ʳ: 'in 100 annis gradu vno'.

40 *whose . . . slake*] J. Faber's corrected table gives 49,000 years. Scott refers to W's inconsistency. In l. 35 the primum mobile is the 9th sphere; but in ll. 39–40 W includes the secundum mobile, and therefore has the 'ten sphere hypothesis' in mind.

44 *In . . . sixtene*] Sacrobosco: 30 years. Faber: 29 years, 16 days (see headnote).

48 *twelff yere*] Sacrobosco: 12 years. Faber: 11 years, 314 days.

51–2 *The fift . . . wayes*] Sacrobosco: 2 years. Faber: 1 year, 322 days.

53 *A . . . six*] Sacrobosco and Faber: 1 year, 6 hours.

57 *like*] 'similiter' (Faber).

58 *so doth*] 'similiter' (Faber).

62 *In . . . one*] Sacrobosco and Faber: 27 days, 8 hours.

11. Satires

CV. Source:

Io ui dirò poi che d' udir ui cale
　Thommaso mio gentil, perch' amo, & colo
　Piu di tutti altri il lito Prouenzale.
Et perche qui cosi pouero & solo,
　Piu tosto che 'l seguir Signiori & Regi　　　　　　5
　Viuo temprando 'l mio infinito duolo.
Ne cio mi uien perch' io tra me dispregi
　Quei, ch' han dalla Fortuna in mano il freno
　Di noi, per sangue, & per ricchezze egregi.
Ma ben' è uer ch' assai gli estimo meno　　　　　　10
　Che 'l uulgo, & quei ch' à cio ch' appar di fuore
　Guardan, senza ueder che chiugga il seno.
Non dico gia che non mi scaldi amore
　Talhor di gloria, ch' io non uo mentire
　Con chi biasmando honor, sol cerca honore.　　　15
Ma con qual pie potrei color seguire
　Che 'l mondo pregia; ch' io non so quell' arte
　Di chi le scale altrui conuien salire.
Io non saprei Sertin porre in disparte
　La uerità, colui lodando ogni hora　　　　　　　20
　Che con piu danno altrui dal ben si parte.
Non saprei reuerir chi soli adora
　Venere & Bacco, ne tacer saprei
　Di quei che 'l uulgo falsamente honora.
Non saprei piu ch' à gli immortali Dei　　　　　　25
　Rendere honor con le ginocchia inchine
　À piu ingiusti che sian, fallaci, & rei.
Non saprei nel parlar courir le spine
　Con simulati fior, nell' opre hauendo
　Mele al principio, & tristo assentio al fine.　　30
Non saprei no, doue 'l contrario intendo
　I maluagi consigli usar per buoni,
　Dauanti al uero honor l' util ponendo.
Non trouare ad ogni hor false cagioni
　Per abbassare i giusti, alzando i praui　　　　　35
　D'auaritia, & di 'nuidia hauendo sproni.
Non saprei dar de miei pensier le chiaui
　All' ambition, che mi portasse in alto
　Alla fucina delle colpe graui.
Non saprei 'l core hauer di freddo sinalto　　　　40
　Contro à pieta, talhor nocendo à tale,
　Ch' io piu di tutti nella mente esalto,
Non di loda honorar chiara immortale
　Cesare & Sylla, condannando à torto
　Bruto, & la schiera che piu d' altra uale.　　　45
Non saprei camminar nel sentier corto

Dell' impia iniquità, lasciando quello
Che reca pace al uiuo, & gloria al morto.
Io non saprei chiamar cortese & bello
   Chi sia Thersite, ne figliuol d' Anchise   50
   Chi sia di senno & di pietà rubello.
Non saprei chi piu 'l cor nell' oro mise
   Dirgli Alessandro, e 'l pauroso & uile
   Chiamarlo il forte, ch' i Centauri ancise.
Dir non saprei Poeta alto, & gentile   55
   Meuio, giurando poi che tal non uide
   Smirna, Manto, & Fiorenza ornato stile.
Non saprei dentro all' alte soglie infide
   Per piu mostrar' amor, contri' à mia uoglia
   Imitar sempre altrui se piange, o ride.   60
Non saprei indiuinar quel ch' altri uoglia,
   Ne conoscer saprei quel che piu piace
   Tacendo il uer che le piu uolte addoglia.
L'amico lusinghier, doppio, & fallace
   Dir non saprei gentil, ne aperto & uero   65
   Chi sempre parli quel che piu dispiace:
Non saprei l' huom crudel chiamar seuero,
   Ne chi lascia peccar chiamarlo pio,
   Ne che 'l tyranneggiar sia giusto impero.
Io non saprei ingannar gli huomini & Dio,   70
   Con giuramenti & con promesse false,
   Ne far saprei quel ch' è d' un' altro mio.
Questo è cagion che non mi cal, ne calse
   Anchor gia mai, di seguitar coloro
   Ne quai Fortuna piu che 'l senno ualse.   75
Questo fa che 'l mio regnio, e 'l mio thesoro
   Son gli 'nchiostri & le carte, & piu ch' altroue
   Hoggi in Prouenza uolentier dimoro.
Qui non ho alcun, che mi domandi doue
   Mi stia, ne uada, & non mi sforza alcuno   80
   À gir pe'l mondo quando agghiaccia & pioue.
Quando e' gli è 'l ciel seren, quando e' gli è bruno
   Son quel medesmo, & non mi prendo affano,
   Colmo di pace, & di timor digiuno.
Non sono in Francia à sentir beffe & danno   85
   S' io non conosco i uin, s' io non so bene
   Qual uiuanda è miglior di tutto l' anno.
Non nella Hispagnia oue studiar conuiene
   Piu che nell' esser poi nel ben parere,
   Oue frode, & menzognia il seggio tiene,   90
Non in Germania oue 'l mangiare e 'l bere
   M' habbia à tor l' intelletto, & darlo in preda
   Al senso, in guisa di seluagge fere.
Non sono in Roma, oue chi 'n Christo creda,
   Et non sappia falsar, ne far ueneni   95
   Conuien ch' a casa sospirando rieda.
Sono in Prouenza, oue quantunque pieni
   Di maluagio uoler ci sian gli 'ngegni,
   L' ignioranza e 'l timor pon loro i freni.

Che benche sian di 'nuidia & d' odio pregni   100
Sempre contro i miglior per ueder poco
Son nel mezzo troncati i lor disegni.
Hor qui dunque mi sto, prendendo in gioco
Il lor breue sauer, le lunghe uoglie
Con le mie Muse in solitario loco.   105
Non le gran Corti homai, non l'alte soglie
Mi uedran gir co i lor seguaci à schiera,
Ne di me hauran troppo honorate spoglie
Auaritia, & liuor, ma pace uera.
  Alamanni, Satire X, 'À Thommaso Sertini',

Opere Toscane (Lyons, 1532–3), 400–4

The source was identified by Nott (562). W translates long passages in which Alamanni's sentiments match his own. Thus the whole attack on the court and on worldliness in favour of a free private life is congenial to him, as is the attack on the vices of foreign lands (ll. 89–99). He adapts Alamanni's personal statements to himself, addresses his satirical epistle to his own friend John Poyntz, in place of Tommaso Sertini (see ll. 1–6, 82, 100) and introduces an appropriate English reference to Chaucer (ll. 50–1). He omits some passages (e.g. Alamanni's ll. 37–9, 98–104, 106–9), and makes a few additions (e.g. ll. 58–63). He reproduces the main effects of Alamanni's tirades, especially their rhetorical repetition: the *Non saprei* series (l. 19 f.) supplies his *I cannot* (l. 19f.), and the *Non sono* series (l. 85 f.) supplies his *I ame not* (l. 89f.). But W also moderates the literary and lofty tone of his original. He uses some unpretentious references to fables (ll. 27 and 46), some colloquialisms (ll. 77–9), and proverbial phrases (ll. 18 and 100), which have no counterparts in the style of the original.

Alamanni's Provençal satires were first published in 1532–3. The favoured date for W's imitation is the latter part of 1536, after, in June, he was released from the Tower and sent home to Allington Castle with 'warnynges' to learn, under his father's supervision, 'to adres hym better' (*L*, 35). The references to his learning to curb *will and lust* (l. 6) and to the *clogg . . . at my hele* (l. 86), which have no counterparts in Alamanni, fit in well with this. The inference, in the opening lines, that W's withdrawal from court was voluntary, though it does not fit the facts of 1536, may well be explained by both natural pride and inclination. The executions of Anne Boleyn and her supposed 'lovers', W's imprisonment and conviction of his own innocence (see CLXXVI), are sufficient to supply these ideas. The date 1536 is accordingly agreed by F (11.100–1), Rollins (11.218), Baldi (54), and Mason (203). Nott (563) differs from the majority in preferring the autumn of 1541, following W's second imprisonment in the Tower. Little is known of John Poyntz, the friend to whom W addresses this satire and CVI. He was at court from about 1520, and there with W at Christmas 1524–5 (see *L*, 4).

W imitates Alamanni's terza rima, though without necessarily enclosing the tercets, as Italian poets normally did. It is probable that Alamanni's example also explains the choice of terza rima for the other two satires (CVI and CVII). With the doubtful exception of Chaucer's 'Complaint to his Lady', these poems provide the first English examples in this form. That the form was considered difficult is shown by the comment of W's contemporary Lord Morley, who, translating Petrarch's 'Trionfi' from terza rima into couplets, remarked on the rhyme of his original 'whiche is not possible for me to folow in the translation' (*The Tryumphes of Fraunces Petrarcke*, London, n.d. (? 1565), sig. A 3ᵛ).

F. D. Hoeniger reports on the version in a commonplace book, Cambridge University MS. Ff. 5, 14, ff. 5ᵛ–7ʳ: see *NQ*, ccii (1957), 103–4. Title in T: 'Of the Courtiers life written to Iohn Poins.'

Comment and criticism: Paolo Bellezza, 'Il Primo Poeta Satirico Inglese e le sue Imitazioni Italiane', Rendiconti: *Reale Instituto Lombardo di Sciense e Lettere*, Series II, vol. xxx. (Milan, 1897), 523–33.

R. M. Alden, *The Rise of Formal Satire in England under Classical Influence* (Philadelphia, 1899), 52f.

Sidney Lee, *The French Renaissance in England* (Oxford, 1910). Alamanni's place in the French Renaissance (pp. 116–17). W's debt to him (pp. 118–19).

Carlo Segré, 'Due Petrarchisti Inglesi del Secolo XVI', *Relazioni Letterarie fra Italia e Inghilterra* (Florence, 1911), 99–105.

Berdan (477–9) has some harsh comments on both Alamanni and W, and on the latter's poor terza rima.

Tillyard (44–8) considers the satires 'experimental' and the tercets unsuccessful.

Hallett Smith (*HLQ*, ix (1946), 337–41) defines W's satires by their vigour.

Baldi (199–201) considers the adaptation of Alamanni as mature work.

R. O. Evans (*JEGP*, liii (1954), 197–213) tabulates irregular lines in CV and CVI, with the object of showing that they are not so irregular syllabically as has been supposed by exponents of the 'pausing line' theory, such as Alan Swallow (*MP*, xlvii (1950), 1–11).

Mason (221–5) considers W's satire as the work of 'the true Humanist', and, with a few reservations, praises his transformation of Alamanni.

John Thompson, *The Founding of English Metre* (London, 1961). The metre of the satires, T's regularization, and W's use of the iambic pentameter line (pp. 17–29).

Donald L. Guss (*Journal of the Rutgers University Library*, xxvi (1962), 6–13) discusses CV as an example of Renaissance 'imitation'.

Thomson (238–70). W's neo-classical satire and imitation of Alamanni.

1 *Myne owne John Poyntz*] Substituted for *Thommaso mio gentil*, i.e. 'Tommaso Sertini'. Cf. l. 19.

sins ye delight to know] Translation of *poi che d' udir ui cale* (l. 1).

2–3] Suggested by *perch' amo . . . Prouenzale* (ll. 2–3), Alamanni's reference to his love for his home in Provence, which served him as a retreat from politics and from the court of Francis I.

3 *wher soo they goo*] Probably a gap-filler, though Nott (562) refers it to the court progresses.

4–6] Suggested by Alamanni's ll. 4–6, which supply chiefly the preference for an alternative to living in thrall to Lords. W discards the reference to poverty, renders *solo* as *wrappid within my cloke*, and 'tempers' *will and lust* instead of *infinito duolo*.

5 *wrappid within my cloke*] Horace's 'mea/virtute me involvo' (*Odes*, III, xxix, 54–5) is cited as W's source by Nott (562).

7–9] A free translation of ll. 7–9.

7 *It is not*] Corresponds structurally to *Io ui dirò* (l. 1), as well as, in sense, to *Ne cio mi uien* (l. 7).
skorne or moke] Cf. *dispregi* (l. 7).

9 *of Right*] Suggested by the more particularised *per sangue, & per ricchezze* (l. 9).
to strike the stroke] Substituted for Alamanni's 'rein' metaphor (l. 8).

10–13] Translation of ll. 10–12, which show that W's meaning is 'But it is true that I have always esteemed the great less than do the common people, who judge by outward appearances, without regard for the inner reality'. Contrast J. Buxton's interpretation in *A Tradition of Poetry*, London, 1967, pp. 2, 48.

10 *ment*] W's addition.

14–16] Translation of ll. 13–15.

15–16 *me lyst . . . desyar*] W's meaning is explained by *io non uo mentire/Con chi biasmando honor, sol cerca honore* (I do not want to lie, with the man who, while blaming honour, seeks nothing but honour). (ll. 14–15).

17–18] Suggested by ll. 16–18. W discards the reference to worldliness, and substitutes his own metaphor for Alamanni's 'stair climbing'. He repeats *honour* to give continuity with l. 16.

18 *dy the coloure blake*] Proverbial; see Tilley, B436; 'They saie, black will take none other hew', Heywood, *Prouerbes*, 1546.
coloure] Guss (op.cit., p. 7) suggests that W mistook the meaning of *color* (i.e. read it as *colore* instead of as *coloro*).

19–21] Translation of ll. 19–21.

19 *My Poyntz*] Substituted for *Sertin* (l. 19). Cf. l. 1.

20 *To cloke the trothe for praisse*] i.e. to flatter (Cf. *lodando*, l. 20).
withowt desart] Substituted for *ogni hora* (l. 20).

22–3] Translation of ll. 22–4.

22 *settes their part*] Cf. *adora*.

23 *all their lyf long*] Corresponds to *soli*.

24 *alltho I smart*] Substituted for *che 'l uulgo falsamente honora*.

25–7] Free translation of ll. 25–7.

25 *crowche, knele*] Cf. *con le ginocchia inchine*.

26 *God on erthe alone*] Used in place of the more literary and rhetorical *gli immortali Dei*.

27] W's terms from parable or fable are substituted for the abstract terms of disapprobation used in Alamanni's l. 27. Cf. ll. 43–5.

28–30] In rendering ll. 28–30, W transmutes the metaphors (flowers, thorns, honey, wormwood) into literal statements. He also draws out more fully and explicitly the implications of *spine* and *tristo assentio* in his own series, *complayne and mone, suffer, smart, complaynt. I cannot . . . torne the worde* is probably, as suggested by Nott (562), dependent on Horace's 'nescit vox missa reverti' (*Ars Poetica*, 390), with *torne*, like 'reverti', used figuratively.

31–3] Free translation of ll. 31–3.

31 *lyke a saynct*] W supplies the simile, which accords with his earlier introduction of religious terms (ll. 26–7), the idea being derived from Alamanni's description of his inability to behave hypocritically.

32, 33 *wyles, deceyt, crafft, counsell*] All, especially the last two, connect with *maluagi consigli.*

33 *for proffett styll to paint*] W supplies the paint metaphor (? from the whited sepulchre, or make-up), the idea being suggested by Alamanni's l. 33. Cf. his use of *colours* (l. 59).

34–6] Correspond to ll. 34–6, but with ideas taken from earlier passages, and from ll. 40–2. At this point W omits one of Alamanni's tercets (ll. 37–9).

34 *I cannot*] Added by W at this point, to strengthen the *Non saprei/I cannot* series.
wrest the law] Cf. *trouare . . . false cagioni/Per abbassare i giusti.*
to fill the coffer] W's concrete rendering of the abstract *auaritia.*

35] W bases the idea on Alamanni's description of his inability pitilessly to do evil to those whom he most respects (ll. 40–1). The metaphor is supplied by his own earlier use of wolves and lambs (l. 27).

36] Supplied by the earlier allusions to hypocrisy (e.g. ll. 31–3).

37–42] Correspond to ll. 43–5. W rejects the condemnation of Sulla, dictator and oppressor of the Roman people, and the praise of Brutus and his party, which by the murder of Caesar, struck a blow for political liberty. He substitutes Livy's story of Brutus's uncle, Cato of Utica, who also fought for freedom against Caesar, and who committed suicide after the battle of Thapsus in 46 B.C. (*History*, cxiv).

43–4] At this point W omits the tercet (ll. 49–51) contrasting Thersites and Aeneas. His own illustration is from a more popular source, the traditional animal lore. Cf. l. 27.

45–6] W continues in the same independent vein, but probably has in mind *pauroso & uile . . . ancise* (ll. 53–4), the idea of which he inverts.

46] Cf. CVI, where W retells Aesop's fable of the cat and mice.

47–8 *And he . . . Alessaundre*] Translation of *Non saprei . . . Allessandro* (ll 52–3).

48–9 *and say . . . manyfolld*] Largely independent, but perhaps suggested by Alamanni's ll. 55–7.

50–1] W's allusion to the difference between Chaucer's 'Sir Thopas' and 'Knight's Tale' is substituted for the allusion (ll. 55–7) to the difference between Maevius (the poetaster of Virgil's third eclogue and Horace's tenth epode) and Homer (supposedly born at Smyrna), Virgil (of Mantua), and Dante (of Florence).

52–4] A free elaboration of the idea of 'imitating' and toadying to the great in ll. 58–60. *Grynne when he laugheth* (cf. *Imitar sempre altrui se . . . ride*) is the only specific detail taken over.

55] Cf. Alamanni's l. 61.

56] W's addition, substituted for Alamanni's l. 63. Possibly a quibble on *points/Poyntz*.

57] Cf. Alamanni's l. 62.

58–63] W adds this transitional passage, which is a generalization suggested by Alamanni's ll. 64–72, illustrating the cloaking of vices in their nearest virtues. W's statements here are still dependent on *I cannot lerne the waye* (l. 57).

59 *colours of devise*] i.e. deceptions (cf. the metaphor in l. 33).

62] 'And likewise as it shall be opportune'.

64–75] Translation, with a few omissions and additions, and some rearrangement, of Alamanni's list of vices cloaked as virtues (ll. 64–72).

64] W's addition. Cf. his earlier reference to drunkenness (l. 52).

65–8 *The frendly ffoo . . . eloquence*] Translation of ll. 64–6. W carries forward the ideas of flattery and duplicity from the first statement to the second, expressing them through the common medieval personification *Favell*. He doubles *gentil* in *gentill and courtois*, and defers *quel che piu dispiace* to l. 72.

68–9 *and crueltie . . . Justice*] Translation of Alamanni's l. 67.

69 *and chaunge in tyme and place*] W's addition, intended to represent the reason, change of circumstance, why cruelty may parade as justice.

70–1 *And he . . . pitefull*] An adaptation of l. 68. W means that he refuses to call the man who allows offences to be perpetrated (whether by himself or others) compassionate.

71–2 *and him . . . shame*] Translation of *ne aperto . . . dispiace* (ll. 65–6).

73] Suggested by ll. 70–1, in which Alamanni speaks of his own inability to lie.

74 *The letcher a lover*] W's addition, possibly suggested by the vague statement in l. 72.

74–5 *and tyrannye . . . reigne*] Translation of l. 69.

76] Introduced by W to form a climax to the *Non saprei/I cannot* series, and based on Alamanni's earlier doubling of the negative, *Non saprei no* (l. 31). On 'this common repetition of the pronoun', see Rollins (II.218).

77–9] Translation of ll. 73–5. W supplies his own metaphors, i.e. *Hang on their slevis* (for the colourless *seguitar*) and *that way* [i.e. *weigh*] . . . *A chippe of chaunce more then a pownde of witt* (for the abstract statement in l. 75).

80–8] Render, with variations to suit W's tastes and circumstances, ll. 76–84, in which Alamanni describes the various private pleasures of his home life in Provence.

80] W's addition.

81] Suggested by *e 'l mio thesoro . . . carte* (ll. 76–7), and *& non mi sforza . . . pioue* (ll. 80–1).

82] Suggested by *& non mi sforza . . . agghiaccia* (ll. 80–1). Whereas Alamanni prefers to stay at home in frosty weather, W prefers stalking. But the point made, that the poet can do as he likes, is identical.

83–4] Free translation of *Qui non ho . . . uada* (ll. 79–80).

84 *lees*] i.e. leas, meadows (*leases* (A, P) is from *lease*, meadow-land).

85 *newes*] Novelties (rather than tidings): see Baldi (237).
I fele nor wele nor woo] Suggested by *& non . . . digiuno* (ll. 83–4). For the phrasing, see LXXVI.8 and note.

86–8] W's addition: see introductory note.

86 *a clogg doeth hang yet at my hele*] Proverbial; cf. 'I am with the gayler, with a clogge upon myn hele' (*Paston Letters*, No. 414 (1461)).

89–99] W renders accurately Alamanni's list of places where he 'is not', and whose vices he deplores.

89–90] Translation of ll. 85–7. W omits *à sentir beffe & danno* (the sneers of the French at those who know nothing of wines and food), and adds the detail of savoury sauce.

89] F (II.103) notes a possible application to W, who, when serving in Calais in September 1529, was granted a licence to import wine (*L*, 25).

91–3] Translation of ll. 88–90. W gives a free and much more moderate version of l. 90, which refers outright to Spanish fraud and vice.

94–6] Translation of ll. 91–3, with *Flaunders* in place of *Germania*, *il mangiare e 'l bere* neatly reduced to *chiere*, and the *black and white* metaphor introduced to enliven the account of the drunkard's fuddled mind.

96 *they beestes do so esteme*] A possible emendation is 'they beestes do so seeme' (cf. *in guisa di seluagge fere*), but this has no support from any MS. The obscurity perhaps explains the numerous early textual variants. Tillyard (176) paraphrases 'they think so highly of beasts that they think fit to make beasts of themselves'.

97–9] Based on ll. 94–6. T's emendations were necessary because in 1557 England had reverted to Rome.

97 *geven in pray*] Taken over from *darlo in preda* (l. 92).

98 *mony*] W's addition.
poisen] Cf. *ueneni*.
traison] Cf. *falsar*.

99] Substituted for l. 96.

100] Based on *Sono in Prouenza* (l. 97). W naturally substitutes his own home Kent for Provence.

100 *in Kent and Christendome*] Proverbial; see Tilley, K16, and cf. Spenser, *S.C.*, Nov. 153, with E. K.'s gloss explaining how Kent remained unconverted under King Ethelbert, and was therefore 'counted no part of Christendome'.

101] Free translation of l. 105, W having omitted ll. 98–104.
where I rede and ryme] Substituted for *in solitario loco*.

102–3] Substituted for ll. 106–9. W may have found their sentiments repetitious, and have wished to reintroduce Poyntz.

cvi. As Nott (cxlii) suggested, this satire is based on Horace's tale of the Town and Country Mouse in the second half of satire II.vi (in which the mice are disturbed by dogs, not cats); and he also suggested that W was influenced by Henryson's 'Taill of the Uponlondis Mous and the Burges Mous'. But the story was told by Aesop and W probably knew several versions of it. See Thomson (259–67) for a full discussion. She concludes that 'It therefore seems unlikely that W was imitating Horace's satire'. Mason (229) stresses the influence of Chaucer. T entitles it: 'Of the meane and sure estate written to *Iohn Poins.*'

42 *Pepe*] Cf. Henryson, op.cit., l. 26. 'Cry peip anis'.

48 *as to pourpose*] 'As it fell into conversation' (Nott).

50 *befell a sorry chaunce*] Cf. *T & C*, ii, 464 (Nott).

53 *stemyng*] Cf. Chaucer, *CT, Prol.*, 201–2 (F).

66] Cf. Tilley, H474 (WMT).

79 *Cannot . . . should*] Nott compares Horace, *Odes*, II, 16.

93–4 *bare . . . affectes*] 'Free from the dominion of all passion' (Nott).

97 *owte . . . fynd*] Nott compares Persius I, 7. 'Nec te quæsiveris extra'.

105–12] Cf. Persius, III, 35–8 (Nott).

> Magne pater divum, saevos punire tyrannos
> haut alia ratione velis, cum dira libido
> moverit ingenium ferventi tincta veneno:
> virtutem videant intabescantque relicta.

105 *dome*] doom, with a possible quibble.

cvii. Entitled in T: 'How to vse the court and him selfe therin, written to syr *Fraunces Bryan*'. Nott (564) and F (11.108) speak of it as an imitation of Horace's satire 11.5. Baldi (237) finds only a generic resemblance. Thomson (268) thinks that W 'might well be taking his cue' from Horace's manner and matter. Mason (231) stresses 'the personal urgency' which makes this satire 'the most fully contemporary of W's poems and the most dramatic'.

Sir Francis Brian, to whom W addressed an epigram from prison, was a poet, translator, and diplomat, some ten years W's senior. But he was nicknamed 'vicar of hell' by Henry VIII and Cromwell; he had a reputation for dissoluteness; he had married a wealthy widow, Lady Fortescue, in 1517 (cf. ll. 60 ff.); and he retained the King's favour by sycophancy. See Thomson (274–5). Rollins (11.82) mentions that Brian collected proverbial sayings, and Thomson suggests that W in this satire 'seems to poke fun at the contemporary liking for proverbs'. W was perhaps criticizing Brian by assuming ironically that he shared his views on the arts necessary for success at court, even though he admired him in other ways.

3–4 *And . . . mosse*] Cf. Tilley, S885 (WMT).

14 *were*] wear.

16 *noyns*] nonce.

21 *Then . . . sownd*] Cf. Tilley, A366. Cf. Chaucer, *Boethius*, 'Artow like an asse to the harpe', and *T & C*, i, 730–5 (Nott).

22 *So . . . cloyster*] Altered by T because such a reference to Monasteries was impossible in Mary's reign.

47 *Lerne at Kittson*] Learn of Kittson. Nott (11.365) suggested that the reference was to Sir Thomas Kitson, Sheriff of London in 1533; Rollins that W referred to Anthony Kitson, a wealthy bookseller.

54 *and . . . sore*] Cf. Horace, *Satires* II, v, 106 (Nott).

> siquis
> forte coheredum senior male tussiet . . .

56 *pikes*] picks. Hughey compares Chaucer, *CT*, A 587–622.

65 *Let . . . bridill*] Cf. Tilley, B670 (WMT).
mule] Cf. xxxv.1.
if . . . mydell] if she has a good figure.

75 *Pandare*] In Chaucer's *T & C*.

91] Cf. Tilley, W111 (WMT).

111. Penitential Psalms

CVIII. W's source material is too bulky to print in full, and selections from it are distributed in the notes below. Aretino's prologues are quoted in full as prefaces to the notes on W's, and these are analysed stanza by stanza. In the case of the Psalms themselves, the verses of the Latin Vulgate head each section, and are followed by other source material.

Sources, with the editions from which they are quoted:

(1) The Latin Vulgate: *Biblia Magna* (Lyons, 1525).

(2) Pietro Aretino's paraphrase of the Penitential Psalms, first published 1534: *I Sette Salmi de la Penitentia di David* (Venice, 1536). This source of W's Psalms and their prologues was identified by Arundell Esdaile (see F, 11.133, and Hughey, 11.212).

(3) *Enchiridion Psalmorum. Eorundum ex ueritate Hebraica uersionem, ac Ioannis Campensis e regione paraphrasim, sic ut uersus uersui respondeat, complectens* (Lyons, 1533). Campensis's paraphrase was first published in Nüremberg in 1532, but appears in the 1533 edition with Zwingli's, on which W also drew. This source was identified by H. A. Mason (*TLS*, 27 February 1953, p. 144).

An English translation of Campensis, *A Paraphrasis vpon all the Psalmes of Dauid* (Antwerp, 1535), also published in W's lifetime, is quoted below from the edition printed in London in 1539. W appears to draw exclusively on the Latin text, but see note to XCIV.

(4) The Great Bible: *The Byble in Englyshe* (London, 1539). (Coverdale's revision, done under Cromwell's auspices, of earlier translations.)

(5) *The Psalter of Dauid*, trans. Johan Aleph; Francis Foxe (Strassburg); or rather M de Keyser (Antwerp, 1530).

(6) Other sources: the Biblical and religious literature on which W drew obviously cannot all be precisely identified. Mason (*Humanism and Poetry*, 179–235) cites a number of influences, including those of Fisher (see note to ll. 94–5) and Tyndale. The chief metrical influence, accounting for W's choice of terza rima, is probably Alamanni, who also rendered the Penitential Psalms in this form, and whose work W had before him in composing cv.

W varies between close translation of his main sources, the Vulgate and Aretino's prose paraphrase, and almost complete abandonment of them. Sometimes it is impossible to tell which source is uppermost in his mind, since the phrasing of the biblical paraphrases and translations he uses is itself often biblical. It is certain, however, that the Bible itself provides his framework for the Psalms (as distinct from the prologues). For he not only often translates direct from it, but also inserts in the MS. the numbers of the verses. This numbering is not found, for instance, in Aretino. Aretino's influence is nevertheless strong. He accounts for all W's prologues, even including the very free seventh one, and for large sections of the Psalm paraphrases. Starting in his first prologue with the story of David's love for Uriah's wife Bathsheba, the warnings of the prophet Nathan, and his repentance, as told in 2 *Samuel*, 11–12, Aretino provides W's context. On Aretino's situation, David's repentance in the cave, W bases his own. The narrative, such as it is, as well as its psychology, therefore depends ultimately on Aretino's. W's handling of Aretino's language is extremely variable. He retains some of the descriptions, similes, and other elaborations, but also frequently cuts such things drastically. His own rhetoric, even when inspired by Aretino's, is unlike it in effect. His favourite rhetorical device in the Psalms is repetition of words or phrases. But even where, as in the opening of the *De profundis*, this has support from Aretino, the result is different. W's repetitions are much denser than those of his source. He is usually briefer in all respects. The long, smooth sentences of Aretino's prose are changed into the much shorter, jerkier ones of W's terza rima.

W's habit of deserting Aretino for Campensis has been discussed by Mason. It operates spasmodically, however, and Campensis can hardly be said to supersede the Bible and Aretino as a major influence on W. The appeal of Campensis, a modern Hebrew scholar, to W's generation is brought out not only by Mason but by H. P. Clive, who demonstrates the prestige of the *Enchiridion* in France and the possibility that it influenced Clément Marot's translation of the Psalms (*Bib. D'Humanisme et Renaissance*, xxvii (1965), 80–95).

Date: W's paraphrase belongs between the publication of Aretino's *Sette Salmi* in 1534 and his death in 1542. The assumption that he wrote it in prison has made 1536 and 1541 the most favoured dates. Mason (204–5) argues the issue between them, concluding with a preference for 1536; and to this David

Scott (*TLS*, 13 September 1963) has lent some support. Baldi (55) and others have preferred 1541.

Scansion: R. O. Evans (*JEGP*, liii (1954), 197–213) gives a table of irregular lines from the first and fifth Psalms, with the object of showing that the Psalms are not, in fact, so irregular as exponents of the pausing line theory have supposed.

Comment and Criticism:

A. K. Foxwell, *Study*, 90–9.

Hallett Smith, 'English Metrical Psalms in the Sixteenth Century and their Literary Significance', *HLQ*, ix (1946), 249–71. (On W, 262–3.)

H. A. Mason, 'Wyatt and the Psalms – I', *TLS*, 27 February 1953, p. 144. (On W's first Psalm in relation to Campensis and other sources.)

H. A. Mason 'Wyatt and the Psalms – II', *TLS*, 6 March 1953, p. 160. (On Surrey's debt to W's Psalms and to Campensis.)

H. A. Mason, *Humanism and Poetry in the Early Tudor Period* (London, 1959), 204–21.

Lily B. Campbell, *Divine Poetry and Drama in Sixteenth Century England* (C.U.P., 1959). (See especially chapter V on 'The Psalms as English Poetry under Edward VI', and pp. 35–40 on W and Surrey.)

Donald M. Friedman, 'The "Thing" in Wyatt's Mind', *EC*, xvi (1966), 375–81. (On W's transporting of 'his secular stoic doctrine into the devotional atmosphere of the psalm translations'.)

PROLOGUE TO THE FIRST PENITENTIAL PSALM

Source:

Standosi Amore a dar legge a le persone gentili ne gliocchi di Bersabe, si trasformò in uno sguardo crudelmente pietoso, e trapassato al Rè Dauid, prima gli abbagliò la uista, poi gli spirò in bocca del suo ueleno, e toccandogli soauemente i sensi corse ne le ossa, e spartogli sopra del suo fuoco, tosto che le uide accese di humido tosco si gli ficcò nel core non sanza spauento de l'anima, che s'inchinò a la effigie, che nel primo apparire le rimase impressa nel seno, onde l' animo di cotanto huomo riuolto ad adorare la nuoua imagine s'infiammò sì di lei, che obliato tutto quel senno, che guai à i Regni quando i Rè ne mancano, ardendo di desiderio, e d' amore, non riguardando ne la Maestà d' Iddio, ne a la sua, sotto inganno di mandarlo à una secura uittoria, diede Vria Etheo marito de lo Idolo suo in preda a le spade inimiche, acciò che mandato lui, egli potesse diuenire sposo de la Donna, che piu che Dio, e che se medesimo amaua. Et adempito cotal uoto godendosi di quel diletto lasciuo, che con dispiacer del mondo ha messo tante uolte sottosopra gli Imperij, e i Regni, affisse il guardo nel fallo suo Nathan Propheta, & hauendone compassione gli pose dinanzi al uiso la ingiuria, che con l' homicidio, e con lo adulterio haueua fatto al suo Fattore; e spauentatolo con la pena, che il Cielo apparecchiaua a la sua colpa, sentissi il buon Vecchio e da l' anima, e dal core, e da i sensi dileguare il desio, il fuoco, & il piacere non altrimenti che si dilegui il caldo da le membra, & il color dal uolto ne lo incontrar cosa, che tutto scuota altrui di paura, e di horrore; e trattosi di testa, e di dosso la corona, e la porpora, gittato in terra lo scettro, humiliando la superbia de la sua dignità con l' humilitade del pentimento, ricoperta la uergogna de le carni con un poco di panno ruuido, scompigliata la chioma, e la barba uenerabil per la canuta

candidezza, che in loro splendeua con graue honore de la sua etade, rimembrandosi
di esser peccatore, e non Rè, sembraua nel sembiante essa penitentia; e presa la
cetera, la quale immollaua tuttauia il pianto, che distillaua il core per bear l' anima;
si auiò in un luogo oscuro, che si staua sotterra come carcere del suo peccato, nel
quale entrando il suo errore fu spauentato da le tenebre de lo speco; & egli nulla
prendendo di indugio a quello che doueua fare per placare Iddio, postosi inginoc-
chioni, recatosi lo stormento al petto, composto il uiso in alto, acquetato il suono de
i sospiri, toccando le corde con tenero feruore, mosse a Dio queste parole.

Aretino, B 1ʳ⁻ᵛ

st. 1. ll. 1–8. Translation of *Standosi . . . fuoco.*

1 *subiect hertes*] Substituted for *persone gentili,* and perhaps infiuenced by *legge/
law.*

2 *the bryght*] W's addition.

6 *sofftly as he myght*] Expansion of *soauemente.*

7–10 *ouer ronnis . . . launcyd*] Surrey's debt in 'In Cypres springes' (ll. 4–6) is
indicated by Mason (*TLS,* 6 March 1953, p. 160).

8 *sparplid*] Cf. *sparto.* See note to xi1.6 on *sperklyng* and *sparpling.* The reading
sparkl'd in A, R, and Q further indicates that the ME *sparple* is an alterna-
tive for *sparkle.*
for the nonis] W's gap-filling addition.

st. 2. ll.9–16. Translation of *tosto . . . di lei* in Aretino's first sentence, with
ideas (e.g. *ardendo di desiderio, e d'amore*) taken from the passage immediately
following. The translation in ll. 11–16 is free.

14 *those fayre Iyes*] Cf. l. 2 (and the corresponding *gliocchi*).

st. 3. ll. 17–24. Translation of *che obliato . . . inimiche* in Aretino's first sentence.

17 *wisdome and fore-cast*] Doubling of *senno.*

st. 4. ll. 25–32. The first two lines of this stanza complete the translation of
Aretino's first sentence (from *acciò che*). W then translates *Et adempito . . .
Regni* from the second sentence, adding his own comment on David's
blindness (ll. 31–2). He omits *con dispiacer del mondo.*

25 *enjoy*] Substituted for *diuenire sposo,* perhaps with the intention of heighten-
ing David's sin.

30 *kyndomes and cytes*] Cf. *gli Imperij, e i Regni.*

st. 5. ll. 33–40. Translation of *affisse il guardo . . . Vecchio* in Aretino's second
sentence.

34 *rufull chere*] Cf. *hauendone compassione.*

35] W strengthens and amplifies the comparatively unemphatic *ingiuria.*

36 *as in this Case*] W's gap-filling addition.

st. 6. ll. 41–8. Translation of *e da l'anima . . . scettro* in Aretino's second sen-
tence.

48] W's addition.

st. 7. ll. 49–56. Translation of *humiliando . . . penitentia* in Aretino's second sentence.

56] W expands *e non Rè.*

st. 8. ll. 57–64. Translation of *e presa . . . speco* in Aretino's second sentence, some of it strikingly literal (e.g. *distilless/distillaua*). But W also expands and intensifies the descriptive detail.

57 *to be his guyde*] W's addition.

60 *dark Cave*] W conflates *luogo oscuro* and *speco.* Cf. l. 201.

61–2 *wherin . . . lyght*] W's addition, though implied by Aretino.

62 *grave*] W's addition. Cf. l. 205.

st. 9. ll. 65–72. Translation of *& egli* to the end of Aretino's prologue.

65 *prolonging or delay*] Doubling of *indugio.*

66 *Rof*] The reading, which has been much debated, is supported by *prendendo.*

66 *his lord, his god*] Doubling of *Iddio.*

67 *I say*] W's gap-filling addition.

68–9 *frawtyd . . . clay*] W's addition, partly suggested by an earlier detail (l. 43).

70 *Dressyd vpryght*] Erect (*composto il uiso in alto*). Cf. 'dressed hym upward' (Chaucer, *T & C*, iii, 71).
sekyng to conterpese] W's correction involves an attempt to approximate more closely to *acquetato* etc., though he still does not render it exactly: Aretino's David quiets his sighs before playing.

The first Penitential Psalm. Psalm 6. *Domine ne in furore.*
Preamble: ll. 73–80. Translation of Aretino's preamble:

> Signore poi che il tuo nome si lascia proferire de la mia lingua, e da che tu le concedi che ella possa anchor chiamare il Signor suo, il core, che prende felice augurio perciò, fauorisce la speranza, che il suo pentirsi ha preso in quella clemenza, con la quale consoli coloro, che si contristano per hauerti offeso; onde io ardisco con la uoce, e co 'l pianto di scongiurati per la tua bontà, che . . . (B 2ʳ)

vs. 1. ll. 81–9. Domine ne in furore tuo arguas me: neque in ira tua corripias me.

81] On coming to the first verse, W, as Mason indicates, deserts Aretino for Campensis: 'Domine ne pro ira tua, quam aduersum me licet meritò, concepisti, castiga me.' Thus *my deserving* is closer to Campensis than to the equivalent phrase (*nostri falli*) in Aretino.

82] W reverts to Aretino: 'secondo la forza de la tua giusta ira'. (B 2ᵛ)

83–5 *O lord . . . bred*] Translation of a further passage from Aretino's preamble: 'O Iddio io ti temo, e di non hauerti temuto mi pento, e di uolerti temere mi delibero.' (B 2ʳ)

85–7 *I open . . . bred*] W's free elaboration.

88–9 Repetition of the substance of ll. 81–2.

vs. 2. ll.90–102. Miserere mei domine quoniam infirmus sum: sana me domine quoniam conturbata sunt ossa mea.

90–3] Translation of Aretino: 'Tempra Signore gli sdegni, che in te hanno accessi i mali, che io feci, co beni, che io m' apparecchio a fare; e uengati pietà di me, che son tutto infermo.' (B 2ᵛ) The phrasing *and rather*, etc., is probably influenced, as Mason indicates, by Campensis: 'Quin potius misereat te mei Domine, æger enim sum.'

94–5] Influenced, as Mason indicates, by John Fisher's sermon on this Psalm: 'It is wryten in the gospell. *Non hiis qui sani sunt opus est medico sed qui male se habent.* They that be hole nedeth no physycyen/but a physycyen is nedefull vnto them that be seke.' (*This Treatise concernynge the Fruytfull Saynges of Dauyd the Kynge* (London, 1508), aa 8ᵛ)

96–102] W follows at a distance Aretino's detailed description of the ills of the flesh, etc. (B 2ᵛ–3ʳ), selecting from it: 'Il core è ferito da lo strale che l'arco del timor de la sua dannatione ha scoccato in lui l'anima languisce gemendo.' (B 2ᵛ)

97] *sek*] i.e. sick.

99] Taken, as Mason indicates, from Zwingli: 'sana me Domine quoniam totus despero'.

vs. 3. ll.103–15. Et anima mea turbata est valde: sed tu domine vsquequo. Translation of Aretino:

> Signore l'anima mia è oltra modo turbata, tante, e tali sono le tentationi che la assalgano; ella si stà rinchiusa dentro a le mura de la carne inferma, e le armi de la uanita mondane gli hanno congiurato contra, & i sensi che si risanano a le lusinghe loro corrotti dal uedere le pompe . . . onde la miseria si ricoura sotto la ombra de la speme. (B 3ʳ⁻ᵛ)

103 *Moche more*] Mason compares Campensis's phrasing: 'Et animus meus conturbatus est *multo magis.*'

104 *as thick as hayle*] W's addition.

113] Closer to Campensis's 'quando tandem respicies miseriam meam?' than to the equivalent passage in Aretino ('Infino a quanto indugierai à uolgere in me quegliocchi' (B 3ᵛ).)

114–15] There is no obvious source for this elaboration.

vs. 4. ll.116–30. Conuertere domine et eripe animam meam: saluum me fac propter misericordiam tuam.

116–17] Translation of the opening of Aretino's paraphrase of this verse: 'Riuolgiti a l'anima mia Signor mio con quel benigno sembiante.' (B 3ᵛ)

116 *O Lorde*] The repetition is W's.

118–25] Having omitted a long passage, W turns to the end of Aretino's paraphrase, and renders it freely:

> hora Signore metti in concordia l'anima, la qual mira il corpo con occhio inimico; mercè de gli appetiti suoi, ella si uede uicina a le croci de lo inferno; & il corpo mio, che di e notte è morso da la sua conscientia, caderà tosto, e tosto si farà cenere, se tu no 'l sostieni, e morendo in cotale stato l'anima andrà doue a pensarlo trema.' (B 4ʳ)

118 *Leche*] W's contribution. Cf. l. 95.

126–30] W moves back to paraphrase the passage immediately preceding the above extract from Aretino: 'ma se lo error non fusse la tua clemenza non sarebbe ciò che ella è: e non essendo la clemenza, in che modo i peccatori conoscerebbero Iddio?' (B 4ʳ)

vs. 5. ll.131–41. Quoniam non est in morte qui memor sit tui: in inferno autem quis confitebur tibi.

131–3] W uses the third person of the Bible, in place of Aretino's first person, but his reflections on God's name are based on Aretino: 'Ma se io muoio Signore non sendo fra i morti che si possa ricordare di te, come potrò io far memoria del tuo nome? ... Il tuo nome addolcisce i fastidi de gli afflitti, et accresce i piaceri de i consolati.' (B 4ʳ)

134–41] W picks up 'Ma se io muoio' (cf. *Then if I dye*) from the above passage and hitches it onto a later one:

> Horsu io morrò, & andrò a lo inferno; Et andandoci non essendo lecito che iui niuno ti ami, perche non uuoi da tali essere amato, come potrò io a quelli che qui rimangano predicare la bontà tua? che à uoler dire quanto ella sia sarebbe un prescriuere il fino a lo infinito. Come potrò io esprimere ne la mia perditione la tua misericordia? la quale co 'l consenso de la tua bontade sofferisce non pur di solleuare, ma di sublimare chi l' hà ingiurata cento anni co 'l pentimento di un' attimo.' (B 4ᵛ)

134–5 *wheare ... thearon*] W's subjective periphrasis for *a lo inferno*.

136] W's metaphor replaces Aretino's literal *a quelli che qui rimangano predicare.*

vs. 6. ll.142–9. Laboraui in gemitu meo: lauabo per singulas noctes lectum meum: lachrymis meis stratum meum rigabo.

142–7] Translation of Aretino:

> Quali sieno state le fatiche mie in auezzarmi a piangere lo sà questo corpo, che per mille promesse che mi habbia fatto di esser continente, niuna me ne hà osseruata. Egli consentiua per gli miei prieghi a mezo il uerno di uscir de le piume su 'l far del dì per confessarti le colpe sue con l'oratione, ne prima haueua fuor de gli agi il piede, che si ritornaua a couare il caldo temprato da la sua pigritia. (B 4ᵛ)

148–9] W departs from Aretino's 'se mai corcherò queste membra nel letto lo righerò in modo con la pioggia de gliocchi miei' (C 1ʳ), and draws instead on one of the following:
(1) The Latin as above.
(2) 'euery nyght wash I my bedde, and water my couche with my teares.' (The Great Bible.)
(3) 'I shall water my bed euery night with my teares.' (1530 Psalter.)
(4) 'lectum meum laui singulis noctibus, & lachrymis meis cubile meum humectaui.' (Campensis.)

There is little to choose between these sources, though W's use of *wasshe* and of the present tense would favour the claims of the Great Bible.

148 *in stede of pleasures olde*] W's addition is influenced by the long central section of Aretino's paraphrase, in which he describes various *delitie* (food, wine, etc.) which no longer appeal to him.

vs. 7. ll. 150–66. Turbatus est a furore oculus meus: inueteraui inter omnes inimicos meos.

150–1] Closer to Campensis's 'Caligine obductus est præ nimio mœrore oculus meus, hebetata est acies eius præ metu tante' than to Aretino's 'gliocchi miei nel piangere hanno perduta la luce.' (C 1ʳ)

152–5] Though not verbally very close to it, this is based on Aretino's paraphrase, which describes how David's enemies 'tentando nuoui lacciuoli a la mia penitentia stanno tuttauia congregati insieme, consigliandosi in che modo io habbia a finir gli anni nel grembo de la lasciuia loro.' (C 1ᵛ)

156–66] Translation of Aretino, with reduction of some of the detail:

> Alcuno mi rapresenta a gliocchi la imagine di colei, le cui maniere, e le cui bellezze han colmato il souerchio de i miei falli; altri mi fa udire la dolcezza di quelle sue parole, che hora cosi amaramente mi suonano ne l' anima; altri mi mostra i trophei, & le spoglie che debbeno conquistare le mie arme; chi promette al capo mio doppio diadema; chi a la mia destra nuouo scettro; alcuno mi uuol cerchiare il collo di pretioso monile; alcuno mi pone inanzi il seggio d'oro; i superbi palazzi; i ricchi pauimenti, & le altre pompe Reali; & cosi ciascuno s'ingegna di inebriarmi di gloria uana. Et io, che faccio schermo a gli hami, et a l' esche de i loro inganno co 'l fiume di questi occhi, chiudendo le orecchie a le Sirene del mondo, spero abattergli in mezo i loro assalti; e da le reti, che hanno distese insidiosamente spero scampare non per arte mia, ma per la cura che hà la tua bontade ... (C 1ᵛ)

vs. 8. ll. 167–71. Discedite a me omnes qui operamini iniquitatem: quoniam exaudiuit dominus vocem fletus mei.

167–8] W's addition, perhaps suggested by Aretino's paraphrase, which says much of grace.

169–71] It is difficult to tell which is the dominant source of this passage. W's *avoyd* and *complaint* derive from the 1530 Psalter: 'Avoide from me ye workers of wikednes: for the lorde hath harde my complaintis powerd oute with wepinges.' His *voyce* could derive either from the Bible (above) or from Aretino: 'Allontanateui da me lusinghieri iniqui . . . perche il Signore hà esaudito la uoce del mio pianto.' (C 2ʳ) In l. 171 the Bible is perhaps to be preferred as source, since *engins* suggests the influence of *operamini* rather than of *lusinghieri*.

vs. 9. ll. 172–7. Exaudiuit dominus deprecationem meam: dominus orationem meam suscepit.

Paraphrase of Aretino:

> Dal mio Signor dico, che hà udito la oration mia, con la quale hò disperso il martiro, che mi haueuano apparecchiato gli errori miei ... Et la bontà sua s'è uendicata meco con le armi de la pietade; & il senso uinto da quella ragione, che tante uolte ha menata su'l carro del suo triompho, è confusamente smarrito.'
> (C 2ʳ⁻ᵛ)

W shifts from *your* (l. 173) to *my* (l. 174) to *yowr* (l. 176), but refers through-
out to his enemies (i.e. his senses).

176 *yowr glosing baite*] W's addition, based on Aretino's paraphrase of the
preceding verse (see l. 165).

*vs. 10. ll.178–84. Erubescant et conturbentur vehementer omnes inimici mei conver-
tantur erubescant valde velociter.* W draws on the Bible for *Sodayne* (*velociter*),
but otherwise paraphrases Aretino:

> Hor uergogninsi, e conturbinsi lo stuolo fallace di tutti i nimici miei, e ripie
> gando l'insegne, che come uincitore de la mia libertade teneuano spiegate nel
> mezo de la mia fronte, conuertansi, & arrossiscansi de la uita loro, e non se ne
> glorijno piu; perche la bontà del mio Signore merita che ritornino a lui. (C 2ᵛ)

PROLOGUE TO THE SECOND PENITENTIAL PSALM

Source:

Chi mai hà uisto uno infermo subito che egli hà fatto tregua co 'l caldo, o co' l gelo
de gli accidenti suoi, & quando è piu rapacificato con la doglia, che languidamente lo
teneua oppresso, uede il giustissimo Dauid, che fattogli prò la oratione, stagnato l'
humore, che egli uersaua da le luci, quasi consolato fa punto a le querele sue; e
deposta alquanto la cetera, l' horrore del peccato non ispauentaua piu la speranza ch'
egli haueua ne la misericordia del Signore con le minaccie con cui la soleua impaurire
inanzi che si deliberasse di piangere le sue colpe. E già il luogo de la penitentia sua
sembraua la casa de la diuotione, e mirandolo il Pastor de i popoli Hebrei con gliocchi
bagnati dal pianto lo faceua degno di reuerentia, e di riguardo come ne sono degne le
cose sacre, e sante. Ma tosto che egli hebbe ripreso lena, raccolti gli spiriti, e scioltigli
con un sospiro formato nel profondo del core, disgiungendo le labbra, e con l'
harmonia del plettro accordato il suono de la uoce, disgroppando le dita su per lo
legno cauo cosi disse.   Aretino, C 3ʳ

st. 1. ll.185–92. Translation of *Chi mai . . . cetera* in Aretino's first sentence,
with the omission of *che fattogli prò la oratione* and *quasi consolato.*

185 *in his fevour*] W's addition, suggested by the context and by *accidenti*
(rendered as *fitt* in l. 187).

186 *treux*] i.e. truce (*tregua*).

187 *past off her faruour*] past its height, a free rendering of *piu rapacificato con
la doglia.*

188 *Draw faynting syghes*] W's addition, suggested by *languidamente lo teneua
oppresso.* Cf. *langour* (l. 189).
I say] W's addition.

189 *Sorowfull*] Substituted for *giustissimo.*

192] W's addition.

st. 2. ll.193–200 Translation and expansion of *l' horrore . . . colpe* in Aretino's
first sentence.

193 *It semid now*] Added by W to introduce his new sentence, and suggested
by the later *sembraua.*

195–6 *whereoff . . . space*] W's rendering strengthens the horror and despair implied in *con cui la soleua impaurire*.

197–200] W's expansion of *inanzi che si deliberasse di piangere le sue colpe*, the disease image being suggested by the passage already translated in st. 1.

st. 3. ll. 201–8. Translation of Aretino's second sentence, with details deriving from the first prologue.

201 *the dark Cave*] Substituted for *il luogo de la penitentia*, and suggested by the description in Aretino's first prologue, and W's rendering of it: see l. 60.

202] W's addition.

203–4 *or refuge . . . socourles*] W's expansion of *la casa de la diuotione*.

205 *who had sene*] W's introduction of the imaginary onlooker is probably not the result of his misunderstanding of the Italian. In Aretino's paraphrase it is David who 'looks' (*mirandolo*, etc.).
grave] A further detail from W's first prologue: see l. 62.

206 *chieff*] W's addition.
assemble] i.e. assembly (cf. *popoli*).

st. 4. ll. 209–16.

209] Translation of *mirandolo . . . con gliocchi bagnati* in Aretino's second sentence.
vapord iyes] Hughey (11.221) claims that Surrey, in 'When Windesor walles' (l. 12), was the first to use this phrase.

210–16] Translation of Aretino's third sentence.

211 *that were dismayd for fere*] W's addition.

212] W's addition.

213] W seems to mean that David tunes his instrument by ear, whereas Aretino says that he pitches his voice to it.

215 *the holow tre*] A literal translation of *lo legno cauo*, Aretino's periphrasis for the harp.

216 *With straynid voyce*] W's usage is cited in *N.E.D.* (3) as the first example of *strained* used of the voice, etc., with the meaning 'exerted by an abnormal effort to an abnormal degree'. It is, however, equally possible that he uses strain (i.e. tighten strings to raise pitch of instrument) metaphorically, so that the phrase here means 'with the pitch of his voice matched to his harp'. Cf. *strains* in l. 425.

The second Penitential Psalm. Psalm 32 (in the Great Bible, etc., 31 in the Latin Vulgate). *Beati quorum remisse sunt iniquitates.*

vs. 1. ll. 217–31. Beati quorum remisse sunt iniquitates: et quorum tecta sunt peccata.

217–24] The opening *Oh* shows that W has Aretino, rather than the Bible, in mind at the outset. He then translates the rest of Aretino's introductory statement:

O Beati coloro le cui iniquità perdona Iddio, lasciandole impunite, non per le opere de la contritione, ne de la penitentia, se ben senza esse le colpe nostre non hanno remissione, ma per beneficio de la gratia sua; la bontà de la quale nel cor rintenerito riguarda, e per la compuntion sua moue a ricoprirgli i peccati col lembo de la misericordia. (C 3ᵛ)

218–21 *not by* . . . *same*] W's obscurely worded account of the remission of sin is clarified by the Italian. Forgiveness 'is not obtained by penitence but by grace (*meryt/gratia*), although no offence will obtain forgiveness without penitence'. The clause *wych recompensyth not* attaches more logically to *penitence* than to *meryt*.

225–31] Paraphrase of the following part of Aretino's paragraph on secret sin:

Beati sono ueramente quegli che si accorgono che Iddio non gli punisce de gli errori; perche eglino conoscendo il demerito, per tema di non cadere ne la ira del Signore, con occulto freno ritengano le sceleratezze, che occultamente poneuano in opra con dishonesti desiderij, onde lo sdegno che sopra di loro tende Iddio non appare, e per cotal modo le colpe, e i peccati che in altrui non inducano mali essempi rimangano impuniti e ricoperti. (C 3ᵛ)

vs. 2. ll. 232–6. Beatus vir cui non imputauit dominus peccatum: nec est in spiritu eius dolus.

232–5] Translation of Aretino: 'Beato l' huomo a cui il Signore non imputa il piacer del peccato, anzi lo uede mondare dal fango del mondo scorzandosi dal uitio in guisa di serpe che pur hora ha deposto la spoglia uecchia.' (C 3ᵛ–4ʳ)

233 *by knoleging his syn*] W's addition, probably derived from the sense of the next verse.

236] W's version is closer to the Bible, both in its sense and in its brevity, than to Aretino's elaborate expansion ('il suo spirito . . . si siede lucente come colomba candida', etc.: C 4ʳ).

vs. 3. ll. 237–44. Quoniam tacui inueterauerunt ossa mea: dum clamarem tota die.

237–43] Paraphrase of Aretino:

Perche in fin a questo tempo hò taciuto non confessando il mio peccato mi noce, e sembro colui che uergognandosi di mostrar le piaghe, si sente perire per hauerli celate, come si sentira sanare per hauerle palesate. Oime Signore che le ossa mie sono inuecchiate ne la infermità, et al male incrudelito non è mestiero di riparo humano perche la medicina de la salute sua è ne lo olio de la tua misericordia. (C 4ʳ)

239] Hughey (11.223) thinks that W may have imitated the phrasing of Surrey's 'The sonne hath twyse brought forthe' (l. 5).

244] Derived from the Bible, as *dayly* indicates, but perhaps also influenced by Aretino's description of David's excessive passion: 'Et io nel patir . . . non hò mai restato di esclamare'. (C 4ʳ)

vs. 4. ll. 245–9. Quoniam die ac nocte grauata est super me manus tua: conuersus sum in erumna mea dum configitur spina. W deserts Aretino for the Bible.

246–7 *and held . . . rest*] Appears to be W's independent elaboration.

248–9] Influenced by Campensis's 'ex succulento factus sim aridior, quam sunt aristæ in media messe' and Zwingli's 'uertebatur succus meus in siccitatem æstiua'. That the English translation of Campensis also uses *wythered* is probably coincidental. W's *grene* may be intended for grain (cf. *aristæ*) rather than green.

vs. 5. ll. 250–7. Delictum meum cognitum tibi feci: & iniustitiam meam non abscondi. Dixi confitebor aduersum me iniustitiam meam domino: et tu remisisti impietatem peccati mei. W draws not only on the Bible but on Campensis: 'Quare aliud inij consilium, & statui peccatum meum non amplius celare, sed aperire tibi iniquitatem, quam admiseram: quod quam primum fecissem, abstulisti continuo iniquitatem peccati mei. Ita factum est profecto.'

250–3] Translates Campensis, paraphrasing *iniquitatem* as *fawt*, *fere*, and *filthines*.

254] Closer to the Bible than to Campensis.

257 *of trowght ryght thus it is*] Based on Campensis's *Ita factum est profecto* (the 'Sela' of the Great Bible and 1530 Psalter).

vs. 6. ll. 258–62. Pro hac orabit ad te omnis sanctus in tempore oportuno. Uerumtamen in diluuio aquarum multarum ad eum non approximabunt.
Based on the Bible.

261 *fluddes of harme*] Influenced by Campensis's 'malorum inundationes'.

vs. 7. ll. 263–71. Tu es refugium meum a tribulatione que circundedit me: exultatio mea erue me a circundantibus me. W returns to Aretino, shortening drastically and purposefully his long descriptions both of the joy of liberation and of the storm from which the seaman escapes:

> Ma tu che solo sei il mio rifugio, e il fine de le speranze mie, e mio sol conforto ne la tribulatione che fino hora mi ha circondato, ne la maniera che circonda il timor de la morte uno che si uede giunto su l' ultimo grado del supplitio, fammi homai lieto di quella incomprensibile allegrezza che trabocca pel seno allagato da la gioia che esce dal core, e da l' anima di coloro che fuor d' ogni credenza son liberati da i legami, dal carcere, e da tormenti in cui gli hanno lungo spatio di tempo tenuti i nimici loro; i quali restano scornati nel uedere rotti i lacci.
> [Aretino continues with more about liberation; then, prefaces the following with a description of the return to tranquillity after a storm.]
> Signore io ueggio farmi da la tua bontade il sentiero pel quale io debbo condurmi dinanzi a te, onde io affigo i miei occhi, ne gliocchi tuoi, quasi nocchiero a le due stelle che gli son guida nel nauicare per i pericoli de le onde.   (D 2ʳ)

264 *the place*] This does not match the equivalent phrase in Aretino (*fino hora*), and is presumably intended to intensify *compasse me*.

265–6] Based largely on the latter part of the first extract from Aretino.

267 *joy*] Picked up from l. 265. W's repetition is based on Aretino's *lieto*, *allegrezza*, and *gioia*.

268–71] Paraphrase of the second extract from Aretino.

vs. 8. ll. 272–5. Intellectum tibi dabo et instruam te in via hac qua gradieris: firmabo super te oculos meos. Based on the Latin, probably with hints from the translation in the Great Bible: 'I will enfourme the, and teach the in the waye wherin thou shalt go: and I wyll gyde the wyth myne eye.'

274] W's addition.

vs. 9. ll. 276–80. Nolite fieri sicut equus et mulus quibus non est intellectus. In chamo et freno maxillas eorum constringe: qui non approximant ad te. The ingratitude of horse and mule is not openly stated in the Bible, and this W derives from Campensis: 'Tantum ne similes efficiamini equo, uel mulo, qui non solum nihil intelligit beneficiorum in se collatorum: sed capistro uel freno os eius constringere oportet, ne appropinquet & mordeat uos'. Aretino also mentions 'la ingratitudine de la natura loro' and their habit of biting (D 2ᵛ). But W's grammar, which is unlike Aretino's, shows that he had his eye on Campensis: e.g. in his use of *uel* and *non solum . . . sed.*

276] W's addition.

277 *that man doth ryde*] W's addition.

278–9] 'That not only does not know his master, but also, in return for the good you do him, has to be tied.'

280 *guyd*] Substituted for Campensis's *uos.*
throw] Substituted for Campensis's *appropinquet.*

vs. 10. ll. 281–8. Multa flagella peccatoris: sperantem autem in domino misericordia circundabit.

281–6] W simplifies and selects from Aretino's paraphrase of the first statement in the Bible:

> Si come il numero de le stelle, de le arene, e de le frondi è senza numero, cosi sono innumerabili i flagelli, che soprastanno al peccatore. Nel percuotere di un piede, nel mouer di una mano, ne lo spurgarsi, nel sonno, nel cibo, ne lo andare, e ne lo stare, è il pericolo pronto a far inciampare chi erra ne la sua punitione; & la afflittione del corpo, & il languire del core, & le occupationi de la mente presaga del suo male, non restano mai di molestar chi uiue in peccato.   (D2ᵛ–3ʳ)

281 *dyuerse*] Neatly reduces the rhetoric in Aretino's first phrase.

285 *new and new*] W's own form of rhetoric, repetition.

287–8] W's translation of the second statement, though it could have been distilled out of Aretino's longer version, is perfectly well accounted for by the Bible.

vs. 11. ll. 289–92. Letamini in domino et exultate iusti: et gloriamini omnes recti corde. W's use of *just, glory,* and *vpright* shows that he is drawing directly on the Latin Vulgate, and not on the versions of it in the Great Bible, the 1530 Psalter, or the paraphrases by Aretino and Campensis.

289 *I say*] W's addition.

290] W's expansion of *in domino.*

PROLOGUE TO THE THIRD PENITENTIAL PSALM

Source:

Tacquesi Dauid tosto ch' egli hebbe cantato le sopradette parole, & in quel santo tacere pareua che il suo silentio raggionasse con la spelunca doue era rinchiuso, de la pace ch' egli haueua fatta con Dio; & egli quasi seruo che scorge ne gliocchi del suo Signore la remissione del fallo pur dianzi da lui commesso, uersaua alcune lagrime che gli traheua dal core la letitia per il merito de la sua penitentia; onde sembraua standosi con le luci, e con le palme leuate al Cielo la figura di un Vecchio pieno di riuerentia intagliato in un sasso, il quale la man de l' arte fa respirare, e piangere. Intanto un raggio di quel Sole che mai non tramonta penetrò ne lo speco, e lo alluminò con si chiare tempre che ricreò il luogo, come ricrea la sua stagione aprile, & la sua aria il sereno, e percotendo su le corde de la cetera, che egli si haueua riposta in grembo, la fece lampeggiare ne la guisa che lampeggia l' oro al cui splendore accresce luce il lume; e feriti i suoi occhi dal lampo, sentì da quello confortarsi l'anima, tutta lieta per la còntritione del core del suo Rè homai piu infiammato de lo amor di Dio che non fu di quel di Bersabe. Per la qual cosa ratto da la certa speranza de la salute sua, posato il ginocchio destro sul uiso de la terra; e con la pianta del piede sinistro nel pauimento, fermatosi tutto nel manco lato, essendo anchora lo instrumento accordato, come huomo che mentre si trastulla col suono ua cercando ne la mente ciò che la obliuione gli hà inuolato, spurgatosi alquanto, disse con moderata uoce.

Aretino, D 4ʳ

st. 1. ll. 293–300. Translation of *Tacquesi . . . Dio* in Aretino's first sentence, with a coda added by W.

294] W's addition.

296-7 *His sylence . . . Apon this pees*] The Italian shows that W means this literally; 'David's silence seemed to converse or reason with the cave about the peace he had made with God'.

296 *argew and replye*] Cf. *raggionasse.*

297–300 *this pees . . . withstand*] W elaborates freely on *la pace ch' egli haueua fatta con Dio,* with characteristic repetition of words.

st. 2. ll. 301–8. Translation of *& egli quasi seruo* to the end of Aretino's first sentence.

304 *Glad*] W's addition, derived, with *gladsome*, from *letitia.*

306 *Marble*] W's addition.

308 *crafft*] Cf. *la man de l' arte.*

308 *to plaine, to sobbe, to sygh*] W's free version of *respirare, e piangère.*

st. 3. ll. 309–16. Translation of *Intanto un raggio . . . contritione* in Aretino's second sentence, omitting the descriptions of the sun's illuminating the cave and of David's holding the harp on his knees.

310] W's variation on Aretino's description of the sun which never sets.

314 *tryde*] W's addition. Cf. XCIX.2.

315] The equivalent statement by Aretino is to the effect that David's eyes were 'wounded' with the flash of light.
torne] i.e. reflection.

316 *Surprisd*] W's addition, suggested by the context.

st. 4. ll. 317–24. Translation of the passage from *homai piu infiammato* to the end of Aretino's second sentence, with the omission of a few phrases.

319–21] David kneels on his right knee, with his weight thrown on to his left.

322 *and harpe*] W's addition, though implied by Aretino.

323] 'His hand sought his tune, and his mind his lay'. Aretino compares David to one who, while 'playing with sound', searches his mind for what he has forgotten.

The third Penitential Psalm. Psalm 38 (in the Great Bible, etc., 37 in the Latin Vulgate). *Domine ne in furore tuo arguas me.*

Preamble: *ll. 325–8.* Paraphrase of parts of Aretino's introductory paragraph:

> Deh Signore si come io ti ho pregato, & si come ti riprego, non mi riprendere nel tuo furore . . . Ma conuertasi il furor tuo tutto ne la pietà tua, benche sempre fusti sempre se, e sempre sarai pietoso, e quello che in te stimiamo furore, è una seuerità di giustitia prescritta de la tua bontade. (D 4ᵛ)

326–8] W seems to mean that 'there is no alteration in God, except what we men, being men, think we see, judging His justice by human standards of changeability'. Aretino supplies the ideas that God is always consistently good, and that the severity of His justice is itself a form of goodness.

vs. 1. ll. 329–30. Domine ne in furore tuo arguas me: neque in ira tua corripias me. Translation of the Latin, W's *castigation* being, perhaps, influenced by Campensis's *castiges* or Aretino's *castigo*.

vs. 2. ll. 331–5. Quoniam sagitte tue infixe sunt mihi: et confirmasti me manum tuam. Translation, with a few omissions, of Aretino:

> Perche le tue saette, perche i tuoi sdegni, & i tuoi terrori, i quali sbigottiscono altrui come i folgori, perciò che essi hanno i raggi di fuoco, di ferro, di morbo, di carestia, di cordoglio, e di morte, si sono profondati in me, io mi sono rileuato à i suoi colpi da la miseria del peccato come a le percosse de gli sproni si rileua il cauallo traboccato nel fango. (E 1ʳ)

335 *such is thi hand on me*] Cf. the second part of the verse in the Latin Vulgate. The grammar of the following lines suggests that W intended to incorporate this in his paraphrase of the third verse, which would be grammatically incomplete without it.

vs. 3. ll. 336–41. Non est sanitas in carne mea a facie ire tue: non est pax ossibus meis a facie peccatorum meorum. W's debts are difficult to settle here. He seems to be building chiefly on the Bible's *non est pax*. Aretino's opening, 'Non è punto di sanita' (E 1ʳ), definitely supplies the phrasing of l. 337. It is unlikely that W misread 'sanita' as 'stabilita', but his account of stability, steadfastness, and mutability may have been influenced by Aretino's later use of a striking 'stability' image: 'e per non esser pace ne le ossa mie che sostengano il corpo, come sostengano le colonne i theatri, temo anzi che io sia riconciliato teco.' (E 1ᵛ) D. M. Friedman, referring to the use of such terms as *stabilite* and *mutabilite*, comments on 'W's reinterpretation of the drama of David's repentance in the concepts and vocabulary of his secular poetry' (*EC*, xvi (1966), 378).

vs. 4. ll. 341–4. Quoniam iniquitates mee supergresse sunt caput meum: et sicut onus graue grauate sunt super me. The first part of W's verse (ll. 341–2) paraphrases

either the Bible or Aretino; the second part (ll. 343–4) at least started as a
version of Aretino:

> Perche tutte le mie iniquità . . . si son poste sopra il capo mio; . . . e ciò oprano
> i miei falli che si aggrauano su la testa mia quasi pondo immobile, onde io mi
> piego sotto il carico come si piega uno arco molestato da la uiolentia di chiunque
> il tira. (E 1ᵛ)

343–4] W at first used Aretino's image of the bow; then, changed to the
willow (cf. LX.7). This seems to be his own contribution to the paraphrase,
though it may be influenced by Aretino's version of vs. 6, in which he uses
the simile of boughs bent by force to the ground: see note to ll. 349–51.

vs. 5. ll. 345–8. Putruerunt et corrupte sunt cicatrices mee: a facie insipientie mee.
The substance of W's verse in ll. 345–6 could be derived from either the
Bible or Aretino. He then makes use, in ll. 347–8, of points supplied by
Aretino: 'e ciò mi auiene perche la mia contritione, e 'l mio pentimento con
cui mi faccio scudo contra i colpi suoi, non mi hanno saputo coprirsi, che
io non tema che egli mi riapra le piaghe che sotto il uelo di dilettarmi mi
fece.' (E 1ᵛ–2ʳ)

*vs. 6. ll. 349–52. Miser factus sum et curuatus sum vsque in finem: tota die constris-
tatus ingrediebar.*

349–51 *Perceyving . . . pryd*] The details of W's paraphrase cannot be fully
explained without both Campensis and Aretino, though the possibility that
some are his independent elaborations on the Bible cannot be ruled out.
Either Campensis or Aretino, drawing out *curuatus sum*, could have supplied
W's *wheit* and *humblid*. Campensis could also have supplied *deprest*, and
Aretino *pryd*:

> Peccati pondere depressus supra modum humiliatus sum. (Campensis)

> la superbia del mio animo alzatosi sopra le ali de la felicità . . . si è humiliata come
> si humiliano i rami leuati al Cielo quando il pastore si delibera inchinargli a terra;
> & essendo io diuentato curuo sotto il peso de i piaceri de la mia perditione,
> uoglio finirmi di ricuruare sotto la soma de i dispiaceri de la mia saluatione fino
> al mio fine. (Aretino, E 2ʳ)

351–2 *by gruging . . . rest*] W's independent paraphrase of the second part of
the verse. Koeppel (78) compares Dante's introduction of 'gran vermo'
into his version of this Psalm.

*vs. 7. ll. 353–5. Quoniam lumbi mei impleti sunt illusionibus: et non est sanitas in
carne mea.* Largely W's independent paraphrase of the Bible.

353] Influenced by Campensis's 'Intestina enim mea feruenti plaga plena
sunt'.

354] W's addition.

vs. 8. ll. 356–7. Afflictus sum et humiliatus sum nimis: rugiebam a gemitu cordis mei.
W's free translations of the Bible.

vs. 9. ll. 358–61. Domine ante te omne desyderium meum: et gemitus meus a te non est absconditus. W selects from Aretino, who supplies, particularly, the idea of inwardness and the phrasing of l. 361. He discards Aretino's colourful images (*tenebre, christallo,* etc.), exploiting, in the repetition of *knowst,* the rhetoric characteristic of his own paraphrase:

> Signore dinanzi a te, che ne le piu folte tenebre uedi ciò che ad altrui è impossibile di uedere, & ne profondi de i cori trapassa l' occhio tuo quasi sole in christallo, si è translato ogni mio desiderio, il qual per non hauere altra uoce che quella del pianto non puo esprimere in seruigio de le mie colpe tutto quello che doueria, et che io uorria. (E 3ʳ)

361 *restraintes*] Literally, what is restrained (in the heart, and which ought to be expressed: cf. the latter part of Aretino's paraphrase).

vs. 10. ll. 362–3. Cor meum conturbatum est dereliquit me virtus mea: et lumen oculorum meorum et ipsum non est mecum. Paraphrase of the Bible, with perhaps some influence from the Great Bible, the 1530 Psalter, or Campensis.

362 *pantyth*] Also used to translate *conturbatum est* in the Great Bible and 1530 Psalter, while Campensis uses *palpitat* (*panteth* in the English version).

vs. 11. ll. 364–8. Amici mei et proximi mei: aduersum me appropinquauerunt et steterunt. Et qui iuxta me erant de longe steterunt. W seems to hover between the Bible and Aretino.

364] Possibly influenced by Aretino, who introduces the idea of enemies at this stage, anticipating vs. 12.

366] Influenced by Aretino, who sees the attacks of enemies as attacks on David's virtue: e.g. 'mille uarietà di inganni sopra la mia innocentia' (E 4ᵛ). The later correction in E, of *vertus* to 'acquaintance', moves closer to the *proximi* of the Bible.

367 *reson and witt vniust*] W's addition: see D. M. Friedman in *EC*, xvi (1966), 378.

vs. 12. ll. 369–71. Et uim faciebant qui querebant animam meam. Et qui inquirebant mala mihi locuti sunt vanitates: et dolos tota die meditabantur.

369] W's independent paraphrase of the Bible.

370–1] Influenced by Campensis's paraphrase of the second and third statements in the Bible, '& studentes incommodare mihi loquebantur scelerata, & fraudes assidue machinabantur'.

vs. 13. l. 372. Ego autem tanquam surdus non audiebam et sicut mutus non aperiens os suum. Paraphrase of the Bible.

vs. 14 and vs. 15. ll. 373–6. Et factus sum sicut homo non audiens: et non habens in ore suo redargutiones. Quoniam in te domine speraui: tu exaudies me domine deus meus. Free translation and expansion of the Bible. W runs one verse into the next. It is difficult to tell whether *knowyng . . . procede* belongs with vs. 14 or vs. 15. Probably it goes with *and thow o lord shalt supplye* to form a free and expanded version of *tu exaudies me domine deus meus* (vs. 15).

376 *trust*] Since W more than once translates the Italian *speranza* as 'trust',

this is perhaps an obvious choice for the Latin *speraui*. It may, however, have been suggested by the 'trust' of the Great Bible.

vs. 16. ll. 377–9. Quia dixi nequando supergaudeant mihi inimici mei: et dum commouentur pedes mei super me magna locuti sunt.
Paraphrase of the Bible and Campensis.

377] Based on Campensis who paraphrases the first part of the verse 'Valde metuebam me nanciscerentur ipsi ansam gloriandi aduersum me'. He also brings fear into his paraphrase of vs. 17 – 'Causam habebam metuendi' – and this seems to have suggested W's actual phrasing.

vs. 17. ll. 380–3. And therwithall ... chere. Quoniam ego in flagella paratus sum: et dolor meus in conspectu meo semper. Paraphrase of Campensis: 'Causam habebam metuendi, quod ferendis uerberibus destinatus essem: quodque uulnus meum cogerer circumferre mecum iugiter.'

vs. 18. ll. 383–4 ffor I ... dashe. Quoniam iniquitatem meam annunciabo: et cogitabo pro peccato meo. Paraphrase of the Bible.

384 *desert*] i.e. lack of desert (cf. *peccato*).
doth all my confortt dash] Perhaps suggested by Campensis's paraphrase of the second part of the verse: 'nec dolorem remittere sinit recordatio peccati mei'.

vs. 19. ll. 385–7. Inimici autem mei viunt et confirmati sunt super me: et multiplicati sunt qui oderunt me inique. Paraphrase of the Bible, with no obvious influence from other sources.

vs. 20. ll. 388–9. Qui retribunt mala pro bonis detrahebant mihi: quoniam sequebar bonitatem. Paraphrase of the Bible.

vs. 21. ll. 390–2. Ne derelinquas me domine deus meus: ne discesseris a me. Based largely on Campensis: 'Vides Domine quo in loco sint res meæ, quare auxilio sis mihi Domine mi Deus, & ne relicto me in his periculis tu procul hinc abscesseris a me.'

390–1] Preamble built up from Campensis's opening statement.

392] This line, giving the substance of the verse, could have been derived direct from the Latin Vulgate. But the Great Bible, with its very similar phrasing, was perhaps in W's mind: 'Forsake me not (O Lorde my God). Be not thou farre fro me.'

vs. 22. ll. 393–4. Intende in adiutorium meum: domine deus salutis mee. Paraphrase of the Bible.

PROLOGUE TO THE FOURTH PENITENTIAL PSALM
Source:
Tosto che Dauid si spedì da la terza Canzone, parue un peregrino che misurando con la mente la lunghezza del camino, & hauendone già buona parte fornito, si arresta a la ombra, al cui fresco lo hanno inuitato l' aure, riprendendo alquanto di quella lena che gli hà tolto la fatica de lo andare. Et si come il peregrino hà riuolto tutto lo animo nel uiaggio che far dee, cosi egli era tutto conuerso a Dio, & tuttauia sonando senza punto auuedersi del suono, il qual sentendolo nol sentiua, posato il mento sul petto si
CC

lasciaua cadere da glioccho il piu caldo, e il piu amaro pianto, che mai piouesse dal
uiso di niuna persona dolente, accorgendosi tanto de lo stillarsi ne le lagrime, quanto
si accorge di restare esangue chi con le uene aperte si giace in una ampia conca di
acqua tepida; e con il gran pianto si mescolauano alcuni sospiri si cocenti, che sendosi
undito il cadere di cotali acque, e il sonare di cosi fatti sospiri, si saria giurato chene le
spelunca fosse una pioggia uentosa, e certamente se i uenti ui fussero potuti entrar
dentro gli hauerieno inuolate le querele de gliocchi, de la lingua, e del petto, &
portandole e le orecchie di tutto il popolo di Israel, ciascuno saria corso a confortare
il suo Rè, il quale ingozzate alcune grosse, e graui lagrime sighiozzando torse di
subito le luci quasi huomo spauentato da lo istesso pensiero; e parendogli che la
horribile ombra del suo peccato uolesse rapirlo esclamando cantò.   Aretino, F 3ᵛ

st. 1. ll. 395–402. Free translation of Aretino's first sentence, and of the first
    part of his second (up to *conuerso à Dio*). In applying the pilgrim image, W
    throws stronger emphasis onto David, his weariness, etc.

396 *Fayntyng for hete*] W's addition.

397 *at mydes off day*] Substituted for *hauendone già buona parte fornito.*

399 *off syghes*] W's addition.

399 *when he had song this lay*] Renders Aretino's opening clause.

402 *to mercy still pretend*] W's more specific statement renders *tutto conuerso a
    Dio.*

st. 2. ll. 403–10. A concentrated version of *& tuttauia . . . cocenti* in Aretino's
    second sentence. Of essentials, W omits only *posato il mento sul petto.*

403 *sonour*] i.e. sonorous.

405 *storme*] W's metaphor is suggested by *piouesse* and by Aretino's later des-
    cription of the *pioggia uentosa* which seems to be in David's cave.

406 *that trykill on the grownd*] W's amplification of *cadere.*

407–8] Aretino explains W's rather obscure statement. His David is no more
    aware of the dropping of his tears than the man who bleeds to death in a
    warm bath is aware of his bloodlessness. There is a transposition of, or
    change in, his senses.

410] W's addition, based on the earlier *tutto conuerso a Dio*, and assisting the
    explanation of how David's thoughts are fixed not on his tears but on God.

st. 3. ll. 411–18. Paraphrase of *che sentendosi . . . suo Rè* in Aretino's second
    sentence.

413 *owt off the sowth*] W's addition.

414 *smoky rayne*] Cf. *T & C*, iii, 628.

415–16] W's addition, though implied by Aretino's statement to the effect
    that had it been possible for David's laments to be carried outside the cave,
    all Israel would have run to comfort him.

st. 4. ll. 419–26. Translation and amplification of *il quale ingozzate* to the end of
    Aretino's second and last sentence.

419 *some part*] i.e. of his tears (Aretino's David swallows his tears).

422–3 *agayne . . . lade*] W's expansion of *uolesse rapirlo.*

424] W's addition, repeating the idea of ll. 420–3.

425–6] W's expansion of *esclamando cantò*.

425 *strains*] See note to l. 216.

The fourth Penitential Psalm. Psalm 51 (in the Great Bible, etc., 50 in the Latin Vulgate). *Miserere mei domine.*

vs. 1. ll. 427–35. Miserere mei deus secundum magnam misericordiam tuam. Et secundum multitudinem miserationum tuarum dele iniquitatem meam. W distils his version of the first part of the verse out of Aretino's, generalizing his ideas, and omitting all the concrete detail of natural phenomena. He is not translating, and hardly even paraphrasing. The two parts of the verse are set out separately below.

427–33] Aretino supplies the ideas of God's goodness, grace, and bountifulness. *Repugnant natures* probably derives from his list of contrasting aspects of nature, heaven, mountain, sea, earth, the abyss, etc., over which God's mercies *extend* (cf. *auanzi*). Two details, *hevin and yerth*, are supplied by *cielo* and *terra*.

> Habbi misericordia di me Iddio, non secondo il picciol merito del mio digiuno, del mio orare, del mio cilicio, del mio flagello, & del mio pianto, ma secondo quella tua gran misericordia, con la quale auanzi di grandezza il uolto del cielo, il petto de i monti, il seno de i mari, il grembo de la terra, i piedi de lo abisso, e la mesura de lo immenso. (F 4ʳ)

429 *brace*] i.e. embrace.

434–5] Taken either from the Bible or from Aretino: 'Aitami Signore, e secondo la moltitudine de la tue compassioni, che sono piu che le falde de la neue, et che le goccioli de la pioggia, scancella le iniquità mie.' (F 4ʳ)

434 *much more then man can synn*] 'which are far greater than man's sins'. This qualifies *marcys*, and paraphrases *multitudinem/moltitudine.*

435 *that so thy grace offend*] W's addition, giving further emphasis to *grace* (cf. l. 427).

vs. 2. ll. 436–41. Amplius laua me ab iniquitate mea: et a peccato meo munda me. W's independent paraphrase of the Bible.

437 *that thus makth me affrayd*] W's addition.

438 *as ay thy wont hath byn*] W's addition.

439–41] W's addition, perhaps suggested by Aretino's and his own versions of vs. 1, with their stress on the multitudinousness of God's mercy.

439 *layd*] i.e. laid down, imposed.

vs. 3. ll. 442–4. Quoniam iniquitatem meam ego cognosco: et peccatum meum contra me est semper. Translation and expansion of the Bible.

442 *my neclegence*] W's addition.

444] W's addition, possibly influenced by Aretino's paraphrase, with its comment on 'la pacientia de la mia penitentia'. (G 1ʳ)

vs. 4. ll. 445–55. Tibi soli peccaui et malum coram te feci: vt iustificeris in sermonibus tuis et vincas cum iudicaris. W draws on the first part of Campensis's paraphrase, but also makes independent additions:

> In te, in solum te peccaui, & abominabile scelus hoc admisi, non reueritus conspectum tuum: quare si hanc iniquitatem mihi condonaueris, & promissa seruaueris perfido mihi, merito aequissimus iudicaberis, & in seruandis promissis constantissimus, & in damnandis illis qui respicere nolunt iustissimus.

445] The repetition of *the* seems to depend on Campensis's repetition of *te*, though, just possibly, it was suggested by the *Tibi . . . te* of the Bible.

446] W's addition, with *fawte* suggested by either the Bible's *malum* ('faulte' in the English trans.) or Campensis's *scelus.*

447–8 *For in . . . offend*] From Campensis's *non reueritus conspectum tuum*, with some of the phrasing perhaps suggested by the Great Bible's 'and done this euell in thy syght'.

448–50 *juging . . . gone*] W's addition, an elaboration of the immediately preceding statement.

451] Paraphrase of Campensis's *hoc admisi* and *quare si hanc iniquitatem mihi condonaueris.*

452–5] Largely W's independent paraphrase of the second part of the Bible's verse, but with hints from Campensis. Thus *kepe still thi word stable* is supplied by Campensis's *promissa seruaueris*, while the series *justice, justly, just, justice*, may have been suggested by his *iustissimus.*

vs. 5. ll. 456–60. Ecce enim in iniquitatibus conceptus sum: et in peccatis concepit me mater mea. Paraphrase of the Bible, with a coda from Aretino.

456] W's addition. Cf. his use of *stable* in l. 452.

459–60] Based on Aretino's introduction to his paraphrase of this verse: 'Non per iscusare il mio fallo Signore, ma per dimostrare quanto bisogno io hò de la tua misericordia, [dico che io sono concetto ne la nequitia,' etc.] (G 1ᵛ)

vs. 6. ll. 461–8. Ecce enim veritatem dilexisti incerta et occulta sapientie tue manifestasti mihi. Paraphrase of the Bible, with some help from Aretino and a great deal from Campensis.

> Ecco che per hauer tu amata la uerità, e la giustitia, non pur mi hai fatto conoscere che niun fallo, e niun merito mai è lasciato da te senza pena, ne senza guiderdone; ma con lo hauermi fatto riconoscer me stesso, il che è difficile assai a l' huomo per cagion di questa carne, me hai anchora manifestate le cose incerte, e occulte de la tua sapientia. (Aretino, G 2ʳ)

> Quanquam ergo uitiatæ carnis impulsu fœdissime lapsus sum, tu fidem tamen & candorem, qui in penetralibus pectoris situs est, maximè amare soles, a quo non omnino sum alienus: non enim tam malitia hoc scelus admissi, quam concupiscentia uictus: quare iterum occultis inspirationibus docere me solidam sapientam, sicut soles, non dedignaberis. (Campensis)

461] W's *Ffor lo thou loves the trowgh* suggests a debt to Aretino's opening. His *inward hert* could also derive from *con lo hauermi fatto riconoscer me stesso*. But it more strikingly resembles Campensis's *penetralibus pectoris*.

462–5] Based on Campensis. Aretino also mentions the weakness of the flesh, and, in an earlier passage, gives a picture of the struggling, faithful servant of God, referring to 'quella constantia, che io ti hò sempre domandata solo per poter perseuerare in seruirti, e in astenermi di non ti offendere.' (G 1ʳ) But W's grammar, with *Tho* (cf. *Quanquam*), and his use of *fydelite* (*fidem*) and *malice* (*malitia*), show that the influence of Campensis is dominant.

466–7] W could have built this up from the Bible. But his *Wherfore* (cf. *quare*) suggests that Campensis is still the dominant influence.

vs. 7. ll. 469–72. Asperges me domine hysopo et mundabor: lauabis me: et super niuem dealbabor. W's independent paraphrase of the Bible. His *liepre sore* is not fully accounted for by any known source, but possibly he was influenced by Aretino who draws out the idea of the healing God, who gives David hyssop 'a bere come phisico che uede il male intorno'. (G 2ʳ)

472 *how*] Probably 'however' (though it could be intended to introduce an exclamation grammatically independent of the preceding statement).

vs. 8. ll. 473–6. Auditui meo dabis gaudium et leticiam: et exultabunt ossa humiliata. Paraphrase of the Bible.

vs. 9. ll. 477–8. Auerte faciem tuam a peccatis meis: et omnes iniquitates meas dele. Free translation of the Bible.

vs. 10. ll. 479–80. Cor mundum crea in me deus: et spiritum rectum innoua in visceribus meis. Free translation of the Bible.

480 *voydyd from fylthye lust*] W's addition, suggested by *visceribus meis*, and the general sense of the second part of the verse.

vs. 11. ll. 481–2. Ne proijicias me a facie tua et spiritum sanctum tuum ne auferas a me. Free translation of the Bible.

481 *Iys cure*] W's metaphor is suggested by *facie*.
vnrest] W's addition. Cf. his addition of *rest* in l. 483.

vs. 12. ll. 483–4. Redde mihi leticiam salutaris tui: et spiritu principali confirma me. Free translation of the Bible, with, perhaps, a hint from Aretino.

483 *rest*] W's addition. Cf. his addition of *vnrest* in l. 481.

484 *spryte off stedfastnesse*] Aretino's is the only other version which connects the second part of the verse specifically with steadfastness (*fermezza*). Thus, having described 'lo spirito principale' as the good spirit of reason, he continues 'Conserua adunque in me quel buono [spirito] che mi inuia al bene, & dandogli fermezza, e uertù concedigli che si rimanga uincitore' (G 4ʳ). By contrast, Campensis paraphrases the statement '& principe illo spiritu muni me'.

vs. 13. ll. 485–7. Docebo iniquos vias tuas: et impij ad te conuertentur. Free translation of the Bible.

485] This line, which is W's addition suggested by Campensis's opening to vs. 13, 'Hoc ubi præstiteris mihi', hangs between his versions of verses 12

and 13. It seems more acceptable as an introduction to vs. 13 than as a coda
to vs. 12.

*vs. 14. ll. 488–92. Libera me de sanguinibus deus deus salutis mee: et exultabit lingua
mea iustitiam tuam.* W's independent paraphrase and expansion of the Bible,
the two parts of the verse being inverted.

489] W, elaborating the second part of the verse, also anticipates *os meum
annunciabit laudem tuam* of vs. 15.

492] W's addition, suggested by *iustitiam*.

vs. 15. ll. 493–4. Domine labia mea aperies et os meum annunciabit laudem tuam.
Translation of the Bible. W contributes the *flood* metaphor.

*vs. 16. ll. 495–9. Quoniam si voluisses sacrificum dedissem vtique holocaustis non
delectaberis.* Paraphrase of Aretino. W follows out his sentence structure,
if thou hadst . . . I wold have corresponding to *se tu hauessi . . . io te lo haurei
fatto.* He increases the stress on the futility of outward ceremonial also
found in Aretino. (Campensis, too, mentions 'externis sacrificijs', but his
phrasing is unlike W's.)

> Laude, e gloria con la bocca, e col core ti hò sacrificato Signore, & se tu hauessi
> uoluto altro sacrificio certamente io te lo haurei fatto; ma io ueggio in spirito che
> tu non ti diletterai de gli holocausti; e uerra tempo che no hauerai agrado cotal
> sacrificare, perche sono cerimonie che appaiano di fuora. (H 1ʳ)

495–6 *plesant . . . disclose*] Anticipates *cerimonie che appaiano di fuora.* Cf. l. 499.

497 *the sacryfice*] i.e. the 'outward' sacrifice, Aretino's *altro sacrificio.*

498 *in no such glose*] Substituted for *de gli holocausti.*

499 *as men dreme and devyse*] W's addition.

*vs. 17. ll. 500–2. Sacrificium deo spiritus contribulatus: cor contritum et humiliatum
deus non despicies.* Paraphrase of the Bible.

vs. 18. ll. 503–5. Benigne fac in bona voluntate tua syon: vt edificentur muri hierusalem.
Translation and expansion of the Bible.

504] W's addition is dictated by the earlier mention of the inward (l. 461), or
by Aretino's or Campensis's paraphrase of vs. 19, in both of which the out-
ward is distinguished from the inward offering: '& tutte quelle dimostra-
tioni di fuore saranno riceuute da la tua bontà in segno di quelle interne, &
uere de l' animo, & del core' (Aretino, H 2ʳ); 'Tum grata tibi erunt sacri-
ficia, quæ signa sunt iustitiæ internæ' (Campensis).

505 *Off hertes*] W's addition, intended to bring out more fully the 'inward'
significance of the biblical terms. It is not directly dependent on Aretino,
though his interpretation of Jerusalem as a symbol of peace and union may
have encouraged W to supply a similar directive to meaning.
strength] i.e. strengthen.

*vs. 19. ll. 506–8. Tunc acceptabis sacrificium iustitie oblationes et holocausta: tunc
imponent super altare tuum vitulos.* Paraphrase of the first part of the verse in
the Bible.

506 *vttward dedes*] W's rendering of *oblationes et holocausta* is dictated by his earlier version of similar terms in vs. 16: see ll. 495–9 and note. He may again have been influenced by Aretino and Campensis: see note to l. 504.

PROLOGUE TO THE FIFTH PENITENTIAL PSALM

Source:

Poscia che Dauid hebbe scongiurata la gran misericordia di Dio ad hauere misericordia de la colpe sue, si rimase inginocchioni; e temendo di non riuedere la imagine del suo peccato che gli mostrasse lo abisso, non ardiua di leuare il uiso dal cielo, il quale egli contemplaua piu con gliocchi occulti che non faceua co palesi. Et standosi immobilmente replicaua col core a Dio, non mouendo punto le labbra tutto il salmo sopradetto; e chi lo hauesse ueduto composto in quel uenerabile gesto hauerebbe non pur uisto un peccatore ueramente pentito, ma haueria anco imparato; come uno si dee ueramente pentire di hauer peccato; & perche gli parea di essere indegno di perdono, si lo aggrauaua il pensare à i suoi falli, gemeua, e sospiraua non altrimenti, che se hauesse udito sbandire da Dio fuor de la gratia sua in eterno; & mentre astratto mesuraua col braccio del pensiero la larghezza del corpo del suo errore, trouandolo fuor di misura, tutto si scosse tremando, e in quello scuotersi, e in quel tremare parue uno infermo sopraggiunto da i rigori de la morte; e temendo di non hauere hauuta ne gli sparsi preghi udientia da Dio, raddoppiando contritione al suo cor contrito, ritoccate le corde, & rauuiuate le uoci, le quali haueuano già commossa a pietà la magione de la sua penitentia humilemente disse.

Aretino, H 2ᵛ

st. 1. ll. 509–16. W builds on the ideas of mercy, sin, hidden truths, and entreaty, as well as the tone of awe, in Aretino's first sentence. He also anticipates, in *repete* (cf. *replicaua*), the second sentence. Otherwise he works independently, summarizing the content of the fourth Penitential Psalm far more fully than Aretino, and using direct speech instead of description to dramatize David's situation.

st. 2. ll. 517–24. Based on *Et standosi . . . eterno* in Aretino's second sentence. W follows the opening fairly closely in ll. 517–19; then omits *e chi lo hauesse . . . peccato*; and finally returns to Aretino for hints for ll. 520–4. His *worthilesse desert* is influenced by *indegno di perdono* and his *graces* by *gratia*. But he makes David very much more hopeful of grace, omitting the fear of being cast out of God's mercy and expressing instead wonder at the extent of it.

st. 3. ll. 525–33. A similar modification of Aretino.

525–7] Based on *& mentre astratto . . . misura* in Aretino's second sentence. It supplies, particularly, W's repetition, *mesure, mesureles*. W takes over the idea of *fawte* (cf. *errore*), but the emphasis on *confort, marcys*, and *tresure* is his own.

528–33] W omits the ensuing passage of Aretino's, which describes David's trembling with fear at the magnitude of his sin. As in st. 2 he substitutes a hopeful account of God's mercy.

531–2 *by whome . . . kay*] By means of mercy remission of sins is the key to the gates of Heaven.

st. 4. ll.533–40. This has very little relation to the corresponding passage (from *e temendo* to the end) of Aretino's prologue, except that, inevitably, W's David is like Aretino's in renewing his contrite song. W continues to throw the stress on hope, where Aretino's is primarily on fear.

538–9 *For . . . labour*] 'For he well knows that such labour is referred to mercy.' W's *Respectles* is cited in *N.E.D.* as the first example of the adjective in the sense of 'regardless, heedless,' etc. W may be referring to David's labour as valueless (which, without grace, it is), or using the word adverbially, with the meaning 'regardless'.

The fifth Penitential Psalm. Psalm 102 (in the Great Bible, etc., 101 in the Latin Vulgate). *Domine exaudi orationem meam.*

vs. 1. ll.541–2. Domine exaudi orationem meam: et clamor meus ad te veniat. Since Aretino's phrasing is biblical, it is difficult to tell whether W translates from the Italian or Latin. His *withowt impediment*, which has no counterpart in the Bible, does, however, derive from Aretino's 'ne me lo impacci la distantia del luogo' (H 3ʳ).

vs. 2. ll.543–50. Non auertas faciem tuam a me in quacunque die tribulor: inclina ad me aurem tuam. In quacunque die inuocauero te: velociter exaudi me. W's independent paraphrase and expansion of the Bible.

544] W's addition.

546 *and thyn Intent*] W's addition.

548] W's amplification is possibly influenced by Campensis's '& uotis meis cito responde' ('agree soone to my desyres', in the English translation).

549–50] W's addition.

vs. 3. ll.551–2. Quia defecerunt sicut fumus dies mei: et ossa mea sicut cremium aruerunt. Translation of the Bible.

vs. 4. ll.553–5. Percussus sum vt fenum et aruit cor meum: quia oblitus sum comedere panem meum. The gist of W's verse comes from either the Bible or Aretino's close translation of it. The latter is more likely, since l. 555 is clearly an amplification of *il uero pane de la uita nostra*. The alteration in E from *foode* to *brede* represents an attempt at more literal accuracy.

> Il cor mio e stato percosso, & è seccato in me come il freno, e tutto questo mi auuiene, perche io mi sono dimenticato di mangiare il mio pane; il uero pane de la uita nostra (Aretino, H 4ʳ).

553 *my mynd*] W's addition. See D. M. Friedman in *EC*, xvi (1966), 379.

vs. 5. ll.556–9. A voce gemitus mei: adhesit os meum carni mee. W's paraphrase is based on a selection of ideas from Aretino's the phrasing of which he shortens drastically:

> Per la continua uoce del mio pianto le mie ossa si sono accostate a la carne mia . . . & questo mi auuiene per non hauer nodrito l' anima del cibo suo, per la qual cosa si sono destrutte le ossa mie, la fortezza mia, e dilenquandosi ognihora piu le uertù de la mia anima . . . son diuentato quasi huomo che si giace in terra con

piu morte che uita, e per cotal debilezza hò si poca lena ne le membra, che temo
di non potere aprire la bocca per confortarmi col pane de la salute, il quale mi
porge la speranza che hanno in te le lagrime che uersa il cor mio per farti dimen-
ticare il fallo suo (H 4ʳ⁻ᵛ).

556 *and my drede*] W's addition.

557 *my strenght, my very force of mynde*] Cf. *la fortezza mia* and *le uertu de la mia
anima*.

558 *Cleved*] Possibly influenced by *cleue* in the Great Bible.
and from thi spryte were flede] Cf. *& questo . . . cibo suo*.

559] Cf. *che temo . . . fallo suo*.

*vs. 6. ll. 560–3. Similis factus sum pellicano solitudinis: factus sum sicut nictorax in
domicilio*. Paraphrase and expansion of the Bible, with perhaps a hint from
Aretino.

562 *Lyght of the day*] Perhaps influenced by Aretino's description of the owl
which 'non uede se non tenebre' (H 4ᵛ).

vs. 7. ll. 564–6. Uigilaui et factus sum sicut passer solitarius in tecto.

564 *waker care*] Cf. XCVIII.1.

*vs. 8. ll. 567–8. Tota die exprobabant mihi inimici mei: et qui laudabant me aduersum
me iurabant*. W's paraphrase of the Bible is very free, since he hardly renders
the idea of reviling, and *conspird* does not bring out fully the idea that
David's enemies laud him to his face, while plotting together behind his
back.

*vs. 9. ll. 569–72. Quia cinerem tanquam panem manducabam: et poculum meum cum
fletu miscebam*. Free translation of the Bible.

570] W's addition, perhaps inspired by Aretino's attack on 'aperti nimici de
la tua giustitia, e de la tua uerità' (I 1ᵛ).

vs. 10. ll. 573–7. A facie ire indignationis tue: quia eleuans allisisti me. Paraphrase
of the Bible, with a hint from Aretino. The idea of self-knowledge and the
image of drowning are W's contributions.

574] *Provokt* and *disdayne* are suggested by Aretino's 'Da la presentia de la ira,
e de lo *sdegno* tuo, mosso in te per colpo del peccato che io . . . commessi',
and 'noi stessi *prouocandoti* con nuoue colpe' (I 1ᵛ).

577] This line appears to be part of W's paraphrase of vs. 10, rather than an
introduction to his vs. 11.
helples] i.e. without (God's) help.

vs. 11. l. 578. Dies mei sicut vmbra declinauerunt: et ego sicut fenum arui. Translation
of the Bible, with the omission of *sicut fenum*.

*vs. 12. ll. 579–80. Tu autem domine in eternum permanes: et memoriale tuum in
generatione et generationem*. Free translation of the Bible.

*vs. 13. ll. 581–8. Tu exurgens domine misereberis syon: quia tempus miserendi eius:
quia venit tempus.*

Paraphrase of Aretino:

> Risurgendo haurai misericordia di Sion. Signore benche i falli del primo padre, e i nostri sieno infinite, quando tu risusciterai son certo che harai pietà di Sion, il qual figuro per la humana generatione: e perche homai è uenuto il tempo di hauergli misericordia, rallegrinsi i peccatori (I 2ʳ).

581] The reference is to original sin, as W's correction brings out. Cf. *i falli del primo padre, e i nostri.*

583–4 *that as I . . . law*] a more precise definition than Aretino's *il qual figuro per la humana generatione.*

585–6] W's repetition of *tyme* was perhaps suggested by the Bible, but it is in any case a typical rhetorical effect.

586–7] W's picture of eager servants of God renders very freely Aretino's *rallegrinsi i peccatori.*

588] The idea of Redemption, implied in the Bible, is drawn out by Campensis ('tempus . . . redemptionis') as well as by Aretino, who, following the passage quoted above, pursues the theme of Christ and Redemption.

vs. 14. ll. 589–90. Quoniam placuerunt seruis tuis lapides eius: et terre eius miserebuntur. W's paraphrase is built largely on the second part of the biblical verse. He transposes *lapides* from the first part, but ignores *placuerunt.*

vs. 15. ll. 591–2. Et timebunt gentes nomen tuum domine: et omnes reges terre gloriam tuam. Translation of the Bible.

591 *gentilles*] Gentiles, in the sense of 'Heathen' (the term used in the Great Bible).

vs. 16. ll. 593–4. Quia edificauit dominus syon: et videbitur in gloria sua. Paraphrase of the Bible, with assistance from Aretino, who reads the account of the building of Sion as an anticipation of the New Testament and the building of Christ's Church.

593 *thi grace, redemeth*] Cf. Aretino's description of 'la misericordia de la redentione' (I 3ʳ).

594 *thy myghty powre*] Probably suggested by Aretino's description of the damnation of sinners at the Last Judgement: 'in tale atto la sua potenza si mostrerà a tutti quelli che . . . non si sono mai consolati con la speranza di saluarsi' (I 3ʳ).

vs. 17. ll. 595–6. Respexit in orationem humilium et non spreuit precem eorum. Free translation of the Bible.

vs. 18. ll. 597–600. Scribantur hec in generatione altera: et populus qui creabitur laudabit dominum. Paraphrase of the Bible, probably influenced by Aretino's version of the second part of the verse, which brings out the idea of regeneration: 'Ma il popolo gentile che sarà creato in te, in cui sarà translato questa uerità lauderà il Signore' (I 3ᵛ).

598] W's addition.

600 *both most and lest*] W's addition, an adjectival phrase attached to *thei* (l. 599).

vs. 19. ll.601–2. Quia prospexit de excelso sancto suo: dominus de celo in terram aspexit. Translation of the Bible. W's introduction of the third person plural (*vs*) may be dependent on Aretino's use of it throughout his paraphrase of this verse (I 4ʳ).

vs. 20. ll.603–5. Ut audiret gemitus compeditorum: vt solueret filios interemptorum. Translation, with some expansion, of the Bible.

604 *fowle*] W's addition.

vs. 21. ll.606–8. Ut annuntient in syon nomen domini: et laudem eius in hierusalem. Translation, with some expansion, of the Bible.

606 *gracius*] W's addition.
607 *holy*] W's addition.
608 *lastyng ay*] W's addition.

vs. 22. ll.609–11. In conueniendo populos in vnum et reges vt seruiant domino. Translation, with some expansion, of the Bible. W's *chirche* may be influenced by Aretino, who has already stressed the founding of Christ's Church, and, in his paraphrase of this verse, continues to do so: 'Ma alhora che fia predicato il nome del Signore per tutta la terra, ne ragunare la speculatione, e la pace in uno, e i Rè, e i popolo acciò che seruino a Dio, la chiesa christiana, in cui si ragunaranno insieme i popoli, e i Rè.' (I 4ᵛ)

609 *off the lond*] W's addition.
610 *to lawd, to pray*] W's amplification of *serve/seruiant.*
611 *aboue . . . mercyfull*] W's addition.

vs. 23. ll.612–17. But to . . . lord. Respondit ei in uia virtutis sue: paucitatem dierum meorum nuncia mihi. Based on the Bible.

612–13] It is unlikely that W misunderstood the sense of the first part of the verse, for, though scholars consider it obscure, the sixteenth-century versions agree on some such meaning as 'He brought downe my strength in my journey' (The Great Bible: cf. 1530 Psalter and Campensis.) W seems deliberately to have deviated from the Bible, and to have established a connection with the gathering of the faithful in one Church, mentioned in the previous verse. Thus his meaning is: 'But as I run in the journey to this assembly (*samble*), my strength fails so that I do not quite reach it.'

616–17 *Altho . . . lord*] It is difficult to tell whether these words form W's coda to vs. 23 or his introduction to vs. 24. They make a more logical and grammatical statement if taken with vs. 23.

vs. 24. ll.616–19. take . . . dekay. Ne reuoces me in dimidio dierum meorum: in generatione et generationem anni tui. Paraphrase of the Bible.

vs. 25. l.620. Initio tu domine terram fundasti: et opera manuum tuarum sunt celi. A slightly shortened version of the Bible.

vs. 26. ll.621–4. Ipsi peribunt tu autem permanes: et omnes sicut vestimentum veterascent. Et sicut operatorium mutabis eos et mutabuntur. Paraphrase of the Bible.

624 *Tourne, and translate*] W's amplification of *chainge/mutabis.*

vs. 27. ll. 625–6. Tu autem idem ipse es: et anni tui non deficient. Free translation of the Bible.

vs. 28. ll. 627–31. Filij seruorum tuorum habitabunt et semen eorum in seculum dirigetur. The preamble (ll. 627–8) seems to be W's own, the rest his slightly expanded paraphrase of the Latin Vulgate. The Great Bible's 'in thy syght' possibly supplies *Byfore thy face.*

629 *dere*] W's addition.

630 *That in thy word ar gott*] W's addition, probably suggested by *semen* (which he does not use as the subject of a new statement).

631 *all in fere*] W's addition.

PROLOGUE TO THE SIXTH PENITENTIAL PSALM

Source:

Cantato c' hebbe Dauid la sopradetta oratione l' ultimo suono de le uoci sue creò un mormorio simile a quello che si ode in cielo quando egli comincia a tonare, e risoluendosi a poco a poco ne la guisa che si risoluano i tinniti de gli stormenti in quel che l' arte del musico resta de affaticargli, il pentito Rè riceuette ne l' anima una disusata consolatione, per cui egli conobbe che Iddio haueua aperte le orecchie al pregar suo, e in quelle raccoltolo con la clemenza con cui esse raccoglie i preghi de i Santi suoi. Ma non gli parendo che la penitentia fusse anchor giunta al termine de la remissione del suo peccato, non rimouendo punto lo animo dal considerare la misericordia del Signore, si staua tutto sospeso in se stesso, riprendendo con la mente il suo uiuer di prima, & ringratiando seco quel giusto pensiero che lo mosse a dar credenza à i consigli, e a le minaccie di Nathan, per la qual cosa s' era sotterrato uiuo ne le tenebre de la spelunca, plorando i suoi falli con lo affetto che Iddio chiede al peccatore dilettatosi il tempo dietro ne piaceri che ci da il mondo, perche noi lo amiamo come doueremmo amare il Cielo; ma statosi alquanto con la mano destra ne la barba, e col dito ch' è allato al piu grosso attrauersato a la bocca, essendo certo che solo il salmeggiare la sua penitentia lo poteua riporre in gratia di Dio, ritornato a lui col core, col uolto, con le parole, e col suono prontamente disse.

Aretino, K 2ᵛ

st. 1. ll. 632–9. Paraphrase and simplification of Aretino's first sentence up to *consolatione.*

632–3] Based on the idea of *Cantato ... tonare,* but omitting the thunder image.

634–7] Based on *e risoluendosi ... affaticargli,* retaining the comparison with music.

637 *fyld*] i.e. filed.

638] The repetition in W's.

639] Paraphrase of *il pentito ... consolatione.*

st. 2. ll. 640–7. Paraphrase of the passage from *per cui egli* to the end of Aretino's first sentence, with some phrases from the beginning of his second.

640–5] W transmutes Aretino's comparison between the reception of David's prayers and that of *i Santi suoi* into a contrast between David's attitude and that of the beasts and the wicked.

645 *this cace*] i.e. the case of the beasts and the wicked.

646–7] W makes a confident claim out of Aretino's statement to the effect that David is still in doubt as to whether his penance has yet earned full remission of his sins. He reserves the doubt for the next stanza.

st. 3. ll. 648–55. Paraphrase of Aretino's second sentence up to *di prima*, with ideas also supplied by the passage immediately following it.

648–50] Based on *Ma non gli . . . se stesso.*

649 *his dede*] Cf. *il suo uiuer di prima.*

651–5] W's distinction between true penitence, the contrite heart, and 'outward' penitential acts, at best merely a sign of inward penitence, is largely his own. But it has been suggested by Aretino's distinctions between David's private penance in the cave and the pleasure of the past and of the world, and between the pleasures of the world and the love of Heaven.

st. 4. ll. 656–63. Paraphrase, in the first part very free, of *& ringratiando* to the end of Aretino's prologue.

656–60] W freely elaborates on ideas implicit in the passage (*& ringratiando . . . Cielo*), in which David expresses his thankfulness that he followed Nathan's counsel and repaired to true penance in the cave, thus stilling his earlier doubts.

656–7] David wards off the suggestion that his belief in the validity of his penance is vain (cf. l. 647).

660] (?) David finds merit in his lack of merit because he has done penance for it and earned forgiveness.

662 *susteind*] Cf. Surrey's usage in 'When Windesor walles' (l. 1).

661–3] A shortened version of *ma statosi* to the end of Aretino's prologue. W alters, though not in essentials, the description of David's posture, and subsumes *penitentia, gratia*, etc., under *thes thinges*.

The sixth Penitential Psalm. Psalm 130 (in the Great Bible, etc., 129 in the Latin Vulgate). *De profundis clamaui.*

vs. 1. ll. 664–7. De profundis clamaui ad te domine. W's verse, though not a translation or even a paraphrase of Aretino's version, is indebted to its imagery and ideas. His selection of detail from it is masterly, and because he writes more concentratedly, his repetition of *depth* and *diepe* is more impressive than Aretino's repetition of *profondi:*

> Dai profondi io hò esclamato a te Signore; Signore essaudisci la oratione mia, perche io te ne prego hora come te ne hò piu uolte pregato, e questa preghiera che io ti porgo nasce da i profondi de la commesse colpe, le quali per hauermi quasi sepolto l' anima ne profondi del core, & ne i profondi di questa grotta formati, solo per muouere la misericordia tua a perdonarmi tutto quel peccato che ti hò confessato da l' hora che io cominciai a riconoscermi fino a questo punto. Si che registra l' oratione mia nel libro doue noti i falli rimessi a quelli che sanno peccare, & pentirsi (K 3ʳ).

664 *Ffrom depth off sinn*] Cf. *da i profondi de le commesse colpe.*

665 *depth off hertes sorow*] Cf. *profondi del core.*

666 *this diepe Cave*] Cf. *i profondi de questa grotta.*
    off darknes diepe repayre] The deep haunt or resort of darkness. In recon-
    structing the phrase in E, W obviously wished to bring it into line with the
    repeated 'of' structure (cf. l. 665): he changed *repayre* from verb to noun (a
    legitimate ME usage, involving no distortion).

667 *to be my borow*] Perhaps suggested by the last sentence of the passage from
    Aretino quoted above.

*vs. 2. ll. 668–74. Domine exaudi vocem meam. Fiant aures tue intendentes in vocem
deprecationis mee.* The first part (ll. 668–71) is W's independent elaboration
of the Bible, the coda (ll. 672–4) a short paraphrase of the opening of
Aretino's:

> Le tue orecchie sieno fatte intendenti a la uoce de la preghiera mia, perche non è
> niun centro si profondo che ti uieti lo ascoltare, e l' udire coloro che ti inuocano
> col core; le parole Signore create da coloro che hanno gelosia de la gratia tua non
> si risoluano in uento per la distantia che è da la altezza tua al nostro profondo.
>
> (K 3ʳ)

668 *perceyve and here*] W's doubling of *exaudi.*

669–70 *My hert, my hope, my ouerthrow, My will to ryse*] W's additions, estab-
lishing continuity with the ideas and images in his vs. 1.

670 *by graunt*] W's addition.

673] As in vs. 1 W concentrates the repetition of *profondo.*

674 *here then my wofull plaint*] W's repetition of the second part of the biblical
verse.

*vs. 3. ll. 675–80: Ffor ... large. Si iniquitates obseruaueris domine: domine quis
sustinebit?* Though l. 675 could be derived direct from the Bible rather than
from Aretino's literal rendering of the first part of the verse, there is no
doubt that W is for the most part paraphrasing Aretino's statement to the
effect that none is so perfect as to stand the test of God's justice, without
His mercy. He shortens the statement considerably, and does not this time
exploit the opportunity, given by *giustitia, giusto, giudichi*, etc., for a series of
repetitions: *just exaction* summarizes Aretino's series. The main feature of
W's rhetoric here is the doubling of the single question in the Bible and
Aretino.

> Ma se tu osseruerai le iniquità Signore, Signore chi sarà atto a sostenerti? niuno
> certo sarà che possa sopportare la giustitia tua se non ti dimentichi de peccati
> nostri; perche non è alcuno tanto giusto, ne si perfetto in questo horribil mare
> di tribulationi che possa, se tu lo giudichi solo con la seuerità de la tua giustitia,
> sostenere ... i colpi che sopra il capo di chi erra lascia cadere il tuo horribil
> flagello. (Aretino, K 3ᵛ)

676] Probably suggested by *se non ti dimentichi de peccati nostri.*

679–80 *dred . . . large*] Dread is obviously suggested by Aretino's sensational terms in the last phrase quoted above. W supplies the contrast with reverence.

vs. 4. and vs. 5. ll. 680–7. But thou . . . pretence. Quia apud te propiciatio est: et propter legem tuam sustinui te domine. Sustinuit anima mea in verbo eius: sperauit anima mea in domino.
W conflates the two verses of the Bible and freely elaborates them, without any obvious reference to Aretino's paraphrase (an account of salvation through Christ and grace).

vs. 6. ll. 688–91. A custodia matutina vsque ad noctem: speret israel in domino. The first part of W's verse (ll. 688–90) is a paraphrase of Campensis: 'Anima mea ardentius expectat aduentum Domini, que uigiles nocturni tempus matutinum: uigiles inquam, qui somno grauati, matutinum expectant tempus, quo dormire liceat ipsis.' The second part of W's verse (l. 691) is a translation of the Bible. (This part is, in many versions of the Psalter, including W's and Campensis's, run into the next verse.)
690 *thrust*] A's reading *thurst* is dictated by the metaphor *quenche*.

vs. 7. ll. 692–3. Quia apud dominum misericordia: et copiosa apud eum redemptio. Free translation of the Bible.

692 *his propertie*] Probably influenced by Campensis's paraphrase of the first part of the verse, which brings out the meaning of *apud dominum* in a similar way: 'est enim natura misericordissimus'.

693 *I say*] Added to secure a rhyme.

vs. 8. l. 694. Et ipse redimet israel: ex omnibus iniquitatibus eius. Free translation of the Bible, with the omission of *israel*.

PROLOGUE TO THE SEVENTH PENITENTIAL PSALM

Source:

Se mai a Dio furono grate le orationi de i suoi serui, gli fu grata questa di Dauid, perche egli la suelse dal profondo core, non altrimenti che il uento suelga dal profondo terreno le radici de l' arbore che per la uiolentia de la tempesta abbatte. E ben ne fece segno che gli fusse aggradata Iddio, che aperto le benigne orecchie à i suoi feruidi uoti, lo toccò di una così fatta letitia nata à un tratto ne l' anima sua, non sapendo egli come, che pareua uno huomo a cui cade quel non so che ne l' animo che lo fa diuentar giocondo, ne la guisa che son coloro ascesi al sommo de la beatitudine desiderata. E in quella subita allegrezza il suo spirito fitto ne le diuine contemplationi, uide quasi in uisione scender la parola di Dio dal Cielo, e uscir de la bocca de lo Angelo, incarnandosi ne la Vergine, uide nascere Christo, uiddelo adorar da i Magi, uiddelo disputare nel Tempio, lo uide fuggir con la Madre in Egitto, lo uide battezare nel Giordano, uiddelo con gli Apostoli, uiddelo sanar gli Infermi, risuscitare i Morti, e cacciare i Demoni, e astratto ne la prophetica Visione, lo uide ungere da la Maddalena, uiddelo a la ultima cena co Discepoli, uiddelo lauargli i piedi, uiddelo orare nel orto, uiddelo tradire, uiddelo flagellare, uiddelo coronato di spine, udillo sententiare a la morte, uiddelo porre in Croce, e nel uedergli rompere le porte del Limbo, si conuerse in quella gioia che doueua sentire, subito che Christo lo trasse de le tenebre insieme con i Padri suoi. E standoso santificato ne suoi meriti, uide risuscitarlo, e nel uederlo ascendere in Cielo, e sedere a la destra del Padre mosse di nuouo queste uoci.

Aretino, L 1ʳ

Of all W's prologues this is the least dependent on its Italian counterpart. There is no verbal following of Aretino's prologue, but the happy, confident tone is derived from it. In the first two stanzas W builds on the substance of his original. Thus ll. 695–8, describing David's *traunce*, are based on Aretino's description. (They may also be influenced by earlier prophetic passages, as, for example, Aretino's paraphrase of the fourth Penitential Psalm.) The following passage (ll. 688–710) is based on the description, in Aretino's prologue, of David's prophetic vision of the Word made flesh, and, though W omits the outline of Christ's life, he draws on the account of His triumph over death. The last two stanzas are independent of Aretino, with W drawing on the Bible and his own imagination.

st. 1. ll. 695–702.

697] Cf. *una . . . letitia nata à un tratto ne l' anima sua* and *il suo spirito fitto ne le diuine contemplationi.*

698] Cf. *ne la guisa che son coloro ascesi al sommo de la beatitudine desiderata.*

699–702] Cf. the passage from *E in quella* to *nascere Christo* in Aretino's third sentence.

700 *humble ere*] W probably means that the Virgin Mary by listening to the Word, became the mother of Christ. Cf.

> Blessed be, ladi, thy Riht Ere:
> The holygost, he liht in there
> fflesh and Blod to take.

(*Minor Poems of the Vernon MS.*, pt. I, ed. C. Horstmann, E.E.T.S., o.s. 98 (London, 1892) 126).

702 *in mortall vaile to shade*] 'in mortal veil to shroud' (cf. the use of 'veil' to describe that which divides mortal from eternal life in *Hebrews* 6: 19).

st. 2. ll. 703–10.

703–5] Cf. *udillo sententiare a la morte*, etc.

706–7] The idea and image were probably suggested by *subito che Christo lo trasse de le tenebre insieme con i Padri suoi.*

710 *assurance*] i.e. certainty of forgiveness.

st. 4. ll. 719–26.

721–4] When Nathan tells David that God has 'put away' his sin, he also prophesies that, as a result of it, his son by Bathsheba will die: 2 *Samuel* 12: 14–19.

721 *poursuys me*] 'pursues me with punishment' (cf. *poursuyt*, l. 724).

The seventh Penitential Psalm. Psalm 143 (in the Great Bible, etc., 142 in the Latin Vulgate). *Domine exaudi orationem meam.*

vs. 1. ll. 727–32. Domine exaudi orationem meam: auribus percipe obsecrationem meam: in veritate tua exaudi me in tua iustitia. Paraphrase and expansion of the Bible.

729 *Not by desert*] W's addition is either an anticipation of vs. 2 of the Bible or the result of Aretino's paraphrase of vs. 1, in which he points a strong contrast between what the sinner legally deserves and what as penitent he hopes for (a reception 'non secondo la uerità e la giustitia de le leggi, le quali condannano, e puniscano di subito il peccato *secondo la grauezza del demerito* (L 1ᵛ)).

vs. 2. ll.733–6. Et non intres in iudicium cum seruo tuo: quia non iustificabitur in conspectu tuo omnis viuens. Paraphrase of the Bible. W's emphasis on the *law* may be his own development of *iudicium.* Or it may derive from Aretino's remarks on the law in his paraphrase of vs. 1 (see note to l. 729), a theme he continues with in his paraphrase of vs. 2 (e.g. 'e perciò oblia parte de le colpe nostre, & non le uoler por tutte dauanti il tribunale del tuo giustissimo giuditio' (L 1ᵛ–2ʳ)). Campensis also provides a possible source: 'Nec uelis summo iure cum seruo tuo agere' (in the English translation: 'And handle not with thy seruant after thy strayte lawe').

734 *thrall bond slave*] W's strengthening of *seruo* (cf. his translation of *seruus* in l. 775).

vs. 3. ll.737–43. Quia persequutus est inimicus animam meam: humiliauit in terra vitam meam. Collocauit me in obscuris sicut mortuos seculi. Paraphrase and expansion of the Bible.

737–9] These lines, though they could be W's coda to vs. 2, are probably his preamble to vs. 3, anticipating the enemy's pursuit, and in *bestlynes,* the idea of *lustynes.* They are possibly inspired by Aretino, who, omitting the first two clauses of the verse, proceeds immediately to draw out the idea, implicit in the third, of David's own sin: 'O Signore & Dio mio lo effetto del peccato mi ha posto ne i luoghi oscuri come quelli che sono morti al secolo.' (L 2ʳ)

vs. 4. ll.744–5. Et anxiatus est super me spiritus meus: in me turbatum est cor meum. Paraphrase of the Bible.

vs. 5. ll.746–50. I had . . . mercys were. Memor fui dierum antiquorum: meditatus sum in omnibus operibus tuis: in factis manuum tuarum meditabar.

747 *in all my dred*] W's addition.

748–50 *that . . . were*] W's additions.

vs. 6. ll.750–2: Then . . . grace. Expandi manus meas ad te: anima mea sicut terra sine aqua tibi. Paraphrase of the Bible, with a hint from Aretino.

750 *in hast*] W's addition.

752 *off thy grace*] The interpretation of *aqua* as grace, though sufficiently obvious, was probably suggested by Aretino's 'l' anima mia è apunto come una terra senza acqua auanti a te, spargimi dico sopra de la gratia tua' (L 3ʳ).

vs. 7. ll.753–7: Hast . . . pitt. Uelociter exaudi me domine defecit spiritus meus. Non auertas faciem tuam a me: et similis ero descendentibus in lacum. Free translation of the Bible.

753 *afore I fall*] Substituted for *Uelociter.*

754 *I fele, a pace*] W's additions.

DD

755–6 *layd/In compt off*] Reckoned among.

vs. 8. ll. 757–61: Shew . . . mynd. Auditam fac mihi mane misericordiam tuam: quia in te speraui. Notam fac mihi viam in qua ambulem: quia ad te leuaui animam meam. Free translation of the Bible.

759] W's addition.

vs. 9. ll. 762–4. Eripe me de inimicis meis domine: ad te confugi. The first part of W's verse is a free translation of either the Bible or Campensis, the second a translation of Campensis: 'Eripe me ab hostibus meis Domine, tuæ enim protectioni occultæ iam olim concredidi me.'

762 *that that do entend*] W's addition.

vs. 10. ll. 765–8. Doce me facere voluntatem tuam: quia deus meus es tu. Spiritus tuus bonus deducet me in terram rectam. Free translation of the Bible, the first statement being expanded.

vs. 11. ll. 769–71. Propter nomen tuum domine viuicabis me in equitate tua. Educes de tribulatione animam meam. Paraphrase of the Bible.

770] W's expansion of *in equitate tua*.

vs. 12. ll. 772–5. Et in misericordia tua disperdes omnes inimicos meos. Et perdes omnes qui tribulant animam meam: quoniam ego seruus tuus sum. Free translation of the Bible. In revision W inverted the order of the first two statements, and differentiated them by the use of past and future tenses.

773 *That vext my sowle*] Perhaps influenced by the Great Bible's 'that vexe my soule'.

775 *ay most bownd*] W's addition (cf. his translation of *seruo* in l. 734).

iv. Poems from the Blage Manuscript

CIX. The relationship of this poem to CL and to the version in Z is obscure. Z seems to be a partial conflation of the other two poems.

On an earlier page of the MS. (f. 58) is a riddle, probably by Blage:

> Whan shall the cruell stormes be past?
> Shall not my truthe thy rigor shake?
> I wyll no more whyle lyue doth last
> Medel wythe loue but yt forsake,
> Wythe out you answer ande rehers
> The fourst wourde of euery verse.

The answer to the riddle – 'when shall I meddle with thee?' – is provided by the initial words of each line of the second stanza, otherwise largely illegible: 'Whan tyme doth sarue you shall'.

CX. This poem, and Nos. CXI–CXXX, CXXXII–CXLI, are in the same handwriting as that of the fragmentary index. The poems are copied in approximately alphabetical order of first lines. A number of poems listed in the index are missing and the poems after CXLI are in a variety of hands. It was presumably intended to make fair copies of them all.

W uses the same stanza form in LXXXVI but the poem may well be earlier than the sixteenth century.

1 *Alone musyng*] Cf. Robbins, *Secular Lyrics* (1935), 173.1 'Alone walkyng', and Greene, *Early English Carols*, 462.13 'Musyng myselffe alone' (WMT).

4 *Then sore sythyng*] Cf. Robbins, op.cit., 173.3 'And sore syghyng' (WMT).

18 *neuer to depart*] Cf. CLXXXVI.15.

CXI. W uses this stanza form in LI, but it is not uncommon.

3 *solas*] solace.

20 *pryson stronge*] Cf. CLIV.25.

CXII

1 *fortune . . . the*] Cf. CLXI.1.
   what alith the] Cf. CXIII.1. B. Pattison, *Music and Poetry of the English Renaissance* (1948), p. 164, lists examples of the use of this refrain.

CXIII. F (11.164) calls this 'A refrain song imitated from Serafino': a statement which puzzles Baldi (235). She might have had in mind simply a general technical resemblance between W's song, which uses the opening line as refrain, and Serafino's barzellette.

CXIV. Source:

Voi mi poneste in foco,
  Per farmi anzi 'l mio di Donna perire:
Et perche questo mal ui parea poco,
  Col pianto raddoppiaste il mio languire.
Hor io ui uo ben dire.   5
  Leuate lun martire;
  Che di due morti [i] non posso morire.
Pero che da l'ardore
  L' humor, che uen de gliocchi mi difende:
Et chel gran pianto non dilegue il core;   10
  Face la fiamma, che l' asciuga e 'ncende.
Cosi, quanto si prende
  Lun mal, laltro mi rende;
  Et quel stesso mi gioua, che m' offende.
Che se tanto a uoi piace   15
  Veder in polue questa carne ardita,
Che uostro et mio mal grado è si uiuace;
  Perche darle giamai quel, che l' aita?
Vostra uoglia infinita
  Sana la sua ferita: 20
  Ond' io rimango in dolorosa uita.
Et uoi non mi doglio,
  Quanto d' Amor, che questo ui comporte;
Anzi di me, ch' anchor non mi discioglio.
  Ma che poss' io? con leggi inique et torte   25
Amor regge sua corte.
  Chi uide mai tal sorte,
  Tenersi in uita un huom con doppia morte [?]
Bembo, *Gliasolani* (Venice, 1505), sig. b 8r–v

The source of W's paraphrase was identified, and his handling of it discussed by R. Gottfried (*NQ*, cxcix (1954), 278–80). Characteristically, W chooses, not one of the 'platonising' poems generally associated with Bembo's name, but a witty Petrarchan love complaint, Perottino's canzonetta in Book I of *Gli Asolani*. It belongs in a context in which Perottino argues against love, as cause of many evils. W's first and last stanzas are relatively independent of the original, but throughout, and especially in the second and third stanzas, he follows Bembo's argument closely. Bembo's theme is *doppia morte*, W's *dowble deth:* the lover cannot die, because the two causes of death, the fire of desire and water of tears, counteract each other. This kind of witty conceit would be familiar to W. Thus Serafino opens a strambotto

> Se drento porto una fornace ardente
> Et spargo ognhor da gliocchi un largo fiume,
> (*Opere* (1516), f. 125ʳ)

and goes on to show that by miracle fire and water can live alongside each other. (Cf. W's own 'contraries' poem, LXXVII, and especially ll. 6–10.) Nevertheless Gottfried's comment that 'in expanding the background of Bembo's paradox', W 'robs it of its wit' is correct. W's emphasis is misogynistic. He introduces explicit references to his mistress's cruelty (ll. 1 and 32). He omits the passage (ll. 22–6) in which Perottino blames Love and his iniquitous laws for his suffering, so that the responsibility rests solely on the mistress. But something of the Italian complexity remains. It is of interest that Nott (581), writing before the source was known, should remark that 'We are even surprised to find W, at so early a period of our literature, able to express so complicated a thought with so much ease and perspicacity.'

W could have known Bembo's canzonetta in a musical setting, and his own version of it has, in I. L. Mumford's opinion, the appearance of a 'lyric for musical setting': see *EM*, xiv (1963), 24.

Form: Though, as Gottfried notes, W uses 'a looser, less continuous rhyme scheme' than Bembo, he does make some attempt to imitate the interwoven quatrain and couplet/triplet of the canzonetta. Thus Bembo's ababbbb becomes W's ababccddd. In this imitation of a canzonetta W's metrical policy obviously differs from the one he adopts in imitating the more complex and ambitious canzoni of Petrarch: see VIII and note, XCVIII, CII, CLVIII.

1–9] Largely W's, but with the main idea, and some detail, from Bembo.

1 *withdraw youre crueltye*] Cf. *Leuate lun martire* (l. 16).

2] Cf. Bembo's l. 2.

5] Cf. *Tenersi in uita* (l. 28).

10–18] Paraphrase of Bembo's second and third stanzas.

10–13] Built up from Bembo's ll. 8 and 11, with *ashes* taken from *polue* (l. 16).

14–16] Built up from Bembo's ll. 9–10.

17–18] Render Bembo's ll. 20–1.

17 *redresse*] Renders *Sana* (l. 20), and also conveys the idea of counteraction

in the central water/fire conceit. The later correction in B, *opres*, is less true to the original.

19–27] Further paraphrase of Bembo's second and third stanzas.

19–20] A closer rendering of Bembo's ll. 9–10, already used in ll. 14–16.

21–2] Cf. Bembo's l. 11.

23–4] Virtually a repetition of ll. 21–2, and also based on Bembo's l. 11.

25–7] Built up from Bembo's ll. 14 and 20–1.

28–36] Largely W's but with the main idea, and some detail, from Bembo.

28 *you*] B's reading is closer to the Italian, and makes more sense than D's *he*.

30–1] Returns to the idea of W's ll. 1–2: cf. Bembo's ll. 2 and 6–7.

33] Based on the idea in Bembo's l. 7. R. C. Harrier (*NQ*, cxcviii (1953), 235) argued for the retention of *doubles*, the reading of D; but he wrote before the discovery of B which supported M's emendation.

34–6] W's first attempt to deal with Bembo's fourth stanza. He omits ll. 22–6, and renders only ll. 27–8.

34 *yt*] Gottfried prefers to take as an expletive, equivalent to 'there', and not to equate it meaninglessly with *youre cruelnes*.
In A and P there is a poem by John Harington which appears to be based on this. It begins:

> At least withdraw your creweltie
>   Or force the tyme to worke your will.
> Yt is to moche extreamytie
>   To kepe me pent in pryson styll,
>   Free from all fawte, voyd of all cawse,
>   Without all right, agaynst all lawse;
>   How can you use more crewell spight
>   Than offre wrong and promes right,
>   Yet can not accuse nor will acquyght?

Harington was imprisoned after the rebellion of Sir Thomas Wyatt, the younger.

cxv. This resembles xxii in style and theme.

9 *grounded in gryff*] Cf. lxxxvii.5.

10 *rotte*] root.
  portred] portrayed.

19 *wormes*] glow-worms.

21 *agaynst my wyll*] Cf. xxv.9 (WMT).

22–8] Cf. xxii.8–14.

33 *wellyng*] wailing.

cxvi. This acrostic, destroyed by revisions in T, was addressed to Lady Anne Stanhope, the wife of Henry VIII's Master of the Horse. Ethel Seaton, *Sir Richard Roos* (1961), 503, argued that the poem was addressed by Roos to

Alice Stanhope; but she wrote before the publication of the B text. T entitles the poem: 'The louer suspected of change praieth that it be not beleued against him.'

4 *Entended*] This spelling is necessary for the acrostic.

8 *Exstew*] estew.

CXVII. Probably a sonnet, with the omission of a line after 4, and possibly a translation.

12 *Deptyst*] Deepest.

CXVIII. Possibly a portrait of Elizabeth Darrell, as Chambers (141) suggests. T entitles the poem: 'A description of such a one as he would loue.'

CXIX. W uses the same stanza form, with the first line of each stanza repeating the last line of the previous one, in CXCII, CCXXXI.

30 *abyde Extremytie*] Cf. CCXXIV.21-2 (WMT).

CXX. The rhythm of this sonnet and the varying length of lines are difficult to parallel in W's known work.

1 *belstred*] Corrected to *bolsterd* by a later hand.
borne in hand] Cf. XIV.13.

11 *poer*] power.

12 *wasted wynd*] Cf. XLVIII.1.

CXXI

6 *Dulphull*] Doleful.

7 *Paciens, parforce*] Cf. XXXIX.1-3 (Patience, ... of force); XL.13 (Paciens, no force), CCXXIX.1 (Patiens, for I have wrong), and CXCI.5 (Pacyence to suffer wrong).

15 *redres*] One of W's favourite words (e.g. 11.12, VI.6, XV.3, XXII. 12) although common in the love poetry of the period (WMT).

CXXII

17 *Comforthles*] Comfortless.

CXXIII

1 *Comeforthe*] Comfort.

24 *In hope*] The line in the MS. is extra-metrical, and either *In* or *soo* appears to be a scribal error. Probably the scribe was influenced by *soo* in ll. 4, 18, and 19.

This poem is followed in B by some weak verses in octosyllabic terza rima:

> Cursyd be he that furst began
>   To make thys Loue be bowght by pryse;
>   Ther ys no man that well tell can

The harm that therby doth aryse.
  The faythfull lover ys put backe,   5
  And who hath most he hath most pryse.
Wytt, manners, manhod thowgh he lacke
  What fors for that yf he can gyve.
  O love, alas, why art th[o]u slacke
Vengance to take on them that lyve   10
  Vnder thy law In such vnryght
  To by and sell that shuld releve
Them that by proffe and by best ryght
  Deserve to haue thy hey reward.
  Alas, yt ys a pytuus spyte   15
To suffer thys withowt regard
  Ffor perle, for stone, for goold, for gyft
  To thy grett shame we be debard
That haue for vs no nother shyft
  But honor the allway with trwth   20
  Theys gooldyn shepe do vs so lyft
From all owr ryght and that ys ruth
  But In thys case on cumfort ys
  When goold doth fayle by gyft that suyth
Anon he shall hys purpos mys   25
  And wold to god he were as sure
  Alsolens kys also to kysse.
Cursyd be she that made that luer;
  Cursyd be she that doth consent;
  Folyd be he that doth Indure   30
For such lyke ware so great turment.
  What dyvyll put in theys womens hedes

     *   *   *

  To sell for rynges, brochys and bedes
The plesant gyft of sacryd love.
  Covytusnes yt ys that ledes   35
  To such vnryght that doth them move.
O Lord yf ryght be in hevyn or hell,
  Grvnt, as thu mast althyng abowe
  That the that In ther yowth do sell
The thyng that shuld be fre and playn   40
  That the In age may bey as well
  By dubbyl prysse the same agayn.
     [l. 27 refers to Chaucer's 'Miller's Tale'.]

cxxiv. Neither B nor V gives a satisfactory text and the present one is a conflation of the two.

4 *Why . . . breke*?] Cf. lxxiv.4.

6 *The . . . Leke*] The B reading 'voide' makes the line a foot too long.

cxxv

1 *Do way*] See Glossary.
  prat] See Glossary.

10 *Or ... countefet*] Cf. Tilley, H60 (WMT), and Chaucer, *T & C*, iv, 1457–8 (S).

14 *to ...yes*] Cf. Chaucer, *CT*, A 3865 (WMT).

21 *make ... muse*] Cf. CCX.7.

22–3 *Ye ...ys*] Cf. CXXXVII.9–10 (WMT).

27 *Leue of, therfore*] Cf. VII.7 (WMT).

CXXVI

2 *incressyng my Smart*] Cf. LXXXIX.5.

3–4] Cf. CXCI.23–4.

5 *put hym self in prese*] Cf. LXXI.9 (WMT).

13 *stryve ... tyde*] Cf. Tilley, S927 (WMT). and LVIII.5–6, XCI.27, CCXXV. 18–20.

CXXVII. The rhythm of this poem does not suggest W's authorship, although there are parallels of phrasing in a poem in D, often ascribed to W.

3 *Gylty, I graunt that I haue don amys*] Cf. CXCVIII.6 'Gyllty I graunt'; CXCV-III.27–8 'And foly framd my thought amyss, The faute wherof now well I ffynd.'

5–6 *Betrayed ... defyled*] Presumably the poet gave away his mistress' name to a friend under pledge of secrecy. Cf. l. 1 'sylens vnkept'.

11–12 *Onles ... amys*] Unless your own conduct is impeccable.

CXXVIII. Only the first stanza of seven lines appears in D. The remaining stanzas, of eight lines, may have been added by another poet, perhaps in imitation of XXXIV. But it is more likely that the B scribe ran two poems together by mistake.

14 *To ... sowen*] Cf. Tilley, S210 (WMT).

30] Cf. XXXIV.10.

31] Cf. XXXIV.12 (WMT).

CXXIX. The alliteration in ll. 1, 5, 7, 8 and elsewhere is unlike W's usual style.

1 *a drad*] adread.

2 *Bitwene ... ground*] Cf. Tilley, S900 (WMT).

6 *at ... bound*] Cf. XXI.11, CCXXXI.32.

9 *Dought*] Doubt.

CXXX. In the same style as CXXIX.

3 *Thancked be fortune*] Cf. XXXVII.8, CXCVIII.23.

5 *traught*] truth.

CXXXI. This epigram is translated from a poem which was included in six-teenth-century editions of Ausonius, though written by a Renaissance poet.

> Illa ego sum Dido, vultu, quem conspicis, hospes,
>   Assimilata modis pulchraque mirificis.
> Talis eram; sed non, Maro quam mihi finxit, erat mens
>   Vita nec incestis feta cupidinibus
> Namque nec Aeneas vidit me Troius unquam,
>   Nec Lybiam aduenit classibus Iliacis,
> Sed furias fugiens atque arma procacis Hiarbae
>   Seruaui, fateor, morte pudicitiam;
> Pectore transfixo costas quod perculit ensis,
>   Non furor aut laeso crudus amore dolor:
> Sic cecidisse iuuat vixi sine vulnere famae,
>   Veta virum positis moenibus oppetii.
> Inuida cur in me stimulasti, Musa, Maronem,
>   Fingeret ut nostrae damna pudicitiae?
> Vos magis historicis, lectores, credite de me,
>   Quam qui furta deum concubitusque canunt
> Falsidici vates, temerant qui carmine verum
>   Humanisque deos assimilant vitiis.

It was afterwards translated by Ralegh in his *History of the World:*

> I am that Dido which thou here do'st see,
> Cunningly framed in beauteous Imagrie.
> Like this I was, but had not such a soule
> As Maro fained, incestuous and foule.
> Æneas neuer with his Troian host
> Beheld my face, or landed on this coast.
> But flying proud Iarbus villanie,
> Not mou'd by furious loue or iealousie;
> I did with weapon chast, to saue my fame,
> Make way for death vntimely, ere it came.
> This was my end; but first I built a Towne,
> Reueng'd my husband's death, liu'd with renowne.
> Why didst thou stirre vp Virgil, enuious Muse,
> Falsely my name and honour to abuse?
> Readers, beleeue Historians; not those
> Which to the world Ioues thefts and vice expose.
> Poets are liers, and for verses sake
> Will make the Gods of humane crimes partake.

The epigram is very much in W's style (cf. LXXX, LXXXI) and the point of the original is made more forcibly by W's characteristic condensation.

There follows in the MS:

> Danger thy selff led for nothyng,
> Thou nedyst not then no remedy,
> So that th[o]u mast att sum tyme styng
> Thos that lov thy adversyte
> Hardely lern thys before at me
> Lyve vnder law and cache at goold
> Who make a nenny bowght and sold.

What makes the dogge to fere the bell,
But the sharp wypp that longes therto,
Without reason he markes hyt well,
And he ons bett wyll kno hys foo
Sens thys ys ryght do thu evye[n] sso
Lern to kepe the owt of prisson
Lyberte ma quyte sum seson.

Tho that sum rejoyst at thys
Thy trubbyll and adversyte,
The[y] gaynd nott much at that ywys,
Tho thu wert In extremite.
Yet art thu not past remedy.
But we thy fryndes be off good chere
And hope for better the next yere.

Even as thu dost thy enmys glad
When thu dust stayn thyn honeste,
Lyke wyse thy fryndes for the be sad
And do lament thy workes and the.
Leve now such yowth that we ma see
Thy fooys Lament that thu dost well,
So shalt thu then both by and sell.

For fryndes there be off sundry kynde[s]
Sum for game, sum for the tabyll
Sum for to content mens mynd[s]
Sum for a tyme, few are stabyll
And sens mens kynd ys warryabyll
Trust to thy self and nott offend
So then thou nedyst nott to amend.

CXXXII. This poem is in atrocious handwriting – the same as CXLIX – and with some very odd spellings.

7 *hieraufter coums not yet*] Cf. Tilley, H439 (WMT) and CCXXIX.6.

13 *Onys I was he*] Cf. CXLVI.6.

15 *rot*] rote.

16 *nyd*] need.

19–20 *What . . . awey*] Cf. Tilley, B683 (WMT).

CXXXIII

1 *Had I wiste*] Cf. Tilley, H8 (WMT).

4 *fayned faith*] A phrase used by W (CCXXVI.15 and CCXXX.22) but it is not, of course, peculiar to him.

8 *pas on*] See Glossary.

This poem is followed in B by two which are not worth printing:

(a) From Adams fall to Noes noy full floudd
(b) O Iove geve eare vnto my cry

cxxxiv. This rather absurd dialogue between the ghost of a murdered man and a despairing lover is a curious mixture of alliterative and rhymed verse. The second and fourth stanzas rhyme ababbcc, but the others are irregular.

16 *ters*] tears.

22 *Cum of*] Come on?

cxxxv. For similar quibbling on 'hap', cf. xxiii, xxxvi, cclvi.

31 *And . . . hy*] Cf. clvi.4.

cxxxvi. Although this jingle is in the section of D which contains a large number of W poems, there is nothing in it particularly characteristic of his work. It is followed in the MS. by Blage's verses, 'A voyce I have and yk a will to wayle', first printed in *L*, 273–6.

cxxxvii. This poem is out of sequence alphabetically, presumably because the pages have been disarranged. It is entitled in T: 'The louers case can not be hidden how euer he dissemble.' Some of the T readings are attractive (e.g. l. 14) but in view of the usual unreliability of the T text, it has been thought advisable to follow B.

cxxxviii. This is not an answer to cxxxvii (which is in a different hand). There are several of W's poems to which it might be a reply, or it may be an answer to one of the lost poems listed in the index to B.

3 *new or old*] i.e. lovers.

5 *profferd seruice*] Cf. clxxxii.1 'hart and servys to yow profferd'.

25–6 *As . . . wisely*] The lady implies as in ll. 21–2 that the lover has been promiscuous.

cxxxix. An undistinguished poem of doubtful authorship.

cxl. R. L. Greene, *RES* (1964), 175–80, showed that a poem in the University of Pennsylvania Library (MS. Latin 35, f[iii]r) contains a shorter version in carol form of this poem:

[burden]

I ham as I ham *and* so will I be
but howe I ham none knowethe truly.

[1]

I lede my lyff indifferntly.
I mean nothinke but honeste.
Though folkex Iugge diversly.
Yet I ham as I ham *and* so will I be.

[2]

Sum that there be that dothe mystrowe.
sum of pleasure and sum of woo.
Yet for all that no thinke they knowe.
For I ham as I ham wher euer I goo.

[3]
Sum ther be that dothe delyght.
to Iugge folkex for envy and spythe.
but whether they Iuge wronge or ryght.
I ham as I ham *and* soo will I wryght

['envoy']

A dew sewte Syster neve[r]
    departinge is A payne
But myrthe renewithe. . .
    when Louyars meate Agen.

These verses correspond to ll. 1–2, 5–8, 13–16, 25–8. Greene suggests that W 'appropriated and expanded into a longer poem' the earlier carol, 'eliminating both the burden and the envoy'. But W's authorship is very uncertain.

3 *evill*] The rhythm and sense would be improved if this word were emended to 'ill'.
    bonde . . . fre] 'may well be a literal reference to W's own second imprisonment or to the fear of it' (Tillyard).

CXLI. A rough version of four stanzas of this poem was printed in Robbins' *Secular Lyrics* from Huntington MS. EL 1160. The handwriting is of the early sixteenth century. There are two copies in the MS, which differ considerably and they probably represent attempts to recall a longer poem; but it is possible that the B text was an adaptation and expansion of an earlier poem. In one Huntington version the refrain varies from 'And all for one' to 'And all for ffer of on' and 'And all ffor lowe off on'. In the other version the refrain in st. 1 and 3 is the same as in B.

F. W. Sternfeld (*TLS* (1961), 433) mentions a tune for virginals by William Byrd entitled 'The woods so wild' and that the same melody is given in Playford's *English Dancing Master* (1651) under the title 'Greenwood'. In Ravenscroft's *Pammelia* (1609) there is a song containing the lines:

Follow me, my sweet heart, follow me where I goe
Shall I goe walke the woods so wild,
Wandering here and there,
As I was once full sore beguiled,
What remedy though alas for love I die with woe.

6 *banysshed from my blys*] Cf. LXXVIII.5.

8 *without offens*] Cf. XXXIX.23, LIII.32 (WMT).

21 *runnyng stremes*] Cf. CCXLV.6 (WMT).

27 *row*] roe.

32 *To turkylles*] two turtle-doves.

66] Cf. LXVI.27.

67] There is a blank in the MS. Possibly we should read 'storms'.

74] *causers of this stryfe*] Cf. XXVI.14.

CXLII

1] Cf. LIII.1.

4 *fervent ffyere*] Cf. XLI.17, LXXXVII.33 (WMT).

11 *weryede lyfe*] Cf. XCVIII.94 (WMT).

27 *weryed breast*] Cf. CLXXII.17.

CXLIII. In H the poem is entitled 'A Balad of Will'. It is preceded by three W poems (CCXLIV, CCXLV, LXXXVI) and followed by one ascribed to him in H. This is followed by some feeble verses beginning 'When shall my lyeue'.

CXLIV

3] Cf. CXLI.63.

11 *betyrnes*] bitterness.

15 *yerthe*] earth.

22 *nys*] is not.

CXLV. Possibly based on a poem in Add. MSS. 31922:

> I have been a foster
> Long and many a day
> My locks ben hore.

16 *clok my wo*] Cf. CXLVI.2 and III.14.

22 *A nothyr had my place*] Cf. CXCV.21 (WMT).

40 *beleve*] belief.

CXLVI. This elegy on Anne Boleyn's alleged paramours (Lord Rochford, Henry Norris, William Brereton, Francis Weston, and Mark Smeaton), who were executed while W was in the Tower of London, must have been written after his release (see l. 28) or by some other acquaintance of the victims. See *L*, 27–36, for an account of the situation.

5 *vmble*] humbly.

12 *those*] i.e. those who.

35 *exsept*] accept.

46 *her*] hear.

51 *my ny*] mine eye.

53 *aboue thy poore degre*] Cf. CLXXXV.28 (WMT).

55 *Rottyn twygge*] Cf. XIII.14, CCXXIV.33, and Tilley, B557 (WMT).

61 *hepe*] help.

This poem is followed by an alliterative and rhyming poem entitled 'Jealosy' (printed by D. S. Brewer in *EPS*, ix (1965), 85–7), given below, and some moralizing verses comparing England to Sodom.

'Jealosy'

In soumer seson as soune as the sonne
Had breydid his bemes on beris and bouddes
Affter longe rest for recreacionne
My wyl was to walke in to the wyld wouddes
And by a bery bushe I bend me to ly
Whyche was under a ok where akornes dyd gro
Ryght by me ran a ryuer mouche plesantly
A symlyer syght neuer sawe man I tro
As I lay lo and loukyd up abowe
Yff i myght ony byrd on bushe or on bryer
I was waer of the lued lad, the lorde of loue
Cursyd Cupid that foul faut hym euer
Blynd as a bytel wythe his bowe in his hande
His shafte[s] were shot awey and shyuerd in sounder
I wounderd what wynde woud hym to thys land
And shaftles to see hym yt symyd me wounder
For savie a blount bolt whyche he baer ounder his belt
Shafte had he noen and that sawe I wel
For magre and malys my hart gan to melt
And my mynd mouyd me wythe hym to mel
To venge the vronge he wraughte me in my youthe
My yes sed they sawe hym that sor had causyd me sob
My tounge told me to that al that was truethe
My reson remembryd that oft he dyd hym rob
And bad me be bold to bet hym and bynd him fast
For ounarmyd to hawe hym aien it weer but a hap
I agied therto and was nothinge agast
And reknyd to reche hym aryght and to lend him a rap
To mak fre my felous wyche be fast feteryd
Bound in the bonds of that blynde bousard
I ros up at the last and loud luryd
And cryed hou Cupid thow Kursyd Coward
He hard me and harkenings ston styl he stoud
And seyd soum of my saruants he symythe to be
That I send to syek my shaftes in the woud
I maruel me mouche he marchethe not to me
I hyed me wythe haste to hyt hym on the hed
Wythe a browde bat I bar on my bak
But whan he dru near for dryd I was nyer ded
I foltered for feere and feynted alak
I maruel mouche seyd hee and ther on I muse
Off jelosy my iowell I done me he bed
Ded seyd he no dowt the not the dyuell hym deer
I wot wher he wonnythe ounder thys would syd
Dow yow so syr he seyd and dru hym soumdel neer
I shawl gyffe you a goud thynge yff yow wyl be my gyd
Nay quodthe I for al Kent I would not cum in his Klaws
Myt he cache me in his coupe he would carwe me as a kapon
He lyuethe lwedly and lovythe no lawes
He is cursed and crabbyd of colloryke complexion
His Lady lyuethe in a loft and lakythe lyberte

> She may synge sorow that euer she saw hym I sey
> But yff I wend the wey do won thynge for me
> Aske campos of that kenel that his wyff may go pley
> For affter meles she must mount up in to hyr maner
> And dar not doun cum for the dethe all the lyue dey
> Ther nys in chrystendom a curtisar creatur
> That lyuethe so lamentably my lyffe I dar ley.

*   *   *

The other poem begins:

> If nowe the tyme is this the dulfull daye
> That thowe lyst lord to wreke the of our synne,
> Is this the last? wyll thow no lenger steye
> Vs to destroye? wylt thow now Lord beginne?

CXLVII. There is not much to choose between the texts given in A and B, but perhaps the order of stanzas in A is better.

27 *I . . . fley*] Cf. Tilley, F353, F396 (WMT).

33 *Farewell, vnstabyll*] Cf. CCXV.21, 28 (WMT).

CXLVIII. There are some errors in both texts. The poem is followed by these verses on the superiority of brown bread to white and an answer. It has been suspected that there is an allegorical meaning.

> Love why so wyll whyt bread, I best do love browne,
> Ffor nothinge so well my hongre can Apesse;
> A bytt of that bread ys worthe A kynges crowne;
> Yf my ffyll of that ons I myght ffese
> I wolde thynke my selffe then very well at ease;
> Nor neuer after that any other bread to crave,
> So styll when I lyst that bread I myght have.
>
> It comffortythe the hart as well as dothe the whytt,
> And as holesome ffor the bodye and as sauorye ffor the tast,
> Nothyng so myche my hart doth delyght.
> Here wyll I love whyll my lyff dothe last.
> Brownes of the collor makes not me Agast;
> Redye ffor to love yt, ffor therin ffynd I rest,
> Ouer all other yt goes wythe me the best.

'The Aunswer'

> Alas your ffondnes makys me smylle,
> What cause have you to love browne bread?
> Ye thynk nowe Another to begyle,
> Nay, nay, be gys we knowe where ye are ffed
> In other placys with mylke and whey bread,
> What bread ye may eat without crommes
> Broune bred ys hard ande wyll hurt your gummes.

CXLIX. Although this poem is ascribed to 'T.W.' in the MS., it does not

seem to be in his style. The peculiar handwriting is the same as that of
CXXXII and the spelling in both poems is eccentric.

5 *Make . . . constreynte*] Make a virtue of necessity.

8 *for me*] This emendation makes sense, but one suspects that the first *me* in
'me for me' was a slip for some other word.

9 *Cast . . . cuer*] Cf. Ps. LV.22.

This poem is followed by verses signed 'B.G.' in the same handwriting as
Blage's poems, but the references to Esther, Abigail, Lydia and Sara show
that the poem was written by – or in the person of – a woman.

Let the hethen whiche trust not in the Lorde
beweyl the ded and mourne apon the graue
of Christians Let that wey be cleen abhorde
Lawdynge our god that yt plees hym vouchsaue
the sacred soul from bondage to mak fre
ounclothed of flesche restord to Lyberte

Sho not as tho thys lyffe weere yt you sought
ioy not theryn it is to ful of vyce
Tyek to the Lord, set all the rest at naught
and for his sak from syn louk you aryce
dispise this erthe the flesche is fauls and freyl
Satan is souttel the worlde dothe you aseyl

The tyme is short, so soudeyne is the faul
that of this Lyffe asurance is ther none
it hathe no suit ountemperid wythe gaul
to part from it alas why should we mone
reioyce wythe me ryd of muche kaer and stryffe
in change whereof I lyue a blessyd lyffe

Lerne you of me who alueys lyued to dy
Lerne you of me this worlde for to despyse
Lerne you of me insessantly to cry
for helpe to hym who only is all wyse
Lerne you of me his wourd and laude to knowe
Lerne you therby in vertuus lyffe to growe

Lo wheer I ly to whom the Lord has lent
Assurid hope as iudithe in hym had
Kaer for the cristians he also me sent
Lyke Hester the queen ther danger I drad
As Abigiel wythe dauid of euene weyt
suche fauor found I wythe henry the eyght

Lyke Lidia I louyd the Lordes Lawe
it was my delight my hol ioy and myrthe
wythe faytheful phoebe I had it in awe
Lyke sara he sent me a blessed byrthe
and nowe by dethe I am cum to the place
preparid for me of his abundant grace

Reioyce wythe me lament your owne estat
kled stil yn kaer and cumberd in flesche
wache wythe the bryd groume to enter the gat
that the blud of the Lamme your syns may wesche
prey eche for outher wythe faythefull tru hart
for after dethe therin you haue no part.

B.G.

CL. See note to CIX. According to J. Stevens (445) this poem is to be found
with music in the Ramsden Documents at Huddersfield (*c.* 1560–80).

11 *Rygore*] Cf. LXXIII.6.

13 *dedlye smart*] Cf. LXXIV.3.

CLI. This poem, and the answer to it (CLII), were probably written by the
same author.

CLII

3 *wrast*] wrest.

This is followed by some feeble verses beginning:

'My Lady ys such one to whom our Lord hath lent'.

CLIII. The rhyme to the third line of each stanza is in the middle of the
fourth, and there is a concealed internal rhyme in the second and third lines of
each stanza (e.g. hete/let, game/blame). In the first respect, but not in the
second, it resembles CLXXV, which also has a similar refrain.

18 *mene*] men.

CLIV

13 *knyt the knot*] Cf. CXVIII.8, CLVI.16.

18 *hold the shott*] See Glossary.

25 *prysone strong*] Cf. CXI.20.

CLV

9 *The place of slepe*] Cf. CLXXXVII.6 (WMT).

10 *an vnquyet enymye*] Cf. CLXXXVII.4 (WMT).

13 *borne*] burn.

CLVI. One of the finest poems in B, and, both in style and content, charac-
teristic of W.

5 *ons I was*] Cf. CCXIX.3, 8 (WMT).

CLVII. The poem contains some effective examples of repetition of ideas
from the last line of one stanza to the first line of the next. See ll. 12–13, 16–17,
28–9, 36–7.

21 *ffalshed ffaythe*] Cf. LIII.22.
   ffalshed] falsed.

EE

23 *But . . . knot*] Cf. CXCII.26–7. CLXXII.24, CLVIII.7, CXVIII.8, CCXVI.34.

35 *letters*] The correction, in a different hand, is a more attractive reading. This is followed by a single stanza:

> O faythfull hart plungyd in distres
> Sustaynyng by ffayth thy nowne wond mortall,
> Euer in trothe, playnt and hevynes
> Replet with dollors and payns ouer [euer B] all,
> Ffor ayd and soccer yt botys not the to call.
> Agaynst thy wyll they faythe aspyed shalbe,
> Sethe she the disdaynethe whyche thou lovyth so faythff[ullye].

CLVIII. Source:

> S' i' 'l dissi mai, ch' i' vegna in odio a quella
> Del cui amor vivo e senza 'l qual morrei:
> S' i' 'l dissi, ch' e' miei dí sian pochi e rei,
> E di vil signoria l' anima ancella:
> S' i' 'l dissi, contra me s' arme ogni stella,   5
> E dal mio lato sia
> Paura e gelosia,
> E la nemica mia
> Piú feroce ver' me sempre e piú bella.
> S' i' 'l dissi, Amor l' aurate sue quadrella   10
> Spenda in me tutte e l' impiombate in lei:
> S' i' 'l dissi, cielo e terra, uomini e dèi
> Mi sian contrari, et essa ogni or piú fella:
> S' i' 'l dissi, chi con sua cieca facella
> Dritto a morte m' invia   15
> Pur come suol si stia,
> Né mai piú dolce o pia
> Ver' me si mostri in atto od in favella.
> S' i' 'l dissi mai, di quel ch' i' men vorrei,
> Piena trovi quest' aspra e breve via: 20
> S' i' 'l dissi, il fero ardor che mi desvia
> Cresca in me quanto el fier ghiaccio in costei:
> S' i' 'l dissi, unqua non veggian li occhi mei
> Sol chiaro o sua sorella
> Né donna né donzella,   25
> Ma terribil procella
> Qual Faraone in perseguir li Ebrei.
> S' 'i' 'l dissi, co i sospir, quant' io mai fei,
> Sia pietà per me morta e cortesia:
> S' i' 'l dissi, il dir s' innaspri, che s' udia   30
> Sí dolce allor che vinto mi rendei:
> S' i' 'l dissi, io spiaccia a quella ch' i' tôrrei,
> Sol, chiuso in fosca cella,
> Dal dí che la mamella
> Lasciai fin che si svella   35
> Da me l' alma, adorar: forse el farei.
> Ma, s' io no 'l dissi, chi sí dolce apria
> Meo cor a speme ne l' età novella
> Regg' ancor questa stanca navicella

Co 'l governo di sua pietà natia,   40
Né diventi altra, ma pur qual solia
Quando piú non potei,
Che me stesso perdei,
Né piú perder devrei.
Mal fa chi tanta fé sí tosto oblia.   45
I' no 'l dissi già mai, né dir poria
Per oro o per cittadi o per castella.
Vinca 'l ver dunque e si rimanga in sella,
E vinta a terra caggia la bugia.
Tu sai in me il tutto, Amor: s' ella ne spia,   50
Dinne quel che dir dêi.
I' beato direi
Tre volte e quattro e sei
Chi, devendo languir, si morí pria.
Per Rachel ho servito e non per Lia;   55
Né con altra saprei
Viver; e sosterrei,
Quando 'l ciel ne rappella,
Girmen con ella in su 'l carro d' Elia.

Petrarch, *Rime*, ccvi

The source was first mentioned by Puttenham (213), who quoted W's ll. 1–18 as an example of 'Ecphonisis or the Outcry'. It was later more precisely identified by Nott (550). Cecchini (99) put forward an earlier imitation of Petrarch's canzone, Serafino's strambotto 'Donna si io dixi mai contra tuo honore' (*Opere* (1516), f. 157ᵛ). But this does not contain the reference to Rachel and Leah common to Petrarch (l. 55) and W (ll. 45–6). W paraphrases Petrarch's sense and imitates his structure. The lover has been wrongly accused of loving another, and is justifying himself to his mistress. W's series of rhetorical repetitions, *I sayd hytt not*, *And yff I dyd*, etc., derives from *S' i' 'l dissi mai*, *S' i' 'l dissi*, etc., and his strategic turn *Yf I be clere* from Petrarch's *Ma, s' io no 'l dissi*. The curses he calls down on himself are derivative but W copies only a few of the details (e.g. in ll. 17–20). He adds his own (e.g. in ll. 21–4). And he omits many of Petrarch's (e.g. love's arrows in ll. 10–11, fire and ice in ll. 21–2, Pharaoh in l. 27, the ship in ll. 39–40). W's is, in fact, a much slighter and lighter poem. Chambers (129–30) cites it as an example of his 'economy of speech', and of other qualities characteristic of W and not found in Petrarch's canzone. W introduces no radically new ideas except in ll. 33–40, where he makes Petrarch's issue with his mistress 'a clear-cut question of justice': see Guss (37). See also the comparison of the two poems and of both with CLXXII by Hietsch (198–208).

W may have known the canzone in its popular musical setting by Bartolmeo Tromboncino: see I. L. Mumford in *EM*, xiv (1963), 20. That W's imitation is itself song-like is emphasized by W. Maynard, who, having tried the experiment of matching his poems to suitable settings, finds that it 'goes so eloquently to "Belle qui tient ma vie" that it may indeed have been written for it' (*RES*, xvi (1965), 11).

On W's handling of Petrarch's canzoni, see note to VIII. It is doubtful whether he could have imitated metrically the structure of *S' i' 'l dissi*, which is based on a difficult Provençal one in which three rhymes only are used throughout, and in a changing pattern. He chose to depend, as D. G. Rees points out, 'not on technical intricacy but on extreme simplicity' (*CL*, vii (1955), 22). Title in T: 'The louer excuseth him of wordes wherwith he was vniustly charged.'

1] Cf. *S' i' 'l dissi mai* (l. 1) and its repetition with variations in both Petrarch and W.

7–8] The knot metaphor is W's addition, and a favourite with him: cf. CLVII and note.

17–20] Based on Petrarch's l. 5.

21–4] The Trojan war illustration is W's addition.

25–8] Based on Petrarch's ll. 8–9.

33–40] Correspond to Petrarch's l. 37 both in idea and in structural importance, as representing a turn in the argument, and introducing the lover's claims for redress of his wrongs. W, using terms such as *Ye must* and *Off ryght . . .ye ought*, gives much more emphasis to these claims.

41–8] Expand Petrarch's l. 55, in which he equates Laura with Rachel and the other lady with whom he is supposedly involved with Leah (Genesis, 29).

44–6] W introduces the puns on *lyer*/Leah and *Rakhell*/Rachel.

CLIX. Nott (548) believed that W was recalling Petrarch's 'Ite, caldi sospiri' (*Rime*, cliii) which is the source of xx. The idea of the lover's cries and tears sallying forth to break down the mistress's resistance may have been suggested by Petrarch's poem. T entitles it: 'The louer sendeth his complaintes and teares to sue for grace.'

6 *weet*] wet.

11 *And . . . Longe*] T smooths out the line.

14 *wons*] once.

17–24] The ultimate source of this image is probably Petrarch's *Rime*, cclxv, 9–14 (quoted above LXXXII n.); but it could have come to W, as Nott suggests, via Serafino.

CLX

1 *in . . . gras*] Cf. XCVII.11 (WMT).

2 *nou*] now.

3 *trad the tras*] trod the trace.

10 *Than*] Then.

12 *many whon*] Many a one.

14 *moo*] more, i.e. those not in her favour.

17 *ouer*] hour.

CLXI. This scribbled fragment is out of alphabetical order in B and has to be completed from the notoriously unreliable V.

26 *terrestrial*] Apparently used as a noun, or with 'ball' understood.
The next poem in B is by Sir George Blage, hitherto unpublished:

> Ryd of bondage free from kaer seven yiers space and mor
> I felt no payne and I knue no griffe, as I had doune before:
> I fed ful wel throwe quiet rest in myrthe was my delyght
> I laught the dey at lyberte and soundly I slept the nyght
> no sythes ieldid to loue nor tears as I was wount
> my drowsie days and kaerfull lyffe I changed to hawk and hunt
> in present tyme contendid me the lyffe that I had past
> I cleen dispisid, I quit forgat, and at my bak yt kast
> my chyffe delyght and pleswer was to heyr a louer playne
> to heyr hym curs to hier him cry and wast his wourdes in vayne
> and ofte I seyde ounto my selffe what lyffe was that I ledd
> when lyke thees foules I lyueyd longe and had byne better dedd
> they feel nothinge that dothe them goud ther harme they still desier
> in blast of colde for to exchue they fle into the fyer
> eche lyer eche louke dothe them abuse they tak all to the best
> and streyt aien those selffe same ies do breed aul ther unrest
> theer fleythe no wourd out of the mouthe from wyche they louk for grace
> but that contentid they are fourthwythe to set it out off place
> and tho that this wythe all the rest wyche foulles by loue do wyn
> weer knowen to me and nothinge hid synse loue did furst begyn
> yet stoupid I forsakynge quit the ground wher I stoude suer
> as tho unknowen had beyn to me ther craft ther trayne and luer
> I yeldid streyght deniynge quit eche wourde that I had seydd
> wythe humbell wyll and hart contrit unto loue I obeyd
> that erst espatynge longe I found full of all craft and woo
> suyter then honey symed the souer the fawt was nothinge soo
> yt semyd me I had doune wronge ounreuerent thought to haue
> I dyd repent aiens loueys power that I had beyne so braue
> and fourthe I went to syk for loue his fauor to obtayne
> wythe bowe and shaft yfeteryd feyr I met hym in this playne
> when I hym sawe full lo on kne as to my loue I fell
> wythe piteus louk and karfull playnt my wofull tale to tell
> I dru neyr who is that seyd he forsouthe syr it is I
> my tounge stak fast ounto my teythe as doust my lyppes were dri
> a wrechid wyt your humbel slaue that sykes helpe at your hand
> hys gyrdle slypt his shaftis fel doune and he gaue me thys bande
> go hange thy selffe at wons he seyd go hange the wythe this corde
> and sey to souche as pas tho (the?) by this gifft gaue me my Lorde
> I touke the rope and fourthe I went ounto this laurel tre
> wyche then was green and noue is blak so hathe it mournde for me
> and heyr I hange ensampell playne to kawes loueers despayr
> satan my soull that foules my fleshe my brethe fleyethe in the [air]
> what so thou be that passis by, cut not the rope in sounder
> but let me hange so that the world apon my folly woun[der]
> cursed be thow what so thou art that this dothe sey [. . .
> and yff thou loue unonestly to haue the same endy[ing]
>
> G.B

There follows, after two pious poems of no value, a poem, 'Some men would
thinke of right to haue', originally ascribed to W by T, but transferred in the
second edition to uncertain authors. B has the following variants:

2 their . . . meaning] trewe menynge get B.   5 that] nought B.   6 hatch] the hatche
B.   7 I] that I B.   8 is] thus B.   10 that] thoughe B.   12 and yet] I have and yt B.
14 my] that my B. others] A nothers B.   15 They eat] who eatys B.   17 I . . . dryve]
they draw I dryve B.   21 Till] styll B. I] that I B.   26 slepe, I tosse] syng I typpe B.
28 lo, cruelty] grevlye B.

CLXII

1 *Sche . . . most*] 'perceive' is understood.

4 *theay . . . expert*] experts on love.

10 *other*] i.e. other lovers.

11 *vnvysyd*] unvised, i.e. ill-advised.

13 *thether*] thither.

14 *whether*] whither.

16 *Ther as*] whereas.

17 *ther as*] whereas.

CLXIII

1 *spytt*] spite.

4] Cf. CLXXXII.22 and CLXXII.11.

9–10 *flytt . . . ffroo*] Cf. Tilley, W86 (WMT).

11 *Spytt . . . spytt*] Quibble on *spit* and *spite*.

17 *And . . . sporne*] Cf. Tilley, F433 (WMT).

25 *lyst*] like.
louere] lour.

28 *Out of my brest*] Cf. XLIV.8 (WMT).
seche] seek.

CLXIV

12 *thought*] i.e. thought to find. (In U the word was emended to *sought*.)
brytell glas] Cf. XXXI.12.

22 *my woffull hart*] Cf. CCLI.2 (WMT).

CLXV. The initial letters of the first line of each stanza read SHELTUN,
and in D Mary Shelton's name is written at the foot of the page.

11 *Encreas*] The B spelling spoils the acrostic.

CLXVI

13 *his*] Possibly an error for *is*.

19 *ffell*] feels.

20–2 *gayne . . . tayme*] To make a satisfactory rhyme one could read either
gayme or *tayne;* but the imperfect rhyme makes better sense.

39 *To . . . hand*] Cf. Tilley, B363 (WMT).

This is followed by a poem previously published from the Bannatyne MS. in
S.T.S. XXII.213.

Sustayne, abstayne, kep well in your mynd;
  Bare and fforbeare haue euer in Remembrance;
  Ffor ye shall therby greate quyetnes ffynd
  In all your lyffe, what so euer dothe chaunce.
  Yt ys the only thyng that may you avance,   5
  And mak you to be extemed verelye
  Amongest all other ffor the most happy.

Bere trobles and payne, bere schlaunder and blame,
  Bere wordes displesant, be theay never so sowere;
  Fforber ye in any wyse to other do the same;   10
  Fforber to Revenge, thoughe yt be in your power;
  Lat neuer your Anger Remaygne with you a nowre;
  Fforbere your owne pleasor, ber your nebors mestrye;
  And ye of all other shalbe most happy.

If ye ben gaynsayed, fforbere ffor a season;   15
  Fforbere to resyst when ye thynke to offend;
  Bere others ygnorance, fforber your owne reason,
  Tyll occasions be gyven you them to amend;
  Then ottyr your wyssdome as god shall yt send;
  Obserue your tyme and fforbere dyscretlye,   20
  And ye of all other shalbe most happy.

Ber Crystys crose, when yt ys layd on your backe,
  That ys to say all manner of adversytie;
  Whiche when ye in your owne person dothe lacke,
  Help other to beare that ouerladyn be.   25
  Ber with them that bere with all humynyte,
  So shall this world be veryffyed accordingly,
  That ye of all other shalbe most happy.

Fforbere Rathe judgment tyll the truthe be tryed;
  Fforbere all hastyne, speak wordis of chastyte;   30
  Fforber extreme punnyshment, tho the fawt be descried;
  To myche in all things ys cownted indignitie.
  Temper your Actis with sustayned Abstynancie;
  Betyr fforber, and then shall ye trulye
  Of all othre creators be most happye.   35

[8 Bere] Bere Bere B.   30 chastyte] *original* charyte.   32 cownted] cownted B.]

The next poem, previously published in *Unpublished Poems,* is probably
not by W.

Syns Loue ys founde wythe parfytnes
  And longe tyme growen within your hart,
  I moust therfor, of gentylnes,
  Regarde your paynes and greuous smart.
  My Loue from you shale no wyse part
    In welthe ande woo, in care and Joye:
    Mon cuer aues pense de moy.

Thowgh falce mystrust doth banyshe our presence,
  Wythe priue dysdayne that Loue woulde disseuer,
Yet shal our hartes be true in absence,
  In faythfull Loue styll too perseuer.
Chaunce as yt wyll, thowghe chawnce coume niuer.
  In welthe ande woo, in care and Joye:
  Mon cuer aues pense de moy.

Myne eyes be closyd, I may not see;
  Myne eres be stopt, I may not here;
Yet ys my hart at lyberte
  On you to thynke bothe far ande nere.
No erthely creature shall change my cheyr.
  In welthe ande woo, in care and Joye:
  Mon cuer aues pense de moy.

I sey no more; in chaunce ys alle.
  Sumwhat I thynke, thowghe lytle I saye;
But of one thynge be sure shalbe
  To haue of me as mooche as may,
To be your coumfort nyt and dey.
  In welthe ande woo, in care and Joye:
  Mon cuer aues pense de moy.

CLXVII. Main source:

Ahime tu dormi, & io con alta uoce
  Vó palesando el duol che ognhor mi dai,
Tu dormi, & limpio amor, crudo feroce
  Sempre piú ueglia à raddopiarmi i guai,
Tu dormi quieta, e in me piú doglia atroce
  Solo in te crudeltá non dorme mai,
Anzi crudel per mai pace non darmi,
  Credo che sogni amor de tormentarmi.
Serafino, *Opere* (1516), f. 132^r

Secondary source:

Tu dormi, io ueglio, & uó perdendo ipassi
  E tormentando intorno alle tue mura,
Tu dormi, el mio dolor resueglia isassi,
  Et fó per gran pietá la luna oscura,
Tu dormi, ma non giá questi occhi lassi
  Doue el somno uenir mai se assicura,
Perche ogni cosa da mia mente fugge,
  Se non limagin tua, che mi destrugge.
Ibid., f. 132^v

First printed by Norman Ault, *Elizabethan Lyrics* (1925). The sources were identified, and their handling discussed, by A. M. Endicott (*RN*, xvii (1964), 301–3). The identification makes W's authorship highly probable, since he stands out, in his generation, as translator of Serafino's strambotti. He translates 'Ahime tu dormi' freely, preserving its sense. He also preserves its main structural feature, the repetition of the key phrase at the beginning of ll. 1, 3, and 5, a device sufficiently common in Serafino to be considered typical (cf. 'Biastemo', *Opere* (1516), f. 137ʳ). W adds to its emphasis by reintroducing it at the end of l. 7. He also strengthens the 'Tu dormi' motif by basing his 'Thou slepest ffast' throughout on Serafino's final version of it, 'Tu dormi quieta' (l. 5). The second strambotto, a companion piece to the first, and strikingly similar in sense and structure, contributes detail to W's strambotto (see notes to ll. 2 and 8).

1 *and I with woffull hart*] W's addition.

2] Based on Serafino's picture of the waking lover slackening his pace by his sleeping mistress's house (secondary source, ll. 1–2).

3–4] Free translation of Serafino's ll. 3–4. W's *darte* is an obvious development of Serafino's image of the love god. He omits the detail that the love god too is wakeful.

5–6] Free translation of Serafino's ll. 5–6. W drops the metaphor of wakeful cruelty. His *call and crye* is dependent on *con alta uoce/Vo palesando* (ll. 1–2).

7] W omits Serafino's l. 7, and uses instead *Credo* (cf. *methinkes*) from l. 8, together with the key phrase.
thou that] Ault wrongly emended to 'though thou' and in U, also unnecessarily, it was emended to 'though that thou'.

8] Free translation of Serafino's l. 8. Possibly, as Endicott suggests, *lyf to wast* derives less from the *tormentarmi* of the main source than from the *mi destrugge* of the secondary one. Cf. CCLIII.8.

CLXVIII

2 *spytte*] spite.

3 *noy*] annoy.

7 *grodge who lyst*] Cf. CXX.1.

CLXIX

15] Cf. LII.26

CLXX. The B text is the better, with the possible exception of the last word (l. 16), *loss* (D) being a more perfect rhyme.

3 *yee*] eye.

CLXXI. Presumably not by W. T entitles it: 'When aduersitie is once fallen, it is to late to beware.'

CLXXII. Hietsch (206–8) notes parallels with CLVIII and with the canzone by Petrarch on which it is based. See notes to CLVIII. But this poem is not directly based on Petrarch. The knot image (ll. 1, 24) is to be found, as Hietsch points out, in CLVIII.7; but W uses it elsewhere (e.g. CXVIII.8).

39 *shytt*] shut.

CLXXIII

3 *bot . . . lypp*] bit not then the lip, in sign of displeasure.

5 *in my boke*] Cf. the note on L.

There follows in B a fragment of a poem by Surrey, first printed *NQ* (1960), 368, and this quatrain.

> He that spares to speak hathe hardly his entent;
> He that speaks and speeds, his speakyng is well spent;
> He that speaks and speeds not, his spekyng is but lost;
> And yet speakyng wythe owt spedyng is but a small cost.

The next poem, signed B.G., but in the same handwriting as the other Blage poems, is here printed for the first time:

> *A remembrance of the dethe of the vertuus lady*
> *Quiene Kateryne dowager lat wyffe to the*
> *Lorde thomas seymor vncle to the kynge hys maieste*
>
> Tho I seyme ded unto the daslynge Iy
> of carnal man: who tastys nothynge but cley;
> yet doue I lyue and to the starry sky,
> fled from this fleshe, ful streyt haue tane the wey:
> Vnuourdly worlde thowe wast me to retayne
> wher naught i sawe but syn was had in pryce
> I thought it longe wythe the for to remayne
> and to thy loue thou kouldes me not entyce
> yet gaues thou me what so was in thy power
> as buety, welthe, in honor for to reayne
> ounspottyd fame unto my latys ower
> the raryst gyfte in erthe for to obtayne
> the wourdist prynce on londe that euer lyuyd
> whos famus brut hathe fyllyd the world so wyd
> for vertus sak hym selffe to me ioynyd
> in marriage puer to rest styl by his syd
> ye and for that yt symyd to me sum blot
> no frut to haue, lest that myght me deface
> thowe tydest me wythe a wyfely laweful knot
> to my dyer spouse of seymors wourdy race
> the bareyne wombe wythe blessynge yk was fylld
> fayr fruet browt fourthe yt hathe bothe lym and lyffe
> thus al was doune as I my selue wyld
> leuynge behynde a moulde to mak a wyffe
> yet was not this the game I ran to wyn
> Cryst was my marke and hym now haue I kaut
> whos dethe hathe payd the rannsom for my syn
> vayne is this worlde and all theryn is naut
>
> B.G.

There follow in B Surrey's poem 'Such wayward wayes hathe loue' and a poem which T placed among the poems of uncertain authorship, 'Yf Ryght be rakt and ouerron', but ascribed to Surrey in B.

CLXXIV. This poem is followed in B by the following words: 'finis/ffinis Vaux'. It is, however, quite unlike the known poems of Thomas, Lord Vaux, and the ascription may be mistaken. It belongs to the group of poems in D, generally, if on insufficient evidence, assumed to be W's.

CLXXV. The rhyme to the third line of each stanza is in the middle of the fourth (recure/insuere; blame/gam). The same stanza form, and a similar refrain, are used in CLIII.

4 *insuere*] insure, am assured.

5 *without cause causles*] without an offence and without a disease.

17 *myscheffe*] See Glossary.

25 *Causeles . . . cause me*].

26 *ffell*] feel.

29 *brynne*] burn.

CLXXVI. Written at the time of W's imprisonment in 1536, and referring to the execution of Anne Boleyn, According to *Crónica del Rey Enrico* (1874), 88, W watched the execution of Anne Boleyn and her lovers, expecting to share their fate; but S informs me that W from his cell could have seen only the execution of Anne, the others being executed on Tower Hill.

The Latin inscription at the head of the poem surrounds W's name with innocency, truth, and faith, and the adaptation of Ps. XVII.9 (Ps. XVI in the Vulgate) refers to the enemies that encompassed him. See L. 234.

1–10] These two stanzas are a rough translation of Seneca, *Phaedra*, 1125ff.

5 *circa Regna tonat*] *Phaedra*, 1140.

19 *vauore*] favour; the 'one instance of *v* for initial *f*' (K).

22 *yerne*] earn.

24 *Ber . . . sterne*] Cf. *Bouge of Courte*, ed. Dyce, 250: 'Holde vp the helme, loke vp, and lete God stere' (WMT).

CLXXVII. Possibly an adaptation of an Italian epigram.

3 *stere*] manage.

4 *foys*] foes.

6 *Doway*] Do away with, i.e. put off.

v. Poems from the Devonshire Manuscript

CLXXVIII. F (1.252) claims that the poem is signed with sprawling initials that resemble T.W. S deciphers them as Th W.

14 *yose*] use.

18 *leve . . . lape*] tell you plainly.

CLXXIX. This poem is similar in style, though inferior in quality, to LXVI. Both poems were first published in *The Court of Venus* and both were imitated

by John Hall in *The Court of Vertue*. There is good reason to believe that W
wrote both, but this might have been written by a clever imitator.

14 *other*] others.

CLXXX

1] Cf. Stevens, 360: 'I Love, loved and loved wolde I be' (WMT). But here
'love' is a noun.

4 *To love so will*] A quibble on *well* and *will*.

6 *vnhappe*] unhappy.

12 *leve*] live. Cf. Stevens, 424: 'leve in payne' (WMT).

13 *Thes*] This.

20 *it*] i.e. will or sexual satisfaction.

21 *But . . . causer*] Cf. CXLI.74

23 *greve*] grief.

CLXXXI. F (1.267) says that the poem is followed by the sign denoting W's
composition. Although it is doubtful whether the sign can be interpreted in
this way, and although a woman is supposed to be speaking, it appears to be
in W's style. Nott prints the stanzas in the wrong order.

1 *Farewell all my wellfare*] Cf. Stevens, p. 397; 'Adew, all my welfare!' (WMT).

2 *My . . . awry*] Proverbial: cf. *ODEP*, p. 346 (WMT).

21 *most it grevyd*] The emendation improves the sense and rhythm of the line.

22 *leyde . . . borow*] laid in pledge. Cf. Chaucer, *T & C*, ii, 963, and *CT*, A
1622 (WMT).

23 *falshode*] Nott conj. that W wrote *falsed*.

24] Cf. Chaucer, *LGW*, 666 (WMT).

CLXXXII. F (11.145) praises the freshness of feeling and simplicity of lan-
guage and says that it is obviously W's. But to others the poem is common-
place and its authorship is unknown.

16 *humbly*] Perhaps this should be pronounced with three syllables.

CLXXXIII. C. E. Nelson, *MLR*, lviii (1963), 60–3, suggested that this poem
echoes Ovid, *Amores*, 1.2, 1–4:

> Esse quid hoc dicam, quod tam mihi dura videntur
> strata, neque in lecto pallia nostra sedent,
> et vaccus somno noctem, quam longa, peregi,
> lassaque versati corporis ossa dolent?

1 *What . . . thys?*] Cf. Lydgate, 'Floure of Curtesy', 68 (WMT).

CLXXXIV. This poem, with a varied refrain and lengthening lines, is not
quite regular in form: in half the stanzas the fourth line has five stresses; in
the others, four.

13 *on*] one.

23 *wasse*] was.

28 *preve*] prove.

29 *As . . . leve*] This means either 'as men marry such fickle creatures as women', or, taking the words with the previous line 'as men take their wives on trust and discover what they are like after the marriage ceremony'.

CLXXXV. As four of the neighbouring poems in D are ascribed to W (CLXXXIII, CLXXXIV, CLXXXVI, CLXXXVII) and this one is not, it is unlikely to be his.

11 *Vnwysse*] unwise.

28 *poore degre*] Cf. CXLVI.53.

CLXXXVI. F (II.146) regards this, with some justification, as the 'most beautiful little song' in D.

CLXXXVII. Source:

> O cameretta, che già fusti un porto
>   A le gravi tempeste mie dïurne,
>   Fonte se' or di lagrime notturne
> Che 'l dí celate per vergogna porto!
> O letticciuol, che requie eri e conforto
>   In tanti affanni, di che dogliose urne
>   Ti bagna Amor con quelle mani eburne
> Solo vèr' me crudeli a sí gran torto!
> Né pur il mio secreto e 'l mio rïposo
>   Fuggo, ma piú me stesso e 'l mio pensero,
>   Che, seguendo 'l, tal or levommi a volo;
> E 'l vulgo, a me nemico et odïoso,
>   (Che 'l pensò mai?) per mio refugio chero:
>   Tal paura ho di ritrovarmi solo.
>
>   Petrarch, *Rime*, ccxxxiv

The source seems to have been recognized by Puttenham (176), who cited W's first stanza as an example of *Irmus* (suspension). It was properly identified by I. Zocco (*Petrarchismo e Petrarchisti in Inghilterra* (Palermo, 1906), 26). Possibly Petrarch's ideas reached W through an earlier imitation, the lover's sleeplessness being a very common Petrarchan topic. He builds chiefly on *e 'l mio riposo/Fuggo*, and on the images of *cameretta* and *letticciuol*. W's antitheses have a basis in Petrarch's first quatrain, but he develops them into a long series, so that, in this respect, his poem resembles rather 'Pace non trovo' (the source of XXVI). This is, in fact, like LXXXVI, a very free imitation: see the study by Hietsch (194–9). Title in T: 'The louer to his bed, with describing of his vnquiet state.'

1–7] W's antitheses are an elaboration of the comparatively unemphatic one in Petrarch's ll. 1–2, *porto/tempeste* (which is followed by *notturne/di*, not used by W, in ll. 3–4).

1 *The restfull place*] Corresponds to *cameretta* (l. 1) rather than to *letticciuol* (l. 5). It is also influenced by *requie* (l. 5).

2 *salve*] Cf. *conforto* (l. 5).

6, 7 *place of slepe, bed*] Cf. *letticciuol* (l. 5).

7] W's refrain line is built up from phrases in Petrarch's ll. 3, 7 and *e 'l mio riposo/Fuggo* (ll. 9–10). Cf. Chaucer, 'Complaint unto Pity', 10 (WMT).

8–21] Show practically no further debt to Petrarch except in the refrain lines.

15–16, 20] Hietsch (199) suggests the possible influence of Petrarch's ll. 9–10.

CLXXXVIII. F (II.148) says this poem is in W's style, although she admits that l. 9 'suggests another author'. R. L. Greene, who includes the poem in *The Early English Carols*, points out in *RES* (1964), 178, that the first lines are the burden of the carol.

21 *follow the trace*] Cf. VIII.25 (F).

34 *than . . . tell*] Cf. Chaucer, *T & C*, v, 445 (WMT).

35 *as . . . gospell*] Cf. *ODEP*, p. 672 (WMT).

CLXXXIX. Koeppel (71) suggests that this sounds like a memory of Petrarch, *Rime*, cclii, ll. 1–3; but Baldi (234) rejects the suggestion. W's *syghe* and *synge* closely resemble Petrarch's *piango* and *canto*; but the resemblance could be simply generic. The phrase from l. 2 of Petrarch's sonnet – 'E temo e spero' – is found also in *Rime*, cxxxiv, translated by W (XXVI).

6 *mevyd*] moved.

20 *And . . . new*] Cf. CIX.11. But it was a cliché.

CXC. For a possible source, and the connection between this and other 'patience' poems, see note to XXXIX, etc., above. As a description of *painfull patience*, it is conceivably a continuation, in more querulous terms, of XXXXIX.

1–2] Cf. Serafino's 'Canzona de la Patientia', ll. 1–2, and XXXIX.19–20.

1 *of all my smart*] in all my pain. For this use of *of*, cf. XXXIX.19.

11 *withowt desart*] without having deserved (to 'smart').

25 *ere*] ear.

CXCI. This poem is in the same handwriting as CXC, but is not a continuation. Patience is not mentioned once in the three stanzas, whereas it is mentioned eleven times in CXC.

This is followed in D by 'In faythe methynkes yt ys no Ryght' (Muses No. 119). It was printed as W's by F; but, as S has shown, these two stanzas are part of a poem, continued on the next page, by A.I. – possibly, as F thinks, Sir Anthony Lee.

CXCII

17 *sew*] sue.

30 *fortune ys frayle*] Cf. *ODEP*, p. 221 (WMT).

34 *trowgh*] truth.

CXCIII. Entitled in T: 'The louer describeth his being taken with sight of his loue.'

5–6 *Thorow . . . ranne*] Cf. Chaucer, *CT*, A 1096–7 (WMT).

6] Nott (549) compares Petrarch, *Rime*, ii, 7–8 and iii, 10; but these are commonplaces.

8 *pale and wanne*] Cf. CCXIII.8 and Chaucer, *T & C*, iv, 235 (WMT). Nott again suggests a Petrarchan echo, but without giving a reference.

CXCIV. This was printed as a doubtful poem in M. But it is at least as likely to be W's as many of the D poems printed as his by Nott and F.

CXCV

4 *pene*] pen.

8 *sleper*] Cf. CCXXX.7.

10 *bowrnyng*] burning.

22 *ner*] not.

CXCVI. Padelford (xxxix), shows that this poem belongs to a class derived ultimately from the *chanson à personnages* or *chanson dramatique* in which a poet listens to the complaint of a young woman, or, at a later period, to the complaint of a male lover.

1–4] The song of the jilted man.

6–10] Cf. e.g. a poem quoted by Padelford, op.cit., p. xxxix:

> This other day I hard a may
> ryght peteusly complayne.

46 *Armeles*] Nott, followed by Chambers, plausibly emended to 'Am left'; but the MS. reading, meaning 'defenceless', is not impossible.

CXCVII

3 *wene*] ween.

18 *falshed*] falsehood.

19 *game*] This is the reading of D and may receive some support from XXIX. 11 'twist ernest and game'. But CLXXXVI.4 'greffe and grame' could be used to support the emendation 'grame'.

26 *concyle*] reconcile (K), not 'conceal'.

CXCVIII. F (II.153) states that this poem continues the argument of CXCVII; but the poems appear to be quite unrelated.

16 *reuthe*] ruth.

18 *ones*] once.

23 *Thankyd be fortune*] Cf. XXXVII.8 (F).

25 *or*] ere.

32 *loves*] A dissyllable. The poet is contrasting the grounded grace of a permanent relationship with the philandering of his earlier years.

CXCIX

1 *sew*] sue.

8 *well in worthe*] F interprets 'of good omen, or important'; but it seems to mean 'in good part'.

CC. F (11.76) remarks that this 'Epigram is in the form of a madrigal'; that the 'style and treatment of the poem mark it as a late composition'; and that the 'merits of such poems as these easily procure for W a front place amongst sixteenth-century lyrists'. All three remarks are questionable.

9 *or*] This could introduce the second of two alternatives, but is more likely to be 'ere'.

CCI.

2 *reioyce*] rejoice at.

CCII. F (11.153) suggests that the poem 'may refer to W's parting from Anne Boleyn'; but for this there is no evidence.

2 *weyne*] wean.

8 *womanhede*] womanhood.

15 *cruche*] crouch.

20 *Suche . . . fforget*] F (11.154) regards this line as a prelude to the next poem; but in CCII the poet determines to forget his foolish love, and in CCIII the poet – not certainly the same one – is urging the lady not to forget his long service.

CCIII. The critics are generally agreed that this is one of W's most perfect poems, although there is no direct evidence of his authorship.

CCIV

4 *thether*] thither.

CCV

3 *lake*] lack.

6 *spekes*] i.e. speak: W is thinking of the lute rather than the strings.

18 *wryeke*] wreak.

20 *To*] Most editors accept Nott's emendation 'Do'. But W is contrasting the songs which he writes to punish his mistress with the blameless lute.

23 *nedes*] The copyist intended to write 'nides'.

29 *mysdown*] An odd spelling for 'misdone'.

31 *bygown*] begun.

38–9 *Yet . . . agayne*] W implies that he has found a new mistress.

CCVI. Source:

> Viuo sol di mirarti hai dura impresa,
> Tu te nascondi, e conuerrá che io mora,
> Ma se saluar mi poi con poca spesa,
> À che pur fuggi, fuggi un che te adora,
> Che só, se al uiuer mio non dai difesa
> Io moro, & tu poi me non campi un hora,
> Che lun per laltro uiue, & pasce il core,
> Io del tuo aspecto, & tu del mio dolore,
>
> Serafino, *Opere* (1516), f. 125ᵛ

The source was identified by Koeppel (72–3). Except in l. 4, W adheres closely to Serafino, working line by line. Title in T: 'To his louer to loke vpon him.' Some of T's variants may derive from a better MS. than D.

1] Translation of *Viuo sol di mirarti* (l. 1). W omits *hai dura impresa*. *thi sight*] i.e. the sight of thee (*mirarti*).

2–3] Translation of Serafino's ll. 2–3.

4] Substituted for Serafino's l. 4.

5–6] Translation of Serafino's ll. 5–6, W simplifying the grammar.

7–8] Translation of Serafino's ll. 7–8. W's use of *thy* for *il* in l. 7 seems illogical: Serafino describes a reciprocal living and feeding.

7 *ton*] The one.

The remaining D poems are, with the exception of CCXIX, written in a single hand. Those peculiar to D are interspersed with numerous poems known to be W's. But as was shown, M 256, the poems are not inscribed 'T.V.', as F believed (II.155) but 'FS' = Finis. F also suggested that the poems were copied into the MS. as soon as they were composed. The evidence, however, seems to show that all this group of poems were copied in a short space of time when another MS. became available. There is no reason to think that they were copied in the order of composition. Indeed, since the order of poems common to E differs from that of E, the order of both MSS., if either, cannot be chronological. The first ten poems common to D and E in this part of the MS. are in the following order: I, XIX, XXXVII, III, LVII, XL, LXIX, LXVIII, LV, XXII.

CCVII. F (II.74) suggests that this epigram is a translation. As it is preceded by twelve of W's known poems and followed by four others, it seems probable that he is the author.

3 *he*] Despair.

8 *Amyds my helpe*] Implying, perhaps, that the poet is close to obtaining his desires, though always cheated of them.

CCIX

5 *Boteles for bote*] Without obtaining any reward.

9 *But ... abed*] Cf. CLXXI.23 and Chaucer, 'Complaint of Venus', II.3. 'As wake abedde, and fasten at the table' (WMT).

27 *pleasant game*] Ironical.

ccx. Koeppel (74) mentions parallels, not very substantial, with Serafino.

9 *song*] sung.

10 *Nother*] Neither.

11 +] A line is apparently missing in this stanza.

13 *withouten taste*] Untasted (F).

32 *quite*] quit.

40 *undre miste*]? misunderstood.

43 *For . . . bene*] Cf. Tilley, B118 (WMT).

ccxi. W is urging his former mistress to treat her new lovers as she has treated him.

3 *chaung*] change.

7 *be kinde*] see Glossary.

14 *To*] Too.

ccxii

1 *The . . . nere*] Cf. Chaucer, 'The Parlement of Foules', 1: 'The lyf so short, the crafte so long to lerne'. (WMT).

21 *That . . . remayne*] The poet's pain is undeserved and will continue, though without a cause.

ccxiii. First printed, with some errors, by F, who suspected it was not W's.

7 *prive morninges*] privy mournings.

28 *colde as enye stonne*] Proverbial, see Tilley S 876.

31 *her*] Although this emendation makes better sense than 'our', the suicide of Lucrece was much debated by theologians and it is possible that the author of this poem either did not realize that she lived before the Christian era, or else regarded her as a kind of forerunner of Christian martyrs.

ccxiv. Possible source:

Voi ch' ascoltate in rime sparse il suono
Di quei sospiri ond' io nudriva 'l core
In su 'l mio primo giovenile errore,
Quand' era in parte altr' uom da quel ch' i' sono;
Del vario stile, in ch' io piango e ragiono
Fra le vane speranze e 'l van dolore,
Ove sia chi per prova intenda amore,
Spero trovar pietà non che perdono.
Ma ben veggio or sí come al popol tutto
Favola fui gran tempo, onde sovente
Di me medesmo meco mi vergogno:
E del mio vaneggiar vergogna è 'l frutto,
E 'l pentersi, e 'l conoscer chiaramente
Che quanto piace al mondo è breve sogno.

Petrarch, *Rime*,

The possible source was identified by Baldi (235), who suggested that W freely expanded Petrarch's first sonnet. Hietsch (208–11) then made a detailed comparison. Two questions remain open: whether the poem is by W, and whether its similarity to Petrarch's is more than generic. In favour of W's authorship, is, perhaps, the use of the ottava rima stanza, and against it such archaic phrasing as appears in l. 14. If the poem be his, then evidently he intended, like Petrarch, to collect and 'send abroad' a 'book' of poems. Like Petrarch's the poem is part preface, part envoy, On the other hand, the similarity does not extend much further than this. There is really no marked detail in common between the two which cannot be referred to the traditional palinode or retraction. Thus references to youthful vanity, repented in later years, and pleas for the reader's indulgence, are common stock: see, for example, the *envoy* to Chaucer's 'Complaint of Venus' (ll. 73–82). The poem was first printed by F.

2] Cf. *Voi ch' ascoltate* (l. 1) and *il suono/Di quei sospiri* (ll. 1–2).

3–4 *your herte . . . pytie*] Cf. *Spero trovar pietà* (l. 8).

5–6] Cf. *'l mio primo giovenile errore* (l. 3).

9–16] Hietsch (210) compares W's general drift, his *good entente*, etc., with Petrarch's ll. 12–14.

9 *redres*] readers.

24 *Perdon me then*] Cf. *Spero trovar . . . perdono* (l. 8).
  rudelye tho I indyte] Probably not derived from Petrarch's *vario stile* (l. 5), but rather from the conventional medieval English 'modesty' topic.

29–30] Cf. *'l mio primo giovenile errore* (l. 3), *E 'l pentersi* (l. 13).

CCXV

14 *perte*] part, but with a possible quibble on Fr. *perte*.

CCXVI

16 *eyes*] The emendation avoids a mixed metaphor.

19 *What . . . trothe*] Cf. 11.1

20 *repreffe*] reproof.

31 *hate*] The copyist substituted *crueltye* from the previous line. The emendation is an antithesis of love and rhymes with what appears to be the correct word in l. 33.

CCXVII. This sonnet is metrically smoother than W's translations, but whether this is because he was not translating or because it was written later it is impossible to determine.

1 *hard*] heard.

4 *pease*] appease.

13 *of kinde*] natural.

14 *That . . . minde*] Cf. *ODEP*, p. 724 (WMT). Koeppel (70) compares Petrarch's 'Se 'l dolce sguardo di costei m' ancide' (*Rime*, clxxxiii), ll. 12–14.

Femina è cosa mobil per natura;
Ond'io so ben ch'un amoroso stato
In cor di donna picciol tempo dura.

CCXVIII. First printed, with several misreadings, by F.

4 *peakes*] The meaning is disputed. Harrier, arguing correctly that a woman is saying that it is a small loss to lose a suitor who is put off by a single refusal, concludes that 'peakes' means 'foolish fellows'. M glossed the word as 'piques, vexations'. It is easier to wipe away a vexation than a fool.

CCXIX. The quatrains are linked in pairs by common rhymes; and the third line of the first stanza reappears as the fourth line of the second, etc.

3 *ons I had*] Cf. CLVI.5.

CCXX. First printed by F. The speaker, as she points out (11.165) is a young woman; and, indeed, the poem may be by a woman. R. L. Greene printed the poem in *The Early Carols* (Oxford, 1938). The opening couplet constitutes the burden.

28 *hollye*] wholly (F interpreted the word as *holly* because she had misread *eke* as *oak* in the previous line).

33 *To ... wise*] Cf. *ODEP*, p. 188 (WMT).

CCXXI. First printed by F, who misread *remedye* as *comedye*.

CCXXII. First printed by F. This tissue of wise saws and modern instances could be by W, or by his friend Bryan.

6 *But ... thinckes*] Cf. *ODEP*, p. 199 (WMT).

22 *Fayre ... fayne*] Cf. *ODEP*, p. 188 (WMT).

24 *tyme ... trothe*] Cf. Tilley, T338.

29 *To ... wordes*] Cf. CCXX.33 and note.

36 *lyfles*] Is it a ghost speaking?
at ... place] somewhere or other.

37 *were*] where.

42 *And ... mowse*] ? and has written something to please all tastes.

CCXXIII. The versification of this sonnet is much smoother than that of W's translations. T entitles it: 'The louer abused renownseth loue.'

7–8] 'Giving me no choice not to agree with her that I might remain her man.'
W's mistress, while scorning his love, wanted to keep him in her clutches.

9 *ye*] W moves from the third person to a direct address.

CCXXIV. Probable source:

Fvi serrato nel dolore
Con la morte à canto à canto
Ha ha ha men rido tanto

Chio son uiuo e son difuore.
Viddi casa altiera e illustra,   5
   Che difuor rende splendore,
   Ma ogni arbor non dimostra
   Per la scorza el suo ualore,
   Perche drento con dolore
   Se sospira in ogni canto.   10
      Ha ha ha men rido tanto
Da mia sorte fui conducto
   In questa aspra e ria pregione,
   Fra color che han perso al tucto
   Lintellecto e la ragione,
   Doue è gran confusione   15
   Chiusa stá sotto un bel manto.
      Ha ha ha men rido tanto
Trouai scripto ne lintrata
   Tal parole à lettre doro,
   Quí di stento è gran derrata
   Crudeltate è mio thesoro,   20
   Dono morte per ristoro
   Per seruitio, eterno pianto,
      Ha ha ha men rido tanto
Ò tú chentri in questa stanza
   Che hai la uia smarrita e torta,
   Lassa fore ogni speranza.   25
   Quí uirtú conuien sia morta,
   Prima chentri in questa porta
   Ti dispoglia tutto uanto.
      Ha ha ha men rido tanto
Ne lintrar sii bene accorto
   Che mai piú ritorni al passo,   30
   Gusterai dun uiuer morto
   Dun calar sempre piú basso,
   Ne mai piú ritroui el passo,
   Forse non per uia de incanto.
      Ha ha ha men rido tanto
Giù per linfernale stygge   35
   Non fur mai tanti tormenti,
   Lachrimando ognun saffligge
   Vanno al ciel gliaspri lamenti,
   Ad ognhor per tutto senti
   Miserere con gran pianto,   40
      Ha ha ha men rido tanto
Doue in fume se risolue
   Ogni bon seruir con fede,
   La speranza tutta in poluc
   Fra li uenti ognhor si uede,
   Quanto è misero chi crede   45
   Hauer ben per aspectar tanto.
      Ha ha ha men rido tanto
Non pensar che sia fino oro
   Tutto quel che in terra luce,
   Spesso un bello & degno alloro

Tristo e mal fructo produce,   50
Son piú uoce assai che nuce
Non è bon creder cotanto.
   Ha ha ha men rido tanto
Spesse uolte in un bel prato
Stá fra ifiorla serpe ascosa,
Resta assai spesso gabbato   55
Chi se fida in ogni cosa,
Se la fé me si noiosa
Haueró pur nobil uanto.
   Ha ha ha men rido tanto
Gran thesoro a pretioso
Fra li sterpi e fra li sassi,   60
Spesse uolte stá nascoso
E fra lochi humili e bassi,
Tal per pian mena li passi
Chun gran spino el pié glihá franto.
   Ha ha ha men rido tanto
Ben me accorsi del ueneno   65
Del paese pien di tigna,
Che non era bon terreno
Dá posserui piantar uigna,
Ma la mia sorte maligna
Mi condusse in simil canto.   70
   Ha ha ha men rido tanto
Chio son uiuo e son difore.

Serafino, *Opere* (1516), f. 202^v–204^r

The probable source was identified by Koeppel (73). Common to both poems are the delight in a newly won freedom from grief and pain, the telling contrast of past and present, and, most noticeably, the laughing refrain. A similar refrain, perhaps also known to W, is used in Serafino's derisory attack 'Contra Vna Vecchia':

A ha ha chi non ridesse
Duna si difforme e uecchia etc.

(Opere, (1516), f. 204^v)

Except in the openings there is little similarity of detail between W's poem and Serafino's. W's account of his woes, taken as a whole, is not, except in general tone, particularly like Serafino's more protracted one, with its lurid visit to a Dantesque Hell. In ll. 13–15 he may be generalizing from the detailed illustrations of deception. But the chief difference between them is in the statement of the sources of sorrow. Serafino writes generally of an unspecified sorrow (probably, in fact, his grievance against Cardinal Ascanio), and he makes no reference to love or women. W writes a love complaint, with particular reference to his usual wily mistress. If, as seems probable, this is a free adaptation of Serafino's poem, it is a successful one, deserving the praise conferred on it by Tillyard (159).

1–2 *Tanglid, Opprest with payne*] Cf. Serafino's l. 1.

2–4] These lines, as well as the talk of *wofull dayes*, etc., which follows (l. 8 f.), may be regarded as a free expansion of Serafino's l. 1.

6] Probably a free rendering of Serafino's l. 4.

13–15] Probably a generalization from the various passages in which Serafino describes the deceptiveness of appearances, e.g. in terms of houses and trees (ll. 5–10), the olive and its fruit (ll. 49–52), fields and flowers (ll. 53–8).

19–22] Have little basis in Serafino's, unless *Hope* be based on *speranza* (l. 25).

19 *To*] too.

31–4] A further development of Serafino's ll. 1 and 4.

31] Proverbial: see Tilley, B380.

33] Proverbial: see Tilley, B557, and cf. XIII.14.

CCXXV

15 *so small gaine*] This continues the theme of CCXXIII.

30+] A line is apparently missing.

38 *be kinde*] see Glossary.

CCXXVI. A reader – possibly the owner – of D has written above this poem 'lerne but to syng yt'. In A it is inscribed 'To Smithe of Camden', which, as Hughey (II.8) suggested, was probably the name of a tune. W. Maynard (*RES* (1967), 162–3) has argued that the reference is to a broadside ballad about the suicide of Henry Smith, son of Thomas Smith of Camden, as described in Foxe's *Acts and Monuments*.

The version in A runs together ll. 1 and 2, 4 and 5, in each stanza, thus forming a quatrain with internal rhymes.

CCXXVII. F (II.48) says that this is adapted from Serafino, but there seems no evidence for this.

2 *olde prouerbe*] Cf. Chaucer, *CT*, B 2244: 'He hasteth wel that wisely kan abide' (WMT). F, however, compares:

> Better is it to suffer and fortune abide
> Than hastily to clime and sodenly to slyde.

3 *my lady*] F remarks that this, 'of course, refers to Fortune'. This seems unlikely.

5 *tarrye the tyde*] Cf. *ODEP*, p. 619 (WMT).

6 *ye*] The lady speeds well, but not her lover.

13–14 *to be . . . obtayne*] For you to refuse me bluntly, than to ask me to wait, and never let me obtain my desires.

CCXXVIII. The second and third stanzas are linked by a common rhyme, as are the fourth and fifth, and the fifth and the sixth. The opening lines of each stanza repeat words from the conclusion of the previous one.

CCXXIX. For possible source, and the connection between this and W's other 'patience' poems, see note to XXXIX.

4 *truthe*] i.e. the utterance of truth.

6 *Hereafter . . . yet*] Cf. CXXXII.7 and Tilley, H439 (WMT).

CCXXX

7 *slipper hold*] Cf. CXCV.8 and 'La Belle Dame', 262 (WMT).

16 *or*] ere.

28 *Wythe ... remedye*] Cf. CXXVI.4–5.

29 *on*] one.

CCXXXI

6 *That*] What

CCXXXII. Source:

> Qual piú diversa e nova
> Cosa fu mai in qualche stranio clima,
> Quella, se ben s' estima,
> Piú mi rasembra; a tal son giunto, Amore.
> Là, onde il dí ven fore   5
> Vola un augel, che sol, senza consorte,
> Di volontaria morte
> Rinasce e tutto a viver si rinova.
> Cosí sol si ritrova
> Lo mio voler, e cosí 'n su la cima   10
> De' suoi alti pensicri al sol si volve,
> E cosí si risolve
> E cosí torna al suo stato di prima;
> Arde e more, e riprende i nervi suoi,
> E vive poi con la fenice a prova.   15
> Una petra è sí ardita
> Là per l' indico mar, che da natura
> Tragge a sé il ferro, e 'l fura
> Dal legno in guisa ch' e' navigi affonde.
> Questo prov' io fra l' onde   20
> D' amaro pianto, ché quel bello scoglio
> Ha co 'l suo duro orgoglio
> Condutta ove affondar convien mia vita:
> Cosí l' alma ha sfornita
> (Furando 'l cor, che fu già cosa dura,   25
> E me tenne un, ch' or son diviso e sparso)
> Un sasso a trar piú scarso
> Carne che ferro. O cruda mia ventura,
> Che 'n carne essendo veggio trarmi a riva
> Ad una viva dolce calamita!   30
>
> Petrarch, *Rime*, cxxxv, stanzas 1 and 2

The source was identified by Koeppel (68), who shows that W develops freely the train of thought in the first two stanzas of Petrarch's canzone. Writing a slighter poem, he omits the remaining stanzas in which other wonders of nature are described and the lover compared to them.

1] Nott (586) suggested that W 'unconsciously perhaps imitated' Petrarch's 'Chi vuol veder quantunque po natura' (*Rime*, ccxlviii, 1). But the idea of nature's wonders is also contained in the source discovered by Koeppel.

5–8] Based on Petrarch's ll. 1–4. W introduces *monstruous* in place of *diversa e nova*, deriving it probably from *stranio*.

9–12] Based on Petrarch's ll. 16–19, which describe the effect of the magnetic stone supposed to be in the Gulf of Bengal (mentioned by various ancient authorities, e.g. Ptolemy, *Geography*, vii, 2).

13–16] Based on Petrarch's ll. 20–30.

17–20] Based on Petrarch's ll. 5–8, describing the phoenix.

21–4] Based on Petrarch's ll. 9–15.

CCXXXIII. The version in *The Gorgeous Gallery* is entitled 'The Lover having his beloved in suspition declareth his doutfull minde.' Although not published until 1578, this miscellany contains poems of a much earlier date.

VI. Poems from the Arundel Manuscript

CCXXXIV. This was ascribed to W by Nott, but not included by F.
18] The varied refrain, as given in A, is superior to the unvaried refrain given by D.

CCXXXV. The version of this poem in T is printed among the poems of uncertain authorship with the title 'Of the lovers vnquiet state'. But in A the poem is written on the same page as CCXXXIV. In H the version of the first stanza is entitled 'A Ridle' and it is followed by this answer:

> Love thou hast which thou dost lacke,
>   With goodwill granted of her treuly;
> But yet to graunt her frendes be slacke.
> So ye be doinge and yet schasely:
> Ffor slothe and fere you cane not wyne.
> So you ar readie newe to begyne.

CCXXXVI. Source:

> Rotta è l' alta colonna e 'l verde lauro
>   Che facean ombra al mio stanco pensero;
>   Perduto ho quel che ritrovar non spero
>   Dal borea a l' austro o dol mar indo al mauro.
> Tolto m' hai, Morte, il mio doppio tesauro
>   Che mi fea viver lieto e gire altero;
>   E ristorar no 'l può terra né impero,
>   Né gemma orïental, né forza d' auro.
> Ma, se consentimento è di destino,
>   Che posso io piú se no' aver l' alma trista,
>   Umidi gli occhi sempre e 'l viso chino?
> Oh nostra vita ch' è sí bella in vista,
>   Com' perde agevolmente in un mattino
>   Quel che 'n molti anni a gran pena s' acquista!
>
>   Petrarch, *Rime*, cclxix

The source of W's imitation was identified by Nott (544), who also pointed out that his departures from Petrarch are explained by his own situation.

Modern scholars have not followed T in labelling this a love poem. It has generally been accepted that W adapts Petrarch's lament for the deaths of his patron Giovanni Colonna and of his mistress Laura into his own lament at the fall and execution of his patron Cromwell. Foxwell (11.53) and Tillyard (171–2) are agreed, Chambers (131) thinks it 'not improbable', while only Berdan (471–2) is, as usual, sceptical. For the story of Cromwell's fall in 1540, and W's trial for treason in 1541, see L, 172–210. Mason (197) produces strong evidence from two contemporary MSS. confirming the well-known account of W's shedding tears when, on the scaffold, Cromwell bad him farewell: see *Chronicle of King Henry VIII*, trans. M. A. S. Hume (London, 1889), 104. There can be no doubt of the genuineness of his mourning, which fits in well with Petrarch's. His additions to Petrarch, notably in ll. 7–8 and 12–14, seem to relate to his imprisonment in the Tower (the result of the machinations of Cromwell's and his own enemies) and his anticipation of death. The only remark difficult to explain in personal terms is the self-hatred expressed in l. 11. W certainly was not directly responsible for Cromwell's fall. It could be that the failure of his mission in Spain (1537–9) or his service in France (1539–40), in which he had to collaborate with Cromwell's enemy the Duke of Norfolk, made him feel that he had indirectly contributed to it. W's adaptation has been discussed by Lever (32–3), Mason (196–7), Hietsch (176–81), Muir (L. 230), and Guss (35–6).

F. M. Padelford takes this as an example of a late sonnet in which 'the reformation of the iambic pentameter line has been essentially accomplished' (*The Poems of . . . Surrey*, rev. ed. (Seattle, 1928), 47–8). Title in T: 'The louer lamentes the death of his loue.'

1] Cf. *Rotta è l' alta colonna* (l. 1). W omits *e 'l verde lauro*, a punning allusion to Laura which could have no meaning for him. Baldi (236) also finds an echo of

> Glorïosa columna, in cui s' appoggia
> Nostra speranza . . .
>   (*Rime*, x, 1–2)

This would supply W's *Lent*.

2] An adaptation of Petrarch's l. 2, with *staye* substituted for Petrarch's metaphor *ombra*.

3] A free translation, put into the third person, of Petrarch's personal statement (l. 3).

4 *From East to west*] Cf. *Dal borea a l' austro* (l. 4).
still seking though he went] Substituted for *o dal mar indo al mauro* (l. 4).

5–6] Paraphrase of Petrarch's ll. 5–6. W omits the *doppio tesauro* metaphor, using in its place one which seems to be influenced by Petrarch's earlier tree metaphor (ll. 1–2). His *happe* stands in place of *Morte*, anticipating *destino* (l. 9).

6 *bark and rynde*] Cf. Chaucer, *R of R*, 7169; *T & C*, iv, 1139.

7–8] Substituted for Petrarch's ll. 7–8. Tillyard (172) relates this addition specifically to W's imprisonment 'when he was in fear of death'.

9–10] Translation of ll. 9–10.

11] Paraphrase of l. 11, W's reference to his *penne* and *voyce* being original.

12–14] W's expression of mental and physical pain, of self-hatred and of longing for death is substituted for Petrarch's ll. 12–14 (in which he laments in general elegiac tones that what has taken years to acquire can be lost in half a day).

CCXXXVII. Entitled in T: 'A riddle of a gift given by a Ladie.' The answer to the riddle is 'a kiss'.

CCXXXVIII. This double sonnet is entitled in T: 'The louer describeth his restlesse state.'

11 *place assynd*] Cf. CCXXXI.28 and CCXXXVI.7.

14 *no . . . race*] Cf. CCXLIV.8 and note.

21 *trifling*] This reading, contrasted with 'weightie matters great' (19), makes better sense than 'tasting'.

25 *assigne*] Referring back to l. 11.

CCXXXIX. This is doubtless the argument to a metrical version of a psalm. It is probably addressed to the Earl of Surrey. It follows XCIV in A and it would be an appropriate argument to that psalm. But there are several missing leaves at this point in the MS., and there are several other psalms to which it might refer (e.g. 7, 57, 59, 69).

CCXL. Translated from Seneca's *Thyestes*, 391 ff.

> Stet quicunque volet potens
> Aulæ culmine lubrico:
> Me dulcis saturet quies
> Obscuro positus loco
> Leni perfruar otio
> Nulla nota Quiritibus
> Ætas per tacitum fluat.
> Sic cum transierint mei
> Nullo cum strepitu dies,
> Plebeius moriar senex.
> Illi mors gravis incubat,
> Qui notus nimis omnibus
> Ignotus moritur sibi.

Marvell has a neater, but less powerful, version of the same lines; and Cowley also translated them. T entitles the poem: 'Of the meane and sure estate.'

VII. Poems from Minor Manuscripts

CCXLI. Title in T: 'Of such as had forsaken him.' Written, probably, just before, or during, W's last imprisonment.

1 *Luckes*] Spelt *Lux* in T, possibly quibbling on *lux* and *luck*.

CCXLII. Source:

> Occhi, piangete; accompagnate il core,
> Che di vostro fallir morte sostene. –
> Cosí sempre facciamo; e ne conviene
> Lamentar piú l' altrui che 'l nostro errore. –
> Già prima ebbe per voi l' entrata Amore
> Là onde ancor, come in suo albergo, vene. –
> Noi gli aprimmo la via per quella spene
> Che mosse d' entro da colui che more. –
> Non son, com a voi par, le ragion pari :
> Ché pur voi foste ne la prima vista
> Del vostro e del suo mal cotanto avari. –
> Or questo è quel che piú ch' altro n' attrista;
> Ch' e' perfetti giudicii son sí rari,
> E d' altrui colpa altrui biasmo s' acquista. –
>
> Petrarch, *Rime*, lxxxiv

The source of this adaptation was identified by Padelford (113). The first three lines derive directly from Petrarch's sonnet, the rest being a free development of his attempt to blame the eyes for the fact that he is dying from love and to exonerate the heart. The dialogue form of the original is not used, and so the eyes' counter-accusation is given no voice. The familiar Petrarchan argument (ll. 5–8) that love enters through the eyes and so penetrates to the heart is not fully followed out. The prophecy of suffering is added (ll. 6–8).

1–2] Translation of Petrarch's ll. 1–2.

3] Based on Petrarch's l. 5, in which he blames the eyes for admitting love.
him] i.e. the heart.

CCXLIII. This appears on f. xxxiii in P along with the previous poem and on the page following two known W poems CCXLI and CXVIII.

CCXLIV. Title in T: 'Wiat being in prison, to Brian.' The poem was probably written during W's last imprisonment. See note on l. 8. For Brian see CVII and note.

6 *Mallice . . . have*] W implies that, although a sinner, he was innocent of the charges levelled against him and that Bonner's motives were not those he professed to have. See *L*, 63 ff., 178 ff.

8 *the . . . remayne*] W uses the same proverbial image in his Defence. See *L*, 193.

CCXLV. This poem is ascribed to W in H; but T prints a poem with a number of common stanzas as Surrey's. The version that follows is from P; T omits stanzas 3, 5, and 8, and adds a stanza after 6.

> As oft as I behold and see
> The soveraigne bewtie that me bound,
> The ner [nier T] my comfort is to me,
> Alas! the fressher is my wound.

As flame dothe quench by rage of fier,
And rounyng streames consumes by raine,
So doth the sight that I desire
Apeace my grif and deadly payne.

Like as the flee that seethe the flame,
And thinkes to plaie her in the fier,
That fownd her woe, and sowght her game,
Whose grief did growe by her desire.

When first I saw theise christall streames
Whose bewtie made this mortall wound,
I little thought with in these beames
So sweete a venume to have found.

Wherein is hid the crewell bytt
Whose sharpe repulse none can resist,
And eake the spoore that straynith eche wytt
To roon the race against his list.

But wilful will did prick me forthe;
Blynd cupide dyd me whipp and guyde
Force made me take my grief in worthe;
My fruytles hope my name did hide.

I fall and see my none [mine own T] decaye,
As he that beares flame in his brest
Forgetes, for payne, to cast awaye
The thing that bredythe his vnrest.

And as the spyder drawes her lyne
With labour lost I frame my sewt
The fault is hers, the losse ys myne
Of yll sown seed such ys the frewte.

The following is the stanza peculiar to T:

As cruell waues full oft be found
Against the rockes to rore and cry;
So doth my hart full oft rebound
Ageinst my brest full bitterly.

It is impossible to determine whether W or Surrey was responsible for the poem, or whether both poets had a hand in it. Padelford takes Surrey to be the author, 'the fresh stanzas [in H] being contributed by some reviser'. F (11.175–6) argues that W was the original author.

Nott and Koeppel compare lines from Petrarch with 5–8, 17–24; but the resemblances are generic rather than specific.

CCXLVI. T entitles the poem: 'Whether libertie by losse of life, or life in prison and thraldome be to be preferred.'

23 *lest*] Although C and T both read 'best', Lovelock's (privately communicated) emendation makes better sense and provides a rhyme for l. 25.

VIII. Poems from Tottel's *Songes and Sonettes*

CCXLVII. T entitles it: 'The louer professeth himself constant.'

8 *blow . . . train*] withdraw from every enterprise.

CCXLVIII. T entitles it: 'The louer lamenteth his estate with sute for grace.'

14 *frute*] Refers back to 'frutelesse' (l. 11).

19 *band of payne*] painful bond.

28 *which*] Presumably this relates to 'me' rather than to 'grace', though one would expect 'my' rather than 'his'.

CCXLIX. T entitles it: 'The louer waileth his changed ioyes.'

23 *to*] too.

38 *plage*] plague.

CCL. This sonnet is entitled by T: 'To his ladie cruel ouer her yelden louer.'

CCLI. T entitles it: 'The louer blameth his loue for renting of the letter he sent her.'

12 *This . . . thereby*] She would gain the death of her lover. But it is possible that a final couplet is missing.

CCLII. Possible source:

> Deh per che non mi fur suelti de testa
> Gliochi quel di che fur si intenti e pronti
> Mirar costei: che gli ha conuersi in fonti
> Colmi dun largo humor che mai non resta:
> E lorechia che a odir fu tanto presta
> Gli dolci acenti soi limati e conti
> Che i sassi tracti harían fuor de i dur monti
> E i uenti aquietati e ogni tempesta:
> Per queste uie discese al cor la pena
> Di questo nacque quella uiua face
> Che occultamente ardendo al fin me mena:
> Questo turbo la mia tranquilla pace
> Questa fu lesca gli hami e la catena
> Duna che fa di me quel che gli piace.
>
> Tebaldeo, *Opere* (Venice)? 1500, sonnet
> ix, sig. a 3ʳ

The possible source was identified by Nott (550), who thought that W's poem was 'probably suggested' by ll. 1–8 of Tebaldeo's sonnet. But if he took account of it at all, he took account of the whole. Tebaldeo's first quatrain expresses regret that on the day he was so ready to gaze at his mistress he had not been free of his eyes, and his second makes similar reflections on his ears, which were all too ready to hearken to her sweet accents. This could provide the matter of W's first stanza. Thence, it may be supposed, he proceeds to an independent but logical development of Tebaldeo's idea, extending it to cover the treacheries of his lips and tongue (stanza 2), and his hands and feet (stanza 3). W's transition from stanza 3 to stanza 4 parallels Tebaldeo's transition from octave to sestet. They turn from the outer to the inner parts. Tebaldeo describes the damage done to the heart by the senses of sight and hearing, and W follows a similar line of thought. That both should bring in the heart at this stage might seem mere coincidence were it not that W's image *bayt* (l. 22) echoes Tebaldeo's *esca* (l. 13). The case seems a fair one. Nevertheless objections to it should be noted. W does not imitate Tebaldeo elsewhere, and may not have read his poems. He was, in any case, well versed in Petrarchan 'eye' lore. Compare, for example, Petrarch's sonnet describing how Laura's eyes deliver a blow which passes 'a le mie parti interne' (*Rime*, lxxxvii) with W's poem on the eye as 'traitor of the herte' (XCIII). Tebaldeo (1463–1537) and W are both Petrarchans of roughly the same period, and both delight in conceits in the manner of Serafino. A common literary background and taste could therefore account for the similarities between them. Title in T: 'The louer curseth the tyme when first he fell in loue.' The poem is not divided into stanzas in T.

12 *deale*] i.e. part of the way of love.

CCLIII. Title in T: 'The louer determineth to serue faithfully.' See note to XXXIX and XL for the relation of this poem to Serafino's 'Canzona de la Patientia'. I. L. Mumford, *EM*, xiv (1963), 13, regards this as 'possibly the most successful' of the group.

CCLIV. T entitles it: 'The louer suspected blameth yll tonges.' But it is not a love poem and was probably written during one of the periods when W was in danger from his enemies in 1536, 1538, or 1540.

CCLV. Title in T: 'The louer complaineth and his lady comforteth.'

25 *good*] 'friend' is understood.

32 *Thus . . . mone*] This line is either an aside of the Lover, or a comment by the poet.

CCLVI. T entitles it: 'The louer complayneth his estate.'

CCLVII. Title in T: 'Against hourders of money.' It is a version of an epigram by Ausonius, derived ultimately from one ascribed to Plato. (Cf. Nott 554 and F 11.74.)

> Thesauro invento qui limina mortis inibat
> Liquit ovans laqueum quo periturus erat.
> At qui quod terræ abdiderat non repperit aurum
> Quem laqueum invenit nexuit et periit.

CCLVIII. Title in T: 'Of dissembling wordes.'

CCLIX. Title in T: 'The courtiers life.'

3 *bankets*] banquets.

CCLX. Title in T: 'That speaking or profering bringes alway speding.'

CCLXI. Title in T: 'He ruleth not though he raigne ouer realmes that is subject to his his owne lustes'. The poem is an adaptation of three passages in Boethius (III metres 5, 6, 3). Although it has been assumed that W used Chaucer's translation, Patricia Thomson, 'Wyatt's Boethian Ballade', *RES* (1964), 262–7, has shown that he 'gave few or no glances at Chaucer's *Boece*', but that he modelled his poem on Chaucer's 'Balade de Bon Conseyl'. The following are the relevant passages from Boethius' *De Consolatione Philosophiae* and Chaucer's version (ed. Thynne):

Qui se volet esse potentem,
Animos domet ille feroces,
Nec victus libidine colla,
Fœdis submittat habenis.
Etenim licet Indica longe
Tellus tua iura tremiscat,
Et serviat vltima Thule,
Tamen atras pellere curas,
Miserasque fugere querelas
Non posse, potentia non est.

Who so wol be myghty/he mote daunten his cruel corages/ne putte nat his necke ouercomen/vnder ye foule raynes of lechery. For al be it so/that the lordshyppe strecthe so ferre/that the countrey of Inde quaketh at thy commaundementes/or at thy lawes. And that the last yle in the see/ that hight Tyle/be thrale to the: yet if thou mayst nat putten awaye thy foule derke desyres/and dryuen out fro the/wretched complayntes: Certes it nys no power that thou haste.

Omne hominum genus in terris
Simili surget ab ortu;
Unus enim rerum pater est,
Unus cuncta ministrat.
Ille dedit Phœbo radios
Dedit et cornua Lunæ.
Ille homines etiam terris
Dedit et sidera cœlo.
Hic clausit membris animos
Celsa sed petitos.
Mortales igitur cunctos
Edit, nobile germen.
Quid genus, et proavos strepitis?
Si primordia vestra
Auctoremque Deum spectes,
Nullus degener extat,
Ni vitiis peiora fovens
Proprium deserat ortum.

Al the lynage of men/that ben in erthe ben of semblable byrthe. One alone is father of thynges: one alone mynistreth al thynges: he yafe to the sonne his beames: he yafe to the moone her hornes: he yafe to men the erthe: he yafe the sterres to the heuen: he enclosed with membres the soules that comen from his hye seate. Than comen al mortal folke of noble seed. Why noysen ye or bosten of your elders? For if ye loke your begynning and god your father authour and your master/ Than nys there no forelyued wyght or vngentyl/but if he nourysshe his corage vnto vyces/and forlete his proper byrthe.

Quamvis fluente dives auri gurgite
Non expleturas cogat avarus opes;
Oneretque baccis colla rubri litoris,
Ruraque centeno scindat opima bove
Nec cura mordax deserit superstitem,
Defunctumque leves non comitantur
opes.

Al were it so/y^t a noble couetous man had a ryuer or a gutter fletynge al of golde/yet shulde it neuer staunche his couetyse: and al though he had his necke charged with precious stones of the reed see: & though he do eere his feldes plenteous with an hundred oxen/neuer ne shal his byting besynes forleten him whyle he lyueth/ne the lyght rychesses ne shall not bearen him companye whan he is deed.

IX. Poems from *The Court of Venus*, etc.

CCLXII–CCLXVIII. Both *The Court of Venus* and *A Boke of Balettes* are carelessly printed books. The texts of those poems which are to be found also in MSS. are manifestly inferior; and in several of the poems there are lines and stanzas missing.

CCLXII

14 *proue*] proof.

CCLXIII. Variations on the theme of CXXXVI by W or another.

CCLXIV. All the Z variants are inferior: it omits the best stanza in BB and adds a feeble one between ll. 4 and 5.

CCLXV. F claimed that this was by W.

CCLXVI. Title in T: 'The louer praieth not to be disdained, refused, mistrusted, nor forsaken.'

17–18] V2 runs together the beginning of one line and the end of the next.

21–4] The lines of this stanza begin with the opening words of the previous stanzas.

CCLXVII. There are four lines missing from the second stanza, the last of which was presumably 'To get agayne myne owne', and the first and third rhymed with 'lost'. There is one line missing from the last stanza, probably ending in 'not'.

CCLXVIII.

15 *had*] Possibly a misprint for *lade*.
45 *by once*] Probably a misprint.

Appendices

A. A REJECTED POEM

THE following poem, signed 'W' in H, appears not to be W's, as the only known Sir Thomas Gravener was knighted after W's death.

An Epitaphe of Sir Thomas Gravener, knyght

Vnder this stone ther lyethe at rest
  A frendly man, a worthie knyght,
Whose hert and mynde was euer prest
  To favor truthe, to farther ryght.

The poores defence, his neigbors ayde,
  Most kynde always vnto his kyne;
That stint all stryf that myght be stayed,
  Whose gentell grace great love dyd wyne.

A man that was full ernest sett
  To serve his prince at all assayes;
No sycknes cowlde hym from that lett,
  Which was the shortnynge of his dayes.

His lyf was good, he dyed full well;
  The bodie here, the sowle in blys.
With lenght of wordes whie shoulde I tell,
  Or farther shewe that well knowne is,

Sins that the tears of more and lesse
Rightwell declare his worthynes?

Viuit post funera Virtus.

Another poem ('In faythe methynkes yt ys no Ryght') has been omitted from this edition. It appears to be the opening stanzas of a poem inscribed 'A.I.' in D.

2 man] mane H

B. *THE QUYETE OF MYNDE*

THE text of W's translation of Budé's translation of Plutarch, *De tranquillitate et securitate animi*, is printed from the facsimile of the unique copy in the Huntington Library. Black letter is here printed in roman. Contractions are expanded.

THO. WYATIS TRANSLATYON
OF PLUTARCKES BOKE/OF
THE QUYETE OF
MYNDE.
To the reder.

It shall seme harde vnto the parauenture gentyll reder/this transla-tion/what for shorte maner of speche/and what for dyuers straunge names in the storyes. As for the shortnesse aduyse it wele and it shalbe the plesaunter/whan thou vnderstandest it. As for the straunge names stycke nat in them/ for who that can take no frute in it/without he knowe clerely euery tale that is here touched/ I wolde he shulde nat rede this boke.

Farewell.

To the most excellent and most vertuous
princes Katheryn/quene of Englande and
of Fraunce &c. encrese & contynuaunce
of moche helth and honour.

The boke of Fraunces Petrarch/of the remedy of yll fortune/at the commaundement of your highnesse/I assayd/as my power wold serue me/to make into our englyssh. And after I had made a profe of nyne or ten Dialogues/the labour began to seme tedious/by superfluous often rehersyng of one thyng. which tho parauenture in the latyn shalbe landable/by plentuous diuersite of the spekyng of it (for I wyll nat that my iugement shall disalowe in any thyng so aproued an auctour) yet for lacke of suche diuersyte in our tong/ it shulde want a great dele of the grace. Altho/as me semeth/and as sayth this Plutarch/the plentuousnesse and faire diuersyte of lan-gage/shulde nat so moch be desyred in suche thynges/as the frutes of the aduertysmentes of them/whiche in my opinyon/this sayde Plutarch hath handsomly gadred togyder/without tedyousnesse of length/contay – [a.ii] ning the hole effect/of that your hyghnes desyred of Petrarch in his lytell boke/which he wrate to one of his frendes/of the Quiete of mynde/nerawhyt erryng from the purpose of the sayd Petrarch. which I haue made now of late in to our tong nat precisely (I confesse) without errour as one shulde haue done that had ben of perfite lernyng/but after my rudenesse/seking rather the profite of the sentence than the nature of the wordes. but how soeuer it be/if it may please your hyghnesse to accept it/ it shall nat onely be a defence for the symplenesse of the boke/ agaynst ouer busy serchers of other mennes actes/whan the good wyll shall haue the alowance of so vertuous a iugement/but also corage to the symple endeuour of this hande/towarde better enterprises. And tho the smalnesse of the present be great/in respecte of that/that accordeth to your excellence/the sentence parauenture shall nat be moche vnacceptable/if it greue nat your grace to marke it after your accustomed wysdome. Pleseth than your hyghnesse to pardone thouerboldnesse of your moost humble slaue/where he presenteth you/for the good lucke of [a.iiᵛ] this newe yere/with this his symple labour/and with as moch quietc of mynde as this boke pretendeth/alwayes prayeng god to sende you thonorable desyre of your vertuous hert. At Alyngton the last day of Decembre. M.D. xxvii.

your most humble subiect
and slaue/Tho. wyat.

Of the Quiete of mynde.

I receyued very late thy letter/wherin thou exhortes me that I shulde write somthyng vnto the of the quietnesse of minde and of those thynges/in Timeus/that thou thynkest nedeth more exquisite declaration. Trewly/where as Eros my frende was redy to sayle towardes Rome and I had receyued hastely of Fundanus the honest man the letters/& I had nat therfore leysar to apply me to that that thou desyredest/as I wolde haue done/nor agayne coude I suffre the man to be seen sent fro me with empty handes/certeyn chosen thynges I haue taken forth of the quietnesse of mynde/out of the comentaris that somtyme I made. And (as I thynke) in such declaration thou sekes [a.iii] nat the delicacy of sayeng/and the piked delight of spech/and thou hast consyderatyon onely of some doctryne/to be as helpe for the lyfe to be ordered. & I iuge it very well doone/that where thou hast great priualte with princes/& that nat in commen thinges/& that in the glori of maters of iugement/no man is afore the/yet for all that thou dasyst nat folysshly at the fawnyng of glory/that wonders and exaltes the/as doth Merops in the tragedy. Oftimes also thou remembrest that thou hast herde/that sore toos are nat esed with gorgious showes/ nor the whitthlowe with a ring/nor the hedach with a crowne. For to what purpose is thuse of money for the eschewyng of the sickenesse of the mynde/or for the easy & sure passage of lyfe? Or wherto serueth the vse of glorie/or among courtiers apparence? Onelesse that they to whom these thynges chaunce/can wisely vse them whan they haue them: and agayne whan they want them/ouer suffre the desyres of them. and what any other thyng is that/than reason accustomed and fore thought/to restrayne quickly/& nat to suffre to stray the apasionate parte of the mynde/wan-[a.iiiᵛ.] tyng reason/whan it breketh forth/and to suffre it to forbeare whan it is ouer-twharted/with assayling affections.

Therfore/as Xenophon bad men in prosperous thynges chefely to remembre the goddes/and to worshyp them than best/that whan case required with betre hope what so euer they nede they myght aske of them/therby contented and mercyfull. So those princyples that are most mete for to apese troubles/must be taken and receyued afore hande/onely of them that are hole mynded/ that long afore prepared/they may be long moost profytable. For lyke as feyrs dogges ragyng at euery voyce/yet at one voyce that they are vsed to and knowe/they apese them selfe. So the wood affections of the mynde/it is no lytel busynesse to order and apese/ Onlesse the princyples for that purpose vsed/be familier and redy at hande/that may clerely appese them/whan they are troubled and meued. Fardermore/they that are of opinyon nat to do many thinges/nor priuately nor openly/for the quiet passyng of lyfe. These first of all wyll make vnto vs/quyetnesse of mynde of a dere price/as to be bought/with slug – [a.iv] gardy and slouthfulnesse/ and as tho he were sicke/they warne euery man/as it were with this worde/lye still wretch in thy bed. Trewly where as it is an hurtfull medicin to the body that deedly sluggardy/nerawhit better phisicien for the sickenesse and trouble of the mynde/is slouth and tendernesse/& faynt hert forsaker of frendes/kyn/and countrey. Besydes that it is false/that vnactyfe men lede a quiete lyfe/for els it must be that the lyfe of women were more quietous than that of men/as they that syt watchyng at home/occupied in huswifely occupations. And yet whan somoch/as the north wynde can nat trouble the yonge maydens/as Hesiodus saith/the diseses of the mynde/the troubles/the passyon of an yll thought/by ielousy/ supersticion/ambicyon/and vayne glorie/wherof no man can attayne the nombre/crepe neuerthelesse/in to the house of their occupacion. Laertes lyueng twenty yeres in the countrey (as it is said) only with an olde woman to serue hym of his meate and drinke/fled from his countrey and princely paleys/& had neuertheles sadnesse and frownyng debate in company. what [a.iv.ᵛ] if that same/nothyng to do/hath troubled many from the ryght order of the mynde? as sayth Homere by Achylles/that he sat amonge the shippes folowing his ire/with ferme purpose/flyeng from the fight/& the worthy counsayls of the nobles and the people/and dyuerting the name of men vnactyfe/he fayleth in his hert/and agayne streyght he seketh the batails/and stereth him selfe in the cruell stryffes of Mars. Therfore/whan he coude nat suffre hym selfe to wyther in ydelnesse/he sayth angerly/I sytte lyke a deed lumpe of erthe/as the keper of the shippes. Nor yet Epycure the alower of voluptousnesse/is nat their auctor/that are outher ambitious or desirous of glory by nature/that they shulde gyue them to ydelnesse/but vnto the gouernaunce of commynaltees/as nature ledeth them. for men that are borne to busynesse/ can nat suffre with euyn and vntroubled mynde to be depriued/of that they most desyred: Altho lyke a fole/he calleth them to a common welth/that can nat holde them self from it/and nat rather them that ar mete for the rule of it. Nor trewly the suretie and trouble of the mynde/ought nat to [a.v] be measured/with multytude or scarsty of businesses. For to ouerslip honest thinges/ is no lesse displesaunt & troublous than (as we haue afore said) to do foule thynges. But them also that haue chosen one maner of life to be voyd from trouble/as some do the life of these husbandmen/some of syngle men/and some of kynges. Menander warneth with these wordes/that they err far (as they say) out of the way. I thynke o Phania that these rich men that nede nat to make eschange for gayne/nor to playne in the night/nor in turnyng them vp and downe/to say often alas/slepe the swete and soft slepes. but whan he came and perceyued the rych men/as well as the nedy to be troubled/it is no marueyle/quoth he/they ar of kyn & both borne at a burthen/lyfe & trouble. for it is the felowe of voluptuous lyfe/& of that brought vp by nede it encreseth. And trewly/as fearfull and sicke folke/out of a lytell bote lepe in to a gret shyp and from thens agayne in to a galy/thinkyng euer to be better/tyll they perceyue them selfe nothyng the nere/& (as who sayth) clene done/as they that cary the coler and fearfulnesse euerywhere with [a.v^v] them/so to take another & another kynd of lyfe/can nat delyuer the mynde from combre and troubles/such as ar vnknowledge of thynges vnconsydred auenture/nouther to know nor to can vse a ryght thynges present/for a mater that is happened. These thynges trouble the riche aswell as the nedy/and vexeth with sadnesse the syngle men as well as the maryed. And for these causes/many that thinke moch welth is in opyn places/can nat suffre a secrete restfull lyfe. for these selfe same causes/it repenteth many/of that they haue begon/that with gret labour haue thrust them self in to the courtes of kynges. It is an vnplesaunt thing of sicke men/as Ion sayth/for the wyfe troubleth them/they blame the phecisyen they be angry with the bed/ye and their frende noyeth them visytyng them/and agayne departyng displeaseth them. After that whan the disese forsaketh them and that by returned tempre helth cometh makyng althyng mery and plesaunt/so that he on the ton day that coud nat broke an egge nor fyne bred/on the next day eteth hungerly whetin bred & cresses. such effect & strength is there in resoning/for to [a.vi] chaunge eche purpose of lyfe/for the happy passyng of the same. Alexander whan he herde Anaxarchus argue that there were infynite worldes/it is said that he wept/and whan his frendes asked hym what thing had happened him to be wept for. Is it nat to be wept for/quoth he/syns they say there be infynite worldes/& we are nat yet lorde of one? Crates contrary wyse/wearyng an olde cloke lyued with sport and laughter/as in holydayes tyll his last. Agayne to Agamemnon it was greuous that he ruled so many/ whan he sayd/Thou shalt knowe Attrides Agamemnon/whom aboue all men Iupiter exerciseth and troubleth with labours.

Diogines/whan he was on the stone to be solde/he scoffed with the crier that shuld auaunce the sale/and whan he bad hym aryse/ he wolde nat/sayeng at the laste/what if thou shuldest haue solde a fissh? And Socrates in his bondes dyd dispute of wisdome among his pursuers. Lo on the othersyde/Pheton clymyng in to heuin/ optayning wepingly/that his father shulde take hym his chare and his horse to rule. Trewly as a showe may be wrested to the facion of a dyuers foote/but [a.vi^v] nat the fote lykewise to the facion of the wrested show/So do the passions of the thought make eche maner of life that is offred them conformable & like to them self/ nor vnto them that haue chosen the best lyf custome maketh it nat plesaunt/as some say/but rather wisdom maketh the best life to be also most plesant. Therfore the well of surete of the minde/springing in our self/let vs assay to make most pure & clere/that those thinges that gyue vs foren thinges & chaunceable/we may make mete & according/in suffring with gret vprightnesse of the mynde. For trewly it accordeth nat to be wroth agayn thynges that chaunce amisse. for our angre nothyng pertayneth to them. but he that can amend by craft yll chaunces/he trewly doth more laudably. Therfore Plato compareth mannes lyfe with the dyse/in the which the best cast is to be of the dyser desyred moost. but how soeuer it happen/there shuld be a ware hede/that he vse ryght that that the chaunce gyueth/whereof it is to parceyue that the tone is nat in our power/that is the chaunce of the dyse/the other is/if we be wyse/that we take with euyn minde/that that chaunce gyueth/& to gyue to eche of them his place/that that which [a.vii] chaunceth well/may be most profyte/and that lest hurt that happeth ouertwhartly. But vnconnyng men/and ignoraunt howe to lede their lyfe lyke sickely men/that can nother suffre hete nor colde/as in prosperyte they are with an hye forhed outragious/kepyng no measure. so are they in aduerstye/with knyt & bent browes fouly distempred. So are they troubled of both/or rather in both/of them self/and lykewise in those that are taken for good thynges. Theodorus that was called Atheus/was often wont to say/that* he reched wordes to his herers with his right hande/& they toke them with their lyft hande. Foles oftentymes whan fortune offreth her ryght hande/vncomely turnyng them selfe/set her on their lyft hande. wyse men do better/that lyke as bees make hony a right swete thing/out of drie tyme/an herbe of very bytre tast/so of very vnhandsome thynges/oft tymes they chuse out some handsome and profytable thynges to them. which thing wolde be moche thought on/& laboured with great exercyse of the mynde. For as he that cast a stone at a froward dog/whan he mist the dogge/and hit his step [a.vii^v] mother vnware/It is nat moch amysse quoth he. So may we mende and turne a nother way fortune/when she chaunceth otherwyse than we wolde. Diogynes bycause of his exyle/left his countre/it was nat so greatly yll/for it gaue hym occasyon of lernyng philosophy. Zenon of Citius that

* that] rhat.

had but one shyp/whan he herd that it was perished/the maryners the marchandise/and (as they say) euery crom/Fortune/quoth he/ thou doest very wel with me/that driues me to myn old cloke/and to the porche of philosophy. what therfore shall let vs/that we may nat folowe them? Thou art fallen from some rule or authorite/thou shalt lyue in the countre. Aplyeng thy priuate busynesse with great compasse assayeng to auaunce thy selfe in the princes fauour/thou art refused/thou shalt lyue surely euery where/with no busynesse layd vnto the. Agayne thou art tangled with many cares and busynesses/warme water doth nat cherysh so moch/ tendre membres (as sayth Pyndarus) as honours and glory ioyned with power/doth make labour swete/and suffrable. But som offence dothe trouble the/of backbityng/[a.viii] of enuy/or nouhhty sclaundre/the best remedy is with the muses/or in som place of lernyng to suffre ouer/as it happened vnto Plato/as in a cruel tempest/whan he was taken in to the fauour of Denys. Therfore it is of no lytell effecte/for the quietnesse of mynd/diligently to marke noble and famous men/if they haue suffred any lyke thyng/by those same causes/as by example/want of children maketh the sad/Loke on the Romayn kynges/of whom neuer a one dieng/left his reigne to his childe. Pouerte/thou can nat suffre with euyn mynde/who than had best thou leuer be of al the Boetians rather than Epaminondas/or of al the Romayns/than Fabricius? But sette case thy wyfe be nat chast/knowest thou nat thepygram of Agys in Delphos? Hast thou nat herde how Alcibyades defyled Timea his wife/and how she was wont to name the childe that she bare/priuely to her maydens/Alcibiades? yet that letted nat Agys/ to be a very worthy and a noble man/no more than vnchast doughter of Stylphon dyd let hym to lyue the merylyst of all the philosophers of his tyme. whiche shame whan Metrocles [a.viii^v] layde vnto hym/is it my faut or my doughturs? quoth he/thy doughturs quoth thother/but thy misfortune/howe can that be? quoth he/are nat fautes fallynges? yes quoth tother/and fallynges/ are nat they also the errours/of them that they are the fallynges of? trewe quoth thother/and what be errours? are they nat the mysfortunes of them/that they be errours of? with such a soft and resoning pesable spech he taught the vayn checkis of the dogged man/to be but triflyng barkinges. Lo now/there are many/whom nat onely the vyces of their frendes and kynsfolke/doth vexe/but in goddes name/they also of their enmys. forscoldyng/angre/enuy folies/& combrous riualytees/at the foulyst spottes of them that they be in. yet they trouble foles/like as the angre of neighbors of thimportunat famyliers/or the noughty wyttes of seruauntes*/ wherwithall I thynke thou be oftymes meued. And as it is in Sophocles/the phisiciens wassh away the bytter coler/with a bytter medicyn so that (nat as aparteyneth the) agayn their diseses/and yll affections of the mynde/art angry/and answerest them with lyke sowernesse of the mynde/whi- [b.i] che thynges that thou doest/ar nat meued with gode & thrifty maners/as most metest instrumentes/but for the most parte with sharpe and frowarde condicions. & truly for to correct these thynges/whan it is more than thou canst do/so is it nat esy by any meanes. So that if thou canst vse these thynges whan they growe/no nother wise than these surgiens vse their sharpe scrapynge instrumentes/than if thou vse them thus/beryng alway with the/as case requireth/ softnesse and mesure/truely thou shalt no more vexe thy self/with others wantones & foly/than thou shalt be gladded with the consciens of thyne owne affection. for thou shalte thinke they do it nat without a cause/no more than dogges whan they barke/do naughtly of their nature. or els folowing such wekenesse and feblenesse of mynde/if thou care nat to be troubled with others ylles/they shall disceyue the wrechedly/dayly suckyng vp many troubles/flowing vnto the/as tho thou satest in a low bottome. what? many philosophers haue reproued pyte/with which we ar meued in beholdyng mesurable men/thynking that it is thoffice of a good man to [b.iᵛ] socour neyghbours/that be oppressed in misery/& nat to be sori therwith/or with slacknesse of a low mynde/to gyue place to fortune. ye/and that that euery man wyll say is more/they wolde nat suffre vs/if we parceyue our self to haue done amysse/or to be of naughty mynd/therfore to be troubled in our thought/& to be sory/for without sorinesse/such thynges shuld be mended/whiche whan it is thus/consyder well/how beestly it is to suffre our self to be any thyng wrath or angry/if they that we haue delt with all do nat gentylly & kyndly with vs. Truly I feare me my frende/leest the loue of our self disceyue vs/ nor the frowardnes of yll speche vexeth so moch the mynde/as we prefer it ouer moche deseruyng of our selues/for vehemently/as it were with dasyng/to be affectionate to certeyn thinges/and vncomely to desyre and folowe them/or agayn to be agaynst

* seruauntes] sernauntes.

448   *Appendix*

them & abhorre them/no marueyle if these bringe stryues
and offences among men/whan diuers men take it diuersly/
outher these to be taken from them/or that they are fallen in to
the other/but if any man/as chaunce requireth/vseth hym selfe
with [b. ii] measure to be aplyable/which way so euer he turneth
hym/he surely lerneth/with handsome esynesse to haunt the
company of men. Nowe lette vs take our purpose that we left
of the self thinges/lykewise as to them that ar sycke of agewes/
all thynges tasted/semeth strait/bitter/and lothsome/tyll they
haue sene other take the same thynges/without any token of
vnplesaunt sauour/whiche they lothly haue cast vp/where at laste
they ley the faut in themself & in the sickenesse/and nat in the
mete or drinke. So we/if we consyder other that vse with great
vprightnesse of the mynde and mery chere/that that we passe nat
without playntfull heuynesse/must nedes leaue to be so angre with
the selfe thynges. But truly for to kepe constancy of mynde in
aduersite/it is of great effect/nat to forgete with a wynkyng eye (as
they say) those thynges that somtyme hath happened hapely vnto
vs/as we wolde haue wysshed/and with due medlyng to way the
prosperous thynges/with euery yll chaunce. But where/as we ar*
wont to turne our eyes/that be dased with beholding bright
thinges/vnto fresh and grene colours/for to [b.ii^v] refressh them/
contrary wyse/we tourne our mynde to heuy thynges/and by
force constrayne it to the remembraunce of thinges most of
repentaunce/and we pull it away agayn the wyll of it/from agreable
and suffrable thinges. And here I remembre I may bring in metely/
that that ones was spoken to a busy felowe/medlyng in that that
partayned nothyng to hym/what the myschefe vngracious felowe/
thou seest other mennes vices with kytes eyes/& thyn own thou
lettes passe/with wynkynge owles eyes? To what purpose good
man doest thou consyder so diligently thy harmes/& renewes
them alwayes with busy remembraunce/ and hast no regarde to
that welfulnesse that is present And like as these surgen boringes
suckes out of the flessh the worste blode/so doest thou/all the
worst of thy thynges/gader in to thy selfe/nerawhit better than
Chius the marchaunt/that where he solde moch wyne of the best/
he gadred to hym selfe/the sower and deed wyne. whose seruaunt
whan he ran away from hym/and one asked hym for what cause
he forsoke his mayster/aunswered/for bycause whan he had good

*we ar] wear.

[b. iii] thynges in his handes/he sought for il. Many lyke vnto hym forsakyng swete drinkes/gyue them self to sharpe & bytter drinkes. So dyd nat Aristyppus lene vnto the heuy balaunce of harme/but reched hym selfe to the lyghter. He whan he had lost a plesaunt maner/asked of one of them that shewed them self most sory and angry for his fortune. Knowest thou nat/quoth he/that thou hast but one lytell house/and I haue yet thre good fermes left me? yes quoth thother. Than shulde I/quoth he/rather be sory for thy fortune? for it is lyke madnesse to be sory for thinges lost/nat reioysing in thinges that be safe. And as lytell chyldren/whan one hath taken from them one tryfle among many/castyng away al the rest/they wepe and crye. so lykewise we troubled by fortune in one thyng complayning and lamentyng make all other thynges to vs vnprofytable. But one wyll say/what haue we? ye/rather what haue we nat? He hath glorie/he a house/another a wyfe as he wolde wysshe/and he a faithfull frende. Antipater of Tarsis dyeng/ whan he rekened on his fyngers/the thynges that he had had in his life/he forgate nat the [b.iiiv] good se passage/that he had out Cilicia to Athens. & pardy/these common & light thinges ar nat to be passed/and there is consyderacion to be had of them/that we lyue/that we are in helth/that we se the sonne/that we haue no warre nor rebellyon/that the grounde is erable/& that the sce may be sayled with litell labour. ye/and for the last/that we haue lyberte to speke and to holde our tong/to be busy & ydell. Truely the possession of these thynges/shall gyue vnto vs/a plentous mater of quietyng the mynde/if we fasten in our mynde thimage of the absence and of the desyres of them/therby warnyng our selfes/ how helth is moch desyred of sicke men/peace of them that are combred with warre/how moch desyred vnto a streyer abrode/ and vnto an vnnoble man is glory/and toptayne suche a name in such a cyte. agayne how displesaunt it is/to lese it whan thou hast it. And yet I thynke nat/that any of these thinges or like shuld be so gret/& to be desyred/that whan it is lost/nothing shalbe safe. for it shuld be nowhit more estemed for that it leueth to be. Nor they shulde nat be possessed/as to worthy thynges/[b.iv] nor kept with such busynesse/watching busely/leest we be spoyled of them as so precious thinges/that we shulde therfore set lyght/and nat regarde thynges that we haue safe/as trifles. for these wolde be vsed/and the frute taken of them with gladnesse/most for that cause/that whan chaunce happeneth/we may suffre more pesably and temperatly/the losse of them. But trewly/as Archesilaus sayd/ some thynke it a great thing/with diligent intent of mynde and of eyes/to beholde others enditynges/pyctures and ymages/exquisitely/as they come to their handes and they nat regardyng their owne life/tho they that behold others chaunces/& loke vpon hym that hath many consyderations & aduertysmentes/and they nat vnplesaunt/lyke these adultrers/that lothyng their owne wyues/ folowe other mennes/erre (as the prouerbe sayth) all the worlde out of the waye. For it maketh moche towarde the constaunt state of the mynde. first to esteme hym selfe/& his own thinges/and the particulers of one/if nat/at the lest to tourne thyntent from consyderacion of courser thynges/nat as the common sort of men/ in* dyuers [b.iv^v] maner to wonder on them/whom fortune hath exalted to the heyght of thynges/whan she lysted to sport. as by example/they that are in prison thinke bondmen happy that are losed/they them that be free/they that be free thynke them that haue the lawe of cyties in their handes happy/and they riche men/ & riche folke prouostes & gouernours/and they kynges/and at the last kynges/the goddes/whom (I had nye said) it irketh also of their godheed/outcept they myght haue power of thunder and lightning/so that where they can nat be euyn with their superiours/ they can nat (as they say) rest with in their bondes. I care nat for the goodes of riche Gygis/quoth Thasius/nor yet I wondre greatly at them/nor I enuy the marueylous workes of the goddes/ nor yet gape I gretly after any kingdome/for fer fer are these thinges from my eyes/said this Thasius. Lo now contrariwyse such another as Chius/or another Galates or Bithynus/nat content that he hath gotten glory & maystership among the cytezins/but on goddes name he must aske pleyningly to be a senatour/whan thou hast gyuen him that he [b.v.] must be prouost/and sette case that thou graunt him that/than must he be consull and whan at last thou hast put to that/all is nat worth a pecs/outcept he be pronounced the first. And what other thing I pray the is this/but in gadring causes of vnkyndnesse agayne fortune/to tourment hym self/and hym selfe perpetually to punish him self? Truly a man well assured of his mynde/tho one or other of mortall people (where as we ar sixe. C. tymes/hundred thousande seers of the son/ and chyldren of the erth) passe hym in glory of name/or habundaunce of ryches/sytteth nat abiect or lamentable with wringyng

*men/in] menlin.

handes (as they say) but rather where he seeth hym self better handled/than an infynite multitude of vndone men/as often as he cometh abrode/he reioyseth in his fortune. In the assays of Olympias/there was no vyctour that might refuse to medle with who so euer came fyrst/hauynge no lyberte to chuse his matche. In our lyfe the state of thinges gyueth lyberte to eche man/that compareth hym self & his fortune/with many/& with the fortune of many/to haue an hye and an vpright mynde/& to make [b.v^v] hym therby to be seen and wondred at to other/rather than him self to wonder at other/so that he be nat so folysshe to compare hym to Briareus or to Hercules. So whan thou marueylinge/seest some great man caryed in a lytter/lette down thyn eyes/& loke vpon the berers therof. Agayn whan thou shalt wonder on Xerxes/as very happy/whan he passed the straites of Hellespont/with a brigge shapt of shyppe wood/behold also them/some their noses & some their eres smytten of and mangled/by reason of the brig broken/with shakyng of the furour of the sees rage/brekyng in by Athon/and beleue that they prayse with great commendacion/the and thy fortune. Socrates whan one of his frendes tolde hym/that all thyng was dere in the town/for wyne of Chia was at a pounde/ and purple at thre pounde/and hony at. v. shyllynges the gallon/ toke him by the hande and ledde him in to the meyle house/it is solde/quoth he/for an halpenny the halfe busshell/therfore vitell is good chepe. from thens he brought him in to the oyle house/it is solde/quoth he/for two brasse pens two gallons/al thyng than is nat dere in the [b.vi] towne. So lykewise we/if we here any man say that our fortune is bare & wretched/for that we haue nouther the consulship nor other maistershippe/we may say vnto hym/ that our fortune is fayre and goodly/and that we go nat from dore to dore/and that among porters and berers/we wery vs nat with burdens/nor like flatterers/are constrained to be as parasites to princes. Altho (for we ar now come to that madnesse/that eche of our lyues hangeth vpon other mens/more than our own/and that our nature is so altred/in to a certeyn vnkynde and enuyous affectyon/nat so moch to glad in our owne/as to be troubled with other folkes welthes) if thou loke nat only vpon those wonders/ and famous thynges in them/whom thou wenest very blessed/& (as they say) in Iouis lap/but the curten & the fayr trauers drawen/ lettyng passe their glory and vtter apparence/if aswell thou loke with in them/thou shalt truly fynde many inwardes/sower &

troblous. Pyttacus/whom the sure fame noyseth to haue ben endewed with wysdome/fortitude/and iustyce/whan he was chering gestes that he had/it is sayd his wyfe came [b.vi^v] and angerly ouerthrew the table wherwith whan he sawe his gestes abasshed eche of you/quoth he/is troubled with some yll/I am in this state alway very well. This man that was demed abrode to be very happy/whan so euer he entred his threshold/he semed to be a wretch/I say nat that he was one/where his wyf had all and ruled princely/where oftimes & alway he neded to fyght with her. Many thynges do trouble you/nothyng dothe trouble me. Many such lyke thinges do cleue vnto glory/vnto riches/ye and vnto a kyngdome. but truely of the ignorant multytude vnperceyued/for the pompe is drawen/behynde the which those thinges lye hydden. Happy Attrides glory of grekes/eueriwhere mylde fortune the fauoureth/whyle she exalteth her chylde. This vtward blyssednesse to be compassed with wepyns/horse/and armes/let vs here lykewise/the repentyng voice of an yll troubled mynde/cryeng agaynst suche excesse of glory. Mighty Iupiter hath tangled me with greuous chauncis/& in another place. O happy & blessed that ferre out of danger/vnnoble/and vnglorious haue passed their lyues. By these [b.vii] and sych lyke declaracions/it may be sensably parceyued/the playntfull vnquietnesse of the minde/ scoldyng with fortune and casting away it self with wondring* at other/& to ryse for toppresse it self/and the owne thynges. For of trouth it breketh marueylously the constant & quyet state of the mynde/with hyer entent to stryue aboue the power to get any thing as to sayle with gretter sayles than proporcion/as whan hope shyneth neuer so lytell/promysing folisshly vnto our selfes vnmesurable and great thynges/& than whan chaunce foloweth nat/we accuse wicked fortune and our desteny/whan rather we shulde dam our selfes of foly/as it were to be angry with fortune/ that thou canst nat shote an arowe with a plou/or hunt an hare with an oxe/and that some cruell god shulde be agaynst them/that with vayn indeuour/hunt an hart with a dragge net/and nat that they attempt to do those impossibilytes/by their own madnesse and folysshnesse. Surely the cause of this errour/is the noughti loue of our self. For men/ouermoch deseruing of them self/where as with great stryfe they alowe them selfe best/enhaunced with [b.vii^v] pride/leaue nothyng vnassayed. For it is nat ynough vnto

*wondring] woudring.

them to be ryche & eloquent/and amonge mery & gladsome festes. but that they must be famyliers of princes and in auctorite/ but that they must haue the best horse & the best dogges and (if god wyll) the best cockerels and quayles/or els they can nat be quiete in their mynde. Denys thelder thought it nat ynough to be the grettest tyraunt in his tyme/but yuell content also/that he was nat so good as the poete Phylarenus in poetry/and as Plato in the craft of resonyng/meued with yre/him he put in to a dongion/and thother he solde/and banysshed in to Aeginas. So did nat Alexandre/ that where he was greatly meued with Brison/with whom he stroue in swyftnesse of the chare/with deliberacion semed plesaunt/forberyng his own right. Therfore Homere spake it very well by Achylles/such a one as was not among the grekes in batayle/and after he sayth/but there were other that were more eloquent. Megabysus of Percia on a tyme whan he came in to Appelles shop/he began to bable I wot nat what of the craft of payntyng. Appelles that [b.viii] coude nat suffre his folyes/ afore/quoth he/that thou shewedest thy self with thy wordes/I had a good opinyon in the/by reason of thy golde & purple/auauncyng thy silence/now the prentises and boyes that grinde me my colours/do mocke thy bablynge. There is that thynke that the Stoyik philosophers do mocke vs/in discribyng a wise man after their facion/nat only to be wise/iust/and strong/but also an oratour/an emperour/a poete/ye/& a kyng. and they are nat ashamed to ascribe all these names vnto him/altho if they perceyue them self in dispeyre of them/they are alway il content/ which how it accordeth with reason/they may se whan that they knowe the goddes contented/eche with his godheed to be satis-fied/as to be called Enyalius/that hath auctorite ouer the furour of batayle/another Mantous/that is ouer prophecies. another Cerdous/that is ruler of lucre. So that in Homere/Iupiter forbyd-deth to Venus werly maters/as nothyng perteynyng to her/& byddeth her to take hede to mariage maters. Besydes this/som-thynges of them that seme to vs to be desyred accorde nat togider of their owne [b.viiiᵛ] nature/as by example. He that desyres the study of sayeng & of lernyng/he must be quiete and without busynesse/agayn auctorites and familyarite with princes/ar wont to make busynesses/& to bring often combraunces. Plentous vse of wyne and flessh/maketh a man strong & mighty/and the mynde frayler and weker. Agayn vnmesurable diligence to encrese/

HH

or busy trouble for to kepe/agreeth for the gadring of riches. A tother syde/contempt & dispisyng/is a great instrument for the beginnyng of philosophy/and almost the first and chefyst exercyse of it. So al thinges is nat for euery man/but he that wyll obey the poesy of Appollo/must first knowe him self/and so take aduyse of his owne nature/& as she ledeth to take an order of lyfe/rather than passyng from one to another/to force & constrayn his nature. An horse for the cart/an oxe is mete for the plowe/after a ship that sayleth/a dolphin is mete to swym/and to hunt the bore a feirse dogge. So that if one be troubled/for that a mighty lyon may nat be norisshed in a womans lappe/as well as a lytell whelpe/surely he is a gret fole. And he is nerawhit wy – [c.i] ser that wyll write of the worlde & seke the nature of thynges/both after Empedoclis facion or Platos/or Democritus togider/or to lye with a riche old woman/as Euphorion/and to be lyke those that were wont to banket late with Alexandre/as Medius/and thinke it vncomely and scant to be suffred/outcept he may by riches be as notable as Ismenia/ & by vertue/as noble as Epaminondas. Ronners whan they haue their game/are content that wrestlers haue their reward/if thou haue gotton/sayth Solon/the towne of Sparta/order it with lawes & decrees. we wyll nat chaunge with you/saith the same man/vertue for riches/synes thone is our owne & stable/& riches is but chaunceable/& passeth from one to another. Strato whan he herde that Menedemus had more scolers than he. Lo/quoth he/is it nat to be marueyled/if many had rather be wasshed than perfumed? Aristotle writyng to Antipater/it is mete saith he/to be as glorious for Alexander/and to be consydred/nat onely to raigne ouer many people/but also to haue beside other/a right opinyon of godly thinges/so that they that vnder this maner calle their [c.iv] glad thynges glorious/and nat so lytell to be estemed/they without doute shall nat be troubled/with wondring at straunge thynges. yet now whan none of vs sees a vyne beare fygges/nor an olyue beare grapes/we braule with our selfe neuerthelesse/and with vngentyll gredynesse oppresse our selfes/& are so wery of our selfes/outcept we may attayne to the hyest degre/both of richmen and of lerned men/both at home & in the werres/both of philosophers and of warryers/ye and bothe of flaterers & of them that by trusty and free playnesse/are knowen to be true/and at last/ bothe of nygardes & wasters. Altho that we se nature to tech vs marueylusly. For as it is sene by nature dyuers beestes to feed for

their lyueng dyuersly/nor that she wolde that all shuld be norisshed
with seedes or with flesshe/or with rotes/but as they are dyuers to
ete dyuers meates/so hath the same nature gyuen to mankynde
dyuers orders of lyueng/as pasturyng/plowyng/foulyng/and
fysshing. we must therfore eche of vs chuse that/that we knowe is
most metest for vs/and with all our endeuoir gyue vs to that/& to
parte from the pos – [c.ii] session of that that we parceyue
parteyneth to another/or elles it is to no purpose that Hesiodus
sayd. The potter enuyeth the potter/and ouer the smythes craft
his fellow is enuious. Truly now men are nat ledde with enuy
of the craft or order of their felowes/but riche men with enuy of
lerned men/nobles of riche men/men of lawe/of deceyuers/and
of players and of tomblers/and at the last/free and noble men of
auncient famyles dasyng for wonder at the good fortunes of men
of bondage in the courtes of kynges/while they thinke that all
their own fortunes are to be lothed/they trouble them self/& with
no lytell cure of mynde kyll them selfe. Surely that euery man hath
cofers & receytes/and as who saith springes/of surety & trouble in
his own thought/and Homers tonnes of good & yll/nat as he said
in Iouis dore/but with in his own mynde/the dyuersite of men
proueth gretly/whom we se by affections of the mynde to be
diuersly tempred. for foles let good thynges passe tho they be
present/and regarde them nat whan they perisshe/so moche doth
their thoughtes gape gredily after thynges to come. Con – [c.iiᵛ]
trariwyse/men of wyt with sharpe remembraunce/reducyng them
self to thynges that be present/make those thinges that yet are
nat/to be at hand. For that that is at hande and present/offring it
self to be taken in on onely instant/after that vnremembred/semeth
vnto foles nother to be ours/nor to partein to vs. and as the roper
that is paynted in Plutos house/as moche as he dyd wreth out of
his basket in to his rope/he suffred folisshly an asse that stode by
hym to ete/no notherwyse doth the vnkynde & slouthfull
forgettinge of many/settyng assyde the commodites of thinges
past/the worthy don dedes/the noble actes/the plesant ydelnesse/
the mery and gladsome company/& forgettyng and scrapyng
out all the delyte of the lyfe/suffreth nat their lyfe to be all
one facyoned and weued togyder/with the thinges past & the
thynges present/deuyding yesterdayes lif from that of to day/&
that from that of to morrow/althyng don they make vndon/with
the weryng out of their remembraunce. Truely they that in the

scoles of philosophers toke away encresynges of bodyes/as vanisshing substaunce by wast/they only in [c.iii] their wordes made eche of vs/another & another than our selues. But they that contayn nat thynges passed/as tho memory failed/nor again remembreth them/they do nat now in wordes/but in very dede/ make them selfe dayly more nedy & more voyde/gapyng alwayes on to morowe/as tho thinges of last yere/of late/& of yesterday/ perteyned nothing to them/& as tho thei had neuer chaunced vnto them. So that the constant state of the mynd/by this maner is troubled. And euyn as flyes slyp of whan they crepe vpon smoth glasses/& in rough & rugged places thei cleue esely/so men slyding from gladsome and plesant thinges/holde fast the remembraunce of heuy thynges. And lyke as at Olinthus/ther is a place they say/wherin these horned flies be taken/and whan they be in/ they can nat get out again/but a great whyle flyeng vp and down within/makyng many circles in vayne/they dye at last. so men enwrapped in the remembraunce of ylles/can neuer after get forth nor get socour. Therfore as paynters are wont in tables to vnderlay dym colours to the eyes/and to enterlyne and draw faire and bright colours vpon them [c. iiiᵛ] so shulde men in their owne myndes/all heuy and darke chaunces/ouercouer and ouerthrowe with glorious & fair chaunces/worthy to be remembred. for thinges past can nat clerely be fordone/nor be agayne afterwarde/ by man onely. For so variable/dyuers and reboundable/is the tune of this worlde/as of an harpe/nor in mortall thynges/is there any thynge that is pure/clere/& symple. But as musyke standeth by hye and lowe soundes/and grammer by letters/vowels & mutes/ and that he is nat a musycien or a gramarien/whom eitherlyke of these dothe offende/but he that can vse them & temper them most accordingly/no notherwise it semeth/that he wisely hath stablished his lyfe/that most dyuers chaunces contrary among them self/hath lerned to mingle hansomly/wayeng prosperite with aduersite. for clerely to set aparte/good or yll/mortall comodite wyll nat suffre/ but it behoueth to make a temper with both/if we wyll determyn right of these thynges. It is nat therfore accordyng/in the tone of these to playne/& faynting in the mynde/to fall down as it were vnder to heuy a burden/but the power and [c.iv] thimpression of euery worst chaunce/to repulse with the remembraunce of better thinges alwayes wrapping vp discomodites in comodites/as it were in a napkyn/to make the tenour of the hole lyfe/made & gadered with prosperites & aduersytes/as a certayne accorde/tempred with connyng reason. And truly/nat as Menander thought/a man hath as soone as he is borne/a good spirite/as begynner of his lyfe & techer of right lyueng/but rather as Empedocles thought/two spyrites of diuers condition/to whom he giueth dyuers & many names/doth receyue vs assone as we come in to the light/from thensforth gyuen vnto them/as it were almost by right of seruice. He said that our generation did receyue the seedes of al these affections/& that therfore the draught of our lyfe was nat euyn and leuell/but rather brackish and sower/& therfore the wise man shuld haue the best thinges in his desyre/& loke for the worst/& in the temper of them bothe vse of neither parte to moche. Nor yet shall he come plesantly to to morowe/as Epicurus saith/that with gret debatyng douteth whyder he shall lyue to it/but riches/ glory/power/& authorite/[c.iv^v] gladeth & reioyseth such men most/that with contrary thinges a totherside/if case happen/can be as gode & as vpright. For truly vehement appetit of any thing/ hath alway fere his felow of lesing it/that dulleth the gladnes/& maketh it more to be desyred/as whan flame is resisted with gret wind. whom truly reson hath taught assuredly & vnferfully thus to say to fortun/if thou gyue it I shalbe rigt glad/if thou take it agayn/I shalbe indifferent. this man than can thus vse him self/ without marueyle must nedes vse thinges that happen plesantly/and nat be pulled from thens with feare of that losse rennynge in the thought. Anaxagoras whan he herde that his sonne was deed/I knewe quoth he/whan I begote him that he shuld dye/& I haue suffred ouer that awayting. this affection of Anaxagoras/is asmoch to be folowed of vs/as wondred at. Surely we may stay forthwith ech misfortun/I knew I had slypper riches/nat nayled with sixe peny nayl/as they say in my possession/and that I had them/but to vse them. I knewe wele inough that they that gaue me power/myght also take it from me. I knewe that my wyfe was wyse/but [c.v.] that she was also a woman/and for the last I knew that my frende was a man/that is to say/a lyuely thyng redy of nature to be depraued/as Plato oft sayde. Truely he that compareth thus the reasons of his affections/& byldeth him such rampers of reason/if ought happen otherwise than he wold/or ouerthwartly/yet is it nat to him sodayn/and where as he neuer admitteth those commen thinges/I wolde neuer haue went it/I was in grete hope/I neuer thought it wold be thus/there truely dothe he fordo the vneuynnesse of a stertynge or glyttering hert/& of one that was troubled and meued/he maketh forwith to him self/one pesable and constant. Carneades was wont to warne men most in prosperite of aduersite/for that euery sodain thinges nature is to be receyued all with grutchynge of the mynde/& as a maner meltyng. How great aparte is nowe Macedony/of the romayn Empyre? yet Perses whan he lost it/nat onely accused fortune with foule complayntes/but semed also to dyuers/most infortunate & wretched of all men. Loke on tother syde/Emilius whan he had ouercom him/partyng from the coun − [c.v^v] trey/gyueng place in the lordship of the see and of the lande to the right successour/ was receyued with the garlandes/and reioysynges of all men/and in the sacrifice extolled vnto heuen with praises/and nat vnde-serued/but most deserued. For he remembred hym self to haue gotten a chaunceable kyngdome/the tother by vnwened and vnfor-thought chaunce was put frome the height of his kyngdome. Me thinketh Homer techeth with a proper example/how moch more hurtfull those thynges are that stryke sodenly. Ulixes at his returne home/wept at the sodeyne deth of his dog/and nat to his wyfe that sat by him and wepte. for in commyng/consydringe the wepynge ymage of his wyfe/he had subdued the affection that els now wolde haue broken out/and by former shittyng of the minde/ had reduced it in to his own power/and was troubled with the vnforethought deth of the dogge/for that in the sodeyn thinge he had no space/to let the power of his affection. to conclude shortly/ thynges that chaunce agaynst our myndes/ar scant & herdly suffred/partly by nature/and partly we se thei ar greuous/by cor − [c.vi] rupt custome and naughty opinion/and they be the moste parte. it is of gret effect against them/to haue at hande this sentence of Menander. Thou hast suffred no gret grefe/onles thou make it so thy self/for what toucheth it the/if it nother streyne thy flessh/nor reche to thy soule/as by example thunnoblenesse of thy father/the adultry of thy moder/the dignite of the first place taken from the/the reward of thy victory bereft the/what perteyn these thynges to the? for truely tho these thinges happen/it shuld nat let the in thy body nor in thy mynd to be well/ye & right well. Against these thinges that by nature doth somthing offend/as siknesses/hurtes/& dethis of kinsfolke/this must be set. alas/ wherfore alas? for we haue suffred nothing/that perteyneth nat to man to suffre. For there is no speche that soner rebuketh thaffectionate parte of the mynde/whan it is drawen ouertwhartly with affections/& whan it snatcheth the byt of reson in the teth/than that that warneth vs of our comen & naturall necessites/vnto whiche necessite man is borne/& entangled as the body groweth/ whiche shall gyue vnto stryuing fortune/a knot/sure [c.vi^v] of all other thinges/that ar most chefe & grettest. They say Demetrius whan he sacked the town of Megarensis/asked of Stylpo if any of his goodes was taken from him? to whom he answered. I sawe no body take away myn/for wher as fortune hath suffred/all her thinges to be taken from her/yet haue we no such thinges in vs/as nother the grekes can do nor suffre. it is nat therfore mete so moch to forsak nature/as hauyng no strength nor sufferaunce/to matche fortunes violence. wher as we knowe rightwell/that that/that in man may be hurt with fortune/is but a lytell/and the worst parte of vs frayle & ouerthrowen with euery impression/by deynte tendernesse/and that we our self haue the power ouer the better partes/wherin be set those grettest & good thinges/as in an vnslypper place/and where also true glory/lerninges/& studys pertayning to vertue haue their being/nother mortall nor byreue-able by no strength. thus I say/knowing our selfes of vnuyncible minde/fortrusting to our selfes/it becometh vs to be assured agayn thinges to come/& to saye that to fortune/that Socrates fayning did say by Anitus & Melitus his accusers/truly quoth he/to the iuges Anytus [c.vii] and Melitus may slee me/but to do me hurt or displeasure/they can nat. for tho fortune might ouerthrow hym with dyuers sicknesses/take from him his riches or accuse hym to a tyrant/or to the people/yet might she nat truely make hym yll/or faynt herted/or fearfull/or altred of his mynde/or els make hym malicyous/but onely a good man/endued with manlynesse and corage of the mynde/& at a worde she might nat bereue him the right order of the mynde/whiche truely profiteth more to man/for the ledyng of the lyfe/than the craft of sayling/for to passe the sees. For the maryner be he neuer so conning/can nat by any meanes redresse the fury of the water/nor repulse the assaut of the feirce wynde/no more than get a hauen where he wolde/whan so euer he wolde retourne from the see. No/nor this cometh nat to him by craft that whan he is taken with tempest/constantly and vnferfully to handle the necessite/herto it helph nat/that whilst he dispayreth nat/for place for his craft/takyng in the sayle/driueth as he may with the tempest/the coward now sitteth down with wringing handes from all this gere/[c.vii^v] & whyle the mast is drowned with force of winde/he shaketh with trembling fere. but in a wyse man/an ordred minde with the body bringeth faire wether/that is to say with contynence/and tempre of fode and labour/wipyng away the causes of sicknesse/and if there be any outwarde cause of trouble/in the whiche a mans mynde is ron/as in the roky flattes/ with quicke pullynge vp the sayle yarde (as Asclepiades saith) it passeth ouer. And if so be it encrese and growe more than can be socourd or suffred by man/the hauen is nat fer of/and there resteth to the to swym out of the body/as out of the ship boote/whan it wyll holde no more. Truly foles/nat so moche for the desyre of lyfe/as for the feare of dethe/hanging on the body cleue fast with claspyng handes/no notherwise than Ulixes dyd hang on the wylde figge tree/whan he feared the russhing of the horelpole Caribdis/ whom Homer saith/was so nere taken in the see of Sycill/that he coud nother stoppe by reason of the wynde that shoued hym/nor yet get out/so dyd that let him/and as tho he held the wolfe by the eres/as the prouerbe saith/coud nother [c.viii] hold the tre/for werynesse & discomodite of the chaunce/nor let it go for fere of the dredfull peryll. But if any mann euer so lytell consyder/the nature of our soule/and doth recken with hym selfe/the passage from the state of this lyfe to be to a better/or at the lest to no worse/ by deth truly he hath alredy/no lytell forderaunce for his iourney/ that is to saye/the contempt of deth. For who that/what with valya-unt vertue/whiche is the properte and peculyarite of man/and what with ordring assuredly the mynde/agaynst forrayne and straunge thinges/whiche come besyde nature/mightely to ouerthrowe our proper thynges/may lyue so plesantly that he may say/I may go/I may go my way surely at the first tym/with the good leue of god/whan I wyll/whan I pray the/other greuous or combrous/or troublous thyng can happen vnto him? Of trouth/what soeuer he is that saith this worde/I haue preuented the/o fortune/and all thy entres were they neuer so streyte I haue stopte/this man nat with berres/nor nayles/nor byldinges hath coraged and strengthed hym selfe/but rather with decrees of philosophy/and ru – [c.viii^v] les of wisemen/whiche also be open & so redy for euery man/that they nede but only the takynge. Nor we may nat take away byleue in those thynges/that haue ben left to our remembraunce of our elders/nor dispeyre in nothyng of them/as tho thei were nat possible to be folowd/but as it is mete to loke vpon them/and to marueyle moche of them/as it were by grace wondringe of them/ so must we make our selfes/by confyrmynge vs to their folowing lyklihodes of them/that by beginnynges set in small thynges/ assayeng gretter and gretter/we may profite to the hyest. But we must diligently loke/that we put nat the thoughtes of these thinges out of our mynd/nor that we let to tourne oft these thinges in our thought/and (as they say) to thinke on them with all our hert. Nor this busynesse endeth no gret labour (for as a certeyn swetnesse of the mynde/noyeth vs and hath taught vs with slouthful and vnexercised tendernesse/and hauntynge most proue thynges of lest busynesse/by an naughty fauour hath taught it selfe/out of vndelightsome thynges/to turne it selfe to eche plesant thyng/so lykwise [d.i] if any man vse to fayne in his mynd/ the ymages of sicknesse/of labour/of exyle/& to gader vnto him the strengthes of his reason/to discus diligently eche by hym selfe. this man/this/shall without fayle se that those thynges/for the most part/ar vayn and dispisable/that seme heuy/fereful/and horrible/and to say trouth/threten more with their loke/than they do in the departyng. But many abhorre that worde of Menander/ that any man a lyue may nat glorie/in sayeng/this I wyll nat suffre. for that they knowe nat what it aueyleth for to auoyde heuines/to thynke and to vse to beholde fortune/with vnagreable and feirs eyes/and nat to leue to tendre thoughtes/and trifling delytes/and norisshmentes of esy lyfe/rysyng at euery lytell hope/and fallyng at euery lytell thyng. Altho it may be thus answered to Menander. It can no wyse be sayde/whyle I lyue this I wyll nat suffre/lette it be so/but this I may saye whyle I lyue/this I wyll nat do/I wyl nat lye/I wyll vse no crafty deceites for to compasse men/I wyll nat begyle/I wyll nat disceitfully lye in awayte. this syns it is in vs/ it is a great help to them [d.iv] that lyfte them selfe vp to the surety of mynde/in which maner lyke as botches be in the body/so is a naughty conscience in the soule/as that that leueth repentaunce/ busely prickyng and pulling the minde. For where all other heuinesses ar wont to be taken away by reason/onely this repentaunce it selfe prouoketh by shame/as one that byteth and gnaweth hym self. And truely/as they that shake of a cold ague/or burne of an hote ague/ar more sharply and feruently vexed than they that suffre the same thynges/of vtwarde colde or hete. so casuall and chaunceable thynges/haue more blunter heuynesses/as outwarde and forayn thinges. And this thing/no body is to blame for me but my self/which is wont to be plainynly cried/whan an offence is done/maketh the hurt that is greuous of it selfe/more greuous/and driueth it in deper. So nouther gorgiousnesse of buylding/nor weight of golde/nor noblenesse of kyn/nor greatnesse of empire/ nor eloquence & fayre spekyng/brinketh so moch clerenesse of lyfe/and so plesant quietnes/as bringeth a mynde disceuered from trouble of busynesse/lyueng (as they say) with [d.ii] hym selfe ferre from yll aduyse. whiche hauyng the well of lyfe (I mean wyt & condicions/from whiche commendable dedes do spring) clere and vntroubled/shall bring forth all his dedes/mery & vpright as it were with an heuenly grace/by the remembraunce wherof/he is feed with a more certeyn/than Pyndarus hope/norishment (as he sayth) of old age. And as Carneades was wont to say/the swete fyrres tho they be cutte or pulled vp by the rotes/they kepe a swete sauour a longe whyle/truely in the mynde of a wyse man/honest dedes do euer leue a certeyn fresshe and plesaunt remembraunce. with the whiche remembraunce that same inwarde gladnesse springeth by a contynuall ryuer/as who saithe bering frute/to the great shame of their errour/that so lamentably blame this lyfe/ sayeng it is a congregation of ylles/and a certeyn resort of out-lawes/in to the whiche onely the soules that be banyshed from aboue be put. I reken that worde of Diogines worthy remem-braunce/whiche he sayd/whan he sawe a straunger in Lacede-mona/curiously pyking hym selfe agayn a holyday. what quoth he/is nat euery day ho[d.iiv]lyday with a good man? yes and if we be wyse most gladsom holiday. For this worlde is a certeyne most holy temple/& most mete for god/in to this temple man is admytted whan he is borne/nat to beholde karuyn ymages wantyng senses/but the son/the mone/& the sterres/from whiche cometh mouyng/& the first principles of lyfe/whiche prouidence hath gyuen vnto vs to beholde/that they shulde be sensyble ymages and folowynges of intelligible thynges/as Plato saith. besydes these/the flodes that bring forthe alwayes newe waters/and the erth producyng fode/bothe vnto trees & vnto all kynde of bestes. with this goodlynesse & prospecte begynnyng truely our lyfe/it must be full of surety and of ouerspred gladsomnesse/nor they ar nat to be loked for of vs/Saturnus festes/or Bacchus festes/or Myneruas festes/as many do that receyue these and such other festes with great awaytinge/gladsomnesse and sporte/in whiche they may more lyberally/glad them self with bought laughter gyueng wages vnto mynstrels and tomblers for their minde sake. And what is more vncomly/than that in suche plays [d.iii] we syt with suche pertynax scylence doyng nothing els (as they say) (for there is no man that lamenteth or wepeth/whan he seith Pythia begyn/no more than he is hungry after the feest) and those good-lynesses whereof god hym selfe is auctor vnto vs/and in maner player/with lamentyng and sowernesse of mynde/ledyng a dolor-ous lyfe/we defile and make soroufull. And yet most vnsely is this/whan we delyte in orgaynes played and sounded/and in lytell byrdes songes/and beholde gladly the beestes playng and dauns-yng/and agayne ar offended with their frowarde noyse and their cruell lokes/yet neuerthelesse seyng our owne lyues sadde and heuy/frownyng/& ouerthrowen with most troublous affections and tangled busynesses/and cures/and driuen with vntemperat-nesse/that nat only we can nat gette vs some lyberte and space to take our brethe/but nother here also other exhortyng vs to it. To whose warnynges with clere and opyn eares/if we wolde gyue hede/we shulde vse thinges present as they come without any blame/and shulde rest with the plesaunt remembraunce of thynges past/and at [d.iii^v] the last we shulde drawe towarde thynges to come/vnferefully and assuredly/with sure and gladsome shynyng hope.

Thende.

Imprinted at London in Fletestrete
by Richarde Pynson/printer
to the kynges moost
noble grace.

Cum priuilegio.

[*Note.* Pynson often confuses n and u (e.g. 447.27 *slackuesse*) and omits spaces between words (e.g. 460.20 *manneuer*). Some doubtful readings have been allowed to stand: e.g. 449.22 *sce* (sea); 450.32 *pecs* (pees); 453.11 *chare* (chace).]

GLOSSARY

A', have (CXCIV.15)
Accomberd, encumbered, troubled (XCVIII.51)
Acited, summoned (VIII.2)
Adeue, adieu (CLXXV.26)
Adresse, control, correction (CVIII.274)
Addresse, direct, send (CVIII.486)
Adventure, at, by luck (CCXXII.40)
Advowtrye, adultery (CCXIII.32)
Adwayting, awaiting (CCXLVI.16)
Affect, effect, accomplishment (CXXXV.5)
Affects, affections, passions, lusts
Affrays, makes afraid (CVIII.420)
Aford, provide (CVIII.519)
Agayn, against (XXIV.2)
Agast, horror-struck (CVIII.447)
Ainst, against (CCL.3)
Algate, in every way (CVIII.603)
Alow, admit as valid (CVIII.647)
Alowance, praise (CVIII.657)
Ambs as, double ace (LXXXVII.103)
Among, from time to time (LXII.24)
Amours, amorous or love's (XII.1)
Apaire, damage (XXXV.5)
Appayre, die down (CLIII.13)
Araced, raised (VIII.26n.)
Armeles defenceless (CXCVI.46)
Aspye, espy (CXI.27)
Assays, trials (CCIII.9)
Assented, submitted (V.9)
Astart, escape (CCLXVIII.11 Etc.)
Astate, estate, position (CLXXVI.13)
Asyen, assign (CXCVI.23)
Ataced, see Araced and n.
Avysing, considering (XXIX.1)
Avaunce, advance (LIII.25 Etc.)
Avauncing, advancing (LXII.5)
Avaunt, boast (CCXLIX.1)
Avoo, avow (CXCV.20)

Bankets, banquets (CCLIX.3)
Bate, decrease (XCVIII.42)
Bayned, bathed (CXVII.10)
Beaulte, beauty (CXCIII.11)
Beknow, recognize, confess (CVIII.198, 442,)
Bekinde, by its nature

Beknowyng, see Beknow
Belaye, enclose (CLIII.1)
Belstred, extreme, inflated (CXX.1)
Belt, strap (CXIX.27)
Bering in hand, deception (XIV.13 Etc.)
Beseke, beseech (LXXXIV.39)
Besene, seen (CXLI.29)
Bestad, beset (CLXXXIX.12)
Bolded, emboldened, encouraged (LVI.12)
Boordes, see Bordes
Boote, spoil, reward (LXXXII.18)
Bordes, jests (XXXIV.3, LIII.12 Etc.)
Borne, burn (CLXII.5)
Borne in hand, deceived (CXX.1)
Borow, deliverer from prison, bail (CVIII.667)
Borow, ransom (CLXXXI.22)
Bot, bit (CLXXIII.3)
Bote, remedy (XLVI.4 Etc.)
Boteles, bootless, vain (CCIX.5)
Botles, bootless (LXIII.9)
Bowght, curve, circuit (CIV.45)
Bowrnyng, burning (CXCV.10)
Breade, breadth
Bronds, swords (XCIV.41)
Brute, reputation (CCXXII.11)
Brynne, burn (CLXXV.29)
Bygone, adorned, fashioned (LXXXVI.10)
Bygown, begun (CCV.31)
Byhest, vow (CVIII.729)
Bytyng, consuming (CCLXI.20)

Calcars, calkers, astrologers (CIV.60)
Care, to be filled with care (CLXXXI.3)
Carefull, full of care, sorrowful, anxious (V.2 Etc.)
Carefully, sorrowfully (CXXXIV.7 Etc.)
Carffull, see Carefull
Carrfull, see Carefull
Cater, caterer (CVI.26)
Centaunce, sentence (CXXVIII.15)
Certene, certainty (CXLI.9)
Changyt, changed (CXCIV.18)
Charged, loaded (XXVIII.1)
Chase, drive away (XXXII.9)
Chase, choose (C.1)
Chaung, change (CCXI.3)

Chave, livelihood (CCXXII.37)
Chaw, chew (CVII.19)
Chepe, good, bargain (CCLVIII.3)
Chere, face, mood, disposition (CXIX.7 Etc.)
Clattering, loud-mouthed, boastful (VIII.76)
Clogg, block attached to leg to impede motion (CV.86)
Clyve, cliff (LXXXV.2)
Cold, could (CLI.7)
Coloured, specious (V.18)
Comeforthe, comfort (CXXIII.1)
Comford, comfort (CXXI.5)
Complyshe, accomplish (CVIII.728)
Complysyth, accomplisheth (CVIII.522)
Concyle, reconcile (K) (CXCVII.26)
Condition, disposition (XIX.5)
Conduyt, conduct (XI.4)
Confort, comfort (XXVIII.13)
Counterpese, counterbalance (CVIII.70)
Contrarieng, contradicting (XLV.3)
Contrewaing, balancing (XLV.4)
Consciens, right conduct, tenderness (CXXI.21)
Conster, guess (CCXXXVII.7)
Convert, change (CCLV.4)
Convey, steal
Cost, coast (CLXI.31)
Couitise, greed (CCLXI.19)
Coylye, coy (CCXIX.10)
Croppe, head of plant (XLVI.6)
Cruche, crouch (CCII.15)
Crysped, curled (XCVIII.69)
Cryspid, *see* Crysped (CIV.4)
Cryspyd, *see* Crysped (CXVIII.6)
Cuer, care (CXLIX.9)
Cumley, comely (CXVIII.2)
Cure, care (I.3)

Dartyd, pierced (CXV.12)
Daskard, dastard, dullard (VIII.84)
Daunger, subjection (XXXVII.5)
Deale, part (CCLII.12)
Deceavable, deceptive (VIII.10)
Ded, did (CXCVI.7 Etc.)
Defuse, doubtful (CCX.6)
Dele, part (CCX, 7)
Deles, *see* Dele (VIII.92)
Demayne, demesne, possession (LXXXVI. 21)
Demyng, judging (CCXXXIX.4)
Denays, denials (CCIII.11)
Depart, sever, part with (CXVI.9, CXLII.9)

Departed, divided, separated (LXXXVI.8)
Departure, death (CCXII.2)
Depaynted, painted, portrayed (XII.5)
Depert, allot (CVIII.715)
Deptyst, deepest (CXVII.12)
Deserft, desert (XXV.4)
Desteyne, destiny (CXV.24)
Destyne, destiny (XXIV.13)
Determed, determined (LXXI.1)
Detract, protract (CLI.2)
Devise, desire (XXVI.7)
Discus, set free (CVIII.604)
Dismolde, dismal (XCIV.55)
Dispayred in, despaired of (CXV.11)
Dispere, despair (CXVII.10)
Distayne, discolour (XCVII.3)
Distrast, racked (LXXXVI.3)
Do way, *see* Way
Dought, doubt (CXXIX.9)
Dowblenes, deceit (II.3 Etc.)
Dowt, extinguishing (CXXX.34)
Dressyd, stood (CVIII.70)
Dropy, dropping (CXXXIV.3)
Drowfft, drought (CIV.46)
Drye, drift (LXVII.22)
Dryve, defer (CLXV.7)
Dulphull, doleful (CXXI.6)
During, enduring (CXXIV.1 n.)
Dy, die (CLXXXIV.18)

Elonged, distant from (LXXVIII.15)
Enlarged, swollen (V.8)
Entreath, entreateth (I.14)
Entremete, interpose (XCVIII.38)
Ere, ear (LXVI.6)
Erryng, wandering (XLVIII.10)
Esse, ease (LVIII.2)
Estert, escape (XI.15)
Eschew, avoid (LXXXIV.15)
Estew, avoidance (XCV.8)
Exsept, accept (CXLVI.35)
Extew, avoid (CXVI.8)

Fall, arrive (LX.5)
Falsed, perjured (LIII.22)
Falshed, falsehood (CXCVII.18)
Fantasy, imagination (CXCII.21)
Fantesy, whim (CXXXVIII.4)
Faruent, fervent (CXIV.13)
Fatte, fate (CXV.2)
Faut, fault (CXXVII.2)
Faute, fault (CXCVIII.28)
Fawtles, faultless (CLXI.8)

Faytfull, faithful (XCVIII.36)
Feet, apt, fitting (LXVIII.1)
Fett, fetch (LIII.2)
Ffell, feel (CLXVI.20)
Fley, fly (CXLVII.27)
Flowdes, rivers (XCVIII.38)
Fond, found (CLXIV.12)
Fonds, play the fool (XCIV.45)
Forbicause, because (LIII.37)
Force, of, of necessity (XVI.11)
Force, no, no matter (XL.13)
Fordon, destroyed (CVIII.772)
Forger, liar (CC.4)
Forowse, furrows (CVI.7)
Forse, force (K) but possibly waterfall (XCV.4)
Fortune, chance to (CCXXII.14)
Foyld, trampled down (CVIII.741)
Frame, bring to, set in order (VIII.81)
Frame, shape (XVI.4); succeed, progress (CV.56)
Fro, from (XXV.1 Etc.)
Fytt, attack of illness (CLXXII.41)

Gadlyng, fellow (XLVI.1)
Gadre, gather (CCX.26)
Game, sport, love-making (CCIX.27)
Gatte, gate (CLXXVI.3)
Gaynward, towards, facing (XCIX.4)
Geat, get (CCLII.16)
Gile, guile (XVI.13)
Girninge, showing the teeth (XCIV.37)
Glede, gleed, fire (XXIV.14)
Glose; Glosing, pretence; deceitful (CVIII.176, 498)
Good, wealth, possessions (XLVIII.3)
Greiff, harm, suffering (IX.10)
Greve, grief (CLXXX.23)
Grame, sorrow (CLXXXVI.4)
Groundyd, settled (CXCVIII.22)
Grownder, causer (CXC.12)
Groynes, groans, grunts (CVII.19)
Gruging, troubling, inward complaining (CVIII.351)
Gryff, grief (CXV.9)
Gyse, fashion (XL.3)
Gysse, guise (CLXXXVI.15)

Habundaunce, abundance (XCII.1)
Hapnet, happened (CXCV.23)
Happe, luck
Hard, heard (CCXVII.1)
Harde, heard (CXCVI.8)
Hardelye, certainly (CXXXIX.27)

Hardelye, boldly (CCXXXI.35)
Hardines, audacity, boldness (IV.8 Etc.)
Hase, has (CCXXII.38)
Hase, *see* n. (XXI.10)
Hau, have (LV.20)
Hay, hunting-net (CVI.88)
Heins, refuge (from *hain* = enclosure) *or* departure (from *hine*) (CVIII.742)
Hepe, help (CXLVI.61)
Here, her (CXLVIII.48)
Hernes, hiding-places (CVIII.742 R)
Hett, heat (CLXIX.6)
Hevenes, heavy-heartedness (XXII.11)
Hiere, *see* Hire
Hire, reward (LXXXVII.37)
Hit, it
Ho, who (XXII.18 n.)
Hold, in, in prison (I.10)
Holde, power (CXCII.2)
Hole, whole (LXXVII.27 Etc.)
Hollye, wholly (CCXX.28)
Honeste, honesty (XXIII.11)
Hoppe, hope (CXII.14)
Host, sacrifice (CVIII.52)
Howgy, huge (XXII.13)
Hyer, reward (CXLVIII.46)
Hyt, it

Induse, lead (CXCII.24)
Insuere, guarantee (CLXXV.4)
Intent, thought, way of looking (CV.12)
I-stricken, struck (XLVII.9)
Iyes, eyes

Jeopretie, jeopardy (CVIII.268)

Kant, portion (CVII.45)
Kappurs, colt's, wanton's (XXXV.9)
Karke, carke, fret (CLXXXI.3)
Kaye, key (CCX.15)
Keste, cast (LXXI.21)
Kinde, be, by kind, of its nature (CCXXV.38)
Kinde, of, of its nature
Kitt, cut (CCXXVIII.8)
Knoleging, confessing (CVIII.233)
Koggh, cough (CVII.54)
Kynkoryd, cankered (CLXVI.4)
Kynde, by, of its nature (CXLVII.12)

Lade, led (CXLVII.23, CCLXVIII.15)
Lake, lack (CCXVI.24)

Lape, lap (CLXXVIII.18)
Launcyd, lanced, pierced (CVIII.10)
Layer, lair (XXXV.8)
Leffer, liefer (LXXXV.11)
Leke, like (CXCIII.9)
Leppe, leap (CXXXVIII.22)
Lese, lose (LIII.20, CCXXV.16)
Let, hindered (XCVIII.45)
Leve, live (CXLIV.15)
Lever, preferable (XIII.8)
Ley, lie (CXXIII.4)
Leynght, length (CCXLVI.15)
Liff, life (LXIII.6)
Lome, come into view (CVIII.707)
Louere, lour (CLXIII.25)
Lowe, low (CXXIII.2)
Lust, like (CXXXVIII.1 Etc.); joy, live-
    liness (CLXXVI.12); will (CV.6); desire
    (CVIII.28)
Lustynes, lustfulness (CVIII.248)
Lybyke, Lybian (CIV.2)
Lyff, lief (LXXXV.5)
Lynne, cease (CCXVII.3)
Lyse, lice (CCXLI.5)

Mak, mate (CVIII.22)
Manner, place, manor house (CCXXII.36)
Mashed, immeshed (LIX.8)
Mede, reward (CXLV.28)
Medeway, midway (CXVII.4)
Meued, moved (CCLXI.8)
Ment, intended (CIV.71)
Mew, cage (LXXIX.6)
Mickell, great prize (CXLVII.42)
Mischef, sorrow, distress
Mo, more (LII.7)
Moo, more (XCIII.24)
Morning, mourning (LII.11)
Morte, dead (CCXIII.28)
Mought, might (VIII.4)
Myche, much (CXXII.10)
Myght, would wish to (XCVIII.32)
Mynde, intention, inclination, desire
    (XXVII, 1)
Mysdown, misdone (CCV.29)
Myse, miss (CXLII.21)
Mytt, meet (X.5)

Nar, nearer (CXXXVII.27)
Natiuitie, birth horoscope (XCII.9)
Narr, nearer (LXXXV.14)
Ner, not (CXCV.22)
Noon, A, anon (CXXXVIII.11)

Noppy, nappy, foaming, strong
    (CVII.16)
Not, know not (LVI.14)
Note, not (LXX.4)
Nother, no other (III.13)
Nother, neither (VIII.50)
Nowne, my, mine own (CXXXI.2)
Noy, annoy (CLXVIII.3)
Nyd, need (CXXXII.16)
Nyes, my, mine eyes (CXV.27)
Nys, is not (CXLIV.22)

On, one (CCXXX.29)
Opyne, open (CXLII.26)
Or, before (CXI.26)
Overlye, supreme (CCVIII.9)
Oure, hour (VIII.126)
Ouer, hour (CLX.17)
Overthwart, cross-direction (XL.4)
Overthwart, unfavourable, perverse
    (CLXXXVII.13)
Overthwart, opposed, thwarted
    (CVIII.463)
Owre, hour (VIII.57)
Owre, oar (XXVIII.5)
Owtestert, spring forth (XXV.13)

Pannyers, panniers (XXXV.12)
Pas, *see* Passe on (CXXXIII.8)
Pase, pass (CVIII.756)
Passe on, mind (XIX.6, CXXXIII.8)
Passe, obtain (CXXII.14)
Passe uppon, care for (CCXXVI.24)
Paynefull, full of pain (CXV.30)
Paysith, weighs (CVIII.518)
Peakes, vexations (CCXVIII.4 n.)
Pease, appease (CCXVII.4)
Pene, pen (CXCV.4)
Perdy, by god, verily (V.16, XLV.1)
Pervert, perverse, wicked (LI.26)
Piery, jewellery (LXXXV.9)
Plage, plague (CI.2)
Power, utmost (XXV.2, LXXIII.18); to my
    power to the best of my ability
Poyntes, pauses (CVIII.520)
Prat, prater (CXXV.1)
Prefate, predestined (CXXXV.13)
Prescrybe, limit (CVIII.440)
Prese, in, in the thick of the crowd
    (LXX.19)
Preseth, presses, pushes (IV.3)
Presse, crowd (CCLIX.4)
Presse, in, under pressure (CVIII.246)
Pressions, oppressions (VIII.45)

Prest, ready, lively, prompt (VIII.19)
Pretence, defence (CVIII.687, 726);
pretension display (IV.3)
Pretend, aspire to (CVIII.402, 608)
Preve, prove (CLXXXIV.28)
Price, glory, esteem (VIII.140); money
value (V.24)
Propertie, attribute (CVIII.692)
Propose, purpose (X.3)
Provoke, stimulate (XCVIII.43, 62)
Provoked, invited (CVIII.396)
Pryvate, deprived of (CCXXVIII.17)
Puisshaunte, puissant (CCXIV.14)
Pyctour, picture (CXV.18)

Quyt, requite (CXCV.28)
Qwite, quit (V.29)

Rabates, rebates, brings down (CVIII.50)
Rage, violent passion (XCV.7)
Rajing, raging (LXI.1)
Rape, take away (XCVIII.12)
Rathe, early, soon (CCXLIX.21)
Raught, reached (XXXVI.34)
Reche, reach (LXXXVI.24)
Recheles, careless (XLVI.2)
Recke, Reke, care (CLXX.12 CLXXIII.31)
Record, recalling (XCVIII.42)
Record, witness (CVIII.416)
Recur, *see* Recure (CXLIX.11)
Recure, cure (XI.8)
Recure, recovery, remedy (LXIII.16)
Reduce, make obedient (CVIII.118)
Reducing, recalling (LXXVIII.16)
Refuse, refusal (CLXXX.6)
Reigne, kingdom (VIII.9)
Reke, reck (CCX.43)
Relyff, relief (CXV.11)
Remedyles, without remedy (CXLI.11)
Remembre, remembrer (XXX.1 note)
Remembryng, recalling (CLXXXVII.5)
Remes, realms (CVIII.18)
Rent, rend (CCLI.2)
Repreffe, reprieve (CCXVI.20)
Repugnant, contrary, opposing (CIV.8)
Resolution, answer (VIII.147)
Respect, partiality (CVIII.720)
Respectles, impartial, heedless
(CVIII.539 n.)
Restrayne, confine (LXXXVI.6)
Restore, restoration (CCXXXI.31)
Reuthe, ruth, pity (CXCVIII.16)
Revolted, turned (as applied to a
knife-edge) (LXII.11)

Revoulsed, upset, violently changed
(XVIII.7)
Righteweise, Righturisnes, righteous,
righteousness (CVIII.127; XCIV.16)
Rightwisely, righteously (XXX.10)
Rof, took (CVIII.66)
Rore, tumult (XCVII.8)
Row, roe (CXLI.27)
Rysen, roused (CVIII.739)

Saff, save (CIV.69)
Samble, assembly (CVIII.612)
Sarue, serve (CXCV.26)
Scapp, escape (CXXX.9)
Scole, school (XCIII.17)
Seche, seek (CLXIII.28)
Seith, saith (CXXVIII.18)
Seith, sith, since (CXXXV.28)
Seithe, saith (XC.19)
Semblaunt, appearance (CXCVI.3)
Ses, cease (CXV.32)
Sese, seize (CLXXII.16)
Seson, seize on, embrace (XXVI.4)
Set, sit (CXLI.32)
Sethens, *see* Sithens
Shapen, shaped (V.2)
Shente, scolded (CCXXII.5)
Shitt, excluded (III.5)
Shott, reckoning (CLIV.18)
Shright, shriek (VIII.137, XXV.12)
Shytt, shut (CLXXII.39)
Siche, such (CCX.35)
Sighting, sighing (XII.10)
Sildam, seldom (XXXI.7)
Silie, simple (CXCVI.51)
Sithens, since (VII.8)
Sittes, suits (XCVIII.58)
Skace, scarce (CCXX.9)
Skantlye, scarcely (CXLIV.8)
Skappt, escaped (CXXX.2)
Slake, render less vigorous (CLXVIII.24);
reduce (LXII.5)
Slepe, slip (CLVII.23)
Sleper, slippery (CXCV.8)
Slepyd, slipped (CLXVI.56)
Slipper, slippery (CCXXX.7 Etc.)
Smarte, keen, quick (CCXII.2)
Smartles, those without smart
(CXXX VIII.31)
Smast, smashed ? (CXIX.16)
Solaine, solitary (CVIII.560)
Solas, solace (CXI.3)
Soleyn, sullen (CXXX.1)

II

Sours, source (CIV.15)
Sowne, swoon (CXIX.17)
Sparkill, scatter, disperse (LIII.20)
Sparplid, scattered (CVIII.8)
Spedles, unsuccessful (CCI.11)
Sperklyng, flashing, lively (XII.6)
Spill, kill (XLI.37)
Sporne, spurn (CLXIII.11)
Spytte, sprite (CLXVIII.2)
Staring (XCIV.32 note)
Stemyng, flaming (CVI.53)
Stere, steer (CLXXVII.3)
Sterred, guided, stirred (VIII.101 n.)
Sterred, stirred (IX.8)
Stert, started (CXCIII.13)
Sterue, die (V.25 Etc.)
Still, always (XXV.1)
Stilling, distilling (LXXXII.6)
Stock, tree-trunk (VIII.64)
Stond, stand (CCXL.1)
Stonnyd, struck dumb (CXV.35)
Stowpith, stoops (LX.7)
Straine, bind, oppress (CCIX.23)
Strains, (of voice) raises, pitches (CVIII.425)
Straynably, compulsively (XX.14)
Straynid, 'exerted by an abnormal effort to an abnormal degree' (*N.E.D.* (3)): *but see* n. (CVIII.216)
Strayne, press hard upon, distress, exude (CVIII.412)
Strenes, strains, light from stars (XCVII.70)
Styk, hesitate (CCVI.4)
Surty, surety (CXCV.27)
Suspect, suspicion (CCLIV.2)
Suttyll, subtile, rarefied
Suype, sweep (CXXXII.19)
Swarve, swerve (CCVII.3 Etc.)
Swelting, perishing, swooning (CCXLVIII.7)
Swete, sweat (CXLVIII.45)
Syegh, sigh (CCXXI.16)
Syght, sigh (CVIII.409)
Sykernes, security (CXLIV.12)
Sythens, since (II.4)
Sythyng, sighing (CX.4)

Tamys, Tems, Thames (XXX.7; XCIX.3)
Terrestrial, *see* n. (CLXI.26)
Tery, tearful (XXIV.12)
Than, then (CCXXXIX.6)
Thes, this (CCV.2)

Thevin, the heaven (LXXXIII.5)
Tho, then (CLXIII.8)
Thought, my, methought (CXXXIV.6)
Thowrs, the hours (XCVIII.15)
Throws, throes (XCVIII.51)
Thrust, pressure (CVIII.690)
Tickell, uncertain (CXLVII.44)
To fore, before (CVIII.637)
Ton, the one (CCVI.7)
Tordes, turds (CVII.19)
Tormente, tormented (CCXXIV.2)
Torne off with, consigned to (CVIII.705)
Towerd, to the point (XXV.7)
To yere, this year (LXXXV.6)
Trad, trod (CLX.3)
Train, *see* Commentary (CCXLVII.8)
Traine, stratagem (CCXIII.14)
Trainid, drawn along, led astray (XCVIII.14)
Trance, to be in fear or suspense
Tras, trace (CLX.3)
Trauncyd, *see* Trance (CVIII.12)
Trayed, betrayed (XLV.6)
Traught, truth (CXXX.5)
Trayn, deceit (CXC.20)
Trayne, lure (LXXXVII.11)
Trayne, treachery (CVIII.31)
Troo, trow, believe (CXLVII.1)
Trusse, quiver (C.4)
Trust, hope (tr. *speranza, spene*) (IV.6, XXXI.13, XXXIII.8)
Trusty, hopeful (XXVIII.8)
Truyse, truce (XXXII.2)
Tryd, determined (CVIII.533)
Tryde, refined (CVIII.314)
Tryllyth, trickles (XCV.2)
Turkylles, turtle-doves (CXLI.32)
Tyre, seize (XXXIII.6)

Uncontrefaict, genuine (LXXXV.16)
Underband, conspire (CXX.4)
Undermyndyth, undermine (CVIII.30)
Unfarme, infirm (CVIII.243)
Unhappe, unhappy (CLXXX.6)
Unhappe, misfortune (CCXXXVI.5)
Unkowth, unknown (CVIII.415)
Unmesurable, immeasurable (XXXIII.1)
Unquyt, without punishment (LXVI.24)
Undremiste, overlooked (CCX.40)
Unsaciat, insatiable (XIV.9)
Unsparred, unbarred (CCXLVI.2)
Unto, until (CCXIII.51)
Unvysyd, ill-advised (CLXII.11)

Untwynde, be undone (XCIV.106)
Unware, unaware (LXXIII.25)
Unwarely, unpreparedly (CXCIII.1)
Unwysse, unwise (CLXXXV.11)
Ure, use (XXI.17 Etc.)

Vauoure, favour (CLXXVI.19)
Vaileth, avail (II.1 Etc.)
Vaylyth, *see* Vaileth
Viage, voyage (CIV.48)

Waker, watchful (XCVII.1)
Wanhope, despair (CCXLVIII.4)
Ward, prison (CVIII.265)
Ware, wary (CXCVII.31)
Warte, wert (CCXIX.16)
Way, do, leave off, abandon (XCIV.25)
Wede, weed (CXL.31)
Wele, well-being (LXIII.3)
Weet, wet (CLIX.6)
Wellyng, weeping (CXV.33)
Welt, wealth (CXLVII.30)
Wene, expect (CLXXVIII.11); wean (CXX.8)
Wenist, hopes (CCXIX.7)
Wenys, judges (XCI.16)
Wenyng, intending (XXIII.18)
Were, wear (CLXXIII.15)
Wered, wearied (XXVIII.10)
Werishe, shrivelled, sickly (CCXIII.8)
Whan, when (CCIII.6)
Whereby, wherefore

Whon, a one (CLX.12)
Will, *see* n. (CLXXX.4)
Withsave, preserve (CXCVIII.20)
Witsave, vouchsafe (XCIII.19)
Womanhede, womanhood (CCII.8)
Wonders, wonderfully (CVI.60)
Wone, one (CXXIX.12)
Worth, betide (VIII.139)
Worth, in, in good part (CVIII.624 Etc.)
Wo worth, may evil betide (VIII.139)
Worth, yn, *see* Worth, in
Wow, woe (C.8)
Wrast, wrest (CLII.3)
Wreake, expend (CXLII.9)
Wrek, avenge; injury
Wry, conceal (CXXXVII.26 T)
Wull, will (LVII.17)
Wysse, I, certainly (CXXX.8)

Ycharged, burdened (CCLXI.19)
Yede, went (CVIII.372)
Yelden, yielded (CCL.4)
Yen, eyes (XXIV.12)
Yerne, earn (CLXXVI.22)
Yerth, earth (XCIV.8)
Yes, eyes
Yet, hitherto (XCVIII.13)
Yie, eye
Yose, use (CLXXVIII.14)
Ywys, certainly (CXCII.6)

Zyns, five (LXXXVII.102)

INDEX

OF FIRST LINES

Absence absenting causeth me to complain	*poem* CCXXVIII	*page* 231
Absence, alas	CXI	127
Accused though I be without desert	CXVI	132
A face that should content me wonders well	CXVIII	132
After great storms the calm returns	LXXXIII	61
Against the rock I climb both high and hard	CXVIII	132
Ah! my heart, ah! what aileth thee?	CXIII	129
A lady gave me a gift she had not	CCXXXVII	238
Alas, fortune, what aileth thee	CXII	128
Alas, dear heart, what hap had I	CIX	126
Alas, madame, for stealing of a kiss	XLIV	33
Alas, my dear, the word thou spakest	CXIX	133
Alas, poor man, what hap had I	CLXXXV	195
Alas the grief and deadly woeful smart	V	3
All heavy minds	LXXXIV	62
All in thy sight my life doth whole depend	CCVI	214
All ye that know of care and heavyness	CXV	131
Alone musing	CX	127
Although thou see th' outrageous climb aloft	XCIV	75
And if an eye may save or slay	XCIII	73
And wilt thou leave me thus?	CLXXXVI	196
A! Robyn	LV	41
A spending hand that alway poureth out	CVII	95
As power and wit will me assist	CLXXXVIII	198
At last withdraw your cruelty	CXIV	129
At most mischief	LI	36
Avising the bright beams of these fair eyes	XXIX	22
Because I have the still kept fro lies and blame	XXV	20
Behold, love, thy power how she despiseth	I	1
Being as none is I do complain	CXXI	134
Blame not my lute, for he must sound	CCV	212
But sithens you it essay to kill	VI	4
By belstred words I am borne in hand	CXX	134
Caesar, when that the traitor of Egypt	III	2
Comfort at hand, pluck up thy heart!	CXXIII	136

Comfort thyself, my woeful heart   *poem* LXXIV   *page* 56
Complaining, alas, without redress   CXXII   135

Deem as ye list upon good cause   CCXXXIII   235
Defamed guiltiness by silence unkept   CXXVII   139
Desire, alas, my master and my foe   LXXV   57
Desire to sorrow doth me constrain   CXXVI   138
Dido am I, the founder first of Carthage   CXXXI   141
Disdain me not without desert   CCLXVI   257
Disdain not, madam, on him to look   CXXXII   142
Divers doth use as I have heard and know   CCXVII   222
Double, diverse, sullen and strange   CXXX   141
Do way, do way, ye little wily prat!   CXXV   138
Driven by desire I did this deed   CXXVIII   139
Driven to desire, adread also to dare   CXXIX   140
Driven by desire to set affection   CCLXII   254
Duresse of pains and grievous smart   CXXIV   137

Each man me telleth I change most my devise   X   11
Even when you lust ye may refrain   CXXXVIII   146
Ever mine hap is slack and slow in coming   XXX   23

Farewell all my welfare   CLXXXI   192
Farewell, love, and all thy laws for ever   XIII   12
Farewell the reign of cruelty   XI   11
Forget not yet the tried intent   CCIII   211
For shamefast harm of great and hateful need   CCLVII   252
For to love her for her looks lovely   XV   14
Fortune doth frown   CCXXI   225
Fortune, what aileth thee?   CLXI   173
For want of will, in woe I plain   CCXLVIII   245
From these high hills as when a spring doth fall XCV   78
From thought to thought, from hill to hill love
                                doth me lead   CII   84
Full well it may be seen   CXCVII   207

Give place all ye that doth rejoice   CCXVI   221
Go burning sighs unto the frozen heart   XX   16
Greeting to you both in hearty wise   CCXXII   225
Grudge on who list, this is my lot   CCXX   224

Had I wist that now I wot   CXXXIII   142
Hap happith oft unlooked for   CXXXV   144

Hate whom yet list, I care not   *poem* CXXXVI   *page* 145
Heart oppressed with desperate thought   CCXXXIV   237
Heaven and earth and all that hear me plain   LXXIII   55
He is not dead that sometime had a fall   LX   45
Help me to seek, for I lost it there   XVII   15
Horrible of hue, hideous to behold   CXXXIV   143
How oft have I my dear and cruel foe   XXXII   24
How should I   CXVI   205

I abide and abide and better abide   CCXXVII   231
I am as I am and so will I be   CXL   148
I am ready and ever will be   CXXXIX   147
If armour's faith, an heart unfeigned   XII   12
If chance assigned   LXVII   50
If ever man might him avaunt   CCXLIX   246
If fancy would favour   XLIII   32
I find no peace and all my war is done   XXVI   20
If I might have at mine own will   CXLII   152
If in the world there be more woe   LXXXIX   70
If it be so that I forsake thee   XVIII   15
If thou wilt mighty be, flee from the rage   CCLXI   253
If waker care, if sudden pale colour   XCVII   78
If with complaint the pain might be expressed   CCVIII   214
I have been a lover   CXLV   155
I have sought long with steadfastness   LXIX   51
I know not where my heavy sighs to hide   CXLIV   154
I lead a life unpleasant, nothing glad   LXXXVIII   70
I have loved and so doth she   CLXXX   191
I may by no means surmise   CCLXVII   258
I must go walk the woods so wild   CXLI   150
In court to serve decked with fresh array   CCLIX   252
In doubtful breast whilst motherly pity   LXXX   60
In eternum, I was once determed   LXXI   53
In faith I wot not well what to say   XXIII   19
In mourning wise since daily I encrease   CXLVI   157
I see my plaint with open ears   CCXLIII   242
I see that chance hath chosen me   CCLVI   251
I see the change from that that was   CXCV   204
Is it possible   CLXXXIV   194
It burneth yet, alas, my heart's desire   CCLV   250
It may be good, like it who list   XXI   17
It was my choice, it was no chance   CXCII   201
I will, although I may not   CXLIII   153

Lament my loss, my labour and my pain   *poem* CCXIV   *page* 219
Like as the bird in the cage enclosed   CCXLVI   243
Like as the swan towards her death   LXX   52
Like as the wind with raging blast   CCXLV   242
Like to these unmeasurable mountains   XXXIII   24
Live thou gladly, if so thy may   CXLIX   162
Lo! how I seek and sue to have   CXCIX   209
Longer to muse   CCXXV   228
Longer to trow ye   CXLVII   159
Love and fortune and my mind remember   XXXI   23
Love hath again   CXLVIII   161
Love to give law unto his subjects' hearts   CVIII   98
Love whom you list and spare not   CCLXIII   255
Lo! what it is to love   LXXXVII   66
Lux, my fair falcon, and your fellows all   CCXLI   241

Madame, I you require   CLI   163
Madame, withouten many words   XXXIV   25
Marvel no more although   LII   38
Me list no more to sing   CCX   215
Might I as well within my song belay   CLIII   164
Mine old dear enemy, my froward master   VIII   5
Mine own John Poins, since ye delight to know   CV   88
Mistrustful minds be moved   CCLIV   250
Mourning my heart doth sore oppress   CL   163
Most wretched heart, most miserable   XCI   71
My galley charged with forgetfulness   XXVIII   21
My heart I gave thee not to do it pain   XIV   13
My hope, alas, hath me abused   LXII   45
My love is like unto th'eternal fire   CC   210
My love took scorn my service to retain   CCXXIII   227
My lute, awake, perform the last   LXVI   48
My mother's maids, when they did sew and spin   CVI   91
My pen, take pain a little space   CLXXIX   190
My sweet, alas, forget me not   CLIV   165

Nature that gave the bee so feat a grace   LXVIII   51
Now all of change   CCXXVI   230
Now must I learn to feign   CCLXVIII   259
Now must I learn to live at rest   CCII   211

O cruel heart, where is thy faith?   CLVII   168
Of Carthage he that worthy warrior   LXXXI   60

Of purpose love chose first for to be blind	*poem* C	*page* 83
O goodly hand	LXXXVI	65
O miserable sorrow withouten cure!	CCIV	212
Once as methought fortune me kissed	LXV	47
Once in your grace I know I was	CLVI	167
O what undeserved cruelty	CLV	166
Pain of all pain, the most grievous pain	CCXIII	218
Pass forth my wonted cries	CLIX	171
Patience for I have wrong	CCXXIX	232
Patience for my device	XL	29
Patience of all my smart	CXC	200
Patience though I have not	XXXIX	29
Perdy I said it not	CLVIII	170
Plain ye mine eyes, accompany my heart	CCXLII	241
Process of time worketh such wonder	LXXXII	61
Prove whether I do change, my dear	XCVI	78
Quondam was I in my Lady's grace	CLX	172
Resound my voice, ye woods that hear me plain	XXII	18
Right true it is, and said full yore ago	XLIX	35
Shall she never out of my mind	CCLXIV	255
She sat and sewed that hath done me the wrong	LIV	40
She that should most perceiveth least	CLXIII	174
Sighs are my food, drink are my tears	CCXLIV	242
Since love is such that, as yet wot	CXCVIII	208
Since love will needs that I shall love	CCLIII	249
Since so ye please to hear me plain	CCI	210
Since ye delight to know	LXXII	54
Since you will needs that I shall sing	CCIX	215
Sith I myself displease thee	CLXVI	177
Sith it so that I am thus refused	CLXIV	175
So feeble is the thread that doth the burden stay	XCVIII	79
Some fowls there be that have so perfect sight	XXIV	19
Some time I fled the fire that me brent	LIX	44
Some time I sigh, some time I sing	CLXXXIX	199
Some time the pride of my assured troth	CCXXXIX	240
So unwarily was never no man caught	CXCIII	202
Speak thou and speed where will or power	CCLX	253
Spite hath no power to make me sad	CCXIX	223
Spite of the spite which that in vain	CLXIII	174

Stand who so list upon the slipper top   *poem* CCXL   *page* 240
Such is the course that nature's kind hath wrought CCL   247
Such hap as I am happed in   XXXVI   26
Such vain thought as wonted to mislead me   LVI   42
Suffering in sorrow in hope to attain   CLXV   176
Sufficed it not, Madame, that you did tear   CCLI   248

Tagus, farewell, that westward with thy streams   XCIV   82
Take heed betime lest ye be spied   CLXXVIII   189
Tangled I was in love's snare   CCXXIV   227
That time that mirth did steer my ship   CLXXIII   184
The answer that ye made to me, my dear   XC   70
The enemy of life, decayer of all kind   LXIV   47
The flaming sighs that boil within my breast   CCXXXVIII   239
The furious gun in his raging ire   LXI   45
The fruit of all the service that I serve   CCVII   214
The heart and service to you proferred   CLXXXII   193
The joy so short, alas, the pain so near   CCXII   217
The knot that first my heart did strain   CLXXII   183
The lively sparks that issue from those eyes   XLVII   35
The long love that in my thought doth harbour   IV   3
The loss is small to lese such one   CCXVIII   223
The pillar perished is whereto I lent   CCXXXVI   238
The restful place, reviver of my smart   CLXXXVII   197
There was never file half so well filed   XVI   14
There was never nothing more me pained   XXXVIII   28
The wandering gadling in the summer tide   XLVI   34
They flee from me that sometime did me seek   XXXVII   27
Though I cannot your cruelty constrain   LVII   42
Though I myself be bridled of my mind   XXVII   21
Though of the sort there be that feign   CLXIX   180
Though some do grudge to see me joy   CLXVIII   179
Though this thy port and I thy servant true   LXXVIII   59
Thou hast no faith of him that hath none   XIX   16
Thou sleepest fast; and I with woeful heart   CLVII   179
Throughout the world, if it were sought   CCLVIII   252
Thy promise was to love me best   CXCIV   203
To cause accord or to agree   LXXVII   58
To make an end of all this strife   CCXXXI   233
To my mishap alas I find   CLXXI   181
To rail or jest, ye know I use it not   CCXI   217
To seek each where, where man doth live   LXXXV   64
To wet your eye withouten tear   CLXX   181

To whom should I sue to ease my pain? *poem* CCLXV *page* 256
To wish and want and not obtain LVIII 43

Under this stone there lieth at rest — 439
Unstable dream, according to the place LXXIX 59

Venemous thorns that are so sharp and keen LXXVI 57
Venus, in sport, to please therewith her dear CLXXVII 188
Vulcan begat me, Minerva me taught CIII 84

Was I never yet of your love grieved LX 45
What death is worse than this LXIII 46
What meaneth this when I lie alone? CLXXXIII 193
What needeth these threatening words and
                                   wasted wind XLVIII 35
What no perdy ye may be sure XLV 34
What rage is this? What furour of what kind? CI 83
What should I say CCXV 220
What thing is that, that I both have and lack CCXXXV 237
What vaileth truth or by it to take pain II 1
What word is that that changeth not L 36
What would ye more of me, your slave, require CLXXV 186
When Dido feasted first the wandering Trojan
                                         knight CIV 84
When first mine eyes did view and mark CCLII 248
When that I call unto my mind CCXXX 252
Where shall I have at mine own will LIII 39
Who hath heard such cruelty before XLII 32
Who list his wealth and ease retain CLXXVI 187
Who would have ever thought CXCI 201
Whoso list to hunt I know where is an hind VII 5
Will ye see what wondrous love hath wrought? CCXXXII 234
Within my breast I never thought it gain CCXLVII 245
With serving still CLXXIV 185

Ye know my heart, my lady dear XLI 30
Ye old mule that think yourself so fair XXXV 25
Your foolish feigned heart CLII 164
Your looks so often cast CXXXVII 145
You that in love find luck and abundance XCII 73

INDEX
OF VERSE IN COMMENTARY

Alas your fondness makes me smile   *page* 403

Cursed be he that first began   394

Danger thyself led for nothing   397

He that spares to speak hath hardly his intent   414

In summer season as soon as the sun   402

Let the heathen which trust not in the Lord   404
Love who so will white bread, I best do love brown   403

O faithful heart plunged in distress   406
Of few words, sir, you seem to be   298

Rid of bondage, free from care, seven years space and more   409

Since love is found with perfectness   411
Sustain, abstain, keep well in your mind   411

Though I seem dead unto the dazzling eye   414

When shall the cruel storms be past?   390